Contemporary
Research in Personality

second edition

edited by
IRWIN G. SARASON
Associate Professor of Psychology
University of Washington

D. VAN NOSTRAND COMPANY, INC.
Princeton, New Jersey   Toronto   London   Melbourne

To My MOTHER and FATHER

Van Nostrand Regional Offices: *New York, Chicago, San Francisco*

D. Van Nostrand Company, Ltd., *London*

D. Van Nostrand Company (Canada), Ltd., *Toronto*

D. Van Nostrand Australia Pty. Ltd., *Melbourne*

Published simultaneously in Canada by
D. Van Nostrand Company (Canada), Ltd.

Library of Congress Catalog Card No. 69–11743

PRINTED IN THE UNITED STATES OF AMERICA

Preface

DAVID G. SCHROT

CONCEPTS OF PERSONALITY propounded over the years would fill a good-sized volume. Most of them involve, at least implicitly, the assumptions that (1) personality refers to some kind of hypothetical internal organization or structure, and (2) since each person is a complex organism, this organization should encompass an intricate interlocking of tendencies and forces. Were one actually to take on the rather formidable task of developing an anthology of concepts of personality, it would be found that most of those put forth represent relatively pure instances of armchair psychology. That is, they are products of the thinking of writers interested in comprehending the determinants of individuality and the interaction between personal characteristics and the world about the individual.

What is the best way to achieve such a comprehension? One of the most clearly distinguishing characteristics of the modern study of personality is that a degree of armchair theorizing is felt to be perhaps a necessary but not sufficient ingredient in an objective approach to the study of the individual. It is useful because it provides orientations which may serve the function of directing objective inquiry to significant problems. It is not sufficient because students of personality increasingly have expressed their intention to contribute to a science of psychology. This requires not only ideas, but also a strong emphasis on observation and evidence prior to propounding formal theories. From this standpoint, the armchair study of personality that is unrelated to any objective observations must be regarded as simply speculation. This does not necessarily mean a rejection of speculation. It does suggest the need to go beyond speculation in order to link speculation to reality.

Yet another characteristic of the modern study of personality is the need felt by its students to relate their research activities to those of the general psychological researcher. The personality researcher uses many methods of general psychology. It is interesting, also, that the general psychologist more and more seeks to integrate knowledge of individual difference variables gathered by the personality researcher with his own work. Sanford has recently commented on this interpenetration of personality and other areas of psychology:

> If general psychology has . . . been stretching itself to embrace more and more of what used to belong to the personality field, so has research in personality . . . served to bring 'variables of personality' to an increasingly prominent place in the attention of the experimentalist in general psychology. There have been literally hundreds of researches undertaken by personality psychologists and devoted to showing that variables of personality were predictive of individual differences in the performance of laboratory tasks. (Sanford, N., Personality: Its Place in Psychology. In S. Koch (Ed.), *Psychology: The Study of a Science,* New York: McGraw-Hill, 1963, Vol. 5, p. 566.)

The material presented in this collection is both the product of prior speculation and prior research. Hopefully, in it some of the seeds of scientific theory of the future may be found. The aim of gathering together this material is to provide for the student interested in the study of individuality examples of how personality psychologists proceed from ideas to hard data. What techniques do they employ? How do they go about their work? How do they carry out objective research dealing with the internal events experienced by persons? What balance of speculation, theory, and data-gathering characterizes their work? It is hoped that a review of the material in this book will provide at least beginnings of answers to these questions for the student.

It will certainly reveal that the two predominant methods in modern personality research are those of assessment and experimentation. These methods are directed toward the delineation of significant personal characteristics and conditions which influence observed behavior. Many of the characteristics of people are neither self-evident nor obvious. Some of them have been described as traits, tendencies, and attributes which must be inferred from behavior. Much of the work of personality assessment has to do with attempts to infer personal characteristics from objective observations of people. Researchers in the area of personality assessment concern themselves with the measurement of personal characteristics because they believe that objectively assessed personal characteristics can aid in understanding and predicting human behavior.

In Part I we shall see examples of the way in which assessment researchers go about their work. We shall see some of their attempts at defining and inferring personal characteristics. We shall see, also, how they seek to establish the validity of the methods which they employ, and how they interpret the results of their research. When doing assessment work, the personality researcher usually does not manipulate independent variables. Instead, he seeks to measure a person's responses under conditions as uniform as possible. He, then, relates the assessed behavior to a variety of criteria, such as achievement while in school and after graduation, and personal adjustment.

The experimentalist adopts a different tack. An experimental is different from, but complementary to, an assessment approach to behavior. Both the assessor and the experimentalist seek to observe and record behavior under carefully controlled conditions. But the experimentalist goes beyond simply the control of extraneous influences over behavior. He, also, manipulates the conditions under which behavior occurs. Thus, experiments permit observation of behavior under carefully controlled *special* behavior-influencing conditions. These special conditions constitute the independent variables of experiments. The dependent variables are the behavioral indices recorded during or after the special conditions have been administered.

In Part II we shall examine several attempts made by personality researchers to use the laboratory in their work. We shall, also, see some of the problems that beset the personality researcher in his efforts to create meaningful experiments. Finally, we shall see how inferences can be drawn from experimental evidence.

This book provides several illustrations of the joint application of assessment and experimental methods to problems in the area of personality. This complementary relationship between assessment and experimental methods is demonstrated clearly in the study of human development. Assessment methods are useful because they provide vehicles for comparing persons at different points in the life cycle. An experimental approach is useful in analyzing reactions of particular groups of people to special situations. One might be interested in assessing personality differences among high school and college students. One might also be interested in finding out how high school and college students differ in their reactions to certain kinds of environmental conditions, such as conditions requiring different levels of independence on the part of the student.

Part III deals with the application of assessment and experimental methods to the study of personality development. A complex variant of an assessment approach, the longitudinal study, will also be seen in Part III. Longitudinal research not only assesses individuals at a particular time, but follows them over what might be a very long time span. Articles in Part III demonstrate the broad range of groups which are studied in order to contribute to a truly comprehensive picture of development. They show that contributions to knowledge of personality development can be made through the study of the preschool child, the retired worker, and various points between these developmental markers.

One problem to which many students of personality have been drawn is that of the development and maintenance of deviant behavior. One of the goals of the field of personality is a contribution to knowledge about human variability. Only through an arbitrary act of exclusion can a distinction be made between "normal" human variability and "abnormal" human variability. It is an interesting fact that the study of deviant behavior has been the context in which many influential general theoretical orientations to personality have been developed (e.g., Freud's, Sullivan's, and Rogers' positions). Part IV deals with efforts to understand deviant devalued behavior and behavior which grows out of significant social problems. Personality researchers have interested themselves in a variety of important problems within these areas. These include the assessment of personality maladjustment, the analysis of effects of cultural deprivation on personality, and the development of rehabilitative techniques applicable to persons with special problems. As is the case in research on human development, so also is it true in the study of individual and social problems, that assessment and experimental approaches play important roles.

The four parts of this book are strongly research-oriented. They reflect the need felt by contemporary students of personality to develop information and techniques upon which theories of personality can be built. As suggested above, this point of view does not necessarily mean a rejection of speculation. It does reflect a willingness to defer theoretical breadth in order to establish firmly the techniques, data, and relationships which can provide the basis for broad generalizations in the future. Contemporary personality research has been influenced by broad theoretical orientations such as Freud's, but it has felt the need to break out on its own in a variety of directions. It seems intent on placing the study of personality on as empirically valid and testable a basis as is possible.

The present collection of readings is predicated on the assumption that personality research, as reflected in current journals, is frequently of quite a different order of investigation than that which would be suggested by "traditional" personality theories. For example, Freud's writings dwelt at length on hypothesized interrelationships among a psychic apparatus: the id, ego, and superego. These hypothesized interrelationships have been of great stimulational value. But scientific research requires unambiguous operational definitions and objective measurements. To meet these requirements the generalities of "traditional" personality theories must give way to less global and more pin-downable concepts.

The aim of this book is to provide the student with examples of empirical and theoretical issues, problems, and methods characteristic of much current research in personality. This aim does not carry with it the assumption that, at the present time, there is a tightly-organized and well-delineated body of verified relationships within the field. Were this the case, one could, in good conscience, refer to a science of personality. But this would be a serious exaggeration. It would not be a distortion, however, to view the field of personality as a science in the making. Indeed, the intent of this collection is to document some of the beginnings which are being made in this direction.

Acknowledgments

I AM INDEBTED to many individuals for their suggestions, criticisms, and reactions. Victor J. Ganzer reviewed a large number of the articles considered for inclusion in this edition. His incisive and wise ideas were especially helpful to me. The many contributions of my wife, Barbara, are deeply appreciated. Virginia Hendrix's major contribution also merits special comment. Her secretarial skills were but one aspect of that contribution.

I owe a debt to the authors and to the following publishers for permission to reprint selections: Academic Press, American Psychiatric Association, American Psychological Association, American Speech and Hearing Association, Journal of Clinical Psychology, and Melbourne University Press.

Contents

PART I

Personality Assessment

THE WIDE VARIABILITY from person to person in response tendencies, inclinations, and attitudes is a "fact of life" for the researcher interested in behavior. Individual differences may be of secondary importance in the study of certain types of problems, e.g., in general, what is the shape of the learning curve? They may, at times, even be viewed as "getting in the way" of more relevant variables or processes. However, for the researcher interested in personality assessment, individual differences are the major focus of his work. Individual differences and the nature of individuality are his subject matter.

The aim of personality assessment might be described as the development of a meaningful vocabulary with which to describe the individual. Certain individual difference variables present few definitional problems for the describer of behavior, e.g., sex, height, and weight. But individual differences relating to people's concepts of themselves and others, their goals, and their fears are much less susceptible to simple and unambiguous definition. The personality assessor deals with these latter differences in an effort to contribute to the scientific description and, ultimately, prediction of behavior. One important result of work in this field has been the development of reliable indices of psychologically significant individual differences. Researchers are now seeking to identify those methods of personality assessment which result in high yields in determinants and predictors of behavior.

Researchers in personality assessment have made the greatest use of persons' own verbal and written behavior as sources of significant individual difference variables. This use grows out of the assumption that what a person says about himself and others provides valuable information about him. Indeed, many methods of personality assessment emphasize the analysis of self-descriptive responses of individuals. Thus, paper and pencil tests of the true-false type often ask the subject to describe the kind of person he is. Self-description can also be elicited using less restricted formats, e.g., in an interview a person may spend many minutes in constructing his own self-description. The freer format of the interview, however, poses different and often more complex methodological problems than does the paper and pencil test.

Efforts to develop vocabularies relevant to human individuality have not been limited to self-descriptions. Projective techniques, for example, have sought to describe individuals in terms of their responses to inkblots, word association stimuli, pictures, and sentence stems. Thus, the Thematic Apperception Test requires that the subject describe characters and scenes presented to him, while the Rorschach test elicits reactions to inkblots.

Yet another approach has been the use of behavior samples as a means of developing a vocabulary of personality. This might be done, for example, in a play situation in which a child is given access to toys. Aspects of the child's behavior and attitude in the play situation are then noted by an observer. A similar technique can be employed with adults by presenting them with problems to be solved; e.g., a person might be asked to act out a particular scene or play a specified role. The measures of individual difference in this case would have to do with the different ways in which a person goes about performing the task presented to him. An example of the use of behavior samples for both assessment and experimental purposes is described in the article by Patterson in Part II.

It is widely agreed that the ultimate judgment of the success of personality assessment must be in terms of its validity. Just as a variety of ways can be used to assess behavior, so can a variety of criteria be employed in judging the contribution of assessment techniques to an understanding of behavior. In some situations, deciding upon a criterion poses no problem whatever. For example, in using a score on an attitude questionnaire as a predictor of academic success in college, grade-point average would be an obvious candidate for the job of serving as a criterion of the validity of the questionnaire. Similarly, if we believed that assessed personality characteristics are related to physical health and longevity, these measurable conditions of life would serve as criteria in terms of which our personality measures could be evaluated. (The article by Riegel, Riegel, and Meyer in Part III presents an empirical attempt along these very lines.)

But what if we believed that one of the goals of personality assessment is to predict persons' levels of happiness and adjustment to life? What would our criteria of "happiness" and "adjustment" be? While longevity and health can be measured rather directly and easily, there is no measure of "happiness" that is as simple and reliable as is the measurement of the length of a person's life. Neither "happiness" nor "hostility" nor "anxiety" nor "submissiveness" can be defined in simple operational terms. Since there are no single, easily agreed-upon definitions of these qualities, it is obvious that the validity of any assessment device designed to predict them cannot be determined in a simple and direct way.

Cronbach and Meehl have used the term "construct validity" to refer to the problem of validating an assessment device for which there is no simple criterion available:

> *Construct validation* is involved whenever a test is to be interpreted as a measure of some attribute or quality which is not "operationally defined." The problem faced by the investigator is, "What constructs account for variance in test performance?" Construct validity calls for no new scientific approach. . . . A construct is some postulated attribute of people, assumed

to be reflected in test performance. In test validation the attribute about which we make statements in interpreting a test is a construct. We expect a person at any time to possess or not possess a qualitative attribute (amnesia) or structure, or to possess some degree of a quantitative attribute (cheerfulness). A construct has certain associated meanings carried in statements of this general character: Persons who possess this attribute will, in situation X, act in manner Y (with a stated probability). The logic of construct validation is invoked whether the construct is highly systematized or loose, used in ramified theory or a few simple propositions, used in absolute propositions or probability statements.

. . . An admissible psychological construct must be behavior relevant. For most tests intended to measure constructs, adequate criteria do not exist. This being the case, many such tests have been left unvalidated, or a finespun network of rationalizations has been offered as if it were validation. Rationalization is not construct validation. One who claims that his test reflects a construct cannot maintain his claim in the face of recurrent negative results because these results show that his construct is too loosely defined to yield verifiable inferences.

A rigorous (though perhaps probabilistic) chain of inferences is required to establish a test as a measure of a construct. . . . When a construct is fairly new, there may be few specifiable associations by which to pin down the concept. As research proceeds, the construct sends out roots in many directions, which attach it to more and more facts or other constructs. (Cronbach, L. J., and Meehl, P. E. Construct validity in psychological tests. *Psychological Bulletin,* 1955, Vol. 52, 281–302.)

Personality assessment is not an activity for the fainthearted. The personality assessor must be technique-oriented, in the sense of being aware of the methodology involved in developing measures of individuality; construct-oriented, in that he is concerned with the degree to which the techniques he develops are related to meaningful concepts and events; and payoff-oriented, in that he wishes to show the relevance of his assessment approach to the understanding of human behavior. The articles of Part I have been selected to reflect efforts and issues in the above three areas which are currently at the forefront in the field of personality assessment.

Were personal characteristics always definable and directly observable, personality research could be more easily conducted but it would be much less interesting and challenging. While the personality assessor does make use of direct factual information such as a person's work history, his physical characteristics, and his family constellation, he usually perceives, as Cronbach and Meehl point out, the necessity for reference to internal events as well. These internal events may be referred to as traits, response tendencies, or habits; but regardless of the particular semantic terms employed, they require validation.

The paper by Allport comes to grips with the basic problem of developing a vocabulary of personality. It emphasizes the inferential quality of attributes uncovered in the process of personality assessment. Allport's contribution represents a plea for balance between too much timidity in recognizing the reality of the internal life of the individual and uncritical acceptance of the reality of internal events such as traits and motives. In the course of his quest for balance, Allport raises two important questions: (1) How many traits or constructs must be hypothesized to describe adequately the life of a person? and (2) Should traits be regarded as primarily motivational in character?

Many personality researchers, along with Allport, feel a need to better delineate underlying attributes of persons. Among these researchers are those factor analysts who operate within the framework of a particular statistical methodology. This methodology has been used in an effort to describe complex events in terms of the smallest number of variables or factors required for the task. One widely employed use of factor analysis is to determine the minimum number of variables in terms of which persons' responses to psychological tests and inventories can be explained. Another use of factor analysis is in analyzing very general concepts into their specific components, e.g., the concept of intelligence has often been used to describe a wide diversity of abilities. With factor analysis, it becomes possible to move from an indefinite notion of general intelligence to explicit intellective factors or components such as verbal ability, conceptual ability, and visual-motor ability. It is necessary to bear in mind, however, that the success of such an analytical job depends upon the quality of the data under study. Thus, unreliable and fuzzy data will not result in psychologically meaningful relationships no matter how sophisticated the statistical treatment to which they are subjected.

Considerable advanced training is required to master and use the methodological intricacies of factor analysis. For our purposes, it is sufficient to be aware in a general way of what factor analysis can do for the personality researcher.

One of the questions that might be asked is: What is the smallest number of independent factors in which responses to a personality questionnaire, such as the true-false Minnesota Multiphasic Personality Inventory (MMPI), can be described? In carrying out a factor analysis, a researcher usually begins with a large number of responses. These responses are intercorrelated and the resulting correlations are factor analyzed. The products of this procedure are clusters of items which cohere. These clusters are called factors. Factors can be treated as independent variables with which other variables can be correlated. But even when he has derived his factors, the researcher's work has just begun. He must then proceed to the task of establishing validity and the relationship of his factors to significant aspects of behavior.

One factor analyst, Guilford, has especially addressed himself to the possible application of factor analysis to a variety of psychological domains. His approach is based on the assumptions that (1) personality may be defined in terms of individual differences and (2) factor analysis is not simply a statistical procedure for determining which of the items in an inventory or questionnaire go together. The following comments by Guilford suggest the point of view of the factor analyst:

. . . the traditional experimentalist focuses his interest upon stimulus-response relationships. The stimulus-response model is basic to his thinking and to his planning of investigations. The factorist, on the other hand, directs his attention primarily upon responses and the concomitances among responses. From the intercorrelation of response values the factorist looks for signs of traits, not for stimulus-response relations. Traits are properties of individuals. To the student of personality, their determination of behavior is just as real a phenomenon as the determination by stimuli. Some experimentalists are now recognizing this general principle, as indicated in studies of the relation of characteristic anxiety levels to various measured effects in behavior. In such an experiment, one independent variable is not a stimulus variable or even a transitory personal variable such as a mental set. It is individual differences on an enduring attribute, in other words a trait.

. . . In the context of personality theory, a trait is any relatively enduring way in which one person differs from others. On a scalable trait, which can be represented by a straight line, each person has a characteristic position. If individuals have different positions on a common scale, the scale represents some quality or property that each person possesses to some degree, in common with other persons. If the quality is a unique one, such as may be discovered by factor analysis, it is some significant component of the individual's constitution. . . .

In one sense, factor analysis is analogous to the atomic physicist's cloud-chamber procedures. The physicist draws a conclusion regarding things that he cannot observe, from observed events remotely connected with them. From such scattered sources of observation he builds up a model of the atom and of its nucleus. From test scores and the ways in which they are interrelated, the factor analyst constructs conceptions of human nature. The one seems as objective as the other. (Guilford, J. P., Factorial angles to psychology, *Psychological Review,* 1961, Vol. 68, pp. 1–20.)

The article by Smith provides an interesting illustration of the application of factor analysis to problems of personality. Smith's research is concerned with such questions as: What can personality assessment contribute to describing the Peace Corps volunteer? Can personality assessment provide a means of measuring the impact of involvement in the Peace Corps on the individual?

Smith's study of Peace Corps volunteers in Ghana made use of a variety of assessment techniques. One of these was factor analysis. Another was the Q-sort. A Q-sort usually begins with a collection of statements or items. Each statement might be typed on a card and the cards arranged in a deck. A subject or "judge" is asked to read the statements and to sort them according to some rule which prescribes how many statements may be placed in a particular pile. There might be nine piles into which the subject is asked to sort statements. If the sorting were to approximate a normal distribution, the subject would be free to place many items in the middle piles but very few in the extreme ones. The Q-sorts can be used in a variety of dimensions, e.g., the subject could be asked to sort a collection of statements in terms of how characteristic the statements are of himself, or of some other person. Smith's research used selected judges who sorted statements which they thought were descriptive of Peace Corps volunteers. The judges' sorts were based on careful study of tape-recorded interviews conducted with Peace Corps volunteers. Smith's study illustrates the application of factor analysis to quantitative measures of personality derived from interviews.

Researchers in personality assessment have made valuable applications of their current methods to many types of problems. They are, however, continually concerned with perfecting and better understanding these methods. Meehl and Edwards, in their papers, illustrate the relevance of methodological investigations to broader issues surrounding the concept of personality. These writers have worked extensively on problems which deal with the nature of an important assessment vehicle, the paper and pencil questionnaire.

Meehl's first paper is directed against a too rigid dichotomy between tightly organized or structured and less tightly organized or unstructured instruments. An example of the former would be the MMPI and, an example of the latter would be the Rorschach inkblots. Meehl does not deny the differences between these two methods of assessment, but he does point out that questionnaire assessment devices may not be quite as structured as some would imagine them to be. While the items on the MMPI are answered by either true or false, these items may nevertheless have important projective aspects. The subject's answers may be viewed not so much as direct responses to items written in a test booklet, but rather as products of his interpretation of the meanings of the items. Meehl's comments represent a caution to a simplistic interpretation of the "simple" true-false item, and raise questions about the oft-made distinction between so-called objective (paper and pencil) and projective tests.

Fisher has recently complemented Meehl's analyses of objective tests with an analysis of projective techniques. It is interesting that while Meehl's identification has been primarily with paper and pencil devices, Fisher's has been primarily with projective techniques. Responding to the diversity of methods which have been labeled "projective tests," Fisher has commented:

> There has been continuing uneasiness about how to include under one rubric measures which range from perceptual to motor, responses that vary from spontaneous to those elicited by direct questioning, interpretative frameworks which argue opposingly for the paramount importance of the form versus the content of the response, and orientations which see validity only in patterned interpretation of responses as contrasted to views that the future of projective tests depends upon isolating simply unidimensional variables. The diversity is so great that it is not an exaggeration to say that some "projective tests" resemble the MMPI more than they do other "projective tests." . . . It is intriguing that most of the hard questions which have been raised about projective tests have turned out to apply equally well to the class of so-called "objective" personality tests. For example, the oft repeated criticism that we do not know the source or level of the response elicited by a projective stimulus is now obviously mirrored in our realization that we do not know what level of response is tapped by "straightforward" questions found in the average "paper and pencil" inventory. Problems of social desirability, lying, and acquiescence have dramatized this fact forcefully. It is doubtful whether in

the long run there will be much profit in assuming that the problems facing the development of projective tests are fundamentally different from those encountered in fashioning any class of techniques for measuring personality traits and sets. The apparently simpler and less complicated conditions of measurement obtaining for "objective tests" have proven to be largely illusory. (Fisher, S. Projective methodologies. In P. R. Farnsworth, O. McNemar and Q. McNemar [Eds.] *Annual Review of Psychology,* Vol. 18, 1967, pp. 165–190.)

Meehl in his article also cautions against the temptation to make interpretations about personality from an individual's response to a particular item. The caution grows out of a conception of personality tests which has attained some influence. This is the view that interpretation of scores on particular scales should be based on statistical expectancies rather than on inferred meanings of particular items. Thus, employing this conception, one might compare an undiagnosed person's scores on the Schizophrenia scale of the MMPI with the scores of known schizophrenics. The statistical similarity of the individual to particular reference groups, and not his responses to discrete items, determines inferences about him. Users of this statistical approach feel that it makes the question of the "correctness" or "truth" of a person's answers an irrelevant one. On the other hand, many psychological tests have been based on the assumption that the individual is capable of responding accurately to appropriately written items.

Edwards' empirical study of the relationship between judged desirability of a trait and the probability that that trait will be endorsed has proved a seminal one. His work (and the work of others) has shown that a person's self-description is a function not only of his own personal characteristics, but also of the way in which a request for self-description is presented to him and interpreted by him. Specifically, in connection with a true-false item, a person may endorse or not endorse an item as a result of his interpretation of the desirability of the characteristic referred to in the item. His endorsement might be quite at variance with the degree to which the individual actually possesses the characteristic referred to in the item. Responding on the basis of the judged social or personality desirability of a particular attribute is one example of what are called response sets and test-taking attitudes. Another example of a set which might influence a person's self-description is the tendency to acquiesce or agree with statements regardless of their actual content.

The research by Jung is, in a sense, a projective test parallel to Edwards' research. Jung asks: What are the determinants of responses to word association stimuli? Just as Edwards suggests that a subject's interpretation of a test item will influence his response to it, Jung suggests, in a review of word association literature, that a subject's perception of the task of word association will influence his verbal behavior. The task of word association, like the true-false questionnaire, has often been regarded as a "simple" one. Jung's article shows the falsity of this view and suggests some directions for increasing an understanding of the word association technique as a personality assessment vehicle. He also demonstrates the valuable contribution which experimental methodology can make to the development and refinement of an assessment technique.

Responses to word association stimuli can be influenced by individual differences among subjects in their ability to associate. They may also be influenced by a variety of nonassociative variables, such as the tester's manner and the way in which the subject is oriented to perform the word association task. These nonassociative variables are especially potent in situations which are ambiguous or unfamiliar to the subject. Thus, reactions to the Rorschach inkblots may be determined as much by the particular situation in which the subject is tested as by underlying trends in his personality. Of especially great relevance is the interpersonal relationship established between the subject and the examiner or tester. Masling has described the roles of situational and interpersonal variables in projective techniques in these terms:

> There is considerable evidence that subjects in an unstructured situation will utilize all available cues to complete their assigned task. The subject in the projective test setting will not only use those cues furnished by the ink blot or picture, but also those supplied by his feelings about the examiner, those furnished by his needs, attitudes and fears, those implied in the instructions, the room, and previous knowledge of the test, and those cues supplied consciously or unconsciously by the experimenter. When the experimenter faces the ambiguous situation of supplying meaning to a series of isolated, discrete responses, he will not only rely on the subject's responses, but also on those cues furnished by his training and theoretical orientation, his own needs and expectations, his feelings about the subject and the constructions he places on the subject's test behavior and attitudes. In short, . . . that the experimenter and the subject behave as we should expect, considering our knowledge of behavior in ambiguous settings.
>
> Thus, the procedure that many clinicians hoped would serve as an X ray proves, on close examination, to function also as a mirror, reflecting impartially the subject, the experimenter, the situation and their interactions. This need not be a cause for despair, except for those who feel that the experimenter and situational influences contaminate a protocol. These influences are not sources of error, however, but indications of adaptation to the task. (Masling, J. The influence of situational and interpersonal variables in projective testing. *Psychological Bulletin,* 1960, Vol. 57, 65–85.)

Most of the Part I articles mentioned thus far have dealt with the conceptual underpinnings and methodology of personality assessment. They leave one with an appreciation of the complexity of the process of describing behavior. We are still far from solutions to many of the methodological and conceptual problems which beset the field of personality. Indeed, one could argue that we are still in the stage of identifying these problems. In addition to the search for better means of assessment, however, personality researchers are also seeking to establish the ends to be obtained from such an assessment.

The value of not becoming so preoccupied with the minutiae of methodology that one loses sight of long-term goals is suggested by Wallace's article. One implication of this article is that the field of personality assessment must go beyond a simple enumeration of the many characteristics of people. It must adopt, Wallace contends, a constructive response-capability conception. This conception permits a close and important linkage between the activities of the assessor and of the therapist. According to it, the assessor can contribute directly to modifying deviant or undesirable behavior by determining new forms of adaptive behavior of which a client may be potentially capable.

This emphasis on the responses of which individuals may be potentially capable seems related to a concept of competence offered by White. As he presents it, competence is not just technical skill; it is also a psychological need to use and acquire capabilities:

> According to Webster, competence means fitness or ability, and the suggested synonyms include capability, capacity, efficiency, proficiency, and skill. It is therefore a suitable word to describe such things as grasping and exploring, crawling and walking, attention and perception, language and thinking, manipulating and changing the surroundings, all of which promote an effective—a competent—interaction with the environment. It is true, of course, that maturation plays a part in all these developments, but this part is heavily overshadowed by learning in all the more complex accomplishments like speech or skilled manipulation. I shall argue that it is necessary to make competence a motivational concept; there is a *competence motivation* as well as competence in its more familiar sense of achieved capacity. The behavior that leads to the building up of effective grasping, handling, and letting go of objects, to take one example, is not random behavior produced by a general overflow of energy. It is directed, selective, and persistent, and it is continued not because it serves primary drives, which indeed it cannot serve until it is almost perfected, but because it satisfied an intrinsic need to deal with the environment. (White, R. W. Motivation reconsidered: The concept of competence. *Psychological Review,* 1959, Vol. 66, 297–333.)

From Wallace's point of view, the assessor's attention should be directed not only to man "as he really is" but also to that "of which he is capable." Wallace reacts strongly against the tendency to see assessment as a vehicle primarily for uncovering an individual's defects, e.g., his complexes and symptoms. It is equally important—indeed, it may prove more important—to focus on human potentiality than on human frailty.

McClelland's work on the need for achievement seems related to Wallace's response-capability conception. McClelland's research began as a rather limited effort to assess the need for achievement in persons. It led to important laboratory efforts at relating scores on a projective measure of need for achievement to performance in a variety of situations. It has culminated in the work reported in the paper presented in Part I.

One inference to be drawn from McClelland's research is that it is important both to assess a person's present level of need for achievement and to delineate the conditions under which it might be possible to influence his motivation to achieve.

It is evident from McClelland's work that one of the positive contributions of personality assessment is its ability to uncover human attributes which can be modified through laboratory and field experiments, e.g., in the case of enhancement of the need for achievement. As McClelland makes clear, personality assessment is not limited to identifying individual difference variables; it can also have a very potent action component.

The paper by Lindzey and the commentary by Meehl bring to the fore an important factor in personality assessment: the role of the assessor or clinician as an integrator of assessment data. Meehl, in 1956, suggested the possibility that a clinician or assessor might not be as reliable or valid a describer or predictor of behavior as a mechanical information storage and retrieval system:

> . . . for a rather wide range of clinical problems involving personality description from tests, the clinical interpreter is a costly middleman who might better be eliminated. An initial layout of research time could result in a cookbook whose recipes would encompass the great majority of psychometric configurations seen in daily work. I am fully aware that the prospect of a "clinical clerk" simply looking up Rorschach pattern number 73 J 10–5 or Multiphasic curve "Halbower Verzeichnis 626" seems very odd and even dangerous. I reassure myself by recalling that the number of phenotypic and genotypic attributes is, after all, finite; and that the number which are ordinarily found attributed or denied even in an extensive sample of psychological reports on patients is actually very limited. A best estimate of a Q-sort placement is surely more informative than a crude "Yes-or-No" decision of low objective confidence. I honestly cannot see, in the case of a *determinate trait domain* and a *specified clinical population,* that there is a serious intellectual problem underlying one's uneasiness. I invite you to consider the possibility that the emotional block we all experience in connection with the cookbook approach could be dissolved simply by trying it out until our daily successes finally get us accustomed to the idea. (Meehl, P. E. Wanted—a good cookbook. *American Psychologist,* 1956, Vol. 11, 263–272.)

How does the individual clinician weigh the various bits of information available to him? What might he have to contribute to describing and predicting the behavior of persons? How might an especially effective clinician compare as a predictor with a purely actuarial or "cookbook" approach? What cognitive processes are involved in the functioning of the human assessment data processor? What can the individual human clinician contribute to the prediction of behavior which is not already contributed by data stored in a computer? Lindzey's research strongly indicates the need for objective inquiry into the role of the assessor in the processes of description and prediction.

Lindzey's and Meehl's articles suggest that the validity of a clinician as a predictor of behavior depends on a number of variables. These include the experience, skill, personality, and set of the clinician, the situation in which he makes his predictions, the data on which he bases his predictions, and the person about whom predictions are to be made. Some therapists are more effective in handling one kind of problem than another and some clinicians may be excellent diagnosticians—but only within a special range of problems.

A crucial question about the human predictor is: What makes for his level of effectiveness? More specifically, how does he go about solving the problem confronting him? We may not be certain at the present time whether valid assessors are artists or orderly scientists. But it is possible to study scientifically the human assessor and such study is of importance, both from practical and theoretical standpoints.

The field of personality assessment appears to be making progress along a number of fronts. One of these is the area with which Lindzey is concerned: the assessor as a variable in the assessment process. As other articles in Part I suggest, progress can be seen as well in the development of assessment techniques and the concepts upon which they are based. The reliable and meaningful description of the personality is becoming a reality.

TRAITS REVISITED *
Gordon W. Allport

Years ago I ventured to present a paper before the Ninth International Congress at New Haven (G. W. Allport, 1931). It was entitled "What Is a Trait of Personality?" For me to return to the same topic on this honorific occasion is partly a sentimental indulgence, but partly too it is a self-imposed task to discover whether during the past 36 years I have learned anything new about this central problem in personality theory.

In my earlier paper I made eight bold assertions. A trait, I said,

1. Has more than nominal existence.
2. Is more generalized than a habit.
3. Is dynamic, or at least determinative, in behavior.
4. May be established empirically.
5. Is only relatively independent of other traits.
6. Is not synonymous with moral or social judgment.

* Reprinted with permission from the American Psychological Association. In *The American Psychologist*, 1966, Vol. 21, pp. 1–10.

7. May be viewed either in the light of the personality which contains it, or in the light of its distribution in the population at large.

To these criteria I added one more:

8. Acts, and even habits, that are inconsistent with a trait are not proof of the nonexistence of the trait.

While these propositions still seem to me defensible they were originally framed in an age of psychological innocence. They now need reexamination in the light of subsequent criticism and research.

CRITICISM OF THE CONCEPT OF TRAIT

Some critics have challenged the whole concept of trait. Carr and Kingsbury (1938) point out the danger of reification. Our initial observation of behavior is only in terms of adverbs of action: John behaves aggressively. Then an adjective creeps in: John has an aggressive disposition. Soon a heavy substantive arrives, like William James' cow on the doormat: John has a trait of aggression. The result is the fallacy of misplaced concreteness.

The general positivist cleanup starting in the 1930s went even further. It swept out (or tried to sweep out) all entities, regarding them as question-begging redundancies. Thus Skinner (1953) writes:

When we say that a man eats *because* he is hungry, smokes a great deal *because* he has the tobacco habit, fights *because* of the instinct of pugnacity, behaves brilliantly *because* of his intelligence, or plays the piano well *because* of his musical ability, we seem to be referring to causes. But on analysis these phrases prove to be merely redundant descriptions [p. 31].

It is clear that this line of attack is an assault not only upon the concept of trait, but upon all intervening variables whether they be conceived in terms of expectancies, attitudes, motives, capacities, sentiments, or traits. The resulting postulate of the "empty organism" is by now familiar to us all, and is the scientific credo of some. Carried to its logical extreme this reasoning would scrap the concept of personality itself—an eventuality that seems merely absurd to me.

More serious, to my mind, is the argument against what Block and Bennett (1955) called "traitology" arising from many studies of the variability of a person's behavior as it changes from situation to situation. Every parent knows that an offspring may be a hellion at home and an angel when he goes visiting. A businessman may be hardheaded in the office and a mere marshmallow in the hands of his pretty daughter.

Years ago the famous experiment by La Piere (1934) demonstrated that an innkeeper's prejudice seems to come and go according to the situation confronting him.

In recent months Hunt (1965) has listed various theories of personality that to his mind require revision in the light of recent evidence. Among them he questions the belief that personality traits are the major sources of behavior variance. He, like Miller (1963), advocates that we shift attention from traits to interactions among people, and look for consistency in behavior chiefly in situationally defined roles. Helson (1964) regards trait as the residual effect of previous stimulation, and thus subordinates it to the organism's present adaptation level.

Scepticism is likewise reflected in many investigations of "person perception." To try to discover the traits residing within a personality is regarded as either naive or impossible. Studies, therefore, concentrate only on the *process* of perceiving or judging, and reject the problem of validating the perception and judgment. (Cf. Tagiuri and Petrullo, 1958.)

Studies too numerous to list have ascribed chief variance in behavior to situational factors, leaving only a mild residue to be accounted for in terms of idosyncratic attitudes and traits. A prime example is Stouffer's study of *The American Soldier* (Stouffer et al., 1949). Differing opinions and preferences are ascribed so far as possible to the GI's age, marital status, educational level, location of residence, length of service, and the like. What remains is ascribed to "attitude." By this procedure personality becomes an appendage to demography (see G. W. Allport, 1950). It is not the integrated structure within the skin that determines behavior, but membership in a group, the person's assigned roles—in short, the prevailing situation. It is especially the sociologists and anthropologists who have this preference for explanations in terms of the "outside structure" rather than the "inside structure" (cf. F. H. Allport, 1955, Ch. 21).

I have mentioned only a few of the many varieties of situationism that flourish today. While not denying any of the evidence adduced I would point to their common error of interpretation. If a child is a hellion at home, an angel outside, he obviously has two contradictory tendencies in his nature, or perhaps a deeper genotype that would explain the opposing phenotypes. If in studies of person perception the process turns out to be complex and subtle, still there would be no perception at all unless there were something out there to perceive and to judge. If, as in Stouffer's studies, soldiers' opinions vary with their marital status or length of service, these opinions are still their own. The fact that my age, sex, social status help form my outlook on life does not change the fact that the outlook is a functioning part of me. Demography deals with distal forces—personality study with proximal forces. The fact that the innkeeper's behavior varies according to whether he is, or is not, physically confronted with Chinese applicants for hospitality tells nothing about his attitude structure, except that it is complex, and that several attitudes may converge into a given act of behavior.

Nor does it solve the problem to explain the variance in terms of statistical interaction effects. Whatever tendencies exist reside in a person, for a person is the sole possessor of the energy that leads to action. Admittedly different situations elicit differing tendencies from my repertoire. I do not perspire except in the heat, nor shiver except in the cold; but the outside temperature is not the mechanism of perspiring or shivering. My capacities and my tendencies lie within.

To the situationist I concede that our theory of traits cannot be so simpleminded as it once was. We are now challenged to untangle the complex web of tendencies that constitute a person, however contradictory they may seem to be when activated differentially in various situations.

ON THE OTHER HAND

In spite of gunfire from positivism and situationism, traits are still very much alive. Gibson (1941) has pointed out that the "concept of set or attitude is nearly universal in psychological thinking." And in an important but neglected paper—perhaps the last he ever wrote—McDougall (1937) argued that *tendencies* are the "indispensable postulates of all psychology." The concept of *trait* falls into this genre. As Walker (1964) says trait, however else defined, always connotes an enduring tendency of some sort. It is the structural counterpart of such functional concepts as "expectancy," and "goal-directedness."

After facing all the difficulties of situational and mood variations, also many of the methodological hazards such as response set, halo, and social desirability, Vernon (1964) concludes, "We could go a long way towards predicting behavior if we could assess these stable features in which people differ from one another [p. 181]." The powerful contributions of Thurstone, Guilford, Cattell, and Eysenck, based on factor analysis, agree that the search for traits should provide eventually a satisfactory taxonomy of personality and of its hierarchical structure. The witness of these and other thoughtful writers helps us withstand the pessimistic attacks of positivism and situationism.

It is clear that I am using "trait" as a generic term, to cover all the "permanent possibilities for action" of a generalized order. Traits are cortical, subcortical, or postural dispositions having the capacity to gate or guide specific phasic reactions. It is only the phasic aspect that is visible; the tonic is carried somehow in the still mysterious realm of neurodynamic structure. Traits, as I am here using the term, include long-range sets and attitudes, as well as such variables as "perceptual response dispositions," "personal constructs," and "cognitive styles."

Unlike McClelland (1951) I myself would regard traits (i.e., some traits) as motivational (others being merely stylistic). I would also insist that traits may be studied at two levels: (*a*) dimensionally, that is, as an aspect of the psychology of individual differences, and (*b*) individually, in terms of *personal dispositions*. (Cf. G. W. Allport, 1961, Ch. 15.) It is the latter approach that brings us closest to the person we are studying.

As for factors, I regard them as a mixed blessing. In the investigations I shall soon report, factorial analysis, I find, has proved both helpful and unhelpful. My principal question is whether the factorial unit is idiomatic enough to reflect the structure of personality as the clinician, the counselor, or the man in the street apprehends it. Or are factorial dimensions screened so extensively and so widely attenuated—through item selection, correlation, axis manipulation, homogenization, and alphabetical labeling—that they impose an artifact of method upon the personal neural network as it exists in nature?

A HEURISTIC REALISM

This question leads me to propose an epistemological position for research in personality. Most of us, I suspect, hold this position although we seldom formulate it even to ourselves. It can be called a *heuristic realism*.

Heuristic realism, as applied to our problem, holds that the person who confronts us possesses inside his skin generalized action tendencies (or traits) and that it is our job scientifically to discover what they are. Any form of realism assumes the existence of an external structure ("out there") regardless of our shortcomings in comprehending it. Since traits, like all intervening variables, are never directly observed but only inferred, we must expect difficulties and errors in the process of discovering their nature.

The incredible complexity of the structure we seek to understand is enough to discourage the realist, and to tempt him to play some form of positivistic gamesmanship. He is tempted to settle for such elusive formulations as: "If we knew enough about the situation we wouldn't need the concept of personality"; or "One's personality is merely the way other people see one"; or "There is no structure in personality but only varying degrees of consistency in the environment."

Yet the truly persistent realist prefers not to abandon his commitment to find out what the other fellow is really like. He knows that his attempt will not wholly succeed, owing partly to the complexity of the object studied, and partly to the inadequacy of present methods. But unlike Kant who held that the *Ding an Sich* is doomed to remain unknowable, he prefers to believe that it is at least partly or approximately knowable.

I have chosen to speak of *heuristic* realism, because to me special emphasis should be placed on empirical methods of discovery. In this respect heuristic realism goes beyond naive realism.

Taking this epistemological point of view, the psychologist first focuses his attention on some limited slice of personality that he wishes to study. He then selects or creates methods appropriate to the empirical testing of his hypothesis that the cleavage he has in mind is a trait (either a dimensional trait or a personal disposition). He knows that his present purposes and the methods chosen will set limitations upon his discovery. If, however, the investigation achieves acceptable standards of validation he will have progressed far toward his identification of traits. Please note, as with any heuristic procedure the process of discovery may lead to important corrections of the hypothesis as originally stated.

Empirical testing is thus an important aspect of heuristic realism, but it is an empiricism restrained throughout by rational considerations. Galloping empiricism, which is our present occupational disease, dashes forth like a headless horseman. It has no rational objective; uses no rational method other than mathematical; reaches no rational conclusion. It lets the discordant data sing for themselves. By contrast heuristic realism says, "While we are willing to rest our case for traits on empirical evidence, the area we carve out for study should be rationally conceived, tested by rational methods; and the findings should be rationally interpreted."

THREE ILLUSTRATIVE STUDIES

It is now time for me to illustrate my argument with sample studies. I have chosen three in which I myself have been involved. They differ in the areas of personality carved out for study, in the methods employed, and in the type of traits established. They are alike, however, in proceeding from the standpoint of heuristic realism. The presentation of each study must of necessity be woefully brief. The first illustrates what might be called *meaningful dimensionalism;* the second *meaningful covariation;* the third *meaningful morphogenesis.*

Dimensions of Values

The first illustration is drawn from a familiar instrument, dating almost from the stone age, *The Study of Values* (Allport & Vernon, 1931). While some of you have approved it over the years, and some disapproved, I use it to illustrate two important points of my argument.

First, the instrument rests on an a priori analysis of one large region of human personality, namely, the region of generic evaluative tendencies. It seemed to me 40 years ago, and seems to me now, that Eduard Spranger (1922) made a persuasive case for the existence of six funda-

TABLE 1

MEAN SCORES FOR OCCUPATIONAL GROUPS OF WOMEN: STUDY OF VALUES

	Female collegiate norms $N = 2,475$	Graduate nurses training for teaching $N = 328$	Graduate students of business administration $N = 77$	Peace Corps teachers $N = 131$
Theoretical	36.5	40.2	37.3	40.6
Economic	36.8	32.9	40.4	29.9
Esthetic	43.7	43.1	46.8	49.3
Social	41.6	40.9	35.0	41.2
Political	38.0	37.2	41.8	39.7
Religious	43.1	45.7	38.7	39.2

mental types of subjective evaluation or *Lebensformen.* Adopting this rational starting point we ourselves took the second step, to put the hypothesis to empirical test. We asked: Are the six dimensions proposed—the *theoretic,* the *economic,* the *esthetic, social, political,* and *religious*—measurable on a multidimensional scale? Are they reliable and valid? Spranger defined the six ways of looking at life in terms of separate and distinct ideal types, although he did not imply that a given person belongs exclusively to one and only one type.

It did not take long to discover that when confronted with a forced-choice technique people do in fact subscribe to all six values, but in widely varying degrees. Within any pair of values, or any quartet of values, their forced choices indicate a reliable pattern. Viewed then as empirical continua, rather than as types, the six value directions prove to be measurable, reproducible, and consistent. But are they valid? Can we obtain external validation for this particular a priori conception of traits? The test's *Manual* (Allport & Vernon, 1931) contains much such evidence. Here I would add a bit more, drawn from occupational studies with women subjects. (The evidence for men is equally good.) The data in Table 1 are derived partly from the *Manual,* partly from Guthrie and McKendry (1963) and partly from an unpublished study by Elizabeth Moses.

For present purposes it is sufficient to glance at the last three columns. For the *theoretic* value we note that the two groups of teachers or teachers in preparation select this value significantly more often than do graduate students of business administration. Conversely the young ladies of business are relatively more *economic* in their choices. The results for the *esthetic* value probably reflect the higher level of liberal arts background for the last two groups. The *social* (philanthropic) value is relatively low for the business group, whereas the *political* (power) value is relatively high. Just why nurses should more often endorse the *religious* value is not immediately clear.

Another study of external validation, showing the long-range predictive power of the test is an unpublished investigation by Betty Mawardi. It is based on a follow-up of Wellesley graduates 15 years after taking the Study of Values.

Table 2 reports the significant deviations (at the 5% level or better) of various occupational groups

workers in *esthetic;* social workers in *social;* and religious workers in *religious* values.

One must remember that to achieve a relatively high score on one value, one must deliberately slight others. For this reason it is interesting to note in the table the values that are systematically slighted in order to achieve a higher score on the occupationally relevant value. (In the case of social workers it appears that they "take away" more or less uniformly from other values in order to achieve a high social value.)

Thus, even at the college age it is possible to forecast in a general way modal vocational activity 15 years hence. As Newcomb, Turner, and Converse (1965) say, this test clearly deals with "inclusive values" or with "basic value postures" whose generality is strikingly broad. An evaluative posture toward life saturates, or guides, or gates (choose your own metaphor) specific daily choices over a long expanse of years.

One reason I have used this illustration of trait research is to raise an important methodological issue. The six values are not wholly independent. There is a slight tendency for theoretic and esthetic values to covary; likewise for economic and political values; and so too with social and religious. Immediately the thought arises, "Let's factor the whole matrix and see what orthogonal dimensions emerge." This step has been taken several times (see *Manual*); but always with confusing results.

TABLE 2

SIGNIFICANT DEVIATIONS OF SCORES ON THE STUDY OF VALUES FOR OCCUPATIONAL GROUPS OF WELLESLEY ALUMNI FROM WELLESLEY MEAN SCORES

Occupational groups	N	Theoretical	Economic	Esthetic	Social	Political	Religious
Business workers	64	Lower	Higher				
Medical workers	42	Higher	Lower			Lower	
Literary workers	40	Higher	Lower	Higher			
Artistic workers	37			Higher	Lower		
Scientific workers	28	Higher		Lower			
Government workers	24	Higher			Lower		Lower
Social workers	26				Higher		
Religious workers	11					Lower	Higher

from the mean scores of Wellesley students. In virtually every case we find the deviation meaningful (even necessary) for the occupation in question. Thus women in business are significantly high in *economic* interests; medical, government, and scientific workers in *theoretical;* literary and artistic

Some investigators discover that fewer than six factors are needed—some that we need more. And in all cases the clusters that emerge seem strange and unnamable. Here is a case, I believe, where our empiricism should submit to rational restraint. The traits as defined are meaningful, reliably measured, and validated. Why sacrifice them to galloping gamesmanship?

Covariation: Religion and Prejudice

Speaking of covariation I do not mean to imply that in restraining our empirical excesses we should fail to explore the patterns that underlie covariation when it seems reasonable to do so.

Take, for example, the following problem. Many investigations show conclusively that on the broad average church attenders harbor more ethnic prejudice than nonattenders. (Some of the relevant studies are listed by Argyle, 1959, and by Wilson, 1960.) At the same time many ardent workers for civil rights are religiously motivated. From Christ to Gandhi and to Martin Luther King we note that equimindedness has been associated with religious devoutness. Here then is a paradox: Religion makes prejudice; it also unmakes prejudice.

First we tackle the problem rationally and form a hypothesis to account for what seems to be a curvilinear relation. A hint for the needed hypothesis comes from *The Authoritarian Personality* (Adorno, Frenkel-Brunswik, Levinson, and Sanford, 1950) which suggests that acceptance of institutional religion is not as important as the *way* in which it is accepted. Argyle (1959) sharpens the hypothesis. He says, "It is not the genuinely devout who are prejudiced but the conventionally religious [p. 84]."

In our own studies we have tentatively assumed that two contrasting but measurable forms of religious orientation exist. The first form we call the *extrinsic* orientation, meaning that for the churchgoer religious devotion is not a value in its own right, but is an instrumental value serving the motives of personal comfort, security, or social status. (One man said he went to church because it was the best place to sell insurance.) Elsewhere I have defined this utilitarian orientation toward religion more fully (G. W. Allport, 1960, 1963). Here I shall simply mention two items from our scale, agreement with which we assume indicates the extrinsic attitude:

What religion offers me most is comfort when sorrows and misfortune strike.

One reason for my being a church member is that such membership helps to establish a person in the community.

By contrast the *intrinsic* orientation regards faith as a supreme value in its own right. Such faith

strives to transcend self-centered needs, takes seriously the commandment of brotherhood that is found in all religions, and seeks a unification of being. Agreement with the following items indicates an intrinsic orientation:

My religious beliefs are what really lie behind my whole approach to life.

If not prevented by unavoidable circumstances, I attend church, on the average (more than once a week) (once a week) (two or three times a month) (less than once a month).

TABLE 3

CORRELATIONS BETWEEN MEASURES OF RELIGIOUS ORIENTATION AMONG CHURCHGOERS AND VARIOUS PREJUDICE SCALES

Denominational sample	N	r
Unitarian	50	
Extrinsic—anti-Catholicism		.56
Intrinsic—anti-Catholicism		−.36
Extrinsic—anti-Mexican		.54
Intrinsic—anti-Mexican		−.42
Catholic	66	
Extrinsic—anti-Negro		.36
Intrinsic—anti-Negro		−.49
Nazarene	39	
Extrinsic—anti-Negro		.41
Intrinsic—anti-Negro		−.44
Mixed[a]	207	
Extrinsic—anti-Semitic		.65

[a] From Wilson (1960).

This second item is of considerable interest, for many studies have found that it is the irregular attenders who are by far the most prejudiced (e.g., Holtzmann, 1956; Williams, 1964). They take their religion in convenient doses and do not let it regulate their lives.

Now for a few illustrative results in Table 3. If we correlate the extrinsicness of orientation with various prejudice scales we find the hypothesis confirmed. Likewise, as predicted, intrinsicness of orientation is negatively correlated with prejudice.

In view of the difficulty of tapping the two complex traits in question, it is clear from these studies that our rationally derived hypothesis gains strong support. We note that the trend is the same when different denominations are studied in relation to differing targets for prejudice.

Previously I have said that empirical testing has the ability to correct or extend our rational analysis of patterns. In this particular research the following unexpected fact emerges. While those who approach the intrinsic pole of our continuum are on the average less prejudiced than those who approach the extrinsic pole, a number of subjects show themselves to be disconcertingly illogical. They accept both intrinsically worded items and extrinsically worded items, even when these are contradictory, such as:

My religious beliefs are what really lie behind my whole approach to life.

Though I believe in my religion, I feel there are many more important things in my life.

It is necessary, therefore, to inspect this sizable group of muddleheads who refuse to conform to our neat religious logic. We call them "inconsistently proreligious." They simply like religion; for them it has "social desirability" (cf. Edwards, 1957).

The importance of recognizing this third mode of religious orientation is seen by comparing the prejudice scores for the groups presented in Table 4. In the instruments employed the lowest possible prejudice score is 12, the highest possible, 48. We note that the mean prejudice score rises steadily and significantly from the intrinsically consistent to the inconsistently proreligious. Thus subjects with an undiscriminated proreligious response set are on the average most prejudiced of all.

Having discovered the covariation of prejudice with both the extrinsic orientation and the "pro"

TABLE 4

TYPES OF RELIGIOUS ORIENTATION AND
MEAN PREJUDICE SCORES

	Mean prejudice scores			
	Consistently intrinsic	Consistently extrinsic	Moderately inconsistent (proreligion)	Extremely inconsistent (proreligion)
Anti-Negro	28.7	33.0	35.4	37.9
Anti-Semitic	22.6	24.6	28.0	30.1

Note.—N = 309, mixed denominations. All differences significant at .01 level.

response set, we are faced with the task of rational explanation. One may, I think, properly argue that

these particular religious attitudes are instrumental in nature; they provide safety, security, and status —all within a self-serving frame. Prejudice, we know, performs much the same function within some personalities. The needs for status, security, comfort, and a feeling of self-rightness are served by both ethnic hostility and by tailoring one's religious orientation to one's convenience. The economy of other lives is precisely the reverse: It is their religion that centers their existence, and the only ethnic attitude compatible with this intrinsic orientation is one of brotherhood, not of bigotry.

This work, along with the related investigations of Lenski (1963), Williams (1964), and others, signifies that we gain important insights when we refine our conception of the nature of the religious sentiment and its functions. Its patterning properties in the economy of a life are diverse. It can fuse with bigotry or with brotherhood according to its nature.

As unfinished business I must leave the problem of nonattenders. From data available it seems that the unchurched are less prejudiced on the average than either the extrinsic or the inconsistent churchgoers, although apparently more prejudiced on the average than those who religious orientation is intrinsic. Why this should be so must form the topic of future research.

Personal Dispositions: An Idiomorphic Approach

The final illustration of heuristic realism has to do with the search for the natural cleavages that mark an individual life. In this procedure there is no reference to common dimensions, no comparison with other people, except as is implied by the use of the English language. If, as Allport and Odbert (1936) have found, there are over 17,000 available trait names, and if these may be used in combinations, there is no real point in arguing that the use of the available lexicon of a language necessarily makes all trait studies purely nomothetic (dimensional).

A series of 172 published *Letters from Jenny* (G. W. Allport, 1965) contains enough material for a rather close clinical characterization of Jenny's personality, as well as for careful quantitative and computational analysis. While there is no possibility in this case of obtaining external validation for the diagnosis reached by either method, still by employing both procedures an internal agreement is found which constitutes a type of empirical validation for the traits that emerge.

The *clinical* method in this case is close to common sense. Thirty-nine judges listed the essential characteristics of Jenny as they saw them. The result was a series of descriptive adjectives, 198 in number. Many of the selected trait names were obviously synonymous; and nearly all fell readily into eight clusters.

The *quantitative* analysis consisted of coding the letters in terms of 99 tag words provided by the lexicon of the General Inquirer (Stone, Bales, Namenwirth, and Ogilvie, 1962). The frequency with which these basic tag words are associated with one another in each letter forms the basis for a factor analysis (see G. W. Allport, 1965, p. 200).

Table 5 lists in parallel fashion the clusters obtained by clinical judgment based on a careful reading of the series, along with the factors obtained by Jeffrey Paige in his unpublished factorial study.

In spite of the differences in terminology the general paralleling of the two lists establishes some

TABLE 5

CENTRAL TRAITS IN JENNY'S PERSONALITY AS
DETERMINED BY TWO METHODS

Common-sense traits	Factorial traits
Quarrelsome-suspicious ⎫	
Aggressive ⎭	Aggression
Self-centered (possessive)	Possessiveness
Sentimental	⎧Need for affiliation
	⎩Need for family acceptance
Independent-autonomous	Need for autonomy
Esthetic-artistic	Sentience
Self-centered (self-pitying)	Martyrdom
(No parallel)	Sexuality
Cynical-morbid	(No parallel)
Dramatic-intense	("Overstate")

degree of empirical check on both of them. We can say that the direct common-sense perception of Jenny's nature is validated by quantification, coding, and factoring. (Please note that in this case factor analysis does not stand alone, but is tied to a parallel rational analysis.)

While this meaningful validation is clearly present, we gain (as almost always) additional insights from our attempts at empirical validation of the traits we initially hypothesize. I shall point to one instance of such serendipity. The tag words (i.e., the particular coding system employed) are chiefly substantives. For this reason, I suspect, *sexuality*

can be identified by coding as a minor factor; but it is not perceived as an independent quality by the clinical judges. On the other hand, the judges, it seems, gain much from the running style of the letters. Since the style is constant it would not appear in a factorial analysis which deals only with variance within the whole. Thus the common-sense traits *cynical-morbid* and *dramatic-intense* are judgments of a pervading expressive style in Jenny's personality and seem to be missed by factoring procedure.

Here, however, the computer partially redeems itself. Its program assigns the tag "overstate" to strong words such as *always, never, impossible,* etc., while words tagged by "understate" indicate reserve, caution, qualification. Jenny's letters score exceedingly high on overstate and exceedingly low on understate, and so in a skeletonized way the method does in part detect the trait of dramatic intensity.

One final observation concerning this essentially idiomorphic trait study. Elsewhere I have reported a small investigation (G. W. Allport, 1958) showing that when asked to list the "essential characteristics" of some friend, 90% of the judges employ between 3 and 10 trait names, the average number being 7.2. An "essential characteristic" is defined as "any trait, quality, tendency, interest, that you regard as of major importance to a description of the person you select." There is, I submit, food for thought in the fact that in these two separate studies of Jenny, the common-sense and the factorial, only 8 or 9 central traits appear. May it not be that the essential traits of a person are few in number if only we can identify them?

The case of Jenny has another important bearing on theory. In general our besetting sin in personality study is irrelevance, by which I mean that we frequently impose dimensions upon persons when the dimensions fail to apply. (I am reminded of the student who was told to interview women patients concerning their mothers. One patient said that her mother had no part in her problem and no influence on her life; but that her aunt was very important. The student answered, "I'm sorry, but our method requires that you tell about your mother." The *method* required it, but the *life* did not.)

In ascribing a list of traits to Jenny we may seem to have used a dimensional method, but such is not the case. Jenny's traits emerge from her own personal structure. They are not imposed by predetermined but largely irrelevant schedules.

CONCLUSION

What then have I learned about traits in the last 4 decades? Well, I have learned that the problem cannot be avoided—neither by escape through positivism or situationism, nor through statistical interaction effects. Tendencies, as McDougall (1937) insisted, remain the "indispensable postulates of all psychology."

Further, I have learned that much of our research on traits is overweighted with methodological preoccupation; and that we have too few restraints holding us to the structure of a life as it is lived. We find ourselves confused by our intemperate empiricism which often yields unnamable factors, arbitrary codes, unintelligible interaction effects, and sheer flatulence from our computers.

As a safeguard I propose the restraints of "heuristic realism" which accepts the common-sense assumption that persons are real beings, that each has a real neuropsychic organization, and that our jobs is to comprehend this organization as well as we can. At the same time our profession uniquely demands that we go beyond common-sense data and either establish their validity or else—more frequently—correct their errors. To do so requires that we be guided by theory in selecting our trait slices for study, that we employ rationally relevant methods, and be strictly bound by empirical verification. In the end we return to fit our findings to an improved view of the person. Along the way we regard him as an objectively real being whose tendencies we can succeed in knowing—at least in part—beyond the level of unaided common sense. In some respects this recommended procedure resembles what Cronbach and Meehl (1955) call "construct validation," with perhaps a dash more stress on external validation.

I have also learned that while the major foci of organization in a life may be few in number, the network of organization, which includes both minor and contradictory tendencies, is still elusively complex.

One reason for the complexity, of course, is the need for the "inside" system to mesh with the "outside" system—in other words, with the situation. While I do not believe that traits can be defined in terms of interaction effects (since all tendencies draw their energy from within the person), still the vast variability of behavior cannot be overlooked. In this respect I have learned that my earlier views seemed to neglect the variability induced by ecological, social, and situational factors. This oversight needs to be repaired through an adequate theory that will relate the inside and outside systems more accurately.

The fact that my three illustrative studies are so diverse in type leads me to a second concession: that trait studies depend in part upon the investigator's own purposes. He himself constitutes a situation for his respondents, and what he obtains from them will be limited by his purpose and his method. But this fact need not destroy our belief that, so far as our method and purpose allow, we can elicit real tendencies.

Finally, there are several problems connected with traits that I have not here attempted to revisit. There are, for example, refinements of difference between trait, attitude, habit, sentiment, need, etc. Since these are all inside tendencies of some sort, they are for the present occasion all "traits" to me. Nor am I here exploring the question to what extent traits are motivational, cognitive, affective, or expressive. Last of all, and with special restraint, I avoid hammering on the distinction between common (dimensional, nomothetic) traits such as we find in any standard profile, and individual traits (personal dispositions) such as we find in single lives, e.g., Jenny's. (Cf. G. W. Allport, 1961, Ch. 15, also 1962.) Nevitt Sanford (1963) has written that by and large psychologists are "unimpressed" by my insisting on this distinction. Well, if this is so in spite of 4 decades of labor on my part, and in spite of my efforts in the present paper—I suppose I should in all decency cry "uncle" and retire to my corner.

REFERENCES

Adorno, T. W., Frenkel-Brunswik, Else, Levinson, D. J., and Sanford, R. N. *The authoritarian personality.* New York: Harper, 1950.

Allport, F. H. *Theories of perception and the concept of structure.* New York: Wiley, 1955.

Allport, G. W. What is a trait of personality? *Journal of Abnormal and Social Psychology,* 1931, 25: 368–372.

Allport, G. W. Review of S. A. Stouffer et al., *The American soldier. Journal of Abnormal and Social Psychology,* 1950, 45: 168–172.

Allport, G. W. What units shall we employ? In G. Lindzey (Ed.), *Assessment of human motives.* New York: Rinehart, 1958.

Allport, G. W. Religion and prejudice. In *Personality and social encounter.* Boston: Beacon Press, 1960. Ch. 16.

Allport, G. W. *Pattern and growth in personality.* New York: Holt, Rinehart and Winston, 1961.

Allport, G. W. The general and the unique in psychological science. *Journal of Personality,* 1962, 30: 405–422.

Allport, G. W. Behavioral science, religion and mental health. *Journal of Religion and Health,* 1963, 2: 187–197.

Allport, G. W. (Ed.) *Letters from Jenny.* New York: Harcourt, Brace and World, 1965.

Allport, G. W., and Odbert, H. S. Trait-names: A psycholexical study. *Psychological Monographs,* 1936, 47: (1, Whole No. 211).

Allport, G. W., and Vernon, P. E. *A Study of values.* Boston: Houghton-Mifflin, 1931. (Reprinted: With G. Lindzey, 3rd ed., 1960.)

Argyle, M. *Religious behaviour.* Glencoe, Ill.: Free Press, 1959.

Block, J., and Bennett, Lillian. The assessment of communication. *Human Relations,* 1955, 8: 317–325.

Carr, H. A., and Kingsbury, F. A. The concept of trait. *Psychological Review,* 1938, 45: 497–524.

Cronbach, L. J., and Meehl, P. E. Construct validity in psychological tests. *Psychological Bulletin,* 1955, 52: 281–302.

Edwards, A. L. *The social desirability variable in personality assessment and research.* New York: Dryden Press, 1957.

Gibson, J. J. A critical review of the concept of set in contemporary experimental psychology. *Psychological Bulletin,* 1941, 38: 781–817.

Guthrie, G. M., and McKendry, Margaret S. Interest patterns of Peace Corps volunteers in a teaching project. *Journal of Educational Psychology,* 1963, 54: 261–267.

Helson, H. *Adaptation-level theory.* New York: Harper and Row, 1964.

Holtzman, W. H. Attitudes of college men toward non-segregation in Texas schools. *Public Opinion Quarterly,* 1956, 20: 559–569.

Hunt, J. McV. Traditional personality theory in the light of recent evidence. *American Scientist,* 1965, 53: 80–96.

La Piere, R. Attitudes vs. actions. *Social Forces,* 1934, 230–237.

Lenski, G. *The religious factor.* Garden City, N. Y.: Doubleday, 1961.

McClelland, D. C. *Personality.* New York: Dryden Press, 1951.

McDougall, W. Tendencies as indispensable postulates of all psychology. In, *Proceedings of the XI International Congress on Psychology: 1937.* Paris: Alcan, 1938. Pp. 157–170.

Miller, D. R. The study of social relationships: Situation, identity, and social interaction. In S. Koch (Ed.), *Psychology: A study of a science.* Vol. 5. *The process areas, the person, and some applied fields: Their place in psychology and the social sciences.* New York: McGraw-Hill, 1963. Pp. 639–737.

Newcomb, T. M., Turner, H. H., and Converse, P. E. *Social psychology: The study of human interaction.* New York: Holt, Rinehart and Winston, 1965.

Sanford, N. Personality: Its place in psychology. In S. Koch (Ed.), *Psychology: A study of a science.* Vol. 5. *The process areas, the person, and some applied fields: Their place in psychology and the social sciences.* New York: McGraw-Hill, 1963. Pp. 488–592.

Skinner, B. F. *Science and human behavior.* New York: Macmillan, 1953.

Spranger, E. *Lebensformen.* (3d ed.) Halle: Niemeyer, 1922. (Translated: P. Pigors. *Types of men.* Halle: Niemeyer, 1928.)

Stone, P. J., Bales, R. F., Namenwirth, J. Z., and Ogilvie, D. M. The general inquirer: A computer system for content analysis and retrieval based on the sentence as a unit of information. *Behavioral Science,* 1962, 7: (4), 484–498.

Stouffer, S. A., et al. *The American soldier.* Princeton: Princeton University Press, 1949. 2 vols.

Tagiuri, R., and Petrullo, L. *Person perception and interpersonal behavior.* Stanford: Stanford University Press, 1958.

Vernon, P. E. *Personality assessment: A critical survey.* London: Methuen, 1964.

Walker, E. L. Psychological complexity as a basis for a theory of motivation and choice. In D. Levine (Ed.), *Nebraska symposium on motivation: 1964.* Lincoln: University of Nebraska Press, 1964.

Williams, R. M., Jr. *Strangers next door.* Englewood Cliffs, N. J.: Prentice-Hall, 1964.

Wilson, W. C. Extrinsic religious values and prejudice. *Journal of Abnormal and Social Psychology,* 1960, 60: 286–288.

EXPLORATIONS IN COMPETENCE:
A STUDY OF PEACE CORPS TEACHERS
IN GHANA *
M. Brewster Smith [1]

One of the hopeful aspects of our affluent society—and I persist in believing that there are many—is our increasing concern with psychological effectiveness and fulfillment. Like the hierarchy of needs that Abraham Maslow (1954) has proposed, there seems to be a hierarchy of human goals that underlie fashions of value-oriented research. When people are undernourished and die young, as they still do in much of the world, research and action on public health is the first order of business. Achievements in this initial sphere have brought us to realize belatedly that successful attack on the "underdeveloped syndrome" requires knowledge and action on two additional fronts: economic development, to provide a better livelihood for the growing and now impatient numbers who survive; and population control, lest economic gains dissolve into net losses. Psychologists are beginning to find a challenge for research in the former topic (McClelland, 1965); they have still to rise to the need and the opportunity in regard to the second.

All the same, psychologists are beginning to bring psychological research to bear upon the forms and conditions of more positive aspects of human functioning, under such rubrics as "positive mental health," psychological effectiveness, creativity, and competence. These may still be middle-class luxuries, but it is now politically astute, not merely visionary, to conceive of a "great society" in which such phrasings of the good life become relevant for everybody.

I therefore grasped the opportunity to make an intensive study of a group of promising young people who were faced with a challenging assignment: the first group of Peace Corps volunteers to go overseas, who trained in Berkeley in the summer of 1961 and served for 2 years as secondary school teachers in Ghana.

There were 58 young people who entered training in Berkeley, 50 of whom completed 1 year [2] and 45 completed 2 years of overseas service. Our most intensive data are for 27 men and 17 women who finished the 2-year term. I met my obligations to the Peace Corps with a technical report (Smith, 1964), and since then have been working on a volume that intends to illuminate the statistical findings with a series of illustrative case studies.

Here I must be selective. I shall draw on our findings to develop several themes that represent things I think I have learned about competence in this special Peace Corps setting.

My major points will be four. First, in regard to the nature of competence in this group, time, and setting: Our data support the view that competence has a coherent core of common psychological attributes. But, second, competent performance takes various forms, which people reach by different psychological routes. Third, in regard to the prediction of competent performance: Two reasonable possibilities, grounded in the respective thought patterns of social psychologists and of psychiatrists and clinical psychologists, turn out not to work at all, while a third predictor, introduced on a hunch, shows promise. Both the failures and the relative success have something to say about the psychological nature of competence. Finally, we have some evidence about the maturing effects of Peace Corps service, which lends itself to speculation about motivational aspects of the Peace Corps experience.

* Reprinted and abridged with permission from the American Psychological Association. In *American Psychologist*, 1966, Vol. 21, pp. 555–566.

[1] Invited address, Division 8, American Psychological Association, Chicago, September 1965; written during tenure as Fellow of the Center for Advanced Study in the Behavioral Sciences and Special Research Fellow of the National Institute of Mental Health. The data reported are based on a study at the Institute of Human Development, University of California, Berkeley, under contract No. PC-(W)-55 with the Peace Corps, which of course is not responsible for the opinions and judgments that I have ventured to express. A fuller report of the study will be presented in a book in preparation, to be published by John Wiley and Sons. I am especially indebted to my closest associates in this research, Raphael S. Ezekiel and Susan Roth Sherman; to George Carter, the initial Peace Corps Representative in Ghana; and to the volunteers themselves whose tolerance and hospitality made my research both possible and gratifying.

[2] Their mean age of entry was 24.0 (range, 19–34); subsequent groups averaged about a year younger. Forty-six percent had had a year or more of teaching experience; subsequent groups were less experienced.

FROM FIELD INTERVIEWS TO *Q* SORT PATTERNS

Before I can turn to the first of these topics, a word is needed about the kind of data that we will be dealing with. Of course we had a kit of pencil-and-paper tests, some of them administered both before and after overseas experience. We also had various staff ratings from the training period and from the field. Our central information about the experience and performance of the volunteers, however, came from long and detailed interviews that R. S. Ezekiel and I recorded with the volunteers at their schools in the early summer of 1962 and 1963.

We planned the guide for the first-year interviews on the basis of my quick reconnaisance during the volunteers' first Christmas in Ghana. As it turned out, the roughly 4 hours of interviewing apiece the first year, and 2½ the second, gave a highly informative picture of what the volunteer had made of his job and Peace Corps role and of his qualities as a person as they were brought out in this novel and challenging setting. We were well satisfied with the quality of our interviews. But how to process them to preserve their richness yet assure the maximum degree of objectivity that we could attain?

Our first and crucial decision on behalf of objectivity was made at the onset: to record and transcribe the interviews in full. Following the lead of my colleague Jack Block (1961), we then invested major effort in constructing two decks of *Q* sort items that "judges" could use to extract and quantify the meat of the interview transcripts. One deck, of 65 items in the final version, dealt with the volunteer's role perceptions, personal agenda, and role performance. The second, of 64 items, permitted judges to characterize the volunteer's personality structure and processes.[3] These sets of items were in development over much of a year. Our procedure was to hold "clinical" conferences in the attempt to formulate what the interviews could tell us about the personality and performance of particular volunteers, then to translate our intuitive insights into items.

Once the decks had been refined to our satisfaction, we had 12 advanced graduate students in

[3] A third *Q* deck characterizing the volunteer's view of his situation, its challenges and limitations, and aspects of morale and job satisfaction was also developed; results depending on this deck are drawn upon in the larger study, but will not be cited here.

psychology use them to characterize each volunteer after studying the transcript of his interviews. Their task in each case was to sort the items of a given deck in a prescribed 9-point distribution, ranging from the three items that appeared to be most saliently characteristic or newsworthy about the volunteer (given a rating of 9) down to the three that seemed most saliently uncharacteristic of him (a rating of 1).

We will be concerned here with *Q* sorts made on the basis of reading *both* years' interviews with a particular volunteer.

The composite ratings of each volunteer on the two *Q* sets allow us to identify distinguishable major patterns of personal orientation and performance in Peace Corps service.

SOME PATTERNS OF COMPETENCE

A Picture of General Competence

Let us first look at the evaluative first principal components, beginning with the one based on *Q* sorts with the personality deck. Table 1 lists the items that were especially characteristic of volunteers who received high loadings on this factor: items with factor scores a standard deviation or more above the mean. The items defining what is *un*characteristic of these volunteers—those with distinctively low factor scores, are given in Table 2. Inspection of the tables shows a pattern of self-confidence, high self-esteem, energy, principled responsibility, optimistic realism, and persistence with flexibility, among other virtues. We felt justified in labelling this P-1 pattern "Self-Confident Maturity."

The corresponding first factor based on the role performance deck really gives us an alternative perspective on the same facts, since it is based on the same interviews and much the same people obtained high loadings. Table 3 shows the items that have high scores on this factor. Commitment to and competence in the teaching role top the list, with liking for one's students a close third. Other items emphasize qualities both of the volunteer's teaching and of his involvement with Africa. In Table 4 are given the *un*characteristic items, with low factor scores. These items paint a picture of low competence and commitment, and of a variety of ways in which a volunteer might perform his role less than well. We label this P-1 performance pattern "Competent Teaching in Africa."

TABLE 1

ITEMS WITH HIGH FACTOR SCORES ON PERSONALITY
FACTOR P-1: SELF-CONFIDENT MATURITY

Item	Factor score
Generally self-confident.	73
A genuinely dependable and responsible person.	69
The values and principles which he holds directly affect what he does.	65
Feels his own life is important, that it matters what he does with his life.	65
Open to experience, ready to learn.	62
Tolerant and understanding.	61
Characteristically maintains a highly articulate, intellectual formulation of his situation and problems.	60

The pictures that emerge from the two *Q* sort decks readily coalesce. We find a pattern defined on its good side by qualities of warranted self-con-

TABLE 2

ITEMS WITH LOW FACTOR SCORES ON PERSONALITY
FACTOR P-1: SELF-CONFIDENT MATURITY

Item	Factor score
Feels a lack of worth; has low self-esteem.	24
Basically a dependent person; characteristically leans upon others for support.	33
Has had a characteristically high level of anxiety during the time in Ghana.	33
Tends to expect little of life, pessimistic.	33
Seems generally to lack energy, to operate at a markedly low key.	35
Tends to be suspicious of others.	35
Tends to give up easily when faced with setbacks.	36
Would be unable to accept help from others when in need.	37
When things go badly, would tend to let them drift.	37
Tends to be preoccupied with matters of physical health.	38
Irritable and overresponsive to petty annoyances.	38
Engages in "posturing" to self and others; concerned with maintaining "face."	39
Tends unrealistically to minimize or deny the difficulties that he faces.	40

fidence, commitment, energy, responsibility, autonomy, flexibility, and hopeful realism together with other skills and attitudes more specifically appropriate to the role of Peace Corps teacher. The pattern has psychological coherence, in that having some of these virtues should make it easier to have the others. (If you lack most of them, it is very

hard to get a start on acquiring any of them—as we are learning from efforts to relaunch culturally deprived youth.) Undoubtedly, raters' halo exaggerates the coherence of our data: To a degree that we cannot ascertain, raters will have attributed miscellaneous virtues to the volunteers of whom they came to think well, on whatever grounds. We will assume, all the same, that this syndrome of general competence rests on underlying psychological fact. Other coherences in our data tend to lend to this assumption at least some support.

TABLE 3

ITEMS WITH HIGH FACTOR SCORES ON PERFORMANCE
FACTOR P-1: COMPETENT TEACHING IN AFRICA

Item	Factor score
Committed to carrying out his job as Peace Corps teacher to the best of his ability.	72
Is, all-in-all, a good competent teacher.	71
Generally likes his students, treats them with warmth and understanding.	66
Values his Peace Corps assignment as relevant to his career plans.	63
Views his teaching in terms of its contribution to the personal welfare or development of his students.	62
In his appraisal of Ghanaian life and institutions, is sympathetically critical; forms his own judgments with due regard to historical and cultural differences.	62
As a teacher emphasizes challenging students to think.	61
His African experiences have increased his concern with race relations in the United States.	61
Judges Ghanaian governmental policies and actions in terms of the needs of Ghana (regardless of approval or disapproval).	61
His approach to teaching integrates the formal curricular and examination requirements with his own sense of proper educational objectives.	60
Has shown consideration in his dealings with adult Ghanaians.	60

Patterns of Role Performance

Turn now to the discriminable patterns of role performance that emerge from varimax rotation. For the sake of economy, we will look only at the items with distinctively high factor scores. Under rotation, the generally evaluative dimension of Competent Teaching in Africa pulls apart into two distinct patterns, one emphasizing involvement with Africa, the other an exclusive commitment to teaching.

Table 5 shows the items with high scores on Factor V-1, "Constructive Involvement with Africa." They emphasize good personal relations with students and with other Africans, and a thoughtful integration of the experience of Africa, coupled with commitment to the teaching job.

Quite in contrast is the picture of Factor V-2, "Exclusive Teaching Commitment" (Table 6). Volunteers who loaded high on this factor were skillfully devoted to their teaching almost to the exclusion of other involvements with Africa: their

TABLE 4

ITEMS WITH LOW FACTOR SCORES ON PERFORMANCE FACTOR P-1: COMPETENT TEACHING IN AFRICA

Item	Factor score
Incompetent in his understanding of the major subject matter that he has to teach.	25
Feels mostly negative about Ghanaians he has met, really doesn't like them very much.	27
Overidentified with Ghana, attempts to "go native."	30
Has little real interest in Ghana.	31
Shows a lack of tact in relations with students.	33
Imposes own educational objectives at expense of preparing student for formal curricular and examination requirements.	34
Sees his school job as one restricted almost entirely to the classroom—the "9 to 5" attitude.	36
Tends to be condescending toward his students.	36
His personal problems of finding himself take priority for him over the tasks of the Peace Corps assignment.	37
Reacts to his students as a category or as types, rather than as individuals (N.B. regardless of degree of warmth or liking).	39

contact with Africa was deep but narrow, through their school and students.

Our third varimax performance factor looks the opposite of "gung-ho." From the items with high factor scores in Table 7, we see that this pattern characterizes volunteers who, by and large, were good teachers, but were low in commitment both to modern Africa and to the teaching job. They were "9-to-5ers" who nevertheless often made a substantial contribution to their schools. The negative correlation of —.50 between factor loadings on "Limited Commitment" and on the P-1 competence factor reflects the relatively low evaluation they tended to receive from the Q sort judges; they did not fare so badly in administrative evaluation.

TABLE 5

ITEMS WITH HIGH FACTOR SCORES ON PERFORMANCE FACTOR V-1: CONSTRUCTIVE INVOLVEMENT WITH AFRICA

Item	Factor score
His African experiences have increased his concern with race relations in the United States.	68
Generally likes his students, treats them with warmth and understanding.	65
Has established intimate, continuing relationships with adult africans.	64
Enjoys or admires Ghanaian style of living.	64
In his appraisal of Ghanaian life and institutions, is sympathetically critical; forms his own judgments with due regard to historical and cultural differences.	63
Is on friendly terms with many Ghanaians (apart from his students). (N.B. Disregard depth of the relationship.)	63
Has developed close, personal relationships with some of his students.	61
Committed to carrying out his job as Peace Corps teacher to the best of his ability.	61
In anticipating his return he is concerned with interpreting Ghana and/or West Africa to Americans.	61
Judges Ghanaian governmental policies and actions in terms of the needs of Ghana (Regardless of approval or disapproval).	61
Views his teaching in terms of its contribution to the personal welfare or development of his students.	60
Views his teaching in terms of its contribution to the development of Ghana.	60
As a result of his experience in Ghana, his thoughts and feelings about America show increased depth and perspective.	60

Note.—Twenty-seven percent of communality; r with P-1 (performance) =.84, r with P-1 (personality) =.68.

The results so far carry a message of some practical importance. They show that although a syndrome of general competence in the Peace Corps role can be identified, two quite different patterns of competent performance emerged, both "good." We will see that different personality patterns accompanied these distinctive performance styles. Selection policies based on a stereotyped conception of the ideal volunteer could readily go astray.

Personality Patterns in the Field Interviews

Since six intelligible patterns appeared in the varimax analysis of the personality Q sorts, I must hold myself to a summary treatment. The labels we gave them appear in Table 8, together with the correlations between loadings on each of them and

TABLE 6

ITEMS WITH HIGH FACTOR SCORES ON PERFORMANCE
FACTOR V-2: EXCLUSIVE TEACHING COMMITMENT

Item	Factor score
His whole life has centered on the school compound.	78
Absorbed in his work.	70
Committed to carrying out his job as Peace Corps teacher to the best of his ability.	69
Is, all-in-all, a good competent teacher.	69
Spends much time preparing lessons, correcting papers, etc.	67
As a teacher emphasizes challenging students to think.	64
Has well defined teaching goals and objectives.	62
Has worked out a balance between informality and closeness to students, on the one hand, and the requirements of discipline and authority on the other.	62
Generally likes his students, treats them with warmth and understanding.	61
His approach to teaching integrates the formal curricular and examination requirements with his own sense of proper educational objectives.	61
Concerned with setting Ghanaians a good personal example.	61

Note.—Nineteen percent of communality; *r* with P-1 (performance) =.32, *r* with P-1 (personality) =.31

loadings on the evaluative first principal components. The table also shows their relationships to the varimax performance factors, again correlating factor loadings taken as scores.

Three of the patterns are associated with competent performance. V-1, Interpersonally Sensitive Maturity, differs little from the P-1 factor based on the same *Q* sort, except that it gives greater emphasis to interpersonal openness, nurturance, empathy, and intensity of self-involvement. Women were more likely than men to fit this pattern. The other two "good" patterns were more characteristic of men: V-2, Intellectualizing Future Orientation, and V-5, Controlling Responsibility.

One pattern, when it appeared, strongly tended to be incompatible with good performance: V-4, Dependent Anxiety. Finally, there were two well-defined patterns that showed little correlation with loadings on the evaluative P-1 factors: V-3, Self-Reliant Conventionality, and V-6, Self-Actualizing Search for Identity.

The right-hand column of the table shows the

TABLE 7

ITEMS WITH HIGH FACTOR SCORES ON PERFORMANCE
FACTOR V-3: LIMITED COMMITMENT

Item	Factor score
Most of his time outside of class is spent in reading, recreation, or other activities unrelated to work.	71
Establishing relationships with the opposite sex has been an important aspect of his period of Peace Corps service.	68
Is, all-in-all, a good competent teacher.	67
Sees his school job as one restricted almost entirely to the classroom—the "9 to 5" attitude.	66
His approach to teaching integrates the formal curricular and examination requirements with his own sense of proper educational objectives.	65
Was quick to become aware of difficulties in communicating with students in the classroom and to adapt his teaching accordingly.	65
Has many, or close, contacts with expatriates (off school compound).	63
Interested in traditional Ghanaian life and customs.	61
Meets his teaching obligations day-by-day with little long-term planning.	61
Concerned with introducing American educational approaches and techniques.	60

Note.—Nine percent of communality; *r* with P-1 (performance) = −.50, *r* with P-1 (personality) = −.39.

main lines of relationship between these personality patterns and the varimax performance factors. Let us note the major correlates of each of these performance patterns in turn. We see that performance factor V-1, Constructive Involvement with Africa, is positively linked with Interpersonally Sensitive Maturity and with Intellectualizing Future Orientation—alternative routes toward getting involved with Africa—and negatively with Dependent Anxiety. V-2, Exclusive Teaching Commitment, is closely tied with Controlling Responsibility, and negatively linked with Self-Actualizing Search for Identity. Finally, V-3, Limited Commitment, is associated with both Self-Reliant Conventionality and with Dependent Anxiety, as alternative psychological bases, and is negatively related to Interpersonally Sensitive Maturity and to Controlling Responsibility. Diverse personal styles are indeed involved in the patterns of performance that our method has discerned in the interviews.

We can put a little meat on these bones by looking at the items that define patterns V-5 and V-6, to which we will have occasion to refer subse-

TABLE 8

PERSONALITY PATTERNS DERIVED FROM INTERVIEW Q SORTS AND SOME OF THEIR CORRELATES

Pattern	% communality	r with P-1 loadings		Closest correlates among role performance factors
		Perf.	Pers.	
V-1, Interpersonally sensitive maturity	27%	.80	.82	V-1 (Involv. in Afr.): .74
				V-3 (Limited commit.): −.43
V-2, Intellectualizing future orientation	13%	.48	.57	V-1 (Involv. in Afr.): .40
V-3, Self-reliant conventionality	12%	−.07	.08	V-3 (Limited commit.): .50
V-4, Dependent anxiety	11%	−.76	−.87	V-1 (Involv. in Afr.): −.58
				V-3 (Limited commit.): .40
V-5, Controlling responsibility	11%	.46	.50	V-2 (Exclus. teach.): .62
				V-3 (Limited commit.): −.51
V-6, Self-actualizing search for identity	7%	−.15	−.11	V-2 (Exclus. teach.): −.38

quently. Factor V-5, Controlling Responsibility, is presented in Table 9. Volunteers who were high on this factor tended, we remember, also to be high on Exclusive Teaching Commitment. They were steady, somewhat rigid people, self-contained but given to intense involvement. Highly *uncharacter-istic* items (not shown) indicate that self-control was as importnat to them as control over the situations that they faced. They tended to be low in emphatic sensitivity but high in nurturance. They had considerable personal resources.

In contrast to them are the interesting volunteers who showed the pattern to which we have given the perhaps pretentious but nevertheless descriptive label, Self-Actualizing Search for Identity. The defining items with high factor scores appear in Table 10. These volunteers, like those who were high on V-2 (Intellectualizing Future Orientation), appear to have been in good communication with themselves and to have found the topic interesting; the search for identity was still a prominent part of their agenda of young adulthood. But whereas the volunteers who were high on Intellectualizing Future Orientation seem in general to have gained the upper hand in the struggle for self-definition, those who were high on V-6 were clearly in the midst of a postadolescent turmoil. The Q sort items describe them as intense, unconventional, and impulsive, a bit confused and chaotic, not at all sure of themselves or of what the future might offer. But they were working hard and constructively, if somewhat erratically, on the problem: Self-cultivation and improvement stood high on their personal agenda.

TABLE 9

ITEMS WITH HIGH FACTOR SCORES ON PERSONALITY FACTOR V-5: CONTROLLING RESPONSIBILITY

Item	Factor score
Control of his situation is important to him.	75
A genuinely dependable and responsible person.	69
Engages in "posturing" to self and others; concerned with maintaining "face."	67
Preoccupied with the power aspects of relations.	66
Intense, tends to involve self deeply.	65
Is uneasy when the situation is not clearly defined.	65
The values and principles which he holds directly affect what he does.	65
High in initiative; active rather than reactive.	65
Nurturant; enjoys helping the younger or less adequate.	62
A major component of his stance has been his assumption that one meets one's daily obligations as a matter of course.	61
Generally self-confident.	60

Note.—Eleven percent of communality; r with P-1 (personality) =.50, r with P-1 (performance) =.46.

SOME PROBLEMS OF PREDICTION

It is one thing to explore, as we have been doing, the relationship between patterns of role performance and of personality overseas, both derived from judgments of the same field interviews. This is to extract, as objectively and sensitively as we can, what the interviews have to say. To do so has obviously been informative. But to *predict* performance from independent measures of personality is quite another matter, in regard to which the entire experience of personnel psychology must

TABLE 10

ITEMS WITH HIGH FACTOR SCORES ON PERSONALITY
FACTOR V-6: SELF-ACTUALIZING
SEARCH FOR IDENTITY

Item	Factor score
Feels his own life is important, that it matters what he does with his life.	73
Devotes much of his energy to a deliberate program of self-improvement (creative activity, study, etc.).	73
Intense, tends to involve self deeply.	72
Is aware of his own feelings and motives.	68
The values and principles which he holds directly affect what he does.	65
Copes with the novelty of the Ghanaian experience by seeking relationships, activities and settings that let him continue important personal interests.	64
Unsure just who he is or who he ought to be or how he fits into the world.	63
Impulsive; undercontrolled (N.B. opposite implies over-controlled).	60
Is actively striving toward a clearer, more complex or mature sense of identity.	60

Note.—Seven percent of communality; r with P-1 (personality) $= -.11$, r with P-1 (performance) $= -.15$.

caution us against optimism. I now turn to three attempts at prediction of competence, two of them failures, one a qualified success.

Authoritarianism

Persons high in authoritarianism, I would have supposed, should be hampered by traits of ethnocentrism and rigidity, among others, from performing well as teachers in Africa. To make a long story short,[4] we employed two measures of authoritarianism: one, a 24-item version identical to that used by Mischel (1965) and closely similar to the versions employed in *The Authoritarian Personality* (Adorno, Levinson, Sanford, and Frenkel-Brunswik, 1950); the other a more sophisticated 100-item instrument carefully balanced to eliminate the effect of response sets. We obtained surprisingly good evidence that these measures, particularly the more sophisticated one, sorted the volunteers out at the time they were in training along a composite dimension, the ingredients of which were essentially as the authors of *The Authoritarian Personality* had claimed, including

[4] A full account of methods and results is given in Smith (1965a).

intolerance of ambiguity, over-control, moralism, projectivity, conservatism, distrustfulness of others, and repressiveness. Yet scores on authoritarianism showed essentially null correlations with loadings on the general competence patterns and with administrative evaluations. The only appreciable correlations involving our better measure of authoritarianism were with V-2, Intellectualizing Future Orientation (—.38, $p < .05$) and with V-6, Self-Actualizing Search for Identity (—.26, $p < .10$), both patterns that involved good communication with and about the self.

Second thoughts after direct experience in the field suggest that the prediction was naive in giving insufficient weight to a job analysis of the requirements on a teacher in an essentially authoritarian educational setting.[5] In any case, it is apparent that although our measure did relate sensibly to certain personality patterns overseas, it did *not* contribute to the prediction of competent performance.

Psychiatric Ratings

Early in the training period at Berkeley, each volunteer was seen in two 50-minute appraisal interviews by psychiatrists from the Langley-Porter Neuropsychiatric Institute.[6] Each of the seven participating psychiatrists made a variety of predictive ratings. The most reliable of these required the psychiatrist to rate the "predicted psychological effectiveness" of the 16 or 17 trainees that he had seen, on a 7-point scale with a prescribed distribution. [Other evidence showed that these ratings were based on an estimate of "mental health" status.]

The psychiatrists' "mental health" ratings had a close to 0 correlation with our criterion measures of competent performance. Within the admittedly restricted range of volunteers actually sent overseas, the degree to which a person's adjustment as

[5] It would be particularly interesting to know the predictive value of measures of authoritarianism for performance in community development settings, where higher levels of flexibility and tolerance for ambiguity would seem to be essential than in classroom teaching.

[6] This procedure was tried out by the Peace Corps for experimental purposes, and does not represent current practice. I am grateful to M. Robert Harris for making the results of the psychiatric interviews available to me.

appraised by the psychiatrists approximated the "optimal" pattern simply had nothing to do with the adequacy with which he performed in the Peace Corps role.[7]

Dimensions of the Personal Future

After this dismal but familiar story of predictive failure, now for a modest success! At the time the Ghana volunteers were in training at Berkeley, Raphael Ezekiel, then a beginning graduate student, was working with me on the psychology of time perspectives. It occurred to him that a subject's view of his own personal future should have a clearer psychological significance than indices derived from Thematic Apperception Test stories and the like. We adapted a procedure that he was currently trying on other groups, and included in the battery for the trainees the assignment of writing three essays: one about their alternative immediate plans if they were not accepted in the Peace Corps, one a brief "mock autobiography" covering the three years after return from Peace Corps service, and the third a similar mock autobiography covering the year in which they would be 40 years old.[8]

These essays were rated with satisfactory reliability by independent judges on three 7-point scales: *Differentiation,* the extent to which each essay showed complex and detailed mapping of the future; *Agency,* the extent to which the essays as a whole showed the future self as the prime agent in determining the course of the person's future life; and *Demand,* the extent to which they described a life viewed by the respondent as demanding long-term, continuing effort. Each of these correlated dimensions has its own distinctive pattern of correlates, but we will be concerned here only with correlates of a sum score across all of them.

The sum score correlated .41 ($p < .01$) with the overall administrative evaluation of the volunteers' effectiveness as of the second year.

TABLE 11

ITEMS THAT ARE CHARACTERISTIC OF VOLUNTEERS
WITH HIGH SUM SCORES ON
MOCK AUTOBIOGRAPHIES

Item	p[a]
Personality Q sort	
Envisions a challenging and demanding personal future.	.05
Characteristically maintains a highly articulate intellectual formulation of his situation and problems.	.05
Shows inventiveness, ingenuity.	.05
Has developed a well-balanced, varied, and stable program for self of work, relaxation, relief or escape.	.05
Devotes much of his energy to a deliberate program of self-improvement (creative activity, study, etc.).	.10
High in initiative; active rather than reactive.	.10
Performance Q sort	
Elaborates his performance of teaching duties in non-routine imaginative ways; invests self creatively in teaching job in and out of class.	.01
Values his Peace Corps assignment as relevant to his career plans.	.05
Actively employs self in useful, school-related activities outside of class.	.10
Concerned with using his Peace Corps experience to test himself.	.10

[a] By t test comparing extreme thirds of distribution.

We may gain a fuller picture of the psychological meaning of the sum scores by looking at the Q sort items from the personality and role performance decks that discriminate high scorers from low scorers significantly by t test. The ones that are more characteristic of high scorers are given in Table 11. Apart from items that constitute further construct validation of the index, the picture of inventiveness, initiative, job-elaboration, and self-testing or responsiveness to challenge indicates that the procedure has indeed tapped qualities that should contribute to a more than routine performance.

Ezekiel interprets his measures as tapping the volunteer's readiness to commit himself to demanding tasks and to take active initiative in bringing

[7] Apart from self-selection by the volunteers and preselection by the Peace Corps on the basis of letters of reference, 8 of 58 volunteers in training were not sent overseas. Of these, 1 fled training in panic; for 4 others, judgments regarding personal adjustment played a substantial role in deselection. My present hunch, for what it is worth, is that 2 or 3 of these would have been quite successful had they been sent to Ghana. The really dubious case would have been deselected by nonprofessionals relying on the naked eye.

[8] A fourth essay, an imaginary letter from Ghana to a friend describing the volunteer's life and activities, was dropped from analysis when it appeared to evoke a highly stereotyped regurgitation of official doctrine received in training.

about desired futures, the pathways to which he sees with some clarity—dispositions exceedingly relevant to the core content of competence as we are beginning to conceive of it. True, there is a bias toward the intellectualizer; but our small sample of strategically evoked verbal behavior does seem to have caught some of the motivational basis for response to the challenge of the Peace Corps assignment with commitment, initiative, and effort. We seem to be on the right track here.[9] Maybe mental health or adjustment (except at the sick extreme) and authoritarianism really were blind alleys.

The Peace Corps and Personality Change

Since our data concerning personality change over the period of Peace Corps service are complex and untidy, I will summarize them cavalierly. In regard to short-run changes, analysis of the field interviews indicated a degree of shift from initial all-out enthusiasm in the first year to more of a "veteran" mentality in the second, in which the volunteers came to be sustained more by their principles than by sheer enthusiasm. In the second year there seems to have been some decrease in involvement on all fronts, a partial withdrawal from full engagement with the opportunities and challenges of the situation. But there were also indications of greater self-insight and raised aspirations for the future. As for the longer run, comparisons are available on two pencil-and-paper questionnaires taken in training and at termination. Consistent shifts in response would appear to indicate that the volunteers became more tough-minded and realistic, more autonomous and independent of authority, and much more concerned with the plight of the American Negro. This was at the time of Birmingham; in the absence of a control group, we cannot assess the importance of the fact that it was from Africa that the volunteers were indignantly viewing events at home.

Messy data aside, my personal impression from knowing a number of the volunteers rather well was that important personality changes in the direction of maturity were frequent. I think I know why. My reconstructed account is at least consistent with our data, though it goes considerably beyond what I could use them to establish. It will

[9] For a full discussion and analysis of the Mock Autobiography technique as used in this research, see Ezekiel (1964).

also serve to put in context some of the themes with which we have been concerned.

When they joined the Peace Corps, many of this initial group of volunteers were not very clear as to why they did so: This was one of the reasons why they prickled when psychologists, psychiatrists, journalists, friends, and casual passers-by insistently asked them the question. Toward the end of their service, one could get a better and I think more accurate answer. The most frequent motivational mix, as I interpret it, was composed in varying proportions of two major ingredients and some minor ones. First, they needed a "psychosocial moratorium," in Erikson's (1956) sense. They were more often than not somewhat unclear about where they were heading, perhaps somewhat dissatisfied with their current directions. Two years' time out for reassessment and self-discovery was welcome, not a major sacrifice. (How the volunteers resented talk of the sacrifices they were making!) But second, and this must be stressed in almost the same breath to give a fair picture, the volunteers wanted to earn and justify this moratorium by doing something that seemed to them simply and instrinsically worthwhile, cutting through the complexities and hypocrisies of modern life and international relations. The Peace Corps as an opportunity for direct personal action toward good ends was strongly appealing. And third—less important—the appeal of adventure and foreign exposure was a factor for some, and the possibility of career-relevant experience for others.

But this account of the volunteers' private motives for joining the Peace Corps does not fairly describe the motivation that *sustained* them in their efforts. Once in, most of them saw and were captured by the challenges of the job and role: students and schools that needed everything they could give, a window on Africa that invited exploration. Their effective motivation was emergent: a response to opportunities and difficulties as challenges to be met, not as frustrations to be endured or "adjusted" to. If this reaction was typical of the group as a whole, it was truest of volunteers who were rated high in competence, and least true of those rated low or characterized by the Limited Commitment pattern.

How did the volunteers' particularly engrossing commitment to the job come about? It was not prominent in their motivation for joining, although their attraction to worthwhile activity as such obviously foreshadows it. Partly, to be sure, it must have been induced by the example and precept of the excellent training staff and Peace Corps leadership in the field. Given the volunteers' initial need to find themselves while doing something valuable intrinsically in simple human terms, however, I think the definite 2-year limit may have been important, though for most it was not salient. One can afford to make a fuller, less reserved or cautious investment of self in an undertaking if the demand is explicitly time limited.

It was this high degree of committed but disinterested investment in a challenging undertaking, I think, that was so auspicious for psychological change in the direction of maturity. Experiences from which the self is held in reserve do not change the self; profit in growth requires its investment.

Largely by self-selection, the volunteers who came to training fortunately contained a majority who were predisposed to respond to the Peace Corps challenge with high commitment. Our experimental Mock Autobiographies seem to have sampled this predisposition, though only crudely. In contrast, the "mental health" orientation, which received considerable weight during selection-in-training, turned out to be essentially irrelevant to the prediction of competent performance—and even of the volunteers' ability to carry on as teachers given the unforeseen press of stresses and supports that Ghana presented. Psychologists who assume responsibility for Peace Corps selection: please note!

This opportunistic study in the Peace Corps has suggested certain common strands in competence, and also illustrated that in this setting, there were various psychological routes to competent performance. We have not asked, how can young people be raised and educated to cultivate the emergence of competence? What social innovations are needed to capitalize upon existing potentials of competence? How can social and psychological vicious circles be reversed to allow the socially deprived to gain in competence? These questions should stand high on our agenda.[10] Our experience

with the Peace Corps as an imaginative social invention carries some suggestions worth pursuing.

REFERENCES

Adorno, T. W., Levinson, D. J., Sanford, R. N., and Frenkel-Brunswik, E. *The authoritarian personality.* New York: Harper, 1950.

Block, J. *The Q-sort method in personality assessment and psychiatric research.* Springfield, Ill.: Charles C. Thomas, 1961.

Erikson, E. H. The problem of ego identity, *Journal of the American Psychoanalytic Association,* 1956, 4: 55–121.

Ezekiel, R. S. *Differentiation, demand, and agency in projections of the personal future. A predictive study of the performance of Peace Corps teachers.* Unpublished doctoral dissertation, University of California, Berkeley, 1964.

Maslow, A. H. *Motivation and personality.* New York: Harper, 1954.

McClelland, D. C. Toward a theory of motive acquisition. *American Psychologist,* 1965, 20: 321–333.

Mischel, W. Predicting the success of Peace Corps volunteers in Nigeria. *Journal of Personality and Social Psychology,* 1965, 1: 510–517.

Smith, M. B. Research strategies toward a conception of positive mental health. *American Psychologist,* 1959, 14: 673–681.

Smith, M. B. Mental health reconsidered: A special case of the problem of values in psychology. *American Psychologist,* 1961, 16: 299–306.

Smith, M. B. Peace Corps teachers in Ghana. Final report of evaluation of Peace Corps projects in Ghana. University of California, Institute of Human Development, Berkeley, 1964. (Mimeo)

Smith, M. B. An analysis of two measures of "authoritarianism" among Peace Corps teachers. *Journal of Personality,* 1965, 33: 513–535. (a)

Smith, M. B. Socialization for competence. *Items* (Social Science Research Council), 1965, 19: 17–23. (b)

White, R. W. Motivation reconsidered: The concept of competence. *Psychological Review,* 1959, 66: 297–333.

White, R. W. Ego and reality in psychoanalytic theory. A proposal regarding independent ego energies. *Psychological Issues,* 1963, 3: No. 3.

[10] For a preliminary scouting of these questions, see Smith (1965b), where I report on a conference at which these topics were discussed.

THE DYNAMICS OF "STRUCTURED" PERSONALITY TESTS *

PAUL E. MEEHL

In a recent article in this Journal, Lt. Max L. Hutt (1945) of the Adjutant General's School has given an interesting discussion of the use of projective methods in the army medical installations. This article was part of a series describing the work of clinical psychologists in the military services, with which the present writer is familiar only indirectly. The utility of any instrument in the military situation can, of course, be most competently assessed by those in contact with clinical material in that situation, and the present paper is in no sense to be construed as an "answer" to or an attempted refutation of Hutt's remarks. Nevertheless, there are some incidental observations contained in his article which warrant further critical consideration, particularly those that have to do with the theory and dynamics of "structured" personality tests. It is with these latter observations rather than the main burden of Hutt's article that this paper is concerned.

Hutt defines "structured personality tests" as those in which the test material consists of conventional, culturally crystallized questions to which the subject must respond in one of a very few fixed ways. With this definition we have no quarrel, and it has the advantage of not applying the unfortunate phrase "self-rating questionnaire" to the whole class of question-answer devices. But immediately following this definition, Hutt goes on to say that "it is assumed that each of the test questions will have the same meaning to all subjects who take the examination. The subject has no opportunity of organizing in his own unique manner his response to the questions."

These statements will bear further examination. The statement that personality tests assume that each question has the same meaning to all subjects is continuously appearing in most sources of late, and such an impression is conveyed by many discussions even when they do not explicitly make this assertion. It should be emphasized very

* Reprinted with permission from the Journal of Clinical Psychology. In *Journal of Clinical Psychology*, 1945, Vol. 1, pp. 296–303.

strongly, therefore, that while this perhaps has been the case with the majority of question-answer personality tests, it is not by any means part of their essential nature. The traditional approach to verbal question-answer personality tests has been, to be sure, to view them as self-ratings; and it is in a sense always a self-rating that you obtain when you ask a subject about himself, whether you inquire about his feelings, his health, his attitudes, or his relations to others.

However, once a "self-rating" has been obtained, it can be looked upon in two rather different ways. The first, and by far the commonest approach, is to accept a self-rating as a second best source of information when the direct observation of a segment of behavior is inaccessible for practical or other reasons. This view in effect forces a self-rating or self-description to act as surrogate for a behavior-sample. Thus we want to know whether a man is shy, and one criterion is his readiness to blush. We cannot conveniently drop him into a social situation to observe whether he blushes, so we do the next best (and often much worse) thing and simply ask him, "Do you blush easily?" We assume that if he does in fact blush easily, he will realize that fact about himself, which is often a gratuitous assumption; and secondly, we hope that having recognized it, he will be willing to tell us so.

Associated with this approach to structured personality tests in the construction of items and their assembling into scales upon an *a priori* basis, requiring the assumption that the psychologist building the test has sufficient insight into the dynamics of verbal behavior and its relation to the inner core of personality that he is able to predict beforehand what certain sorts of people will say about themselves when asked certain sorts of questions. The fallacious character of this procedure has been sufficiently shown by the empirical results of the Minnesota Multiphasic Personality Inventory alone, and will be discussed at greater length below. It is suggested tentatively that the relative uselessness of most structured personality tests is due more to *a priori* item construction than to the fact of their being structured.

The second approach to verbal self-ratings is rarer among test makers. It consists simply in the explicit denial that we accept a self-rating as a feeble surrogate for a behavior sample, and substitutes the assertion that a "self-rating" constitutes an intrinsically interesting and significant bit of verbal behavior, the non-test correlates of which must be discovered by empirical means. Not only is this approach free from the restriction that the subject must be able to describe his own behavior accurately, but a careful study of structured personality tests built on this basis shows that such a restriction would falsify the actual relationships that hold between what a man says and what he *is*.

Since this view of question-answer items is the rarer one at the present time, it is desirable at this point to elucidate by a number of examples. For this purpose one might consider the Strong Vocational Interest Blank, the Humm-Wadsworth Temperament Scales, the Minnesota Multiphasic Personality Inventory, or any structured personality measuring device in which the selection of items was done on a thoroughly empirical basis using carefully selected criterion groups. In the extensive and confident use of the Strong Vocational Interest Blank, this more sophisticated view of the significance of responses to structured personality test items has been taken as a matter of course for years. The possibility of conscious as well as unconscious "fudging" has been considered and experimentally investigated by Strong and others, but the differences in possible interpretation or *meaning* of items have been more or less ignored—as well they should be. One is asked to indicate, for example, whether he likes, dislikes, or is indifferent to "conservative people." The possibilities for differential interpretation of a word like *conservative* are of course tremendous, but nobody has worried about that problem in the case of the Strong. Almost certainly the strength of verbs like "like" and "dislike" is variably interpreted throughout the whole blank. For the present purpose the Multiphasic (referred to hereinafter as MMPI) will be employed because the present writer is most familiar with it.

One of the items on the MMPI scale for detecting psychopathic personality (Pd) is "My parents and family find more fault with me than they should." If we look upon this as a rating in which the *fact* indicated by an affirmative response is crucial, we immediately begin to wonder whether the testee can objectively evaluate how much other people's parents find fault with them, whether his own parents are warranted in finding

as much fault with him as they do, whether this particular subject will interpret the phrase "finding fault" in the way we intend or in the way most normal persons interpret it, and so on. The present view is that this is simply an unprofitable way to examine a question-answer personality test item. To begin with, the empirical finding is that individuals whose past history and momentary clinical picture is that of a typical psychopathic personality tend to say "Yes" to this much more often than people in general do. Now in point of fact, they probably should say "No" because the parents of psychopaths are sorely tried and probably do not find fault with their incorrigible offspring any more than the latter deserve. An allied item is "I have been quite independent and free from family rule" which psychopaths tend to answer *false*—almost certainly opposite to what is actually the case for the great majority of them. Again, "Much of the time I feel I have done something wrong or evil." Anyone who deals clinically with psychopaths comes to doubt seriously whether they could possibly interpret this item in the way the rest of us do (*cf.* "semantic dementia," Cleckley, 1941), but they *say* that about themselves nonetheless. Numerous other examples such as "Someone has it in for me" and "I am sure I get a raw deal from life" appear on the same scale and are significant because psychopaths tend to *say* certain things about themselves, rather than because we take these statements at face value.

Consider the MMPI scale for detecting tendencies to hypochondriasis. A hypochondriac says that has headaches often, that he is not in as good health as his friends are, and that he cannot understand what he reads as well as he used to. Suppose that he has a headache on an average of once every month, as does a certain "normal" person. The hypochrondriac says he often has headaches, the other person says he does not. They both have headaches once a month, and hence they must either interpret the word "often" differently in that question, or else have unequal recall of their headaches. According to the traditional view, this ambiguity in the word "often" and the inaccuracy of human memory constitute sources of error; for the authors of the MMPI they may actually constitute sources of discrimination.

We might mention as beautiful illustrations of

this kind of relation, the non-somatic items in the hysteria scale of MMPI (McKinley and Hathaway, 1944). These items have a statistical homogeneity and the common property by face inspection that they indicate the person to be possessed of unusually good social and psychiatric adjustment. They are among the most potent items for the detection of hysterics and hysteroid temperaments, but they reflect the systematic distortion of the hysteric's conception of himself, and would have to be considered invalid if taken as surrogates for the direct observation of behavior.

As a last example one might mention some findings of the writer, to be published shortly, in which "normal" persons having rather abnormal MMPI profiles are differentiated from clearly "abnormal" persons with equally deviant profiles by a tendency to give statistically rare as well as psychiatrically "maladjusted" responses to certain other items. Thus a person who says that he is afraid of fire, that windstorms terrify him, that people often disappoint him, stands a better chance of being normal in his non-test behavior than a person who does not admit to these things. The discrimination of this set of items for various criterion groups, the intercorrelations with other scales, and the content of the items indicate strongly that they detect some verbal-semantic distortion in the interpretation and response to the other MMPI items which enters into the spurious elevation of scores achieved by certain "normals." Recent unpublished research on more subtle "lie" scales of the MMPI indicates that unconscious self-deception is inversely related to the kind of verbal distortion just indicated.

In summary, a serious and detailed study of the MMPI items and their interrelations both with one another and non-test behavior cannot fail to convince one of the necessity for this second kind of approach to question-answer personality tests. That the majority of the questions seem by inspection to require self-ratings has been a source of theoretical misunderstanding, since the stimulus situation seems to request a self-rating, whereas *the scoring does not assume a valid self-rating to have been given.* It is difficult to give any psychologically meaningful interpretation of some of the empirical findings on the MMPI unless the more sophisticated view is maintained.

It is for this reason that the possible differences in interpretation do not cause us an *a priori* concern in the use of this instrument. Whether any structured personality test turns out to be valid and useful must be decided on pragmatic grounds, but the possibility of diverse interpretations of a single item is not a good *theoretical* reason for predicting failure of the scales. There is a "projective" element involved in interpreting and responding to these verbal stimuli which must be recognized, in spite of the fact that the test situation is very rigidly structured as regards the ultimate response possibilities permitted. The objection that all persons do not interpret structured test items in the same way is not fatal, just as it would not be fatal to point out that "ink blots do not look the same to everyone."

It has not been sufficiently recognized by critics of structured personality tests that what a man says about himself may be a highly significant fact about him even though we do not entertain with any confidence the hypothesis that what he says would agree with what complete knowledge of him would lead others to say of him. It is rather strange that this point is so often completely passed by, when clinical psychologists quickly learn to take just that attitude in a diagnostic or therapeutic interview. The complex defense mechanisms of projection, rationalization, reaction-formation, etc., appear dynamically to the interviewer as soon as he begins to take what the client *says* as itself motivated by other needs than those of giving an accurate verbal report. There is no good *a priori* reason for denying the possibility of similar processes in the highly structured "interview" which is the question-answer personality test. The summarized experience of the clinician results (one hopes, at least) in his being able to discriminate verbal responses admissible as accurate self-descriptions from those which reflect other psychodynamisms but are not on that account any the less significant. The test analogue to this experience consists of the summarized statistics on response frequencies, at least among those personality tests which have been constructed empirically (MMPI, Strong, Rorschach, etc.).

Once this has been taken for granted we are prepared to admit powerful items to personality scales regardless of whether the rationale of their appearance can be made clear at present. We do not have the confidence of the traditional personality test maker that the relation between the behavior dynamics of a subject and the tendency to respond verbally in a certain way must be psychologically obvious. Thus it puzzles us but does not disconcert us when this relation cannot be elucidated, the science of behavior being in the stage that it is. That "I sometimes tease animals" (answered *false*) should occur in a scale measuring symptomatic depression is theoretically mysterious, just as the tendency of certain schizophrenic patients to accept "position" as a determinant in responding to the Rorschach may be theoretically mysterious. Whether such a relation obtains can be very readily discovered empirically, and the wherefore of it may be left aside for the moment as a theoretical question. Verbal responses which do not apparently have any *self*-reference at all, but in their form seem to request an objective judgment about social phenomena or ethical values, may be equally diagnostic. So, again, one is not disturbed to find items such as "I think most people would lie to get ahead" (answered *false*) and "It takes a lot of argument to convince most people of the truth" (answered *false*) appearing on the hysteria scale of the MMPI.

The frequently alleged "superficiality" of structured personality tests becomes less evident on such a basis also. Some of these items can be rationalized in terms of fairly deep-seated trends of the personality, although it is admittedly difficult to establish that any given depth interpretation is the correct one. To take one example, the items on the MMPI scale for hysteria which were referred to above as indicating extraordinarily good social and emotional adjustment can hardly be seen as valid self-descriptions. However, if the core trend of such items is summarily characterized as "I am psychiatrically and socially well adjusted," it is not hard to fit such a trend into what we know of the basic personality structure of the hysteric. The well-known *belle indifference* of these patients, the great lack of insight, the facility of repression and dissociation, the "impunitiveness" of their reactions to frustration, the tendency of such patients to show an elevated "lie" score on the MMPI, may all be seen as facets of this underlying structure. It would be interesting to see experimentally whether to the three elements of Rosenzweig's "triadic hypothesis" (impunitiveness, repression, hypnotizability) one might add a fourth correlate—the

chief non-somatic component of the MMPI hysteria scale.

Whether "depth" is plumbed by a structured personality test to a lesser extent than by one which is unstructured is difficult to determine, once the present view of the nature of structured tests is understood. That the "deepest" layers of personality are not verbal might be admitted without any implication that they cannot therefore make themselves known to us via verbal behavior. Psychoanalysis, usually considered the "deepest" kind of psychotherapy, makes use of the dependency of verbal behavior upon underlying variables which are not themselves verbalized.

The most important area of behavior considered in the making of psychiatric diagnosis is still the form and content of the *speech* of the individual. I do not mean to advance these considerations as validations of any structured personality tests, but merely as reasons for not accepting the theoretical objection sometimes offered in criticizing them. Of course, structured personality tests may be employed in a purely diagnostic, categorizing fashion, without the use of any dynamic interpretations of the relationship among scales or the patterning of a profile. For certain practical purposes this is quite permissible, just as one may devote himself to the statistical validation of various "signs" on the Rorschach test, with no attempt to make qualitative or really dynamic personological inferences from the findings. The tradition in the case of structured personality tests is probably weighted on the side of non-dynamic thinking; and in the case of some structured tests, there is a considerable amount of experience and clinical subtlety required to extract the maximum of information. The present writer has heard discussions in case conferences at the University of Minnesota Hospital which makes as "dynamic" use of MMPI patterns as one could reasonably make of any kind of test data without an excessive amount of illegitimate reification. The clinical use of the Strong Vocational Interest Blank is another example.

In discussing the "depth" of interpretation possible with tests of various kinds, it should at least be pointed out that the problem of validating personality tests, whether structured or unstructured, becomes more difficult in proportion as the interpretations increase in "depth." For example, the validation of the "sign" differentials on the Rorschach is relatively easier to carry out than that of the deeper interpretations concerning the basic personality structure. This does not imply that there is necessarily less validity in the latter class of inferences, but simply stresses the difficulty of designing experiments to test validity. A very major part of this difficulty hinges upon the lack of satisfactory external criteria, a situation which exists also in the case of more dynamic interpretations of structured personality tests. One is willing to accept a staff diagnosis of psychasthenia in selecting cases against which to validate the Pt scale of the MMPI or the F% as a compulsive-obsessive sign on the Rorschach. But when the test results indicate repressed homosexuality or latent anxiety or lack of deep insight into the self, we may have strong suspicions that the instrument is fully as competent as the psychiatric staff. Unfortunately this latter assumption is very difficult to justify without appearing to be inordinately biased in favor of our test. Until this problem is better solved than at present, many of the "depth" interpretations of both structured and unstructured tests will be little more than an expression of personal opinion.

There is one advantage of unstructured personality tests which cannot easily be claimed for the structured variety, namely, the fact that falsehood is difficult. While it is true for many of the MMPI items, for example, that even a psychologist cannot predict on which scales they will appear nor in what direction certain sorts of abnormals will tend to answer them, still the relative accessibility of defensive answering would seem to be greater than is possible in responding to a set of ink-blots. Research is still in progress on more subtle "lie" scales of the MMPI and we have every reason to feel encouraged on the present findings. Nevertheless the very existence of a definite problem in this case and not in the case of the Rorschach gives the latter an advantage in this respect. When we pass to a more structured method, such as the T.A.T., the problem reappears. The writer has found, for example, a number of patients who simply were not fooled by the "intelligence-test" set given in the directions for the T.A.T., as was indicated quite clearly by self-references and defensive remarks, especially on the second day. Of course such a patient is still under pressure to produce material

and therefore his unwillingness to reveal himself is limited in its power over the projections finally given.

In conclusion, the writer is in hearty agreement with Lieutenant Hutt that unstructured personality tests are of great value, and that the final test of the adequacy of any technique is its utility in clinical work. Published evidence of the validity of both structured and unstructured personality tests as they had to be modified for convenient military use does not enable one to draw any very definite conclusions or comparisons at the present time. There is assuredly no reason for us to place structured and unstructured types of instruments in battle order against one another, although it is admitted that when time is limited they come inevitably into a very real clinical "competition" for use. The present article has been aimed simply at the clarification of certain rather prevalent misconceptions as to the nature and the theory of at least one important structured personality test, in order that erroneous theoretical considerations may not be thrown into the balance in deciding the outcome of such clinical competition.

REFERENCES

Benton, A. C. The interpretation of questionnaire items in a personality schedule. *Archiv. Psychol.*, 1935, No. 190.

Cleckley, H. *The Mask of Sanity,* St. Louis: Mosby, 1941.

Hathaway, S. R., and McKinley, J. C. A multiphasic personality schedule: I. Construction of the schedule. *J. Psychol.,* 1940, 10: 249–254.

McKinley, J. C., and Hathaway, S. R. A multiphasic personality schedule: II. A differential study of hypochondriasis. *J. Psychol.,* 1940, 10: 255–268.

Hathaway, S. R., and McKinley, J. C. A multiphasic personality schedule: III. The measurement of sympotomatic depression. *J. Psychol.,* 1942, 14: 73–84.

McKinley, J. C., and Hathaway, S. R. A multiphasic personality schedule: IV. Psychasthenia. *J. appl. Psychol.,* 1942, 26: 614–624.

Hathaway, S. R., and McKinley, J. C. *Manual for the Minnesota Multiphasic Personality Inventory*. Minneapolis: University of Minnesota Press, 1943.

McKinley, J. C., and Hathaway, S. R. The Minnesota Multiphasic Personality Inventory: V. Hysteria, hypomania, and psychopathic deviate, *J. appl. Psychol.*, 1944, 28: 153–174.

Hutt, Max L. The use of projective methods of personality measurement in army medical installations. *J. clin. Psychol.*, 1945, 1: 134–140.

Landis, C., and Katz, S. E. The validity of certain questions which purport to measure neurotic tendencies. *J. appl. Psychol.*, 1934, 18: 343–356.

Landis, C., Zubin, J., and Katz, S. E. Empirical evaluation of three personality adjustment inventories. *J. educ. Psychol.*, 1935, 26: 321–330.

Leverenz, C. W. Minnesota Multiphasic Personality Inventory: An evaluation of its usefulness in the psychiatric service of a station hospital. *War Med.*, 1943, 4: 618–629.

Maller, J. B. Personality tests. In J. McV. Hunt (Ed.), *Personality and the Behavior Disorders*. New York: Ronald Press, 1944, pp. 170–213.

Meehl, P. E. A general normality or control factor in personality testing. Unpublished Ph.D. Thesis, University of Minnesota Library, Minneapolis, 1945.

Mosier, C. I. On the validity of neurotic questionnaires. *J. soc. Psychol.*, 1938, 9: 3–16.

Rosenzweig, S. An outline of frustration theory. In J. McV. Hunt (Ed.), *Personality and the Behavior Disorders*. New York: Ronald Press, 1944.

Strong, E. K. *Vocational Interests of Men and Women*. Stanford University Press, 1943.

THE RELATIONSHIP BETWEEN THE JUDGED DESIRABILITY OF A TRAIT AND THE PROBABILITY THAT THE TRAIT WILL BE ENDORSED *

ALLEN L. EDWARDS [1]

There is a rather common suspicion among many psychologists that subjects tend to give what are considered to be socially desirable responses to items in personality inventories. This

* Reprinted with permission from the American Psychological Association. In *The Journal of Applied Psychology,* 1953, Vol. 37, pp. 90–93.

[1] This paper was presented before the Western Psychological Association, Fresno, California, April 26, 1952. It is part of a research program made possible by an appointment as a Faculty Research Fellow of the Social Science Research Council.

suspicion has been given public expression in a recent article by Gordon (3, p. 407) who comments upon ". . . the motivation of a majority of respondents to mark socially acceptable alternatives to items, rather than those which they believe apply to themselves."

We have here two problems. One concerns the truthfulness of a subject's answers to items in a personality inventory, i.e., whether the response accurately describes the subject. The answer to this question implies that we have available some independent criterion in terms of which the inventory response is to be evaluated. The other problem concerns the relationship between a subject's response to an item and the social desirability of that item, i.e., whether the subject tends to give a positive answer to an item that is socially desirable and a negative answer to an item that is not. The answer to this question implies that we have available some measure of the social desirability of the item to which the response can be related. It is this problem we wish to report upon here.

THE PRESENT STUDY

The hypothesis to be investigated may be stated in this way: If the behavior indicated by an inventory item is socially desirable, the subject will tend to attribute it to himself; if it is undesirable, he will not. This hypothesis may be put more precisely: The probability of endorsement of personality items is a monotonic increasing function of the scaled social desirability of the items.

To study the relationship between the probability of endorsement of personality trait items and the social desirability of the items requires that we determine independently two measures: the probability of endorsement and the social desirability scale value of the items. This study thus consists of two parts: in the first, the scale values of the items are determined; in the second, the probability of endorsement is related to the independently determined scale values.

DETERMINING THE SCALE VALUES

A total of 140 personality trait items, based upon Murray's (4) discussion of needs, were written and edited. The items were selected so that 14 needs were investigated with 10 items supposedly indicative of each need. The items were arranged in 10 sets of 14 items each, so that each set consisted of one item relating to each of the needs. The items were presented to subjects with instructions to judge the degree of social desirability of the behavior indicated by each item in terms of how the behavior would be regarded in others. Judgments were made in terms of nine successive intervals, with the lowest interval representing extreme undesirability and the highest extreme desirability. The rating system was explained in terms of a sample set of four items for which judgments had already been obtained. After these ratings had been discussed, the instructions to the subjects concluded with the following statement:

"Indicate your own judgments of the desirability or undesirability of the traits which will be given to you by the examiner in the same manner. *Remember that you are to judge the traits in terms of whether you consider them desirable or undesirable in others.* Be sure to make a judgment about each trait."

The subjects judging the desirability of the items consisted of 86 men and 66 women, a total of 152 subjects. Twenty-six of the subjects were under 20 years of age, 97 were between 20 and 30 years of age, and 29 were over 30 years of age.

Cumulative distributions of the judgments were made separately by age and by sex groups. For each item we then found the interval in which the median of the distribution of judgments would fall.

In Figure 1, we show the plot of the women's intervals against the corresponding values for the men. It may be noted that in the case of only two items would the medians be separated by as much as two intervals. For 43 of the items the medians might possibly be separated by as much as one interval. For the remaining 95 items the medians would all fall within the same interval.

In the case of many of the items falling outside the principal diagonal of Figure 1, the medians would still be approximately the same for the reason that the medians of both distributions are close to the limit of the interval, but one happens to fall slightly above and the other slightly below the limit.

A similar analysis of the judgments was made in terms of the age variable. Examination of the separate distributions indicated that the scale values that would thus be obtained would be comparable and that little distortion would be introduced by pooling the judgments for all groups.

On the basis of the combined distributions, the scale values of the 140 items were found. The scale values were determined by the *method of successive intervals* (1). This method of scaling does not involve any assumption of equality of the successive rating intervals.

After determining the widths of the successive intervals and the scale values of the items on the psychological continuum of social desirability, an internal consistency test was applied (1). Using the 147 parameters calculated from the data, it was possible to reproduce the 1,120 independent, empirical observations with an average error of .023. This value, it may be mentioned, compares favorably with that usually obtained from internal consistency tests used when stimuli are scaled by the *method of paired comparisons.*

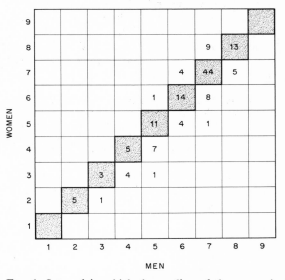

FIG. 1. Interval in which the median of the women's distribution of judgments would fall plotted against the interval in which the median of the men's distribution of judgments would fall.

RELATIONSHIP BETWEEN SCALE VALUES AND PROBABILITY OF ENDORSEMENT

In the second part of this study, a sample of 140 pre-medical and pre-dental students responded to the same set of items for which we had previously determined the scale values on the psychological continuum of social desirability. This time, however, the items appeared in a printed form as a personality inventory. The inventory was part of a test battery which was administered for the Medical and Dental Schools of the University of Washington. The instructions were those that are commonly used with personality inventories. A "Yes" response indicated that the subject believed that a given item was characteristic of himself and a "No" response that it was not.

Item counts were made for each item, by means of IBM equipment, and the per cent responding "Yes" was then found for each item. This per cent is the proportion of the sample indicating that the behavior stated by a particular item is characteristic of themselves. The proportions may be taken as the probability of endorsement of a particular trait item for the sample at hand.

The probability of endorsement of each item was plotted against the previously, and independently, determined social desirability scale value of the item. This plot is shown in Figure 2. On the Y-axis we have the probability of endorsement and on the X-axis the social desirability scale value. It is apparent that the probability of endorsement is a linear function of the scaled desirability of the item.[2] The product-moment correlation coefficient is .871.

[2] There is a slight indication of departure from linearity at the two extremes of the scale value axis. This is probably because of the limit placed upon the plotted points in terms of the Y-axis. The departure from linearity, however, is not statistically significant.

DISCUSSION

The data clearly indicate that the probability of endorsement of an item increases with the judged desirability of the item. This does not necessarily mean that the subjects are misrepresenting themselves on the inventory. It may be that traits which are judged as desirable are those which are fairly widespread or common among members of a culture or group. That is, if a pattern of behavior is prevalent among members of a group, it will be judged as desirable; if it is uncommon, it will be judged as undesirable. We might thus expect items indicating desirable traits to be endorsed more frequently than items indicating undesirable traits.

It is also possible that the behavior indicated by an item with a high social desirability scale value is not common, but that the subject taking the inventory is trying, consciously or unconsciously, to give a good impression of himself. He therefore tends to distort his answers in such a way as to make himself out as having more of the socially desirable traits and fewer of the socially undesirable traits than might be the case if his behavior were evaluated in terms of some other independent criterion.

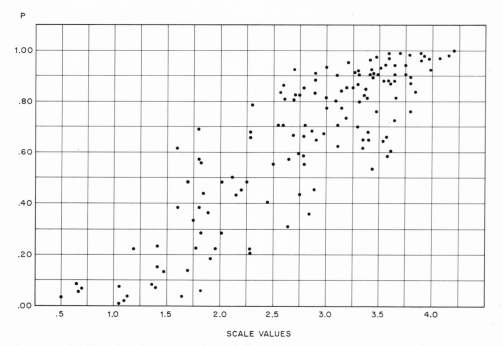

FIG. 2. Probability of endorsement of a trait item plotted against the social desirability scale value of the item. The product-moment correlation coefficient is .871.

Either one or both of the interpretations presented would account for the relationship between probability of endorsement and scaled desirability of the item. I have no data to support the interpretation that the subjects misrepresented themselves on the inventory, but Ellis (2) in his recent review cites quite a few studies which would indicate that this is the case.

If this is true, then in a personality inventory we should attempt to minimize the tendency for a given response to be determined primarily by the factor of social desirability. A suggested solution is to pair items indicative of different traits in terms of their social desirability scale values. If the subject is then forced to choose between the two items, his choice obviously cannot be upon the basis of the greater social desirability of one of the items.

REFERENCES

1. Edwards, A. L. The scaling of stimuli by the method of successive intervals. *J. appl. Psychol.*, 1952, 36: 118–122.
2. Ellis, A. The validity of personality questionnaires. *Psychol. Bull.*, 1946, 43: 385–440.
3. Gordon, L. V. Validities of the forced-choice and questionnaires methods of personality measurement. *J. appl. Psychol.*, 1951, 35: 407–412.
4. Murray, H. A. *Explorations in personality*. New York: Oxford University Press, 1938.

EXPERIMENTAL STUDIES OF FACTORS AFFECTING WORD ASSOCIATIONS *

JOHN JUNG

Sir Francis Galton, the originator of the study of word associations, believed that they "lay bare the foundations of a man's thought with more vividness and truth than he would probably care to publish to the world."

Since Galton's pioneering work in 1879, word association tests (WATs) have had considerable use in psychology. The task has been applied to clinical situations, studies in personality, develop-

* Reprinted by permission from the American Psychological Association. In *Psychological Bulletin*, 1966, Vol. 66, pp. 125–133.

mental studies, and cross-cultural comparisons. They have also been used indirectly in studies of verbal behavior, such as free recall (see Marshall and Cofer, 1963, for a summary of indices of associative strength of lists of words based on WAT technique).

Although WATs have been utilized in a variety of situations, there have been relatively few experimental investigations of factors affecting the WAT performance per se. Due to the early influence of C. G. Jung, the WAT has received extensive use as a projective test in clinical settings. Research employing the WAT outside the clinic has been of a descriptive and comparative nature. Numerous norms have been obtained, and individual differences as a function of age, sex, personality, etc., have been compared.

In view of the widespread use of the WAT paradigm and its variations, it is important that an examination be made of factors affecting WAT performance. This review is centered on discrete free word association and does not include derivative paradigms such as continuous association. The studies to be cited here are limited to those published since the last known summary of this literature, which comprised a chapter in an experimental psychology textbook (Woodworth and Schlosberg, 1954). Studies concerned with individual differences and applications of the WAT are not cited unless they involved or are related to experimentally manipulated variables.

KENT-ROSANOFF TEST

The most commonly employed version of WAT is the test developed by Kent and Rosanoff (1910) which is comprised of 100 common words, mostly nouns and adjectives. Usually, the subject is instructed to give the first word that he can think of in response to each stimulus word presented by the experimenter. He is also instructed to respond as quickly as possible. A constant serial order of list presentation is used for all subjects. The mode of stimulus presentation and response production varies, usually depending on whether the test is given on an individual or group basis. Individual testing usually involves aural stimulus presentation and oral response production, whereas group tests usually involve printed stimulus presentation and written responses.

The popularity of the Kent-Rosanoff (K-R) WAT has doubtless been due in large measure to the existence of norms for the frequencies of occurrence of the individual responses given to each stimulus word over a group of subjects (see Palermo and Jenkins, 1965, for a comparison of the existing sets of norms). In order to enhance the generalizability of such norms to their own data, subsequent investigations have generally involved WAT administration with procedures as similar as possible to those originally employed in obtaining the norms. While this procedure enhances the applicability of norms to new data, it prevents an examination of the effects of administrative procedure on WAT performance. There is a need for the collection of norms under systematically varied conditions.

EFFECTS OF ADMINISTRATIVE PROCEDURES

Variations in test administration procedures may lead to differences in the obtained responses. The Minnesota norms (Russell and Jenkins, 1954), for example, were obtained using a group testing procedure in which 50 stimulus words were printed on each of two pages. Such a procedure increases the chances of some words on the page affecting responses to other words. Even when each stimulus word is presented separately, as under individual testing, the effects of context are still potential factors influencing responses. The context of preceding stimuli and the responses to them may affect responses to subsequent stimuli. If only one constant serial order of the stimuli is used for all subjects, there is the risk of a systematic bias on responses by the preceding context. Since context cannot be eliminated, the best apparent solution would be to use varied serial orders of stimuli so as to obtain responses to given stimuli under varying contexts.

Evidence to support this warning is rare since most studies do not vary serial order of the stimuli. A study by Wynne, Gerjuoy, and Schiffman (1965), however, did compare responses obtained under three different serial orders of the stimuli. The list they used contained stimulus words either with or without opposites. For one condition, the antonyms occurred early in the serial order; for another condition, they were evenly distributed throughout the list; and, in a third condition, they were placed near the end of the list. They obtained significantly more antonyms as responses to stimuli having opposites under the first two types of serial orders than with the last

type. Wynne et al. ascribed these results to the possibility that a set to give antonyms developed in the first two orders but not in the third order. Their findings suggest that norms which are usually collected with a constant serial order of stimulus presentation might differ if some other serial order were used. It may be unwise to compare the response obtained in normative data with a response to the same stimulus word if the serial order of the list differs from that used in the norms.

Several studies (Cofer and Ford, 1957; Cramer, 1964; Jenkins and Cofer, 1957) manipulated the context for each stimulus word in the list individually. Cofer and Ford (1957) compared the free association times for stimulus words presented alone, in the context of a semantically unrelated word, and in the context of a synonym. The only difference found was that of longer association times for words presented in the context of a synonym as compared to words presented in the absence of context.

Cramer (1964) compared indirect forward and reverse priming on word associations. For each stimulus word in the list, a response was selected which occurred infrequently as an associate to that stimulus in the norms. The question was whether or not a context of primer words could increase the frequency with which subjects would give the arbitrarily selected infrequent response as an associate. For example, FLY is an infrequent response to SPIDER. By using forward primer words such as BIRD, MOTH, and EAGLE as a context preceding the stimulus SPIDER, Cramer attempted to increase the frequency of FLY as a response. Since each of the three primer words in this example elicit FLY as an associative response, it was inferred that their presence might increase the occurrence of FLY as a response to SPIDER. In all instances of forward primers, Cramer found that the responses occurred more frequently when preceded by the context than in the norms where primers were not used.

The context of reverse primers, however, did not increase the number of infrequent normative responses to stimulus words. Thus, ANGER is an infrequent response to TROUBLE in the norms. Reverse priming involves the use of words which are themselves frequent associates of ANGER as a context for the stimulus TROUBLE. It had been assumed that such a context would increase the occurrence of ANGER as a response to TROUBLE. No evidence for reverse priming was obtained.

Jenkins and Cofer (1957) presented college subjects with 20 compound stimuli comprised of adjective-noun pairs. A comparison was made between the types of responses obtained from these compound stimuli and those reported in the Minnesota norms to each word comprising a compound separately. The associative responses that were obtained depended on whether the stimulus words were presented alone or as part of a compound stimulus.

Administrative procedures for WATs may involve group written or individual aural tests. Entwisle and Forsyth (1963) compared these two types of WAT administration using fifth grade children. It was found that children with high urban status gave responses of higher commonality under individual aural testing than under group written testing. Only slight differences were found between the two procedures for children of low urban status. Entwisle and Forsyth speculated that the high urban status child tries to impress adults, and the individual test situation is more opportune for this goal than the group test situation.

Buchwald (1957) also reported some differences in the types of responses obtained under visual and auditory test conditions in college subjects. However, this effect was observed for only 2 of the 10 stimulus words in his list.

The possibility that the mode of testing and responding may affect response limits the generalizability of the normative data. It may be unwarranted to compare any data obtained from group administration with that obtained from individual testing or to compare any data obtained from written tests with those obtained from aural tests. The processes and factors affecting responses may differ in these situations.

Responses may also differ as a function of whether the test involves speeded or relaxed responding. The Minnesota norms were collected from subjects under a speeded set. Comparing the two response sets yields conflicting predictions and results. Flavell, Draguns, Fernburg, and Budin (1958) proposed a microgenetic approach. They hypothesized that speeded responses would be more "primitive" or less mature as compared to relaxed conditions. On the basis of the microgenetic analysis, they classified the responses of several widely used categories. Superordinate, subordinate,

and synonyms were considered as mature responses and completion, clang, and repetition responses were viewed as immature responses. Attribute, contrast, and blocking responses were designated as indeterminate. The classification itself has no a priori validity. Their results did not yield clear support for their predictions of the effects of time pressure on responses from college students.

Siipola, Walker, and Kolb (1955) instructed subjects for speeded or relaxed responding. Differences in the grammatical form class similarity of stimuli and responses were found as a function of set. If subjects were under the speeded set, adjective stimuli tended to elicit more adjectives; but with relaxed responding, the adjective stimuli tended to elicit noun responses. Siipola et al. concluded that a speeded set limits the subject to more superficial stimulus-bound responses, whereas relaxed or free conditions permit richer subject-bound responses.

Horton, Marlowe, and Crowne (1963) also compared speeded and relaxed test instructions. It was predicted that more common responses would result under speeded instructions, since verbal habits are so highly overlearned. Less common responses would occur under relaxed conditions, since other factors besides associative factors would have a chance to operate. Results were positive and opposed to the prediction of Flavell et al. that more primitive responses would result with a speeded set.

The situation in which the subject takes the WAT may affect some aspects of his performance. Saltz (1961) made a comparison of commonality as a function of the amount of stress in the situation. Stress was induced by giving the K-R WAT during a period of 1 hour during which subjects were awaiting results of an examination they had just completed. Lack of stress was provided by giving the same WAT during a regular class period without any immediately preceding examination. Half of the subjects were tested under stress, then no stress; the opposite sequence was used for the remaining half. The two administrations were separated by 1 week. Saltz found responses of lower commonality under stress conditions than under nonstress. The loss of commonality under induced stress was attributed to dedifferentiation or loss of differentiation among responses.

Instructional set regarding the purpose of the WAT may also affect the type of responses. Sarason (1959) gave the WAT twice to college subjects differing in level of anxiety. After the first test, the subjects were instructed to give the same response to a given stimulus on the second trial as they had given on the first trial. One group of subjects was given neutral instructions which consisted of procedural details only, while another group was further instructed that the test was a measure of personality. An interaction between Anxiety Level and Instructions was obtained such that with high anxiety, the personality-instructed subjects gave responses which were less common and were unable to give as many same responses to given stimuli in the list on the two trials. Sarason (1961) obtained a similar interaction between Test-Anxiety Level and Instructional Set when one group was instructed that the test measured intelligence. High test-anxiety subjects under the intelligence set instructions gave more same responses to given stimuli on the two administrations of the same list than those with neutral instructions. However, there was no difference between subjects of low test anxiety as a function of instructions on this measure.

Jung (1966) compared the effects of instructions which led subjects to believe a multiple trial WAT reflected either social adjustment or creativity. The same list of 10 words was given as a WAT for five successive trials. No explicit instruction was provided to the subject as to whether he should use the same or different responses to given words on repeated tests. Group tests were used with aural stimulus presentation and written response production. Significantly more different responses and less common responses were obtained under creativity-set than under social-adjustment-set test conditions. These results, like those of Sarason, demonstrate that the subject's perception of the task affects the type of responses he gives on WATs.

However, instructions regarding how to give associations may not be effective. Boyer and Elton (1958) preinstructed subjects by providing examples of common associations for one group, uncommon associations for another group, and no examples for a third group. These differences in treatment led to no differences in association after the first few items on the list. Apparently, the verbal habits of subjects are more powerful than the effects of these types of instructions.

On the other hand, instructions as to the type of responses desired on the test by the experi-menter have been effective (Horton et al., 1963; Jenkins, 1959). In both studies, subjects were given two tests on the same list of stimulus words. On the first test, neutral instructions such as "give the first word that comes to mind" were used; on the retest, subjects were asked to give the responses they thought most other people gave, that is, to give popular responses. Both Horton et al. and Jenkins found that the retest instructions led to more common responses. In Jenkins' study, this increase was greater in subjects who originally gave less common responses. However, it could be maintained that some of the changes in the type of responses occurred as a result of the retesting per se. This possibility is unlikely in view of the fact that the increase in commonality occurred regardless of whether the retest was given 5 minutes or 1 month later (Jenkins, 1959).

In a similar study to that of Jenkins, subjects were instructed to give opposites as responses where possible on the retest (Kjeldergaard, 1962). This set led to larger increases in commonality on the retest compared to the results Jenkins obtained with instructions for giving popular responses.

In summary, experimental evidence of the effects of variations of test administration on WAT responses shows that a number of factors are influential. These findings bring into question the validity of the procedure of comparing data collected by one investigator with those of another or with a set of norms if the test administration procedures differed widely. Evidence is available to show that serial order of stimulus presentation, context of a stimulus, method of responding (oral vs. written), method of testing (group vs. individual), amount of time pressure (relaxed vs. speeded), and instructional set may affect the nature of the resenses on the WAT.

COMMONALITY INDEX

In most early studies of word association, reaction time was a major dependent variable. It was assumed that responses with the greatest associative strength to the stimulus word would have the shortest reaction times. More recently, reaction time has been virtually replaced by commonality as the most widely used measure, especially with the K-R WAT.

Commonality is a measure based on the cultural frequency-of-occurrence norms compiled for the K-R WAT by the Minnesota group (Palermo and

Jenkins, 1964; Russell and Jenkins, 1954). Based on an N of 1,008 college students (Russell and Jenkins, 1954) and an N of 1,000 students at each of grades 4 through 12 and college (Palermo and Jenkins, 1964), norms for the frequencies of occurrence for the various responses to each stimulus word have been tabulated.

Comparisons of these norms taken at different eras in the past have also been made for data of adults (Dörken, 1956; Jenkins and Palermo, 1965; Jenkins and Russell, 1960) as well as for children's data (Koff, 1965; Palermo and Jenkins, 1965). In general, systematic changes toward greater commonality have been found over the past 50 years for both adults and children. The investigators making these comparisons generally conclude that these trends are attributable to the greater mass communication and uniformity in modern society. It is assumed that such environmental conditions lead to the formation of more universal verbal habits.

The commonality index is a score based on the total number of responses given on the K-R WAT which correspond to the cultural norm primaries. A primary is the response which most people in the normative sample gave in response to a stimulus word. This index has the advantage of ease of recording as well as objective, quantifiable scoring.

A major problem with the use of cultural frequency norms is that it involves the application of data based on one group of subjects (the normative sample) who each gave one response to each stimulus word to the data of individual subjects. In other words, the question of the equivalence of group and individual data arises in the extension of group norms to the data of individual subjects.

Jenkins, Russell, and Foss [1] have provided evidence which suggests that group norms can be accurately employed in analyzing individual responses on WAT. They analyzed unpublished data from a 1953 study by Russell and Sacks based on a WAT task involving repeated test trials on the same list. Each subject gave associations to a list of 50 words for eight consecutive trials. This procedure not only afforded comparisons across individuals on a given trial (group data) but also across trials for a given individual (individual

data). Such comparisons of group and individual data for each stimulus word in the list demonstrated the equivalence of the two measures.

WHAT DOES COMMONALITY MEASURE?

A determination of what commonality reflects may aid in determining what a response on WAT represents. One position is that the response given to a stimulus word is the one having the greatest associative strength for that stimulus. A strong form of this position implies that each stimulus word will elicit its strongest associative response in any situation. That is, associative strength would be considered the primary determinant of the response given to a stimulus word on a WAT.

Evidence consistent with this view can be found in a study by Hall and Ugelow (1957), who obtained a direct relationship between the frequency of occurrence of the stimulus words in the language and the speed with which the responses were given. Furthermore, the higher the frequency of occurrence of the stimulus words, the fewer were the different responses obtained over the group to a given word.

Additional support for a strong associationistic interpretation of WAT responses can be found in studies by Brody (1964) and in Jenkins et al.'s (see Footnote 1) analysis of the Russell and Sacks study mentioned above. Both studies employed a variation of the WAT in which the stimulus list was presented on each of several test trials in varying serial orders. A tendency was found for subjects to give the *same* response on repeated tests of a given stimulus word for stimuli with high dominance primaries. Dominance refers to the frequency with which the primary response was given to a stimulus in the cultural frequency norms. Furthermore, it was found that these consistent responses to high dominance stimuli tended to be the primaries themselves. However, with stimuli of low dominance, subjects tended to give *different* or inconsistent responses to given stimuli over repeated administrations of the list.

Saltz (1961) compared the commonality of WAT responses to stimuli differing in dominance levels of their primaries. It was found that the higher the dominance level of the stimuli, the greater the commonality of the responses obtained.

These studies demonstrate that associative mechanisms can account for responses obtained to stimuli on WATs. It does not follow, however,

---

[1] Jenkins, J. J., Russell, W. A., and Foss, D. "Word Association and Behavior: A Report of the Minnesota Studies." Manuscript in preparation for McGraw-Hill.

that one can conclude that associative factors are the only or even the major determinants of WAT responses.

Characteristics of the stimulus words other than their frequencies of association with other words have been found to affect word associations. Deese (1962) examined the relationship between the grammatical form class of the stimuli and the responses they elicited on a WAT. An earlier study (Ervin, 1961) had reported that children tended to give responses which were of the same form class as that of the stimuli. Furthermore, this tendency to give same form-class (paradigmatic) responses rather than different form-class (syntagmatic) responses tended to increase as a function of the age of the children. Similar results were obtained by Brown and Berko (1960). Deese's study was an extension of Ervin's work using college students as subjects. He employed substantially more words of more different grammatical classes as his stimuli. He was interested in whether the tendency to give same or different form-class responses varied as a function of the particular stimulus form classes used. Nouns, verbs, adjectives, and adverbs were found, in increasing order, to produce more responses of different form class from that of the form class of the stimuli.

Fillenbaum and Jones (1965) compared the form class of responses as a function of the form class of stimuli for an even wider variety of grammatical forms than did Deese. They found that the most frequently occurring type of response was of the same form class as that of the stimulus except for articles. However, there were different distributions of total responses on the basis of form class for stimuli of different form classes.

Jenkins (1960) suggested that commonality reflects underlying intraverbal habits in the individual which operate in determining which response will be given to each stimulus word. Thus far, Jenkins' view is essentially the same as the aforementioned associative strength position; however, Jenkins added the important restriction that if other factors are present, the intraverbal or associative factors may be overridden. He viewed the intraverbal factors or habits as fragile determinants of WAT responses which can be knocked out if stronger factors are present. For example, Jenkins (1959) demonstrated that subjects who gave low commonality responses gave more popular responses on a retest when explicitly instructed to do so. Similar findings were reported in a study by Horton, Marlowe, and Crowne (1963). Two groups, differing in set for speed, were given a WAT. One month later, a retest on the same list was given with instructions for popular responses. They obtained higher commonality responses on the retest. Jenkins implied that when no explicit instructions are given, the responses are determined by intraverbal habits; when explicit instructions are given, the associative verbal habits are overridden and other factors come into play.

The views of the writer agree with Jenkins' position that associative factors are readily supplanted, and, in addition, question whether one can ever measure "pure associative habits," uncontaminated by nonassociative factors. Thus, it is questionable as to whether the low commonality subjects in the Jenkins (1959) study were responding primarily on the basis of intraverbal habits in the absence of explicit experimental instructions on their original test. The self-instructions, or set, of the subject may be a more critical factor in determining whether he is a high or low commonality responder than his underlying set of intraverbal habits.

The effectiveness of instructional set on the qualitative aspects of responses is illustrated in the studies cited above (Jung, 1966; Sarason, 1959, 1961). In addition to instructional set, Jung (1966) demonstrated that the subject may "instruct himself" in a manner predictable from the demand characteristics of the situation, which were experimentally manipulated.

In Jung's study, two subjects were always tested in each other's presence on a successive word association test consisting of five repeated tests on a list of 10 stimulus words. Each subject received a different list of stimuli. Testing involved both aural stimulus presentation and oral response production. Half of the first subjects in each pair were instructed by written means to give the *same* response to any given stimulus word on successive tests, and half of the first subjects were instructed to give *different* responses to any given stimulus word on successive tests. All second subjects of each pair, however, were instructed by written means to give "the first word that entered their minds."

The total number of different responses over the list for second subjects tended to match the number produced by the explicitly instructed first subjects who preceded them. Second subjects gave as few or as many different responses as did the first subject with whom they were paired. Such findings demonstrate that the performance of another person on a similar task may serve as an instruction which the second person adopts as a guide for his performance in ambiguous situations such as WATs. This nonassociative factor overrides the associative factors in determining the nature of the responses.

The question of whether or not commonality simply reflects associative strength has also been raised by Carroll, Kjeldergaard, and Carton (1962). These experimenters found that much of the variance attributed to commonality could be due to the fact that the K-R stimuli contained many words with opposites or what Carroll et al. termed opposite-evoking stimuli (OES). Not only were many K-R stimuli classifiable as OES, but a check of the Russell and Jenkins (1954) norms showed that the primary responses given to these OES were usually the opposites and that these types of primaries were stronger (more frequent) than nonopposite primaries. Carroll et al. concluded that the number of opposite responses is a better measure of WAT responses than commonality.

Carroll et al.'s conclusion is further support for the view that other factors beside associative ones determine word associations. The production of an opposite response to a stimulus word is a response of a higher order classification. "Opposites" is a logical classification which may reflect a dominant response set in subjects. Thus, subjects give many primaries which are also opposites since the stimuli of the K-R list contain many OES. This response set increases the commonality as defined by the number of primaries elicited on the list. However, these primaries are elicited not so much by their associative strength but rather as an consequence of the response set to give opposites. This interpretation is similar to the analysis of Wynne et al. (1965) described earlier.

Kjeldergaard's (1962) findings support the above views regarding the basis of commonality. Instructions on a retest to "give opposites as responses if possible" produced greater increases in commonality than in Jenkins' (1959) study where retest instructions asked for popular responses.

The position that the strategy or task orientation of the subject, in addition to or rather than associative habits, is operative on WAT performance agrees with the views of Jenkins (1960). He found that subjects high in commonality also tended to be high on other verbal tasks and other WATs, whereas low commonality subjects were less predictable across tasks. Jenkins hypothesized that intraverbal habits are the primary determinants of the responses of high commonality subjects, whereas the performance of the low commonality subjects is affected by many different factors, such as individual differences in imagination, degree of mental disorder, nonconformity, etc. Thus, for high commonality subjects, it is possible that their characteristic mode of responding is similar across a range of tasks. However, low commonality subjects may display inconsistency or lack of style across a set of tasks. As a result, it is not surprising that no correlation has been found between commonality and certain personality measures (Jenkins, 1960).

Furthermore, as described earlier, Jenkins (1959) found that low commonality subjects, when instructed, were able to provide popular or higher commonality responses. This suggests that the associative habits are similar for subjects at any level of commonality but that nonassociative factors lead to differences in the level of commonality exhibited by different types of subjects.

What, then, is responsible for the level of commonality if one rules out associative factors as the only factors? Jenkins (1960), as well as Moran, Mefferd, and Kimble (1964), has studied styles of individual responding on WATs. Style refers to the individual's characteristic manner of responding and is a nonassociative factor affecting WAT performance.

Moran et al. (1964) administered a WAT of 125 words to separate groups of normals and schizophrenics. A different list was employed on each of 4 successive test days. They found that there was consistency within both types of subjects in the manner in which they responded on all four lists with respect to the style of responding or idiodynamic set employed. Moran et al. referred to implicit instructions or interpretations of the experimenter's instructions by the subject as his idiodynamic set. Factor analyses of the responses on each day revealed three such idiodynamic sets: a concrete attitude toward words (object-referent), an abstract attitude toward words (conceptual-referent), and a set for giving the fastest response (speed). Although individuals differed in the set which they employed, they were self-consistent by using the same set over all four lists. Such intraindividual consistency over lists with different associative characteristics is consistent with the concept of style. Style may be a factor which overrides the associative verbal habits as determinants of WAT responses.

Jung (1966) also obtained evidence of intraindividual consistency of response style. Three different consecutive lists of 10 words each were employed for word association. Each list was presented for five successive trials, and no explicit instructions were provided to the subject as to whether he should give the same or different responses to a given stimulus on successive trials. The number of different responses obtained on each list extended between the maximum of 50 and minimum of 10. More importantly for the concept of style, individuals were consistent in their levels of responding across the three different lists.

CONCLUSIONS

Although the word association technique and data obtained from it have been widely used in many areas, relatively few experimental studies of the WAT itself have been conducted. Such studies are necessary in order to understand the factors influencing WAT performance before it is applied in other research areas. This review of available experiments on WATs supports the position of Jenkins (1960) for the most part. Both associative and nonassociative factors must be considered as operative on WATs; however, the latter factors, which include different types of subject set as well as some aspects of administrative procedure, must be considered stronger factors which easily displace the former factors.

The WAT, by nature of its lack of structure, is subject to the influence of the subject's perception of the task. If he views the WAT as involving only the assessment of verbal associations, then his responses may be adequately predicted by associative mechanisms. However, if his self-instructions or the experimental instructions lead the subject to regard the task as involving personality or clinical measurements, the associative factors may be supplanted.

The extent to which the subject is governed by each type of factor may be a function of test administration procedures. For example, individual aural tests may be more stressful than group written tests. Relaxed testing may allow the subject to monitor responses, which cannot be done under speeded testing. Associative factors may be more prominent under group written or speeded testing, whereas nonassociative determinants may come into play when testing is individual and aural or relaxed.

SUMMARY

Experimental investigations of word association tests per se have been infrequent although the technique itself is widely used in other areas of research. This review cites studies aimed at the determination of variables which affect the nature of responses on word association tests (WATs). Experimental evidence illustrating the role of associative as well as nonassociative factors is reported. It is concluded that although word associations are generally considered to reflect underlying verbal habits primarily, various nonassociative factors such as the set of S and details of administrative procedure may be stronger determinants of responses on a WAT.

REFERENCES

Boyer, R. A., and Elton, C. F. Effect of instructions on free association. *Journal of Educational Psychology,* 1958, 49: 304–308.

Brody, N. Anxiety and the variability of word associates. *Journal of Abnormal and Social Psychology,* 1964, 68: 331–334.

Brown, R., and Berko, J. Word association and the acquisition of grammar. *Child Development,* 1960, 31: 1–14.

Buchwald, A. M. The generality of the norms of word associations. *American Journal of Psychology,* 1957, 70: 233–237.

Carroll, J. B., Kjeldergaard, P. M., and Carton, A. S. Number of opposites versus number of primaries as a response measure in free-association tests. *Journal of Verbal Learning and Verbal Behavior,* 1962, 1: 22–30.

Cofer, C. N., and Ford, T. J. Verbal context and free association-time. *American Journal of Psychology,* 1957, 70: 606–610.

Cramer, P. Successful mediated priming via associative bonds. *Psychological Reports,* 1964, 15: 235–238.

Deese, J. Form class and the determinants of association. *Journal of Verbal Learning and Verbal Behavior,* 1962, 1: 79–84.

Dörken, H., Jr. Frequency of common association. *Psychological Reports,* 1956, 2: 407–408.

Entwisle, D. R., and Forsyth, D. F. Word associations of children: Effect of method of administration. *Psychological Reports,* 1963, 13: 291–299.

Ervin, S. M. Changes with age in the verbal determinants of word-association. *American Journal of Psychology,* 1961, 74: 361–372.

Fillenbaum, S., and Jones, L. V. Grammatical contingencies in word association. *Journal of Verbal Learning and Verbal Behavior,* 1965, 4: 161–169.

Flavell, J. H., Draguns, J., Fernberg, L. D., and Budin, W. A microgenetic approach to word association. *Journal of Abnormal and Social Psychology,* 1958, 57: 1–7.

Hall, J. F., and Ugelow, A. Free association time as a function of word frequency. *Canadian Journal of Psychology,* 1957, 11: 29–32.

Horton, D. L., Marlowe, D., and Crowne, D. P. The effect of instructional set and need for social approval on commonality of word association responses. *Journal of Abnormal and Social Psychology,* 1963, 66: 67–72.

Jenkins, J. J. Effect on word-association of the set to give popular responses. *Psychological Reports,* 1959, 5: 94.

Jenkins, J. J. Commonality of association as an indicator of more general patterns of verbal behavior. In T. S. Sebeok (Ed.), *Style in language.* New York: Wiley, 1960. Pp. 307–330.

Jenkins, J. J., and Palermo, D. S. Further data on changes in word-association norms. *Journal of Personality and Social Psychology,* 1965, 1: 303–309.

Jenkins, J. J., and Russell, W. A. Systematic changes in word association norms: 1910–1952. *Journal of Abnormal and Social Psychology,* 1960, 60: 293–304.

Jenkins, P. M., and Cofer, C. N. An explanatory study of discrete free association to compound verbal stimuli. *Psychological Reports,* 1957, 3: 599–602.

Jung, J. Nonassociative factors on a successive word association test (SWAT). Unpublished manuscript, York University, 1966.

Kent, G. H., and Rosanoff, A. J. A study of association in insanity. *American Journal of Insanity,* 1910, 67: 37–96, 317–390.

Kjeldergaard, P. M. Commonality scores under instructions to give opposites. *Psychological Reports,* 1962, 11: 219–220.

Koff, R. H. Systematic changes in children's word-association norms 1910–1963. *Child Development,* 1965, 36: 299–305.

Marshall, G. R., and Cofer, C. N. Associative indices as measure of word relatedness: A summary and comparison of ten methods. *Journal of Verbal Learning and Verbal Behavior,* 1963, 1: 408–421.

Moran, L. J., Mefferd, R. B., Jr., and Kimble, J. P. Idiodynamic sets in word association. *Psychological Monographs,* 1964, 78: (2, Whole No. 579).

Palermo, D. S., and Jenkins, J. J. *Word association norms. Grade school through college.* Minneapolis: University of Minnesota Press, 1964.

Palermo, D. S., and Jenkins, J. J. Changes in word associations of fourth and fifth grade children from 1916–1961. *Journal of Verbal Learning and Verbal Behavior,* 1965, 4: 180–187.

Russell, W. A., and Jenkins, J. J. The complete Minnesota norms for responses to 100 words from the Kent-Rosanoff Word Association Test. Technical Report No. 11, 1954, University of Minnesota, Contract N8 onr 66216.

Saltz, E. The effect of induced stress on free associations. *Journal of Abnormal and Social Psychology,* 1961, 62: 161–164.

Sarason, I. G. Relationship of measures of anxiety and experimental instructions to word association test performance. *Journal of Abnormal and Social Psychology,* 1959, 59: 37–42.

Sarason, I. G. A note on anxiety, instructions, and word association performance. *Journal of Abnormal and Social Psychology,* 1961, 62: 153–154.

Siipola, E., Walker, W. N., and Kolb, D. Task attitudes in word association, projective and non-projective. *Journal of Personality,* 1955, 23: 441–459.

Woodworth, R. S., and Schlosberg, H. *Experimental psychology.* New York: Holt, 1954.

Wynne, R. D., Gerjuoy, H., and Schiffman, H. Association test antonym-response set. *Journal of Verbal Learning and Verbal Behavior,* 1965, 4: 341–347.

AN ABILITIES CONCEPTION OF PERSONALITY: SOME IMPLICATIONS FOR PERSONALTY MEASUREMENT *

JOHN WALLACE

Anybody who has taught an introductory course in personality theory knows from past experience that the first thing one must do is clarify certain misconceptions that students hold. Among these multifarious naïvetés which instructors anticipate, none is construed as more deserving of rapid extinction than the concept of personality as social skill. In one way or another, our ingenuous students must be led to eschew efficiency-evaluative conceptions of personality, i.e., personalities are "good" or "bad," and come to embrace what must certainly appear to them a bewildering phantasmagoria of putative underlying mediating structures and mechanisms. In exchange for a concept of personality which emphasizes the *efficiency* with which a person can elicit positive statements and actions from others, the student is invited to consider alternative constructs such as needs, traits, drives, cathexes, and a host of energy transformations apparently involving as many structures and mechanisms of change as there are theorists. Occasionally the instructor may encounter a student whose "misconceptions" about personality show considerable resistance to extinction. And perhaps this is as it should be. It may very well be the case that a social-skills conception is not so much wrong as it is narrow and incomplete.

Psychologists much like other scientists have shown a strong penchant for categorization. While cognizant of the arbitrary boundaries which, as a matter of convenience, separate one behavioral domain from another, we frequently *act* as if our categories were indeed mutually exclusive and non-overlapping. Perhaps our preference for neat and unambiguous categories led to the rather humorous subtractive definition of personality as that which remains after intelligence, aptitudes, interests, and attitudes have been removed. The fact that the extant literature in personality research abounds

with an enormous number of studies concerning needs or traits, while the first study which would follow logically from an explicit "abilities" conception of personality remains to be accomplished, certainly attests to the fact that most psychologists have tended to regard the domains of personality and ability as separate. This unfortunate separation has resulted in a necessary confounding of two important response properties in personality research, i.e., *response predisposition* and *response capability*. The present paper comprises an attempt to explore the consequences of conceiving personality as sets of abilities—abilities which, with regard to acquisition, maintenance, and modification, share much in common with other abilities.

RESPONSE PREDISPOSITION VERSUS RESPONSE CAPABILITY

The manner in which we choose to construe personality will obviously affect our research efforts. Construing personality as *essence* leads one to embrace somewhat different sets of theoretical constructs and research operations from those that would result from a construction of personality as response capability. And this is as it should be since the implications for personality measurement, description, and modification are of necessity quite different when we choose to search for *man as he really is* rather than *that of which he is capable*.

The bulk of research in personality has stemmed from essence concepts of personality and has focused upon such concepts as needs which, while accorded hypothetical status, stand in some relationship to underlying physiological processes (Murray, 1938) or traits which presumably possess a reality independent of the construct systems of observers (Allport, 1937). Both needs and traits possess the capacity to initiate and guide behavior, i.e., predispose the individual to respond in certain ways. While many who align themselves with trait or need concepts might reject the extreme critical realism as typified by the thought of Allport and might correspondingly embrace a position of nominalism to some degree or another, the fact remains that it would prove difficult to distinguish such positions from research operations alone. Essence concepts of personality have channelized research activities in directions that appear to have become "functionally autonomous."

In order to clarify the distinction made between response predisposition and response capability, let

* Reprinted with permission from the American Psychological Association. In *American Psychologist,* 1966, Vol. 21, pp. 132–138.

us consider a concrete example. Imagine a situation in which a child is observed striking another child repeatedly and in a forceful and excited fashion. A need theorist might infer the existence of an underlying construct, need for aggression. The trait theorist would probably demand more information and, depending upon the frequency of the behavior, the similarities among struck children, and the number of objectively diverse situations in which striking takes place, might infer the existence of a secondary, central, or cardinal trait of aggressiveness. In both cases, it is assumed that the individual is predisposed to respond aggressively. Curiously enough, neither trait nor need theory takes into account the simple but important matter of whether or not the child is capable of responding in a different way. Equally important but perhaps trivial at first blush is the fact that the child in question is indeed *capable* of an aggressive response in the first place, i.e., he is capable of assuming an aggressive role. Rather than inferences about predisposition in terms of operative needs or traits one can with equal justification assert that given individuals are simply either capable or incapable of certain responses in certain stimulus situations.

Is it possible that accurate knowledge of the breadth and diversity of *extant behavioral repertoires* in conjunction with detailed *knowledge of specific stimulus situations* would render motivational inferences superfluous? In conceiving of situations in which social needs or traits are presumed operative, it seems difficult to think of any in which capability statements appear less justified than predisposition statements. For example, consider the individual who may be described as gregarious or high in need for affiliation. Rather than describe such an individual as possessed of a strong need to "draw near and enjoyably co-operate or reciprocate with an allied other [Murray, 1938, p. 154]," could we not describe him equally well in terms of his utter inability to withstand social isolation or that he is quite incapable of independent effort? Turning to essence conceptions in terms of traits, might we not describe a "shy" person as one who is incapable of making assertive responses in certain situations? Or to take an example from psychopathology, a world of difference exists between the statements, "Patient A *is* schizophrenic" and "Patient A is *capable* of schizophrenic behavior." The first of the state-

ments, an essence concept, is somewhat incongruous with the observation that hospitalized psychotics infrequently show overt psychotic symptoms (Lindsley, 1962). Capability statements, on the other hand, do not imply "continuous pathology" and are not rendered problematic by the intermittent expression of pathological behavior.

Essence conceptions of personality typically involve hierarchical arrangements of personality structure. Thus, for example, needs are thought to vary with regard to intensity or strength. And traits are described as secondary, central, or cardinal. Perhaps the most extreme example of hierarchical organization is found in Freud's bifurcation of mental life into conscious and unconscious. The problems posed by hierarchical conceptions of the organization of personality structure are still unresolved. For example, the assumption that needs are hierarchically arranged in order of increasing strength renders *frequency* of response to projective stimuli a plausible measure of need strength. But, frequency will prove to be a useful measure of response strength and hence of response predisposition if and only if our assumption concerning the organization of needs is reasonable. It is not unreasonable to suppose that "needs" can be organized in other than hierarchical arrangements. For example, consider the extreme case of an individual who possesses relative balance among his operative needs. Of what significance is a given "need-related" response when it is but one of numerous possible need-related responses all of which are equivalent in strength and, hence, in probability of occurrence. Clearly, in such a case, one is in considerable danger of confusing response capability with response predisposition. Moreover, if one assumes a need organization other than a hierarchical one, how can one predict what particular need-related response will occur in response to a projective stimulus? And even more important, how can one ever hope to establish extratest correlates of such responses? As the organization of needs approaches balance within the individual, his responses to projective instruments should more clearly indicate his *capabilities* rather than his predispositions.

In order to allay the reader's fears that the preceding amounts to nothing more than a play upon words, let us now turn to some of the implications of an abilities conception for personality measurement.

IMPLICATIONS FOR PERSONALITY MEASUREMENT

In the measurement of abilities, attempts are made to elicit indices of *maximal* performance under *optimal* conditions of measurement. The phrase optimal conditions of measurement refers to the selection, development, and maintenance of both extratest and test stimuli in a manner considered most favorable for demonstration of the ability in question. Considerable care is exercised in the selection of items such that ambiguity is at a minimum and difficulty levels are known. Moreover, in abilities testing, ambiguity in *the purpose of testing* is generally quite low, i.e., the subject is frequently informed of the nature of the instrument, the possible range of inferences which are permissible from the resulting data, and the type of decisions which may take place either by the subject himself or by some external agent as a consequence of performance in the testing situation. Finally, response uncertainty is reduced since the subject is informed that convergent solutions exist, i.e., there is one and only one correct response to a given item rather than a range of responses.

In order to clarify differences, consider the most extreme example of predisposition measurement, i.e., projective techniques. In contrast to abilities measurement, projective techniques as originally conceived were thought to constitute rather pure measures of response predisposition. While great effort is expended in the construction of abilities measures to avoid ambiguity, the classical view of projective measurement which stemmed from well-known psychoanalytic notions of projection would imply the more ambiguity the better. Deliberate attempts were made to achieve stimuli highly unstructured as well as ambiguous. It was thought that when the subject was presented with stimuli whose components permitted multiple organizations and upon which numerous interpretations could be placed, his responses would reflect central tendencies, i.e., projections. Moreover, since maximum structure in the testing situation itself might obscure response predispositions, efforts were made to disguise the real purpose of testing, i.e., subjects were provided with vague instructional sets such as "tests of imagination," etc. Given the rather novel nature of tasks such as the Rorschach or the Thematic Apperception Test (TAT) as well as the rather wide publicity of projective techniques through educational and mass media channels, few subjects could be expected to accept these explanations of the nature of the task by the examiner. In contrast to abilities measurement, ambiguity in the purpose of testing when projective techniques are employed is quite high.

The subject is free to interpret (and usually does so) the nature of the test as he chooses. In addition, subjects are typically quite uncertain as to the range of inferences which are permissible from the resulting data as well as the type of decisions that might result as function of their performance in the testing situation. Response uncertainty is at a maximum since the subject is typically informed that convergent solutions do not exist, i.e., there are no right or wrong answers.

Obviously, then, predisposition conceptions of personality *can* lead to operations which are clearly at odds with those demanded by an abilities conception. In short, the projective-techniques setting in which highly ambiguous materials are employed comprises the most inefficient and nonoptimal of all possible situations one could imagine for the demonstration by subjects of their *capabilities*. It would follow from an abilities conception of personality that the usefulness of any measuring instrument would *decrease* as ambiguity in the measuring instrument is *increased*. Curiously enough, although some lack of agreement is apparent, this is precisely what research on the matter of ambiguity in the TAT seems to show. Two researches by Kagan (1956, 1959) provide clear support for the notion that the usefulness of TAT-like responses varies as a function of level of stimulus ambiguity. In the first, Kagan (1956) found that fantasy productions to highly structured hostile pictures differentiated aggressive boys from non-aggressive boys while responses to ambiguous pictures did not. In the second study, Kagan (1959) examined the stability of content scores over time. Two content measures, need for achievement and need for aggression, were the only fantasy motives showing stability. Both of these measures were derived from stimulus cards highly structured for these needs. Several researches (Leiman, 1961; Leiman and Epstein, 1961; Strizver, 1961) seem to indicate quite clearly that subjects respond to highly structured stimuli quite in line with a "capability" conception. Leiman and Epstein (1961) obtained self-report measures on their subjects for guilt associated with sexuality. The subjects were divided into low- and high-guilt groups. On pictures highly structured for sexual themes, those who reported themselves high on guilt over sexual matters projected less sexual imagery than those who had reported low guilt. Leiman (1961), in a separate study, found that subjects with conflict over sexual expression responded with less magnitude to high-relevance pictures than subjects with minimal or no conflict. In an experiment which involved induced sexual drive and experimental manipulation of inhibition, Strizver (1961) found that pictures of high relevance coupled with low inhibition yielded considerable sexual imagery. These studies involving highly structured pictures and socially "questionable" behaviors, i.e., hostility and sexuality, seem to suggest that subjects who appear *capable* of responding to the "stimulus pull" of highly structured cards do so while subjects who appear incapable for whatever reason, e.g., guilt, inhibition, do not. Murstein (1963), after reviewing the literature on ambiguity levels and the TAT, reaches a conclusion which is in partial agreement when he asserts that "low and medium-structure cards are most sensitive to the direct expression of drive, *while the highly structured cards* are most diagnostic through the avoidance of stimulus pull [p. 193]."

Considering the fact that projective techniques were once thought (and apparently still are by some) to constitute a "royal road to the unconscious," it seems of great interest to note that such responses become more predictable when *self-reported* guilt over expression of the drive in question is considered. It would appear that some relationship exists between the *ability* to assume roles in a stimulus situation which contains discriminable cues relevant to such roles (the TAT testing situation) and the ability to assume such roles in a second stimulus environment (a self-report testing situation). One may readily rephrase this relationship in terms of a broad general question as follows: What is the relationship between the ability to make certain verbal responses in a make-believe setting and the ability to respond in a similar fashion in overt behavior? In seeking an answer to this question, the ambiguity factor is crucial. In contrast to the classical view of projective techniques, which would imply the more ambiguity the better, an abilities conception would

hold that, as ambiguity is reduced through the addition of discriminable cues highly relevant to the examiner's purpose in testing, optimal conditions for the demonstration of maximal performance are achieved. Following this line of reasoning, one might achieve maximum clarity in projective-technique settings by simply directly requesting responses which correspond to the examiner's purposes in testing.

Murstein (1963) has indicated that a "test the limits" procedure employed by R. S. Lazarus with the TAT has yielded tentative findings of interest. Some observations from a study by the author and Michael Conant currently in progress appear most intriguing. Fraternity boys were presented with two cards from the TAT, Card 7BM and Card 6GF. Card 7BM has been shown to have moderate pull for hostile thema (Murstein, 1963) while Card 6GF seemed to be one which would have at least moderate pull for sexuality. Responses were first gathered under the typical McClelland "predisposition" instructions. After the subjects had written a story to each of the cards, the stimuli were immediately reshown and the subjects were asked to write the "sexiest story" of which they were capable to one and the "most hostile" story of which they were capable to the other. The stories which follow were obtained from two different subjects under the instructions to write the "sexiest" story of which they were capable.

Story 1. Martin leaned over her shoulder and while appearing to look at her face, he was actually viewing the bulge at her chest. He was suddenly overcome with desire wanting to grab them, rip open her dress, put his mouth all over them, suck them, bite them—and lower, yes lower. His hands wanted to roam, to enter secret places, to weave through pubic hairs. But his mouth and tongue too were moist with the desire to lick.

Suddenly he seized, and she let out a moan deep in the throat—half passionate, half-terrified.

But she let him anyway, she wanted it.

She quickly unbuttoned and his hands wormed into the opening.

He pulled her to him, waiting and trying to touch all over as her dress fell.

"Do you want me to touch you too?" she pleaded

Yes, yes!

Here?

Yes!

And here?

Yes!

And here?

Yes, yes!

His hands roamed wildly, seeking hard breasts and dark crevices.

Soon he laid her on the bed and began.

Story 2. The young woman has been living with another man for several weeks. Now she is pregnant and has come to her father for help. The old man is at first shocked since he thought his daughter was away at school. But he advises his daughter not to marry her lover if he does not really love her as she says. He is not a prudish man and understands that this can happen. He sees nothing wrong in keeping the child when it is born even though the mother is unmarried.

Eventually the girl meets a man who loves her for herself and is willing to accept the child. The woman is fully capable of offering sexual fulfillment to this man even though she suffers from a guilt feeling from the previous affair. It is unfortunate that society should force such a guilty complex upon her. She should feel free to give a man sexual fulfillment without marriage if she wants to. She does get married to this man, in this case, but only after she has lived with him long enough to know that she has a good deal more to offer him than sex.

While our research is still in its developmental stages, one cannot help but be impressed with the rather striking differences among subjects with regard to their ability to comply with the instructions. Equally intriguing are the marked differences in what subjects construe as constituting a "sexy" story. Lacking knowledge of the specific instructional set employed, one would hardly conclude that each of these subjects was in fact writing the "sexiest" story of which he was capable. The author of Story 1 appears quite capable of complying with the instructions. His account of the sexual act is liberally sprinkled with a variety of erotic acts. His characters behave with nearly total abandon and the consequences of engaging in sexual behavior for both male and female appear wildly pleasurable. On the other hand, the author of Story 2 omits description of the sexual act itself and concentrates upon unhappy consequences of sexual intercourse, e.g., an illegitimate pregnancy, guilt feelings, etc. Story 2 ends with a strong denial of the importance of sexual relations at all in male-female relationships. While it is obvious that striking differences in story content are obtained by "capability" instructions, it is, of course, necessary to show that such differences are useful in predicting extratest behavior.

In the preceding material, the implications of a response-capability conception of personality for projective measurement has been treated in some detail. It seems reasonable to draw implications for other methods of measurement as well. In fact, one may draw reasonable conclusions as to what methods of measurement may prove of value in personality assessment. The use of role playing in well-defined stimulus situations will most likely be of considerable value as an assessment method. By varying systematically given attributes of the stimulus situations under which roles are assumed, it may prove quite feasible to specify the conditions under which the individual becomes capable of performing given responses. It would appear most reasonable to assume that the closer the approximation of the role-playing situation to the predictive situation, the greater should be the accuracy of the predictions. If an individual can demonstrate response capability under a given set of conditions, he ought to be able to demonstrate the same capability under other highly similar conditions.

RESPONSE DEFICITS OR RESPONSE INHIBITION

Those interested in the assessment of personality in research as well as clinical settings have overlooked an assessment question of considerable importance. Emphasis upon psychodynamics and matters such as "unconscious conflict" dictate a search for internal states which presumably mediate and guide overt behavior. Psychoanalytic theorizing of the classical vintage assumes that powerful but unconscious controlling forces over overt behavior must be made conscious before overt behavior can be changed. Learning-theory conflict models emphasize the importance of lowering the avoidance gradient before approach responses can be made. Both positions are in a sense "subtractive." The classical analytical model emphasis the importance of libidinal discharge, i.e., catharsis. And the learning-theory conflict model indicates the importance of the unlearning of inhibitory tendencies, i.e., extinction of underlying conditioned emotional responses such as "anxiety." Neither position considers the important question of whether or not the alternative responses which are to be performed or the components of these responses are a part of the individual's repertoire of responses in the first place. It is an altogether erroneous assumption to assume that nonperformance of appropriate (as defined by an observer) responses *always* reflects the operation of response inhibition, avoidance, anxiety, or some other internal state. Certainly, it is difficult to see how an individual can perform given responses if he has never learned them, i.e., they are not a part of his response repertoire. A meaningful assessment problem then revolves around the question of the maintaining factors in behavior. It is most conceivable that some behaviors of the individual reflect *inadequate learning,* i.e., response deficits, while others may reflect *overlearning,* i.e., extraordinary conditioned emotional responses. In personality assessment, then, one must bear in mind that response incapability may be attributable to *either* a learning deficit or response inhibition.

RESPONSE CAPABILITY AND PSYCHOPATHOLOGY

An emphasis upon response capability would do much to bring order to one of the most confused areas of psychology, that of psychopathology. The difficulties posed by psychiatric nosology are well known. While many have criticized traditional classificatory schema, a satisfactory and *useful* diagnostic nomenclature has not appeared. The reliability (diagnostic agreement among those who use a given nomenclature) of such systems remains less than adequate. And the validity (demonstrated intraclassification and extraclassification correlates) leaves much to be desired. While some may feel that it is premature to abandon the search for an adequate classificatory system (e.g., Zigler and Phillips, 1961), it may very well be the case that our traditional approaches to psychiatric diagnosis are inherently wrong. The search for "disease entities" is, in actuality, a search for essences. Disease entity conceptions, regardless of the way the "symptomatic pie" is cut, have, without exception, ignored the conditions under which behavior occurs. Thus, for example, while hundreds of studies have been conducted upon the various attributes of persons classified as schizophrenic, few have concerned themselves with the conditions under which such behavior becomes apparent. Considering the fact that Lindsley's (1962) study of hospitalized patients indicated that such patients rather infrequently display overt psychotic behavior, a logical first step might be a careful analysis of given stimulus conditions in the hospital milieu under which the patient becomes capable of hallucinatory behavior, assaultive behavior, etc. Our assumption that schizophrenia is an entity, disease, or disorder has precluded sensitive analysis of situational determinants of the behavior of persons so diagnosed. Szasz's (1957) plea for a situational analysis of psychiatric operations is certainly a step in the right direction.

While clinicians who have embraced psychodynamic models of psychopathology have eschewed traditional nosological efforts in favor of description of underlying dynamics, it would appear that such efforts have simply directed the search for essences to a different level of functioning. The Freudian emphasis upon unconscious determinants of behavior and underlying structure typifies such efforts. It would certainly appear to make a world of difference, both to the patient and his therapist, to construe the patient as capable of homicidal behavior rather than, "underneath it all," a homicidal person. The former would lead to an examination of the conditions under which such behavior might occur. The latter might very well suggest little beyond immediate confinement!

In conclusion, many of the problems in personality assessment with which we are currently faced seem attributable, in large part, to the marked influence of "essence" conceptions of personality which have captured the imaginations of those interested in personality over the past 60-odd years. Conceiving personality in terms of response capability would appear to have meaningful and tangible implications for personality assessment. Certainly, a response-capability conception would do much toward providing the means by which the persistent epistemological quandary inherent in essence conceptions could be resolved. When faced with the inevitably incompatible evidence, how does one decide as to the *level* at which, or the *particular* stimulus situation in which, the "real" person (whatever that may mean) can be found?

In short, whether we choose to search for man "as he really is" or that "of which he is capable" is of utmost importance. Construing personality as response capability reemphasizes the importance of the stimulus conditions under which behavior occurs—something which, in my opinion, has been neglected by those interested in personality description, measurement, and development.

REFERENCES

Allport, G. W. *Personality: A psychological interpretation.* New York: Holt, 1937.

Kagan, J. The measurement of overt aggression from fantasy. *Journal of Abnormal and Social Psychology,* 1956, 52: 390–393.

Kagan, J. The stability of TAT fantasy and stimulus ambiguity. *Journal of Consulting Psychology*, 1959, 23: 226–271.

Leiman, A. H. Relationship of TAT sexual responses to sexual drive, sexual guilt, and sexual conflict. Unpublished doctoral dissertation, University of Massachusetts, 1961.

Leiman, A. H., and Epstein, A. Thematic sexual responses to sexual drive and guilt. *Journal of Abnormal and Social Psychology*, 1961, 63: 169–175.

Lindsley, O. L. Characteristics of the behavior of chronic psychotics as revealed by free-operant conditioning methods. In T. R. Sarbin (Ed.), *Studies in behavior pathology*. New York: Holt, Rinehart and Winston, 1962.

Murray, H. A. *Explorations in personality*. New York: Oxford University Press, 1938.

Murstein, B. I. *Theory and research in projective techniques*. New York: Wiley, 1963.

Strizver, G. L. Thematic sexual and guilt responses as related to stimulus-relevance and experimentally induced drive and inhibition. Unpublished doctoral dissertation, University of Massachusetts, 1961.

Szasz, T. S. The problem of psychiatric nosology: A contribution to a situational analysis of psychiatric operations. *American Journal of Psychiatry*, 1957, 114: 405– 413.

Zigler, E., and Phillips, L. Psychiatric diagnosis: A critique. *Journal of Abnormal and Social Psychology*, 1961, 63: 607–618.

TOWARD A THEORY OF MOTIVE ACQUISITION *

DAVID C. McCLELLAND [1]

Too little is known about the processes of personality change at relatively complex levels. The

* Reprinted with permission from the American Psychological Association. In *American Psychologist*, 1965, Vol. 23, pp. 321–333.

[1] I am greatly indebted to the Carnegie Corporation of New York for its financial support of the research on which this paper is based, and to my collaborators who have helped plan and run the courses designed to develop the achievement motive—chiefly George Litwin, Elliott Danzig, David Kolb, Winthrop Adkins, David Winter, and John Andrews. The statements made and views expressed are solely the responsibility of the author.

empirical study of the problem has been hampered by both practical and theoretical difficulties. On the practical side it is very expensive both in time and effort to set up systematically controlled educational programs designed to develop some complex personality characteristic like a motive, and to follow the effects of the education over a number of years. It also presents ethical problems since it is not always clear that it is as proper to teach a person a new motive as it is a new skill like learning to play the piano. For both reasons, most of what we know about personality change has come from studying psychotherapy where both ethical and practical difficulties are overcome by the pressing need to help someone in real trouble. Yet, this source of information leaves much to be desired: It has so far proven difficult to identify and systematically vary the "inputs" in psychotherapy and to measure their specific effects on subsequent behavior, except in very general ways (cf. Rogers and Dymond, 1954).

On the theoretical side, the dominant views of personality formation suggest anyway that acquisition or change of any complex characteristic like a motive in adulthood would be extremely difficult. Both behavior theory and psychoanalysis agree that stable personality characteristics like motives are laid down in childhood. Behavior theory arrives at this conclusion by arguing that social motives are learned by close association with reduction in certain basic biological drives like hunger, thirst, and physical discomfort which loom much larger in childhood than adulthood. Psychoanalysis, for its part, pictures adult motives as stable resolutions of basic conflicts occurring in early childhood. Neither theory would provide much support for the notion that motives could be developed in adulthood without somehow re-creating the childhood conditions under which they were originally formed. Furthermore, psychologists have been hard put to it to find objective evidence that even prolonged, serious, and expensive attempts to introduce personality change through psychotherapy have really proven successful (Eysenck, 1952). What hope is there that a program to introduce personality change would end up producing a big enough effect to study?

Despite these difficulties a program of research has been under way for some time which is attempting to develop the achievement motive in adults. It was undertaken in an attempt to fill some of the gaps in our knowledge about personality change or the acquisition of complex human characteristics. Working with n Achievement has proved to have some important advantages for this type of research: The practical and ethical problems do not loom especially large because previous research (McClelland, 1961) has demonstrated the importance of high n Achivement for entrepreneurial behavior and it is easy to find businessmen, particularly in underdeveloped countries, who are interested in trying any means of improving their entrepreneurial performance. Furthermore, a great deal is known about the origins of n Achievement in childhood and its specific effects on behavior so that educational programs can be systematically planned and their effects evaluated in terms of this knowledge. Pilot attempts to develop n Achievement have gradually led to the formulation of some theoretical notions of what motive acquisition involves and how it can be effectively promoted in adults. These notions have been summarized in the form of 12 propositions which it is the ultimate purpose of the research program to test. The propositions are anchored so far as possible in experiences with pilot courses, in supporting research findings from other studies, and in theory.

Before the propositions are presented, it is necessary to explain more of the theoretical and practical background on which they are based. To begin with, some basis for believing that motives could be acquired in adulthood had to be found in view of the widespread pessimism on the subject among theoretically oriented psychologists. Oddly enough we were encouraged by the successful efforts of two quite different groups of "change agents"—operant conditioners and missionaries. Both groups have been "naive" in the sense of being unimpressed by or ignorant of the state of psychological knowledge in the field. The operant conditioners have not been encumbered by any elaborate theoretical apparatus; they do not believe motives exist anyway, and continue demonstrating vigorously that if you want a person to make a response, all you have to do is elicit it and reward it (cf. Bandura and Walters, 1963, pp. 238 ff.). They retain a simple faith in the infinite plasticity of human behavior in which one response is just like any other and any one can be "shaped up" (strengthened by reward)—presumably even an "achievement" response as produced

by a subject in a fantasy test. In fact, it was the naive optimism of one such researcher (Burris, 1958) that had a lot to do with getting the present research under way. He undertook a counseling program in which an attempt to elicit and reinforce achievement-related fantasies proved to be successful in motivating college students to get better grades. Like operant conditioners, the missionaries have gone ahead changing people because they have believed it possible. While the evidence is not scientifically impeccable, common-sense observation yields dozens of cases of adults whose motivational structure has seemed to be quite radically and permanently altered by the educational efforts of Communist Party, Mormon, or other devout missionaries.

A man from Mars might be led to observe that personality change appears to be very difficult for those who think it is very difficult, if not impossible, and much easier for those who think it can be done. He would certainly be oversimplifying the picture, but at the very least his observation suggests that some theoretical revision is desirable in the prevailing views of social motives which link them so decisively to early childhood. Such a revision has been attempted in connection with the research on n Achievement (McClelland, Atkinson, Clark, and Lowell, 1953) and while it has not been widely accepted (cf. Berelson and Steiner, 1964), it needs to be briefly summarized here to provide a theoretical underpinning for the attempts at motive change to be described. It starts with the proposition that all motives are learned, that not even biological discomforts (as from hunger) or pleasures (as from sexual stimulation) are "urges" or "drives" until they are linked to cues that can signify their presence or absence. In time clusters of expectancies or associations grow up around affective experiences, not all of which are connected by any means with biological needs (McClelland et al., 1953, Ch. 2), which we label motives. More formally, motives are "affectively toned associative networks" arranged in a hierarchy of strength or importance within a given individual. Obviously, the definition fits closely the operations used to measure a motive: "an affectively toned associative cluster" is exactly what is coded in a subject's fantasies to obtain an n Achievement score. The strength of the motive (its position in the individual's hierarchy of motives) is measured essentially by counting the number of associations belonging to this cluster as compared to others that an individual produces in a given number of opportunities. If one thinks of a motive as an associative network, it is easier to imagine how one might go about changing it: The problem becomes one of moving its position up on the hierarchy by increasing its salience compared to other clusters. It should be possible to accomplish this end by such tactics as: (a) setting up the network—discovering what associations, for example, exist in the achievement area and then extending, strengthening, or otherwise "improving" the network they form; (b) conceptualizing the network—forming a clear and conscious construct that labels the network; (c) tying the network to as many cues as possible in everyday life, especially those preceding and following action, to insure that the network will be regularly rearoused once formed; and (d) working out the relation of the network to superordinate associative clusters, like the self-concept, so that these dominant schemata do not block the train of achievement thoughts—for example, through a chain of interfering associations (e.g., "I am not really the achieving type").

This very brief summary is not intended as a full exposition of the theoretical viewpoint underlying the research, but it should suffice to give a rough idea of how the motive was conceived that we set out to change. This concept helped define the goals of the techniques of change, such as reducing the effects of associative interference from superordinate associate clusters. But what about the techniques themselves? What could we do that would produce effective learning of this sort? Broadly speaking, there are four types of empirical information to draw on. From the animal learning experiments, we know that such factors as repetition, optimal time intervals between stimulus, response, and reward, and the schedule of rewards are very important for effective learning. From human learning experiments, we know that such factors as distribution of practice, repetitions, meaningfulness, and recitation are important. From experiences with psychotherapy (cf. Rogers, 1961), we learn that warmth, honesty, non-directiveness, and the ability to recode associations in line with psychoanalytic or other personality theories are important. And, from the attitude-change research literature, we learn that such variables as presenting one side or two, using

reason or prestige to support an argument, or affiliating with a new reference group are crucial for developing new attitudes (cf. Hovland, Janis, and Kelley, 1953). Despite the fact that many of these variables seem limited in application to the learning situation in which they were studied, we have tried to make use of information from all these sources in designing our "motive acquisition" program and in finding support for the general propositions that have emerged from our study so far. For our purpose has been above all to produce an effect large enough to be measured. Thus we have tried to profit by all that is known about how to facilitate learning or produce personality or attitude change. For, if we could not obtain a substantial effect with all factors working to produce it, there would be no point to studying the effects of each factor taken one at a time. Such a strategy also has the practical advantage that we are in the position of doing our best to "deliver the goods" to our course participants since they were giving us their time and attention to take part in a largely untried educational experience.[2]

Our overall research strategy, therefore, is "subtractive" rather than "additive." After we have demonstrated a substantial effect with some 10–12 factors working to produce it, our plan is to subtract that part of the program that deals with each of the factors to discover if there is a significant decline in the effect. It should also be possible to omit several factors in various combinations to get at interactional effects. This will obviously require giving a fairly large number of courses in a standard institutional setting for the same kinds of businessmen with follow-up evaluation of their performance extending over a number of years. So obviously it will be some time before each of the factors incorporated into the propositions which follow can be properly evaluated so far as its effect on producing motive change is concerned.

The overall research strategy also determined the way the attempts to develop the achievement motive have been organized. That is to say, in order to process enough subjects to permit testing

---

[2] Parenthetically, we have found several times that our stated desire to evaluate the effectiveness of our course created doubts in the minds of our sponsors that they did not feel about many popular courses for managers that no one has ever evaluated or plans to evaluate. An attitude of inquiry is not always an asset in education. It suggests one is not sure of his ground.

the effectiveness of various "inputs" in a reasonable number of years, the training had to be both of *short duration* (lasting 1–3 weeks) and *designed for groups* rather than for individuals as in person-to-person counseling. Fortunately these requirements coincide with normal practice in providing short courses for business executives. To conform further with that practice, the training has usually also been *residential* and *voluntary*. The design problems introduced by the last characteristic we have tried to handle in the usual ways by putting half the volunteers on a waiting list or giving them a different, technique-oriented course, etc. So far we have given the course to develop n Achievement in some form or another some eight times to over 140 managers or teachers of management in groups of 9–25 in the United States, Mexico, and India. For the most part the course has been offered by a group of 2–4 consultant psychologists either to executives in a single company as a company training program, or to executives from several different companies as a self-improvement program, or as part of the program of an institute or school devoted to training managers. The theoretical propositions which follow have evolved gradually from these pilot attempts to be effective in developing n Achievement among businessmen of various cultural backgrounds.

The first step in a motive development program is to create confidence that it will work. Our initial efforts in this area were dictated by the simple practical consideration that we had to "sell" our course or nobody would take it. We were not in the position of an animal psychologist who can order a dozen rats, or an academic psychologist who has captive subjects in his classes, or even a psychotherapist who has sick people knocking at his door every day. So we explained to all who would listen that we had every reason to believe from previous research that high n Achievement is related to effective entrepreneurship and that therefore business executives could expect to profit from taking a course designed to understand and develop this important human characteristic. What started as a necessity led to the first proposition dealing with how to bring about motive change.

Proposition 1. The more reasons an individual has in advance to believe that he can, will, or should develop a motive, the more educational attempts designed to develop that motive are likely to succeed. The empirical support for this proposition from other studies is quite impressive. It consists of (*a*) the prestige-suggestion studies showing that people will believe or do what prestigeful sources suggest (cf. Hovland et al., 1953); (*b*) the so-called "Hawthorne effect" showing that people who feel they are especially selected to show an effect will tend to show it (Roethlisberger and Dickson, 1947); (*c*) the "Hello-Goodbye" effect in psychotherapy showing that patients who merely have contact with a prestigeful medical authority improve significantly over waiting list controls and almost as much as those who get prolonged therapy (Frank, 1961); (*d*) the "experimenter bias" studies which show that subjects will often do what an experimenter wants them to do, even though neither he nor they know he is trying to influence them (Rosenthal, 1963); (*e*) the goal-setting studies which show that setting goals for a person particularly in the name of prestigeful authorities like "science" or "research" improves performance (Kausler, 1959; Mierke, 1955); (*f*) the parent-child interaction studies which show that parents who set higher standards of excellence for their sons are more likely to have sons with high n Achievement (Rosen and D'Andrade, 1959). The common factor in all these studies seems to be that goals are being set for the individual by sources he respects—goals which imply that his behavior should change for a variety of reasons and that it *can* change. In common-sense terms, belief in the possibility and desirability of change are tremendously influential in changing a person.

So we have used a variety of means to create this belief: the authority of research findings on the relationship of n Achievement to entrepreneurial success, the suggestive power of membership in an experimental group designed to show an effect, the prestige of a great university, our own genuine enthusiasm for the course and our conviction that it would work, as expressed privately and in public speeches. In short, we were trying to make every use possible of what is sometimes regarded as an "error" in such research—namely, the Hawthorne effect, experimenter bias, etc., because we believe it to be one of the most powerful sources of change.

Why? What is the effect on the person, theoretically speaking, of all this goal setting for him? Its primary function is probably to arouse what exists of an associative network in the achievement area for each person affected. That is, many studies have shown that talk of achievement or affiliation or power tends to increase the frequency with which individuals think about achievement or affiliation or power (cf. Atkinson, 1958). And the stronger the talk, the more the relevant associative networks are aroused (McClelland et al., 1953). Such an arousal has several possible effects which would facilitate learning: (*a*) It elicits what exists in the person of a "response" thus making it easier to strengthen that response in subsequent learning. (*b*) It creates a discrepancy between a goal (a "Soll-lage" in Heckhausen's—1963—theory of motivation) and a present state ("Ist-lage") which represents a cognitive dissonance the person tries to reduce (cf. Festinger, 1957); in common-sense terms he has an image clearly presented to him of something he is not but should be. (*c*) It tends to block out by simple interference other associations which would inhibit change—such as, "I'm too old to learn," "I never learned much from going to school anyway," "What do these academics know about everyday life?" or "I hope they don't get personal about all this."

After the course has been "sold" sufficiently to get a group together for training, the first step in the course itself is to present the research findings in some detail on exactly how n Achievement is related to certain types of successful entrepreneurial performance. That is, the argument of *The Achieving Society* (McClelland, 1961) is presented carefully with tables, charts, and diagrams, usually in lecture form at the outset and with the help of an educational TV film entitled the *Need to Achieve*. This is followed by discussion to clear up any ambiguities that remain in their minds as far as the central argument is concerned. It is especially necessary to stress that not all high achievement is caused by high n Achievement—that we have no evidence that high n Achievement is an essential ingredient in success as a research scientist, professional, accountant, office or personnel manager, etc.; that, on the contrary, it seems rather narrowly related to entrepreneurial, sales, or promotional success, and therefore should be of particular interest to them because they hold jobs which either have or could have an entrepreneurial component. We rationalize this activity in terms of the following proposition.

Proposition 2. The more an individual perceives that developing a motive is consistent with the demands of reality (and reason), the more educational attempts designed to develop that motive are likely to succeed. In a century in which psychologists and social theorists have been impressed by the power of unreason, it is well to remember that research has shown that rational arguments do sway opinions, particularly among the doubtful or the uncommitted (cf. Hovland et al., 1953). Reality in the form of legal, military, or housing rules does modify white prejudice against Negroes (cf. Berelson and Steiner, 1964, p. 512). In being surprised at Asch's discovery that many people will go along with a group in calling a shorter line longer than it is, we sometimes forget that under most conditions their judgments conform with reality. The associative network which organizes "reality"—which places the person correctly in time, place, space, family, job, etc.—is one of the most dominant in the personality. It is the last to go in psychosis. It should be of great assistance to tie any proposed change in an associative network in with this dominant schema in such a way as to make the change consistent with reality demands or *"reasonable"* extensions of them. The word "reasonable" here simply means extensions arrived at by the thought processes of proof, logic, etc., which in adults have achieved a certain dominance of their own.

The next step in the course is to teach the participants the n Achievement coding system. By this time, they are a little confused anyway as to exactly what we mean by the term. So we tell them they can find out for themselves by learning to code stories written by others or by themselves. They take the test for n Achievement before this session and then find out what their own score is by scoring this record. However, we point out that if they think their score is too low, that can be easily remedied, since we teach them how to code and how to write stories saturated with n Achievement; in fact, that is one of the basic purposes of the course: to teach them to think constantly in n Achievement terms. Another aspect of the learning is discriminating achievement thinking from thinking in terms of power or affiliation. So usually the elements of these other two coding schemes are also taught.

Proposition 3. The more thoroughly an individual develops and clearly conceptualizes the associative network defining the motive, the more likely he is to develop the motive. The original empirical support for this proposition came from the radical behaviorist Skinnerian viewpoint: If the associative responses are the motive (by definition), to strengthen them one should elicit them and reinforce them, as one would shape up any response by reinforcement (cf. Skinner, 1953). But, support for this proposition also derives from other sources, particularly the "set" experiments. For decades laboratory psychologists have known that one of the easiest and most effective ways to change behavior is to change the subject's set. If he is responding to stimulus words with the names of animals, tell him to respond with the names of vegetables, or with words meaning the opposite, and he changes his behavior immediately and efficiently without a mistake. At a more complex level Orne (1962) had pointed out how powerful a set like "This is an experiment" can be. He points out that if you were to go up to a stranger and say something like "Lie down!" he would in all probability either laugh or escape as soon as possible. But, if you say "This is an experiment! Lie down!" more often than not, if there are other supporting cues, the person will do so. Orne has demonstrated how subjects will perform nonsensical and fatiguing tasks for very long periods of time under the set that "This is an experiment." At an even more complex level, sociologists have demonstrated often how quickly a person will change his behavior as he adopts a new role set (as a parent, a teacher, a public official, etc.). In all these cases an associative network exists usually with a label conveniently attached which we call set and which, when it is aroused or becomes salient, proceeds to control behavior very effectively. The purpose of this part of our course is to give the subjects a set or a carefully worked out associative network with appropriate words or labels to describe all its various aspects (the coding labels for parts of the n Achievement scoring system like Ga+, I+, etc.; cf. Atkinson, 1958). The power of words on controlling behavior has also been well documented (cf. Brown, 1958).

It is important to stress that it is not just the label (n Achievement) which is taught. The person must be able to produce easily and often the new associative network itself. It is here that our research comes closest to traditional therapy which could be understood as the prolonged and laborious formation of new associative networks to replace anxiety-laden ones. That is, the person

over time comes to form a new associative network covering his relations, for example, to his father and mother, which still later he may label an "unresolved Oedipus complex." When cues arise that formerly would have produced anxiety-laden associations, they now evoke this new complex instead, blocking out the "bad" associations by associative interference. But all therapists, whether Freudian or Rogerian, insist that the person must learn to produce these associations in their new form, that teaching the label is not enough. In fact, this is probably why so-called directive therapy is ineffective: It tries to substitute new constructs ("You should become an achiever") for old neurotic or ineffective ones ("rather than being such a slob") without changing the associative networks which underlie these surface labels. A change in set such as "Respond with names of vegetables" will not work unless the person has a whole associative network which defines the meaning of the set. The relation of this argument is obvious both to Kelly's (1955) insistence on the importance of personal constructs and to the general semanticists' complaints about the neurotic effects of mislabeling or overabstraction (Korzybski, 1941).

But, theoretically speaking, why should a change in set as an associative network be so influential in controlling thought and action? The explanation lies in part in its symbolic character. Learned acts have limited influence because they often depend on reality supports (as in typewriting), but learned thoughts (symbolic acts) can occur any time, any place, in any connection, and be applied to whatever the person is doing. They are more generalizable. Acts can also be inhibited more easily than thoughts. Isak Dinesen tells the story of the oracle who told the king he would get his wish so long as he never thought of the left eye of a camel. Needless to say, the king did not get his wish, but he could easily have obeyed her prohibition if it had been to avoid *looking* at the left eye of a camel. Thoughts once acquired gain more control over thoughts and actions than acquired acts do because they are harder to inhibit. But why do they gain control over actions? Are not thoughts substitutes for actions? Cannot a man learn to think achievement thoughts and still not act like an achiever in any way? The question is taken up again under the next proposition, but it is well to remember here that thoughts are symbolic acts and that practice of symbolic acts facilitates performing the real acts (cf. Hovland, 1951, p. 644).

The next step in the course is to tie thought to action. Research has shown that individuals high in n Achievement tend to act in certain ways. For example, they prefer work situations where there is a challenge (moderate risk), concrete feedback on how well they are doing, and opportunity to take personal responsibility for achieving the work goals. The participants in the course are therefore introduced to a "work" situation in the form of a business game in which they will have an opportunity to show these characteristics in action or more specifically to develop them through practice and through observing others play it. The game is designed to mimic real life: They must order parts to make certain objects (e.g., a Tinker Toy model bridge) after having estimated how many they think they can construct in the time allotted. They have a real chance to take over, plan the whole game, learn from how well they are doing (use of feedback), and show a paper profit or loss at the end. While they are surprised often that they should have to display their real action characteristics in this way in public, they usually get emotionally involved in observing how they behave under pressure of a more or less "real" work situation.

Proposition 4. The more an individual can link the newly developed network to related actions, the more the change in both thought and action is likely to occur and endure. The evidence for the importance of action for producing change consists of such diverse findings as (*a*) the importance of recitation for human learning, (*b*) the repeated finding that overt commitment and participation in action changes attitudes effectively (cf. Berelson and Steiner, 1964, p. 576), and (*c*) early studies by Carr (cf. McGeoch and Irion, 1952) showing that simply to expose an organism to what is to be learned (e.g., trundling a rat through a maze) is nowhere near as effective as letting him explore it for himself in action.

Theoretically, the action is represented in the associative network by what associations precede, accompany, and follow it. So including the acts in what is learned *enlarges* the associative network or the achievement construct to include action. Thus, the number of cues likely to trip off the n Achievement network is increased. In common-sense terms, whenever he works he now evaluates what he is doing in achievement terms, and whenever he thinks about achivement he tends to think of its action consequences.

So far the course instruction has remained fairly abstract and removed from the everyday experiences of businessmen. So, the next step is to apply what has been learned to everyday business activities through the medium of the well-known case-study method popularized by the Harvard Business School. Actual examples of the development of the careers or firms of business leaders or entrepreneurs are written up in disguised form and assigned for discussion to the participants. Ordinarily, the instructor is not interested in illustrating "good" or "bad" managerial behavior—that is left to participants to discuss—but in our use of the material, we do try to label the various types of behavior as illustrating either n Achievement and various aspects of the achievement sequence (instrumental activity, blocks, etc.), or n Power, n Affiliation, etc. The participants are also encouraged to bring in examples of managerial behavior from their own experience to evaluate in motivational terms.

Proposition 5. The more an individual can link the newly conceptualized association-action complex (or motive) to events in his everyday life, the more likely the motive complex is to influence his thoughts and actions in situations outside the training experience. The transfer-of-training research literature is not very explicit on this point, though it seems self-evident. Certainly, this is the proposition that underlies the practice of most therapy when it involves working through or clarifying, usually in terms of a new, partially formed construct system, old memories, events from the last 24 hours, dreams, and hopes of the future. Again, theoretically, this should serve to enlarge and clarify the associative network and increase the number of cues in everyday life which will rearouse it. The principle of symbolic practice can also be invoked to support its effectiveness in promoting transfer outside the learning experience.

For some time most course participants have been wondering what all this has to do with them personally. That is to say, the material is introduced originally on a "take it or leave it" objective basis as something that ought to be of interest to them. But, sooner or later, they must confront the issue as to what meaning n Achievement has in their own personal lives. We do not force this choice on them nor do we think we are brainwashing them to believe in n Achievement. We believe and we tell them we believe in the "obstinate audience" (cf. Bauer, 1964), in the ultimate capacity of people to resist persuasion or to do in the end what they really want to do. In fact, we had one case in an early session of a man who at this point decided he was not an achievement-minded person and did not want to become one. He subsequently retired and became a chicken farmer to the relief of the business in which he had been an ineffective manager. We respected that decision and mention it in the course as a good example of honest self-evaluation. Nevertheless, we do provide them with all kinds of information as to their own achievement-related behavior in the fantasy tests, in the business game, in occasional group dynamics session—and ample opportunity and encouragement to think through what this information implies so far as their self-concept is concerned and their responsibilities to their jobs. Various devices such as the "Who am I?" test, silent group meditation, or individual counseling have been introduced to facilitate this self-confrontation.

Proposition 6. The more an individual can perceive and experience the newly conceptualized motive as an improvement in the self-image, the more the motive is likely to influence his future thoughts and actions. Evidence on the importance of the ego or the self-image on controlling behavior has been summarized by Allport (1943). In recent years, Rogers and his group (Rogers, 1961; Rogers and Dymond, 1954) have measured improvement in psychotherapy largely in terms of improvement of the self-concept in relation to the ideal self. Indirect evidence of the importance of the self-schema comes from the discussion over whether a person can be made to do things under hypnosis that are inconsistent with his self-concept or values. All investigators agree that the hypnotist can be most successful in getting the subject to do what might normally be a disapproved action if he makes the subject perceive the action as consistent with his self-image or values (cf. Berelson and Steiner, 1963, p. 124).

The same logic supports this proposition. It seems unlikely that a newly formed associative network like n Achievement could persist and influence behavior much unless it had somehow "come to terms" with the pervasive superordinate network of associations defining the self. The logic

is the same as for Proposition 2 dealing with the reality construct system. The n Achievement associations must come to be experienced as related to or consistent with the ideal self-image; otherwise associations from the self-system will constantly block thoughts of achievement. The person might be thinking, for example: "I am not that kind of person; achievement means judging people in terms of how well they perform and I don't like to hurt people's feelings."

Closely allied to the self-system is a whole series of networks only half conscious (i.e., correctly labeled) summarizing the values by which the person lives which derive from his culture and social milieu. These values can also interfere if they are inconsistent with n Achievement as a newly acquired way of thinking. Therefore, it has been customary at this point in the course to introduce a value analysis of the participants' culture based on an analysis of children's stories, myths, popular religion, comparative attitude surveys, customs, etc., more or less in line with traditional, cultural anthropological practice (cf. Benedict, 1946; McClelland, 1964). For example, in America we have to work through the problem of how being achievement oriented seems to interfere with being popular or liked by others which is highly valued by Americans. In Mexico a central issue is the highly valued "male dominance" pattern reflected in the patriarchal family and in the *macho* complex (being extremely masculine). Since data show that dominant fathers have sons with low n Achievement and authoritarian bosses do not encourage n Achievement in their top executives (Andrews, 1965), there is obviously a problem here to be worked through if n Achievement is to survive among thoughts centered on dominance. The problem is not only rationally discussed. It is acted out in role-playing sessions where Mexicans try, and often to their own surprise fail, to act like the democratic father with high standards in the classic Rosen and D'Andrade (1959) study on parental behavior which develops high n Achievement. Any technique is used which will serve to draw attention to possible conflicts between n Achievement and popular or traditional cultural values. In the end it may come to discussing parts of the *Bhagavad Gita* in India, or the *Koran* in Arab countries, that seem to oppose achievement striving or entrepreneurial behavior.

Proposition 7. The more an individual can per-

ceive and experience the newly conceptualized motive as an improvement on prevailing cultural values, the more the motive is likely to influence his future thoughts and actions. The cultural anthropologists for years have argued how important it is to understand one's own cultural values to overcome prejudices, adopt more flexible attitudes, etc., but there is little hard evidence that doing so changes a person's behavior. What exists comes indirectly from studies that show prejudice can be decreased a little by information about ethnic groups (Berelson and Steiner, 1963, p. 517), or that repeatedly show an unconscious link between attitudes and the reference group (or subculture to which one belongs—a link which presumably can be broken more easily by full information about it, especially when coupled with role-playing new attitudes (cf. Berelson and Steiner, 1963, pp. 566 ff.).

The theoretical explanation of this presumed effect is the same as for Propositions 2 and 6. The newly learned associative complex to influence thought and action effectively must somehow be adjusted to three superordinate networks that may set off regularly interfering associations—namely, the networks associated with reality, the self, and the social reference group or subculture.

The course normally ends with each participant preparing a written document outlining his goals and life plans for the next 2 years. These plans may or may not include references to the achievement motive; they can be very tentative, but they are supposed to be quite specific and realistic; that is to say, they should represent moderate levels of aspiration following the practice established in learning about n Achievement of choosing the moderately risky or challenging alternative. The purpose of this document is in part to formulate for oneself the practical implications of the course before leaving it, but even more to provide a basis for the evaluation of their progress in the months after the course. For it is explained to the participants that they are to regard themselves as "in training" for the next 2 years, that 10–14 days is obviously too short a time to do more than conceive a new way of life: It represents the residential portion of the training only. Our role over the next 2 years will be to remind them every 6 months of the tasks they have set themselves by sending them a questionnaire to fill out which will serve

to rearouse many of the issues discussed in the course and to give them information on how far they have progressed toward achieving their goals.

Proposition 8. The more an individual commits himself to achieving concrete goals in life related to the newly formed motive, the more the motive is likely to influence his future thoughts and actions.

Proposition 9. The more an individual keeps a record of his progress toward achieving goals to which he is committed, the more the newly formed motive is likely to influence his future thoughts and actions. These propositions are both related to what was called "pacing" in early studies of the psychology of work. That is, committing oneself to a specific goal and then comparing one's performance to that goal has been found to facilitate learning (cf. Kausler, 1959), though most studies of levels of aspiration have dealt with goal setting as a result rather than as a "cause" of performance. At any rate, the beneficial effect of concrete feedback on learning has been amply demonstrated by psychologists from Thorndike to Skinner. Among humans the feedback on performance is especially effective if they have high n Achievement (French, 1958), a fact which makes the relevance of our request for feedback obvious to the course participants.

The theoretical justification for these propositions is that in this way we are managing to keep the newly acquired associative network salient over the next 2 years. We are providing cues that will regularly rearouse it since he knows he is still part of an experimental training group which is supposed to show a certain type of behavior (Proposition 1 again). If the complex is rearoused sufficiently often back in the real world, we believe it is more likely to influence thought and action than if it is not aroused.

As described so far the course appears to be devoted almost wholly to cognitive learning. Yet this is only part of the story. The "teachers" are all clinically oriented psychologists who also try to practice whatever has been learned about the type of human relationship that most facilitates emotional learning. Both for practical and theoretical reasons this relationship is structured as warm, honest, and nonevaluative, somewhat in the manner described by Rogers (1961) and recommended by distinguished therapists from St.

Ignatius[3] to Freud. That is to say, we insist that the only kind of change that can last or mean anything is what the person decides on and works out by himself, that we are there not to criticize his past behavior or direct his future choices, but to provide him with all sorts of information and emotional support that will help him in his self-confrontation. Since we recognize that self-study may be quite difficult and unsettling, we try to create an optimistic relaxed atmosphere in which the person is warmly encouraged in his efforts and given the opportunity for personal counseling if he asks for it.

Proposition 10. Changes in motives are more likely to occur in an interpersonal atmosphere in which the individual feels warmly but honestly supported and respected by others as a person capable of guiding and directing his own future behavior. Despite the widespread belief in this proposition among therapists (except for operant conditioners), one of the few studies that directly supports it has been conducted by Ends and Page (1957) who found that an objective learning-theory approach was less successful in treating chronic alcoholics than a person-oriented, client-centered approach. Rogers (1961) also summarizes other evidence that therapists who are warmer, more empathic, and genuine are more successful in their work. Hovland et al. (1953) report that the less manipulative the intent of a communicator, the greater the tendency to accept his conclusions. There is also the direct evidence that parents of boys with high n Achievement are warmer, more encouraging and less directive (fathers only) than parents of boys with low n Achievement (Rosen and D'Andrade, 1959). We tried to model ourselves after those parents on the theory that what is associated with high n Achievement in children might be most likely to encourage

[3] In his famous spiritual exercises which have played a key role in producing and sustaining personality change in the Jesuit Order, St. Ignatius states: "The director of the Exercizes ought not to urge the exercitant more to poverty or any promise than to the contrary, nor to one state of life or way of living more than another . . . [while it is proper to urge people outside the Exercizes] the director of the Exercizes . . . without leaning to one side or the other, should permit the Creator to deal directly with the creature, and the creature directly with his Creator and Lord."

its development in adulthood. This does not mean permissiveness or promiscuous reinforcement of all kinds of behavior; it also means setting high standards as the parents of the boys with high n Achievement did but having the relaxed faith that the participants can achieve them.

The theoretical justification for this proposition can take two lines: Either one argues that this degree of challenge to the self-schema produces anxiety which needs to be reduced by warm support of the person for effective learning to take place, or one interprets the warmth as a form of direct reinforcement for change following the operant-conditioning model. Perhaps both factors are operating. Certainly there is ample evidence to support the view that anxiety interferes with learning (cf. Sarason, 1960) and that reward shapes behavior (cf. Bandura and Walters, 1963, pp. 283 ff.).

One other characteristic of the course leads to two further propositions. Efforts are made so far as possible to define it as an "experience apart," "an opportunity for self-study," or even a "spiritual retreat" (though that term can be used more acceptably in India than in the United States). So far as possible it is held in an isolated resort hotel or a hostel where there will be few distractions from the outside world and few other guests. This permits an atmosphere of total concentration on the objectives of the course including much informal talk outside the sessions about Ga^+, Ga^-, I^+, and other categories in the coding definition. It still comes as a surprise to us to hear these terms suddenly in an informal group of participants talking away in Spanish or Telugu. The effect of this retreat from everyday life into a special and specially labeled experience appears to be twofold: It dramatizes or increases the salience of the new associative network and it tends to create a new reference group.

Proposition 11. Changes in motives are more likely to occur the more the setting dramatizes the importance of self-study and lifts it out of the routine of everyday life. So far as we know there is no scientific evidence to support this proposition, though again if one regards Jesuits as successful examples of personality change, the Order has frequently followed the advice of St. Ignatius to the effect that "the progress made in the Exercizes will be greater, the more the exercitant withdraws from all friends and acquaintances, and from all worldly cares." Theory supports the proposition in two respects: Removing the person from every-day routine (*a*) should decrease interfering associations (to say nothing of interfering appointments and social obligations), and (*b*) should heighten the salience of the experience by contrast with everyday life and make it harder to handle with the usual defenses ("just one more course," etc.). That is to say, the network of achievement-related associations can be more strongly and distinctly aroused in contrast to everyday life, making cognitive dissonance greater and therefore more in need of reduction by new learning. By the same token we have found that the dramatic quality of the experience cannot be sustained very long in a 12–18-hour-a-day schedule without a new routine attitude developing. Thus, we have found that a period somewhere between 6 to 14 days is optimal for this kind of "spiritual retreat." St. Ignatius sets an outside limit of 30 days, but this is when the schedule is less intensive (as ours has sometimes been), consisting of only a few hours a day over a longer period.

Proposition 12. Changes in motives are more likely to occur and persist if the new motive is a sign of membership in a new reference group. No principle of change has stronger empirical or historical support than this one. Endless studies have shown that people's opinions, attitudes, and beliefs are a function of their reference group and that different attitudes are likely to arise and be sustained primarily when the person moves into or affiliates with a new reference group (cf. Berelson and Steiner, 1963, pp. 580 ff.). Many theorists argue that the success of groups like Alcoholics Anonymous depends on the effectiveness with which the group is organized so that each person demonstrates his membership in it by "saving" another alcoholic. Political experience has demonstrated that membership in small groups like Communist or Nazi Party cells is one of the most effective ways to sustain changed attitudes and behavior.

Our course attempts to achieve this result (*a*) by the group experience in isolation—creating the feeling of alumni who all went through it together; (*b*) by certain signs of identification with the group, particularly the language of the coding system, but also including a certificate of membership; and (*c*) by arranging where possible to have par-

ticipants come from the same community so that they can form a "cell" when they return that will serve as an immediate reference group to prevent gradual undermining of the new network by other pressures.

In theoretical terms a reference group should be effective because its members constantly provide cues to each other to rearouse the associative network, because they will also reward each other for achievement-related thoughts and acts, and because this constant mutual stimulation, and reinforcement, plus the labeling of the group, will prevent assimilation of the network to bigger, older, and stronger networks (such as those associated with traditional cultural values).

In summary, we have described an influence process which may be conceived in terms of "input," "intervening," and "output" variables as in Table 1. The propositions relate variables in Column A via their effect on the intervening variables in Column B to as yet loosely specified behavior in Column C, which may be taken as evidence that "development" of n Achievement has "really" taken place. The problems involved in evaluation of effects are as great and as complicated as those involved in designing the treatment, but they cannot be spelled out here, partly for lack of space, partly because we are in an even earlier stage of examining and classifying the effects of our training 1 and 2 years later preparatory to conceptualizing more clearly what happens. It will have to suffice to point out that we plan extensive comparisons over a 2-year period of the behaviors of our trained subjects compared with matched controls along the lines suggested in Column C.

What the table does is to give a brief overall view of how we conceptualize the educational or treatment process. What is particularly important is that the propositions refer to *operationally defined* and *separable* treatment variables. Thus, after having demonstrated hopefully a large effect of the total program, we can subtract a variable and see how much that decreases the impact of the course. That is to say, the course is designed so that it could go ahead perfectly reasonably with very little advanced goal setting (P1), with an objective rather than a warm personal atmosphere (P11), without the business game tying thought to action (P9), without learning to code n Achievement and write achievement-related stories (P3),

TABLE 1

VARIABLES CONCEIVED AS ENTERING INTO THE MOTIVE CHANGE PROCESS

A Input or independent variables	B Intervening variables	C Output or dependent variables
1. Goal setting for the person (P1, P11)	Arousal of associative network (salience)	Duration and/or extensiveness of changes in:
2. Acquisition of n Achievement associative network (P2, P3, P4, P5)	Experiencing and labeling the associative network	1. n Achievement associative network
3. Relating new network to superordinate networks	Variety of cues to which network is linked	2. Related actions: use of feedback, moderate risk taking, etc.
reality (P2)	Interfering associations assimilated or bypassed by reproductive interference	3. Innovations (job improvements)
the self (P6)		4. Use of time and money
cultural values (P7)		5. Entrepreneurial success as defined by nature of job held and its rewards
4. Personal goal setting (P8)		
5. Knowledge of progress (P3, P4, P9)		
6. Personal warmth and support (P10)	Positive affect associated with network	
7. Support of reference group (P11, P12)		

Note.—P1, P11, etc., refer to the numbered propositions in the text.

without cultural value analysis (P7), or an isolated residential setting (P1, P11, P12). The study units are designed in a way that they can be omitted without destroying the viability of the treatment which has never been true of other studies of the psychotherapeutic process (cf. Rogers and Dymond, 1954).

But is there any basis for thinking the program works in practice? As yet, not enough time has elapsed to enable us to collect much data on long-term changes in personality and business activity. However, we do know that businessmen can learn to write stories scoring high in n Achievement, that they retain this skill over 1 year or 2, and that they like the course—but the same kinds of things can be said about many unevaluated management training courses. In two instances we have more objective data. Three courses were given to some 34 men from the Bombay area in early 1963. It proved possible to develop a crude but objective and reliable coding system to record whether each one had shown *unusual* entrepreneurial activity in the 2 years prior to the course or in the 2 years after course. "Unusual" here means essentially an unusual promotion or salary raise or starting a new business venture of some kind. Of the 30 on whom information was available in 1965, 27% had been unusually active before the course, 67% after the course ($\chi^2 = 11.2$, $p < .01$). In a control group chosen at random from those who applied for the course in 1963, out of 11 on whom

information has so far been obtained, 18% were active before 1963, 27% since 1963.

In a second case, four courses were given throughout 1964 to a total of 52 small businessmen from the small city of Kakinada in Andhra Pradesh, India. Of these men, 25% had been unusually active in the 2-year period before the course, and 65% were unusually active immediately afterwards ($\chi^2 = 17.1$, $p < .01$). More control data and more refined measures are needed, but it looks very much as if, in India at least, we will be dealing with a spontaneous "activation" rate of only 25%–35% among entrepreneurs. Thus we have a distinct advantage over psychotherapists who are trying to demonstrate an improvement over a two-thirds spontaneous recovery rate. Our own data suggest that we will be unlikely to get an improvement or "activation" rate much above the two-thirds level commonly reported in therapy studies. That is, about one-third of the people in our courses have remained relatively unaffected. Nevertheless the two-thirds activated after the course represent a doubling of the normal rate of unusual entrepreneurial activity— no mean achievement in the light of the current pessimism among psychologists as to their ability to induce lasting personality change among adults.

One case will illustrate how the course seems to affect people in practice. A short time after participating in one of our courses in India, a 47-year-old businessman rather suddenly and dramatically decided to quit his excellent job and go into the construction business on his own in a big way. A man with some means of his own, he had had a very successful career as employee-relations manager for a large oil firm. His job involved adjusting management-employee difficulties, negotiating union contracts, etc. He was well-to-do, well thought of in his company, and admired in the community, but he was restless because he found his job increasingly boring. At the time of the course his original n Achievement score was not very high and he was thinking of retiring and living in England where his son was studying. In an interview, 8 months later, he said the course had served not so much to "motivate" him but to "crystallize" a lot of ideas he had vaguely or half consciously picked up about work and achievement all through his life. It provided him with a new language (he still talked in terms of standards of excellence, blocks, moderate risk, goal anticipation, etc.), a new construct which served to organize those ideas and explain to him why he was bored with his job, despite his obvious success. He decided he wanted to be an n-Achievement-oriented person, that he would be unhappy in retirement, and that he should take a risk, quit his job, and start in business on his own. He acted on his decision and in 6 months had drawn plans and raised over $1,000,000 to build the tallest building in his large city to be called the "Everest Apartments." He is extremely happy in his new activity because it means selling, promoting, trying to wangle scarce materials, etc. His first building is partway up and he is planning two more.

Even a case as dramatic as this one does not prove that the course produced the effect, despite his repeated use of the constructs he had learned, but what is especially interesting about it is that he described what had happened to him in exactly the terms the theory requires. He spoke not about a new motive force but about how existing ideas had been crystallized into a new associative network, and it is this new network which *is* the new "motivating" force according to the theory.

How generalizable are the propositions? They have purposely been stated generally so that some term like "attitude" or "personality characteristic" could be substituted for the term "motive" throughout, because we believe the propositions will hold for other personality variables. In fact, most of the supporting experimental evidence cited comes from attempts to change other characteristics. Nevertheless, the propositions should hold best more narrowly for motives and especially the achievement motive. One of the biggest difficulties in the way of testing them more generally is that not nearly as much is known about other human characteristics or their specific relevance for success in a certain type of work. For example, next to nothing is known about the need for power, its relation to success, let us say, in politics or bargaining situations, and its origins and course of development in the life history of individuals. It is precisely the knowledge we have about such matters for the achievement motive that puts us in a position to shape it for limited, socially and individually desirable ends. In the future, it seems to us, research in psychotherapy ought to follow a similar course. That is to say, rather than developing "all purpose" treatments, good for any person and any purpose, it should aim to develop specific treatments or educational programs built on laboriously accumulated detailed knowledge of the characteristic to be changed. It is in this spirit that the present research program in motive acquisition has been designed and is being tested out.

REFERENCES

Allport, G. W. The ego in contemporary psychology. *Psychological Review,* 1943, 50: 451–478.

Andrews, J. D. W. The achievement motive in two types of organizations. *Journal of Personality and Social Psychology,* 1965, in press.

Atkinson, J. W. (Ed.), *Motives in fantasy, action and society.* Princeton, N. J.: Van Nostrand, 1958.

Bandura, A., and Walters, R. H. *Social learning and personality development.* New York: Holt, Rinehart and Winston, 1963.

Bauer, R. A. The obstinate audience: The influence process from the point of view of social communication. *American Psychologist,* 1964, 19: 319–329.

Benedict, Ruth. *The chrysanthemum and the sword.* Boston: Houghton Mifflin, 1946.

Berelson, B., and Steiner, G. A. *Human behavior: An inventory of scientific findings.* New York: Harcourt, Brace, 1964.

Brown, R. W. *Words and things.* Glencoe, Ill.: Free Press, 1958.

Burris, R. W. The effect of counseling on achievement motivation. Unpublished doctoral dissertation, University of Indiana, 1958.

Ends, E. J., and Page, C. W. A study of three types of group psychotherapy with hospitalized male inebriates. *Quarterly Journal on Alcohol,* 1957, 18: 263–277.

Eysenck, H. J. The effects of psychotherapy: An evaluation. *Journal of Consulting Psychology,* 1952, 16: 319-324.

Festinger, L. *A theory of cognitive dissonance.* New York: Harper and Row, 1957.

Frank, J. *Persuasion and healing.* Baltimore: Johns Hopkins Press, 1961.

French, E. G. Effects of the interaction of motivation and feedback on task performance. In J. W. Atkinson (Ed.), *Motives in fantasy, action and society.* Princeton, N. J.: Van Nostrand, 1958. Pp. 400–408.

Heckhausen, H. Eine Rahmentheorie der Motivation in zehn Thesen. *Zeitschrift für experimentelle und angewandte Psychologie,* 1963, X/4: 604–626.

Hovland, C. I. Human learning and retention. In S. S. Stevens (Ed.), *Handbook of experimental psychology.* New York: Wiley, 1951.

Hovland, C. I., Janis, I. L., and Kelley, H. H. *Communication and persuasion: Psychological studies of opinion change.* New Haven: Yale Univer. Press, 1953.

Kausler, D. H. Aspiration level as a determinant of performance. *Journal of Personality,* 1959, 27, 346–351.

Kelly, G. A. *The psychology of personal constructs.* New York: Norton, 1955.

Korzybski, A. *Science and sanity.* Lancaster, Pa.: Science Press, 1941.

McClelland, D. C. *The achieving society.* Princeton, N. J.: Van Nostrand, 1961.

McClelland, D. C. *The roots of consciousness.* Princeton, N. J.: Van Nostrand, 1964.

McClelland, D. C., Atkinson, J. W., Clark, R. A., and Lowell, E. L. *The achievement motive.* New York: Appleton-Century, 1953.

McGeoch, J. A., and Irion, A. L. *The psychology of human learning.* (2nd ed.) New York: Longmans, Green, 1952.

Mierke, K. *Wille und Leistung.* Göttingen: Verlag für Psychologie, 1955.

Orne, M. On the social psychology of the psychological experiment: With particular reference to demand characteristics and their implications. *American Psychologist,* 1962, 17: 776–783.

Roethlisberger, F. J., and Dickson, W. J. *Management and the worker.* Cambridge: Harvard Univer. Press, 1947.

Rogers, C. R. *On becoming a person.* Boston: Houghton Mifflin, 1961.

Rogers, C. R., and Dymond, R. F. (Eds.) *Psychotherapy and personality change.* Chicago: Univer. Chicago Press, 1954.

Rosen, B. C., and D'Andrade, R. G. The psychosocial origins of achievement motivation. *Sociometry,* 1959, 22: 185–218.

Rosenthal, R. On the social psychology of the psychological experiment: The experimenter's hypothesis as unintended determinant of experimental results. *American Scientist,* 1963, 51: 268–823.

Sarason, I. Empirical findings and theoretical problems in the use of anxiety scales. *Psychological Bulletin,* 1960, 57: 403–415.

Skinner, B. F. *Science and human behavior.* New York: Macmillan, 1953.

SEER VERSUS SIGN [*]

GARDNER LINDZEY [1]

The task of the investigator is inextricably linked to the individual observer, and nowhere is this more frustratingly evident than in the study of personality. Although the efforts of psychologists to dehumanize—more positively, to "objectify" —the process of data collection have been many and ingenious, it remains true that behind every validity coefficient or network of justifying concepts and operations there lurks, at some point, an observer, hopefully a sensitive and unbiased observer. Few psychologists have accepted this fact more gracefully than Henry A. Murray and none has labored more diligently and imaginatively to maximize the contribution of the observer and to

[*] Reprinted with permission from Academic Press, Inc. In *Journal of Experimental Research in Personality,* 1965, Vol. 1, pp. 17–26.

[1] This research was supported by a grant from the Ford Foundation and research grant M-1949 from the National Institute of Mental Health. The paper was written while the author was in residence at the Center for Advanced Study in the Behavioral Sciences. Final preparation of the manuscript was facilitated by sage comments from Lee J. Cronbach, Anthony Davids, Edward E. Jones, and David T. Lykken. I received valuable assistance in the collection and analysis of data from Jean Bradford, James Kincannon, and Harvey D. Winston. The late Ephraim Rosen generously served as one of the judges in the second study.

provide him with a respected position within the field of psychology.

The present investigations may be viewed as minor attempts to assess the relative merits of the trained human observer in a particular setting. More specifically, they compare the judgment of one or more unaided clinicians with objective and actuarial methods of prediction under conditions where the special strengths of the clinician are given a reasonable opportunity to manifest themselves. As such they belong to a growing body of investigations concerned with the relative merits of mechanical, objective, and (typically) quantitative methods of prediction as opposed to the relatively subjective and qualitative predictions of the clinician. Such studies have been summarized ably by Meehl (1954), Cronbach (1956), and Gough (1962) among others, and the area of investigation owes much to the earlier writing of Allport (1937, 1942), Sarbin (1941, 1942), and Murray (1938, 1948).

It is worth noting that this issue possesses certain significant links to the idiographic-nomothetic question, and like the latter controversy it has proved sturdily resistant to the frequent suggestion (for example, Holt, 1958; Zubin, 1956) that sophisticated examination of the problem reveals little or no real basis for maintaining such a distinction or issue. Just as species survival may be considered the ultimate test of "fitness," so too the persistence of a conceptual distinction or empirical issue over many years in the face of repeated efforts to obliterate or dissolve it may be considered evidence of theoretical-empirical fitness or significance.

STUDY I

In this study, which already has been reported in part (Lindzey, Tejessy, and Zamansky, 1958), it was possible to compare the predictive (literally, postdictive) effectiveness of a number of objective TAT indices of homosexuality (individually and in combination) with the comparable effectiveness of clinical predictions by an experienced interpreter of the TAT.

Method

Subjects. The Ss consisted of 20 undergraduate male students who had acknowledged overt homosexual acts and a group of 20 undergraduates comparable in sex, age, and educational

level but with no known history of homosexuality. They were volunteers and received no pay for their participation.

Procedure. Five TAT cards (4, 6BM, 7BM, 10, 18BM) were administered individually by an experienced male administrator. The resultant protocols with all identification of individual Ss removed were then scored for 20 different variables or indices that were believed on the basis of prior research or formulation to be indicative of homosexual tendencies (Lindzey, Bradford, Tejessy, and Davids, 1959). The variables, scoring procedures, and reliabilities are described in greater detail in an earlier publication (Lindzey *et al.*, 1958), and they are briefly identified in Table 1.

The TAT protocols were also sorted blindly by an experienced interpreter of the TAT who was generally familiar with all the objective indices used in the study but was permitted to make his classification without justification or specification of the basis for his decision. He also divided the predictions into those of which he was confident and those of which he was uncertain.

Results

The results summarized in Table 1 indicate clearly that the objective indices functioned very well in comparison with similar indices derived from TAT protocols that have been examined in previous studies (Lindzey and Newburg, 1954; Lindzey and Tejessy, 1956). However, it is equally clear that none of the indices serves by itself as a powerful basis for discrimination between the homosexual and normal groups. Indeed, when compared with the judgments of an experienced clinician they fare very poorly. The judge was able to sort the protocols with 95% accuracy—classifying incorrectly one S from each group. Moreover, of the 29 judgments which he considered "confident," there were no incorrect classifications.

The question remains whether it is possible to combine after the fact the information contained in the 20 objective indices and produce findings that parallel, or closely resemble, those produced by qualitative, clinical judgments. The first step in answering this question was simply to arrange all indices (no matter what the prediction or expectation had been) so that a high score was typical of the homosexual group and a low score of the normal group. This involved reversing two variables (15 and 19). We then cumulated raw

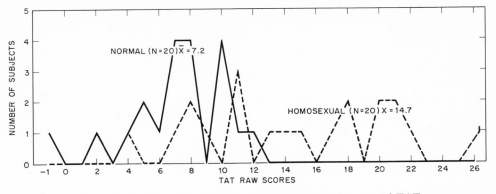

FIG. 1. Comparison of normal and homosexual college students on total TAT scores.

scores across all variables for each *S,* ignoring the different ranges of scores permitted by the various scoring procedures. The resultant distribution of scores for the two groups are reported in Fig. 1. Next we divided the scores for each variable as close to the median as possible so that we had a high and low group. Then for each *S* we simply counted the number of variables in which his score placed him in the high group, and the results for the two groups are summarized in Fig. 2. Both of these procedures functioned effectively; indeed, if we permit ourselves the luxury of maximizing diagnostic accuracy by identifying a cutting point after-the-fact, we are able to identify such a score for each distribution that will correctly classify 34 of the 40 *S*s.

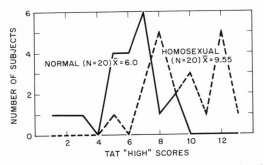

FIG. 2. Comparison of normal and homosexual college subjects on total TAT "high" scores.

A third objective approach used in the attempt to extract the diagnostic information potentially available in these indices emphasized pattern or configural analysis. We employed an ingenious technique devised by Lykken (1956; Lykken and

Rose, 1963) that utilizes dichotomous predictor variables to make up actuarial tables for the various patterns of scores. Each table represents the observed frequency from each criterion group for one particular pattern; for example, for the pattern low,high,high for variables 14, 16, and 17 there were 5 homosexual *S*s and 0 normal *S*s, thus leading to the prediction of homosexuality from this pattern, while for the pattern low,low,low for variables 14, 16, and 17 there were 7 homosexual *S*s and 20 normal *S*s, leading to the prediction of normality. It is also possible to provide a "validity coefficient" for each pattern which is based upon the number of cases in the original group displaying the pattern and the amount of difference between criterion groups in frequency for this pattern.

In the present study we used five actuarial tables, consisting of three variables each, which included most of the individual indices that seemed to function effectively. The variable groups employed were 14–16–17, 12–19–20, 2–12–16, 6–2–11, and 3–4–15. With this method it proved possible to predict correctly (after the fact) 34 out of the 40 cases when the prediction for each case was that indicated by three or more of the five tables. This performance could be increased slightly (36 correct identifications) if the prediction was based upon the difference for each *S* between the summed validity coefficients for the homosexual predictions as opposed to the normal predictions.

In summary, we find that the informed but unfettered and nonquantified clinician functioned slightly better than any of the actuarial combinations of objective scores. The relative similarity

TABLE 1
DIMENSIONAL TAT COMPARISON OF COLLEGE STUDENTS

Variable	Normal (N = 20)		Homosexual (N = 20)		p^a
	M	Freq.	M	Freq.	
1 Misrecognition of sex		3		3	—
2 18BM: Attack from the rear		4		9	< .10
3 Feminine identification	1.05		1.55		< .005
4 Attitude toward marriage	− .32		.48		< .005
5 Man killing woman		0		5	< .02
6 Sexual references	.55		1.25		NS
7 Unstable identification	1.65		2.25		< .005
8 Feminine feelings, emotions	2.10		2.05		NS
9 Shallow heterosexual relations	.90		1.75		< .005
10 Male embrace		0		1	—
11 Attitude toward opposite sex	− .32		.18		NS
12 Tragic heterosexual relations		2		7	.06
13 Attachment to mother		2		4	NS
14 18BM: Symbolism or allegory		0		6	.01
15 Attachment to father		5		1	.18
16 Derogatory sexual terms applied to women		0		7	.004
17 Homosexual content		0		6	.01
18 Incest		0		1	—
19 10BM: No elderly couple		16		11	NS
20 18BM: Positive introduction of female		5		0	.02

[a] Values of p for differences between means are based on t tests. Those for variables 2 and 19 are based on χ^2, and the remainder, on Fisher's Exact Test. Only the variables on which the difference was not in the predicted direction (8, 15, 19) were assigned to a two-tailed test of significance.

in performance of the two approaches must be evaluated against the background of a deliberate maximizing after-the-fact of the information contained in the objective indices, even when this meant reversing the intended direction of scoring. Thus, the clinician made his predictions before the fact while the objective procedure was adjusted to maximize its sensitivity after the fact. Under these circumstances one may naturally expect a great deal of shrinkage when the actuarial procedure is applied to an independent sample of observations. Study II was intended to permit an estimate of just how effectively the two systems would function when applied to a new source of data.

STUDY II

In this study we compared clinical judgment with our actuarial procedures when applied to two groups of Ss that were distinguished from each other in terms of overt homosexual acts but otherwise were quite different from the Ss of the

previous study. We were interested in further evaluating the two different methods of prediction and also in examining the situational generality of findings concerned with the relation between a particular TAT sign or index and an underlying disposition or personal attribute.

Method

Subjects. The Ss consisted of 30 male prisoners in a state maximum security prison. The group was divided into 14 who were known to have been overtly homosexual prior to imprisonment (11 were convicted of sodomy charges) and 16 who provided no evidence of homosexuality prior to imprisonment or during incarceration. The groups were matched in terms of age, education, intelligence, period of imprisonment, and place of residence. The normal group was selected in such a manner as to exclude persons convicted of crimes of violence, and consequently it included predominately persons convicted of charges related to crimes against property. The Ss were paid for their participation in the study and all knew that they were participating in a study that involved, among other things, an interest in homosexuality.

Procedure. The TAT was administered individually (Cards 2, 3BM, 6BM, 9BM, 10, 12, 13 MF, 18 BM) by two male administrators who were unaware of the group to which any S belonged. Each examiner tested an equal number of normal and homosexual Ss.

The stories were scored for 20 variables according to the procedures developed in the earlier studies by two raters who were unaware of the group to which any S belonged. Discrepancies between the two sets of scores were eliminated by discussion between the two raters so that the final score represented a composite rating. The scoring was the same as in the previous study except that the larger number of cards increased the range of scores for a number of variables, and for two variables (4, 11) the numerical score assigned for the five categories was changed from (—2 to +2 to (0 to +4).

The Ss were classified by two judges independently as being homosexual or nonhomosexual on the basis of the TAT stories and knowledge of the true distribution of cases in the two categories. One judge (A) was unfamiliar with the objective indices and the findings of the previous studies, but the other judge (B) was intimately familiar with these findings although he did not make any systematic effort to use this information. Judge B was the same judge who had made the comparable ratings in the first study. Each judge divided his predictions into those of which he was confident and those of which he was uncertain.

Results

Examination of the findings summarized in Table 2 indicates a consistent failure of the objective indices to differentiate between normal and homosexual Ss in a manner comparable to that revealed in the first study. Of 20 comparisons only one achieved conventional significance in the predicted direction; there were four reversals in the expected direction of the difference, and most of the 10 group differences in the predicted direction were minute. It seems clear that these indices, even though "validated" in several previous studies (Davids, Joelson, and McArthur, 1956; Lindzey *et al.*, 1958), have little merit when applied under the conditions of the present study.

Not surprisingly, in view of the results for the individual variables, the application of the actuarial procedures used in the previous study to combine these indices were highly ineffective. Whether we use raw scores cumulated (Fig. 3), number of high scores (Fig. 4), or the configural scoring method, we arrive at the same "hit rate" of 17 out of 30, or 57%. Even an additional, and more complicated application of Lykken's technique

TABLE 2

DIMENSIONAL TAT COMPARISON OF PRISONERS

Variable	Normal (N = 16)		Homosexual (N = 14)	
	M	Freq.	M	Freq.
1	2.31		1.86	
2		2		4
3	3.50		3.79	
4	15.75		15.00	
5		4		4
6	1.75		1.93	
7	1.44		1.43	
8	1.94		1.79	
9	.56		.64	
10		0		0
11	15.94		15.86	
12		5		5
13		3		8
14		1		1
15		0		0
16		4		4
17		0		0
18		0		2
19		6		6
20		14		12

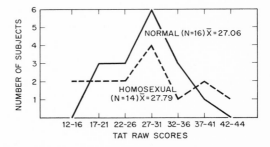

FIG. 3. Comparison of normal and homosexual prisoners on total TAT scores.

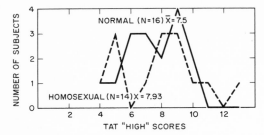

FIG. 4. Comparison of normal and homosexual prisoners on total TAT "high" scores.

failed to improve upon the 57% figure. In this
method each S was compared with all 40 of Ss in
the previous study, and for each pair-comparison
a deviation score was computed that represented
the number of times the two Ss were discrepant on
a variable (one high and the other low). Then
those Ss in the comparison group who had deviation scores of six or less were identified, and a
prediction was made based upon whether the majority of these similar patterns had been drawn
from homosexual or normal Ss.

TABLE 3

ACCURACY OF JUDGES' PREDICTIONS FOR NORMAL
AND HOMOSEXUAL PRISONERS

| | | Per cent correct | |
Predictions	N	Judge A	Judge B
Over-all	30	80	60
Confident	14	71	86
Uncertain	16	88	38

In contrast, the judges' performance (Table 3,
although variable, appears distinctly better. The
most efficient of the judges was able to identify
group membership with 80% success. While the
less successful judge was able to identify correctly
only 60% of the cases, of those 14 judgments in
which he indicated confidence he was correct in
86% or 12 of the cases. Thus Judge A was able
to predict significantly better than chance for all
Ss, and Judge B functioned well above chance for
those predictions of which he was confident; none
of the actuarial methods proved able to function
above the level of chance.

DISCUSSION

Clinical versus Actuarial Prediction. The studies
we have just discussed may be viewed as a direct,
although modest, response to a challenge issued by

Paul Meehl following a comprehensive review of
the clinical-statistical research literature. His survey failed to reveal any clear evidence for the
superiority of the clinical method, and he concluded, "I have reservations about some of these
studies; I do not believe they are optimally designed
to exhibit the clinician at his best; but I submit that
it is high time that those who are so sure that the
'right kind of study' will exhibit the clinician's
prowess, should *do* this right kind of study and
back up their claim with evidence" (Meehl, 1957,
p. 272). Our findings, although far from definitive,
do provide evidence that, at least under some circumstances, clinical judgment may function somewhat more efficiently than objective and actuarial
prediction.

For such findings to be of more than glancing
importance, however, it must be possible to state
something about the conditions that may have
played a role in producing these discrepant results.
In the present study it seems to us the events predisposing in favor of the sensitive and informed
clinician relate to the psychometric intractability
of the TAT. In brief, we have here an instrument
that elicits a large amount of complex response
data and which is accompanied by very little in the
way of rules for effectively transforming or en-
capsulating these responses within a finite number
of scores, variables, or indicants. Thus, although
there have been many attempts to establish dimensions or categories for analyzing TAT responses (cf. Lindzey *et al.*, 1959), none of them
has met with spectacular success. It appears that
the massive and unwieldy qualitative data of the
TAT continue to provide predictive cues for the
skilled clinician that are not represented adequately
in the objective indices upon which actuarial prediction must rest. To generalize, it seems reasonable to expect that, under circumstances where
there is little available in the way of sensitive and
objective guidelines, the experienced clinician is
likely to function relatively better than in a psycho-
metrically highly developed terrain.

It may appear that I am suggesting that clinical
predictions function better only in very primitive
areas of psychological measurement. Indeed, over-
looking the role of the clinician as a source of
ideas or hypotheses that may lead to further objectivity and specification, this is precisely what is
implied. Insofar as the objective basis for clinical
prediction's operating better than chance can be
made explicit and verbalized, it will usually prove

possible to devise substitutive methods that are freer of error than the human mind. On the other hand, there is little doubt that much of psychological measurement, defined broadly, is still in a very primitive state and, consequently, it may be no trivial accomplishment to function relatively well under conditions such as those that prevailed in this study.

It is clear, in addition, that conditions in the present study come closer than most studies in this area to meeting the demands that the criterion to be predicted is at least as familiar to the clinician as to the psychometrician. Comparison of the two methods of prediction in connection with academic achievement, or some comparable outcome variable, favors the actuarial method both because this area of behavior is more often studied by psychometrist than clinician and also because the objective indices for predicting such behavior are relatively efficient and readily susceptible to quantitative analysis. McArthur (1956), Meehl (1956), and Cronbach (1960) have pointed to the importance of studying clinical predictions on their home terrain, and all have suggested that here the performance of the clinician may be relatively more encouraging, as indeed it appears to be.

It is worth emphasis that, contrary to a frequent misunderstanding, Meehl has always believed in the probable superiority of the clinician over the actuary under certain circumstances. Indeed, in a recent paper (Meehl, 1959) he has identified six factors that should favor the clinician. The first is *open-endedness,* where the event to be predicted cannot be represented by means of a single dimension or a small number of categories but where the predictor himself is determining the terms or content of the prediction. Second is *unanalyzed stimulus-equivalences,* where the rules for analyzing or classifying the relevant data are not objectively specifiable. Third is the existence of *empty cells,* where particular events or combinations of events have not been observed in the past and consequently have not yet gained a place in the actuarial tables. Fourth is the possible role of *theory-mediation,* where there is an active process of theoretical reasoning and hypothesis formation intervening between the observational data and the particular prediction to be made. Fifth is the situation which offers *insufficient time* for the application of actuarial methods simply because an immediate decision must be made. Sixth is the case

where there is a *nonlinear* and particularly a *configural* or pattern association between the predictor variables and the criterion. The performance of the clinicians in the present studies is presumably consistent with the implications of Meehl's statements in regard to "unanalyzed stimulus equivalences" and "empty cells" as factors favoring the effectiveness of clinical prediction. That is, the clinicians responded to stimuli that had not yet been objectively identified and classified, and among these cues there may even have been some that had not been encountered in previous studies and consequently could not have been used by the actuarial methods. It is impossible to completely rule out the role of theory-mediated hypotheses, but the subjective report of the judges and the state of theory in this area make such a contingency most unlikely.

Our findings are only obliquely related to Holt's (1958) distinctions between pure actuarial, naive clinical, and sophisticated clinical prediction. However, insofar as the distinction between naive clinical and sophisticated clinical can be mapped into this study, we would have to place Judge A in the naive category and Judge B in the sophisticated class, on the basis of the fact that Judge B had made comparable predictions from a similar data base before and was intimately familiar with objective findings in this area. Our evidence suggests that the naive clinical judge did at least as well as the sophisticated clinical judge, contrary to Holt's expectation, although one would not like to generalize far from only two judges.

If we recklessly accept the difference between Judge A and Judge B as a real and stable difference, we are faced with the mild embarrassment of increased experience and sophistication appearing to diminish accuracy or sensitivity. Obviously this is not necessarily the case. Judge A may simply have been a better diagnostician, and with increased experience his advantage might have been even greater than it was. However, it is at least possible that experience with predicting this variable under conditions of the first study, and a thorough knowledge of the TAT literature on homosexuality, might make a negative contribution to prediction in the second study. Remembering how poorly the objective indices functioned in the second study, it seems altogether conceivable that if Judge B was deriving many of his diagnostic cues from these indices he might have operated at a disadvantage.

Utility of Projective Technique "Signs" or Objective Indices. In view of the fact that the indices and related variables studied in the present investigations comprise one of the most successful sets of "signs" in the history of TAT research, their almost total collapse upon further cross-validation might be considered a serious indictment of this entire approach to measurement. On the other hand, such a finding should scarcely come as a surprise in view of the many investigations (for example, Kenny, 1954, 1961; Lindzey and Silverman, 1959; Masling, 1960) and formulations (Lindzey, 1952, 1961; Gleser, 1963) that have made clear the extent to which these instruments are responsive to a wide array of diverse determinants. Given this multiplicity of conditions that determine projective technique response, only a small proportion of which are related to personality variables or dispositions, it is inevitable that strictly empirical findings secured in one situation will not be likely to generalize effectively if we change a great many of the situational factors as well as nonpersonality attributes of the Ss.

Let us consider some of the respects in which the Ss and conditions of test administration differed between our first and second studies. The Ss of the second study were much more heterogeneous than Ss of the first study in age, socioeconomic status, education, intelligence, employment history, indeed on almost any other variable one might care to mention other than criminality. Not only was the second group more variable on these attributes but also there were sizeable differences in the group average for most variables, including verbal facility, intelligence, and socioeconomic status. The differences in situational determinants of test performance were at least as striking as the differences in demographic and personal attributes. To mention only the most salient of these differences, one group of tests was given in a maximum security prison and another in an institution of higher learning; one group of Ss was paid for participation and the other was not; one group of homosexual Ss knew the examiner was aware of their homosexual behavior while the other group did not; one group of homosexual Ss included a large number who had been harshly punished by society for homosexual acts while the comparable group in the other study included no such Ss. A large number of studies have been conducted that demonstrate projective technique responses to vary

with conditions such as those just described. Many of these investigations are described or referred to in recent publications by Masling (1960) and Lindzey (1961).

Generalizations of the sort dealt with in this study must be accompanied by a statement of the parametric limits within which they operate, and among the group differences mentioned above there are undoubtedly many such parameters that must be attended to in order to permit effective generalization of findings. To cite only a single illustration, a great deal of the research and clinical literature on projective techniques has tended to ignore the difference between the situation in which the S sees the examiner as sympathetically involved in a cooperative and supportive enterprise and the situation in which the S, accurately or not, perceives the examiner as hostile, as a barrier to some desired goal, or as the potential revealer of some deeply defended aspect of the S's inner world. There seems little doubt that one of the reasons for the failure of the second study to even approach a replication of the findings of the first study concerns just this difference. Indeed, when reporting the initial results of the first study we indicated that " . . . most of the indices of homosexuality that functioned successfully tended to be relatively directly related to homosexuality and thus might be expected to be readily subject to censoring or inhibition" (Lindzey *et al.,* 1958, p. 74). Given this observation it is altogether predictable that, with less cooperative Ss, the TAT indices would fare more poorly.

What has just been said concerning the parametric limits within which one may expect a given relation between projective technique sign and personality disposition to be maintained might be considered banal if it were not for the fact that the majority of studies concerned with such diagnostic relationships fail even to mention the importance of such parameters. Thus, much of the existing interpretive lore, both that based upon controlled research and that derived from clinical observation, is certain to be misleading because there has been no attempt to state the reasonable bounds within which the interpretation or relationship is likely to be sustained.

The sensitivity of the TAT to situational variation is obviously a serious problem for the person interested in enduring and personological traits, albeit the problem is equally perplexing with structured tests and other techniques for assessing personality. Until and unless we are able to identify objective cues that prove to be linked with personality traits in an invariant manner over many different situations, the clinician or investigator must be exceedingly cautious in attempting to make personality inferences concerning respondents who are examined in a novel setting.

SUMMARY

Thematic Apperception Test (TAT) protocols from homosexual and normal college Ss and homosexual and normal prisoners were employed in two consecutive studies concerned with clinical and actuarial prediction. In the first study a clinician blindly predicted the criterion from TAT protocols with 95% accuracy. Twenty objective TAT indices, when combined after-the-fact using actuarial methods, functioned nearly as well as the clinician. When applied to the prison population, the actuarial methods were totally ineffective, while two clinicians were more successful in predicting the criterion. The findings are discussed in terms of their implications for the clinical-actuarial prediction controversy as well as the probable utility of objective "signs" derived from projective technique protocols.

REFERENCES

Allport, G. W. *Personality: a psychological interpretation.* New York: Holt, 1937.

Allport, G. W. *The use of personal documents in psychological science.* Social Science Research Council Bull. No. 42, 1942.

Cronbach, L. J. Assessment of individual differences. In P. R. Farnsworth and Q. McNemar (Eds.), *Annual review of psychology.* Vol. 7. Stanford, Calif.: Annual Reviews, 1956. Pp. 173–196.

Cronbach, L. J. *Essentials of psychological testing.* New York: Harper, 1960.

Davids, A., Joelson, M., and McArthur, C. Rorschach and TAT indices of homosexuality in overt homosexuals, neurotics, and normal males. *Journal of Abnormal and Social Psychology,* 1956, 53: 161–172.

Gleser, Goldine C. Projective methodologies. In P. R. Farnsworth (Ed.), *Annual review of psychology.* Vol. 14. Palo Alto, Calif.: Annual Reviews, 1963. Pp. 391–422.

Gough, H. G. Clinical versus statistical prediction in psychology. In L. Postman (Ed.), *Psychology in the making.* New York: Knopf, 1962. Pp. 526–584.

Holt, R. R. Clinical and statistical prediction: A reformulation and some new data. *Journal of Abnormal and Social Psychology,* 1958, 56: 1–12.

Kenny, D. T. Transcendence indices, extent of personality factors in fantasy responses, and the ambiguity of TAT cards. *Journal of Consulting Psychology,* 1954, 18: 345–348.

Kenny, D. T. A theoretical and research reappraisal of stimulus factors in the TAT. In J. Kagan and G. Lesser (Eds.), *Contemporary issues in thematic apperceptive methods.* Springfield, Ill.: Thomas, 1961. Pp. 288–310.

Lindzey, G. Thematic Apperception Test: Interpretive assumptions and related empirical evidence. *Psychological Bulletin,* 1952, 49: 1–25.

Lindzey, G. *Projective techniques and cross-cultural research,* New York: Appleton-Century-Crofts, 1961.

Lindzey, G., and Newburg, A. S. Thematic Apperception Test: A tentative appraisal of some "signs" of anxiety. *Journal of Consulting Psychology,* 1954, 18: 389–395.

Lindzey, G., and Silverman, M. Thematic Apperception Test: Techniques of group administration, sex differences and the role of verbal productivity. *Journal of Personality,* 1959, 27: 311–323.

Lindzey, G., and Tejessy, Charlotte. Thematic Apperception Test: Indices of aggression in relation to measures of overt and covert behavior. *American Journal of Orthopsychiatry,* 1956, 26: 567–576.

Lindzey, G., Tejessy, C., and Zamansky, H. Thematic Apperception Test: An empirical examination of some indices of homosexuality. *Journal of Abnormal and Social Psychology,* 1958, 57: 67–75.

Lindzey, G., Bradford, Jean, Tejessy, Charlotte, and Davids, A. Thematic Apperception Test: An interpretive lexicon for clinician and investigator. *Journal of Clinical Psychology, Monograph Supplement,* 1959, No. 12.

Lykken, D. T. A method of actuarial pattern analysis. *Psychological Bulletin,* 1956, 53: 102–107.

Lykken, D. T., and Rose, R. Psychological prediction from actuarial tables. *Journal of Clinical Psychology,* 1963, 19: 139–151.

McArthur, C. Clinical versus actuarial prediction. In *Proceedings of the 1955 invitational conference on testing problems.* Princeton, N.J.: Educational Testing Service, 1956. Pp. 99–106.

Masling, J. The influence of situational and inter-personal variables in projective testing. *Psychological Bulletin,* 1960, 57: 65–85.

Meehl, P. E. *Clinical versus statistical prediction.* Minneapolis: Univer. of Minnesota Press, 1954.

Meehl, P. E. Clinical versus actarial prediction. In *Proceedings of the 1955 invitational conference on testing problems.* Princeton, N.J.: Educational Testing Service, 1956. Pp. 136–141.

Meehl, P. E. When shall we use our heads instead of the formula? *Journal of Counseling Psychology,* 1957, 4: 268–273.

Meehl, P. E. A comparison of clinicians with five statistical methods of identifying psychotic MMPI profiles. *Journal of Counseling Psychology,* 1959, 6: 102–109.

Murray, H. A. *Explorations in personality.* New York: Oxford Univer. Press, 1938.

Murray, H. A., *et al. Assessment of man.* New York: Rinehart, 1948.

Sarbin, T. Clinical psychology—art or science? *Psychometrika,* 1941, 6: 391–400.

Sarbin, T. A contribution to the study of actuarial and individual methods of prediction. *American Journal of Sociology,* 1942, 48: 593–602.

Zubin, V. Clinical versus actuarial prediction. In *Proceedings of the 1955 invitational conference on testing problems.* Princeton, N.J.: Educational Testing Service, 1956. Pp. 107–128.

SEER OVER SIGN:
THE FIRST GOOD EXAMPLE *

PAUL E. MEEHL

Ten years ago I made a rather unsuccessful attempt to arouse clinical practitioners from their dogmatic slumbers (Meehl, 1954). I call the attempt unsuccessful because, while it mobilized emergency emotions and made some sparks fly, I have not as yet been able to detect any significant impact upon clinical practice. In his daily decision-making the clinician continues to function, usually quite unabashedly, as if no such book had ever been written. However, I can perhaps lay claim to having focused attention on a research problem

* Reprinted with permission from Academic Press, Inc. In *Journal of Experimental Research in Personality,* 1965, Vol. 1, pp. 27–32.

of both theoretical interest and practical importance, thereby generating numerous research studies. Monitoring of the literature in the decade since the book appeared yields a current bibliography of some fifty empirical investigations in which the efficiency of a human judge in combining information is compared with that of a formalized ("mechanical," and "statistical") procedure. The design and the range of these investigations permits much more confident generalization than was true on the basis of the eighteen studies available to me in 1954. They range over such diverse substantive domains as success in training or schooling, criminal recidivism and parole violation, psychotherapy (stayability and outcome), recovery from psychosis, response to shock treatment, formal psychiatric nosology, job success or satisfaction, medical (non-psychiatric) diagnosis, and general trait ascription or personality description. The current "box score" shows a significantly superior predictive efficiency for the statistical method in about two-thirds of the investigations, and substantially equal efficiency in the rest. (In 1954 I mistakenly classified one paper as favoring nonformalized judgment, because I failed to detect its use of a spuriously inflated chi-square.)

It would be difficult to mention any other domain of psychological controversy in which such uniformity of research outcome as this would be evident in the literature. Since Professor Lindzey's paper is the first and *only* empirical comparison of the relative efficiency of the two methods showing clear superiority for the clinical judge, it is deserving of special attention.

Since, as Lindzey points out, commentators have tended to polarize and oversimplify my own views, in reacting to his paper I should like first to say clearly that I incline strongly to accept his results and interpretation. It would be my judgment that we have here the first clear instance of somebody's accepting the statistical challenge and exhibiting a significantly superior predictive performance by the human judge. What I have to say by way of further comment or questions should not, therefore, be construed as meaning that I disagree with the author's essential conclusions.

I take it as not in controversy that the clinical judge (proceeding informally or impressionistically) and the "sign" list (employed mechanically) do not differ significantly in the hit-rate achieved on a college population. While the statistical method is given an advantage through the lack of cross-validation, I would be inclined not to assign this factor as much weight as the author does. Cross-validation shrinkage (in the narrow sense) is a very important influence for prediction systems such as regression equations where the actual magnitude of a rather unstable statistic like a beta-weight is used with the idea of maximizing predictive power. But this effect is very considerably reduced when a simple count of signs, based on a median cut or similar dichotomous procedure such as the author employed, is involved. I have seen some striking examples where such an unweighted sign-counting procedure results in negligible cross-validating shrinkage. Presumably the reason for this is that the discriminating *power* of a dichotomous sign is not being weighted, so as long as the signs are at least scored "in the right direction," an unweighted sign-count is not a statistic greatly biased by capitalizing on random error in the criterion sample. (This is especially true, of course, when the selected signs do not represent a small minority of a large potential set such as the MMPI item pool.)

On the clinician's side, we have no accurate means within the data of estimating how much of the fluctuation in hit-rate between the two samples (a drop from 95% hits in Sample I to 80% hits in Sample II) is attributable to random sampling error and how much to the (presumably much more important) factor of validity generalization to a different population. That is, we have no good means, either from theoretical considerations or estimators calculable from the data, of deciding whether there is a difference between the efficiency of the statistical method and the judges in the first study. If we were dealing with the first study taken by itself, we would have to record it in the box score as "no substantial difference." I shall therefore confine my discussion to the striking superiority of the clinical judges in Study II.

In explaining the clinical judges' marked superiority over the statistical sign-combination in Study II, the fascinating question is, of course, "What were the clinical judges *doing*?" I put it this way because the data make it quite clear that the difference in results between Studies I and II lies in the failure of the sign-statistical method to hold up, while the clinical judges did almost as well as in Study I. It is important to realize that we deal here not with shrinkage on *cross-validation* in the strict sense, i.e., that attributable to random sampling fluctuation within the same population, but the very different situation of *validity generalization*, i.e., the extent to which predictor variables function in the same way in a different population. Granted that in theory it will never be the case that any two clinical populations are mathematically identical in their parameters, in practice one can usually assume that shrinkage in passing from one VA Mental Hygiene Clinic sample, say, in Minnesota in 1956 to one in Michigan in 1958 will be largely attributable to sampling fluctuations; whereas moving from a population of college students to a population of prisoners involves a rather marked change in a number of presumably critical variables (demographic, intellectual, psychiatric, test-attitudinal, stylistic). A hard-line protagonist of the statistical method might be tempted to view this fact as a defect of the experimental design, saying that it is "not fair to the statistician" to expect him to make estimates of parameters in a prediction function for a population which he has not yet sampled. I am sure that Lindzey would accept the substance of that observation as a statistical truism. However, as regards the "fairness" aspect, I think that this line of rebuttal would be improper, for the same reason that I think it improper when clinicians dismiss the adverse studies by saying it is "unfair" to expect the clinician to know in advance whether a certain predictor variable is relevant to a certain criterion. If the clinician makes judgments under the erroneous impression that the current state of psychological theory or the generalizability of his accumulated clinical experience is such as to permit him to make powerful predictions of a given criterion, this error is part of the clinician's weakness as a predictive instrument. Similarly, I would insist that given the pragmatic context in which the whole issue makes sense—and it is only, I believe, in the pragmatic context that it can be properly formulated as a competition between techniques—then it seems obvious that the ability of a clinician to move successfully into a new population, when the statistical method collapses upon attempting such movement, must be viewed as a manifestation of the clinician's pragmatic superiority under the particular circumstances.

The data indicate that, whereas the clinical

judges suffered some loss of predictive power in moving to the prisoner population, their attrition was not nearly as great as the attrition suffered by the sign-statistics, which collapsed to a clinically useless magnitude. That the latters' collapse is mainly a matter of validity generalization rather than pure sampling-error shrinkage is shown by the data in Table 2,* where we see that the component signs in the sign-statistic had individually no discrimination power, with a couple of exceptions. Thus we deal here not with a situation in which purportedly "optimal weights" fail because they capitalize excessively upon random error in the initial sample; rather we deal with a situation in which the very *dimensions* being utilized for prediction are for the most part predictively irrelevant within the new population.

On first reading the paper I was impelled to criticize the emphasis in its first two paragraphs upon the clinical judge as "observer," but I think I understand on further thought why the author emphasizes the "observer" aspect as he does. It seems the most parsimonious interpretation of the data to say that the clinical judges were able to do almost as good a job on the prisoner sample as on the college sample, in spite of the fact that the samples differ so greatly in respect to the variables used as statistical signs, because the clinical judges were relying largely, perhaps almost wholly, upon other aspects of the protocol than those aspects represented in the signs. Hence I would myself look upon the author's comments on the "psychometric refractoriness" of the TAT protocol as getting closest to the heart of the matter. Of the (practically) unlimited number of facets or aspects of the verbal behavior recorded in a TAT protocol, it seems that those which the research, and even the articulated clinical tradition, have fixed upon as TAT "signs" of homosexuality are just not the best ones, i.e., "best" in the sense of possessing high validity generalizability.

If we inquire into what these superior aspects might be, we leave the realm of the data for speculation. But if it is permissible to record a hunch, I would hazard a guess that we deal here with some subtle aspects—subtle because highly configural—of a stylistic-expressive nature. I do

* This table has been omitted from the selection.— ED.

not, of course, mean something crude like sentence length or verb-adjective quotient or what not, but I do mean some features of the patient's discourse which are relatively closer to the *formal* than to the *contentual* aspects of the stream of speech. It is a pity that the article does not report any introspective account by the judges of what they at least *thought* they were attending to in making the discrimination. But this general line is what has made me more comfortable with the author's "observer" emphasis, because pending further investigation of the inferential process in this situation, I would opt for the working hypothesis that the judges were scanning the material with responsiveness to features of it that have as yet eluded anything like an adequate reduction to scoring categories.

This latter point perhaps renders the investigation somewhat less central in regard to the clinical-statistical issue than it would otherwise be. As I formulated the distinction (Meehl, 1954, pp. 15–18) the question of relative efficiency is most appropriately asked having first settled upon a defined class of data, whether these data are rockbottom epistemologically or are themselves, strictly speaking, inferences, constructions, or behavior summaries. Thus, for example, in predicting academic success one would normally treat the student's Stanford-Binet IQ as part of the "data." But a little reflection upon the process of administering an individual intelligence test makes it obvious that "clinical judgments" already occur close to the behavior level, as when the examiner must decide how a patient's definition of a word is to be scored when precisely that definition cannot be found among the scored samples in the manual. There is, admittedly, an arbitrary element here because of the ambiguity of the verb "observed" in ordinary language and even in conventional scientific usage. In moving from the patient's stream of behavior to the scored signs, two reductions of data occur: First, only the words are recorded and such behavioral features as rate, tone, expressive movements, and the like are ignored, a factor not relevant in the present study. Second, only certain features of the word sequence as found in the protocol are selected for attention and classified with respect to specified properties, i.e., "scored." Here again, I can understand a temptation on the part of the actuarial protagonist to say that the study does not quite fulfill the criteria for a meaningful test because the two predictive methods do not "start with the same body of data." While this is true in one sense, a sense of which Lindzey is fully cognizant, it is not true in that sense which is pragmatically important. The fact is that the skilled judge reading the protocol impressionistically and the statistical system putting together scores obtained by attending selectively to prespecified features of the record, *do* have access to the "same data," namely a transcript of verbal behavior. At the risk of overstressing a methodological abstraction, one could say as a matter of strict logic or epistemology that, when the statistical method does not begin by scoring the aspects of verbal behavior which the judge responds to impressionistically, from the mathematical point of view this amounts in effect to the actuarial method's assigning a zero weight to those aspects and meanwhile assigning non-zero weights to other aspects which are less predictive, or at least less generalizably so.

I think it is less important to argue the semantic merits of a broad versus narrow use of the verb "observe" than it is to get as conceptually clear as we can about what is actually going on in the situation. There is an interesting symmetry here between the special disadvantages of the two predictive methods, in that Holt's distinction (1958) between the "naive" and the "sophisticated" clinical judge finds its counterpart in the "naive" versus "sophisticated" actuary. Holt wants to make sure, before he will be happy with a comparison of the two methods' efficiencies, that the clinical judge has had an adequate opportunity to consult actuarial experience (including actuarial experience with his own previous judging behavior) so that he can adjust and hopefully improve his subjective weights by whatever psychological means clinical judges do this. Similarly, it will not do much good for the statistician to employ formally powerful mathematical methods of combining scored dimensions if those dimensions are not the right ones to start with. Noting this symmetry, we must nevertheless give due recognition within the pragmatic context of predictive efficiency to a finding that the efforts of clinically knowledgeable investigators to identify the predictively relevant and *population-generalizable* aspects of the stream of TAT speech, and to subject them to a semiobjec-

tive response classification procedure ("scoring"), has thus far apparently failed. I should think that the observational and classificatory problem involved here would partake to a considerable degree of the same elements that enter into skillful functioning as a psychotherapist and, therefore, that many of the theoretical considerations I raised in that respect would be relevant in understanding the findings of the present study (Meehl, 1954, Chapters 6 and 7). I am also inclined to agree with the author's identification of two of my proposed six "pro-clinical" factors (Meehl, 1957) as being most likely operative in this predictive situation.

As must be evident from the character of my comments, I find very little in the paper with which to disagree. I am not entirely happy about the terminology adopted to describe the two clinical judges, especially since the judge characterized as "naive" paradoxically did the better job in both samples and, I take it, significantly better in the prisoner sample. This judge, the late Ephraim Rosen of the Minnesota Psychology Department, was trained by Nevitt Sanford and was an unusually gifted clinician. As the author points out, the other judge's "sophistication," consisting in his own research experience and familiarity with the statistical sign list, may actually have worked to his disadvantage. There is the further consideration that, whereas the explicit identification of predictive signs can never systematically reduce the power of an actuarial method, it may sometimes reduce power when the signs are not treated actuarially but are filtered through the thinking process of a clinical judge. This possibility arises because one of the changes that is likely to occur when a judge succeeds in making explicit a proper subset of the cues to which he is potentially responsive is that his subjective beta-weights on these cues will increase, to the disadvantage of the residual subset of cues which he has not yet brought to the reporting level. Thus Sarbin, in his classical study (1942), found that the well-recognized scholastic predictors HSR and CAT were being subjectively assigned a *larger* proportion of criterion variance by counselors than these two variables actually accounted for. A beautiful instance of this effect can be found in the fascinating article by Berne (1949) in which an intuitively gifted psychoanalyst who had been doing remarkably well diagnosing certain occupations of inductees "at sight" suffered a marked decline in his efficiency as a result of identifying only a *portion* of the cue-family to which he had been originally responding unconsciously.

The only other partial disagreement I would have with the author is based upon literature not extensively known to him, in that he lays some stress upon the relative lack of studies in which the clinician is operating on his own terrain and attempting to predict a criterion with which he has some meaningful clinical familiarity. This criticism has been considerably reduced by the studies appearing since 1954, and I am not convinced that on the basis of the total body of presently available evidence one can plausibly attribute the highly consistent and sometimes marked superiority of the statistical method to the use of an inappropriate setting and criterion for assessing the clinician's predictive skills.

Finally, I believe it is needful to enter a *caveat* with regard to the general application of these findings in the pragmatic context of daily clinical decision-making. I have little doubt, on the basis of my long personal acquaintance with them, that both of these clinical judges would be superior to the modal practitioner in a number of dimensions that I can hardly think irrelevant in this task, particularly abstract intelligence, good common-sense judgment, flexibilty, and responsiveness to subtle nuances. [While revising the draft of this paper, I received a research report on counselor predictions in which 12 accurately predicting counselors differed from 12 inaccurately predicting ones by 27 raw score points on the Miller Analogies Test, a mean difference of approximately two sigma. No other counselor variable showed any such large differentiation as this measure of "Ph.D.-type brains"; see Watley and Vance (1964).] Investigations involving several clinicians characteristically show significant differences in predictive skill. The average judge does no better than the statistical method and usually somewhat worse; a minority of judges will sometimes succeed in bettering the actuarial procedure. While the functioning of a consistently superior judge is of great theoretical interest, and also could presumably provide one basis for refurbishing the less adequate average judge who performs below the actuarial method, unless individual judges are empirically calibrated with respect to their predictive efficiency over the range of recurring clinical tasks, the present empirical demonstration that these two judges were doing something validly that the scoreable signs were not doing does not help us much in adopting an over-all administrative policy with regard to the optimal method of clinical decision-making. As I have earlier pointed out, a pretty strong case can be made for an overarching decision-policy *to predict by actuarial methods, except when empirical information is available as to the predictive efficiency of the clinicians functioning in an installation;* and the specificity of abilities surely makes it dangerous to assume that these can be assessed by an indirect general method (except perhaps general intelligence) instead of carrying out a major predictive study on each clinic's personnel (Meehl, 1954, pp. 114–116).

With these minor reservations and qualifications, let me conclude by saying that, so far as I am concerned, Professor Lindzey has successfully responded to my "challenge" to do the right kind of study enabling the clinical judge to emerge victorious.

SUMMARY

Professor Lindzey's study is the first (in some fifty published) which demonstrates a clear superiority of the clinical judge over formalized (actuarial) methods of data combination. These clinicians' superiority lay in validity generalization, the semi-objectified "signs" derived from research on college students having negligible validity singly and collectively when applied to a population of maximum-security prison inmates. The data indicate that the clinical experts were not employing the "signs" reported in the research literature. It is suggested that TAT-skilled judges rely on subtle stylistic features of the protocol, which are refractory to scoring categories. Because of their atypicality and the crucial role played by moving to a very different population, the findings should not be generalized to other prediction tasks, kinds of data, or an unselected population of clinicians.

REFERENCES

Berne, E. The nature of intuition. *Psychiatric Quarterly,* 1949, 23: 203–226.

Gough, H. G. Clinical versus statistical prediction in psychology. In L. Postman (Ed.), *Psychol-*

ogy in the making. New York: Alfred A. Knopf, 1962. Pp. 526–584.

Holt, R. R. Clinical and statistical prediction: A reformulation and some new data. *Journal of Abnormal and Social Psychology,* 1958, 56: 1–12.

Meehl, P. E. *Clinical versus statistical prediction: A theoretical analysis and a review of the evidence.* Minneapolis: Univer. of Minnesota Press, 1954.

Meehl, P. E. When shall we use our heads instead of the formula? *Journal of Counseling Psychology,* 1957, 4: 268–273.

Sarbin, T. R. A contribution to the study of actuarial and individual methods of predicition. *American Journal of Sociology,* 1942, 48: 593–602.

Watley, D. J., and Vance, F. L. Clinical versus actuarial prediction of college achievement and leadership activity. *U. S. Office of Education Cooperative Research Project No. 2202.* Minneapolis: Univer. of Minnesota, 1964.

PART II

Experimental Study of Personality

WHILE THE ASSESSMENT approach to personality seeks to uncover the individual difference variables that underlie observed behavior, the experimental study of personality deals with the determinants of individual differences. It is important to realize that these may be as scientifically significant as the individual differences themselves. In Part II we shall deal with the experimental approach to personality. It will be evident that it represents an important complement to an assessment approach. In Part III, we shall see how a developmental approach to personality can provide insight into the genesis of behavior and that this approach entails the use of both assessment and experimental methods.

The experimental study of personality involves the manipulation of objectively definable conditions. By carefully controlling stimulus situations and changing only a small number of independent variables, it becomes possible to determine systematically how these variables influence behavior. An experimental approach to personality deals with such questions as: How do people react to various types of emotionally arousing or ego-involving conditions? What kinds of spoken or written communications influence people's performance on different types of tasks? How does the interaction of assessed personality characteristics with specially created experimental conditions influence behavior? Can an experimenter isolate and manipulate the variables that significantly affect individuals' attitudes and behavior in interpersonal situations?

One of the challenges confronting the experimenter in personality study is the translation of ideas into operational terms. These are the conditions of the experiment; how these conditions are created is a matter of great importance. Controversy over a particular experiment may come about for a variety of reasons: Was the experimental situation as well controlled as it should have been? Were the experimentally manipulated variables as relevant as they should have been to the concept under study? Were the methods of measurement the most appropriate ones available? Was the experimenter's concept so vague as to make the interpretation of his experiment difficult or impossible? Were the conditions of the experiment the most effective ones for testing a particular hypothesis? Were the dependent variables, the aspects of behavior which the experimental conditions were to measure, as appropriate as they might have been for investigating the concept under study?

Disputes surrounding these questions often stem from different theoretical orientations among both researchers and readers of the reports. In general, the experimenter's theoretical orientation influences the way in which he conducts his experiments: a behavioristic orientation could lead one experimenter to attend to and manipulate certain kinds of variables such as changing the reinforcement conditions associated with the learning of a skill; a psychoanalytic orientation could lead another experimenter to research primarily concerned with the relationship between anxiety, selective forgetting, and repression; and a physiological orientation could lead one to be concerned with the influences of certain experimental variables on autonomic reactivity.

Part II begins with two articles which illustrate the general nature of an experimental approach to personality and the relevance of this approach to problems of assessment. In the first one, Lazarus deals with an important question: Can a psychological experiment, in some sense, represent significant events that occur in everyday life? He argues that the laboratory can be used to evaluate constructs relevant to these events. He further states that the work of the laboratory, because it occurs under controlled circumstances, need not be artificial. Indeed, Lazarus believes, the purpose of carefully controlling conditions in the laboratory is to place in bold relief the "outside" processes and events whose understanding the experimenter seeks to enhance.

Lazarus' research illustrates how experiments can be both simple and complex at the same time. For example, the procedure can be simple in that the subject's task is common, ordinary, or easy to perform while the hypothesis or area to be investigated can be quite complex. In Lazarus' experiment, all the subject had to do was watch a movie; the experimenter had to measure changes in physiological reactivity and attitude as a function of the subject's cognitive appraisal of the movie. Lazarus' hypothesis was that changes in physiological, biochemical, and psychological processes can best be understood in terms of the personal threat perceived by an individual in a given situation. Lazarus' attempt to relate the scores on personality tests to the reactions of subjects to potentially threatening film stimuli illustrates well the fact that assessment and experimental approaches are complementary. It is interesting that through his experiment he was able to demonstrate that groups differing in certain characteristics did, in fact, react differently to a psychologically threatening situation.

Reviewing Lazarus' work, one sees that an experiment is not simply a matter of manipulating independent variables in order to find out what effects they might have on dependent variables. Both independent variables, which it is hoped will influence behavior, and dependent variables, the aspects of behavior which are influenced, grow out of constructs whose validity the experimenter seeks to establish. Lazarus' paper illustrates how personality researchers seek to link constructs such as stress and defense to concrete operations such as showing movies to experimental subjects and recording their physiological and psychological reactions.

The research reported by Lazarus employed measures of individual differences of the type described in Part I. In Part I we saw that most assessment work involves the quantification of verbal behavior recorded at a particular point in time. Patterson, in the second article of Part II, deals with assessment from a somewhat different standpoint. He argues for greater use of experimental methods in assessing people.

Patterson's methodology involves change in behavior, a much studied variable in experimental work. He asks the question: Can the changes in behavior due to certain events be predictive of future behavior? In approaching this, Patterson used rate of response, a variable frequently studied in operant conditioning experiments. He employed this by measuring changes of rates of lever-pressing to predict the frequency with which subjects (children) would be victimized by an aggressor. His finding, a significant correlation between change in rate of subjects' lever pressing and victimization, is highly suggestive. The use of behavior samples obtained in relatively simple but controlled experimental situations is one which has not been sufficiently explored in previous research on assessment.

Further exploration of this approach to assessment will require study of a number of questions. Important among these is the relationship between assessment based on verbal behavior and assessment based on nonverbal behavior, as exemplified by lever-pressing responses, physiological reactivity, or the characteristics of brain waves. For example, in examining Patterson's experimental approach tc assessment, the reader may wonder what the subjects were thinking and feeling while they engaged in lever pressing. The reader may also wonder about the ability and motivational variables which may have affected the subjects' rates of motor responding. These are reasonable points. They demonstrate that the determinants of nonverbal behavior require careful experimental examination. The same can be said about the determinants of verbal behavior.

The experiment reported by Sarason and Harmatz deals simultaneously with the relationships among individual differences, experimental conditions, and behavior. These investigators studied the reactions of persons, preselected on the basis of test anxiety and sex, to the learning of difficult verbal material. The conditions of learning varied. Some groups received reports about their level of performance, while other groups did not. Previous research has shown that the test-anxiety variable is related to learning and performance in a variety of tasks. Interestingly, the experiment by Sarason and Harmatz failed to show differences between groups varying in test anxiety scores. Males and females, however, showed striking differences in performance.

Lazarus has emphasized that a person's cognitive interpretation of a situation can be a crucial determinant of his behavior. The Sarason and Harmatz study suggests that the "simple" variable of sex may be related to a person's cognitive interpretation and, thus, ultimate performance in a learning situation. It also shows the necessity of determining which individual difference variables, in interaction with which experimental conditions, influence behavior in specified types of situations. To simply state that individual differences and experimental conditions influence behavior is not enough.

The Lindzey, Lykken, and Winston experiment illustrates the relevance of research on animals to the study of human personality. There are two major values in animal research. One is that animals may be subjected to experimental conditions which would be neither feasible nor ethically defensible when used with human subjects. The other is that the histories and environments of animals can be more carefully controlled than the pre-experimental experiences of humans. Lindzey, Lykken, and Winston point out that Freud was emphatic in discussing the important effects of heredity and early experiences on adult behavior. How do you investigate these effects experimentally? Lindzey, Lykken, and Winston attempted to do so with animals and while the experiment was not a direct outgrowth of psychoanalytic concepts, the authors suggest that it did relate to certain Freudian ideas.

Though there has been considerable curiosity about animal behavior as a scientific phenomenon in its own right, there is still a significant body of research with animals designed to shed light on human problems. Hebb and Thompson have observed that animal research may:

> . . . clarify a human problem without "proving" anything. It may draw attention to facets of human behavior one has not noticed; it may point to a trouble-making but implicit assumption; it may suggest a new principle of human behavior. Furthermore, animal experiment in the past has repeatedly shown that the treatment of some human problem or other has been oversimplified. (Hebb, D. O. and Thompson, W. R. The social significance of animal studies. In G. Lindzey (Ed.) *Handbook of Social Psychology,* Vol. 1, Cambridge, Mass: Addison-Wesley Publishing Co., 1954, p. 533.)

Lindzey, Lykken, and Winston used mice to study the effects of infantile trauma and genetic factors on adult behavior. In the experiment, offspring of four strains of mice were assigned to experimental and control conditions. It was shown that, at least for mice, infantile trauma and genetic factors must be studied simultaneously to obtain the best prediction of adult emotionality. (In Part III there is another example of animal research: Harlow deals with affectional and social aspects of the lives of monkeys reared under special laboratory conditions.)

The work of Lindzey, Lykken, and Winston also illustrates the renaissance of sorts that the variable of hereditary background is experiencing. For a variety of historical reasons, behavioral scientists paid little attention to the hereditary antecedents of observed behavior; but now, a behavior-genetic attack on the biological properties of man and animals is under way. Since it is estimated that there are over 10,000 human genes, the task of uncovering the genetic underpinning of observed behavior is a formidable one indeed. It represents no less than an effort to comprehend truly the evolution of behavior.

Hirsch has been one of the most forceful advocates of a behavior-genetic approach:

> Though lip service has been paid to the study of behavior and evolution ever since Darwin pointed the way, there has been little progress in the description and understanding of either the units of behavioral evolution or the role of behavior in evolution . . .
>
> Man . . . has evolved through natural selection. But, as we now study his behavior in civilization, there is no comparable face validity permitting us to call natural most of the units we observe. In contemporary behavioral science far more attention is paid to man's social roles than to his biological properties. In industrial psychology, for example, tests are devised to select individuals who will perform most skillfully those tasks for which industry needs them. Because of the speed of cultural evolution, man cannot possibly have been subjected to intense natural selection for his technological skills. Though man must employ the capacities he has evolved in the exercise of skills, the great challenge now before behavioral science lies in the behavior-genetic analysis of man's biological properties and the elucidation of their modus operandi in a sociotechnological context. This is a far more fundamental scientific question than the one usually asked by pretending that all "normal" individuals are essentially alike, that mastery of a small number of "conditions" (=?) permits shaping "The Behavior of Organisms," and that, for a typological abstraction called behavior, such "conditions" can be discovered by an "experimental analysis" yielding a representative curve for some mythical representative organism—the lure of that engineering paradise, a prediction-and-control technology. (Hirsch, J. Behavior-genetic or "experimental" analysis: The challenge of science versus the lure of technology, in *Proceedings of the 74th Annual Convention of the American Psychological Association, 1966*. Washington, D. C.: American Psychological Association, pp. 7 and 8.)

As the social, ethnic, and economic barriers to education are removed throughout the world, and as the quality of education approaches a more uniformly high level of effectiveness, heredity may be expected to make an ever larger contribution to individual differences in intellectual functioning and consequently to success in our increasingly complex civilization. Universally compulsory education, improved methods of ability assessment and career counseling, and prolongation of the years of schooling further into the reproductive periods of life can only increase the degree of positive assortative mating in our population. From a geneticist's point of view, our attempt to create the great society might prove to be the greatest selective breeding experiment ever undertaken. (Hirsch, J. Behavior-genetic, or "experimental" analysis: The challenge of science versus the lure of technology. *American Psychologist*, 1967, Vol. 22, #2, p. 128.)

Researchers interested in personality have very strong ties with the field of social psychology, particularly in research on reactions to group pressure and influence. Social psychology is the study of social behavior; the study of personality involves the analysis of personal characteristics. Clearly, both are needed in the effort to obtain an understanding of the intricacies of interpersonal relationships. The presence of others, their reactions to us, and our expectations about these reactions all influence our interpersonal behavior.

The Orne and Scheibe study shows how the expectations (demand characteristics) and the cues provided in a situation in which persons are deprived of social companionship and norms can influence these people's subjective reactions and overt behavior. For over a decade psychologists have sought to explore experimentally what have come to be known as sensory deprivation situations. In these situations, individuals are deprived of both social companionship and the usual perceptual experiences of everyday life. Sensory deprivation has been shown to result in distinguishable and sometimes dramatic impacts on behavior, such as hallucinations and distortions of reality. By intent, the conditions of the Orne and Scheibe experiment did not fully meet the customary definition of sensory deprivation; yet, through experimental manipulations, the subjects' attitudes and expectations were influenced enough to result in some effects that were similar to what is usually called sensory deprivation effects. The Orne and Scheibe experiment suggests the necessity of considering both sensory and interpersonal factors in interpreting the findings of sensory deprivation experiments.

In terms of interpersonal factors, it is worthwhile to note that Orne and Scheibe did not investigate the influence of individual difference variables in their experimental situation. Might the individual differences in assessed test anxiety that were nonsignificant in the Sarason-Harmatz experiment be relevant to an Orne-Scheibe situation? Or might reactions to that situation be especially strong for persons with tendencies toward suggestibility and conformity? It is interesting that these tendencies have been found to be related significantly to the ease with which persons could be hypnotized. Thus, might reactions to both hypnosis and social deprivation situations be related to the variables of suggestibility and need to conform? All good experiments raise as many questions as they answer. This is certainly true for the Orne and Scheibe experiment.

The Bandura, Grusec, and Menlove experiment represents an interesting contrast to the Orne and Scheibe study. Orne and Scheibe studied the effects of attitudes and expectations on behavior in a situation in which interpersonal contact was considerably reduced. Bandura, Grusec, and Menlove, on the other hand, sought to change attitudes and, ultimately, overt behavior, through the presence of interpersonal contact. They demonstrated, in their study of young children's fears of dogs, the importance of observational opportunities as modifiers of behavior. They also showed one way in which experimental methodology can be applied to the study of the behavior of children.

The significance of observational opportunities cannot be over-emphasized (although it is noteworthy that until recently they were sorely neglected by behavioral researchers). Observing models such as parents, teachers, and friends, can powerfully influence the socialization process and personality development. Models provide us with figures with whom we can identify. Through controlled laboratory study it becomes possible to isolate variables implicated in modeling and identification.

There are three classes of variables that are likely to serve as important determiners of modeling processes. The first of these is the nature of the relationship between the model and the observer. Among the numerous relationship factors that have received attention, the nurturant or rewarding quality of the model, which tends to increase interpersonal attraction, has been shown to be influential in facilitating identificatory outcomes. . . .

The extent to which a model's behavior will be reproduced by others may also be greatly influenced by the reinforcing consequences associated with the critical response patterns. There is little question but that children would conform to the standards of achievement exemplified by a model if extrinsic incentives of sufficient positive valence were made contingent upon matching behavior. Of greater social and theoretical significance, however, is the spontaneous emulation of models that results from witnessing reinforcing consequences, usually in the form of social approval and public recognition, accruing to the model. . . .

In naturalistic situations individuals are typically confronted with a multiplicity of modeling influences, many of which operate in opposing directions. Theoretical speculations about the effect of multiple modeling on social learning generally give considerable emphasis to the conflicting identifications occurring in relation to adult and peer models. In the case of achievement standards and self-reinforcing patterns of behavior, there are several factors that might predispose children toward peer modeling when they are confronted with a conflict in standards between adults and peer members. If adult achievements and criteria for self-reward are relatively high, as is usually the case, then children will be reluctant to emulate such high aspirations because to do so would result in frequent negative self-reinforcement of their performances. In addition, according to social comparison theory, adults are likely to be viewed by children as too divergent in ability to serve as meaningful reference models. However, it is possible that conditions serving to reduce receptivity of adult modeling cues might be effectively counteracted by the simultaneous operation of opposing influences arising from strong affective ties to the model, and from vicarious positive reinforcement of high standard-setting behavior. (Bandura, A., Grusec, J. E., and Menlove, F. L. Some social determinants of self-monitoring reinforcement systems, *Journal of Personality and Social Psychology,* 1967, Vol. 5, pp. 449–455.)

Reinforcement procedures, either by themselves or allied with modeling techniques, can be powerful vehicles for achieving behavior modification. Numerous articles in this book directly or indirectly involve the reinforcement of particular aspects of behavior. For example, the article by Isaacs, Thomas, and Goldiamond in Part IV dramatically illustrates the role which reinforcers can play in shaping the behavior of disturbed individuals and the experiment in the article by Sarason and Harmatz in Part II could be said to deal with reinforcement in a laboratory verbal learning situation. Unfortunately, reinforcers may be quite subtle. The cheers of the crowd after a touchdown has been scored serve as an obvious reinforcer to successful football players. But what of the slight head nod given at just the right point in a conversation, or the gesture of interest shown by a student to his teacher, or the little signs of liking which one friend shows to another? We need the specification of what makes for a reinforcing state of affairs. A similar need applies to modeling where we need to know the characteristics of the effective model.

The model in the Bandura, Grusec, and Menlove study was a peer who was not afraid of dogs. Knowledge of the presumed reactions of a peer or group of peers can influence judgmental processes. Crutchfield has shown this in his work on conformity. A significant point in the article by Crutchfield (and this has been substantiated by the subsequent research of others) is that it is possible in a controlled laboratory situation to create social pressures which appear to be every bit as powerful as those seen in everyday life. Crutchfield sought to investigate the possibility that individual differences in personality might influence the degree to which conformity under social pressure will occur; his results suggest that this is so. Furthermore, it appears to be possible, through personality assessment, to objectively measure some of these individual differences. We do not, at the present time, know whether the influence of assessed personality characteristics is universal for all kinds of conformity situations. We also do not know how enduring experimentally-induced conformity responses can be. A future task is to determine how general are the behavior and attitudes of the conformist or persuadable person.

Sampson's experiment, like Crutchfield's, deals with the process of social influence. Sampson focused his attention on the variable of birth order and its relationship to resistance to social influence. This subject had been raised in an earlier series of experiments. In 1959, Schachter reported research he had conducted on the need to affiliate. He asked the question: Is it possible to specify the conditions which either increase or decrease the likelihood of individuals making affiliative responses? In his experiment, subjects' affiliative behavior was measured by asking each of them individually if they would like to spend a ten minute interval prior to receiving electric shocks alone or in a room with other people. In the course of experimentally studying this kind of affiliative behavior, Schachter focused on what seems, after the fact, to be a very simple individual difference variable, that of ordinal position in the family. He found that while family size was unrelated to affiliative responses under anxiety-provoking conditions, ordinal position was strongly related to the incidence of affiliative responses. The later an individual's position in the family's birth order sequence, the less the likelihood that an affiliative response would be made under anxiety-provoking experiences. In one study, 80% of all first-born subjects chose to wait with other people prior to a shock experiment, while only 31% of later-borns chose to wait with others.

Sampson's experiment relating birth order, need for achievement, and conformity extends the problem investigated by Schachter from affiliative behavior to behavior under conditions conducive to social conformity. Sampson's findings indicate that birth order by itself may not be significantly related to certain aspects of social behavior. This is really not surprising, since it is unlikely that any variable, even an extremely powerful one, could by itself influence all forms of social behavior. Sampson has shown that combining birth order with relevant individual difference variables (e.g., sex) can clarify persons' social behavior under controlled experimental conditions. Might birth order also function as a clarifying variable in conformity experiments of the type described by Crutchfield?

A comment is in order concerning the "simple" variable of birth order. While complex investigative techniques are not necessary for the assessment of birth order, unrefined techniques can obscure important relationships. For example, it may, for particular purposes, be crucial to know not only the birth order position of an individual, but also the age differentials between himself and his siblings and the age of his mother at the time of his birth. It is known that younger and older mothers create rather different intra-uterine and home environments.

It is worthwhile emphasizing the point that relatively straightforward variables such as birth order and sex are as significant objects of research as are more complex and elusive constructs. One inference which might be drawn from recent research on birth order is that experimenters may unwittingly ignore such "obvious" variables. The paper by Rosenthal suggests another "obvious" variable often ignored by experimenters: the experimenter himself. Does the experimenter have certain hypotheses, expectations, and wishes about the outcome of the experiment he is conducting? Do his personality characteristics influence subjects' behavior? Rosenthal has contributed to experimental psychology generally, as well as to the experimental study of personality, by emphasizing and empirically showing that characteristics of the experimenter and his behavior can be as potent shapers of behavior as formally defined and experimentally manipulated variables. The empirical work summarized in his paper suggests that, wherever possible, manipulation of experimenter variables should be carried out in order to clarify the influence process in experimental situations.

When considering the experimenter variable it is useful to bear in mind that it may be related to another often confounding factor, the placebo effect. It has been shown that giving a placebo, an inert substance which cannot affect a subject physiologically, can bring about noticeable changes in behavior. The link between the experimenter and placebo variables is that the experimenter's and doctor's characteristics may influence the degree to which a treatment, which per se may be innocuous, brings about observable behavior change. Rosenthal's analysis of covert communication in the psychological experiment, and the need suggested earlier for specification of the characteristics of effective reinforcers and models, reflect a larger need for understanding the psychology of interpersonal situations.

Milgram's research bears on a problem that has long perplexed mankind: Why does man commit shocking aggressive acts, such as war atrocities? Milgram did not expect to perform a single experiment which would provide an answer to this question. Indeed, it might well be said that his paper represents essentially a methodological report. He did succeed in demonstrating the feasibility of eliciting obedient and emotionally-arousing aggressive responses from civilized and, presumably, nonvicious people. He showed the willingness of many people to be obedient and to meet arbitrary requirements set for them. This obedience may occur even though the requirements are in conflict with usual ways of thinking.

Milgram's demonstration, the comments by Baumrind, and the rejoinder by Milgram raise important ethical questions relating to the protection of the rights of subjects who serve in experiments. These questions cannot be answered with empirical data because they are matters of value and of opinion. All researchers and students would agree that experiments cannot be judged simply in terms of their intellectual provocativeness and creativity. Ethical and human considerations must be carefully taken into account, be the subjects animals or humans. As Milgram's and Baumrind's comments suggest, there is not yet complete agreement about the explicit definition of standards for treatment of subjects.

The Milgram-Baumrind dispute involves several dimensions of a general problem which is created by the need to weigh two factors: the theoretical desirability of gathering certain kinds of data in psychological research, on the one hand, and the rights of subjects to be treated in a humane and dignified manner, on the other. Our consideration of this problem has been within the context of experimentation. It is equally applicable to research on personality assessment.

As we saw in Part I, research on personality assessment involves obtaining data about individual differences. Are there limits to the assessment researcher's inquiries into the lives of people? It seems obvious that there are. One of the most basic of these is that subjects have a right to privacy. Another is the subject's right to assume that information provided by him will be held in confidence. These rights mean that an assessment researcher, in conducting his investigations, must not limit himself to defining the information he seeks to gather about the behavior and thoughts of people, but that he must also consider the impact on the subject of asking for certain kinds of information.

The following views are those of a group appointed by the Federal government to review carefully the matter of privacy and behavior research:

> The root of the conflict between the individual's right to privacy and society's right of discovery is the research process. Behavioral science seeks to assess and to measure many qualities of men's minds, feelings, and actions. In the absence of informed consent on the part of the subject, these measurements represent invasion of privacy. The scientist must therefore obtain the consent of the subject.
>
> To obtain truly informed consent is often difficult. In the first place, the nature of the inquiry sometimes cannot be explained adequately because it involves complex variables that the nonscientist does not understand. Examples are the personality variables measured by questionnaires, and the qualities of cognitive processes measured by creativity tests. Second, the validity of an experiment is sometimes destroyed if the subject knows all the details of its conduct. Examples include drug testing, in which the effect of suggestion (placebo effect) must be avoided, and studies of persuasability, in which the

subjects remain ignorant of the influences that are being presented experimentally. Clearly, then, if behavioral research is to be effective, some modification of the traditional concept of informed consent is needed.

Such a change in no sense voids the more general proposition that the performance of human behavioral research is the product of a partnership between the scientist and his subject. Consent to participate in a study must be the norm before any subjects embark on the enterprise. Since consent must sometimes be given despite an admittedly inadequate understanding of the scientific purposes of the research procedures, the right to discontinue participation at any point must be stipulated in clear terms. In the meantime, when full information is not available to the subject and when no alternative procedures to minimize the privacy problem are available, the relationship between the subject and the scientist (and between the subject and the institution sponsoring the scientist) must be based upon trust. This places the scientist and the sponsoring institution under a fiduciary obligation to protect the privacy and dignity of the subject who entrusts himself to them. The scientist must agree to treat the subject fairly and with dignity, to cause him no inconvenience or discomfort unless the extent of the inconvenience and discomfort has been accepted by the subject in advance, to inform the subject as fully as possible of the purposes of the inquiry or experiment, and to put into effect all procedures which will assure the confidentiality of whatever information is obtained.

Occasionally, even this degree of consent cannot be obtained. Naturalistic observations of group behavior must sometimes be made unbeknownst to the subjects. In such cases, as well as in all others, the scientist has the obligation to insure fully confidentiality of the research records. Only by doing so, and by making certain that published reports contain no identifying reference to a given subject, can the invasion of privacy be minimized. (Privacy and behavioral research: Preliminary summary of the report of the Panel on Privacy and Behavioral Research, *Science,* 1967, #3762, pp. 536–537.)

The experimental study of personality has failed to resolve the many problems and disagreements it has aroused involving questions of both ethics and theory. On balance, however, its overall impact has been distinctly positive. The diversity of the approaches it uses, the variables it has uncovered, and the methods it employs have all helped to clarify understanding of significant aspects of behavior and in so doing have placed the spotlight of scientific inquiry on important processes and events.

A LABORATORY APPROACH
TO THE DYNAMICS OF
PSYCHOLOGICAL STRESS *

RICHARD S. LAZARUS [1]

The importance of the topic of stress is reflected in the tremendous quantity of relevant multidisciplined experimentation in recent years. Whether the term used to describe this work is emotion, stress, threat, defense, anxiety, or conflict, to name a few of the more common terms designating the broad problem area, scarcely an issue of a psychological journal goes by without containing at least one experimental article on this subject. An attempt at a general review of this work would be beyond the scope of this paper. Some of the problems posed by such a review include the multitude of different issues addressed by the research, the variety of variables studied and methods used which make comparison of the experiments difficult if not impossible, and the grossly different meanings given to the term stress.

This paper undertakes two somewhat limited tasks: (a) an analysis of some of the key problems in experimentation, and (b) the presentation of a brief account of some research from the author's own laboratory which was designed to throw light on some of the psychological mechanisms underlying stress reactions.

A great portion of the experimentation in the field of stress does not add significantly to our knowledge of the psychological principles underlying the problem. If we are to understand the reasons for this, we need to recognize that, to be valuable, laboratory experiments must be effective analogues of postulated processes in the naturalistic phenomena of stress. These phenomena come to our attention through observations of people in real life. Our concern with stress phenomena arises from such observations as the behavior of people

in disasters (Baker and Chapman, 1962), of mourning following bereavement (Lindermann, 1944), of various forms of psychopathology (Hambling, 1959), of the nature and effects of concentration camps (Bettelheim, 1943) and military combat (Grinker and Spiegel, 1945), and of patients anticipating surgery (Janis, 1958), to mention a few of the more prominent examples of field studies which have enriched the recent literature.

As a first step in understanding these phenomena, they are placed in a loose way under the rubric of stress. Thus, for example, various somatic symptoms such as ulcers and hypertension are conceived to be the result of stress processes, as are the symptoms of battle fatigue or schizophrenia, or the deterioration of skilled performance in battle, and the disorganization of social systems in disaster. Analytic statements are then evolved which identify the antecedent conditions of the so-called stress reactions, and the processes involved. An examination of the field-study literature reveals abundant conceptualizations about the sources of threat, the mechanisms of threat production, the coping processes following threat, and the behavioral and physiological consequences. Some of the most significant of these conceptualizations may be found in the work of Janis (1958, 1962).

Now the laboratory makes it possible for us to test the adequacy of our conceptualizations by making the relevant processes happen under conditions of careful control and measurement. Although it is not always strictly the case, laboratory experimentation usually depends upon the definition of problems originating in our observations of nature and the development of theories about the processes which underlie what is observed.

What then is a laboratory analogue? First of all, it is an experiment performed under controlled conditions so that a variable, or several variables can be unequivocally related to some effect that one measures. But what about the term *analogue*? This refers to the manipulations in the experiment which parallel, or are similar to, the processes that are postulated to take place in nature. We are never really interested in the limited conditions of the experiment itself. Rather, we assume that these conditions represent those in real life, and that the findings can be generalized to conditions like them in nature. If an experimenter creates

* Reprinted with permission from American Psychological Association. In *American Psychologist,* 1964, Vol. 19, pp. 400–411.

[1] This paper is a slightly modified version of one given at a symposium of the American Psychiatric Association, on "Human Reaction to the Threat of Impending Disaster," at American Association for the Advancement of Science, Philadelphia, December 27, 1962.

stress by exposing his experimental subjects to an experience of failure by doing or saying certain things to him, he expects to generalize his results to all those situations in life which involve such failure. The laboratory experiment on stress is but a miniature of these life experiences, and most importantly, one whose procedures, by analogy, are thought to correspond to or be isomorphic with the processes we postulate as taking place in nature.

All laboratory experiments are, in a sense, analogues, although they are not necessarily good analogues to postulated processes, nor are they necessarily well designed to identify the relationships between the variables which confirm or disconfirm the postulated process. Experiments which serve to advance our understanding depend upon a clear conceptual analysis of a problem. Very little of the recent experimental work on the problem of psychological stress falls into this category, sometimes because of the painful absence of a clear conception, sometimes because of the failure of adequate design.

These critical statements can be brought home by turning to substantive problems in the field, emphasizing the question of what psychological processes mediate stress reactions. We must ask when a stimulus will produce stress reactions, and what factors determine whether it will or will not.

In raising this question, the temptation must be resisted to digress into the equally important problem of what reactions define stress. An enormous variety of measures are employed to this end, ranging from biochemical studies of adrenal-cortical or medulla secretions in the blood, to autonomic nervous system indicators of arousal such as skin conductance, heart rate and respiration, as well as a large class of behavioral reactions including reports of affect, observations of behavioral and cognitive disorganization, and motor and postural manifestations. These indicators reflect, for one thing, different levels of analysis, physiological as well as psychological. Little is known about the relationships between them. In fact, what is known suggests that stress indicators are poorly correlated (Lazarus, Speisman, and Mordkoff, 1963), and it is difficult to identify the conditions under which stress should be indexed by one or the other. And yet, the many measures employed are all identified as stress reactions. However, the many problems inherent in the definition of stress

and stress reactions must be excluded here as beyond the possibility of the present discussion.

Returning to the matter of what produces stress reactions, experimenters have employed a remarkable variety of procedures. Included are efforts to attack the self-esteem of subjects, or other significant personal needs such as achievement or affiliation, frightening subjects by making them believe that they are in danger of electrocution from a malfunctioning electrical instrument, employing insulting remarks to induce anger, making ego-threatening interpretations in a psychiatric interview, presenting movies dealing with threatening experiences, blowing a loud horn behind the subject's head, requiring the performance of intellectual tasks such as mental arithmetic, producing sensory deprivation, and having subjects plunge their arm into a bucket of ice-cold water. This list is by no means exhaustive, but it is fairly representative of the kinds of experimental conditions used in laboratory research. Often, great ingenuity is employed by the experimenter in setting up the conditions producing stress, as in a recent study by Korchin and Herz (1960), in which the subject is made to think he has autistically misperceived the contents of perceptual stimuli by a clever ruse.

Now what about the mechanism by which the stimulus condition results in the measured stress reaction? By what reasoning does plunging the arm into ice-cold water or doing mental arithmetic get placed in the same category of stressor stimuli as do conditions designed to threaten self-esteem? It is true that heart rate changes, elevation of skin conductance, and other autonomic indices of stress reaction can be demonstrated to occur as a consequence of each of these procedures, and of many more, including an experience of failure or watching a disturbing movie. It can also be demonstrated that increased hydrocortisone may be found in the blood following an experience of failure, attacks on the subjects' ability to perceive correctly, living in a strange environment, or watching threatening movies. Experiments merely demonstrating that autonomic, behavioral, and adrenal-cortical responses follow the use of some specific, so-called stressor procedure, have proliferated.

What is missing from much of this work is a clear set of notions about why this diverse variety of stimulus conditions produces the reactions identified as stress. Without an analysis of the psychological or physically noxious nature of these stimulus conditions, and the processes that intervene between them and the measured stress reaction, the only link between them must remain the response measure, say hydrocortisone or skin-conductance elevation, which is found to be a common response to all of these stimuli.

But is the reason why plunging the arm into ice water produces such responses the same as is assumed to be the case for mental arithmetic or for assaults on the self-esteem? In the latter case, the intervening process is often assumed to be the production of threat in the psychological sense. Do we then assume also that plunging the arm into ice-cold water is threatening, or is there a more direct, homeostatic mechanism of temperature regulation involved in that procedure which is not true in assaults on self-esteem? Similarly, does mental arithmetic produce stress responses because of potential psychological threats involved in performing such a task, or is it merely a matter of activation or mobilization of effort?

It is possible that both the state of being threatened and physical demands upon the tissues tend to activate the organism and produce similar autonomic and biochemical changes, and that even nonthreatening kinds of experiences such as watching a funny movie, or running up and down a hillside or golf course in sheer pleasure have similar effects. The changes that are called stress reactions may not be at all specific to psychologically threatening conditions, and perhaps positive affective experiences might produce the same reaction although in lesser degree. If this is true, then on what grounds do we identify all such reactions as stress? Similarly with the adrenal-cortical reactions emphasized by Selye (1956), serum-hydrocortisone elevation may follow any biological demand, rather than necessarily being associated with the psychological state of being threatened. Have we not begged here the key question, that concerning the mechanisms by which these effects are produced?

There are many variables confounded in the data alluded to above which leave indeterminate the bases, physiological and psychological, on which the so-called stress reactions depend. Perhaps the easiest one to recognize is the confounding between physiological and psychological levels of explanation. The process of having a tooth pulled results in increased hydrocortisone in the

blood. Shannon and his colleagues (Shannon, Isbell, and Hester, 1962) have shown, however, that merely anticipating such dental work will lead to the same results. In the latter case, the mechanisms intervening between the threat of dental surgery and the stress reaction are psychological, since there is no direct assault on the tissue system at all, merely the recognition by the patients of a danger to come. To return to another stress situation, it is possible that plunging the arm into cold water has psychological implications that are connected with the stress reactions, but this is not the explanation that would normally be accepted. Rather, what is assumed is the direct disturbance of the tissue system, that and the natural defensive or homeostatic reactions of the body to such noxious conditions, referred to by Selye (1956) as "the adaptation syndrome," are called into play. But the levels of explanation are entirely different in instances of threat and direct tissue damage. While it is true that the ultimate physiological mechanisms may be the same once the subject has been threatened psychologically or once a directly noxious stimulus has assaulted a tissue system, the key psychological questions are begged unless the researcher attempts to specify the psychological processes which determine whether these changes will indeed be activated.

Most of the experiments performed on stress simply ignore this question of psychological process, and serve merely as demonstrations that such and such a condition results in some stress reaction, usually defined by a single measure. They are not analogues of psychological stress at all, in the sense that they permit evaluation of some postulated process of stress production. Strangely enough, most are not even psychological in character at all, since typically one cannot find a single psychological question that has been elucidated. And often, even the physiological mechanism by which the hydrocortisone, skin-conductance change, or whatever, comes about is not clarified, so that such studies are not even physiological analogues of the kinds of processes Selye (1956), Lindsley (1957), or other physiologically oriented theorists were so concerned with.

The impression that all experimental studies ignore psychological questions should not be created, although those that tackle them are often woefully inadequate to the task. A good example is the recent paper by Alexander and his colleagues (Alexander, Flagg, Foster, Clemens, and Blahd, 1961) dealing with the psychological mechanism of stress production in patients suffering from hyperthyroidism. Alexander started with two assumptions. One, of less interest here, was that hyperthyroid disorder leads to specificity of reaction to stress, for such patients the preferred organismic response being in the category of heightened thyroid activity. The other, dealing more with the psychodynamics of stress production, was that the hyperthyroid patient is especially vulnerable to threat in situations engendering fear of biological survival. This fear then is the postulated fundamental source of stress in the hyperthyroid patient.

Here is a postulate about the mechanism underlying stress in a particular group, a postulate which Alexander attempted to check by an experimental analogue. The analogue consisted of employing as a stimulus a movie called "The Wages of Fear" which was thought to deal with the theme of threat to biological survival. The film was presented to a group of untreated thyrotoxic patients, a treated group, and a group of normal controls. Thyroid functioning was found to be elevated in the untreated patient group as a result of viewing the film.

While the Alexander study did attempt to identify the psychological mechanism underlying stress in the hyperthyroid patient, it failed for design reasons. The trouble is that there is no way of knowing from this study whether the reactions of the patients were specific to this film with its particular contents revolving around the theme of biological survival threats. Maybe any disturbing film would have had the same effects regardless of theme. To support the hypothesis about the specific kind of threat production in these patients, it was necessary to demonstrate that the stress reaction of heightened thyroid activity did not occur when another film was used—a film which, because of other kinds of threatening content, could indeed produce stress reactions in another type of population.

Still, the study of Alexander goes in the right direction in its attempt to spell out and test psychodynamic factors in stress production. It failed simply for methodological reasons to demonstrate that fear for biological survival is the necessary and sufficient condition of stress production in a hyperthyroid group. It is an analogue of stress because it was designed to test, empirically, a postulate about the mechanism of stress production by creating conditions that could be considered appropriate for this mechanism. Such process-oriented studies exist but are disturbingly rare. Without them, and without systematic research programs based upon well-articulated theories of psychological stress, laboratory studies continue to proliferate without leading to significant advances in our generalizable knowledge.

Attention should now be shifted from general statements about the field of experimentation as a whole, to a presentation of some work from the author's laboratory in which a research group has been seeking to test and elaborate certain theoretical principles of psychological stress production.[2] While this program is many faceted and deals with a number of key theoretical issues in psychological stress, one particular concept which has led to some extremely interesting findings will be touched on in the remainder of this paper.

An important feature of stress in the psychological sense is seen in the literature on disaster. In that literature, it is often implied that stress depends on the *anticipation* of something harmful in the future, and that it requires an interpretation by the person about the personal significance of the stimulus situation. Janis (1962), for example, discusses this problem in the concept of "anticipatory fear." This anticipation of potential harm or motive thwarting is the key to the concept of *threat*. Threat can be regarded as the central intervening variable in psychological stress.

Just before the 1953 Worcester tornado, the spring storm with thunder and lightning and dark clouds preceding the disaster did not communicate threat to the residents. There was no expectation of harm and hence no threat until the tragic event happened. Subsequently, however, after the experience of the tornado, ordinary storms carried an ominous quality. People were subsequently frightened by summer storms that had previously carried no threat. The crucial issue here in the production of threat is the process of discrimination of dangerous or threatening conditions from benign ones.

It is this idea of the dependence of threat upon a discrimination, a judgment, or an interpretation

[2] The research findings reported here are based on investigations supported by Research Grant No. MH-02136 from the National Institute of Mental Health, United States Public Health Service.

that will be developed briefly now. For this process the term *cognitive appraisal* is used. The process of appraising which circumstances are harmful and which are benign is crucial to the production of stress reactions at least at the psychological level of analysis. In fact, as Arnold (1960) has recently argued most persuasively, any emotion implies an evaluation of a stimulus as either harmful or beneficial. But Arnold has not described the conditions that determine the appraisal, and without such analysis, experimental studies of the process are not possible. Among other things, beliefs or expectations about events, based both upon past experience and the present stimulus configuration, determine whether or not a stimulus will be reacted to as threatening.

Let us consider a moment what the concept of cognitive appraisal means concerning the production of threat. For one thing, it means that the same stimulus can be threatening or not, depending upon the interpretation the person makes concerning its future personal significance. This is an important point. The threat is not simply out there as an attribute of the stimulus. Rather it depends for its threat value on this appraisal process, which in turn depends upon the person's beliefs about what the stimulus means for the thwarting of motives of importance to him.

In the research project [3] which forms the basis of this discussion, experimental analogues of cognitive appraisal have been created and the factors that determine this appraisal manipulated. A stimulus which is normally threatening to most experimental subjects has been made relatively benign by influencing the way in which subjects interpret it.

The basic method of producing threat has been the use of motion-picture films, the orientation toward which is manipulated by introductory statements and/or sound tracks during the film which cast the events viewed in the way we choose (Lazarus, Speisman, Mordkoff, and Davison, 1962). One of these films shows a primitive ritual of an Australian Stone Age tribe. It involves a series of crude operations on the genitals of the native boys when they have reached puberty. The

operation is called "subincision." The film is generally quite disturbing to watch. This same film has previously been employed by Aas (1958) and Schwartz (1956) as a means of studying the Freudian concept of castration anxiety, although unpublished experimental studies in our laboratory suggest that there are other sources of threat in the film as well as the mutilation- or castration-relevant content.

In the typical experiment using the subincision film, subjects watch the film individually. Continuous recordings are made of autonomic variables such as skin conductance, heart rate, respiration, and motor activity, depending upon our interests at the moment, and at the end of the film reports of the subject's affective state are solicited, usually by an interview or an adjective check list of mood. Merely watching the film produces marked stress reactions, some of which can be occasionally quite severe with symptoms of disgust, nausea and anxiety (Lazarus et al., 1962). To give you some picture of the ebb and flow of the typical stress reaction to this film, Figure 1 portrays the pattern of skin conductance shown by 50 subjects over the entire 17 minutes of the subincision film.

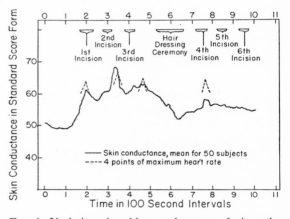

FIG. 1. Variation in skin conductance during the subincision film for 50 subjects.

You will notice in Figure 1 the ups and downs: high points in skin conductance signifying arousal or threat, low points indicating more benign states. The peak periods occur when the surgical operations are taking place, especially the first three which seem to be the most disturbing to watch.

[3] The author's colleagues and students whose work is referred to here, or who have participated in this project, include: Joseph C. Speisman, Arnold M. Mordkoff, Leslie A. Davison, Cliff A. Jones, Jr., and Elizabeth Alfert.

In the second operation for example, the native boy is obviously distressed and in pain, immediately following which he sobs and appears to suffer considerably. The deep trough in skin conductance in the middle of the film occurs in relation to the relatively benign ceremonial activity of hair tying, in which one native binds the hair of another who has recently been operated upon. It might be noted also that this curve of autonomic reactivity is extremely stable in reflecting the stimulus impact, since in each new study with a sizable sample the same basic pattern is generated. This shows how desirable continuous recording of skin conductance is in indicating the ups and downs of stress reaction.

It has been said that this same film stimulus, which is so disturbing, could be made relatively benign by altering the interpretation which the subject places upon the events which are portrayed, presumably by eliminating the threatening significance (Speisman, Lazarus, Mordkoff, and Davison, 1964). How can threatening material be viewed so as to nonthreatening? One kind of answer to this question can be found in the theory of ego defense, which postulates, in a rather loose way, certain mental operations which are conceived of as ways of reducing threat. Such mechanisms can be thought of as resulting in altered cognitive appraisal of threatening stimuli, be they internal or environmental.

Two very general kinds of defensive orientation were chosen as especially suitable for the subincision film: intellectualization on the one hand, and denial and reaction formation, employed together on the other. In intellectualization one gets detachment from threatening experiences by taking an analytic, impersonal viewpoint. In denial one denies the threatening implications, and in reaction formation the negative aspects are reversed entirely so that only positive, rosy qualities are allowed expression and emphasized.

Two sound tracks were created for the subincision film, one called intellectualization, the other denial and reaction formation. The sound tracks contained a brief introductory statement, followed by a narrative, like a travelogue that ran simultaneously with the film itself. In intellectualization the orientation of the anthropologist was taken who, like the viewer, is observing an interesting specimen of human behavior and describing it analytically. In it no reference is made to feelings of any kind. In the denial and reaction formation statement, the idea that the operative procedures damaged the functioning of the natives, threatened their health, or resulted in significant pain was denied. It was further suggested that the native boys had looked forward all their lives to this happy experience which permitted them to join their brothers as emerging adults and full members of the society. Everything that happened, however gruesome, was given a rosy glow.

A third control sound track was also created to compare with both the silent film and the two defensively oriented sound tracks. This was euphemistically called the trauma track, since it pointed up all of the major sources of threat in the film, the filth, the pain, the danger of the operation, and the sadism of the procedure, although this presentation was made in the same calm tone of the narrator's voice as that used in the other two sound tracks.

Two groups of subjects were employed in this experiment with the defensive sound tracks, one a college student group, the other consisting of middle-level airline executives who graciously consented to participate in the study. The reasoning behind the choice of groups had to do with an interest in defensive dispositions, that is, the habitual way in which the subjects coped with threat. One might assume that a person who usually denies threat would be most responsive to the denial and reaction formation sound track, while the person whose preferred mode of defense is intellectualization would get the most threat reduction from the intellectualization sound track, which was more compatible with his "natural" way of coping.

The assumption was made that college students, aside from whatever dispositional qualities led them into the system of higher education in the first place, are continually exposed to intellectualized modes of thought. Every facet of the world, physical, biological, psychological, social, and artistic, is placed in the context of analysis and intellectual understanding. For example, in an anthropology class one is taught about how people in other cultures live. In physiology one gets accustomed to examining and even discussing tissues and inspecting the anatomies of human and infrahuman species. The entire content of higher education poses a continual force toward intellectualized modes of thought.

With business executives the matter would appear to be quite different. The educational back-ground of the group was, in the main, high-school level. The activities of life of the executive are more action oriented. Decision is emphasized rather than intellectual introspection. Managerial people are apt to be subjected far more to the social atmosphere which emphasizes such denial slogans as "the power of positive thinking," and the conviction that, if you believe in yourself, chances of success are good. Understanding and knowledge are favorably seen less for their own sake and more for their power to produce desired results.

As it turns out, some personality-test data on both groups of subjects were available, and this appeared to support our assumption that students were more apt to be intellectualizers, and the executives more disposed to denial-type defenses. Two scales of the Minnesota Multiphasic Personality Inventory (MMPI) were most relevant. One, identified as Psychasthenia (*Pt*) could be regarded as a measure of anxiety and obsessive compulsive tendencies which are considered a consequence of intellectualized defenses. The other, a derived scale of the MMPI called Hysteria Denial (*Hy Dn*), is presumed to measure tendencies to deny threatening or unacceptable thoughts, impulses and the threatening aspects of events. The college-student group was found to be significantly higher than the executives on the *Pt* scale, while the executives showed significantly higher scores than the students on the *Hy-Dn* scale.

The results of the study showed that the defensive sound tracks, in general, significantly reduced the threatening impact of the subincision film, while the trauma track increased it (Speisman et al., 1964). This is shown in Figure 2 illustrated, as before, for the autonomic nervous system variable of skin conductance. In the figure are presented the skin-conductance results for the subincision film without any sound track, the film accompanied by the trauma track, and the film accompanied by either the denial-and-reaction-formation track or the intellectualization track.

While both defensive sound tracks reduced threat, their effectiveness did appear to depend, as expected, on compatability with the natural defensive dispositions of the subject populations. Intellectualization was most effective in reducing stress reaction in the student group, and less effective with the executives. In contrast, denial and reaction formation worked best with the execu-

tives but was far less successful with the students. It is as if the students simply did not accept as fully as the executives the orientation provided in the denial-and-reaction-formation sound track.

This interaction between the subject groups and the two defensive sound tracks is shown in Figure 3. Examination of the figure reveals that the students who heard the denial-and-reaction-formation sound track showed only a slight reduction in stress reaction over the silent version, compared with that found when students heard intellectualization, and with denial and reaction formation in the executive group.

Lest these findings with respect to personality and the effectiveness of different modes of cognitive appraisal be taken as more pat than they really are, a perplexing sour note must be introduced into the discussion. Up to this point in the analysis, there seemed no reason to doubt that whatever was being measured by the *Pt* and *Hy-Dn* scales of the MMPI accounted for the interesting and sensible differences between the students and executives. If this were true, then the interaction between defensive disposition and sound-track effects could also be shown, and even strengthened, if we ignore the social group to which the subject belongs and array the data entirely on the basis of the MMPI scales. That is, the effectiveness of the sound tracks could be compared between those subjects scoring high in *Hy Dn* and those scoring low, and between subjects scoring high in *Pt* and those scoring low. When this was done, the interaction found earlier simply disappeared.

This latter finding somewhat embarrasses the interpretation of the interplay between defensive disposition and effects of the defensive sound tracks. At least it tells us that the differences between the students and executives are not accounted for on the basis of the *Hy-Dn* and *P't* personality scales. The original interpretation is still reasonable, however, that executives are more prone to denial-and-reaction-formation modes of thought and students more oriented toward intellectualization as part of the social pattern to which they are exposed. And additional data have been appearing which further support the original interpretation. In any event, the findings on the general success of the defensive sound tracks in reducing the threat normally conveyed by the subincision movie are not in doubt.

The above findings have been replicated and extended in another study (Lazarus and Alfert,

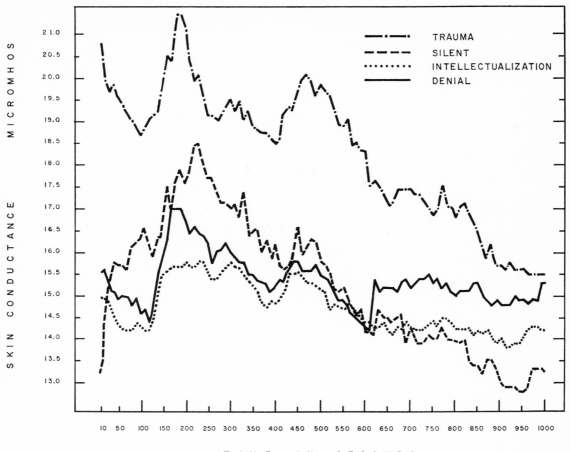

FIG. 2. Skin-conductance patterns during the subincision film as determined by the various sound-track conditions.

1964) which is even more dramatic in showing the power of cognitive appraisal. This time there was no sound track at all, merely a prior orientation session, and still subjects could view the silent film with equanimity once they had been led to interpret the events portrayed in a benign way. In this study only the denial-and-reaction-formation statements were used, and they were presented to subjects as orienting instructions before the film began. Figure 4 shows that the lowest stress reactions occur in this condition, compared with either a sound-track condition involving denial and reaction formation, or a silent film version with no effort to manipulate appraisal. Stress reaction, as we would expect, is greatest in the latter case. It should be added also that psychological assess-

ments of the beliefs of the subjects about the film events made at the end of the film conditions follow what might be expected from the levels of stress reaction found. The cognitive appraisal of threat is indeed lowest in the denial-and-reaction-formation conditions, with the most threatening interpretations found in the untreated group.

Finally, the study of Lazarus and Alfert (1964) tends to confirm the principle that the defense-oriented communication must be compatible with defensive dispositions in the subject in order to reduce stress reaction. As assessed by scales of the MMPI considered to tap the disposition toward denial as a defense, subjects high in denial tendency showed marked stress reduction as a result of the denial communications, while subjects low

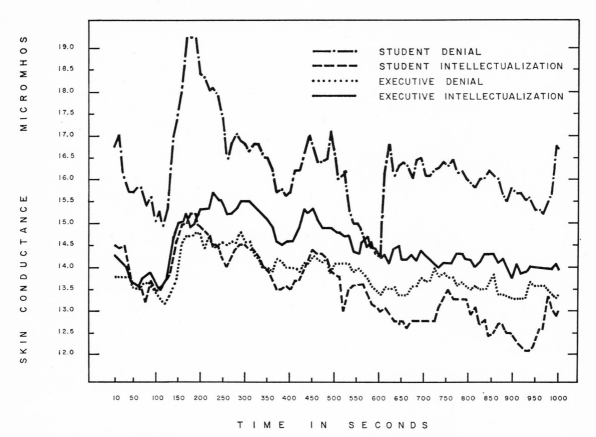

Fig. 3. Interaction effects on skin-conductance patterns of subject groups and defensive sound-track conditions.

in denial tendency were not so influenced. The personality dispositions determined whether or not the denial communications, presented either prior to or along with the threatening film as a sound track, would reduce the usual stress reaction to the film.

It has been shown here that threat, or at least stress reactions mediated psychologically, depend upon the cognitive appraisal of a stimulus. This is another way of talking about the interpretation of the personal significance of the stimulus. Moreover, two kinds of appraisal, intellectualized on the one hand, and that based on denial and reaction formation on the other, result in the short-circuiting of the expected threat arousal. These modes of viewing a potentially threatening stimulus, based on the theory of ego defense, are not as

readily accepted by all persons, but if they are, they make for a nonthreatening appraisal.

The experimental analogue involves two steps. One is the assumption that the subject, in watching a motion-picture film, identifies himself with the actors in the film as though he were one of them, and can be thus threatened by what is happening to them. The second stage in the analogue concerns the process of cognitive appraisal, in effect, that the orienting instructions and sound tracks produce varying appraisal processes of the sort involved in the concepts of denial and reaction or intellectualization, and that these, in turn, correspond to what occurs in the natural context.

It should be made absolutely clear that, although the discussion has referred to ego-defense

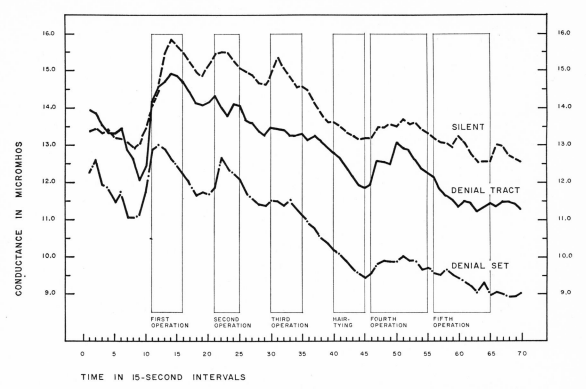

FIG. 4. Effects of experimental treatments on skin conductance during the subincision film.

theory and employs the terms *intellectualization* and *denial and reaction formation,* in describing the sound tracks, the experiments are analogues of cognitive appraisal and not ego defense. We have merely borrowed from defense theory in constructing our appraisal statements. Defense is usually considered to involve first the arousal of threat, and then, by principles that are still not clear to us, the activation of certain self-induced modes of thought which reduce the threat that has once been aroused. In these experiments, the modes of thought that short-circuit threat are encouraged by manipulation of the situation; they do not follow the generation of threat in the subject, nor are they self-induced by the subject. We cannot consider our findings as resulting from defensive processes, although we can learn something about the threat-reducing effectiveness of various defensive modes of thought from systematic manipulation of the kinds of statements we give orienting the subjects. Thus, indirectly they contribute to the theory of ego defense.

Those familiar with the literature on ego defense will recognize the vague condition of these concepts, even though the general idea of defensive reappraisal has wide acceptance. The specific mental operations involved are not clearly understood, their comparative effectiveness is not known, nor is their relationship with each other. From the point of view of the experimental analogue, some key questions can be phrased in this way: What are the necessary and sufficient mental operations for the successful defensive reappraisal of various kinds of threatening events? And what are the conditions under which these coping processes will be activated and successful? By means of the experimental paradigm described above, it is possible to subject a variety of carefully defined modes of defensive appraisal to the test of effectiveness in reducing the physiological as well as behavioral manifestations of threat. By the proper analysis of such maneuvers as intellectualization, for example, we can separate out of this global and poorly articulated concept, the precise elements of thought which are capable of making a threatening stimulus less threatening or benign.

About the experiments themselves, I would say at the present time that when the belief is created that the surgical procedures in the subincision film are neither painful nor harmful, and are viewed by the natives with joy, then, assuming that the subject has placed himself in their shoes, there is no threat associated with vicariously undergoing the subincision experience. Similarly, from the vantage point of intellectualized detachment, the same events which are normally threatening can be looked at without emotionalized, empathic involvement, and can be placed in the context of a neutral conceptual framework.

In making this latter point about intellectualization, one may think of the experience of Hamlet in coming upon the grave digger unearthing a skull. Hamlet says poignantly, "Alas, poor Yorick, I knew him." This emotional statement is the dramatist's way of involving Hamlet and therefore the audience with the image of a friend, a fellow human being, dead, now nothing more than bones. If we follow the kind of arguments made about intellectualization, he might have said with far less emotional impact, "Isn't this an interesting specimen of primate bone?" In fact, is this not exactly what the anatomist or surgeon does when he dons his scientist hat and observes pathology? Yorick as a dead friend is a threatening thought, but Yorick as a nameless primate bone short-circuits the threat by employing a nonthreatening framework within which to view the same event which could be most disturbing from another point of view.

At this point again, the temptation is strong and must be resisted to digress to the issues inherent in using the vicarious procedure of motion-picture films to produce threat, issues concerned with advantages and disadvantages, and with the assumed processes by which marked stress reactions can be so easily produced by this laboratory method. But these questions themselves are complex and require extensive exposition. Moreover, the purpose of illustrating the laboratory analogue of stress processes has been fulfilled in the presentation of some studies dealing with processes of threat production and reduction.

It must be clear by now that, implicitly or explicitly, laboratory analogues of stress must start from some conceptualization of the very processes underlying the phenomena observed. In the film technique the analogue involves assumptions about the process of identification with the actors in the film, to mention one. In the sound track procedures there is available an analogue of the process of cognitive appraisal, the different sound tracks representing different frames of reference within which the film events are viewed.

It is remarkable that, in the quarter of a century that has seen interest in stress phenomena grow so greatly, pyschological stress theory has had so little influence on experimental research on the subject. Some researchers seem to believe that Selye's (1956) work on the adaptation syndrome has solved our problems concerning the psychology of stress, when, in reality, it leaves all the psychological questions untouched. Selye has added perhaps to the measures indexing stress, and to our sophistication about the physiological mechanisms underlying these measures, but not to the understanding of the psychological processes which determine when a stress reaction will or will not occur.

The current work on the physiology of arousal tends to confuse psychological threat with activation, to confuse the jumping up and down in happy enthusiasm, and the physiological mobilization involved in this, with the state of being threatened by the sight of something, by the thought of something, by a small change in environment which betokens a potential harm. The theoretical and methodological problems inherent in the field of psychological stress will never be solved merely by repeated demonstrations that this or that condition will result in a blood chemistry effect, a change in affect, or an autonomic nervous system reaction—unless at the same time attention is given to the psychological processes involved, and to the empirical conditions which identify these processes. In the experimental laboratory what we need are more carefully though out analogues of these psychological processes.

REFERENCES

Aas, A. *Mutilation fantasies and autonomic response*. Oslo, Norway: Oslo Univer. Press, 1958.

Alexander, F., Flagg, G. R., Foster, S., Clemens, T., and Blahd, W. Experimental studies of emotional stress: 1. Hyperthyroidism. *Psychosom. Med.*, 1961, 22: 104–114.

Arnold, Magda B. *Emotions and personality*. Vol. 1. New York: Columbia Univer. Press, 1960.

Baker, G. W., and Chapman, D. W. *Man and society in disaster*. New York: Basic Books, 1962.

Bettelheim, B. Individual and mass behavior in extreme situations. *J. abnorm. soc. Psychol.*, 1943, 38: 417–452.

Grinker, R. R., and Spiegel, J. P. *Men under stress*. New York: Blakiston, 1945.

Hambling, J. The nature of stress disorder. In, *Conference of the Society for Psychosomatic Research held at the Royal College of Physicians, May, 1958*. Springfield, Ill.: Charles C Thomas, 1959.

Janis, I. L. *Psychological stress*. New York: Wiley, 1958.

Janis, I. L. Psychological effects of warnings. In G. W. Baker and D. W. Chapman (Eds.), *Man and society in disaster*. New York: Basic Books, 1962.

Korchin, S. J., and Herz, M. Differential effects of "shame" and "disintegrative" threats on emotional and adrenocortical functioning. *AMA Arch. gen. Psychiat.*, 1960, 2: 640–651.

Lazarus, R. S., and Alfert, Elizabeth. Short-circuiting of threat by experimentally altering cognitive appraisal. *J. abnorm. soc. Psychol.*, 1964, 69: 195–205.

Lazarus, R. S., Speisman, J. C., and Mordkoff, A. M. The relationship between autonomic indicators of psychological stress: Heart rate and skin conductance. *Psychosom. Med.*, 1963, 25: 19–30.

Lazarus, R. S., Speisman, J. C., Mordkoff, A. M., and Davison, L. A. A laboratory study of psychological stress produced by a motion picture film. *Psychol. Monogr.*, 1962, 76:(34, Whole No. 553).

Lindemann, E. Symptomatology and management of acute grief. *Amer. J. Psychiat.*, 1944, 101: 141–148.

Lindsley, D. B. Psychophysiology and motivation. In M. R. Jones (Ed.), *Nebraska symposium on motivation: 1957*. Lincoln: Univer. Nebraska Press, 1957.

Schwartz, B. J. An empirical test of two Freudian hypotheses concerning castration anxiety. *J. Pers.*, 1956, 24: 318–327.

Seyle, H. *The stress of life*. New York: McGraw-Hill, 1956.

Shannon, I. L., Isbell, G. M., and Hester, W. R. Stress in dental patients. Report, April 1962, School of Aerospace Medicine, Brooks Air Force Base, Texas.

Speisman, J. C., Lazarus, R. S., Mordkoff, A., and Davison, L. Experimental reduction of stress based on ego-defense theory. *J. abnorm. soc. Psychol.*, 1964, 68: 367–380.

PREDICTION OF VICTIMIZATION FROM AN INSTRUMENTAL CONDITIONING PROCEDURE *

G. R. PATTERSON [1]

Traditionally, assessment devices have presented the subject with a set of stimuli (items) and, after grouping the elicited responses into a subset (scale), have made predictions to external criteria of various kinds. For discussion purposes, it is reasonable to view this approach as a poorly controlled variant of standard laboratory procedures. The traditional assessment procedures are viewed as poorly controlled because the variables determining the behavior of the subjects are relatively unspecified. Although the subject's behavior may consist of a quantifiable response such as marking a question as "true" or "false," the variables controlling the response may be the content of the item, or any one of a half dozen response sets. Occasionally, the self-report behavior is random. It is not surprising that such data rarely account for more than 10% of the criterion variance. In spite of the fact that these procedures seldom account for a large amount of variance for any single criterion, some of these devices such as the Minnesota Multiphasic Personality Inventory can account for small amounts of variance across an impressive array of criteria. It is evident that whatever assessment devices might be constructed

* Reprinted with permission from the American Psychological Association. In *Journal of Consulting Psychology*, 1967, Vol. 31, pp. 147–152.

[1] This research was financed in part by United States Public Health Service Grants M-4063, M-5429, and MH08009. H. Schumacker and H. Munsinger were instrumental in instigating the earlier stages of this research. The writer also wishes to express his appreciation to the undergraduate National Science Foundation students who collected the data: B. Hodges, Sandra Anderson, L. Bowlin, and Ronda Frazer. The writer owes a particular debt to Lew Goldberg for his persistent refusal to "understand" earlier translations of this manuscript.

for the clinician they must eventually make provision for a similar range of criterion coverage. The writer proposes that some traditional laboratory procedures might be adapted to assessment problems. The eventual utility of such an application would be a function of its ability to provide measures which can make predictions to a significant range of criterion behaviors.

The present report summarizes the last in a series of six pilot studies designed to explore a possible contribution of one type of laboratory procedure to the assessment process. For example, operant technology could provide better controls by limiting the number of variables which are operating in determining the behavior of the subject. Presumably, these better controls should provide better response data which in turn could account for more of the variance in the criterion measures than has been the case for the traditional assessment devices.

Aside from the allure of tighter controls, there seems to be little else about operant technology that immediately recommends it to the assessment enterprise. For example, it is possible to conceive of changes in rate of response as a substitute for marking "true" or "false" to items. However, it is not always clear what the appropriate independent variables might be in the laboratory-assessment procedure which would provide for predictions across a wide range of social behaviors. What is required before seriously entertaining the possibility of such an approach is a general paradigm for systematically programming independent variables within the operant framework. To have maximal general utility, the laboratory procedures would have to lend themselves to great flexibility in the programming of independent variables. Flexible programming would imply that some provision be made for systematically sampling a wide range of stimuli to be used as reinforcers in the operant task. Presumably, each set of reinforcers would make it possible to predict a different set of criteria. Given that a clinical psychologist can specify a list of criterion behaviors for which predictions would be of some value, then some hypothetical "systematic framework" would be used to specify the subsets of reinforcer stimuli to be used in the laboratory task in order to make prediction to each criterion. The effect of these stimuli in controlling the behavior of the subjects would be precisely measured and would provide the basis

for making predictions to the criterion. For present purposes, the immediate question concerns the framework which will be used to select the stimuli to be introduced in the laboratory setting. The main purpose of the present report was to provide one possible approach to this problem together with a preliminary set of data testing its effectiveness.

First, it was necessary to introduce the obvious assumption that there are individual differences in subjects' responsiveness to any given class of reinforcing stimuli. These differences in responsiveness should reflect, in part, differences in past conditioning histories. Presumably, the criterion behaviors which we wish to predict are also outcomes of a similar conditioning history. For example, for any individual there are a number of social behaviors which are likely to become associated with aversive stimuli. Although the specifics may vary from individual to individual, such pairings occur in the life of most people living in this culture. For most, the sight of the dentist's uniform and his drill becomes conditioned stimuli (CS) for pain reactions. However, individuals differ in terms of the number of such pairings and intensity of the unconditioned stimuli (UCS) characterizing these associations. If, in an operant conditioning procedure, a picture of the dentist's drill were made contingent upon lever pressing, it would be expected that such a contingency might have a mild suppressing effect upon the rate of responding (Church, 1963; Solomon, 1964). It would also be expected that individuals who had had a large number of these associations of the CS to pain would show a greater suppression of rate of responding than would individuals who had had fewer, or less intense, original pairings. As a general case, it was assumed that there was a linear, monotonic function holding for the relation between the frequency and intensity of the pairings for CS and UCS on the one hand, and the effect of CS in suppressing the rate of responding when made contingent upon a response in an instrumental conditioning task.

The criterion used in the present study consisted of a set of behaviors which occur rather frequently in the socialization of most children. The criterion was "frequency of victimization." In an observational study reported by Bricker and Patterson (1964), data were collected on the frequency with which children were attacked by other children. The data showed impressive individual differences in the number of occasions, on any given day, in which a child would be "victimized" by other children. For example, some children were struck as often as 70 times, while others were not assaulted at all. The data also showed moderate stability in the frequency with which individual children were victimized. The correlations between the median rankings of victim status were .54 for a 6-week period and .40 for a 9-month period.

The behavior displayed by the attacker was most frequently such responses as "hit with hand," "push," or "hit with object." These behaviors of the attacker were viewed as CS's for the pain which followed. It was predicted that for some children pictures of children hitting or pushing other children would function as being mildly aversive. In an instrumental conditioning procedure, if lever pressing produced displays of such pictures, it would be predicted that for some children the rate of lever pressing would be moderately impaired. More to the point, it was predicted that the magnitude of the impairment effect would correlate significantly with the number of times a child had been observed to have been victimized.

Method

Sample

The subjects were 23 children from two nursery schools. Their ages ranged from 3 to 4 years. The sample was equally divided as to sex. Most of these subjects were from middle- and upper-class families.

Procedures

The laboratory apparatus consisted of a slide projector which was programmed to present a stimulus on a fixed interval schedule (5 seconds). The schedule was operative only if the child continued responding. The instructions to the child were as follows:

> There are pictures in this machine and you can make them come in this window by tapping the button on the desk like this [experimenter demonstrates]. You can tap the button and you will see pictures in the window. When a picture comes, look at it, but keep pressing the button. Keep tapping and looking at the different pictures in the window until I tell you to stop.

A series of studies has been carried out with the apparatus (Patterson and Littman, 1963). These studies have shown that if pictures which are generally of interest to children are presented on the screen at a fixed ratio schedule there is a significant increase in rate of responding. These findings are in keeping with the research findings by Munsinger (1964) to the effect that any meaningful stimulus can function as a reinforcer and that reinforcer effectiveness varies as a function of the "amount" of meaning. In the pilot study, 15 children from the first grade showed an increase of 1.0 response per slide.

In the next pilot study, eight children from the present sample participated in the procedure under conditions of nonreinforcement. Only those children were selected who had been observed to display neither extreme aggressiveness nor extreme passivity. In the procedure, 40 slides were presented which depicted lines tilted at various angles. The first question raised concerned the sampling of behavior necessary to establish a stable estimate for rate of responding. The data showed that the median rate of responding based upon Slides 6 through 10 correlated .87 with the median rate of key pressing during the remainder of the trial. The young child seemed to require a certain amount of participation in the procedure as a settling down or adaptation period. As might be expected, under conditions of nonreinforcement there was a marked decrease in the rate of responding. The median difference between the block of Slides 5–10 and the remainder of the trial was —1.0 (responses per slide).

The 15 subjects remaining in the sample were used for the experimental study. Ten slides depicting tilted lines constituted the base operant period. During the conditioning period, 18 slides were presented. These latter slides presented aggressive interactions among children. These slides were cartoons taken from an objective test designed to predict aggressive behaviors in children (Patterson, 1960). The number of key-tapping responses was recorded for each slide. The difference between the median number of key taps for the base operant slides (6–10) and conditioning slides (11–28) constituted a measure of behavior change.

The criterion estimate of "frequency of victimization" was obtained during a 5-week period of observation. An observer was present in each classroom for each of the periods and recorded each aggressive episode including the aggressor, the aggressive response, the name of the victim, and the consequence provided by the victim. The total number of times in which a child was attacked provided an estimate of the occurrence of these events for each child.

RESULTS

Because the cartoons had associative value (were meaningful), it was expected that some children would respond to them as if they were positive reinforcers and display an increase in rate. For other children, the cartoons were associated with aversive stimuli. This latter group of children would be expected to respond to the pictures with a moderate decrease in rate. The average change in rate for the total group was $-.37$ responses per slide. A t test of the distribution of difference scores showed this value was not significantly different from zero.

As pointed out in the volume edited by Harris (1963), the measurement of change is an extremely complex problem. When using difference scores of the type provided in this study, there will undoubtedly be a correlation between baseline rate and the magnitude of the difference score. Correlations of $-.63$ were reported for an instrumental conditioning procedure which was similar in many respects to the one being presented in the present report (Patterson and Hinsey, 1964). For this reason, a simple correlation between the change score and the criterion measure would be confounded by baseline differences. As recommended in Harris (1963), the partial correlation coefficient was used to partial out the baseline rate.

In spite of the weak general conditioning effect, the data from both schools showed that the more frequently a child had been victimized, the more the aggressive stimuli disrupted his rate of responding. The partial correlation for one school was .52 ($N = 7$); the comparable correlation for the other school was .70 ($N = 8$).

These data constitute an impressive beginning. Not only do they offer support for the general assumptions being made here, but the magnitude of the correlations suggested a relation which is at least comparable to the findings obtained by traditional psychometric devices.

DISCUSSION

The data presented in this report provide support for the general feasibility of constructing laboratory procedures to fulfill traditional assessment functions. The procedure described in the present paper is clearly exploratory. However, the results showed that it was possible to make predictions to a criterion of social behavior. The level of success in making these "predictions" about concurrent behavior was better than might have been expected.

Extrapolating a bit, it seems plausible to assume that one could sample other sets of social behaviors which had been conditioned to various UCS's in the lives of most individuals. For example, in the case of children it is a frequent and prime insult to accuse another child of being "a baby," or to accuse a boy of being "a sissy." Photographs of older children dressed as infants or of young boys dressed as girls would probably serve as aversive stimuli. For some younger children, being left by the parent is another conditioned stimuli associated with fear. In all three cases, it would be predicted that making such classes of stimuli contingent upon a lever-pressing response should result in a mildly suppressive effect upon the rate of responding for some children. It is also reasonable to assume that there would be individual differences among children in terms of the magnitude of this impairment effect upon the rate of the instrumental response. In the examples given above, the criterion to which one would relate these differences in effect would not be difficult to imagine.

In keeping with the procedures outlined thus far, it should be possible to make predictions to a wide spectrum of those social behaviors which in the past have been frequently associated with pain or discomfort. However, this line of reasoning would also provide its own set of limitations. For example, one could conceive of the set of social behaviors subsumed under the terms "achievement" or "responsible" as being associated with aversive stimuli, but more likely such contingencies played a rather minor role for the acquisition of such behaviors in the conditioning histories of most people. To the extent that aversive associations played a minor role in the acquisition and maintenance of the criterion behaviors, the laboratory assessment procedures described thus far would be of limited value.

With these limitations in mind, it might be of some interest to consider a set of conditions in which assessment devices could be constructed that would have broader generality. The laboratory studies completed by Munsinger (1964) in our laboratory may provide a basis for extending the assessment paradigm. He showed that the reinforcing effectiveness of stimuli varied as a function of the associative value of the stimulus. In general, the more meaningful a stimulus the greater its effect in strengthening a response. The stimulus which elicited a large number of associations proved to be a more effective reinforcer when this stimulus was made contingent upon a motor response in an instrumental conditioning procedure.

These findings provide an interesting basis for speculation about possible differences among individuals. For example, it seems likely that there are broad classes of social behaviors which would elicit a large number of associations from all individuals. By the same token, descriptions of these behaviors would function as effective reinforcers for most individuals if these descriptions were made contingent upon a response in an instrumental conditioning task. It seems doubtful that a laboratory procedure could be devised which would be sensitive enough to differentiate among individuals using stimuli which were uniformly of high associative value. However, it is likely that there are some social behaviors which are rather unique to the individual and which would concomitantly be of high associative value to him, for example, terms such as "hackle," "caddis," or "coachman" would have some additional associations for the fly fisherman. Presumably, visual representations of such stimuli would be more effective as reinforcers for these individuals.

When presented with a particular criterion of social behavior to which predictions are to be made, the experimenter may decide then to sample only those behaviors which would be rather unique to the criterion. Presumably, these behaviors would be uniquely reinforcing (high association value) to a small group of subjects. For example, if the criterion to be predicted was delinquent behavior it would seem plausible to construct photographs of behaviors relating to a variety of social behaviors, for example, riding motorcycles very fast, siphoning gas, stealing hub caps, stealing cigarettes from a store, fighting, violating traffic signals, showing disrespect for a teacher. Undoubtedly, some of these would be reinforcers for the nondelinquent adolescent, but the delinquent has quite likely a broader hierarchy of such behaviors. For the latter, the stimulus set should function as more effective reinforcers.

Before considering extensive testing of the general assumptions, there are several problems which must be met. Part of the difficulty lies in identifying the most effective measure of response strength to be used in the laboratory task. There is no single, best measure of response strength. As shown in the review by Parton and Ross (1965), time-dependent measures of response strength tend to be rather unstable. Time-independent measures, while they are more reliable, are also more likely to be confounded by the effects of the structure of responding which occurred just prior to the advent of the reinforcer (Patterson and Hinsey, 1964). In addition, if the reinforcement schedules are simple one-to-one contingencies, there is little reason to doubt that the mediational processes will determine some of the variance in measures of reinforcement effect (Farber, 1963; Kanfer, 1966).

This listing of a number of potential contributors to variance is intended to give pause to investigators who might believe that to solve the problems of assessment it is only necessary to "condition" a subject and to correlate the laboratory measure with a criterion. It is the impression of the writer that some of these problems in the measurement of reinforcement effect can be met, and that the possible contribution to assessment by these laboratory procedures merits the effort. For example, subjects could be classified as to the kind of response structure occurring prior to the introduction of the reinforcement contingencies (Patterson and Hinsey, 1964). The different classes could then be analyzed separately to determine the relations holding between measures of reinforcement effects and criterion variables. Also it should be possible to use more complex conditioning technologies of the kind described by Hefferline, Keenan, and Birch (1963) in which the ostensible contingency, for example key tapping to produce pennies, was irrelevant and the "real" contingency involved an eye-blink response.

Investigators should be encouraged to undertake these problems not with the object that laboratory procedures will provide a panacea for the problems besetting modern day assessment but rather as an approach which is potentially able to feed a very different kind of data into the assessment model.

SUMMARY

The report presents a description of an instrumental conditioning apparatus designed to serve as a personality assessment procedure. In this procedure, a visual stimulus was made contingent upon a lever-pressing response. The magnitude of the change in rate of responding constituted the dependent measure. The stimuli consisted of cartoons portraying social behaviors that had in the past for the children studied been associated as conditioned stimuli for pain. Each of the Ss was observed over a 5-wk. period in a nursery school setting. The number of occasions on which each child was victimized by an aggressor was recorded. It was predicted that children who had been more frequently victimized would show a greater impairment in the rate of responding when such stimuli were made contingent upon lever pressing. The prediction was confirmed.

REFERENCES

Bricker, W., and Patterson, G. R. Peer group reactions as a determinant of aggressive behavior in nursery school children. In B. McCandless (Chm.), Peer influence on social behavior. Symposium presented at American Psychological Association, Los Angeles, September 1964.

Church, R. M. The varied effects of punishment on behavior. Psychological Review, 1963, 70: 369–402.

Farber, I. E. The things people say to themselves. American Psychologist, 1963, 18: 185–197.

Harris, C. W. (Ed.) Problems in measuring change. University of Wisconsin Press, 1963.

Hefferline, R. F., Keenan, B., and Birch, J. D. Conditioning small events in human subjects without their observation by means of secondary reinforcement. Cited in A. J. Bachrach (Ed.), Experimental foundations of clinical psychology, Basic Books, 1963. Pp. 96–138.

Kanfer, F. H. Verbal conditioning: A review of its current status. Paper read at Conference on

Verbal Behavior sponsored by the University of Kentucky, 1966.

Munsinger, H. L. Meaningful symbols as reinforcing stimuli. Journal of Abnormal and Social Psychology, 1964, 68: 665–669.

Parton, D. A., and Ross, A. O. Social reinforcement of children's motor behavior: A review. Psychological Bulletin, 1965, 64: 65–73.

Patterson, G. R. A non-verbal technique for the assessment of aggression in children. Child Development, 1960, 31: 643–653.

Patterson, G. R., and Hinsey, C. Investigations of some assumptions and characteristics of a procedure for instrumental conditioning in children. Journal of Experimental Child Psychology, 1964, 1: 111–123.

Patterson, G. R., and Littman, I. Methodological studies on imitation. Unpublished paper, University of Oregon, 1963. (Mimeo)

Solomon, R. Punishment. American Psychologist, 1964, 19: 239–254.

SEX DIFFERENCES AND EXPERIMENTAL CONDITIONS IN SERIAL LEARNING *

Irwin G. Sarason and
Morton G. Harmatz [1]

Research on motivational factors in verbal learning has largely been directed to the study of two classes of variables: individual differences in subjects' personalities and experimentally created motivational conditions. Scores on personality tests have typically been employed to assess individual differences (Sarason, 1960). Orienting instructions (such as ego-involving communications and failure reports) have been the most commonly used means of experimentally manipulating motivation (Lazarus, Deese, and

* Reprinted with permission from the American Psychological Association. In Journal of Personality and Social Psychology, 1965, Vol. 1, pp. 521–524.

[1] This research was supported by grants (M-3889) from the National Institute of Mental Health, United States Public Health Service, and the State of Washington Initiative 171 Fund for Research in Biology and Medicine.

Osler, 1952; Sarason, 1960). Available evidence suggests that the simultaneous study of both individual difference variables and experimental manipulation of subjects' set is superior to the study of either of them alone in accounting for the performance of subjects (Sarason, 1960). Thus, for example, it has been found that lightly motivating or achievement-orienting preliminary instructions often have different effects on the verbal learning of subjects differing in test anxiety (Mandler and Sarason, 1952; Nicholson, 1958; Sarason, 1957). The learning of low-anxious subjects appears to be facilitated by these instructions, while the speed of learning of high test-anxious subjects is slowed down by them.

While instructions and failure reports have been the most widely used methods of experimentally approaching motivation in relation to learning, they do not exhaust the methods available. Both preperformance instructions and failure reports have in common the characteristic that they serve to orient the subject to perform at as high a level as possible. These cues to the subject have typically been given either at the outset of the experimental session (as in the case of preperformance instructions) or at some intermediate point in the course of learning (as in the case of failure reports administered between lists of verbal stimuli). Another approach, largely unexplored in the verbal learning literature, involves events occurring while the subject is performing the task assigned to him. However, reinforcement procedures have been widely used in the study of operant conditioning and verbal behavior. A review of the verbal conditioning literature indicates that events such as reinforcements are effective in influencing the subjects' emission of a variety of operant responses (Krasner, 1962). Similar effects have been obtained in studies of the effects of the experimenter's emission of "right" and "wrong" on response repetition in Thorndikian associative learning situations (Postman, 1962).

Two studies bear quite directly on the relationship of events occurring during performance to subjects' attained level of performance. In experiments conducted by Hetherington and Ross (1963) and by Sarason and Harmatz (1965) subjects performed on verbal learning tasks. Subjects were assigned to "good" and "try harder" conditions. The former condition involved encouraging, supportive comments to the subject by the experimenter during learning. The latter involved comments by the experimenter designed to increase the subjects' effortfulness in performance. The evidence provided by these studies indicates that multiple performance events such as reinforcements can significantly affect the subjects' attained performance levels and suggests that future research might well benefit from attempts to manipulate the subjects' motivation *during* their performance.

The present experiment was designed to contribute to knowledge of the effects of experimentally controlled events during performance on learning. In an effort to reduce the confounding of characteristics associated with the experimenter and the administration of a success-failure condition, light signals, rather than verbal reports by the experimenter, were used to inform the subject about his performance. The experimental design encompassed three variables. One of these was that of reports of performance. Following one-third of the trials, through light signals, the subject was given a report concerning his level of performance. One-fourth of the subjects were informed that their performance level was above average; to one-fourth of the subjects it was indicated that their performance was average; and one-fourth was informed that they were performing below average. The remaining subjects constituted a control group in that they were given no reports.

Two organismic variables were incorporated into this research. One of these was questionnaire-inferred test anxiety. The measure employed has been shown to relate to subjects' performance on verbal learning and other tasks (Sarason, 1960; Sarason and Ganzer, 1962). The second organismic variable was sex. This variable has, also, been found to relate to verbal learning under motivational conditions. The experimental design called for three levels of test anxiety (high, middle, and low scores), four experimental conditions (three light conditions and a control one), and sex of subject.

METHOD

Subjects

The subjects were 60 male and 60 female undergraduates enrolled in introductory psychology courses at the University of Washington. Prior to and independent of the experiment the students had been administered the Test Anxiety Scale (TAS) (Sarason and Ganzer, 1962). High TAS scores ranged between 8 and 15. Middle TAS scores ranged between 3 and 7, while the low TAS group consisted of subjects with scores between

TABLE 1

M<small>EAN</small> N<small>UMBER</small> <small>OF</small> C<small>ORRECT</small> R<small>ESPONSES</small> <small>FOR</small> G<small>ROUPS</small> <small>OF</small>
S<small>UBJECTS</small> C<small>LASSIFIED</small> <small>IN</small> T<small>ERMS</small> <small>OF</small>
S<small>EX</small> <small>AND</small> C<small>ONDITIONS</small>

| | Light conditions | | | |
	Above average	Average	Below average	Control
Male	264.60	240.27	254.00	167.73
Female	248.87	226.07	228.80	278.93

Note.—N = 15 per group.

0 and 2. The high, middle, and low TAS groups corresponded to the upper 22%, middle 54%, and lower 24% of the TAS score distribution.

Procedure

The task employed was a serial learning one requiring the anticipation of dissyllabic words. The material to be learned consisted of 17 items of low m value drawn from Noble's list (Noble, 1952). The mean m value of the list was 1.22 and the range was .99–1.50. The dissyllables were presented by means of a memory drum with an exposure time of 2 seconds. Following Item 17 there were three blank spaces. The list was presented for 35 trials without interruption.

The subjects were met by the experimenter, a male graduate student in psychology, and were seated at a table facing a black wooden screen. The memory drum was located in a space at the bottom of the screen. Above the drum were located in clear view of the subjects the three lights. At the left was a green light with a template underneath which said ABOVE AVERAGE. In the middle was a blue light with a template reading AVERAGE. On the right, there was a red light for the BELOW AVERAGE condition. The subjects in the control group had the same stimulus situation as the subjects in the three light-condition groups, except that the lights were omitted.

All subjects were given necessary introductory instructions. In addition, the subjects in the three light-condition groups were told:

> Since everyone wants to know how they are doing, I will indicate this to you.
> As you can see on the panel in front of you, there are three lights. A green one marked above average, a blue one marked average, and a red one marked below average. One of these three lights will be turned on during the rest space at the end of every third trial informing you of how you are doing.

For the subjects in the three light-condition groups, a light went on at the end of every third trial. Which of the three lights that was turned on was determined by the condition to which the subject had been assigned. The light went on at the beginning of the first of the three blank spaces which constituted the intertrial interval, and went off at the end of the second blank space.

R<small>ESULTS</small>

The results were analyzed in terms of a 3 × 2 × 4 × 35 analysis of variance design (TAS × Sex × Conditions × Trials) with five subjects in each of the experimental groups. The 35 trials constituted a repeated measurements variable.

The results of the analysis performed on the number of correct responses showed a significant Sex × Conditions interaction ($F = 4.79$, $df = 3/96$, $p < .005$). Table 1 presents means relevant to this interaction. Under the control condition in which no lights were employed, females performed at a higher level than did males. Just the opposite was the case for the three light conditions. In each instance, males performed at a higher level than did females. A breakdown of the Sex × Conditions interaction in terms of anxiety levels indicated that the nature of the interaction was essentially the same for high, middle, and low TAS groups. The trials effect was, of course, highly significant ($F = 390.91$, $df = 34/3264$, $p < .005$). There was a tendency towards significance for the Lights × Trials interaction ($p < .10$), with a more steeply accelerated learning curve for the above average light condition than the other three conditions. The Sex × Conditions × Lights interaction was found to be highly significant ($F = 1.77$, $df = 102/3264$, $p < .005$). The learning curve for males showed better performance over trials under the three light conditions than under the control condition. Just the opposite result obtained for females. This finding, together with the significant Sex × Conditions effect shows that the condition (absence of feedback) which led to the best performance for females resulted in the poorest performance for males. Although it was not statistically significant ($p < .25$), there was a tendency for the middle and low TAS groups to perform at a higher level ($Ms = 241.78$ and 256.38, respectively) than the high TAS group ($M = 219.77$). A Duncan's test indicated that the low TAS group performed at a higher level than did the high TAS group ($p < .05$).

An analysis of variance was also performed on the number of anticipatory errors, i.e., errors in which subjects emitted terms on the list but in the wrong order. The difference between males and females was found to be significant ($Ms = 27.69$ and 20.79, respectively, with $p < .025$). The rise and, then, decline in anticipatory errors led to a significant Trials effect ($p < .005$). An analysis of variance performed on intrusive errors (subject's responding with words which were not on the list used) yielded only one significant F, that for Trials ($p < .005$). The trial means on which this F was based followed a course similar to that mentioned for anticipatory errors.

The final analysis of variance was done using as the dependent variable the number of occasions on each trial on which the subject made no response, correct or incorrect. The Sex × Conditions interaction was found to be significant ($p < .01$). This result was due to the performance of male subjects under the neutral condition. This group made more nonresponses ($M = 386.33$) than did all other groups (overall $M = 316.54$). The Trials effect was significant ($p < .005$) and was due, as one would expect, to the decline in nonresponses over trials. The Sex × Conditions × Trials effect was found to be statistically significant ($p < .005$). This result was attributable to the slower decline in nonresponses for male subjects under the control condition than all other groups.

DISCUSSION

The striking differences between males and females under the experimental conditions would appear to be the most provocative findings of this research. Two worthwhile problems for future investigation suggested by them relate to differences among the conditions and between the sexes.

In general, it did not appear to matter very much under which report condition subjects performed. The decisive factor seemed to be, simply, whether or not any reports at all were given. On *a priori* grounds one might well have expected that the three meanings which were attached to the light conditions would differentially influence subjects' performance. An important question would appear to be the nature of the subjects' interpretations of the reports of performance which were given to them.

Associated with this problem is the need to shed light on the basis for males' and females' different reactions to the light conditions. It would appear that, as it were, leaving female subjects alone during learning is relatively facilitative, but that absence of feedback does not lead to a high level of performance for males. One possibility that comes to mind is that females, at least, in certain situations, may have a greater capacity for self-motivation than do males.

Previous research on anxiety in relation to verbally administered performance reports appeared to provide a basis for anticipating an interaction between the conditions of this experiment and TAS scores (Sarason, 1960). That there was no evidence in support of this expectation seems somewhat surprising. It may be that the interpersonal aspects of the experimenter-subject interaction (which were minimized in this study) have contributed to the previously reported significant results using experimenter-administered motivational instructions and failure reports.

SUMMARY

This experiment dealt with the relationship of 3 independent variables to serial learning. Male and female Ss differing in test-anxiety scores performed under 4 conditions. Three of these conditions involved evaluative reports to Ss, by means of light signals, of their performance at several points in learning. There were no reports of level of performance under a control condition. The major finding was a significant difference between the sexes under these conditions. Under the control condition, females performed at a higher level than did males. Just the opposite was the case for the 3 light conditions.

REFERENCES

Hetherington, Mavis, and Ross, L. E. Effect of sex of subject, sex of experimenter, and reinforcement condition on serial learning. *Journal of Experimental Psychology*, 1963, 65: 572–575.

Krasner, L. The therapist as a social reinforcement machine. In H. H. Strupp and L. Luborsky (Eds.), *Research in psychotherapy*. Vol. 2. Washington, D. C.: American Psychological Association, 1962. Pp. 61–94.

Lazarus, R. S., Deese, J., and Osler, Sonia, F. The effects of psychological stress upon performance. *Psychological Bulletin*, 1952, 49: 293–317.

Mandler, G., and Sarason, S. B. A study of anxiety and learning. *Journal of Abnormal and Social Psychology*, 1952, 47: 166–173.

Nicholson, W. M. The influence of anxiety upon learning. *Journal of Personality*, 1958, 26: 303–319.

Noble, C. E. An analysis of meaning. *Psychological Review*, 1952, 59: 421–430.

Postman, L. Rewards and punishments in human learning. In L. Postman (Ed.), *Psychology in the making*. New York: Knopf, 1962. Pp. 331–401.

Sarason, I. G. Effect of anxiety and two kinds of motivating instructions on verbal learning. *Journal of Abnormal and Social Psychology*, 1957, 54: 166–171.

Sarason, I. G. Empirical findings and theoretical problems in the use of anxiety scales. *Psychological Bulletin*, 1960, 57: 403–415.

Sarason, I. G., and Ganzer, V. J. Anxiety, reinforcement, and experimental instructions in a free verbalization situation. *Journal of Abnormal and Social Psychology*, 1962, 65: 300–307.

Sarason, I. G., and Harmatz, M. G. Test anxiety and experimental conditions. *Journal of Personality and Social Psychology*, 1965, 1: 499–505.

INFANTILE TRAUMA, GENETIC FACTORS, AND ADULT TEMPERAMENT [*]

GARDNER LINDZEY, DAVID T. LYKKEN, AND HARVEY D. WINSTON [1]

In spite of a welter of empirical and theoretical activity centering upon the role of infantile experience as a determinant of adult personality it is evident that there are few important issues in this area that have been satisfactorily resolved. Prominent among these open issues is the potential contribution of gene structure to the relation between infantile experience and adult temperament. Although King (1958) has identified gene factors as one of seven major parameters to be considered in studying the relation between infantile experience and adult effects, there is little in the way of compelling empirical findings concerning the role of genetic factors in this setting.

This sparse activity in the world of observation exists in spite of a history of theoretical interest in this issue. There are few general theories of behavior that fail to take into consideration, at least implicitly, the potential impact of constitutional or genetic factors upon early experience and its consequences. Perhaps the most influential and persistent emphasis upon the role of heredity in this context has been provided by Freud (1905) with his discussions of the determinants of fixation, but his position differs from other personality theorists on this issue primarily in regard to explicitness.

The present study was designed to provide further evidence relevant to this general issue. Because of traditional difficulties involved in using human subjects for studies spanning the life history of the organism and the additional requirement that genetic variation be controlled, it was

[*] Reprinted with permission from the American Psychological Association. In *Journal of Abnormal and Social Psychology*, 1960, Vol. 61, pp. 7–14.

[1] From the Center for Personality Research. This investigation was supported by a grant from the Ford Foundation. We are deeply grateful to John J. Bittner for his generous assistance and detailed advice concerning the care and breeding of mice. Mary Ahlquist, Samuel Berman, and Arthur Hill all rendered valuable aid at various stages in this study.

necessary to use subjects drawn from inbred strains of mice.

While the most unusual aspect of this study inquired into the interaction between gene factors and the effects of infantile trauma, it would be a rash investigator indeed who risked his all on an interaction term. Consistent with this premise is the fact that our study also provides information concerning the general effects of infantile trauma, their situational generality and duration, as well as further evidence regarding the influence of genetic factors upon various measures of temperament.

A word should be said concerning previous results that are relevant to the relation between infantile trauma and emotionality, for here, as well as in connection with the interaction effect we have just discussed, we have made specific predictions prior to the study. Clear evidence of an increase in emotionality in mice as a result of infantile trauma has been demonstrated by Hall and Whiteman (1951), while other investigators working with mice (Stanley and Monkman, 1956) and with rats (Griffiths and Stringer, 1952) have failed to find any significant differences in emotionality between control and traumatized animals. One investigator (Ader, 1957) actually has reported results indicating that treated rats were *less* emotional than control animals. Although these studies have led to conflicting results, the firmness of the findings of Hall and Whiteman (1951), coupled with consistent evidence from human investigations (Bowlby, 1951) and a boost from psychoanalytic theory, led us to predict that early traumatic experience would produce an increase in emotionality (timidity).

In summary, this study was designed to provide information concerning:

1. The importance of genetic factors as determinants of emotionality, timidity, and activity.

2. The general effects of infantile trauma, their situational generality, and the duration of these effects through time.

3. The influence of genetic factors upon the relation between infantile trauma and adult temperament.

METHOD

Subjects

The (Ss) of this investigation were offspring of breeding animals belonging to four different inbred strains of mice. The parent animals were obtained from a colony maintained by John J. Bittner of the Cancer Biology Laboratories of the University of Minnesota and represent the outcome of many generations of brother-sister matings. The conventional labels for these strains and the approximate number of generations of controlled brother-sister matings are as follows: C57BL/1 or B/1 (51 generations); C3H (93 generations); DBA/8 or D/8 (27 generations); JK (71 generations). The first three strains were selected on the basis of prior information (Lindzey, 1951) indicating diversity in emotionality, while the JK strain was selected because observation of them in the colony suggested that their behavior was quite different from the other strains. They were also selected so that all four strains could be identified easily by their distinctive coat color.

Within each strain the successive litters at birth were assigned alternately to either the experimental or the control group with the restriction that when the second litter by a particular mother was born that it would be given a different assignment than the first litter. This shifting procedure was continued through all litters until the desired number of animals in either the control or experimental group was achieved, and all subsequent litters were then assigned to the other group until the necessary number was reached. Because of the impossibility of predicting survival rates precisely for a period of almost four months, a variable number of animals resulted in the different experimental groups. The smallest number in any single group was 23 while the largest number was 36. The total number of animals included in the study was 259.

Each litter was raised in a separate cage with the mother until 24 days of age, at which time the young were weaned and segregated by sex. Animals were individually identified by an ear punch code, but this operation was not carried out until completion of the first consequent measure in order to avoid the possibility that this relatively traumatic procedure would wipe out the effects of our experimental treatment.

Infantile Trauma

Control and experimental animals were raised under the same conditions except that at four days of age those animals assigned to the experimental group were on four successive days exposed to an extremely loud, high frequency, auditory stimulus. The procedure followed was essentially the same as that described by Hall and Whiteman (1953) and involved placing the mice on a thin cardboard container in a #1 12-gal. wash tub with a doorbell (#504 Eclipse) fixed to the side. After a 2-min. interval the doorbell was rung for 2 min., following which the mice were left in the tub for another two minutes before being returned to their cages. On the first three trials all animals were placed together in the tub, but on the fourth trial they were separated. The procedure for the control animals was precisely the same except that the bell was not rung while they were in the tub.

Consequent Measures

30-Day Open Field Test. Beginning at 30 days of age each mouse was placed for 2 min. in the same type of wash tub in which the auditory trauma had been administered. The tub was brightly lighted by a shielded 150-w. glazed bulb that was placed directly over the tub at a height of approximately 1½ ft. The mouse was left in the tub for 2 min. at the end of which time the incidence of defecation and urination was recorded and the mouse returned to his living cage. This measure was repeated on 10 successive days. The measure of emotionality was simply presence or absence of defecation and/or urination during each trial.

Stovepipe Test. This instrument was devised by Stone (1929) as a measure of timidity or of the "dominance of hiding tendency over hunger," (p. 36) and was used by Hall and Whiteman (1951) in the study referred to earlier. In this measure the mouse was placed in a starting box connected with a U-shaped stovepipe (each unit approximately 2 ft. in length) that led to a goal box containing a food receptacle holding wet mash. Thus, all that the mouse had to do to reach the food was to enter the stovepipe, follow the passage, and leave the dark pipe for the more brightly illuminated goal box. The mice were again given 10 trials on successive days, commencing at 70 days of age, and they were run under 22½ hrs. of food deprivation. The measure employed was the total time that it took on the 10 trials for the mouse to enter the goal box. The few mice that on particular trials failed to leave the starting box within 5 min. were on these trials arbitrarily as-

signed the same time as the mouse that took the longest time in reaching the goal box.

100-Day Open Field Test. Commencing at 100 days of age the open field test was repeated for 10 trials with the measure of emotionality consisting of presence or absence of defecation and/or urination summed across the 10 trials for each *S*. In addition a measure of motility was secured by dividing the wash tub into 12 spaces of equal area and counting the number of spaces that each mouse moved through during the two minute trial and again summing the results of the individual trials over the 10 days.

Analysis of Data

The obvious method of statistical analysis for our data was a 2 × 4 analysis of variance and this technique was used for all data except those derived from the first open field test. In the latter case the absence of individual identification made it impossible to summate scores over the 10 trials and, in general, made it virtually impossible to devise a sensitive measure of the interaction hypothesis. Demonstration of strain differences and treatment effects was not particularly difficult, in part because they were relatively evident, and here we have relied upon descriptive presentation and the use of such simple devices as the sign test. The best estimate of interaction that could be devised, however, was to adapt the chi square test and then to apply this test separately to the data for each of the 10 days. This is obviously a somewhat unsatisfactory test of the interaction. We have not hesitated to apply one-tailed tests of significance to data related to directional hypotheses stated in advance of the study.

For purposes of analysis of variance we reduced all groups to the size of the smallest group in order to avoid the complexities of disproportionality. *S*s were eliminated on a chronological basis beginning with the animals that were last to complete the procedures. In the case of descriptive presentation of results we have included all animals studied with an appropriate indication of the number in each group.

RESULTS AND DISCUSSION

Gene Determinants of Temperament

Here we are concerned with strain differences

in two open field measures of emotionality, the stovepipe measure of timidity, and an open field measure of motility. The findings are clear and dramatic. No sentient person could observe the data reported in Tables 1–6 and conclude for any one of these attributes that the animals in all the strains could have been drawn from a single common population. In some instances the strains are so different as to show virtually no overlap. In view of the fact that the only known difference between these strains lies in their genetic constitution, it seems a prudent conclusion that genetic factors make a considerable contribution to each of our three measures of temperament.

Our findings are given added weight when coupled with the results of a number of earlier investigations using both rats (Hall, 1938; Broadhurst, 1958) and mice (Lindzey, 1951; Thompson, 1953, 1956; McClearn, 1959), all of which demonstrate wide strain differences on comparable

strain in the present study, are compared. The figures are highly constant in spite of the fact that the data were collected with more than a decade of time intervening, with considerable variation in the details of the open field test, with different persons collecting the data, and with animals that are not even known to belong to the same subline within the various strains. Even worse, we *do* know that the two samples were drawn from colonies that have been separated long enough to provide ample opportunity for "genetic drift" as well as spontaneous mutation. Given all of these sources of potential variation it is quite surprising to find the consistency of the strains and the measure so great. Thus, we are afforded the luxury of simultaneously gaining confidence in the stability of the organism we are studying and the reliability of our measure.

In general, these findings serve to emphasize again the pervasive impact upon behavior of ge-

TABLE 1

Percentage of Animals Defecating Daily on 30-Day Open Field Test

| Strain | Treatment | N | Day | | | | | | | | | | Average |
			1	2	3	4	5	6	7	8	9	10	
C57BL/1	Control	28	28.6	28.6	32.1	53.6	35.7	39.3	46.4	32.1	28.6	17.9	34.3
C57BL/1	Experimental	25	32.0	36.0	40.0	40.0	60.0	52.0	36.0	40.0	36.0	32.0	40.4
C3H	Control	34	85.3	88.2	82.3	64.7	73.5	70.6	85.3	73.5	73.5	73.5	77.1
C3H	Experimental	39	92.3	92.3	92.3	79.5	82.0	84.6	92.3	94.9	94.9	100.0	90.5
DBA/8	Control	37	64.9	81.1	73.0	70.3	62.2	64.9	62.2	64.9	59.5	67.6	67.0
DBA/8	Experimental	35	54.3	80.0	82.9	80.0	82.9	82.9	74.3	57.1	77.1	71.4	74.3
JK	Control	29	58.6	79.3	82.8	86.2	100.0	89.6	96.5	72.4	93.1	86.2	84.5
JK	Experimental	32	90.6	87.5	84.4	90.6	93.8	96.9	90.6	87.5	87.5	93.8	90.3

measures. More interesting than this general congruence is a specific examination of the incidence of defecation on the part of the three strains included in both the present study and the previous investigation by Lindzey (1951). In each study, C57, DBA, and C3H strains were employed and in each case an open field test of emotionality was utilized. In Table 2 the percentage of animals defecating in each strain in the earlier study, and the percentage of defecation over 10 trials in each

netic factors and thus strongly suggest the inadequacy of attempts to formulate or account for behavior that do not direct careful attention to the role of hereditary factors. It is interesting to note that it is not necessary to inbreed selectively for particular characteristics in order to produce clear evidence for the influence of genic factors upon behavior. Inbreeding of the present animals was uninfluenced by the temperament characteristics of interest in the present study, and, in spite of

TABLE 2

CONSISTENCY OF EMOTIONALITY MEASURE
IN 1951 STUDY AND PRESENT STUDY

	C57BL	C3H	DBA
Percent defecation (1951)	37 (N = 100)	72 (N = 100)	68 (N = 100)
Percent defecation (present study)	34 (N = 28)	77 (N = 34)	67 (N = 37)

TABLE 3

ANALYSIS OF VARIANCE OF STOVEPIPE TEST

Source	df	Sum of Squares	Mean Square	F	P
Treatment	1	2,350,782	2,350,782	1.93	<.10*
Strain	3	241,013,412	80,337,804	65.96	<.0001
Interaction	3	10,241,048	3,413,682	2.80	<.05
Within (error)	176	214,356,579	1,217,935		
Total	183	467,961,821			

* One-tailed test.

this, we find the particular genetic patterns that have been isolated are dramatically different in their behavioral consequences.

Influence of Infantile Trauma upon Temperament

What exactly were the effects of the auditory, infantile trauma? The reader will recall our prediction that this experience would lead to an increase of emotionality and timidity. Examination of the data summarized in Table 1 reveals that in spite of the awkwardness resulting from our inability to identify individual animals, there is little doubt that the experimental treatment led to an increase in emotionality as measured by the 30-day test. Inspection of the proportion of experimental and control animals defecating on each of the 10 trials within the four strains reveals that 32 of the 40 comparisons point to the greater emotionality of the traumatized animals. This incidence of "hits" is well beyond the 1% level of significance, even utilizing the relatively insensitive sign test. Actually, the within-strain results for the C3H animals (on all 10 trials the experimental animals showed a greater proportional defecation) are by themselves significant at below the 5% level using the sign test, while results for the other strains (7 or 8 trials out of 10 in which experimentals defecate more) approach significance.

The results of the stovepipe test, summarized in Table 3, provide suggestive evidence ($p < .10$) for a treatment effect indicating greater timidity (slower in getting to reward) on the part of the traumatized mice. Consistently, we find in Table 4 that at the 100-day open field test there is also a difference in emotionality indicating that the treated animals were more emotional. Only in the case of motility, as revealed in Table 5, do we find little indication of treatment effects upon behavior.

To summarize, there seems little doubt that subjecting infant mice to a noxious, auditory stimulus of high intensity leads to an increase in emotionality in adulthood and there is some basis for believing that there is also an increase in timidity.

TABLE 4

ANALYSIS OF VARIANCE OF 100-DAY OPEN
FIELD TEST: EMOTIONALITY

Source	df	Sum of Squares	Mean Square	F	P
Treatment	1	16.5093	16.5093	2.86629	<.05*
Strain	3	679.4458	226.4819	39.3211	<.0001
Interaction	3	2.1082	.7027	—	—
Within (error)	176	1013.7287	5.7598		
Total	183	1711.7920			

* One-tailed test.

TABLE 5

ANALYSIS OF VARIANCE OF 100-DAY OPEN
FIELD TEST: MOTILITY

Source	df	Sum of Squares	Mean Square	F	P
Treatment	1	14,635.2	14,635.2	1.29	<.50
Strain	3	1,421,619.4	473,873.1	41.8	<.0001
Interaction	3	24,268.4	8,089.5	.071	—
Within (error)	176	1,994,390.6	11,331.8		
Total	183	3,454,213.6			

There is no evidence, however, that this experience influences motility in an open field setting.

These findings confirm our prior expectations and fit very neatly with the results reported by Hall and Whiteman (1951) on the basis of similar experimental operations. However, our results directly contradict the conclusion of Ader (1957), based upon an investigation dealing with rats, and are inconsistent with the findings of Griffiths and Stringer (1952), and Hunt and Otis (1955) based

TABLE 6
MEANS AND SDs FOR STOVEPIPE TEST AND 100-DAY OPEN FIELD TEST

Strain	Treatment	Stovepipe		100-Day Emotionality		100-Day Motility	
		Mean (N = 24)	SD	Mean (N = 23)	SD	Mean (N = 23)	SD
C57BL/1	Control	2301	1339	4.26	3.40	401.2	135.3
C57BL/1	Experimental	2069	882	4.57	3.19	355.0	165.1
C3H	Control	3322	1669	8.43	1.58	198.2	110.7
C3H	Experimental	4312	1039	9.35	1.05	188.1	85.9
DBA/8	Control	773	436	6.39	2.84	272.5	63.3
DBA/8	Experimental	778	407	6.96	2.71	287.7	99.7
JK	Control	1480	1061	8.87	1.51	163.3	67.1
JK	Experimental	1601	1007	9.48	1.02	133.0	53.7

on observation of rats, as well as the findings of Stanley and Monkman (1956) derived from the study of mice. There are so many parametric differences between all of these studies (species of animal, nature of trauma, age at trauma, age at consequent measure) that it is probably useless to attempt a rational analysis of the basis for these experimental differences. It is worth note, however, that there is actually no evidence in any study for infantile trauma *decreasing* emotionality. Although Ader has suggested this possibility, his own data, in the only study in which he employed stimuli that could reasonably be considered noxious or traumatic (Ader, 1959), suggest a heightening of emotionality as a result of infantile trauma. Moreover, Ader's attempts to account for the findings of Hall and Whiteman on the basis of the fact that they used seizure-susceptible mice and an infantile trauma identical to that used in producing audiogenic seizures, is not supportable in view of the fact that the present study led to comparable results with strains such as the C57BL/1 and C3H, which are very low in seizure incidence (Lindzey, 1951).

Duration of traumatic effects. Because of the imprecision of our measures and the differences in the form of our data at age 30 days and age 100 days, it is impossible to make any exact estimate of the extent to which the experimental effects may have diminished with the passage of time. However, it is evident that at 30 days, at 70 days, and at 100 days, the influence of the infantile trauma is clearly observable. Whatever may have been lost in intensity, the main effect is

still manifest at the time of the last measure. Actually, a close descriptive inspection of the results of the present study, and the results contained in the Hall and Whiteman paper, suggest that there may have been some diminishing of treatment effects by the time of the 100-day test, but there is no firm evidence to support this contention.

Generality of traumatic effects. One obvious and important question has to do with the narrowness with which the effects of the infantile trauma are linked to situations resembling the original traumatic setting. Obviously, the implications of the trauma for the organism are very different if it leads to a generalized response disposition that is elicited in many settings, rather than leading to effects that can be observed only in situations very similar to the original one. Both Beach and Jaynes (1954) and Ader (1959) attempt to account for the increased emotionality following infantile trauma reported by Hall and Whiteman on the basis of the similarity between the traumatic setting and the setting in which emotionality was measured. The results of the present study are quite specific in refuting this proposal, as we secured consistent empirical findings in connection with both Stone's measure of timidity and Hall's open field measure. The stimulus differences between the stovepipe test and the open field test are so profound that if we are willing to concede the possibility of stimulus generalization from the original setting to the stovepipe test, we have already granted tremendous generality to the effects of the trauma. In brief, then, our findings suggest that the results of the infantile trauma are of a relatively general nature and should be discernible in a wide variety of different settings.

Impact of Genetic Variation upon Effects of Infantile Trauma

We have already seen that our behavioral measures of temperament are heavily influenced by genetic variation and that these same measures covary with traumatic, infantile experience. The essential question remaining is whether these two sets of determinants show any interaction. Are the changes in temperament that can be attributed to early infantile experience in part dependent upon the gene structure of the organism undergoing the experience?

It was impossible to devise a completely satisfactory test of the interaction effect for the 30-day open field test of emotionality because the individual animals were not identified. Consequently, the best we could do was to measure the interaction between strain and treatment effects for each of the 10 trials individually. The resulting χ^2 coefficients provide no evidence to support the hypothesis of interactions. It is true that we would have preferred to use a single more sensitive measure of emotionality (incidence of defecation summed over 10 days), and it is possible to speculate that with this increased sensitivity we would have been able to detect an interaction. There is, however, no direct evidence to support this contention.

Our second measure of interaction between strain and treatment effects deals with the stovepipe measure of timidity and, as the results summarized in Table 3 indicate, we found clear evidence for the existence of an interaction. These results suggest that changes in timidity resulting from the infantile trauma are in part dependent upon the strain (genetic makeup) of the mouse. In particular, the C57BL/1 mice seemed much less influenced by the experimental treatment than the other strains. The third test of the interaction hypothesis is presented in Tables 4 and 5, where we find no evidence for an interaction between strain and treatment in effects upon emotionality or motility at the 100-day test.

The simplest conclusion that can be derived from these findings is that there is an interaction between gene factors and infantile trauma for timidity, as measured by the stove pipe test, but not for emotionality or motility. While this finding may ultimately be substantiated, there are certain unsatisfactory aspects to our test of the interaction of strain and infantile trauma in the case of the two emotionality measures and the measure of motility. The test for the 30-day data had to be carried out upon single observations rather than observations cumulated over 10 days and the test of interaction for the 100-day data may have suffered from a diminishing of treatment effects at this stage. It is known that the analysis of variance measure of interaction is not a powerful test and it is possible that interaction could be demonstrated only with more powerful treatment effects or a larger number of Ss. Our failure to find treatment effects upon motility made our interaction measure in this area relatively meaningless.

So far as our hypothesis is concerned, we have obtained evidence for the existence of interaction between strain and infantile treatment effects as predicted, but this relationship was not so general as we had expected. Our conviction concerning the existence of some degree of interaction is strengthened by the results obtained by King (1959), demonstrating an interaction between the effects of infantile handling and membership in different subspecies, and Valenstein, Riss, and Young (1955), suggesting a relationship between the effects of isolation upon sexual behavior and membership in a particular inbred strain. An additional study by King (1957) also provides evidence suggestive of such an interaction, although the experimental treatment (isolation) did not take place in this case until after weaning. The findings indicate that changes in aggressive behavior that were produced by isolation in one mouse strain were not duplicated in a second strain. There is unfortunately, no direct test of the difference between the two strains in treatment effects. Joint consideration of all of these findings provides a relatively firm basis for concluding that the consequences of infantile trauma are in part dependent upon the genetic structure of the organism experiencing the trauma.

What are the implications of such a finding for psychological theory? One may contend that these results, even secured in connection with mere mice or guinea pigs, provide a type of confirmation of Freud's assertion that any attempt to map early experience into adult behavior must allow for the contribution of genetic factors. While such a statement has a rather hollow sound at the level of human behavior because of the little that is known concerning the gene structure of man, it does have some specific empirical implications. For example, our results would suggest that when an investigator works with Ss of unknown or uncontrolled heredity, it is altogether possible to conduct an otherwise exemplary study of the effects of infantile experience and fail to find evidence for such effects. Or, more generally, we may expect that a variety of different empirical findings might be observed in similar studies as a consequence of investigators dealing with Ss of various genetic backgrounds, rather than as a result of faulty experimental technique. In general, this is a finding that makes life more complex for both investigator and theorist, and in an area where there has never been any shortage of complexity.

SUMMARY

This investigation was concerned with the effects of infantile trauma upon adult temperament, the influence of genetic factors upon temperament, and the possibility of an interaction between early experience and gene structure in their influence upon adult behavior.

Four strains of homozygous mice were used in the study, with the infant offspring assigned by litter to either an experimental or control group. In all, 259 mice were studied. The experimental mice, beginning at four days of age, were exposed on four successive days to a noxious, auditory stimulus while the control animals were treated in an identical manner except that they were not exposed to the traumatic stimulus. At 30 days of age all mice were examined for 10 successive days in an open field test of emotionality and beginning at 70 days of age the mice were again observed for 10 successive days in a stovepipe test of timidity. A final measure of emotionality, and a measure of motility, were secured from 10 days of observation in an open field test beginning at 100 days of age.

The data obtained provide clear and compelling evidence for the importance of genetic factors as determinants of emotionality, timidity, and motility. The four strains displayed marked differences in all three attributes. There was also direct evidence for the influence of infantile trauma upon emotionality and suggestive evidence in regard to timidity, but no evidence for such an influence upon motility. The effects of the infantile trauma were enduring, extending at least to an age of 100 days, and were not limited to stimulus situations closely similar to the orginal traumatic situation. We found evidence of an interaction between the effects of infantile trauma upon stovepipe timidity and genetic factors, but there was no evidence for such an interaction in the case of emotionality. All of our positive findings are supported by evidence supplied by other investigators.

These findings not only demonstrate the central developmental importance of genetic factors and infantile trauma, they also underline the relative complexity of the relationship between infantile experience and adult behavior. Given an interaction between gene factors and infantile trauma it is readily understandable that inconsistent results might be observed by investigators working with heterozygous Ss of unknown gene structure. Finally, we have pointed to the consistency between the present findings and Freud's formulations concerning the role of constitutional factors in the developmental process.

REFERENCES

Ader, R. Effects of early experience on emotionality. *Amer. Psychologist,* 1957, 12: 410.

Ader, R. The effects of early experience on subsequent emotionality and resistance to stress. *Psychol. Monogr.,* 1959, 73: (2, Whole No. 472).

Beach, F. A., and Jaynes, J. Effects of early experience upon the behavior of animals. *Psychol. Bull.,* 1954, 51: 239–264.

Bowlby, J. *Maternal care and mental health.* Geneva: World Health Organization, 1951.

Broadhurst, P. L. Determinants of emotionality in the rat: III. Strain differences. *J. comp. physiol. Psychol.,* 1958, 51: 55–59.

Freud, S. Three essays on the theory of sexuality. (Originally published 1905.) In *The standard edition of the complete psychological works of Sigmund Freud.* Vol. 7. London: Hogarth, 1953. Pp. 125–248.

Griffiths, W. J., Jr., and Stringer, W. F. The effects of intense stimulation experienced during infancy on adult behavior in the rat. *J. comp. physiol. Psychol.,* 1952, 45: 301–306.

Hall, C. S. The inheritance of emotionality. *Sigma Xi Quart.,* 1938, 26: 17–27.

Hall, C. S., and Whiteman, P. H. The effects of infantile stimulation upon later emotional stability in the mouse. *J. comp. physiol. Psychol.,* 1951, 44: 61–66.

Hunt, H. F., and Otis, L. S. Restricted experience

and "timidity" in the rat. *Amer. Psychologist,*
1955, 19: 432.

King, J. A. Relationships between early social experience and adult aggressive behavior in inbred
mice. *J. genet. Psychol.,* 1957, 90: 151–166.

King, J. A. Parameters relevant to determining the
effect of early experience upon the adult behavior of animals. *Psychol. Bull.,* 1958, 55:
46–58.

King, J. A., and Eleftheriou, B. E. Effects of early
handling upon adult behavior in two subspecies
of deermice, *Peromyscus maniculates. J. comp.
physiol. Psychol.,* 1959, 52: 82–88.

Lindzey, G. Emotionality and audiogenic seizure
susceptibility in five inbred strains of mice. *J.
comp. physiol. Psychol.,* 1951, 44: 389–393.

McClearn, G. E. The genetics of mouse behavior
in novel situations. *J. comp. physiol. Psychol.,*
1959, 52: 62–67.

Stanley, W. C., and Monkman, J. A. A test for
specific and general behavioral effects of infantile stimulation with shock in the mouse.
J. abnorm. soc. Psychol., 1956, 53: 19–22.

Stone, C. P. Wildness and savageness in rats of
different strains. In K. S. Lashley (Ed.), *Studies
in the dynamics of behavior.* Chicago: Univ.
Chicago Press, 1932. Pp. 3–55.

Thompson, W. R. The inheritance of behavior:
Behavior differences in fifteen mouse strains.
Canad. J. Psychol., 1953, 7: 145–155.

Thompson, W. R. The inheritance of behavior:
Activity differences in five inbred mouse strains.
J. Hered., 1956, 47: 147–148.

Valenstein, E. S., Riss, W., and Young, W. C.
Experiential and genetic factors in the organization of sexual behavior in male guinea pigs. *J.
comp. physiol. Psychol.,* 1955, 48: 397–403.

THE CONTRIBUTION OF NONDEPRIVATION FACTORS IN THE PRODUCTION OF SENSORY DEPRIVATION EFFECTS: THE PSYCHOLOGY OF THE "PANIC BUTTON" *

MARTIN T. ORNE AND KARL E. SCHEIBE [1]

It seems reasonable to view the subject in a
psychological experiment as a social as well as an
experimental animal. To do so, however, makes
necessary a distinction between that part of the
subject's behavior which is a function of the experimental variable under analysis and that part
which is tied to his perception of the experiment
as a social situation.

To support this view, Orne (1959b) has shown
that subjects in hypnosis experiments behave in a
way that is largely congruent with their precon-
ceptions of hypnosis. Orne (1959a; 1962), in
developing the concept of "demand characteristics," has also suggested that the results of many
psychological experiments are liable to be biased
by those cues, both implicit and explicit, that
communicate to the subject what is expected of
him in the experimental situation.

The results of any experiment involving human
subjects are seen to include at least two distinct
components. The first, which may be called the
true experimental effect, is entirely contingent
upon the antecedence of the independent variable.
The second is induced by the social cues that attend the experimental situation and is unrelated
to the independent variable. An analogy may aptly
be drawn to the distinction between "real" and

* Reprinted with permission from the American
Psychological Association. In *Journal of Abnormal
and Social Psychology,* 1964, Vol. 68, pp. 3–12.

[1] This sudy was supported in part by Contract
AF49(638)-728 from the Air Force Office of Scientific
Research and in part by Public Health Research
Grant M-3369, National Institute of Mental Health,
United States Public Health Service. We would like
to thank Ronald Shor for his help in the analysis of
the data and in the exposition of our findings. We are
grateful also to Donald N. O'Connell, Emily C. Orne,
and M. Brewster Smith for their many valuable suggestions and comments.

"placebo" effects in pharmacological research, where it is first necessary to discern the extent and direction of the placebo component before a meaningful conclusion can be drawn about the real effect.

Research findings on sensory deprivation are likely to be subject to the kind of bias here described. Little attempt has been made to separate those aspects of the reactions to sensory deprivation actually due to the diminution of sensory input from those due to the matrix of social cues surrounding the experimental situation.[2]

Since the first studies at McGill University in 1951, there have been many attempts to delineate and account for the effects of prolonged sensory deprivation. Experimental techniques have been devised to reduce insofar as possible all forms of external stimulation. The McGill research employed a sound-damped cubicle: the subject rests on a soft bed, wearing translucent goggles over his eyes and cardboard gauntlets over his forearms and hands (Bexton, Heron, and Scott, 1954). Another technique involves placing normal subjects in tank-type respirators, so that movement is restricted and external sources of stimulation are rendered fairly homogeneous (Leiderman, Mendelson, Wexler, and Solomon, 1958). A third technique consists of prolonged total immersion in a tank of water at body temperature, with the subject using a face mask for breathing (Lilly, 1956). With a very few exceptions (Vernon and McGill, 1957; Zubek, Sansom, and Prysiazniuk, 1960) these procedures have produced significant changes in behavior, usually in the form of a decrement in psychological efficiency.

Bexton et al. (1954) report a general cognitive deterioration under the McGill conditions. Deprivation subjects showed decrements on a number of pre- and postisolation cognitive tasks. Subjects reported an intenseness of visual imagery, an inability to concentrate, and spatial and temporal disorientation. Scott, Bexton, Heron, and Doane (1959) and Doane, Mahatoo, Heron, and Scott (1959) provide further evidence on several more testing instruments, including some of the perceptual-motor variety. The findings of Vernon,

McGill, Gulick, and Candland (1961) have been less striking, but the general tenor of their conclusions is the same. Likewise, studies by Zubek et al. (1960) and Zubek, Pushkar, Sansom, and Gowing (1961) show an impairment of mental functioning along the lines noted above. A remark by Hebb (1958) perhaps best epitomizes the findings of these studies: "Without physical pain, without drugs, the personality can be badly deformed simply by modifying the perceptual environment [p. 110]."

An alternative view of these data would be that at least in part the dramatic effects could be a function of the demand characteristics of the experimental situation. Thus, the cues in the experimental procedure itself would communicate to the subject the behavior expected of him.

There is evidence in an experiment by Kandel, Myers, and Murphy (1958) that preparing a subject for probable hallucinations significantly affects the frequency of hallucinations. This preparation was accomplished by verbal instructions. However, such devices as "panic buttons" in experiments (Vernon et al., 1961; Zubek et al., 1961) are in a sense eloquent "instructions." The use of such a device increases the subject's expectation that something intolerable may occur, and, with it, the likelihood of a bad experience.

Indeed, it is possible to refer to many potential role cues of greater or lesser subtlety. In an experiment by Freedman, Grunebaum, and Greenblatt (1961), subjects were required to sign a forbidding release form prior to participation. Psychiatric screenings have been commonly used to single out individuals who might be harmed by an experiment, and physical examinations have been given to make sure of the subject's ability to withstand experimental stress. Even the existence of such experimental accouterments as observation windows and microphones have a potential cue value. As one of our own subjects remarked, "If you didn't expect to see or hear something unusual, why were you looking and listening?"

It should be made clear that the experiment to be described was *not* designed to test any hypothesis about the *nature* of sensory deprivation. Rather it was aimed at calling attention to a set of variables which must be considered in evaluating that phenomenon. The postulate that certain cues increase the likelihood of occurrence of a predicted effect is easily converted into an em-

---

[2] One notable exception is the work of Jackson (1960; Jackson & Kelly, 1962) who explored the role of "indirect suggestion" in the production of sensory deprivation effects.

pirical question: If the cues attending the typical sensory deprivation experiment are retained *while no sensory deprivation takes place,* is it still possible to produce effects similar to those produced in such an experiment?

METHOD

Subjects

Subjects were recruited for "a psychological experiment in Meaning Deprivation" through the placement services of colleges and universities in the Boston area. Each subject was paid $2 an hour plus transportation costs. In order to correspond more closely with the practice in most previous sensory deprivation experiments, only male college students ranging in age from 18 to 25 were used. Subjects were excluded who had previously participated in sensory deprivation experiments or who were too familiar with sensory deprivation experiment results.[3] Twenty subjects in all took part; each was assigned alternately to the experimental and control groups, with 10 subjects comprising each group.

Procedure for Experimental Group

All subjects who called to volunteer were told that the experimental session would last an indefinite period of time, and that in order for the subject to participate, it would be necessary for him to reserve an entire day or entire evening. He was also told that the experiment was to be performed at a psychiatric hospital.

When the subject arrived there he was greeted by the experimenter, dressed in a white medical coat. Prior to giving instructions, the experimenter asked the subject briefly about his medical history, asked him whether he had a history of dizziness, or fainting spells, and so on. An aura of great seriousness and importance was maintained throughout this introductory period. As a prop to reinforce the subject's notion that great caution was necessary in the experiment, a tray of drugs and medical instruments, labeled "Emergency Tray" was in full view. No direct reference was

[3] Four subjects were thus eliminated. One further subject was dropped because he was not only unable to perform two of the pretests—one involving a reversible figure and the other a mirror tracing task —but had great difficulty even in understanding the instructions.

ever made to this tray unless the subject asked, and then he was told that this was one of the precautionary measures taken for the experiment, and that he had nothing to worry about.

At the conclusion of the introductory remarks, the following set of instructions, a composite of the instructions used in other sensory deprivation experiments, was read to the subject:

> The experiment for which you have volunteered has as its object the determination of the psychological consequences of a special kind of deprivation procedure.
> There are three parts to the experiment: Testing Period I, the Experimental Deprivation Condition, and Testing Period II. You will receive special instructions in the testing periods.
> During the deprivation period, which will last an undisclosed length of time, you will have an optional task involving adding numbers, the full instructions for which will be explained once we enter the chamber.
> While you are in the chamber, you will be under constant observation. Also, there will be a microphone through which anything you might say will be recorded. It is important that you report your experiences freely and completely. You are not expected to talk a great deal, but you should report any visual imagery, fantasies, special or unusual feelings, difficulties in concentration, hallucinations, feelings of disorientation, or the like. Such experiences are not unusual under the conditions to which you are to be subjected.
> If at any time you feel very discomforted, you may obtain release immediately by pressing the button which I will show you once we enter the chamber ["by knocking on the window," for control subjects]. Do not hesitate to use this button if the situation becomes difficult [this sentence deleted for control subjects]. However, try to stick it out if you can.
> Should you feel upset, or should anything untoward develop, a physician is immediately at hand [this sentence deleted for control subjects].
> Remember, I should like you to pay special attention to any special visual or other sensations, or feelings of disorientation, and to report these experiences as they happen.
> Do you have any questions?

At the conclusion of the instructions, questions were answered if at all possible by referring to portions of the written instructions. The subject was then asked to sign a release form that was almost identical in detail with the one used by Freedman et al. (1961). It was worded so as to relieve the Massachusetts Mental Health Center and all affiliated organizations and personnel from legal responsibility for consequences of the experiment. All experimental subjects signed the form, although some were a little reluctant to do so.

Next, the subjects' blood pressure and pulse count were recorded. These measures were also taken for control subjects, who were told, however, that it was being done only because it was part of the procedure for experimental subjects. After this, subjects were given the pretest battery to be described below. At the conclusion of the battery they were allowed to go to the bathroom, after which they were accompanied by the experimenter to the "isolation chamber."

The isolation chamber was a quiet room 6 × 7 × 8 feet in dimension. It was furnished simply with a large oak desk and two comfortable chairs. Beige drapes covered a small, shaded window above the desk, but the room was amply lighted by a circular fluorescent fixture. One wall was fitted with a 2 × 4 foot observation window, the function of which was explained to the subject upon entering.

On the desk were a number of objects: a thermos of ice water, a glass, and a sandwich; a microphone; a stack of approximately 2,000 sheets of paper containing numbers; a red pushbutton mounted on a board and labeled "Emergency Alarm."

In the instruction period the subject was informed that the food and water were for his convenience, and that he could partake of them at any time. He was told further that the microphone was sensitive enough to pick up anything said in the room, and that he should comment upon the experience whenever he felt so inclined.

Each sheet of paper containing numbers was made up of eight columns of single random digits. The subject was told that, as an optional task, he could add the adjacent digits in the columns, and record the sum in the space between them. It was made clear to him that he might do as much or as little of this task as he pleased, and that he did not have to do it at all if he did not want to. He was instructed, however, to confine his use of paper and pencil to the prescribed optional activity. In addition, he was requested to remain awake throughout the period, but was assured that if he really became sleepy, it was permissible to go to sleep.

The subject was finally informed that by pressing the pushbutton, which was shown to activate a loud alarm, he would obtain release from the experiment.

Upon completing the instructions, the experimenter asked the subject if everything was clear to him; if it was, the experimenter left, audibly locking the door behind him.

The room, it should be pointed out, could hardly be construed as a sensory deprivation environment. Voices and footsteps could be heard from other parts of the building, and at various times the sounds of automobiles, airplanes, and the chirping of birds outside were clearly audible. The room was well lighted and large enough for the subject to move about freely; movements were not prohibited by the instructions.

After the subject had been in the room for exactly 4 hours, the experimenter returned to carry out an interview of the type to be described below, and to run the subject again through the testing procedure: his blood pressure and pulse were rechecked; he was asked for further comments or questions at the conclusion, paid for his services, and released after he had promised not to relate details of the experiment to others. The entire procedure from the time the subject arrived to the time he left generally took 6 hours.

Procedure for Control Group

Control subjects were treated in exactly the same manner as experimental subjects except for the following particulars. First, when greeting the subject the experimenter wore business clothes and acted in a less officious manner. The testing room, or office, was not equipped with an emergency tray, nor was the medical history interview conducted. In lieu of this, the subject was told that he was part of a control group for a sensory deprivation experiment. The usual conditions of such an experiment—translucent goggles, white noise, arm gauntlets, soft bed, and restriction of activity—were described to the subject. He was informed that he would be given exactly the same tests and receive the same instructions, with minor modifications, that experimental sensory deprivation subjects received. He was told that it was necessary to place him in the same chamber for the same period of time, so that the effects of the more restrictive sensory deprivation conditions could be differentiated from the effects of simply being left alone in a room for a period of time. He was urged to report his experiences freely and completely, and was told that recordings were being made of all his comments. After these introductory remarks, the same set of instructions was read to the control subject as was read to the experimental meaning deprivation subject (with the modifications noted in the section on procedure for the experimental group).

The cubicle was outfitted in exactly the same way, except that there was no "Emergency Alarm." Control subjects were told that if they wanted to gain release they could do so by knocking on the window.

The postexperimental treatment was the same for both groups, except that the experimenter wore a white coat for the experimental subjects.

Tests and Criteria

Several criteria were used in the selection of tests. First, the choice was made from among the approximately 75 tests that have been used by previous investigators of sensory deprivation. Second, only those tests were considered which were reported as positive indicators of sensory deprivation; that is, the results of which were significantly different for control and experimental groups. From the 25 tests that met these criteria, 10 were selected on the basis of ease and speed of administration, ease and objectivity of scoring, and availability of testing materials. Tests of both cognitive and perceptual abilities were included. Whenever possible, exactly the same tests were used as were used by previous investigators. In some cases approximations were necessary because of a lack of adequate descriptions in the reports or the uniqueness of a test. The battery which emerged was as follows. Tests are listed in order of administration. Unless otherwise noted, tests were given in exactly the same way before and after isolation.

Mirror Tracing. Subjects were instructed to trace a line around the .25-inch border of a six pointed star on a conventional mirror drawing apparatus. The score was the number of times the traced line went out of the border. Vernon et al. (1961) found a significant decrement in the performance of this task after deprivation.

Spatial Orientation. Subjects were asked to draw a figure in response to specific commands, without seeing the paper on which they drew. For this purpose, a mirror drawing shield without the mirror was used. Instructions were as follows:

Draw a line three inches to your left and stop. Now 90 degrees to the right of the direction you were moving, draw a line two inches and stop. Now 90 degrees to the right again, draw a line three inches and stop. Now 90 degrees to the left, draw a line three inches and stop. Now 90 degrees to the right, draw a line two inches and stop. Now 90 degrees to the right again, draw a line one inch and stop. Finally, draw a line back to your original starting position.

Figures were scored for both linear and angular deviation from the figure thus described. Doane et al. (1959) found experimental subjects exhibited significantly more angular deviation on this task, while linear deviation was apparently not scored. Linear deviation scores were included in the present experiment with the expectation that experimental subjects would also do worse on this aspect of spatial orientation.

Word Recognition. Subjects were given 90 seconds to study a list of 20 words that had been taken from words classified as AA (highest) frequency in the Thorndike-Lorge (1944) tabulation. Immediately at the conclusion of this period, subjects were instructed to circle, on a list of 70 words of similar frequency, as many of the original 20 as they recognized. After isolation, the recognition test was administered without additional opportunity for study. The score was the number of correct recognitions. This procedure was adapted from that of Zubek et al. (1960), who found significantly poorer recognition scores for experimental subjects.

Reversible Figure. Subjects were instructed to press a counter key every time there was a shift in a reversible figure. A 4×6 inch reproduction of the reversible staircase figure was used for this test. The score was the number of alterations in 1 minute. Significantly faster alternation cycles were found for experimental subjects by Freedman et al. (1961) and by Freedman and Greenblatt (1961).

The Digit-Symbol subtest of the Wechsler Adult Intelligence Scale. Standard administration and scoring procedures were used. Scott et al. (1959) and Davis, McCourt, and Solomon (1960) found a significant superiority in accuracy of control subjects in this task.

MacQuarrie-Morris Test of Mechanical Ability. Standard administration and scoring procedures were used. Zubek et al. (1960) and Vernon et al.

(1961) found decrements for sensory deprivation subjects on motor coordination tasks very closely related to this test.

Simple Form perception. Six simple geometrical forms, completely regular, were cut from black construction paper and pasted on 10×10 inch neutral gray cards. These forms were: a plus sign, two parallel lines, a circle, a single straight line, an equilateral triangle, and a square. The cards were held one at a time in front of the viewer, at a distance of 12 feet. In the pretesting, subjects were asked to describe what they saw on the cards, and to note any irregularities. In the posttesting, the following instructions, identical to those used by Freedman and Greenblatt (1961), were given:

I am going to show you some simple charts [cards], and I would like to have you tell me what each one looks like to you—not what you think it really is, but what it looks like subjectively.

Scores were obtained by subtracting the number of distortions reported in pretesting from the number reported in posttesting. No more than a single distortion was counted for each card. This test was given immediately after the subjects emerged from isolation, in congruence with the Freedman and Greenblatt procedure. These investigators found significantly more simple form distortions in experimental than in control subjects.

Size Constancy. Fifteen light gray circular disks of graduated diameter were pasted on a large sheet of dark gray cardboard and shown, from a distance of 12 feet, to the subjects who were asked to estimate which disk most approximated in size the standard disk, mounted on a similar background, and held 2 feet from the eyes. Scores were assigned in terms of the number and direction of step deviations from the standard. Doane et al. (1959) report that the subjects tend to see figures larger after deprivation. This test was pulled out of order and given right after the simple form perception test when the subject came out of the isolation chamber. This is in accord with the procedures of Doane et al. and also of Freedman and Greenblatt (1961).

Spiral Aftereffect. An 8-inch Archimedes spiral rotating at about 40 rpm was viewed at a distance of 3 feet for 90 seconds. At a signal from the experimenter, the subject shifted his vision to an identical spiral which was stationary. Subjects were instructed to say "stop" upon cessation of the movement aftereffect thus induced. The score was the number of seconds that the effect persisted. Doane et al. (1959) report a greater duration of this effect after isolation.

Logical Deductions. Subtest 3 of the Watson-Glaser Appraisal of Critical Thinking was administered after isolation only. Standard administration and scoring procedures were used. Goldberger and Holt (1958) found that the performance of sensory deprivation subjects on this test was significantly poorer than was that of controls.

The postisolation interview was conducted in exactly the same manner for all subjects. The experimenter first called upon the subject to express, at whatever length was agreeable to him, the general nature of his experience, his feelings thoughts, and so forth. After these comments, the experimenter asked him to estimate the time he had spent in isolation and to make an affective evaluation of the experience; the experimenter questioned the subject on the presence of anxiety, of temporal or spatial disorientation, of distortions perception, or of perceptions of doubtful origin; finally the experimenter asked the subject to elaborate upon some of the subject's opening remarks. The information gained in this interview, together with the notes made on visual observations of the subject and recording of his spontaneous remarks, was used in forming general clinical evaluations of his behavior in the experimental situation.

RESULTS

In Table 1 is presented summary information on the battery of 10 tests. The table includes determinations of statistical significance. Note the multiple methods of scoring for a few of the measures.

Although the pre-experimental performances of the experimental and control groups did not test significantly different, the analysis of covariance technique was used to take into account any systematic influence of initial values on the postexperimental comparisons. For comparisons without preexperimental components, simple t tests were used. In one instance the plotting of the data appeared so grossly abnormal that the distribution-

TABLE 1

SUMMARY AND ANALYSIS OF 10 TESTS FOR CONTROL AND EXPERIMENTAL GROUPS

Test and group	Pretest M	Posttest M	Difference statistic
Mirror Tracing (errors)			
Experimental	28.1	19.7	$F = 1.67$[a]
Control	35.8	15.2	
Spatial Orientation			
Angular deviation			
Experimental	45.7	53.9	$F = .25$[a]
Control	52.5	59.1	
Linear deviation			
Experimental	5.3	5.4	$F = 3.34$*
Control	6.4	5.7	
Word Recognition (N correct)			
Experimental	17.3	15.6	$t = .50$
Control	15.2	12.3	
Reversible Figure (rate per minute)			
Experimental	29.0	35.0	$F = 1.54$[a]
Control	20.1	25.0	
Digit Symbol (N correct)			
Experimental	98.2	109.9	$F = .05$[a]
Control	99.2	111.9	
Mechanical Ability			
Tapping speed (N completed)			
Experimental	33.9	32.2	$F = 2.26$
Control	32.9	35.0	
Tracing speed (N completed)			
Experimental	55.6	52.3	$F = 4.57$*
Control	53.1	58.4	
Visual pursuit (N completed)			
Experimental	5.7	8.9	$F = .22$[a]
Control	5.7	9.2	
Simple Forms (N increment distortions)			
Experimental	—	3.1	$U = 19$**
Control	—	0.8	
Size Constancy (change in steps)			
Experimental	—	0.6	$t = 1.03$[a]
Control	—	0.0	
Spiral Aftereffect			
Duration, seconds			
Experimental	24.4	27.1	$F = .99$[a]
Control	15.6	16.1	
Absolute change			
Experimental	—	7.0	$t = 3.38$***
Control	—	2.7	
Logical Deduction (N correct)			
Experimental	—	20.3	$t = 1.64$
Control	—	22.1	

Note.—F = adjusted postexperimental scores, analysis of covariance; t = t tests; U = Mann-Whitney U test, where plot of data appeared grossly abnormal.

[a] Indicates differences between groups were in predicted direction.

* $p < .05$, one-tailed.

** $p = .01$, one-tailed.

*** $p < .001$, nondirectional measure.

free Mann-Whitney U test was used on difference scores. One-tailed statistical probabilities are reported (except for the one statistically insignificant instance of a mean difference in the direction opposite prediction, that is, Word Recognition). Since this report is concerned with a critical appraisal of factors involved in prior findings rather than an initial setting-forth of evidence, the 10% confidence level was selected as an appropriate alpha.

It can be observed that 6 of the 14 criteria achieve statistical significance. Note again that the mean differences of 13 of the 14 criteria are in the direction predicted.

A Mann-Whitney U test was performed on the summation ranks of all the 14 measures as a convenient method for summarizing the overall differences. The one-tailed probability which emerges is $p = .001$, a clear demonstration of expected effects.

TABLE 2

OCCURRENCE OF SENSORY DEPRIVATION SYMPTOMS IN CONTROL AND EXPERIMENTAL SUBJECTS

Subject and group	Perceptual aberrations	Intellectual dullness	Affectively unpleasant	Anxiety fears	Spatial disorientation	Restlessness	Irritability	Total number of symptoms
Experimental								
E_1	X	X	O	O	X	O	O	3
E_2	X	O	X	X	X	X	X	6
E_3	X	X	X	O	O	X	O	4
E_4	O	X	X	X	X	X	O	5
E_5	X	X	X	X	X	X	X	7
E_6	X	X	X	X	O	X	X	6
E_7	O	X	O	O	O	O	O	1
E_8	O	O	O	O	O	O	X	1
E_9	X	X	X	X	X	X	X	7
E_{10}	X	X	O	X	X	X	X	6
Control								
C_1	O	O	O	O	O	O	O	0
C_2	X	O	O	X	O	O	O	2
C_3	O	O	O	O	O	O	O	0
C_4	O	O	O	O	O	O	O	0
C_5	X	O	X	X	X	X	O	5
C_6	O	O	O	O	O	O	O	0
C_7	X	O	O	X	O	O	X	3
C_8	O	O	O	O	O	O	X	1
C_9	O	O	O	O	O	O	O	0
C_{10}	X	X	X	X	X	X	X	7
Summary and significance								
Frequency Experimental	7	8	6	6	6	7	6	
Frequency Control	4	1	2	4	2	2	3	
Fisher exact p	.11	<.01	.06	.33	.06	<.05	.35	

Note.—See text for discussion of categories.
Mean positive entries: Experimental group, 4.5; Control group, 1.8.
$U = 16.5$, $p < .01$, one-tailed.

Subjects' Reports and the Experimenter's Clinical Impressions

That expected differences exist between the groups is further demonstrated in Table 2, which shows for each subject the number and kind of sensory deprivation "symptom" observed or reported. Following is a brief elaboration of the criteria in the column headings. An analysis of the data reported in Table 2 indicates that experimental subjects exhibited a significantly greater number of sensory deprivation "symptoms" than did control subjects ($p = .01$, one-tailed, Mann-Whitney U test).

Perceptual aberrations. Various reports of unusual perceptions or imaginal activity were obtained, both in subjects' spontaneous remarks and in the interview. Some examples are: "the walls of the room are starting to waver"; "the objects on the desk are becoming animated and moving about"; "the lighting in the room is growing gradually dimmer and yellower"; "the buzzing of the fluorescent light is growing alternately louder and softer, so that at times it sounds like a jack-hammer"; "there are multicolored spots on the wall"; and "the numbers on the number sheets are blurring and assuming various inkblot forms." None of these experiences was especially upsetting to the subjects, nor did they appear in most cases to be more than mildly compelling. An exception is the one experimental subject who terminated by pressing the panic button, and who gave "disorganization of senses" as one of his reasons for ending the experiment.

Intellectual dullness. Generally, this refers to a report by the subject that he experienced marked difficulty in concentration. Typically, those who complained of this said that there was little difficulty at first, but that after about half the period they became unable, even with considerable effort, to think for more than a few seconds on any serious topic. Also included in this category are reports of "blank periods" when the subject could not remember thinking of anything, and which he characterized as being extremely vague and abstract.

Affectively unpleasant. In the interview, subjects

were asked to make an overall evaluation of the pleasantness or unpleasantness of the experience. Reports ranged from extremely unpleasant to extremely pleasant. Positive entries in this column indicate a report of mildly unpleasant or worse.

Anxiety or fears. Positive entries in this column denote a report of thoughts of being forgotten, or of being inadvertently left in the room for a long time, or of being trapped while the building burned down. Several subjects reported claustrophobic anxiety.

Spatial disorientation. Included here are reports of the relative dimensions of the room seeming to change, or of the size of the subject in relation to the room seeming to change, or more general comments of confusion or amnesia regarding the location of the room in the building or of the building in the city.

Restlessness. Ratings of restlessness were based on reports by some subjects that they began wondering whether the experiment was worth the money, entertaining semihostile thoughts regarding the experimenter, or having serious impulses to end the experiment. Usually, the reports indicated that such irritability was rather short-lived and not serious, and none of the subjects was overtly hostile to the experimenter upon completion of the experiment.

It will be noted in Table 2 that there are two apparent reversals in each group. An example of these is the final subject in the control group who was in fact quite upset by the experience, and terminated it by knocking on the window 3 minutes before the end of the 4-hour period. Excepting these two reversals, however, the resulting clinical impressions for the two groups were distinct and consistent.

The control group subject typically started his isolation period by inspecting the room, looking through the drawers in the desk, then settling in one of the chairs, and beginning to add the numbers. After this, the pattern of activity would generally consist of long periods of repose interspersed with moderate amounts of activity on the serial additions. These subjects gave the impression, while in the chamber, of being in every way relaxed and in a pleasant frame of mind. The rate of verbalization was lower for control than for experimental subjects; typically there was but a single rather long comment at the beginning telling the experimenter how the subject intended to occupy his time while in the chamber.

In marked contrast to the repose of the controls was the general behavior of the experimental subjects. They usually began the experiment in much the same way as controls: inspection followed by some adding of numbers. But, after the first hour there would ensue a marked restlessness, a decrease in the performance of serial additions, frequent comments of displeasure at some aspect of the experience, or remarks indicating concern over lack of time sense. Occasionally experimental subjects would try to sleep, but with little success. Some exercised, while others undertook an intense and minute inspection of the room. Viewed in relation to the controls, these subjects gave an impression of almost being tortured. While the control group seemed to alternate between quiet contemplation and work with numbers, experimental subjects seemed to fluctuate between periods of unpleasant restlessness and abstract, vague periods of total inactivity.

Discussion

These findings demonstrate that subjects' behavior can be differentially manipulated by altering the implicit and explicit cues in the experimental situation, and further that subjects may react to social cues, or demand characteristics, in such a way as to confound experimental results.

In the light of our findings, it would seem plausible to suggest that an important confounding variable may be present in much of the reported sensory deprivation research. (Our data yield no evidence, of course, regarding the effect of actual restriction of sensory input. It is possible that many aspects of the reported phenomena in sensory deprivation studies *are* due to the restriction of sensory input.) Our data emphasize the need for further research to determine the actual extent to which the reported "sensory deprivation phenomena" are related to the decrement of sensory input.

In any experiment, the subject's reaction may be viewed as resulting from both the actual treatment (restriction of sensory input by means of gauntlets, goggles, special chambers, etc.) and the social situation created by the setting in which the experiment is conducted, the instructions used, and the cue characteristics of the treatment operations themselves. For example, in our particular experiment the treatment was not that of sensory deprivation, but, rather, of 4-hour isolation. At the same time, the situation (demand characteristics) was deliberately varied for the control and the experimental groups. We interpret our data to mean that four hours of isolation coupled with differing sets of demand characteristics yield different experimental results.

The demonstrated effectiveness of demand characteristics in this or any experiment is not taken to indicate that subjects openly and willfully cooperate with the experimenter. Rather, it is likely that social cues can determine the subject's actual experience in the situation. There is reason to believe that the subjects in the Meaning Deprivation experimental condition actually did experience considerable discomfort. The demand characteristics communicated to the subjects that they would feel discomfort despite any efforts to forestall discomfort. It must be remembered that in order for this communication to be effective, the treatment conditions must be such that they might reasonably be expected to produce just those effects suggested by the pre-experimental cues. This is to say that treatment conditions in themselves communicate crucial social cues and that these are assimilated with the other social cues in the experimental setting to form the demand characteristics of the particular experiment. If both these components of demand characteristics consistently provide an expectation of discomfort and a decrement in performance, then it is likely that the subject's experience as well as his behavior will be constrained by these demands. A distinction is to be made between behavior constrained in this fashion and conscious cooperation (Sarbin, 1950).

The main difficulty in designing definitive sensory deprivation experiments is the inevitable close relationship between the alterations in the physical environment that are necessary to decrease sensory input and the demand characteristics communicated by their use. In order to create the treatment of sensory deprivation, goggles, gauntlets, and various other devices have to be employed. Their use provides obvious cues as to how the subject is expected to behave in the situation.

These considerations suggest that a feasible approach would be to utilize conditions of maximal deprivation while varying the demand characteristics. It is possible to structure the situation so that different groups perceive the restriction as a means to a variety of experimental purposes. It is not possible to eliminate demand characteristics, but they can be varied with relative ease. Cues provided by the deprivation manipulations themselves must remain fairly constant, but the other cues can be systematically varied, thereby creating a variety of totally distinct sets of demand characteristics for different groups. Such studies would go far toward clarifying the actual effects of reduced sensory input.

SUMMARY

From the premise that both social cue factors, or demand characteristics, and sensory deprivation operations combine in producing commonly observed effects of sensory deprivation, an experiment is reported which tests the hypothesis that sensory deprivation effects can be produced by manipulating demand characteristics while holding the effect of the physical environment constant. Experimental Ss were exposed to pre-experimental conditions which were designed to imply to them that sensory deprivation effects were expected to emerge. The same physical conditions were structured for control Ss in such a way as to lead them to expect nothing to happen. Results show that the groups were significantly different on a number of before and after tests, as well as in general clinical appearance, and these results were interpreted as supporting the hypothesis. An interpretation is offered of the operation of demand characteristics as a factor interactiong with treatment conditions. Ways of taking demand characteristics into account in sensory deprivation research are suggested.

REFERENCES

Bexton, W. H., Heron, W., and Scott, T. H. Effects of decreased variation in the sensory environment. *Canad. J. Psychol.*, 1954, 8: 70–77.

Davis, J. M., McCourt, W. F., and Solomon, P. Effect of visual stimulation on hallucinations and other mental experience during sensory deprivation. *Amer. J. Psychiat.*, 1960, 116: 889–892.

Doane, B. K., Mahatoo, W., Heron, W., and Scott, T. H. Changes in perceptual function after isolation. *Canad. J. Psychol.,* 1959, 13: 210–219.

Freedman, S. J., and Greenblatt, M. Studies in human isolation: I. Perceptual findings. *U. S. Armed Forces med. J.,* 1961, 11: 1330–1348.

Freedman, S. J., Grunebaum, H. U., and Greenblatt, M. Perceptual and cognitive changes in sensory deprivation. In P. Solomon et al. (Eds.), *Sensory deprivation: A symposium held at Harvard Medical School.* Cambridge: Harvard Univer. Press, 1961. Pp. 58–71.

Goldberger, L., and Holt, R. R. Experimental interference with reality contact (perceptual isolation): Method and group results. *J. nerv. ment. Dis.,* 1958, 127: 99–112.

Hebb, D. O. The motivating effects of exteroceptive stimulation. *Amer. Psychologist,* 1958, 13: 109–113.

Jackson, C. W. An exploratory study of the role of suggestion in research on sensory deprivation. Unpublished doctoral dissertation, University of Michigan, 1960.

Jackson, C. W., and Kelly, E. L. Influence of suggestion and subjects' prior knowledge in research on sensory deprivation. *Science,* 1962, 135: 211–212.

Kandel, E. J., Myers, T. I., and Murphy, D. B. Influence of prior verbalization and instructions on visual sensations reported under conditions of reduced sensory input. *Amer. Psychologist,* 1958, 13: 334. (Abstract)

Leiderman, P. H., Mendelson, J. N., Wexler, D., and Solomon, P. Sensory deprivation: Clinical aspects. *A. M. A. Arch. intern. Med.,* 1958, 101: 389–396.

Lilly, J. C. Mental effects of reduction of ordinary levels of physical stimuli on intact, healthy persons. *Psychiat. Res. Rep.,* 1956, 5: 1–9.

Orne, M. T. The demand characteristics of an experimental design and their implications. Paper read at American Psychological Association, Cincinnati, September 1959. (a)

Orne, M. T. The nature of hypnosis: Artifact and essence. *J. abnorm. soc. Psychol.,* 1959, 58: 277–299. (b)

Orne, M. T. On the social psychology of the psychological experiment: With particular reference to demand characteristics and their implications. *Amer. Psychologist,* 1962, *17:* 776–783.

Sarbin, T. R. Contributions to role-taking theory: I. Hypnotic behavior. *Psychol. Rev.,* 1950, 57: 255–270.

Scott, T. H., Bexton, W. H., Heron, W., and Doane, B. K. Cognitive effects of perceptual isolation. *Canad. J. Psychol.,* 1959, 13: 200–209.

Thorndike, E. L., and Lorge, I. *The teacher's word book of 30,000 words.* New York: Teachers College, Columbia University, Bureau of Publications, 1944.

Vernon, J. A., and McGill, T. E. The effect of sensory deprivation upon rote learning. *Amer. J. Psychol.,* 1957, 70: 637–639.

Vernon, J. A., McGill, T. E., Gulick, W. L., and Candland, D. K. The effect of human isolation upon some perceptual and motor skills. In P. Solomon et al. (Eds.), *Sensory deprivation: A symposium held at Harvard Medical School.* Cambridge: Harvard Univer. Press, 1961. Pp. 41–57.

Zubek, J. P., Pushkar, Dolores, Sansom, Wilma, and Gowing, J. Perceptual changes after prolonged sensory isolation (darkness and silence). *Canad. J. Psychol.,* 1961, 15: 83–100.

Zubek, J. P., Sansom, Wilma, and Prysiazniuk, A. Intellectual changes during prolonged perceptual isolation (darkness and silence). *Canad. J. Psychol.,* 1960, 14: 233–243.

VICARIOUS EXTINCTION OF AVOIDANCE BEHAVIOR *

ALBERT BANDURA, JOAN E. GRUSEC, AND FRANCES L. MENLOVE [1]

Recent investigations have shown that behavioral inhibitions (Bandura, 1965a; Bandura, Ross, and Ross, 1963; Walters and Parke, 1964) and conditioned emotional responses (Bandura and Rosenthal, 1966; Berger, 1962) can be acquired by observers as a function of witnessing aversive stimuli administered to performing subjects. The present experiment was primarily designed to determine whether preexisting avoidance behavior can similarly be extinguished on a vicarious basis. The latter phenomenon requires exposing observers to modeled stimulus events in which

* Reprinted with permission from the American Psychological Association. In *Journal of Personality and Social Psychology,* 1967, Vol. 5, pp. 16–23.

[1] This research was supported by Public Health Research Grant M-5162 from the National Institute of Mental Health. The authors are indebted to Janet Brewer, Edith Dowley, Doris Grant, and Mary Lewis for their generous assistance in various phases of this research.

a performing subject repeatedly exhibits approach responses toward the feared object without incurring any aversive consequences.

Some suggestive evidence that avoidance responses can be extinguished vicariously is furnished by Masserman (1943) and Jones (1924) in exploratory studies of the relative efficacy of various psychotherapeutic procedures. Masserman produced strong feeding inhibitions in cats, following which the inhibited animals observed a cage mate, that had never been negatively conditioned, exhibit prompt approach and feeding responses. The observing subjects initially cowered at the presentation of the conditioned stimulus, but with continued exposure to their fearless companion they advanced, at first hesitantly and then more boldly, to the goal box and consumed the food. Some of the animals, however, showed little reduction in avoidance behavior despite prolonged food deprivation and numerous modeling trials. Moreover, avoidance responses reappeared in a few of the animals after the normal cat was removed, suggesting that in the latter cases the modeling stimuli served merely as temporary external inhibitors of avoidance responses. Jones (1924) similarly obtained variable results in extinguishing children's phobic responses by having them observe their peers behave in a nonanxious manner in the presence of the avoided objects.

If a person is to be influenced by modeling stimuli and the accompanying consequences, then the necessary observing responses must be elicited and maintained. In the foregoing case studies, the models responded to the most feared stimulus situation at the outset, a modeling procedure that is likely to generate high levels of emotional arousal in observers. Under these conditions any avoidance responses designed to reduce vicariously instigated aversive stimulation, such as subjects withdrawing or looking away, would impede vicarious extinction. Therefore, the manner in which modeling stimuli are presented may be an important determinant of the course of vicarious extinction.

Results from psychotherapeutic studies (Bandura [2]) and experiments with infrahuman subjects (Kimble and Kendall, 1953) reveal that avoidance responses can be rapidly extinguished if subjects are exposed to a graduated series of aversive stimuli that progressively approximate the original intensity of the conditioned fear stimulus. For the above reasons it would seem advisable to conduct vicarious extinction by exposing observers to a graduated sequence of modeling activities beginning with presentations that can be easily tolerated; as observers' emotional reactions to displays of attenuated approach responses are extinguished, the fear-provoking properties of the modeled displays might be gradually increased, concluding with interactions capable of arousing relatively strong emotional responses.

If emotion-eliciting stimuli occur in association with positively reinforcing events, the former cues are likely to lose their conditioned aversive properties more rapidly (Farber, 1948) than through mere repeated nonreinforced presentation. It might therefore be supposed that vicarious extinction would likewise be hastened and more adequately controlled by presenting the modeling stimuli within a favorable context designed to evoke simultaneously competing positive responses.

The principles discussed above were applied in the present experiment, which explored the vicarious extinction of children's fearful and avoidant responses toward dogs. One group of children participated in a series of modeling sessions in which they observed a fearless peer model exhibit progressively longer, closer, and more active interactions with a dog. For these subjects, the modeled approach behavior was presented within a highly positive context. A second group of children was presented the same modeling stimuli, but in a neutral context.

Exposure to the behavior of the model contains two important stimulus events, that is, the occurrence of approach responses without any adverse consequences to the performer, and repeated observation of the feared animal. Therefore, in order to control for the effects of exposure to the dog per se, children assigned to a third group observed the dog in the positive context but with the model absent. A fourth group of children participated in the positive activities, but they were never exposed to either the dog or the model.

In order to assess both the generality and the stability of vicarious extinction effects, the children were readministered tests for avoidance behavior

[2] A. Bandura, "Principles of Behavioral Modification," unpublished manuscript, Stanford University, 1966.

toward different dogs following completion of the treatment series, and approximately 1 month later. It was predicted that children who had observed the peer model interact nonanxiously with the dog would display significantly less avoidance behavior than subjects who had no exposure to the modeling stimuli. The largest decrements were expected to occur among children in the modeling-positive context condition. It was also expected that repeated behavioral assessments and the general disinhibitory effects of participation in a series of highly positive activities might in themselves produce some decrease in avoidance behavior.

METHOD

Subjects

The subjects were 24 boys and 24 girls selected from three nursery schools. The children ranged in age from 3 to 5 years.

Pretreatment Assessment of Avoidance Behavior

As a preliminary step in the selection procedure, parents were asked to rate the magnitude of their children's fearful and avoidant behavior toward dogs. Children who received high fear ratings were administered a standardized performance test on the basis of which the final selection was made.

The strength of avoidance responses was measured by means of a graded sequence of 14 performance tasks in which the children were required to engage in increasingly intimate interactions with a dog. A female experimenter brought the children individually to the test room, which contained a brown cocker spaniel confined in a modified playpen. In the initial tasks the children were asked, in the following order, to walk up to the playpen and look down at the dog, to touch her fur, and to pet her. Following the assessment of avoidance responses to the dog in the protective enclosure, the children were instructed to open a hinged door on the side of the playpen, to walk the dog on a leash to a throw rug, to remove the leash, and to turn the dog over and scratch her stomach. Although a number of the subjects were unable to perform all of the latter tasks, they were nevertheless administered the remaining test items to avoid any assumption of a perfectly ordered scale for all cases. In subsequent items the children were asked to remain alone in the room with the

animal and to feed her dog biscuits. The final and most difficult set of tasks required the children to climb into the playpen with the dog, to pet her, to scratch her stomach, and to remain alone in the room with the dog under the exceedingly confining and fear-provoking conditions.

The strength of the children's avoidant tendencies was reflected not only in the items completed, but also in the degree of vacillation, reluctance, and fearfulness that preceded and accompanied each approach response. Consequently, children were credited 2 points if they executed a given task either spontaneously or willingly, and 1 point when they carried out the task minimally after considerable hesitancy and reluctance. Thus, for example, children who promptly stroked the dog's fur repeatedly when requested to do so received 2 points, whereas subjects who held back but then touched the dog's fur briefly obtained 1 point. In the item requiring the children to remain alone in the room with the dog, they received 2 points if they approached the animal and played with her, and 1 point if they were willing to remain in the room but avoided any contact with the dog. Similarly, in the feeding situation children were credited 2 points if they fed the dog by hand, but a single point if they tossed the biscuits on the floor and thereby avoided close contact with the animal. The maximum approach score that a subject could attain was 28 points.

On the basis of the pretreatment assessment, the children in each nursery school were grouped into three levels of avoidance behavior, with the corresponding scores ranging from 0 to 7, 8 to 17, and 18 to 20 points. There were approximately the same number of children, equally divided between boys and girls, at each of the three avoidance levels. The subjects from each of these groups were then assigned randomly to one of four conditions.

Treatment Conditions

Children who participated in the *modeling-positive context* condition observed a fearless peer model display approach responses toward a cocker spaniel within the context of a highly enjoyable party atmosphere.

There were eight 10-minute treatment sessions conducted on 4 consecutive days. Each session, which was attended by a group of four children, commenced with a jovial party. The children were furnished brightly colored hats, cookie treats, and given small prizes. In addition, the experimenter read stories, blew large plastic balloons for the children to play with, and engaged in other party activities designed to produce strong positive affective responses.

After the party was well under way, a second experimenter entered the room carrying the dog, followed by a 4-year-old male model who was unknown to most of the children. The dog was placed in a playpen located across the room from a large table at which the children were seated. The model, who had been chosen because of his complete lack of fear of dogs, then performed prearranged sequences of interactions with the dog for approximately 3 minutes during each session. One boy served as the model for children drawn from two of the nursery schools, and a second boy functioned in the same role at the third school.

The fear-provoking properties of the modeled displays were gradually increased from session to session by varying simultaneously the physical restraints on the dog, the directness and intimacy of the modeled approach responses, and the duration of interaction between the model and his canine companion. Initially, the experimenter carried the dog into the room and confined her to the playpen, and the model's behavior was limited to friendly verbal responses ("Hi, Chloe") and occasional petting. During the following three sessions the dog remained confined to the playpen, but the model exhibited progressively longer and more active interactions in the form of petting the dog with his hands and feet, and feeding her wieners and milk from a baby bottle. Beginning with the fifth session, the dog was walked into the room on a leash, and the modeled tasks were mainly performed outside the playpen. For example, in addition to repeating the feeding routines, the model walked the dog around the room, petted her, and scratched her stomach while the leash was removed. In the last two sessions the model climbed into the playpen with the dog where he petted her, hugged her, and fed her wieners and milk from the baby bottle.

It would have been of interest to compare the relative efficacy of the graduated modeling technique with bold displays of approach behavior from the outset. However, pretest findings showed that when modeled displays are too fear provoking, children actively avoid looking at the performances and are reluctant to participate in subsequent sessions. The latter approach would therefore require additional procedures designed to maintain strong attending behavior to highly aversive modeling stimuli.

Children assigned to the *modeling-neutral context* condition observed the same sequence of approach responses performed by the same peer model except that the parties were omitted. In each of the eight sessions the subjects were merely seated at the table and observed the modeled performances.

In order to control for the influence of repeated exposure to the positive atmosphere and to the dog per se, children in the *exposure-positive context* group attended the series of parties in the presence of the dog with the model absent. As in the two modeling conditions, the dog was introduced into the room in the same manner for the identical length of time; similarly, the dog was confined in the playpen during the first four sessions and placed on a leash outside the enclosure in the remaining sessions.

Children in the *positive-context* group participated in the parties, but they were never exposed to either the dog or the model. The main purpose of this condition was to determine whether the mere presence of a dog had an adverse or a beneficial effect on the children. Like the third condition, it also provided a control for the possible therapeutic effects of positive experiences and increased familiarity with amiable experimenters, which may be particularly influential in reducing inhibitions in very young children. In addition repeated behavioral assessments in which subjects perform a graded series of approach responses toward a feared object without any aversive consequences would be expected to produce some direct extinction of avoidance behavior. The inclusion of the latter two control groups thus makes it possible to evaluate the changes effected by exposure to modeling stimuli over and above those resulting from general disinhibition, direct extinction, and repeated observation of the feared object.

Posttreatment Assessment of Avoidance Behavior

On the day following completion of the treatment series, the children were readministered the performance test consisting of the graded sequence of interaction tasks with the dog. In order to determine the generality of vicarious extinction effects, half the children in each of the four groups were tested initially with the experimental animal and then with an unfamiliar dog; the remaining children were presented with the two dogs in the reverse order.[3] The testing sessions were separated by an interval of 1½ hours so as to minimize any transfer of emotional reactions generated by one animal to the other.

The unfamiliar animal was a white mongrel, predominantly terrier, and of approximately the same size and activity level as the cocker spaniel. Two groups of 15 children, drawn from the same nursery-school population, were tested with either the mongrel or the spaniel in order to determine the aversiveness of the two animals. The mean approach scores with the spaniel ($M = 16.47$) and the mongrel ($M = 15.80$) were virtually identical ($t = .21$).

Follow-Up Assessment

A follow-up evaluation was conducted approximately 1 month after the posttreatment assessment in order to determine the stability of modeling-induced changes in approach behavior. The children's responses were tested with the same performance tasks toward both animals, presented in the identical order.

After the experiment was completed, the children were told that, while most dogs are friendly, before petting an unfamiliar dog they should ask the owner. This precautionary instruction was designed to reduce indiscriminate approach behavior by children who were in the modeling conditions toward strange dogs which they would undoubtedly encounter.

Measurement Procedure

The same female experimenter administered the pretreatment, posttreatment, and follow-up behavioral tests. To prevent any possible bias, the experimenter was given minimal information about the details of the study and had no knowledge of the conditions to which the children were assigned. The treatment and assessment procedures were further separated by the use of different rooms for each activity.

In order to provide an estimate of interscorer reliability, the performances of 25% of the chil-

[3] The authors are especially indebted to Chloe and Jenny for their invaluable and steadfast assistance with a task that, at times, must have been most perplexing to them.

dren, randomly selected from pretreatment, posttreatment, and follow-up phases of the experiment, were scored simultaneously but independently by another rater who observed the test sessions through a one-way mirror from an adjoining observation room. The two raters were in perfect agreement on 97% of the specific approach responses that were scored.

A dog's activity level may partly determine the degree of fear and avoidance exhibited by the children; conversely, timorous or unrestrained approach responses might differentially affect the animals' reactivity. Therefore, during the administration of each test item, the animals' behavior was rated as either passive, moderately active, or vigorous. The raters were in perfect agreement in categorizing the dogs' activity levels on 81% of the performance tests.

Changes in children's approach-response scores across the different phases of the experiment, and the number of subjects in each treatment condition who were able to carry out the terminal performance task served as the dependent measures.

Results

The percentages of test items in which the animals behaved in a passive, moderately active, or vigorous manner were 55, 43, and 2, respectively, for the model-positive context group; 53, 44, and 2 for children in the model-neutral context condition; 52, 45, and 3 for the exposure-positive context group; and 57, 41, and 2 for the positive-context subjects. Thus, the test animals did not differ in their behavior during the administration of performance tasks to children in the various treatment conditions.

Approach Responses

Table 1 presents the mean increases in approach behavior achieved by children in each of the treatment conditions in different phases of the experiment with each of the test animals.

The children's approach responses toward the two dogs did not differ either in the posttreatment assessment ($t = 1.35$) or in the follow-up phase ($t = .91$) of the study. Nor were there any significant effects ($t = 1.68$) due to the order in which the test animals were presented following completion of the treatment series. A t-test analysis also disclosed no significant change ($t = 1.50$) in mean approach scores between measurements conducted in the posttreatment and the follow-up phases of the experiment. Moreover, analysis of variance of the posttreatment scores revealed no significant Treatment $\times$ Dogs ($F = 2.15$) or Treatment $\times$ Order ($F = .30$) interaction effects. The data were therefore combined across phases and test animals in evaluating the major hypotheses.

An analysis of covariance, in which adjustments were made for differences in initial level of avoidance, was computed for mean approach responses performed by children in the various groups. The results reveal that the treatment conditions had a

increases in approach behavior for children in the modeling-positive context group ($t = 7.71$, $p < .001$) and for those who observed the modeling performance within the neutral setting ($t = 5.80$, $p < .001$). Although the positive-context group showed an increment in approach behavior ($t = 5.78$, $p < .001$), children who were merely exposed to the dog in the positive context achieved a small, but nonsignificant ($t = 1.98$), reduction in avoidance responses.

Terminal Performances

Another measure of the efficacy of modeling

TABLE 1

MEAN INCREASES IN APPROACH RESPONSES AS A FUNCTION OF TREATMENT
CONDITIONS, ASSESSMENT PHASES, AND TEST ANIMALS

Phases	Treatment conditions			
	Modeling—positive context	Modeling—neutral context	Exposure—positive context	Positive context
Posttreatment				
Spaniel	10.83	9.83	2.67	6.08
Mongrel	5.83	10.25	3.17	4.17
Follow-Up				
Spaniel	10.83	9.33	4.67	5.83
Mongrel	12.59	9.67	4.75	6.67
Combined data	10.02	9.77	3.81	5.69

highly significant effect on the children's behavior ($F = 5.09$, $p < .01$). Tests of the differences between the various pairs of treatments indicate that subjects in the modeling-positive context condition displayed significantly more approach behavior than subjects in either the exposure ($F = 9.32$, $p < .01$) or the positive-context ($F = 8.96$, $p < .01$) groups. Similarly, children who had observed the model within the neutral setting exceeded both the exposure ($F = 6.57$, $p < .05$) and positive-context groups ($F = 4.91$, $p < .05$) in approach behavior. However, the data yielded no significant differences between either the two modeling conditions ($F = .04$) or the two control groups ($F = .76$).

Within-Group Analysis of Approach Responses

The approach scores obtained by the different groups of children in preexperimental and subsequent tests are summarized graphically in Figure 1. Within-group analyses of changes between initial performance and mean level of approach behavior following treatment disclose significant

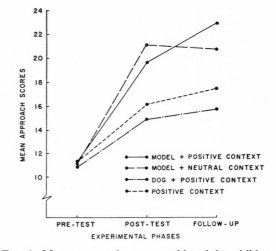

FIG. 1. Mean approach scores achieved by children in each of the treatment conditions on the three different periods of assessment.

procedures is provided by comparisons of the number of children, in each condition who performed the terminal approach behavior at least once during the posttreatment assessment. Since the frequencies within the two modeling conditions did not differ, and the two control groups were essentially the same, the data for each of the two sets of subgroups were combined. The findings showed that 67% of the children in the modeling treatment were able to remain alone in the room confined with the dog in the playpen, whereas the corresponding figure for the control subjects is 33%. The χ^2 value for these data is 4.08, which is significant beyond the .025 level.

Within the control groups, the terminal performances were attained primarily by subjects who initially showed the weakest level of avoidance behavior. The differences between the two groups are, therefore, even more pronounced if the analysis is conducted on the subjects whose pretreatment performances reflected extreme or moderately high levels of avoidance behavior. Of the most avoidant subjects in each of the two pooled groups, 55% of the children in the modeling conditions were able to perform the terminal approach behavior following the experimental sessions, while only 13% of the control subjects successfully completed the final task. The one-tailed probability for the obtained $\chi^2 = 4.74$ is slightly below the .01 level of significance.

The relative superiority of the modeling groups is also evident in the follow-up phase of the experiment. Based on the stringent criterion in which the most fearful task is successfully performed with *both* animals, a significantly larger number of children in the modeling conditions (42%) than in the control groups (12%) exhibited generalized extinction ($\chi^2 = 4.22$, $p < .025$). Moreover, not a single control subject from the two highest levels of avoidance behavior was able to remain alone in the room confined in the playpen with each of the dogs, whereas 33% of the most avoidant children in the modeling conditions successfully passed both terminal approach tasks ($\chi^2 = 4.02$, $p < .025$).

DISCUSSION

The findings of the present experiment provide considerable evidence that avoidance responses can be successfully extinguished on a vicarious basis. This is shown in the fact that children who experienced a gradual exposure to progressively more fearful modeled responses displayed extensive and stable reduction in avoidance behavior.

Moreover, most of these subjects were able to engage in extremely intimate and potentially fearful interactions with test animals following the treatment series. The considerable degree of generalization of extinction effects obtained to the unfamiliar dog is most likely due to similar stimulus properties of the test animals. Under conditions where observers' avoidance responses are extinguished to a single animal, one would expect a progressive decrement in approach behavior toward animals of increasing size and fearfulness.

The prediction that vicarious extinction would be augmented by presenting the modeling stimuli within a highly positive context was not confirmed, although subjects in the latter condition differed more significantly from the controls than children who observed approach behavior under neutral conditions. It is entirely possible that a different temporal ordering of emotion-provoking modeling stimuli and events designed to induce anxiety-inhibiting responses would facilitate the vicarious extinction process. On the basis of evidence from conditioning studies (Melvin and Brown, 1964) the optimal treatment procedure might require repeated observational trials, in each of which aversive modeling stimuli are immediately followed by positively reinforcing experiences for the observers. These temporal prerequisites depend upon the abrupt presentation and termination of the two sets of stimulus events that cannot be readily achieved with live demonstrations. It would be possible, however, to study the effects of systematic variations in the temporal spacing of critical variables if modeling stimuli were presented pictorially. Apart from issues of economy and control, if pictorial stimulus material proved equally as efficacious as live modeling, then skillfully designed therapeutic films could be developed and employed in preventive programs for eliminating common fears and anxieties before they become well established and widely generalized.

Although children in both the exposure and the positive-context groups showed some increment in approach behavior, only the changes in the latter group were of statistically significant magnitude. Apparently the mere presence of a dog had some mild negative consequences that counteracted the facilitative effects resulting from highly rewarding interactions with amiable experimenters, increased familiarity with the person conducting the numerous tests of avoidance behavior, and any inevitable direct extinction produced by the repeated performance of some approach responses toward the test animals without any adverse consequences. As might be expected, the general disinhibitory effects arising from these multiple sources occurred only in the early phase of the experiment, and no significant increases in approach behavior appeared between the posttreatment and follow-up assessments.

The data obtained in this experiment demonstrate that the fearless behavior of a model can substantially reduce avoidance responses in observers, but the findings do not establish the nature of the mechanism by which vicarious extinction occurs. There are several possible explanations of vicariously produced effects (Bandura, 1965b; Kanfer, 1965). One interpretation is in terms of the informative value of modeling stimuli. That is, the repeated evocation of approach responses without any adverse consequences to another person undoubtedly conveys information to the observer about the probable outcomes of close interactions with dogs. In the present study, however, an attempt was made to minimize the contribution of purely cognitive factors by informing children in all groups beforehand that the test animals were harmless.

The nonoccurrence of anticipated aversive consequences to a model accompanied by positive affective reactions on his part can also extinguish in observers previously established emotional responses that are vicariously aroused by the modeled displays (Bandura and Rosenthal, 1966). It is therefore possible that reduction in avoidance behavior is partly mediated by the elimination of conditioned emotionality.

Further research is needed to separate the relative contribution of cognitive, emotional, and other factors governing vicarious processes. It would also be of interest to study the effects upon vicarious extinction exercised by such variables as number of modeling trials, distribution of extinction sessions, mode of model presentation, and variations in the characteristics of the models and the feared stimuli. For example, with extensive sampling in the modeled displays of both girls and boys exhibiting approach responses to dogs ranging from diminutive breeds to larger specimens, it may be possible to achieve widely generalized extinction effects. Once approach behaviors have been restored through modeling, their maintenance and further generalization can be effectively controlled by response-contingent reinforcement administered directly to the subject. The combined use of modeling and reinforcement procedures may thus serve as a highly efficacious mode of therapy for eliminating severe behavioral inhibitions.

SUMMARY

This experiment was designed to investigate the extinction of avoidance responses through observation of modeled approach behavior directed toward a feared stimulus without any adverse consequences accruing to the model. Children who displayed fearful and avoidant behavior toward dogs were assigned to 1 of the following treatment conditions: 1 group of children participated in a series of brief modeling sessions in which they observed, within a highly positive context, a fearless peer model exhibit progressively stronger approach responses toward a dog; a 2nd group of Ss observed the same graduated modeling stimuli, but in a neutral context; a 3rd group merely observed the dog in the positive context, with the model absent; while a 4th group of Ss participated in the positive activities without any exposure to either the dog or the modeled displays. The 2 groups of children who had observed the model interact nonanxiously with the dog displayed stable and generalized reduction in avoidance behavior and differed significantly in this respect from children in the dog-exposure and the positive-context conditions. However, the positive context, which was designed to induce anxiety-competing responses, did not enhance the extinction effects produced through modeling.

REFERENCES

Bandura, A. Influence of models' reinforcement contingencies on the acquisition of imitative responses. *Journal of Personality and Social Psychology,* 1965, 1: 589–595. (a)

Bandura, A. Vicarious processes: A case of no-trial learning. In L. Berkowitz (Ed.), *Advances in experimental social psychology.* Vol. 2. New York: Academic Press, 1965. Pp. 1–55. (b)

Bandura, A., and Rosenthal, T. L. Vicarious classical conditioning as a function of arousal level. *Journal of Personality and Social Psychology,* 1966, 3: 54–62.

Bandura, A., Ross, D., and Ross, S. A. Vicarious

reinforcement and imitative learning. *Journal of Abnormal and Social Psychology,* 1963, 67: 601–607.

Berger, S. M. Conditioning through vicarious instigation. *Psychological Review,* 1962, 69: 450–466.

Farber, I. E. Response fixation under anxiety and non-anxiety conditions. *Journal of Experimental Psychology,* 1948, 38: 111–131.

Jones, M. C. The elimination of children's fears. *Journal of Experimental Psychology,* 1924, 7: 383–390.

Kanfer, F. H. Vicarious human reinforcement: A glimpse into the black box. In L. Krasner and L. P. Ullmann (Eds.), *Research in behavior modification.* New York: Holt, Rinehart and Winston, 1965. Pp. 244–267.

Kimble, G. A., and Kendall, J. W., Jr. A comparison of two methods of producing experimental extinction. *Journal of Experimental Psychology,* 1953, 45: 87–90.

Masserman, J. H. *Behavior and neurosis.* Chicago: University of Chicago Press, 1943.

Melvin, K. B., and Brown, J. S. Neutralization of an aversive light stimulus as a function of number of paired presentations with food. *Journal of Comparative and Physiological Psychology,* 1964, 58: 350–353.

Walters, R. H., and Parke, R. D. Influence of response consequences to a social model on resistance to deviation. *Journal of Experimental Child Psychology,* 1964, 1: 269–280.

CONFORMITY AND CHARACTER *

Richard S. Crutchfield [1]

During the Spring of 1953, one hundred men visited the Institute of Personality Assessment and Research at the University of California, Berkeley, to participate in an intensive three-day assessment

* Reprinted with permission from the American Psychological Association. In *American Psychologist,* 1955, Vol. 10, pp. 191–198.

[1] Adapted from the address of the retiring president of the Division of Personality and Social Psychology, American Psychological Association, New York City, September 4, 1954.

of those qualities related to superior functioning in their profession.[2]

As one of the procedures on the final day of assessment, the men were seated in groups of five in front of an apparatus consisting of five adjacent electrical panels. Each panel had side wings, forming an open cubicle, so that the person, though sitting side by side with his fellow subjects, was unable to see their panels. The experimenter explained that the apparatus was so wired that information could be sent by each man to all the others by closing any of eleven switches at the bottom of his panel. This information would appear on the other panels in the form of signal lights, among five rows of eleven lights, each row corresponding to one of the five panels. After a warm-up task to acquaint the men with the workings of the apparatus, the actual procedure commenced.

Slides were projected on a wall directly facing the men. Each slide presented a question calling for a judgment by the person. He indicated his choice of one of several multiple-alternative answers by closing the appropriately numbered switch on his panel. Moreover, he responded *in order,* that is, as designated by one of five red lights lettered A, B, C, D, E, on his panel. If he were A, he responded first, if B, second, and so on. The designations, A, B, C, D, and E, were rotated by the experimenter from time to time, thus permitting each person to give his judgments in all the different serial positions. No further explanation about the purpose of this procedure was offered.

It may help to convey the nature of the men's typical experiences by giving an illustrative description of what happens concretely to one of the men. The first slide calls for a simple judgment of which of two geometrical figures is larger in area. Since his red light C is on, he waits for A and B to respond before making his response. And, as he is able to observe on the panel, his own judgment coincides with the judgments of A and B who preceded him, and of D and E who follow him. After judgments on several further slides in

[2] The principal study reported here owes much to the collaboration of Dr. Donald W. MacKinnon, director of the Institute of Personality Assessment and Research, and of his staff. Mr. Donald G. Woodworth has contributed especially to the statistical analysis of data.

position C, he is then shifted to position D for more slides, then to A.

The slides call for various kinds of judgments —lengths of lines, areas of figures, logical completion of number series, vocabulary items, estimates of the opinions of others, expression of his own attitudes on issues, expression of his personal preferences for line drawings, etc. He is not surprised to observe a perfectly sensible relationship between his judgments and those of the other four men. Where clear-cut perceptual or logical judgments are involved, he finds that his judgments are in perfect agreement with those of the other four. Where matters of opinion are involved, and some differences in opinion to be expected, his judgments and those of the other four men are sometimes in agreement and sometimes not.

Eventually the man finds himself for the first time in position E, where he is to respond last. The next slide shows a standard line and five comparison lines, of which he is to pick the one equal in length to the standard. Among the previous slides he has already encountered this kind of perceptual judgment and has found it easy. On looking at this slide it is immediately clear to him that line number 4 is the correct one. But as he waits his turn to respond, he sees light number 5 in row A go on, indicating that that person has judged line number 5 to be correct. And in fairly quick succession light 5 goes on also in rows B, C, and D.

At this point the man is faced with an obvious conflict between his own clear perception and a unanimous contradictory consensus of the other four men. What does he do? Does he rely on the evidence of his own senses and respond independently? Or does he defer to the judgment of the group, complying with their perceptions rather than his own?

We will postpone for a moment the answer as to what he does, and revert to the description of our apparatus.

We have been describing the situation as if seen from the perspective of one of the men. Actually his understanding of the situation is wrong. He has been deceived. For the apparatus is *not* really wired in the way that he was informed. There actually is no connection among the five panels. Instead, they are all wired in an identical manner to a control panel where the experimenter sits be-

hind the men. It is the experimenter who sends all the information which appears on the panels, and the wiring is in parallel in such a way that whatever signals are sent by the experimenter appear simultaneously and identically on all five panels. Moreover, the designations of serial order of responding—A through E—are identical at all times for the five panels, so that at a given moment, for instance, all five men believe themselves to be A, or at another time, E.

As we have just said, the responses actually made by the five men do not affect in any way the panels of the others. They do get registered individually on one part of the experimenter's control panel. The *latency* of each individual response to one tenth of a second is also recorded by timers on the control panel.

Hence, the situation as we have described it for our one illustrative man is actually the situation simultaneously experienced by all five men. They all commence in position C, and all shift at the same time to position D, and to A, and finally E. They all see the same simulated group judgments.

The entire situation is, in a word, contrived, and contrived so as to expose each individual to a standardized and prearranged series of group judgments. By this means the simulated group judgments can be made to appear sensible and in agreement with the individual, or, at chosen critical points, in conflict with his judgments.

Most of you will recognize at once the basic similarity of our situation to that invented by Asch (1952) in his extremely important work of recent years on independence of individual judgment under opposing group pressure. In his method, ten subjects announced aloud and in succession their judgments of the relative length of stimulus lines exposed before the group. The first nine subjects were actually confederates of the experimenter, and gave uniformly false answers at pre-established points, thus placing pressure on the single naive subject.

For extensive research use, for instance in personality assessment, Asch's technique is handicapped by the severely unfavorable ratio of confederates to true subjects. The present technique, utilizing the electrical network described above, avoids this difficulty. There are no confederates required; all five subjects are tested simultaneously in a thoroughly standardized situation. The experimenter exercises highly flexible control of the simulated group judgments, and of the serial order of responding. Stimulus material to be judged can be varied as widely as desired by use of different slides.

Now at last come back to our man still sitting before his panel, still confronted with the spurious group consensus, still torn between a force toward independent judgment and a force toward conformity to the group. How he is likely to behave in the situation can best be described by summarizing the results for our study of 50 of the 100 men in assessment.

EFFECTS OF CONSENSUS

All of these men were engaged in a profession in which leadership is one of the salient expected qualifications. Their average age was 34 years. Their educational levels were heterogeneous, but most had had some college training.

Fifty of the men were tested in the procedure as described. Another 40 served as *control* subjects; they simply gave individual judgments of the slides without using the apparatus, and hence without knowledge of the judgments of others. The distribution of judgments of these control subjects on each slide was subsequently used as a baseline for evaluating the amount of group pressure influence on the experimental subjects.

Now as to results. When faced with the dilemma posed by this first critical slide, 15 of the 50 men, or 30 per cent, conformed to the obviously false group consensus. The remaining 70 per cent of the men maintained independence of judgment in face of the contradictory group consensus.

The first critical slide was followed by 20 others, all with the subjects responding in position E. The 20 slides involved a broad sampling of judgmental materials, exploring the question of what would happen to other kinds of perceptions, to matters of factual appraisal and of logic, of opinion and attitude, of personal preference—all under the same conditions of group pressure. Interpolated among them were occasional neutral slides, in which the group consensus was simulated as correct or sensible, in order to help maintain the subjects' acceptance of the genuineness of the apparatus and situation.

The results on several more of the critical slides will give a representative picture of what happens under group pressure. First, take another kind of perceptual judgment. A circle and a star are exposed side by side, the circle being about one third larger in area than the star. The false group consensus is on the *star* as the larger, and 46 per cent of the men express agreement with this false judgment.

On a simple logical judgment of completion of a number series, as found in standard mental tests, 30 per cent of the men conform to an obviously illogical group answer, whereas not a single control subject gives an incorrect answer.

As striking as these influence effects are, they are overshadowed by the even higher degree of influence exhibited on another set of items. These pertain to perceptual, factual, and logical judgments which are designed to maximize the *ambiguity* of the stimulus. There are three such examples: (*a*) two actually equal circles are to be judged for relative size; (*b*) a pair of words are to be judged as either synonyms or antonyms, though actually entirely unrelated in meaning and unfamiliar to all subjects; (*c*) a number series is to be completed which is actually insoluble, that is, for which there is no logically correct completion.

To take the third example, which gives the most pronounced influence effect of all 21 critical items, 79 per cent of the men conform to a spurious group consensus upon an arbitrarily chosen and irrational answer.

Influence effects are found, we see, on both well-structured and poorly-structured stimuli, with markedly greater effects on the latter.

Turning from perceptual and factual judgments to opinions and attitudes, it is clearly evident that here, too, the judgments of many of the men are markedly dependent upon a spurious group consensus which violates their own inner convictions. For example, among control subjects virtually no one expresses disagreement with the statement: "I believe we are made better by the trials and hardships of life." But among the experimental subjects exposed to a group consensus toward disagreement, 31 per cent of the men shift to expressing disagreement.

It can be demonstrated that the conformity behavior is not found solely for attitudes on issues like the foregoing, which may be of rather abstract and remote significance for the person. Among the control sample of men, not a single one expresses agreement with the statement: "I doubt whether I would make a good leader," whereas 37 per cent of the men subjected to group pressure toward agreement succumb to it. Here is an issue relating to appraisal of the self and hence likely to be of some importance to the person, especially in light of the fact already mentioned that one of the salient expected qualifications of men in this particular profession is that of leadership.

The set of 21 critical items ranges from factual to attitudinal, from structured to ambiguous, from impersonal to personal. With only two exceptions, all these items yield significant group pressure influence effects in our sample of 50 men. The very existence of the two exceptional items is in itself an important finding, for it demonstrates that the observed influences are not simply evidence of indiscriminate readiness to conform to group pressure regardless of the specific nature of the judgment involved. The character of the two exceptional items is significant, for they are the two most extremely personal and subjective judgments, namely, those in which the individual is asked which one of two simple line drawings *he prefers*. On these slides there is virtually no effective result of group pressure. Not more than one man of the 50 expresses agreement with the spurious group consensus on the nonpreferred drawing. Such personal preferences, being most isolated from the relevance of group standards, thus seem to be most immune to group pressure.

INDIVIDUAL DIFFERENCES

To what extent do the fifty men differ among themselves in their general degree of conformity to group pressure?

A total "conformity score" is readily obtainable for each individual by counting the number of the 21 critical items on which he exhibits influence to the group pressure. The threshold for influence for each item is arbitrarily fixed on the basis of the distribution of judgments by control subjects on that item.

Considering that we are dealing wtih a fairly homogeneous sample of limited size, the range of individual differences that we obtain is astonishingly large, covering virtually the entire possible scope of our measure. At the lower extreme, several of the men showed conformity on no more than one or two of the critical items. At the upper

extreme, one man was influenced on 17 of the 21 items. The rest of the scores are well distributed between these extremes, with a mean score of about eight items and a tendency for greater concentration of scores toward the lower conformity end.

The reliability of the total score, as a measure of generalized conformity in the situation, is obtained by correlating scores on two matched halves of the items. The correlation is found to be .82, which when corrected for the combined halves gives a reliability estimate for the entire 21-item scale of .90.

To recapitulate, we find large and reliable differences among the 50 men in the amount of conformity behavior exhibited, and there appears to be considerable generality of this conformity behavior with respect to widely varied judgmental materials. Whether such conformity tendencies also generalize to other, quite different behavioral situations is a question for future research.

RELATIONS TO PERSONALITY VARIABLES

Assuming that we are, indeed, measuring conformity tendencies which are fundamental in the person, the question is what traits of character distinguish between those men exhibiting much conformity behavior in our test and those exhibiting little conformity. The assessment setting within which these men were studied provides an unusually fertile opportunity to explore this question, in light of the wide range of personality measurements available.

Correlational study of the conformity scores with these other variables of personality provides some picture of the independent and of the conforming person. As contrasted with the high conformist, the independent man shows more intellectual effectiveness, ego strength, leadership ability and maturity of social relations, together with a conspicuous absence of inferiority feelings, rigid and excessive self-control, and authoritarian attitudes.

A few correlations will illustrate. The assessment staff rating on "intellectual competence" correlates —.63 with conformity score, this being the highest relationship of any found. The *Concept Mastery Test*,[3] a measure of superior mental

[3] Used with the kind permission of Dr. Lewis M. Terman.

functioning correlates —.51 with conformity. An "ego strength" scale, independently derived by Barron (Barron, 1953a), correlates —.33, and a staff rating on "leadership ability," —.30 with conformity. Scales of Gough's *California Psychological Inventory* (Gough, 1954), pertaining to such dimensions as "tolerance," "social participation," and "responsibility," range in correlation from —.30 to —.41 with conformity.

And as for some of the positive correlates, the F scale (1), a measure of authoritarian attitudes, correlates +.39 with conformity, and a staff rating on amount of authoritarian behavior manifested in a standard psychodrama situation correlates +.35 with conformity.

The general appraisal of each man by the assessment staff in the form of descriptive Q sorts further enriches this picture. Those men exhibiting extreme independence in the situation as contrasted with those at the high conformity end are described more often in the following terms by the assessment staff, which was entirely ignorant of the actual behavior of the men in the group pressure procedure:

Is an effective leader.
Takes an ascendant role in his relations with others.
Is persuasive; tends to win other people over to his point of view.
Is turned to for advice and reassurance.
Is efficient, capable, able to mobilize resources easily and effectively.
Is active and vigorous.
Is an expressive, ebullient person.
Seeks and enjoys aesthetic and sensuous impressions.
Is natural; free from pretense, unaffected.
Is self-reliant; independent in judgement; able to think for himself.

In sharp contrast to this picture of the independent men is the following description of those high in conformity behavior:

With respect to authority, is submissive, compliant and overly accepting.
Is conforming; tends to do the things that are prescribed.
Has a narrow range of interests.
Overcontrols his impulses; is inhibited; needlessly delays or denies gratification.
Is unable to make decisions without vacillation or delay.
Becomes confused, disorganized, and unadaptive under stress.

Lacks insight into his own motives and behavior.
Is suggestible; overly responsive to other people's evaluations rather than his own.

Further evidence is found in some of the specific items of personality inventories on which the answers of the high and low conformers are significantly different. Here are some illustrative items more frequently answered "True" by the independent subjects than by the conforming subjects:

Sometimes I rather enjoy going against the rules and doing things I'm not supposed to.
I like to fool around with new ideas, even if they turn out later to be a total waste of time.
A person needs to "show off" a little now and then.
At times I have been so entertained by the cleverness of a crook that I have hoped he would get by with it.
It is unusual for me to express strong approval or disapproval of the actions of others.
I am often so annoyed when someone tries to get ahead of me in a line of people that I speak to him about it.
Compared to your own self-respect, the respect of others means very little.

This pattern of expressed attitudes seems to reflect freedom from compulsion about rules, adventurousness (perhaps tinged with exhibitionism), self-assertiveness, and self-respect.

Turning to the opposite side of the picture, here are some illustrative items more frequently answered "True" by the extreme conformists, which reflect a rather rigid, externally sanctioned, and inconsistent, moralistic attitude.

I am in favor of very strict enforcement of all laws, no matter what the consequences.
It is all right to get around the law if you don't actually break it.
Most people are honest chiefly through fear of being caught.

Another set of items reveals a desire for clarity, symmetry, certainty, or, in presently popular phraseology, "an intolerance of ambiguity."

I don't like to work on a problem unless there is a possibility of coming out with a clear-cut and unambiguous answer.
Once I have made up my mind I seldom change it.
Perfect balance is the essence of all good composition.

Other items express conventionality of values:

I always follow the rule: business before pleasure.

The trouble with many people is that they don't take things seriously enough.

I am very careful about my manner of dress.

Anxiety is revealed in numerous items:

I am afraid when I look down from a high place.

I am often bothered by useless thoughts which keep running through my head.

I often think, "I wish I were a child again."

I often feel as though I have done something wrong or wicked.

And, finally, there are various expressions of disturbed, dejected, and distrustful attitudes toward other people:

When I meet a stranger I often think that he is better than I am.

Sometimes I am sure that other people can tell what I am thinking.

I wish that I could get over worrying about things I have said that may have injured other people's feelings.

I commonly wonder what hidden reason another person may have for doing something nice for me.

People pretend to care more about one another than they really do.

Although there is an unmistakable neurotic tone to many of the foregoing statements, one must be chary of inferring that those high on conformity are measurably more neurotic than the others. There does not in fact appear to be any significant correlation of the conformity scores with obvious standard measures of neuroticism as found, for instance, in scales of the Minnesota Multiphasic Personality Inventory. A similar negative finding has been reported by Barron (1953b) in his study of the personality correlates of independence of judgment in Asch's subjects.

In another area, attitudes concerning parents and children, differences between those high and low on conformity are especially interesting. The extreme conformists describe their parents in highly idealized terms, unrelieved by any semblance of criticism. The independents, on the other hand, offer a more balanced picture of praise and criticism.

Most of the men in the sample are fathers, and it is instructive to see that in their view of child-rearing practices, the conformers are distinctly more "restrictive" in their attitudes, and the inde-

pendents distinctively more "permissive" (Block, 1955).

Finally, there appears to be a marked difference in the early home background of the conformists and independents. The high conformers in this sample come almost without exception from stable homes; the independents much more frequently report broken homes and unstable home environments.

Previous theoretical and empirical studies seem to converge, though imperfectly, on a picture of the overconformist as having less ego strength, less ability to tolerate own impulses and to tolerate ambiguity, less ability to accept responsibility, less self-insight, less spontaneity and productive originality, and as having more prejudiced and authoritarian attitudes, more idealization of parents, and greater emphasis on external and socially approved values.

All of these elements gain at least some substantiation in the present study of conformity behavior, as objectively measured in our test situation. The decisive influence of intelligence in resisting conformity pressures is perhaps given even fuller weight in the present findings.

Conformity Behavior in Different Populations

Two further studies have been made. The first was with 59 college undergraduates, mostly sophomores. Forty were females, 19 males. An additional 40 students served as control subjects.

Using the same procedures and the same items for judgment, the conformity results for this student sample were highly similar to those already reported for the adult men. Here again extensive group pressure effects are found on almost all items. And here again there are wide individual differences, covering virtually the entire score range.

The male students on the average exhibit just about the same level of conformity as do the adult men. The female students, on the other hand, exhibit significantly *higher* amounts of conformity than the male groups. This greater conformity among females is evident across the entire range of items tested. Interpretation of this sex difference in conformity will require further research.

But before male egos swell overly, let me hasten to report the results of a third study, just completed. Fifty women, all college alumnae in their early forties, were tested in the same group pressure procedure, again as part of a larger assessment setting, and under the auspices of the Mary Conover Mellon Foundation.[4] As in the previous populations, virtually the entire range of individual differences in conformity is exhibited by these women. Some of them show no effect at all; others are influenced on almost all items. But the average conformity score for these 50 women is significantly *lower* than that found in the previous populations.

Thus we find our sample of adult women to be more independent in judgment than our adult men. The interpretation is difficult. The two groups differ in many particulars, other than sex. The women are highly selected for educational and socioeconomic status, are persons active in their community affairs, and would be characterized as relatively stable in personality and free of psychopathology. The adult men in our professional group are less advantageously selected in all these respects. Differences in intellectual level alone might be sufficient to account for the observed differences in conformity scores.

PSYCHOLOGICAL PROCESSES

Turn now to questions concerning the nature of the psychological processes involved in these expressions of conformity to group pressure. How, for instance, is the situation perceived by the individual? The most striking thing is that almost never do the individuals under this pressure of a false group consensus come to suspect the deception practiced upon them. Of the total of 159 persons already tested in the apparatus, and questioned immediately afterwards, only a small handful expressed doubt of the genuineness of the situation. Of these not more than two or three really seem to have developed this suspicion while in the actual situation.

Yet all the subjects are acutely aware of the sometimes gross discrepancies between their own inner judgments and those expressed by the rest of the group. How do they account for these discrepancies?

Intensive individual questioning of the subjects immediately following the procedure elicits evidence of two quite different tendencies. First, for

[4] The assessment was under the direction of Dr. R. Nevitt Sanford.

many persons the discrepancies tend to be resolved through self-blame. They express doubt of their own accuracy of perception or judgment, confessing that they had probably misread or misperceived the slides. Second, for many other persons the main tendency is to blame the rest of the group, expressing doubt that they had perceived or read the slides correctly. This is not a neat dichotomy, of course. Most persons express something of a mixture of these explanations, which is not surprising in view of the fact that some slides may tend to favor one interpretation of the difficulty and other slides the opposite interpretation.

As might be predicted, there is a substantial relationship between conformity score and tendency to self-blame; or, putting it the other way, those who remain relatively independent of the group pressure are more likely to blame the discrepancies on poor judgments by the rest of the group.

But this is by no means a perfect relationship. There are many persons who, though retrospectively expressing doubt of the correctness of the group's judgment, did in fact conform heavily while in the situation. And what is even more striking is that a substantial number of the subjects—between 25 and 30 per cent—freely admit on later questioning that there were times when they responded the way the group did *even when they thought this not the proper answer*. It seems evident, therefore, that along with various forms of cognitive rationalization of the discrepancies, there occurred a considerable amount of what might be called deliberate conforming, that is, choosing to express outward agreement with the group consensus even when believing the group to be wrong.

Another noteworthy effect was the sense of increased psychological distance induced between the person himself and the rest of the group. He felt himself to be queer or different, or felt the group to be quite unlike what he had thought. With this went an arousal of considerable anxiety in most subjects; for some, manifest anxiety was acute.

The existence of these tensions within and between the subjects became dramatically manifest when, shortly after the end of the procedure, the experimenter confessed the deception he had practiced and explained the real situation. There were obvious and audible signs of relaxation and relief, and a shift from an atmosphere of constraint to one of animated discussion.

This is an appropriate point to comment on ethics. No persons when questioned after explanation of the deception expressed feelings that they had been ethically maltreated in the experiment. The most common reaction was a positive one of having engaged in an unusual and significant experience, together with much joking about having been taken in.

Undeniably there are serious ethical issues involved in the experimental use of such deception techniques, especially inasmuch as they appear to penetrate rather deeply into the person. My view is that such deception methods ethically require that great care be taken immediately afterwards to explain the situation fully to the subject.

These remarks on ethics of the method are especially pertinent as we move from study of judgmental materials which are noncontroversial to those which are controversial. In the studies of college students and of mature women, many new critical items were introduced and subjected to the pressure. They were intended to explore more deeply the conformity tendencies in matters of opinion and attitude. And they were so chosen as to pertain to socially important and controversial issues involving civil liberties, political philosophy, crime and punishment, ethical values, and the like.

Here are two salient examples. An expression of agreement or disagreement was called for on the following statement: "Free speech being a privilege rather than a right, it is proper for a society to suspend free speech whenever it feels itself threatened." Among control subjects, only 19 per cent express agreement. But among the experimental subjects confronted with a unanimous group consensus agreeing with the statement, 58 per cent express agreement.

Another item was phrased as follows: "Which one of the following do you feel is the most important problem facing our country today?" And these five alternatives were offered:

Economic recession
Educational facilities
Subversive activities
Mental health
Crime and corruption

Among control subjects, only 12 per cent chose "Subversive activities" as the most important. But when exposed to a spurious group consensus which unanimously selected "Subversive activities" as the most important, 48 per cent of the experimental subjects expressed this same choice.

I think that no one would wish to deny that here we have evidence of the operation of powerful conformity influences in the expression of opinion on matters of critical social controversy.

REINFORCEMENT OF CONFORMITY

There is one final point upon which I should like to touch briefly. That is the question of whether there are circumstances under which the power of the group to influence the judgments of the individual may be even more greatly reinforced, and if so, how far such power may extend.

One method has been tried as part of the study of college students. With half of the subjects, a further instruction was introduced by the experimenter. They were told that in order to see how well they were doing during the procedure, the experimenter would inform the group immediately after the judgments on each slide what the correct answer was. This was to be done, of course, only for those slides for which there was a correct answer, namely, perceptual judgments, logical solutions, vocabulary, etc. No announcement would be made after slides having to do with opinions and attitudes.

The experimenter here again deceived the subjects, for the answers he announced as correct were deliberately chosen so as to agree with the false group consensus. In short, the external authority of the experimenter was later added on as reinforcement to the group consensus.

The effect of this so-called "correction" method is striking. As the series of judgments goes on, these individuals express greater and greater conformity to the group pressure on slides which are of the same character as those for which earlier in the series the false group consensus was thus reinforced by the false announcement by the experimenter.

But the more critical issue is whether this enhanced power of the group generalizes also to judgments of an entirely unrelated sort, namely, matters of opinion and attitude, rather than of fact. In other words, will the group, through having the rightness of its judgment supported by the experimenter on matters of perception, logic, and the like, thereby come to be regarded by the individual as more right, or more to be complied with, on entirely extraneous matters, such as social issues?

The answer is absolutely clear. The enhanced power of the group does *not* carry over to increase the effective influence on expression of opinions and attitudes. The subjects exposed to this "correction" method do not exhibit greater conformity to group pressure on opinions and attitudes than that found in other subjects.

This crucial finding throws some light on the nature of the psychological processes involved in the conformity situation. For it seems to imply that conformity behavior under such group pressure, rather than being sheerly an indiscriminate and irrational tendency to defer to the authority of the group, has in it important rational elements. There is something of a reasonable differentiation made by the individual in his manner of reliance upon the group. He may be led to accept the superiority of the group judgment on matters where there is an objective frame of reference against which the group can be checked. But he does not, thereby, automatically accept the authority of the group on matters of a less objective sort.

CONCLUSION

The social psychologist is concerned with the character of conformity, the personologist with conformity of character. Between them they raise many research questions: the comparative incidence of conformity tendencies in various populations; the influence of group structure and the individual's role in the group on the nature and amount of conformity behavior; the effects of reward or punishment for conforming on habits of conformity; the genesis and change of conformity behavior in the individual personality; the determinants of extreme *anti*conformity tendencies.

Contributing to such questions we have what appears to be a powerful new research technique, enabling the study of conformity behavior within a setting which effectively simulates genuine group interaction, yet preserves the essential requirements of objective measurement.

REFERENCES

Adorno, T. W., Frenkel-Brunswik, Else, Levinson, D., and Sanford, R. N. *The authoritarian personality*. New York: Harper, 1950.

Asch, S. E. *Social psychology*. New York: Prentice-Hall, 1952.

Barron, F. An ego-strength scale which predicts response to psychotherapy. *Journal of Consulting Psychology,* 1953, 17: 327–333. (a)

Barron, F. Some personality correlates of independence of judgment. *Journal of Personality,* 1953, 21: 287–297. (b)

Block, J. Personality characteristics associated with fathers' attitudes toward child-rearing. *Child Development,* 1955, 26: 41–48.

Gough, H. G. *A preliminary guide for the use and interpretation of the California Psychological Inventory.* Privately distributed by the Institute of Personality Assessment and Research, University of California, Berkeley, 1954. (Mimeo)

BIRTH ORDER, NEED ACHIEVEMENT, AND CONFORMITY *

EDWARD E. SAMPSON [1]

Although Alfred Adler (1945) suggested the importance of an individual's ordinal position in the family, until recently, very little research had been conducted using ordinal position as an independent variable. A few years ago, Schachter (1959) published a book in which he reported the interesting results of a series of studies on ordinal position, motivation, and behavior in social or experimental situations. In his work, Schachter suggested the hypothesis that first born individuals were more anxious and affiliatively dependent than later born persons. This suggests that the first born individual should be more prone to influence by

* Reprinted with permission from the American Psychological Association. In *Journal of Abnormal and Social Psychology,* 1962, Vol. 64, pp. 155–159.

[1] The author wishes to thank John R. P. French, Jr. for his invaluable contributions in the first experiment, and Ernest Harburg for his collaboration in the third experiment, which he is now preparing for eventual publication.

others; and, in fact, Schachter reports the findings of a study by Ehrlich that supports this hypothesis. Ehrlich found that first born males were less resistant in a social influence situation than later born males.

The data reported in this paper derive from a series of three experiments, two of them directly concerned with social influence, the third more directly concerned with the need for achievement (n Ach). As a routine part of each of these experiments, birth order data were obtained from each subject and analyzed in order to test the relationships between birth order and conformity in two experiments and birth order and n Ach in one experiment.

METHOD

Birth Order

Information was obtained about the individual's order of birth by a simple question on which each subject indicated whether he was the first born, second born, etc. The data were classified into two major groupings: first born versus later born. The former category consisted of first and only and first with sibs. The latter category consisted of all persons second born or later. For the analyses of this study, such factors as age distance between self and sibs or sex of nearest sibs were not controlled because of the small N.

Experimental Situations

There were two experimental situations which yielded data about conformity and birth order. The first situation, A, consisted of an audience-type influence experiment in which a hired assistant, playing the role of a debator, sought to influence the subject to adopt the position which he advocated on an attitude issue about Russia and the United States. The experiment used a 2×3 design, with a condition of negative attraction towards the debator and one of neutral attraction. Within each of these, the debator was a false-expert—that is, he based his influence on an assumed expertness which he actually did not possess; sought to control the subjects' behavior—that is, he told the subjects that he possessed the ability to completely determine their beliefs in this particular situation; or was neither—that is, the control group. The measures of conformity consisted of the direction and distance of the subjects'

change from their preinfluence to their postinfluence position.

The second experimental situation, B, consisted of a four-man group working in separate cubicles on a simple performance task. The task involved drawing circles with dots in the middle for a series of 10-second trials. During the course of the experiment, an individual assumed to be the leader of this four-man group gave instructions to the subjects to increase their performance. The leader promised rewards for conformity to his instructions to half the groups and threatened fines for nonconformtiy to the other half. The rewards and fines consisted of points given or taken away, the points being worth money. The group leader also gave each subject his evaluation of their performance on the task. Upon receiving his group leader's evaluation, each subject was asked to record his own personal evaluation on the same scale employed by the group leader. The measure of conformity in this situation consisted of the discrepancy between the subject's own personal evaluation and the group leader's evaluation of his performance. Thus, as with the conformity measure in Situation A, this involved a judgmental or cognitive conformity rather than an action conformity.

The third experimental situation, C, gave information about birth order and n Ach. It consisted of a digit-symbol task given to groups of persons premeasured on n Ach and test anxiety. The major concern in this situation was to determine differences in digit-symbol performance between persons motivated by the need to achieve as compared with persons motivated to avoid failure.

TABLE 1

THE RELATION BETWEEN BIRTH ORDER
AND THE NEED FOR ACHIEVEMENT

Total	Birth order		Total	Birth order	
	First	Later		First	Later
High n Ach	23	7	High Ach-Low TAQ	13	2
Low n Ach	15	16	Low Ach-High TAQ	6	9
	$\chi^2 = 4.05$[a],			$p = .05$ by	
	$p < .05$			Fisher's	
				exact test	
Males					
High n Ach	12	3	High Ach-Low TAQ	6	0
Low n Ach	9	7	Low Ach-High TAQ	3	3
	$\chi^2 = 1.03$[a]				
Females					
High n Ach	11	4	High Ach-Low TAQ	7	2
Low n Ach	6	9	Low Ach-High TAQ	3	6
	$\chi^2 = 2.17$[a]				

[a] Corrected for continuity.

Subjects

In Experimental Situation A, involving an attitude issue about Russia and the United States, there were 88 female subjects obtained from introductory psychology courses at the University of Michigan. In Experimental Situation B, involving four-man groups, there was a total of 116 male subjects obtained from recruits at the Coast Guard base in Oakland, California. The final set of subjects in Experimental Situation C consisted of 31 males and 30 females who were members of an undergraduate social psychology class at the University of Michigan.

Measurement of n Ach

n Ach was measured by the projective French (1958) Test of Insight.[2] Test anxiety was measured by the Mandler-Sarason test anxiety items (Mandler and Cowen, 1958). These measures were obtained only on persons in Experimental Situation C. The inclusion of the measure of test anxiety enables a further refinement to be made of n Ach and fear of failure. Subjects above the median on n Ach and below the median on test anxiety constitute one "pure" group in contrast to the subjects below the median on n Ach and above it on test anxiety. This is the type of breakdown suggested by Atkinson (1958; Atkinson and Litwin, 1960).

RESULTS [3]

Birth Order and n Ach

The analyses presented in Table 1 permit us to look at the achievement measure alone and the split involving both achievement and anxiety (Experimental Situation C). For the total sample of both men and women, there is a significant tendency for first born persons to have a higher need for achievement than later born persons. This relation is supported in the finer breakdown, employing both the measure of achievement and the measure of anxiety. Both of these relationships are significant at the .05 level. The trend of the relationship is the same for both males and females taken as separate groups, but is not

[2] Ernest Harburg coded the projective test data measuring n Ach.
[3] All statistical tests are two-tailed, as we have no firm basis for making specific directional predictions.

statistically significant ($x^2 = 1.03$ for the males; $x^2 = 2.17$ for the females). There is, however, a slight, nonsignificant indication that this relationship is stronger for females than for males.

Birth Order and Conformity

Experimental Situations A and B each involved an influence situation in which we could measure the conformity or resistance of first and later born persons. Table 2 presents the relevant data from Experimental Situation A. The statistical test is significant at the .10 level, with the direction of the relationship suggesting that first born persons have higher resistance to influence than later born persons.[4] This finding is directly opposite to that Ehrlich has reported by Schachter (1959), but his subjects were males.

Although the sample on which these conformity data were obtained is not the same as that on which the n Ach data were obtained, the groups being compared in each are female undergraduate college students at the University of Michigan, and are, thus, a relatively homogeneous sample. If we look at these results on conformity and the results on n Ach, we note that they are consistent, but only the former approaches significance. That is, in general, first born females are more resistant in a social influence situation and tend to be higher in the need for achievement than later born females.

Table 3 presents the data from Experimental Situation B on birth order and conformity for the Coast Guard recruits under conditions of reward and fine. The direction of the differences in conformity is the same within reward and fine, with first born being *more* conforming than later born. The differences were significant, however, only in the reward conditions ($p = .06$). A comparison of first and later born persons on

[4] Because Experimental Situation A employed an experimental division of groups into those having a neutral debator and those having a disliked debator, we conducted an analysis of birth order and conformity within these two major groupings. For both those having a neutral debator and those having a disliked debator, there is an indication (not statistically significant, however) that later born persons are less resistant than first born persons. This finding is consistent with the findings reported in Table 2 for the total sample.

TABLE 2

THE RELATION BETWEEN BIRTH ORDER OF FEMALES
AND RESISTANCE TO INFLUENCE
ON AN ATTITUDE ISSUE

	Birth order	
	First	Later
Low resistance to influence	18	29
High resistance to influence	24	17
	$\chi^2 = 3.60, p < .10$	

TABLE 3

THE RELATION BETWEEN BIRTH ORDER OF MALES AND
RESISTANCE TO ACCEPTANCE OF THE
GROUP LEADER'S EVALUATION[a]

	Birth order		t
	First	Later	
Reward conditions	3.62	5.67	1.86*
Fine conditions	5.07	5.88	.88

[a] The measure reported is the mean discrepancy between the group leader's evaluation of the subject's performance and the subject's own evaluation of his performance.
* Significant at .06 level.

their conformity in the six experimental conditions of the study supports the overall finding. In six out of six groups, the first born are more conforming than the later born. This finding is directly opposite to our preceding findings from Experimental Situation A, but is quite consistent with the Ehrlich findings.

DISCUSSION

We have presented a series of results which suggest that (a) first born females are more resistant to social influence than later born females and (b) first born males are less resistant to social influence than later born males. There is also a slight, but nonsignificant, indication that first born females have a higher need for achievement than later born females and that this relationship between birth order and need for achievement is stronger for the females than for the males.

Although the influence situations on which these data were obtained were different, we shall make the working assumption that there is sufficient comparability to permit us to draw certain conclusions about the important interactions between birth order, sex, and conformity.

In attempting to explain the original data relating birth order and conformity, Schachter (1959) made the assumption that the first born person who gets dethroned by later born sibs will be anxious about losing his position and losing the love of his parents, and would, thus, be oriented towards seeking attention, approval, and support from others. One could further assume that the first-and-only child—who by definition does not get dethroned by later sibs—is still involved in approval seeking behavior that has its source in the typically intense dependent relationship that parents form with an only child. The parents here may become the major source of support and approval, and anxiety over not pleasing them may become particularly intensified in the first-and-only child. Assuming this approval seeking, dependent behavior generalizes, one would expect the first born to conform more in a social influence situation than the later born. These assumptions are consistent with the Ehrlich data and with our data on males from Experimental Situation B, in which we find first born males less resistant (more conforming) to social influence than later born males.

However, we have reported another set of data—that involving the females from Experimental Situation A, which suggest that the first born female is more resistant to influence than the later born female. Thus, although the data from Experimental Situations A and B and our data and Ehrlich's are not strictly comparable, one could infer from the available data that the first born female is more independent and resistant to influence than the first born male. Accepting for the moment the validity of this inference, let us look at some possible assumptions one could make to explain it, as well as other research findings relevant to these assumptions.

One assumption relates early training in independence to the development of the need for achievement, and from this, to resistance to influence. Winterbottom (1958) reports a relationship between early training in independence and the development of need for achievement. Krebs (1958) offers further data on this point, although his correlation between independence training and n Ach was not significant. The picture becomes more complex when we look at findings relating the need for achievement with conformity. Mc-Clelland's (1953) analysis of the Asch data suggests a relation between high n Ach and independence from influence. Winterbottom reports that subjects high in n Ach less frequently asked for help in a puzzle solving situation. Krebs finds that subjects with the most intense orientation towards achievement are the most resistant to opinion change. He also finds that there is greatest conformity when achievement is low and independence training is late. Similarly, Walker and Heyns (1956 unpublished) find an inverse relation between achievement and conformity. This rather neat picture is somewhat complicated by the work of Samelson (1958) who finds that n Ach and social approach interacted with the experimental treatment, producing *higher conformity* under some conditions for persons high in the need for achievement. In support of this finding, Burdick (1955) suggests that the independent, achievement oriented person should conform in situations in which he perceives conformity as leading to achievement.

It seems fair to conclude that in general there is a positive relationship between early training in independence and the strength of need for achievement, but the apparent positive relationship between high n Ach and resistance to influence may be altered under certain conditions, as when conformity leads to achievement.

Applying these assumed relationships between early training in independence, development of the need for achievement, and resistance to influence to the interpretation of our data, we suggest that the first born female is involved in rearing later born sibs (Koch, 1955), and that this involvement gives the first born female more training in independence than the first born male. This independence training for the first born female could lead to a higher need for achievement and eventually to greater resistance in a social influence situation.

Another related assumption one could make involves the differential significance and timing of independence training for males and for females. The nature of the family situation is such that the young girl is being introduced to her adult role at an earlier age than the young boy. "Helping mother around the house" is more a part of the girl's later role than it is a part of the boy's later adult role. Here we are assuming that the first born male, although expected to assume some forms of responsibility in helping around the house, generally is not expected to be as responsible a person in these home activities as is the female, because these do not form an important part of his later adult role. His later responsibilities will lie within an occupational role in which he is still too young to be expected to form responsible behavior patterns. Some of these assumptions are supported by Koch's (1955) data in which she reports that generally girls are seen as more responsible than boys, and first born girls are rated higher in leadership (perhaps an indication of greater independence) than are first born boys. Koch, however, employed controls on sex of sibs and sib age separation, two conditions that were shown to interact significantly with birth order in effecting other variables such as leadership, ambition, etc.

We may now add to this picture another link in our chain of assumptions. Although the first born male and the first born female may be concerned over dependency and may be involved in seeking parental approval and love, the first born female initially has greater pressures than the male to develop responsibility as part of her role. She can handle both the needs to get parental approval and these pressures by the same activity: that is, by developing responsibility, she is receiving the approval of her parents. This does *not* mean that the male is not approved for exhibiting independent, responsible behavior. It does mean, however, that the parents expect greater responsibility at an earlier age from the female, apply greater pressures to the female to show it, and express greater approval when she exhibits such responsible, independent behavior. Consistent with this is Tuddenham's (1952) finding that in general girls are more approved by elders and peers than are boys.

What we are suggesting by our assumptions is that both the *significance* of the independence training and the *timing* of such training differ for the first born females as compared with first born males. Training in independence is more significant for the female and occurs at an earlier age than for the male.

Although one generally thinks of females as being more dependent than males, we are suggesting that the *first born* female is more independent and has a higher need for achievement than the *first born* male; and this independence results in greater resistance in a social influence situation on the part of the first born female as compared with the first born male. Without an analysis of birth order, the results from the work of Witkin, Lewis, Hertzman, Machover, Meissner, and Wapner (1954) which suggests that females are more field dependent than males, and the work of Crutchfield (1955) which suggests that females conform more than males, cannot be directly integrated into our own scheme. It is interesting to note, however that Crutchfield reports that with a sample of older females, he gets a whole range of conformity and resistance, with the general trend showing the females to be *more* resistant to influence than the adult male sample. It is also interesting to note that in a replication of Witkin's work (Gruen, 1955), there is no significant difference between males and females on some of the tests on which Witkin et al. originally reported a difference. Thus, the picture that females are more dependent and conforming than males is itself more complex than originally thought, as some studies, including our own, suggest that some females are more resistant than some males. It would be of interest to reanalyze the data of Crutchfield, Witkin, and Gruen, controlling the apparently important variable of birth order.

The above set of assumptions provides a source for deriving additional hypotheses which are testable in a more systematic research project. For example, one would expect (*a*) the first born female to have greater responsibility demands from her parents than the first born male, (*b*) parents to perceive early responsibility as being more important for the first born female child than for the first born male child, and (*c*) the first born female to be more resistant to social influence than the first born male. We have inferred support for this third hypothesis from our data. However, a strict test of that hypothesis would involve placing males and females into the *same* influence situation and measuring their resistance to influence.

SUMMARY

The combined results from three separate studies using three separate samples of subjects suggest the following three conclusions: first born persons have a higher need for achievement than later born persons; first born females exhibit greater resistance to influence than later born females; and first born males exhibit less resistance to influence than later born males.

These findings are taken to be consistent with a set of assumptions that the first born female is more significantly involved in independence training than the first born male. This early independence training produces a greater need for achievement and leads to greater resistance to influence for the first born females. First ordinal position for the male, on the other hand, produces greater affiliative dependency and leads to greater conformity in an influence situation.

REFERENCES

Adler, A. *Social interest: A challenge to mankind.* (Trans. by J. Linton and R. Vaughan) London: Faber & Faber, 1945.

Atkinson, J. W. (Ed.) *Motives in fantasy, action, and society.* Princeton: Van Nostrand, 1958.

Atkinson, J. W., and Litwin, G. H. Achievement motive and test anxiety conceived as motive to approach success and motive to avoid failure. *J. abnorm. soc. Psychol.,* 1960, 60: 52–63.

Burdick, H. A. The relationship of attraction, need achievement, and certainty to conformity under conditions of simulated group atmosphere. Unpublished doctoral dissertation, University of Michigan, 1955.

Crutchfield, R. S. Conformity and character. *Amer. Psychologist,* 1955, 10: 191–198.

French, E. G. Development of a measure of complex motivation. In J. W. Atkinson (Ed.), *Motives in fantasy, action, and society.* Princeton: Van Nostrand, 1958. Pp. 242–248.

Gruen, A. The relation of dancing experience and personality to perception. *Psychol. Monogr.,* 1955, 69: (14, Whole No. 399).

Koch, H. L. Some personality correlates of sex, sibling position, and sex of sibling among five- and six-year-old children. *Genet. psychol. Monogr.,* 1955, 52: 3–50.

Krebs, A. M. Two determinants of conformity: Age of independence training and achievement. *J. abnorm. soc. Psychol.,* 1958, 56: 130–131.

McClelland, D. C., Atkinson, J. W., Clark, R. A., and Lowell, E. L. *The achievement motive.* New York: Appleton-Century-Crofts, 1953.

Mandler, G., and Cowen, J. E. Test anxiety questionnaires. *J. consult. Psychol.,* 1958, 22: 228–229.

Samelson, F. The relation of achievement and affiliation motives to conforming behavior in two conditions of conflict with a majority. In J. W. Atkinson (Ed.), *Motives in fantasy, action, and society*. Princeton: Van Nostrand, 1958. Pp. 421–433.

Schachter, S. *The psychology of affiliation*. Stanford, Calif.: Stanford Univer. Press, 1959.

Tuddenham, R. D. Studies in reputation: I. Sex and grade differences in school children's evaluation of their peers. *Psychol. Monogr.*, 1952, 65: (1, Whole No. 333).

Winterbottom, M. R. The relation of need for achievement to learning experiences in independence and mastery. In J. W. Atkinson (Ed.), *Motives in fantasy, action, and society*. Princeton: Van Nostrand, 1958. Pp. 453–478.

Witkin, H. A., Lewis, Helen B., Hertzman, M., Machover, Karen, Meissner, Pearl B., and Wapner, S. *Personality through perception*. New York: Harper, 1954.

COVERT COMMUNICATION IN THE PSYCHOLOGICAL EXPERIMENT *

ROBERT ROSENTHAL [1]

Psychological laboratories and the psychological experiments conducted there are not the only scenes or means whereby we learn of human behavior. There is no doubt, however, that in our discipline as in others, the laboratory experiment is a preferred mode for the observation of nature. It is so preferred because of the greater control it gives us over the inputs to the experimental subject. Unlike the usual situation in the field or in the "real world," when we observe the behavior of the subject of a psychological experiment we

* Reprinted with permission from the American Psychological Association. In *Psychological Bulletin*, 1967, Vol. 67, pp. 356–367.

[1] The research described in this paper has been supported by research grants (G-17685, G-24826, GS-177, GS-714) from the Division of Social Sciences of the National Science Foundation. An earlier version of this paper was presented at the symposium "Ethical and Methodological Problems in Social Psychological Experiments," American Psychological Association, Chicago, September 1965.

are in a position to attribute his behavior to the antecedent conditions we have ourselves arranged.

In the paradigm psychological experiment, there is a subject whose behavior is to be observed and an experimenter whose functions include the control of inputs to the subject. (The experimenter also often functions as a recorder of the subject's output, but this function of the experimenter is not important to the present discussion. It may be assumed for present purposes that the subject's response is recorded directly by an error-free automated system.) As part of the experimenter's function of controlling the subject's inputs, he engages in a variety of intended, programmed, overt communications with the subject. Such communications include the "instructions to subjects." Although the instructions are highly programmed, they, along with aspects of the physical scene (Riecken, 1962) and the overall design of the experiment as perceived by the subject, may unintentionally communicate to the subject something of what the experimenter is after. Such unintended information transmission has been discussed most fully by Orne (1962), who referred to such sources of cues as the *demand characteristics* of the experimental procedures. To the extent that these unintended cues tend to be systematic for a given experiment, and do not depend for their operation on *differential* communication to subjects by experimenters, they are not discussed here. Instead, the focus will be on variations in the covert and unintended communications that occur in the psychological experiment. Such variations are not random and are predictable to some extent from a knowledge of various characteristics of the experimenter and the subject.

One purpose of this paper is to illustrate the fact that unintended covert communications are the norm in psychological experiments. To the extent that the experimenter communicates unintentionally and differentially with his subjects he has lost some measure of control over the inputs. Since such control is a major reason for our reliance on the experimental method, there are serious implications. Serious as these implications may be for our interpretation of the results of experiments, it should not surprise us that different experimenters engage in different covert communication with different subjects. We should, in fact, be more surprised if such covert communication did not occur. Covert communications occur routinely in all other dyadic interactions; why then, should they not occur in the dyad composed of the experimenter and his subject?

The evidence for the experimenter's covert communication with his tacitly understanding subject comes from a program of experiments on experiments (Rosenthal, 1964). One purpose of this research program is primarily methodological. By taking account of the covert communication processes in the psychological experiment, techniques may be developed which will permit the drawing of more valid substantive conclusions about those experimental inputs about whose effects on the subject's behavior we want to learn. Another purpose of this research program is less methodological and more substantive. What we learn about the covert communication between experimenter and subject may teach us something about covert communication processes in other dyadic interactions as well. Laboratories need not simply be those places where we test, in simplified form, the hypotheses derived from the "real world." Laboratories, as Mills (1962) has pointed out, are just as "real" as the rest of the world.

THE EXPERIMENTER AS COVERT COMMUNICATOR

Covert communication between experimenter and subject could be demonstrated simply by showing that different experimenters behave differently toward their subjects in their conduct of a specific experiment and that these individual differences in behavior affect the subject's response. But it seems late in the history of psychology simply to demonstrate individual differences in behavior even when the people happen to be experimenters. It seems more useful, therefore, to concentrate on those cases of covert communication in which we can predict, more or less, just how he will communicate covertly with his subjects, before the experimenter even enters the laboratory.

Experimenter's Sex

There is a good deal of evidence that the sex of the experimenter can affect the responses of the experimental subject (Rosenthal, 1966; Sarason, 1965; Stevenson, 1965). What we have not known, however, is whether the effect of the sex of the experimenter was passive or active. By "passive effect" is meant that subjects respond differently to and for male and female experimenters simply because they are male or female. By "active effect" is meant that subjects respond differently to and for male and female experimenters because male and female experimenters treat the subjects differently. The best way to determine the extent to which any effects of the experimenter are active or passive is to make observations of the experimenter as he or she conducts an experiment.

In our research program we have employed two types of observers. One type of observer has been the subject himself. In several experiments, subjects have been asked to describe the behavior of their experimenter during the experimental transaction. An advantage of such observations by the subject himself is that there is no one closer to the experimenter during the experiment than the subject, and he is in a good position to see what the experimenter does. A disadvantage of such observations by the subjects themselves is that they may be contaminated by the responses subjects made during the experiment itself. Thus, if a subject has made conforming responses during an experiment in verbal conditioning, he may describe his experimenter as a more forceful, dominant person, not because the experimenter really was, but because that would justify to the subject and to others the subject's having conformed.

Another type of observer has been employed who was not a participant in the experiment itself. Instead, graduate and undergraduate students have observed sound motion pictures made of experimenters interacting with their subjects. Neither experimenters nor subjects knew that their interaction was being observed. The films were of five different samples of experimenters and subjects involving altogether 29 experimenters (5 of whom were females) and 86 subjects (of whom 21 were males). The details of the experiments which were filmed are given elsewhere (Rosenthal, Persinger, Mulry, Vikan-Kline, and Grothe, 1964a, 1964b). It is enough to know that in all the experiments filmed the task was the same. The experimenters presented to each of their subjects a series of 10 standardized photos of faces. Each face was to be judged as to how successful or unsuccessful the person appeared to be. All experimenters were to read the same instructions to their subjects and this reading lasted about a minute, on the average.

Before reading the instructions, experimenters asked subjects for their name, age, major field, and marital status. This brief preinstructional period lasted on the average about half a minute.

Analysis of the films showed that even during this brief preinstructional period, male and female experimenters treated their subjects in a significantly different manner. Male experimenters interacting with either male or female subjects were a good deal more friendly in their interaction than were female experimenters ($r_{pb} = .47$; $p < .05$). Support for this finding comes from a different study employing the same experimental task. This time the observers of the experimenters' behavior were the subjects themselves. Suzanne Haley made the data available for this analysis. Her 86 female subjects judged their 12 male experimenters to be more friendly during the course of the experiment than their 2 female experimenters ($r_{pb} = .32$, $p < .005$). Regardless of whether we ask external observers or the subjects themselves, male experimenters are observed to behave differently than female experimenters. Such systematic differences in the treatment of subjects suggest that though experimenters may read the same instructions to their subjects, subjects contacted by male experimenters and subjects contacted by female experimenters are simply not in the same experiment. It should not surprise us, therefore, when male and female experimenters obtain different responses from their subjects. Whenever the warmth or friendliness of the experimenter can affect the subject's response, and that happens often (Gordon and Durea, 1948; Luft, 1953; Reece and Whitman, 1962), we may look also for the effect of the experimenter's sex.

The effect of the experimenter's sex is complicated by the effect of the subject's sex. Male and female subjects evoke different behavior from their experimenters. Neil Friedman (1964) made observations of the smiling behavior of the experimenters who had been filmed which were made available for this analysis. During the brief half-minute preceding the reading of the instructions, female subjects evoked more smiling behavior from their experimenters than did male subjects ($p < .05$). Only 12% of the experimenters smiled even a little at any male subject, but 70% of the experimenters smiled at least a little at their female subjects. From this evidence and from some more detailed analyses which suggest that female

subjects may be more protectively treated by their experimenters (Rosenthal, 1966), it might be suggested that in the psychological experiment, chivalry is not dead. This news may be heartening socially, and it is interesting social psychologically, but it is very disconcerting methodologically. Sex differences are well established for many kinds of behavior. But a question must now be raised as to whether sex differences which emerge from psychological experiments are due to the subject's genes, morphology, enculturation, or simply to the fact that the experimenter treated his male and female subjects differently so that, in a sense, they were not really in the same experiment at all.

Male and female experimenters remember and respond to their subject's sex. They also remember their own sex. Female experimenters show a pattern of behavior which might be called "interested modesty" when interacting with their male subjects, while male experimenters show a pattern which might more simply be called "interested" when interacting with their female subjects. An indirect assessment of this interest comes from an analysis of the time spent in performing the preparations to show the subject the next stimulus photo. The timing of these portions was done by Richard Katz (1964), who made the data available for the present analysis. When male experimenters were contacting female subjects, it took them 16% longer to prepare to present the next stimulus than when they were contacting male subjects ($p < .01$). When female experimenters were contacting male subjects, it took them 13% longer to prepare the next stimulus for presentation than when they were contacting female subjects, though this difference was not significant statistically. Though the absolute amounts of time involved were measured in a few seconds, it appeared that among male experimenters especially, there was a tendency to stretch out the interaction with the opposite-sexed subject. This same finding of a prolongation of opposite sex experimental interactions has also been reported recently by Shapiro (1966) in an experiment on verbal conditioning.

Among our own female experimenters, evidence for their "modesty" in the motor channel of communication comes from observations of the degree to which experimenters leaned toward their subjects during the experimental transaction. (These observations were made by R. Katz, who made them available for this analysis.) Male and female experimenters leaned toward their female subjects to about the same degree. However, when the subjects were males, female experimenters did not lean as close as did their male colleagues ($p < .05$).

Further evidence for this relative modesty of female experimenters when contacting male subjects comes from a different, still preliminary sort of analysis. Observations of experimenters' friendliness were now made by two different groups of observers. One group watched the films but did not hear the sound track. Another group listened to the sound track but did not see the films. From this, a measure of motor or visual friendliness and an independent measure of verbal or auditory friendliness were available. (The correlation between ratings of friendliness obtained from these independent channels was only .29.) The results of this analysis are shown in Table 1. Among male experimenters, there was a tendency, not statistically significant, for their movements to show greater friendliness than their tone of voice, and to be somewhat unfriendly toward their male subjects in the auditory channel of communica-

TABLE 1

EXPERIMENTER FRIENDLINESS IN TWO COM-
MUNICATION CHANNELS AS A FUNCTION
OF EXPERIMENTER AND SUBJECT SEX

Experi-menter sex	Subject sex	Communication channel		
		Visual	Auditory	Difference
Male	Male	3.00	−0.50	3.50
	Female	2.81	1.32	1.49
	Mean	2.90	0.41	
Female	Male	0.44	2.96	−2.52
	Female	1.75	0.25	1.50
	Mean	1.10	1.60	

tion. It was among the female experimenters that the more striking effects occurred. They were quite friendly toward their female subjects in the visual channel but not in the auditory channel. With male subjects, the situation was reversed significantly ($p < .05$). Though not friendly in the visual mode, female experimenters showed remarkable friendliness in the auditory channel when contacting male subjects.

The quantitative analysis of sound motion pic-

tures is not yet far enough developed that we can say whether such channel discrepancy in the communication of friendliness is generally characteristic of women in our culture, or only of advanced women students in psychology, or only of female experimenters conducting experiments in person perception. Perhaps it would not be farfetched to attribute the obtained channel discrepancy to an ambivalence over how friendly they ought to be. Quite apart from considerations of processes of covert communication in the psychological experiment, such findings may have some relevance for a better understanding of communication processes in general.

Other Attributes

We have seen that the sex of the experimenter, a variable shown often to affect subjects' responses, is associated with different patterns of communication in the psychological experiment, patterns which may account in part for the effects on the subjects' responses. Further, we have seen that the sex of the subject affects the experimenters' behavior, so that it is hard to tell whether different responses obtained from male and female subjects are due to the subjects' difference in sex or to the differences in the behavior of their experimenters. There are many other characteristics of experimenters and of subjects which should be analogously investigated. Some beginnings have been made and some results have been reported (Rosenthal, 1966). Here we present brief examples of differences in the experimenter's behavior toward the subject of the experiment, differences which are predictable from a knowledge of various attributes of the experimenter. The examples are chosen from only those experimenter variables which have been shown by various investigators to affect the subjects' responses.

There is considerable evidence that the anxiety of the experimenter, as measured before he enters the laboratory, can be a significant determinant of his subjects' responses (e.g., Rosenthal, 1966; Sarason, 1965). But what does the more anxious experimenter do in the experiment that leads his subjects to respond differently? We might expect more anxious experimenters to be more fidgety, and that is just what they are. Experimenters scoring higher on the Taylor (1953) Manifest Anxiety scale are observed from their films to show a greater degree of general body activity

($r = .41$, $p = .09$) and in addition, to have a less dominant tone of voice ($r = -.43$, $p = .07$). What effects just such behavior on the part of the experimenter will have on the subjects' responses depends no doubt on the particular experiment being conducted and, very likely, on various characteristics of the subject as well. In any case, we must assume that a more anxious experimenter cannot conduct just the same experiment as a less anxious experimenter. It appears that in experiments which have been conducted by just one experimenter, the probability of successful replication by another investigator is likely to depend on the similarity of his personality to that of the original investigator.

Anxiety of the experimenter is just one of the experimenter variables affecting the subjects' responses in an unintended manner. Crowne and Marlowe (1964) have shown that subjects who score high on their scale of need for approval tend to behave in such a way as to gain the approval of the experimenter. Now there is evidence that suggests that experimenters who score high on this measure also behave in such a way as to gain approval from their subjects. Analysis of the filmed interactions showed that experimenters scoring higher on the Marlowe-Crowne scale spoke to their subjects in a more enthusiastic tone of voice ($r = .39$, $p < .10$) and in a more friendly tone of voice ($r = .47$, $p < .05$). In addition, they smiled more often at their subjects ($r = .44$, $p = .07$) and slanted their bodies more toward their subjects than did experimenters lower in the need for approval ($r = .39$, $p < .10$).

THE EXPERIMENTER AS REACTIVE COMMUNICATOR

Experimenter's Experience

The kind of person the experimenter is *before* he enters his laboratory can in part determine the responses he obtains from his subjects. From the observation of experimenters' behavior during their interaction with their subjects there are some clues as to how this may come about. There is also evidence that the kind of person the experimenter becomes *after* he enters his laboratory may alter his behavior toward his subjects and lead him, therefore, to obtain different responses from his subjects.

In the folklore of psychologists who do experiments, there is the notion that sometimes, perhaps more often than we might expect, subjects contacted early in an experiment behave differently from subjects contacted later in an experiment. There may be something to this bit of lore even if we make sure that subjects seen earlier and later in an experiment come from the same population. The difference may be due to changes over the course of the experiment in the behavior of the experimenter. From what we know of performance curves we might, in fact, predict both a practice effect and a fatigue effect on the part of the experimenter. There is evidence for both. In the experiments which were filmed, experimenters became more accurate ($r = .25$, $p = .07$) and also faster ($r = .31$, $p = .03$) in the reading of their instructions to their later-contacted subjects. That seems simply to be a practice effect. In addition, experimenters became more bored or less interested over the course of the experiment as observed from their behavior in the experimental interaction ($r = .31$, $p = .02$). As we might also predict, experimenters became less tense with more experience ($r = -.26$, $p = .06$). The changes which occur in the experimenters' behavior during the course of their experiment affect their subjects' responses. In the experiments which were filmed, for example, subjects contacted by experimenters whose behavior changed as described rated the stimulus persons as less successful ($r = .31$, $p = .02$).

Subjects' Behavior

The experimenter-subject communication system is a complex of intertwining feedback loops. The experimenter's behavior, we have seen, can affect the subject's next response. But the subject's behavior can also affect the experimenter's behavior, which in turn affects the subject's behavior. In this way, the subject plays a part in the indirect determination of his own next response. The experimental details are given elsewhere (Rosenthal, 1966; Rosenthal, Kohn, Greenfield, and Carota, 1965). Briefly, in one experiment, half the experimenters had their experimental hypotheses confirmed by their first few subjects, who were actually accomplices. The remaining experimenters had their experimental hypotheses disconfirmed. This confirmation or disconfirmation of their hypotheses affected the experimenters' behavior sufficiently so that from their next subjects, who were bona fide and not accomplices, they obtained significantly different responses not only to the experimental task, but on standard tests of personality as well. These responses were predictable from a knowledge of the responses the experimenters had obtained from their earlier-contacted subjects.

There is an interesting footnote on the psychology of the accomplice which comes from the experiment alluded to. The accomplices had been trained to confirm or to disconfirm the experimenter's hypothesis by the nature of the responses they gave the experimenter. These accomplices did not, of course, know when they were confirming an experimenter's hypothesis or, indeed, that there were expectancies to be confirmed at all. In spite of the accomplices' training, they were significantly affected in the adequacy of their performance as accomplices by the expectancy the experimenter had of their performance, and by whether the experimenter's hypothesis was being confirmed or disconfirmed by the accomplices' responses. We can think of the accomplices as experimenters and the experimenters as their targets or "victims." It is interesting to know that experimental targets are not simply affected by experimental accomplices. The targets of our accomplices, like the subjects of our experimenters, are not simply passive responders. They "act back."

Experimental Scenes

One of the things that happens to the experimenter which may affect his behavior toward his subject, and thus the subject's response, is that he falls heir to a specific scene in which to conduct his experiment. Riecken (1962) has pointed out how much there is we do not know about the effects of the physical scene in which an experimental transaction takes place. We know little enough about how the scene affects the subject's behavior, we know even less about how the scene affects the experimenter's behavior.

The scene in which the experiment takes place may affect the subject's response in two ways. The effect of the scene may be direct, as when a subject judges others to be less happy when his judgments are made in an "ugly" laboratory (Mintz, 1957). The effect of the scene may also be indirect, as when the scene influences the experimenter to behave differently and this change in the experimenter's behavior leads to a change in the subject's

response. The evidence that the physical scene may affect the experimenter's behavior comes from some data collected with Suzanne Haley. We had available eight laboratory rooms which were varied as to the "professionalness," the "orderliness," and the "comfortableness" of their appearance. The 14 experimenters of this study were randomly assigned to the eight laboratories. Experimenters took the experiment significantly more seriously if they had been assigned to a laboratory which was both more disordered and less comfortable ($R = .73$, $p = .02$). These experimenters were graduate students in the natural sciences or in law school. Perhaps they felt that scientifically serious business is carried on best in the cluttered and severely furnished laboratory which fits the stereotype of the scientist's ascetic pursuit of truth.

In this same experiment, subjects described the behavior of their experimenter during the course of the experiment. Experimenters who had been assigned to more professional appearing laboratories were described by their subjects as significantly more expressive-voiced ($r = .22$, $p = .05$), more expressive-faced ($r = .32$, $p = .005$), and as more given to the use of hand gestures ($r = .32$, $p = .005$). There were no films made of these experimenters interacting with their subjects, so we cannot be sure that their subjects' descriptions were accurate. There is a chance that the experimenters did not really behave as described but that subjects in different appearing laboratories perceive their experimenters differently because of the operation of context effects. The direct observation of experimenters' behavior in different physical contexts should clear up the matter to some extent.

Principal Investigators

More and more research is carried out in teams and groups so that the chances are increasing that any one experimenter will be collecting data not for himself alone. More and more there is a chance that the data are being collected for a principal investigator to whom the experimenter is responsible. The basic data are presented elsewhere (Rosenthal, 1966), but here it can be said that the response a subject gives his experimenter may be determined in part by the kind of person the principal investigator is and by the nature of his interaction with the experimenter.

More specifically, personality differences among

principal investigators, and whether the principal investigator has praised or reproved the experimenter for his performance of his data-collecting duties, affect the subject's subsequent perception of the success of other people and also affect subjects' scores on standardized tests of personality (e.g., Taylor Manifest Anxiety scale).

In one experiment, there were 13 principal investigators and 26 experimenters. When the principal investigators collected their own data it was found that their anxiety level correlated positively with the ratings of the success of others (pictured in photographs) they obtained from their subjects ($r = .66$, $p = .03$). Each principal investigator was then to employ two research assistants. On the assumption that principal investigators select research assistants who are significantly like or significantly unlike themselves, the two research assistants were assigned to principal investigators at random. That was done so that research assistants' scores on the anxiety scale would not be correlated with their principal investigator's anxiety scores. The randomization was successful in that the principal investigators' anxiety correlated only .02 with the anxiety of their research assistants.

The research assistants then replicated the principal investigators' experiments. Remarkably, the principal investigators' level of anxiety also predicted the responses obtained by their research assistants from their new samples of subjects ($r = .40$, $p = .07$). The research assistants' own level of anxiety, while also positively correlated with their subjects' responses ($r = .24$, ns) was not as good a predictor of their own subjects' responses as was the anxiety level of their principal investigator. Something in the covert communication between the principal investigator and his research assistant altered the assistant's behavior when he subsequently contacted his subjects. We know the effect of the principal investigator was mediated in this indirect way to his assistant's subjects because the principal investigator had no contact of his own with those subjects.

Other experiments show that the data obtained by the experimenter depend in part on whether the principal investigator is male or female, whether the principal investigator makes the experimenter self-conscious about the experimental procedure, and whether the principal investigator leads the experimenter to believe he has himself performed well or poorly at the same task the experimenter is to administer to his own subjects. The evidence comes from studies in person perception, verbal conditioning, and motor skills (Rosenthal, 1966).

As we would expect, these effects of the principal investigator on his assistant's subjects are mediated by the effects on the assistant's behavior toward his subjects. Thus, experimenters who have been made more self-conscious by their principal investigator behave less courteously toward their subjects, as observed from films of their interactions with their subjects ($r = -.43$, $p = .07$). In a different experiment, involving this time a verbal conditioning task, experimenters who had been given more favorable evaluations by their principal investigator were described by their subsequently contacted subjects to be more casual ($r = .33$, $p < .01$), and more courteous ($r = .27$, $p < .05$). These same experimenters, probably by virtue of their altered behavior toward their subjects, obtained significantly more conditioning responses from their subjects. All 10 of the experimenters who had been more favorably evaluated by their principal investigator showed conditioning effects among their subjects ($p = .001$) but only 5 of the 9 experimenters who felt unfavorably evaluated obtained any conditioning ($p = 1.00$).

THE EXPERIMENTER AS HYPOTHESIS COMMUNICATOR

Ever since Pfungst's (1911) brilliant series of experiments with Clever Hans, we have known that the experimenter's hypothesis can be communicated quite unintentionally to his subject. Hans, it will be remembered, was that clever horse who could solve problems of mathematics and musical harmony with equal skill and grace, simply by tapping out the answers with his hoof. A committee of eminent experts testified that Hans, whose owner made no profit from his horse's talents, was receiving no cues from his questioners. Of course, Pfungst later showed that this was not so, that tiny head and eye movements were Hans's signals to begin and to end his tapping. When Hans was asked a question, the questioner looked at Hans's hoof, quite naturally so, for that was the way for him to determine whether Hans's answer was correct. Then, it was discovered that when Hans approached the correct number of taps, the questioner would inadvertently move his head or eyes upward—just enough that Hans could discriminate the cue, but not enough that even trained animal observers or psychologists could see it.

The "Clever Hans" phenomenon has also been demonstrated to occur in more ordinary and more recent experiments. The details are found elsewhere (Rosenthal, 1966). Briefly, the expectancy or hypothesis of the experimenter has been shown to be a significant determinant of the results of his research in studies of person perception, verbal conditioning, personality assessment, and animal learning. The basic paradigm for such studies has been to divide a sample of experimenters into two equivalent groups and to create in each an expectancy for the data they would obtain which was opposite in direction to the expectancy induced in the other group of experimenters. Thus in the animal learning studies, half the experimenters were told that their rats were from the special "Berkeley Stock" and were specially bred for maze brightness or "Skinner-box brightness." The remaining experimenters were told that their animals had been specially bred for maze or "Skinner-box dullness." The rats run by experimenters expecting good performance performed significantly better than did the rats run by experimenters expecting poor performance. This was equally true in maze learning and in operant learning experiments.

In the person perception studies, half the experimenters were told that their subjects (humans now) had been selected because they tended to see photos of people as reflecting a great deal of past success, while the remaining experimenters were told that their subjects had been selected for the perception of failure in other people's faces. Subjects were then randomly assigned to their experimenters who subtly communicated their expectancies to their subjects in such a way that subjects expected to be success perceivers became success perceivers while subjects expected to be failure perceivers became failure perceivers. We can safely say that the communication processes whereby subjects learned of experimenter expectations were subtle ones because for the last 5 years we have been analyzing films of such experiments and we have yet to find the specific cues that mediate the Clever Hans phenomenon to human subjects. This is not for want of careful observation. The films have been observed by dozens of psychologists, graduate students, and undergraduate students;

and two doctoral dissertations were based on the analysis of these films (Friedman, 1964; Katz, 1964). We all wish Pfungst were here to help us now, though there is some experimental evidence that human subjects are not using the same sort of cues that Clever Hans employed.

What we do know of the communication to subjects of the experimenter's expectancy has been learned as much from experiments as from the analysis of films. The details of the research are available elsewhere (Rosenthal, 1966). To summarize briefly, we know that both visual and auditory cues are helpful to the subjects in their tacit understanding of the experimenter's covertly communicated messages. We know that the communication of expectancies can occur before the subject makes even his first response so that verbal or nonverbal reinforcements of desired responses will not do as an explanation. There are not yet sufficient data to be sure of this point, but there are indications that experimenters learn during the course of an experiment how better to communicate their expectancies to their subjects. Subjects contacted later in the experiment, therefore, tend to give responses more biased in the direction of their experimenter's hypothesis.[2]

Such a finding makes good sense. It may be asked, if the experimenter is learning to communicate unintentionally, who is the teacher? Most likely, the subject is the teacher. It seems to be rewarding to have one's expectations confirmed (Aronson, Carlsmith, and Darley, 1963; Carlsmith and Aronson, 1963; Harvey and Clapp, 1965; Sampson and Sibley, 1965). Therefore, whenever the subject responds in accordance with the experimenter's expectancy, the likelihood is increased that the experimenter will repeat any covert communicative behavior which may have preceded the subject's confirming response. Subjects, then, may quite unintentionally shape the experimenter's unintended communicative behavior. Not only does the experimenter influence his subjects to respond in the expected manner, but his subjects may well evoke just that unintended

[2] For three experiments with a total of 54 experimenters, the combined p was less than .001, but it must be pointed out that in these studies we could not always be sure that there were no systematic subject differences which could have accounted for a greater effect of the experimenter's expectancy among later-contacted subjects.

behavior which will lead subjects to respond as expected. As the work of Hefferline (1962) suggests, such communication may not fall under what we commonly call "conscious control."

When it was mentioned earlier that the observation of the films of experimenters interacting with their subjects had not solved the modern riddle of Clever Hans, it was not meant that the films had not been worthwhile. There has already been frequent reference to things learned about experiments and experimenters from these movies. There is a good deal more. One of the most exciting findings was that it was possible to predict whether an experimenter would subsequently influence his subjects to respond in accordance with his hypothesis from the experimenter's behavior during the first half-minute of his interaction with the subject. Experimenters who were more likeable, dominant, personal, relaxed, and important-acting during these initial seconds of the interaction and less given to leg movements, later obtained data significantly biased in the direction of their hypothesis (all the correlations exceeded .30 but were less than .43 and all p's were less than .05).

Observations were made of the sound films by one group of observers, of the silent films by another group, and of the sound track alone by a third group. Interestingly, during this phase of the experiment, it did not help the observers at all to have access to the sound track. None of the observations made by the group with access only to the sound track was predictive of subsequent effects of the experimenter's expectancy. The group of observers with access only to the silent films did just as well in predicting subsequent biasing as did the observers who had access to the sound films. During this brief preinstructional phase, then, tone of voice variables seemed to be of little consequence.

Observations of the experimenter's behavior during the instruction-reading period showed much the same pattern of variables to be predictive of subsequent biasing of the subject's responses. Only now there were a great many more predictor variables which reached significance, and the correlations became larger. (The largest of the newly significant predictors of subsequent biasing was the variable of professionalism of manner, $r = .45$, $p < .005$.) The details are presented elsewhere (Rosenthal, 1966), but one interesting phenomenon must be mentioned. During the instruction-

reading period of the experiment, a number of tone of voice variables became significant predictors of the experimenter's subsequent unintended biasing effects. Very often, the direction of the predictive correlation with a variable judged from the sound track alone was in the opposite direction from the correlation with the same variable judged from the films without sound track. One example must do. Experimenters who later biased their subjects' responses more were *seen* as more honest ($r = .40$, $p < .01$) in the films but were *heard* as less honest ($r = -.30$, $p < .05$). Current work in the search for the cues mediating the Clever Hans phenomenon has turned to a closer examination of the implications for unintended communication processes of such channel discrepancy. Such an examination may have consequences for areas other than the social psychology of the psychological experiment. It is, for example, part of clinical lore, though the evidence is scanty (Ringuette and Kennedy, 1966), that such channel discrepancies may have important consequences for the development of psychopathology (Bateson, Jackson, Haley, and Weakland, 1956).

The clinical and social importance of a better understanding of discrepancies among communication channels has been recently implied in a study of the treatment of alcoholism. Tape recordings were made of nine physicians' voices as they talked about their experiences with alcoholic patients. There was no relationship between the amount of hostility judges perceived in the doctors' speech and the doctors' effectiveness in getting alcoholics to accept treatment. However, when the content was filtered out of the tape recordings, the degree of hostility found in the doctors' tone of voice alone was found to correlate significantly and negatively with his success in influencing alcoholics to accept treatment ($r = -.65$, $p = .06$; Milmoe, Rosenthal, Blane, Chafetz, and Wolf, 1967).

Beyond the Experimenter-Subject Dyad

The particular patterns of covert communication which have been described as relevant to the experimenter's communication of his expectancy to his subject are no doubt specific to the type of experiment being performed. We are in no position to speak for the generality of any of these findings across different experiments, much less for their generality in the other "real world," that one outside the laboratory. But there are some conclusions to be drawn from the data presented here and from the program of research which has investigated the effects of the experimenter's expectancy.

Perhaps the most compelling and most general conclusion is that human beings can engage in highly effective and influential unprogrammed and unintended communication with one another. If such communication is responsible in the psychological experiment for the fulfillment of the experimenter's expectancy, it might also be responsible for the fulfillment of other expectancies held by humans outside the laboratory. If rats learn better when their experimenter thinks they will, then children may learn better if their teachers think they will.

The experiment, a longitudinal one, is not yet completed, but the results for the first year can be given (Rosenthal and Jacobson, 1966). The procedure was exactly as in the experiments on the effects of the experimenter's expectancy. All the children in an elementary school were given an intelligence test which was disguised as a test which would predict academic "blooming." There were 18 classes, 3 at each of six grade levels. By the use of a table of random numbers, about 20% of the children in each class were chosen for the experimental condition. The experimental treatment consisted of telling their teachers that they had scored on the predictive achievement test such that they would show unusual intellectual development within the next academic year. At the end of the academic year the children were retested with the same test of intelligence. For the 18 classes combined, children whose teachers expected them to gain in performance showed a significantly greater gain in IQ than did the control children, ($p < .02$), though the mean relative gain in IQ was small (3.8 points). Teachers' expectancies, it turned out, made little difference in the upper grades. But at the lower levels the effects were dramatic. First graders purported to be bloomers gained 15.4 IQ points more than did the control children ($p = .002$), and the mean relative gain in one classroom was 25 points. In the second grade, the relative gain was 9.5 IQ points ($p < .02$), with one of the classes showing a mean gain of 18 points. These effects were especially surprising in view of the large gains in IQ made by the control group, which had to be surpassed by the experimental groups. Thus first graders in the control group gained 12 IQ points and second graders gained 7 IQ points, somewhat larger than might simply be ascribed to practice effects. More likely, the entire school was affected to some degree by being involved in an experiment with consequent good effects on the children's performance.[3]

Experimenters, teachers, probably psychotherapists, and probably "ordinary" people can affect the behavior of those with whom they interact by virtue of their expectations of what that behavior will be. Of course we must now try to learn how such communication takes place—how teachers communicate their expectations to their pupils. Considering the difficulties we have had in trying to answer that same question for the case of experimenters, whose inputs into the experimenter-subject interaction could be much more easily controlled and observed, we should not expect a quick or an easy solution. But there may be consolation drawn from the conviction that, at least, the problem is worth the effort.

SUMMARY

Unintended covert communication by E to S appears to be the norm in psychological experiments. Such communication can (a) affect S's response to the experimental task, and (b) be partially predicted from a knowledge of various E attributes. The nature of E's unintended messages can be affected by (a) E's experience as E, (b) the behavior of his S, (c) the physical scene in which E conducts his research, and (d) E's perception of and relationship with the principal investigator. One particular type of unintended communication is the process whereby E covertly influences S to respond in accordance with E's hypothesis or expectation. Such unintended fulfillments of interpersonal prophecies have also been found beyond the E-S dyad, as when school children show significant IQ gains simply by virtue of their teachers' expectations that such gains will be made.

[3] These findings raise the question of what proportion of the effects of contemporary educational programs are due to the content of the programs rather than to the administrators' and teachers' expectancies. The social importance of these programs, to say nothing of the financial costs, make it appear important that program evaluations employ some form of "expectancy control group" (Rosenthal, 1966).

REFERENCES

Aronson, E., Carlsmith, J. M., and Darley, J. M. The effects of expectancy on volunteering for an unpleasant experience. *Journal of Abnormal and Social Psychology,* 1963, 66: 220–224.

Bateson, G., Jackson, D. D., Haley, J., and Weakland, J. H. Toward a theory of schizophrenia. *Behavioral Science,* 1956, 1: 251–264.

Carlsmith, J. M., and Aronson, E. Some hedonic consequences of the confirmation and disconfirmation of expectancies. *Journal of Abnormal and Social Psychology,* 1963, 66: 151–156.

Crowne, D. P., and Marlowe, D. *The approval motive.* New York: Wiley, 1964.

Friedman, N. The psychological experiment as a social interaction. Unpublished doctoral dissertation, Harvard University, 1964.

Gordon, L. V., and Durea, M. A. The effect of discouragement on the revised Stanford Binet Scale, *Journal of Genetic Psychology,* 1948, 73: 201–207.

Harvey, O. J., and Clapp, W. F. Hope, expectancy, and reactions to the unexpected. *Journal of Personality and Social Psychology,* 1965, 2: 45–52.

Hefferline, R. F. Learning theory and clinical psychology—An eventual symbiosis? In A. J. Bachrach (Ed.), *Experimental foundations of clinical psychology.* New York: Basic Books, 1962. Pp. 97–138.

Katz, R. Body language: A study in unintentional communication. Unpublished doctoral dissertation, Harvard University, 1964.

Luft, J. Interaction and projection. *Journal of Projective Techniques,* 1953, 17: 489–492.

Mills, T. M. A sleeper variable in small groups research: The experimenter. *Pacific Sociological Review,* 1962, 5: 21–28.

Milmoe, S., Rosenthal, R., Blane, H. T., Chafetz, M. E., and Wolf, I. The doctor's voice: Postdictor of successful referral of alcoholic patients. *Journal of Abnormal Psychology,* 1967, 72: 78–84.

Mintz, N. On the psychology of aesthetics and architecture. Unpublished manuscript, Brandeis University, 1957.

Orne, M. T. On the social psychology of the psychological experiment: With particular reference to demand characteristics and their implications. *American Psychologist,* 1962, 17: 776–783.

Pfungst, O. *Clever Hans (the horse of Mr. von Osten): A contribution to experimental animal, and human psychology.* (Trans. by C. L. Rahn) New York: Holt, 1911. (Republished: 1965)

Reece, M. M., and Whitman, R. N. Expressive movements, warmth, and verbal reinforcements. *Journal of Abnormal and Social Psychology,* 1962, 64: 234–236.

Riecken, H. W. A program for research on experiments in social psychology. In N. F. Washburne (Ed.), *Decisions, values and groups.* Vol. 2. New York: Pergamon Press, 1962. Pp. 25–41.

Ringuette, E. L., and Kennedy, T. An experimental study of the double bind hypothesis. *Journal of Abnormal Psychology,* 1966, 71: 136–141.

Rosenthal, R. The effect of the experimenter on the results of psychological research. In B. A. Maher (Ed.), *Progress in experimental personality research.* Vol. 1. New York: Academic Press, 1964. Pp. 79–114.

Rosenthal, R. *Experimenter effects in behavioral research.* New York: Appleton-Century-Crofts, 1966.

Rosenthal, R., and Jacobson, L. Teachers' expectancies: Determinants of pupils' IQ gains. *Psychological Reports,* 1966, 19: 115–118.

Rosenthal, R., Kohn, P., Greenfield, P. M., and Carota, N. Experimenters' hypothesis-confirmation and mood as determinants of experimental results. *Perceptual and Motor Skills,* 1965, 20: 1237–1252.

Rosenthal, R., Persinger, G. W., Mulry, R. C., Vikan-Kline, L., and Grothe, M. Changes in experimental hypotheses as determinants of experimental results. *Journal of Projective Techniques and Personality Assessment,* 1964, 28: 465–469. (a)

Rosenthal, R., Persinger, G. W., Mulry, R. C., Vikan-Kline, L., and Grothe, M. Emphasis on experimental procedure, sex of subjects, and the biasing effects of experimental hypotheses. *Journal of Projective Techniques and Personality Assessment,* 1964, 28: 470–473. (b)

Sampson, E. E., and Sibley, L. B. A further examination of the confirmation or nonconfirmation of expectancies and desires. *Journal of Personality and Social Psychology,* 1965, 2: 133–137.

Sarason, I. G. The human reinforcer in verbal behavior research. In L. Krasner and L. P. Ullman (Eds.), *Research in behavior modifications: New developments and implications.* New York: Holt, Rinehart and Winston, 1965. Pp. 231–243.

Shapiro, J. L. The effects of sex, instructional set, and the problem of awareness in a verbal conditioning paradigm. Unpublished master's thesis, Northwestern University, 1966.

Stevenson, H. W. Social reinforcement of children's behavior. In L. P. Lipsitt and C. C. Spiker (Eds.), *Advances in child development and behavior.* Vol. 2. New York: Academic Press, 1965. Pp. 97–126.

Taylor, J. A. A personality scale of manifest anxiety. *Journal of Abnormal and Social Psychology,* 1953, 48: 285–290.

BEHAVIORAL STUDY OF OBEDIENCE *

Stanley Milgram [1]

Obedience is as basic an element in the structure of social life as one can point to. Some system of authority is a requirement of all communal living, and it is only the man dwelling in isolation who is not forced to respond, through defiance or submission, to the commands of others. Obedience, as a determinant of behavior, is of particular relevance to our time. It has been reliably established that from 1933–45 millions of innocent persons were systematically slaughtered on command. Gas chambers were built, death camps were guarded, daily quotas of corpses were produced with the same efficiency as the manufacture of appliances. These inhumane policies may have originated in the mind of a single person, but they could only be carried out on a massive scale if a very large number of persons obeyed orders.

Obedience is the psychological mechanism that links individual action to political purpose. It is the dispositional cement that binds men to systems of authority. Facts of recent history and observation in daily life suggest that for many persons obedience may be a deeply ingrained behavior tendency, indeed, a prepotent impulse overriding training in ethics, sympathy, and moral conduct. C. P. Snow (1961) points to its importance when he writes:

* Reprinted with permission from the American Psychological Association. In *Journal of Abnormal and Social Psychology,* 1963, Vol. 67, pp. 371–378.

[1] This research was supported by a grant (NSF G-17916) from the National Science Foundation. Exploratory studies conducted in 1960 were supported by a grant from the Higgins Fund at Yale University. The research assistance of Alan C. Elms and Jon Wayland is gratefully acknowledged.

When you think of the long and gloomy history of man, you will find more hideous crimes have been committed in the name of obedience than have ever been committed in the name of rebellion. If you doubt that, read William Shirer's "Rise and Fall of the Third Reich." The German Officer Corps were brought up in the most rigorous code of obedience . . . in the name of obedience they were party to, and assisted in, the most wicked large scale actions in the history of the world [p. 24].

While the particular form of obedience dealt with in the present study has its antecedents in these episodes, it must not be thought all obedience entails acts of aggression against others. Obedience serves numerous productive functions. Indeed, the very life of society is predicated on its existence. Obedience may be ennobling and educative and refer to acts of charity and kindness, as well as to destruction.

General Procedure

A procedure was devised which seems useful as a tool for studying obedience (Milgram, 1961). It consists of ordering a naive subject to administer electric shock to a victim. A simulated shock generator is used, with 30 clearly marked voltage levels that range from 15 to 450 volts. The instrument bears verbal designations that range from Slight Shock to Danger: Severe Shock. The responses of the victim, who is a trained confederate of the experimenter, are standardized. The orders to administer shocks are given to the naive subject in the context of a "learning experiment" ostensibly set up to study the effects of punishment on memory. As the experiment proceeds the naive subject is commanded to administer increasingly more intense shocks to the victim, even to the point of reaching the level marked Danger: Severe Shock. Internal resistances become stronger, and at a certain point the subject refuses to go on with the experiment. Behavior prior to this rupture is considered "obedience," in that the subject complies with the commands of the experimenter. The point of rupture is the act of disobedience. A quantitative value is assigned to the subject's performance based on the maximum intensity shock he is willing to administer before he refuses to participate further. Thus for any particular subject and for any particular experimental condition the degree of obedience may be specified with a numerical value. The crux of the study is to systematically vary the factors believed to alter the degree of obedience to the experimental commands.

The technique allows important variables to be manipulated at several points in the experiment. One may vary aspects of the source of command, content and form of command, instrumentalities for its execution, target object, general social setting, etc. The problem, therefore, is not one of designing increasingly more numerous experimental conditions, but of selecting those that best illuminate the *process* of obedience from the sociopsychological standpoint.

Related Studies

The inquiry bears an important relation to philosophic analyses of obedience and authority (Arendt, 1958; Friedrich, 1958; Weber, 1947), an early experimental study of obedience by Frank (1944), studies in "authoritarianism" (Adorno, Frenkel-Brunswik, Levinson, and Sanford, 1950; Rokeach, 1961), and a recent series of analytic and empirical studies in social power (Cartwright, 1959). It owes much to the long concern with *suggestion* in social psychology, both in its normal forms (e.g., Binet, 1900) and in its clinical manifestations (Charcot, 1881). But it derives, in the first instance, from direct observation of a social fact; the individual who is commanded by a legitimate authority ordinarily obeys. Obedience comes easily and often. It is a ubiquitous and indispensable feature of social life.

METHOD

Subjects

The subjects were 40 males between the ages of 20 and 50, drawn from New Haven and the surrounding communities. Subjects were obtained by a newspaper advertisement and direct mail solicitation. Those who responded to the appeal believed they were to participate in a study of memory and learning at Yale University. A wide range of occupations is represented in the sample. Typical subjects were postal clerks, high school teachers, salesmen, engineers, and laborers. Subjects ranged in educational level from one who had not finished elementary school, to those who had doctorate and other professional degrees. They were paid $4.50 for their participation in the experiment. However, subjects were told that payment was simply for

coming to the laboratory, and that the money was theirs no matter what happened after they arrived. Table 1 shows the proportion of age and occupational types assigned to the experimental condition.

Personnel and Locale

The experiment was conducted on the grounds of Yale University in the elegant interaction laboratory. (This detail is relevant to the perceived legitimacy of the experiment. In further variations,

TABLE 1

DISTRIBUTION OF AGE AND OCCUPATIONAL TYPES IN THE EXPERIMENT

Occupations	20–29 years n	30–39 years n	40–50 years n	Percentage of total (Occupations)
Workers, skilled and unskilled	4	5	6	37.5
Sales, business, and white-collar	3	6	7	40.0
Professional	1	5	3	22.5
Percentage of total (Age)	20	40	40	

Note.—Total $N = 40$.

the experiment was dissociated from the university, with consequences for performance.) The role of experimenter was played by a 31-year-old high school teacher of biology. His manner was impassive, and his appearance somewhat stern throughout the experiment. He was dressed in a gray technician's coat. The victim was played by a 47-year-old accountant, trained for the role; he was of Irish-American stock, whom most observers found mild-mannered and likable.

Procedure

One naive subject and one victim (an accomplice) performed in each experiment. A pretext had to be devised that would justify the administration of electric shock by the naive subject. This was effectively accomplished by the cover story. After a general introduction on the presumed relation between punishment and learning, subjects were told:

> But actually, we know *very little* about the effect of punishment on learning, because almost no truly scientific studies have been made of it in human beings.

For instance, we don't know how *much* punishment is best for learning—and we don't know how much difference it makes as to who is giving the punishment, whether an adult learns best from a younger or an older person than himself—or many things of that sort.

So in this study we are bringing together a number of adults of different occupations and ages. And we're asking some of them to be teachers and some of them to be learners.

We want to find out just what effect different people have on each other as teachers and learners, and also what effect *punishment* will have on learning in this situation.

Therefore, I'm going to ask one of you to be the teacher here tonight and the other one to be the learner.

Does either of you have a preference?

Subjects then drew slips of paper from a hat to determine who would be the teacher and who would be the learner in the experiment. The drawing was rigged so that the naive subject was always the teacher and the accomplice always the learner. (Both slips contained the word "Teacher.") Immediately after the drawing, the teacher and learner were taken to an adjacent room and the learner was strapped into an "electric chair" apparatus.

The experimenter explained that the straps were to prevent excessive movement while the learner was being shocked. The effect was to make it impossible for him to escape from the situation. An electrode was attached to the learner's wrist, and electrode paste was applied "to avoid blisters and burns." Subjects were told that the electrode was attached to the shock generator in the adjoining room.

In order to improve credibility the experimenter declared, in response to a question by the learner: "Although the shocks can be extremely painful, they cause no permanent tissue damage."

Learning task. The lesson administered by the subject was a paired-associate learning task. The subject read a series of word pairs to the learner, and then read the first word of the pair along with four terms. The learner was to indicate which of the four terms had originally been paired with the first word. He communicated his answer by pressing one of four switches in front of him, which in turn lit up one of four numbered quadrants in an answer-box located atop the shock generator.

Shock generator. The instrument panel consists of 30 lever switches set in a horizontal line. Each switch is clearly labeled with a voltage designation that ranges from 15 to 450 volts. There is a 15-volt increment from one switch to the next going from left to right. In addition, the following verbal designations are clearly indicated for groups of four switches going from left to right: Slight Shock, Moderate Shock, Strong Shock, Very Strong Shock, Intense Shock, Extreme Intensity Shock, Danger: Severe Shock. (Two switches after this last designation are simply marked XXX.)

Upon depressing a switch: a pilot light corresponding to each switch is illuminated in bright red; an electric buzzing is heard; an electric blue light, labeled "voltage energizer," flashes; the dial on the voltage meter swings to the right; various relay clicks are sounded.

The upper left-hand corner of the generator is labeled Shock Generator, Type ZLB, Dyson Instrument Company, Waltham, Mass. Output 15 Volts–450 Volts.

Details of the instrument were carefully handled to insure an appearance of authenticity. The panel was engraved by precision industrial engravers, and all components were of high quality. No subject in the experiment suspected that the instrument was merely a simulated shock generator.[2]

Sample shock. Each naive subject is given a sample shock on the shock generator, prior to beginning his run as teacher. This shock is always 45 volts, and is applied by pressing the third switch of the generator. The shock is applied to the wrist of the naive subject, and has its source in a 45-volt battery wired into the generator. This further convinces the subject of the authenticity of the generator.

Shock instructions. The subject is told to administer a shock to the learner each time he gives a wrong response. Moreover—and this is the key command—the subject is instructed to "move one

---

[2] A related technique, making use of a shock generator, was reported by Buss (1961) for the study of aggression in the laboratory. Despite the considerable similarity of technical detail in the experimental procedures, both investigators proceeded in ignorance of the other's work. Milgram provided plans and photographs of his shock generator, experimental procedure, and first results in a report to the National Science Foundation in January 1961. This report received only limited circulation. Buss reported his procedure 6 months later, but to a wider audience. Subsequently, technical information and reports were exchanged.

level higher on the shock generator each time the learner flashes a wrong answer." He is also instructed to announce the voltage before administering a shock. This serves to continually remind subjects of the increasing intensity of shocks administered to the learner.

Preliminary and regular run. Pretests revealed that the procedure of reading words and administering shocks requires some practice before it can be handled smoothly. Therefore, immediately preceding the regular run, the teacher is given a preliminary series of 10 words to read to the learner. There are 3 neutral words in the practice series (i.e., words that the learner answers correctly), so that shocks are administered for 7 of the words, with the maximum shock at 105 volts (moderate shock). Almost all subjects master the procedure by the time the preliminary run is over.

Subjects are then presented with a second list, and are told that the procedure is the same as for the first list; the experimenter adds, however:

When you get to the bottom of the list, repeat it over again, and continue giving shocks, until the learner has learned all the pairs correctly.

The experimenter instructs the subject to,

start from 15 volts and increase the shock level one step each time the learner gives a wrong answer.

Feedback from the victim. In all conditions the learner gives a predetermined set of responses to the word pair test, based on a schedule of approximately three wrong answers to one correct answer. In the present experimental condition no vocal response or other sign of protest is heard from the learner until Shock Level 300 is reached. When the 300-volt shock is administered, the learner pounds on the wall of the room in which he is bound to the electric chair. The pounding can be heard by the subject. From this point on, the learner's answers no longer appear on the four-way panel.

At this juncture, subjects ordinarily turn to the experimenter for guidance. The experimenter instructs the subject to treat the absence of a response as a wrong answer, and to shock the subject according to the usual schedule. He advises the subjects to allow 5–10 seconds before considering no response as a wrong answer, and to increase the shock level one step each time the

learner fails to respond correctly. The learner's pounding is repeated after the 315-volt shock is administered; afterwards he is not heard from, nor do his answers reappear on the four-way signal box.

Experimenter feedback. At various points in the experiment the subject may turn to the experimenter for advice on whether he should continue to administer shocks. Or he may indicate that he does not wish to go on. It was important to standardize the experimenter's responses to these inquiries and reactions.

If the subject indicated his unwillingness to go on, the experimenter responded with a sequence of "prods," using as many as necessary to bring the subject into line.

> Prod 1: Please continue. *or* Please go on.
> Prod 2: The experiment requires that you continue.
> Prod 3: It is absolutely essential that you continue.
> Prod 4: You have no other choice, you *must* go on.

The prods were always made in sequence: Only if Prod 1 had been unsuccessful, could Prod 2 be used. If the subject refused to obey the experimenter after Prod 4, the experiment was terminated. The experimenter's tone of voice was at all times firm, but not impolite. The sequence was begun anew on each occasion that the subject balked or showed reluctance to follow orders.

Special prods. If the subject asked if the learner was liable to suffer permanent physical injury, the experimenter said:

Although the shocks may be painful, there is no permanent tissue damage, so please go on. [Followed by Prods 2, 3, and 4 if necessary.]

If the subject said that the learner did not want to go on, the experimenter replied:

Whether the learner likes it or not, you must go on until he has learned all the word pairs correctly. So please go on. [Followed by Prods 2, 3, and 4 if necessary.]

Dependent Measures

The primary dependent measure for any subject is the maximum shock he administers before he refuses to go any further. In principle this may vary from 0 (for a subject who refuses to administer even the first shock) to 30 (for a subject who administers the highest shock on the generator). A subject who breaks off the experiment at any point prior to administering the thirtieth shock level is termed a *defiant* subject. One who complies with experimental commands fully, and proceeds to administer all shock levels commanded, is termed an *obedient* subject.

Further records. With few exceptions, experimental sessions were recorded on magnetic tape. Occasional photographs were taken through one-way mirrors. Notes were kept on any unusual behavior occurring during the course of the experiments. On occasion, additional observers were directed to write objective descriptions of the subjects' behavior. The latency and duration of shocks were measured by accurate timing devices.

Interview and dehoax. Following the experiment, subjects were interviewed; open-ended questions, projective measures, and attitude scales were employed. After the interview, procedures were undertaken to assure that the subject would leave the laboratory in a state of well being. A friendly reconciliation was arranged between the subject and the victim, and an effort was made to reduce any tensions that arose as a result of the experiment.

RESULTS

Preliminary Notions

Before giving an account of the experimental results, it is instructive to consider how persons predict others will perform when commanded to administer powerful shocks to another person. Fourteen Yale seniors, all psychology majors, were provided with a detailed description of the experimental situation. They were asked to reflect carefully on it, and to predict the behavior of 100 hypothetical subjects. More specifically, they were instructed to plot the distribution of obedience of "100 Americans of diverse occupations, and ranging in age from 20 to 50 years," who were placed in the experimental situation.

There was considerable agreement among the respondents on the expected behavior of hypothetical subjects. All respondents predicted that only an insignificant minority would go through to the end of the shock series. (The estimates ranged from 0 to 3%; i.e., the most "pessimistic" member of the class predicted that of 100 persons,

3 would continue through to the most potent shock available on the shock generator—450 volts.) The class mean was 1.2%. The question was also posed informally to colleagues of the author, and the most general feeling was that few if any subjects would ge beyond the designation Very Strong Shock.

Result of Experiment I

Subjects accept situation. With few exceptions subjects were convinced of the reality of the experimental situation, that they were administering shocks to another person, and the most potent shocks were extremely painful. In the post-experimental interview subjects were asked: "How painful to the learner were the last few shocks that you administered to him?" Subjects were instructed to indicate their answers on a printed 14-point scale ranging from "Not at all painful" to "Extremely painful." The modal response was 14 (Extremely painful) with the mean at 13.42.

Signs of extreme tension. Many subjects showed signs of nervousness in the experimental situation, and especially upon administering the more powerful shocks. In a large number of cases the degree of tension reached extremes that are rarely seen in sociopsychological laboratory studies. Subjects were observed to sweat, tremble, stutter, bite their lips, groan, and dig their fingernails into their flesh. These were characteristic rather than exceptional responses to the experiment.

One sign of tension was the regular occurrence of nervous laughing fits. Fourteen of the 40 subjects showed definite signs of nervous laughter and smiling. The laughter seemed entirely out of place, even bizarre. Full-blown, uncontrollable seizures were observed for 3 subjects. On one occasion we observed a seizure so violently convulsive that it was necessary to call a halt to the experiment. The subject, a 46-year-old encyclopedia salesman, was seriously embarrassed by his untoward and uncontrollable behavior. In the post-experimental interviews subjects took pains to point out that they were not sadistic types, and that the laughter did not mean they enjoyed shocking the victim.

Distribution of scores. It had been conjectured that persons would not, in general, agree to administer shocks beyond the level designated as Very Strong Shock. The distribution of maximum shocks for this experiment is shown in Table 2.

The obtained distribution of scores deviates radically from the prediction.

Upon command of the experimenter, each of the 40 subjects went beyond the expected breakoff point. No subject stopped prior to administering Shock Level 20. (At this level—300 volts—the victim kicks on the wall and no longer provides answers to the teacher's multiple-choice questions.)

Of the 40 subjects, 5 refused to obey the experimental commands beyond the 300-volt level. Four more subjects administered one further shock, and then refused to go on. Two broke off at the 330-volt level, and 1 each at 345, 360, and 375 volts. Thus a total of 14 subjects defied the experimenter. It is instructive to reprint their remarks at the point of defiance, as transcribed from the tape recordings:

> [0124] I think he's trying to communicate, he's knocking. . . . Well it's not fair to shock the guy . . . these are terrific volts. I don't think this is very humane. . . . Oh, I can't go on with this; no, this isn't right. It's a hell of an experiment. The guy is suffering in there. No, I don't want to go on. This is crazy. [Subject refuses to administer more shocks.]
>
> [0123] He's banging in there. I'm gonna chicken out. I'd like to continue, but I can't do that to a man. . . . I'm sorry I can't do that to a man. I'll hurt his heart. You take your check. . . . No really, I couldn't do it.

These subjects were frequently in a highly agitated and even angered state. Sometimes, verbal protest was at a minimum, and the subject simply got up from his chair in front of the shock generator, and indicated that he wished to leave the laboratory.

Of the 40 subjects, 26 obeyed the orders of the experimenter to the end, proceeding to punish the victim until they reached the most potent shock available on the shock generator. At that point, the experimenter called a halt to the session. (The maximum shock is labeled 450 volts, and is two steps beyond the designation: Danger: Severe Shock.) Although obedient subjects continued to administer shocks, they often did so under extreme stress. Some expressed reluctance to administer shocks beyond the 300-volt level, and displayed fears similar to those who defied the experimenter; yet they obeyed.

After the maximum shocks had been delivered, and the experimenter called a halt to the proceedings, many obedient subjects heaved sighs of relief, mopped their brows, rubbed their fingers over their eyes, or nervously fumbled cigarettes. Some shook their heads, apparently in regret. Some subjects had remained calm throughout the experiment, and displayed only minimal signs of tension from beginning to end.

TABLE 2
DISTRIBUTION OF BREAKOFF POINTS

Verbal designation and voltage indication	Number of subjects for whom this was maximum shock
Slight Shock	
15	0
30	0
45	0
60	0
Moderate Shock	
75	0
90	0
105	0
120	0
Strong Shock	
135	0
150	0
165	0
180	0
Very Strong Shock	
195	0
210	0
225	0
240	0
Intense Shock	
255	0
270	0
285	0
300	5
Extreme Intensity Shock	
315	4
330	2
345	1
360	1
Danger: Severe Shock	
375	1
390	0
405	0
420	0
XXX	
435	0
450	26

DISCUSSION

The experiment yielded two findings that were surprising. The first finding concerns the sheer strength of obedient tendencies manifested in this situation. Subjects have learned from childhood that it is a fundamental breach of moral conduct to hurt another person against his will. Yet, 26 subjects abandon this tenet in following the instructions of an authority who has no special powers to enforce his commands. To disobey would bring no material loss to the subject; no punishment would ensue. It is clear from the remarks and outward behavior of many participants that in punishing the victim they are often acting against their own values. Subjects often expressed deep disapproval of shocking a man in the face of his objections, and others denounced it as stupid and senseless. Yet the majority complied with the experimental commands. This outcome was surprising from two perspectives: first, from the standpoint of predictions made in the questionnaire described earlier. (Here, however, it is possible that the remoteness of the respondents from the actual situation, and the difficulty of conveying to them the concrete details of the experiment, could account for the serious underestimation of obedience.)

But the results were also unexpected to persons who observed the experiment in progress, through one-way mirrors. Observers often uttered expressions of disbelief upon seeing a subject administer more powerful shocks to the victim. These persons had a full acquaintance with the details of the situation, and yet systematically underestimated the amount of obedience that subjects would display.

The second unanticipated effect was the extraordinary tension generated by the procedures. One might suppose that a subject would simply break off or continue as his conscience dictated. Yet, this is very far from what happened. There were striking reactions of tension and emotional strain. One observer related:

> I observed a mature and initially poised businessman enter the laboratory smiling and confident. Within 20 minutes he was reduced to a twitching, stuttering wreck, who was rapidly approaching a point of nervous collapse. He constantly pulled on his earlobe, and twisted his hands. At one point he pushed his fist into his forehead and muttered: "Oh God, let's stop it." And yet he continued to respond to every word of the experimenter, and obeyed to the end.

Any understanding of the phenomenon of obedience must rest on an analysis of the particular conditions in which it occurs. The following features of the experiment go some distance in explaining the high amount of obedience observed in the situation.

1. The experiment is sponsored by and takes place on the grounds of an institution of unimpeachable reputation, Yale University. It may be reasonably presumed that the personnel are competent and reputable. The importance of this background authority is now being studied by conducting a series of experiments outside of New Haven, and without any visible ties to the university.

2. The experiment is, on the face of it, designed to attain a worthy purpose—advancement of knowledge about learning and memory. Obedience occurs not as an end in itself, but as an instrumental element in a situation that the subject construes as significant, and meaningful. He may not be able to see its full significance, but he may properly assume that the experimenter does.

3. The subject perceives that the victim has voluntarily submitted to the authority system of the experimenter. He is not (at first) an unwilling captive impressed for involuntary service. He has taken the trouble to come to the laboratory presumably to aid the experimental research. That he later becomes an involuntary subject does not alter the fact that, initially, he consented to participate without qualification. Thus he has in some degree incurred an obligation toward the experimenter.

4. The subject, too, has entered the experiment voluntarily, and perceives himself under obligation to aid the experimenter. He has made a commitment, and to disrupt the experiment is a repudiation of this initial promise of aid.

5. Certain features of the procedure strengthen the subject's sense of obligation to the experimenter. For one, he has been paid for coming to the laboratory. In part this is canceled out by the experimenter's statement that:

> Of course, as in all experiments, the money is yours simply for coming to the laboratory. From this point on, no matter what happens, the money is yours.[3]

6. From the subject's standpoint, the fact that he is the teacher and the other man the learner is

[3] Forty-three subjects, undergraduates at Yale University, were run in the experiment without payment. The results are very similar to those obtained with paid subjects.

purely a chance consequence (it is determined by drawing lots) and he, the subject, ran the same risk as the other man in being assigned the role of learner. Since the assignment of positions in the experiment was achieved by fair means, the learner is deprived of any basis of complaint on this count. (A similar situation obtains in Army units, in which—in the absence of volunteers—a particularly dangerous mission may be assigned by drawing lots, and the unlucky soldier is expected to bear his misfortune with sportsmanship.)

7. There is, at best, ambiguity with regard to the prerogatives of a psychologist and the corresponding rights of his subject. There is a vagueness of expectation concerning what a psychologist may require of his subject, and when he is overstepping acceptable limits. Moreover, the experiment occurs in a closed setting, and thus provides no opportunity for the subject to remove these ambiguities by discussion with others. There are few standards that seem directly applicable to the situation, which is a novel one for most subjects.

8. The subjects are assured that the shocks administered to the subject are "painful but not dangerous." Thus they assume that the discomfort caused the victim is momentary, while the scientific gains resulting from the experiment are enduring.

9. Through Shock Level 20 the victim continues to provide answers on the signal box. The subject may construe this as a sign that the victim is still willing to "play the game." It is only after Shock Level 20 that the victim repudiates the rules completely, refusing to answer further.

These features help to explain the high amount of obedience obtained in this experiment. Many of the arguments raised need not remain matters of speculation, but can be reduced to testable propositions to be confirmed or disproved by further experiments.[4]

The following features of the experiment concern the nature of the conflict which the subject faces.

10. The subject is placed in a position in which he must respond to the competing demands of two persons: the experimenter and the victim. The conflict must be resolved by meeting the demands of one or the other; satisfaction of the victim and the experimenter are mutually exclusive. Moreover, the resolution must take the form of a highly visible action, that of continuing to shock the victim or breaking off the experiment. Thus the subject is forced into a public conflict that does not permit any completely satisfactory solution.

11. While the demands of the experimenter carry the weight of scientific authority, the demands of the victim spring from his personal experience of pain and suffering. The two claims need not be regarded as equally pressing and legitimate. The experimenter seeks an abstract scientific datum; the victim cries out for relief from physical suffering caused by the subject's actions.

12. The experiment gives the subject little time for reflection. The conflict comes on rapidly. It is only minutes after the subject has been seated before the shock generator that the victim begins his protests. Moreover, the subject perceives that he has gone through but two-thirds of the shock levels at the time the subject's first protests are heard. Thus he understands that the conflict will have a persistent aspect to it, and may well become more intense as increasingly more powerful shocks are required. The rapidity with which the conflict descends on the subject, and his realization that it is predictably recurrent may well be sources of tension to him.

13. At a more general level, the conflict stems from the opposition of two deeply ingrained behavior dispositions: first, the disposition not to harm other people, and second, the tendency to obey those whom we perceive to be legitimate authorities.

SUMMARY

This article describes a procedure for the study of destructive obedience in the laboratory. It consists of ordering a naive S to administer increasingly more severe punishment to a victim in the context of a learning experiment. Punishment is administered by means of a shock generator with 30 graded switches ranging from Slight Shock to Danger: Severe Shock. The victim is a confederate of the E. The primary dependent variable is the maximum shock the S is willing to administer before he refuses to continue further. 26 Ss obeyed the experimental commands fully, and administered the highest shock on the geenrator. 14 Ss broke off the experiment at some point after the

[4] A series of recently completed experiments employing the obedience paradigm is reported in Milgram (1964).

victim protested and refused to provide further answers. The procedure created extreme levels of nervous tension in some Ss. Profuse sweating, trembling, and stuttering were typical expressions of this emotional disturbance. One unexpected sign of tension—yet to be explained—was the regular occurrence of nervous laughter, which in some Ss developed into uncontrollable seizures. The variety of interesting behavioral dynamics observed in the experiment, the reality of the situation for the S, and the possibility of parametric variation within the framework of the procedure, point to the fruitfulness of further study.

REFERENCES

Adorno, T., Frenkel-Brunswik, Else, Levinson, D. J., and Sanford, R. N. *The authoritarian personality.* New York: Harper, 1950.

Arendt, H. What was authority? In C. J. Friedrich (Ed.), *Authority.* Cambridge: Harvard Univer. Press, 1958. Pp. 81–112.

Binet, A. *La suggestibilité.* Paris: Schleicher, 1900.

Buss, A. H. *The psychology of aggression.* New York: Wiley, 1961.

Cartwright, S. (Ed.) *Studies in social power.* Ann Arbor: University of Michigan Institute for Social Research, 1959.

Charcot, J. M. *Oeuvres complètes.* Paris: Bureaux du Progrès Médical, 1881.

Frank, J. D. Experimental studies of personal pressure and resistance. *J. gen. Psychol.,* 1944, 30: 23–64.

Friedrich, C. J. (Ed.) *Authority.* Cambridge: Harvard Univer. Press, 1958.

Milgram, S. Dynamics of obedience. Washington: National Science Foundation, 25 January 1961. (Mimeo)

Milgram, S. Some conditions of obedience and disobedience to authority. *Hum. Relat.,* 1964, 18: 57–76.

Rokeach, M. Authority, authoritarianism, and conformity. In I. A. Berg and B. M. Bass (Eds.), *Conformity and deviation.* New York: Harper, 1961. Pp. 230–257.

Snow, C. P. Either-or. *Progressive,* 1961 (Feb.), 24.

Weber, M. *The theory of social and economic organization.* Oxford: Oxford Univer. Press, 1947.

SOME THOUGHTS ON ETHICS OF RESEARCH: AFTER READING MILGRAM'S "BEHAVIORAL STUDY OF OBEDIENCE" *

DIANA BAUMRIND

Certain problems in psychological research require the experimenter to balance his career and scientific interests against the interests of his prospective subjects. When such occasions arise the experimenter's stated objective frequently is to do the best possible job with the least possible harm to his subjects. The experimenter seldom perceives in more positive terms an indebtedness to the subject for his services, perhaps because the detachment which his functions require prevents appreciation of the subject as an individual.

Yet a debt does exist, even when the subject's reason for volunteering includes course credit or monetary gain. Often a subject participates unwillingly in order to satisfy a course requirement. These requirements are of questionable merit ethically, and do not alter the experimenter's responsibility to the subject.

Most experimental conditions do not cause the subjects pain or indignity, and are sufficiently interesting or challenging to present no problem of an ethical nature to the experimenter. But where the experimental conditions expose the subject to loss of dignity, or offer him nothing of value, then the experimenter is obliged to consider the reasons why the subject volunteered and to reward him accordingly.

The subject's public motives for volunteering include having an enjoyable or stimulating experience, acquiring knowledge, doing the experimenter a favor which may some day be reciprocated, and making a contribution to science. These motives can be taken into account rather easily by the experimenter who is willing to spend a few minutes with the subject afterwards to thank him for his participation, answer his questions, reassure him that he did well, and chat with him a bit. Most

* Reprinted with permission from the American Psychological Association. In *American Psychologist,* 1964, Vol. 19, pp. 421–423.

volunteers also have less manifest, but equally legitimate, motives. A subject may be seeking an opportunity to have contact with, be noticed by, and perhaps confide in a person with psychological training. The dependent attitude of most subjects toward the experimenter is an artifact of the experimental situation as well as an expression of some subjects' personal need systems at the time they volunteer.

The dependent, obedient attitude assumed by most subjects in the experimental setting is appropriate to that situation. The "game" is defined by the experimenter and he makes the rules. By volunteering, the subject agrees implicitly to assume a posture of trust and obedience. While the experimental conditions leave him exposed, the subject has the right to assume that his security and self-esteem will be protected.

There are other professional situations in which one member—the patient or client—expects help and protection from the other—the physician or psychologist. But the interpersonal relationship between experimenter and subject additionally has unique features which are likely to provoke initial anxiety in the subject. The laboratory is unfamiliar as a setting and the rules of behavior ambiguous compared to a clinician's office. Because of the anxiety and passivity generated by the setting, the subject is more prone to behave in an obedient, suggestible manner in the laboratory than elsewhere. Therefore, the laboratory is not the place to study degree of obedience or suggestibility, as a function of a particular experimental condition, since the base line for these phenomena as found in the laboratory is probably much higher than in most other settings. Thus experiments in which the relationship to the experimenter as an authority is used as an independent condition are imperfectly designed for the same reason that they are prone to injure the subjects involved. They disregard the special quality of trust and obedience with which the subject appropriately regards the experimenter.

Other phenomena which present ethical decisions, unlike those mentioned above, *can* be reproduced successfully in the laboratory. Failure experience, conformity to peer judgment, and isolation are among such phenomena. In these cases we can expect the experimenter to take whatever measures are necessary to prevent the subject from leaving the laboratory more humiliated, insecure, alienated, or hostile than when he arrived. To guarantee that an especially sensitive subject leaves a stressful experimental experience in the proper state sometimes requires special clinical training. But usually an attitude of compassion, respect, gratitude, and common sense will suffice, and no amount of clinical training will substitute. The subject has the right to expect that the psychologist with whom he is interacting has some concern for his welfare, and the personal attributes and professional skill to express his good will effectively.

Unfortunately, the subject is not always treated with the respect he deserves. It has become more commonplace in sociopsychological laboratory studies to manipulate, embarrass, and discomfort subjects. At times the insult to the subject's sensibilities extends to the journal reader when the results are reported. Milgram's (1963) study is a case in point. The following is Milgram's abstract of his experiment:

This article describes a procedure for the study of destructive obedience in the laboratory. It consists of ordering a naive S to administer increasingly more severe punishment to a victim in the context of a learning experiment. Punishment is administered by means of a shock generator with 30 graded switches ranging from Slight Shock to Danger: Severe Shock. The victim is a confederate of E. The primary dependent variable is the maximum shock the S is willing to administer before he refuses to continue further. 26 Ss obeyed the experimental commands fully, and administered the highest shock on the generator. 14 Ss broke off the experiment at some point after the victim protested and refused to provide further answers. The procedure created extreme levels of nervous tension in some Ss. Profuse sweating, trembling, and stuttering were typical expressions of this emotional disturbance. One unexpected sign of tension—yet to be explained—was the regular occurrence of nervous laughter, which in some Ss developed into uncontrollable seizures. The variety of interesting behavioral dynamics observed in the experiment, the reality of the situation for the S, and the possibility of parametric variation within the framework of the procedure, point to the fruitfulness of further study [p. 371].

The detached, objective manner in which Milgram reports the emotional disturbance suffered by his subject contrasts sharply with his graphic account of that disturbance. Following are two other quotes describing the effects on his subjects of the experimental conditions:

> I observed a mature and initially poised businessman enter the laboratory smiling and confident. Within 20 minutes he was reduced to a twitching, stuttering wreck, who was rapidly approaching a point of nervous collapse. He constantly pulled on his earlobe, and twisted his hands. At one point he pushed his fist into his forehead and muttered: "Oh God, let's stop it." And yet he continued to respond to every word of the experimenter, and obeyed to the end [p. 377].

> In a large number of cases the degree of tension reached extremes that are rarely seen in sociopsychological laboratory studies. Subjects were observed to sweat, tremble, stutter, bite their lips, groan, and dig their fingernails into their flesh. These were characteristic rather than exceptional responses to the experiment.
> One sign of tension was the regular occurrence of nervous laughing fits. Fourteen of the 40 subjects showed definite signs of nervous laughter and smiling. The laughter seemed entirely out of place, even bizarre. Full-blown, uncontrollable seizures were observed in 3 subjects. On one occasion we observed a seizure so violently convulsive that it was necessary to call a halt to the experiment . . . [p. 375].

Milgram does state that,

> After the interview, procedures were undertaken to assure that the subject would leave the laboratory in a state of well being. A friendly reconciliation was arranged between the subject and the victim, and an effort was made to reduce any tensions that arose as a result of the experiment [p. 374].

It would be interesting to know what sort of procedures could dissipate the type of emotional disturbance just described. In view of the effects on subjects, traumatic to a degree which Milgram himself considers nearly unprecedented in sociopsychological experiments, his casual assurance that these tensions were dissipated before the subject left the laboratory is unconvincing.

What could be the rational basis for such a posture of indifference? Perhaps Milgram supplies the answer himself when he partially explains the subject's destructive obedience as follows, "Thus they assume that the discomfort caused the victim is momentary, while the scientific gains resulting from the experiment are enduring [p. 378]." Indeed such a rationale might suffice to justify the means used to achieve his end if that end were of inestimable value to humanity or were not itself transformed by the means by which it was attained.

The behavioral psychologist is not in as good a position to objectify his faith in the significance of his work as medical colleagues at points of breakthrough. His experimental situations are not sufficiently accurate models of real-life experience; his sampling techniques are seldom of a scope which would justify the meaning with which he would like to endow his results; and these results are hard to reproduce by colleagues with opposing theoretical views. Unlike the Sabin vaccine, for example, the concrete benefit to humanity of his particular piece of work, no matter how competently handled, cannot justify the risk that real harm will be done to the subject. I am not speaking of physical discomfort, inconvenience, or experimental deception per se, but of permanent harm, however slight. I do regard the emotional disturbance described by Milgram as potentially harmful because it could easily effect an alteration in the subject's self-image or ability to trust adult authorities in the future. It is potentially harmful to a subject to commit, in the course of an experiment, acts which he himself considers unworthy, particularly when he has been entrapped into committing such acts by an individual he has reason to trust. The subject's personal responsibility for his actions is not erased because the experimenter reveals to him the means which he used to stimulate these actions. The subject realizes that he would have hurt the victim if the current were on. The realization that he also made a fool of himself by accepting the experimental set results in additional loss of self-esteem. Moreover, the subject finds it difficult to express his anger outwardly after the experimenter in a self-acceptant but friendly manner reveals the hoax.

A fairly intense corrective interpersonal experience is indicated wherein the subject admits and accepts his responsibility for his own actions, and at the same time gives vent to his hurt and anger at being fooled. Perhaps an experience as distressing as the one described by Milgram can be integrated by the subject, provided that careful thought is given to the matter. The propriety of such experimentation is still in question even if such a reparational experience were forthcoming. Without it I would expect a naive, sensitive subject to remain deeply hurt and anxious for some time, and a sophisticated, cynical subject to become even more alienated and distrustful.

In addition the experimental procedure used by Milgram does not appear suited to the objectives of the study because it does not take into account the special quality of the set which the subject has in the experimental situation. Milgram is concerned with a very important problem, namely, the social consequences of destructive obedience. He says,

> Gas chambers were built, death camps were guarded, daily quotas of corpses were produced with the same efficiency as the manufacture of appliances. These inhumane policies may have originated in the mind of a single person, but they could only be carried out on a massive scale if a very large number of persons obeyed orders [p. 371].

But the parallel between authority-subordinate relationships in Hitler's Germany and in Milgram's laboratory is unclear. In the former situation the SS man or member of the German Officer Corps, when obeying orders to slaughter, had no reason to think of his superior officer as benignly disposed towards himself or their victims. The victims were perceived as sub-human and not worthy of consideration. The subordinate officer was an agent in a great cause. He did not need to feel guilt or conflict because within his frame of reference he was acting rightly.

It is obvious from Milgram's own descriptions that most of his subjects were concerned about their victims and did trust the experimenter, and that their distressful conflict was generated in part by the consequences of these two disparate but appropriate attitudes. Their distress may have resulted from shock at what the experimenter was doing to them as well as from what they thought they were doing to their victims. In any case there is not a convincing parallel between the phenomena studied by Milgram and destructive obedience as that concept would apply to the subordinate-authority relationship demonstrated in Hitler Germany. If the experiments were conducted "outside of New Haven and without any visible ties to the university," I would still question their validity on similar although not identical grounds. In addition,

I would question the representativeness of a sample of subjects who would voluntarily participate within a noninstitutional setting.

In summary, the experimental objectives of the psychologist are seldom incompatible with the subject's ongoing state of well being, provided that the experimenter is willing to take the subject's motives and interests into consideration when planning his methods and correctives. Section 4b in *Ethical Standards of Psychologists* (APA, undated) reads in part:

> Only when a problem is significant and can be investigated in no other way, is the psychologist justified in exposing human subjects to emotional stress or other possible harm. In conducting such research, the psychologist must seriously consider the possibility of harmful aftereffects, and should be prepared to remove them as soon as permitted by the design of the experiment. Where the danger of serious aftereffects exists, research should be conducted only when the subjects or their responsible agents are fully informed of this possibility and volunteer nevertheless [p. 12].

From the subject's point of view procedures which involve loss of dignity, self-esteem, and trust in rational authority are probably most harmful in the long run and require the most thoughtfully planned reparations, if engaged in at all. The public image of psychology as a profession is highly related to our own actions, and some of these actions are changeworthy. It is important that as research psychologists we protect our ethical sensibilities rather than adapt our personal standards to include as appropriate the kind of indignities to which Milgram's subjects were exposed. I would not like to see experiments such as Milgram's proceed unless the subjects were fully informed of the dangers of serious aftereffects and his correctives were clearly shown to be effective in restoring their state of well being.

REFERENCES

American Psychological Association. Ethical Standards of Psychologists: A summary of ethical principles. Washington, D. C.: APA, undated.

Milgram, S. Behavioral study of obedience. *J. abnorm. soc. Psychol.,* 1963, 67: 371–378.

ISSUES IN THE STUDY OF OBEDIENCE: A REPLY TO BAUMRIND *

STANLEY MILGRAM

Obedience serves numerous productive functions in society. It may be ennobling and educative and entail acts of charity and kindness. Yet the problem of destructive obedience, because it is the most disturbing expression of obedience in our time, and because it is the most perplexing, merits intensive study.

In its most general terms, the problem of destructive obedience may be defined thus: If X tells Y to hurt Z, under what conditions will Y carry out the command of X, and under what conditions will he refuse? In the concrete setting of a laboratory, the question may assume this form: If an experimenter tells a subject to act against another person, under what conditions will the subject go along with the instruction, and under what conditions will he refuse to obey?

A simple procedure was devised for studying obedience (Milgram, 1963). A person comes to the laboratory, and in the context of a learning experiment, he is told to give increasingly severe electric shocks to another person. (The other person is an actor, who does not really receive any shocks.) The experimenter tells the subject to continue stepping up the shock level, even to the point of reaching the level marked "Danger: Severe Shock." The purpose of the experiment is to see how far the naive subject will proceed before he refuses to comply with the experimenter's instructions. Behavior prior to this rupture is considered "obedience" in that the subject does what the experimenter tells him to do. The point of rupture is the act of disobedience. Once the basic procedure is established, it becomes possible to vary conditions of the experiment, to learn under what circumstances obedience to authority is most probable, and under what conditions defiance is brought to the fore (Milgram, in press).

The results of the experiment (Milgram, 1963) showed, first, that it is more difficult for many

* Reprinted with permission from the American Psychological Association. In *American Psychologist,* 1964, Vol. 19, pp. 848–852.

people to defy the experimenter's authority than was generally supposed. A substantial number of subjects go through to the end of the shock board. The second finding is that the situation often places a person in considerable conflict. In the course of the experiment, subjects fidget, sweat, and sometimes break out into nervous fits of laughter. On the one hand, subjects want to aid the experimenter; and on the other hand, they do not want to shock the learner. The conflict is expressed in nervous reactions.

In a recent issue of *American Psychologist,* Diana Baumrind (1964) raised a number of questions concerning the obedience report. Baumrind expressed concern for the welfare of subjects who served in the experiment, and wondered whether adequate measures were taken to protect the participants. She also questioned the adequacy of the experimental design.

Patently, "Behavioral Study of Obedience"' did not contain all the information needed for an assessment of the experiment. But it is clearly indicated in the references and footnotes (pp. 373, 378) that this was only one of a series of reports on the experimental program, and Baumrind's article was deficient in information that could have been obtained easily. I thank the editor for allotting space in this journal to review this information, to amplify it, and to discuss some of the issues touched on by Baumrind.

At the outset, Baumrind confuses the unanticipated outcome of an experiment with its basic procedure. She writes, for example, as if the production of stress in our subjects was an intended and deliberate effect of the experimental manipulation. There are many laboratory procedures specifically designed to create stress (Lazarus, 1964), but the obedience paradigm was not one of them. The extreme tension induced in some subjects was unexpected. Before conducting the experiment, the procedures were discussed with many colleagues, and none anticipated the reactions that subsequently took place. Foreknowledge of results can never be the invariable accompaniment of an experimental probe. Understanding grows because we examine situations in which the end is unknown. An investigator unwilling to accept this degree of risk must give up the idea of scientific inquiry.

Moreover, there was every reason to expect, prior to actual experimentation, that subjects would refuse to follow the experimenter's instructions beyond the point where the victim protested; many colleagues and psychiatrists were questioned on this point, and they virtually all felt this would be the case. Indeed, to initiate an experiment in which the critical measure hangs on disobedience, one must start with a belief in certain spontaneous resources in men that enable them to overcome pressure from authority.

It is true that after a reasonable number of subjects had been exposed to the procedures, it became evident that some would go to the end of the shock board, and some would experience stress. That point, it seems to me, is the first legitimate juncture at which one could even start to wonder whether or not to abandon the study. But momentary excitement is not the same as harm. As the experiment progressed there was no indication of injurious effects in the subjects; and as the subjects themselves strongly endorsed the experiment, the judgment I made was to continue the investigation.

Is not Baumrind's criticism based as much on the unanticipated findings as on the method? The findings were that some subjcets performed in what appeared to be a shockingly immoral way. If, instead, every one of the subjects had broken off at "slight shock," or at the first sign of the learner's discomfort, the results would have been pleasant, and reassuring, and who would protest?

PROCEDURES AND BENEFITS

A most important aspect of the procedure occurred at the end of the experimental session. A careful post-experimental treatment was administered to all subjects. The exact content of the dehoax varied from condition to condition and with increasing experience on our part. At the very least all subjects were told that the victim had not received dangerous electric shocks. Each subject had a friendly reconciliation with the unharmed victim, and an extended discussion with the experimenter. The experiment was explained to the defiant subjects in a way that supported their decision to disobey the experimenter. Obedient subjects were assured of the fact that their behavior was entirely normal and that their feelings of conflict or tension were shared by other participants. Subjects were told that they would receive a comprehensive report at the conclusion of the experimental series. In some instances, additional detailed

and lengthy discussions of the experiments were also carried out with individual subjects.

When the experimental series was complete,

TABLE 1

EXCERPT FROM QUESTIONNAIRE USED IN A FOLLOW-UP STUDY OF THE OBEDIENCE RESEARCH

Now that I have read the report, and all things considered . . .	Defiant	Obedient	All
1. I am very glad to have been in the experiment	40.0%	47.8%	43.5%
2. I am glad to have been in the experiment	43.8%	35.7%	40.2%
3. I am neither sorry nor glad to have been in the experiment	15.3%	14.8%	15.1%
4. I am sorry to have been in the experiment	0.8%	0.7%	0.8%
5. I am very sorry to have been in the experiment	0.0%	1.0%	0.5%

Note—Ninety-two percent of the subjects returned the questionnaire. The characteristics of the nonrespondents were checked against the respondents. They differed from the respondents only with regard to age; younger people were overrepresented in the nonresponding group.

subjects received a written report which presented details of the experimental procedure and results. Again their own part in the experiments was treated in a dignified way and their behavior in the experiment respected. All subjects received a follow-up questionnaire regarding their participation in the research, which again allowed expression of thoughts and feelings about their behavior.

The replies to the questionnaire confirmed my impression that participants felt positively toward the experiment. In its quantitative aspect (see Table 1), 84% of the subjects stated they were glad to have been in the experiment; 15% indicated neutral feelings, and 1.3% indicated negative feelings. To be sure, such findings are to be interpreted cautiously, but they cannot be disregarded.

Further, four-fifths of the subjects felt that more experiments of this sort should be carried out, and 74% indicated that they had learned something of personal importance as a result of being in the study. The results of the interviews, questionnaire responses, and actual transcripts of the debriefing procedures will be presented more fully in a forthcoming monograph.

The debriefing and assessment procedures were carried out as a matter of course, and were not stimulated by any observation of special risk in the experimental procedure. In my judgment, at no point were subjects exposed to danger and at no point did they run the risk of injurious effects resulting from participation. If it had been otherwise, the experiment would have been terminated at once.

Baumrind states that, after he has performed in the experiment, the subject cannot justify his behavior and must bear the full brunt of his actions. By and large it does not work this way. The same mechanisms that allow the subject to perform the act, to obey rather than to defy the experimenter, transcend the moment of performance and continue to justify his behavior for him. The same viewpoint the subject takes while performing the actions is the viewpoint from which he later sees his behavior, that is, the perspective of "carrying out the task assigned by the person in authority."

Because the idea of shocking the victim is repugnant, there is a tendency among those who hear of the design to say "people will not do it." When the results are made known, this attitude is expressed as "if they do it they will not be able to live with themselves afterward." These two forms of denying the experimental findings are equally inappropriate misreadings of the facts of human social behavior. Many subjects do, indeed, obey to the end, and there is no indication of injurious effects.

The absence of injury is a minimal condition of experimentation; there can be, however, an important positive side to participation. Baumrind suggests that subjects derived no benefit from being in the obedience study, but this is false. By their statements and actions, subjects indicated that they had learned a good deal, and many felt gratified to have taken part in scientific research they considered to be of significance. A year after his participation one subject wrote:

This experiment has strengthened my belief that man should avoid harm to his fellow man even at the risk of violating authority.

Another stated:

To me, the experiment pointed up . . . the extent to which each individual should have or discover firm ground on which to base his decisions, no matter how trivial they appear to be. I think people should think more deeply about themselves and their relation to their world and to other people. If this experiment serves to jar people out of complacency, it will have served its end.

These statements are illustrative of a broad array of appreciative and insightful comments by those who participated.

The 5-page report sent to each subject on the completion of the experimental series was specifically designed to enhance the value of his experience. It laid out the broad conception of the experimental program as well as the logic of its design. It described the results of a dozen of the experiments, discussed the causes of tension, and attempted to indicate the possible significance of the experiment. Subjects responded enthusiastically; many indicated a desire to be in further experimental research. This report was sent to all subjects several years ago. The care with which it was prepared does not support Baumrind's assertion that the experimenter was indifferent to the value subjects derived from their participation.

Baumrind's fear is that participants will be alienated from psychological experiments because of the intensity of experience associated with laboratory procedures. My own observation is that subjects more commonly respond with distaste to the "empty" laboratory hour, in which cardboard procedures are employed, and the only possible feeling upon emerging from the laboratory is that one has wasted time in a patently trivial and useless exercise.

The subjects in the obedience experiment, on the whole, felt quite differently about their participation. They viewed the experience as an opportunity to learn something of importance about themselves, and more generally, about the conditions of human action.

A year after the experimental program was completed, I initiated an additional follow-up study. In this connection an impartial medical examiner, experienced in outpatient treatment, interviewed 40 experimental subjects. The examining psychiatrist focused on those subjects he felt would be most likely to have suffered consequences from participation. His aim was to identify possible injurious effects resulting from the experiment. He concluded that, although extreme stress had been experienced by several subjects,

none was found by this interviewer to show signs of having been harmed by his experience.

. . . Each subject seemed to handle his task [in the experiment] in a manner consistent with well established patterns of behavior. No evidence was found of any traumatic reactions.

Such evidence ought to be weighed before judging the experiment.

OTHER ISSUES

Baumrind's discussion is not limited to the treatment of subjects, but diffuses to a generalized rejection of the work.

Baumrind feels that obedience cannot be meaningfully studied in a laboratory setting: The reason she offers is that "The dependent, obedient attitude assumed by most subjects in the experimental setting is appropriate to that situation [p. 421]." Here, Baumrind has cited the very best reason for examining obedience in this setting, namely that it possesses "ecological validity." Here is one social context in which compliance occurs regularly. Military and job situations are also particularly meaningful settings for the study of obedience precisely because obedience is natural and appropriate to these contexts. I reject Baumrind's argument that the observed obedience does not count because it occurred where it is appropriate. That is precisely why it *does* count. A soldier's obedience is no less meaningful because it occurs in a pertinent military context. A subject's obedience is no less problematical because it occurs within a social institution called the psychological experiment.

Baumrind writes: "The game is defined by the experimenter and he makes the rules [p. 421]." It is true that for disobedience to occur the framework of the experiment must be shattered. That, indeed, is the point of the design. That is why obedience and disobedience are genuine issues for the subject. *He must really assert himself as a person against a legitimate authority.*

Further, Baumrind wants us to believe that outside the laboratory we could not find a comparably high expression of obedience. Yet, the fact that ordinary citizens are recruited to military service and, on command, perform far harsher acts against people is beyond dispute. Few of them know or are concerned with the complex policy issues underlying martial action; fewer still become conscientious objectors. Good soldiers do as they are told, and on both sides of the battle line. However, a debate on whether a higher level of obedi-

ence is represented by (*a*) killing men in the service of one's country, or (*b*) merely shocking them in the service of Yale science, is largely unprofitable. The real question is: What are the forces underlying obedient action?

Another question raised by Baumrind concerns the degree of parallel between obedience in the laboratory and in Nazi Germany. Obviously, there are enormous differences: Consider the disparity in time scale. The laboratory experiment takes an hour; the Nazi calamity unfolded in the space of a decade. There is a great deal that needs to be said on this issue, and only a few points can be touched on here.

1. In arguing this matter, Baumrind mistakes the background metaphor for the precise subject matter of investigation. The German event was cited to point up a serious problem in the human situation: the potentially destructive effect of obedience. But the best way to tackle the problem of obedience, from a scientific standpoint, is in no way restricted by "what happened exactly" in Germany. What happened exactly can *never* be duplicated in the laboratory or anywhere else. The real task is to learn more about the general problem of destructive obedience using a workable approach. Hopefully, such inquiry will stimulate insights and yield general propositions that can be applied to a wide variety of situations.

2. One may ask in a general way: How does a man behave when he is told by a legitimate authority to act against a third individual? In trying to find an answer to this question, the laboratory situation is one useful starting point—and for the very reason stated by Baumrind—namely, the experimenter does constitute a genuine authority for the subject. The fact that trust and dependence on the experimenter are maintained, despite the extraordinary harshness he displays toward the victim, is itself a remarkable phenomenon.

3. In the laboratory, through a set of rather simple manipulations, ordinary persons no longer perceived themselves as a responsible part of the causal chain leading to action against a person. The means through which responsibility is cast off, and individuals become thoughtless agents of action, is of general import. Other processes were revealed that indicate that the experiments will help us to understand why men obey. That understanding will come, of course, by examining the full account of experimental work and not alone

the brief report in which the procedure and demonstrational results were exposed.

At root, Baumrind senses that it is not proper to test obedience in this situation, because she construes it as one in which there is no reasonable alternative to obedience. In adopting this view, she has lost sight of this fact: A substantial proportion of subjects do disobey. By their example, disobedience is shown to be a genuine possibility, one that is in no sense ruled out by the general structure of the experimental situation.

Baumrind is uncomfortable with the high level of obedience obtained in the first experiment. In the condition she focused on, 65% of the subjects obeyed to the end. However, her sentiment does not take into account that within the general framework of the psychological experiment obedience varied enormously from one condition to the next. In some variations, 90% of the subjects *dis*obeyed. It seems to be *not* only the fact of an experiment, but the particular structure of elements within the experimental situation that accounts for rates of obedience and disobedience. And these elements were varied systematically in the program of research.

A concern with human dignity is based on a respect for a man's potential to act morally. Baumrind feels that the experimenter *made* the subject shock the victim. This conception is alien to my view. The experimenter tells the subject to do something. But between the command and the outcome there is a paramount force, the acting person who may obey or disobey. I started with the belief that every person who came to the laboratory was free to accept or to reject the dictates of authority. This view sustains a conception of human dignity insofar as it sees in each man a capacity for *choosing* his own behavior. And as it turned out, many subjects did, indeed, choose to reject the experimenter's commands, providing a powerful affirmation of human ideals.

Baumrind also criticizes the experiment on the grounds that "it could easily effect an alteration in the subject's . . . ability to trust adult authorities in the future [p. 422]." But I do not think she can have it both ways. On the one hand, she argues the experimental situation is so special that it has no generality; on the other hand, she states it has such generalizing potential that it will cause subjects to distrust all authority. But the experimenter is not just any authority: He is an authority who tells the subject to act harshly and inhumanely against another man. I would consider it of the highest value if participation in the experiment could, indeed, inculcate a skepticism of this kind of authority. Here, perhaps, a difference in philosophy emerges most clearly. Baumrind sees the subject as a passive creature, completely controlled by the experimenter. I started from a different viewpoint. A person who comes to the laboratory is an active, choosing adult, capable of accepting or rejecting the prescriptions for action addressed to him. Baumrind sees the effect of the experiment as undermining the subject's trust of authority. I see it as a potentially valuable experience insofar as it makes people aware of the problem of indiscriminate submission to authority.

CONCLUSION

My feeling is that viewed in the total context of values served by the experiment, approximately the right course was followed. In review, the facts are these: (*a*) At the outset, there was the problem of studying obedience by means of a simple experimental procedure. The results could not be foreseen before the experiment was carried out. (*b*) Although the experiment generated momentary stress in some subjects, this stress dissipated quickly and was not injurious. (*c*) Dehoax and follow-up procedures were carried out to insure the subjects' well-being. (*d*) These procedures were assessed through questionnaire and psychiatric studies and were found to be effective. (*e*) Additional steps were taken to enhance the value of the laboratory experience for participants, for example, submitting to each subject a careful report on the experimental program. (*f*) The subjects themselves strongly endorse the experiment, and indicate satisfaction at having participated.

If there is a moral to be learned from the obedience study, it is that every man must be responsible for his own actions. This author accepts full responsibility for the design and execution of the study. Some people may feel it should not have been done. I disagree and accept the burden of their judgment.

Baumrind's judgment, someone has said, not only represents a personal conviction, but also reflects a cleavage in American psychology between those whose primary concern is with *helping* people and those who are interested mainly in *learning* about people. I see little value in perpetuating divisive forces in psychology when there is so much to learn from every side. A schism may exist, but it does not correspond to the true ideals of the discipline. The psychologist intent on healing knows that his power to help rests on knowledge; he is aware that a scientific grasp of all aspects of life is essential for his work, and is in itself a worthy human aspiration. At the same time, the laboratory psychologist senses his work will lead to human betterment, not only because enlightenment is more dignified than ignorance, but because new knowledge is pregnant with humane consequences.

REFERENCES

Baumrind, D. Some thoughts on ethics of research: After reading Milgram's "Behavioral study of obedience." *Amer. Psychologist,* 1964, 19: 421–423.

Lazarus, R. A laboratory approach to the dynamics of psychological stress. *Amer. Psychologist,* 1964, 19: 400–411.

Milgram, S. Behavioral study of obedience. *J. abnorm. soc. Psychol.,* 1963, 67: 371–378.

Milgram, S. Some conditions of obedience and disobedience to authority. *Hum. Relat.,* 1964, 18: 57–76.

PART III

Personality Development

EACH OF US is a product of the complex development of our genetic endowment, our bodily structure, and our life experiences. How people develop is the major focus of an area called developmental psychology; why people develop observed individual differences is a major focus of the student of personality. He often attends to more than one stage of development and may seek to analyze the genesis of individuality as it manifests itself at several points in time and in various conditions.

The study of personality development, while often requiring special methodologies and ingenuity in planning research essentially, involves application of the assessment and experimental techniques which were described in Parts I and II. An example of the former would be the assessment of characteristics of a particular group of people, such as high school students, or newlyweds, or persons in retirement. An example of the latter would be a study of the reactions of people with particular experiential histories to certain special conditions, e.g., do the reactions of preschoolers, temporarily separated from their mothers, differ as a function of the type of situation in which separation occurs?

Assessment and experimental approaches to personality development might involve the study of various historical factors. One investigator might compare the personality characteristics of groups of preschoolers, elementary school children, high school students, and college students. Another investigator might prefer to compare these very same groups in terms of their reaction to experimental conditions, e.g., separation from parents or peers. Both of these approaches illustrate a cross-sectional approach to the study of development. Cross-sectional research closes in on many individuals at only one point or at a small number of closely spaced points in time.

Some investigators, however, in order to test their hypotheses, find it necessary to compare the same persons over time rather than to compare groups of people differing in age and other characteristics. Longitudinal research may require following each subject over a period of many years. The challenge of longitudinal research stems from the fact that the researcher seeks to observe and record specific aspects of the natural history of a human life as it unfolds. Unfortunately, some subjects will move without notifying the researcher; others may die. When events such as these occur they constitute impediments to the successful completion of a series of longitudinal observations. Longitudinal research is both significant and difficult. In order to plan his work, the longitudinal researcher usually selects a manageable and relatively small number of variables for intensive study over a period of time.

Whether it be cross-sectional or longitudinal in character, developmental research may pose unusual problems for the investigator. It may require inventive application of on-the-spot techniques of naturalistic observation, e.g., research dealing with behavior in the home or classroom. Observation in ongoing interpersonal situations requires that the researcher attend to a relatively large number of events, some of which may occur simultaneously. The social situations of interest to the developmental researcher are often complex and involve person-person and person-environment events not found in other kinds of empirical investigation, e.g., the nonverbal communication between mother and child. Personal characteristics change over time and the developmental psychologist who is studying these characteristics must determine if the change was due to age and maturation, cultural events relatively independent of the personal life of the individual, or other complex factors. Problems such as these provide the developmental researcher with both challenges and opportunities.

Most students of human development have restricted their interests to relatively narrow bands within the life cycle, e.g., the period of infancy, adolescence, or senescence. Relatively narrow band investigations may be either cross-sectional or longitudinal. Thus, the study of adolescence might involve comparing different groups of freshman, sophomore, junior, and senior high school students. A more complex approach might entail following a group of students throughout their entire high school careers. In Part III, we shall see a number of research methods with which we are already familiar applied to the study of both cross-sectional and longitudinal developmental problems.

The first two authors in Part III used assessment methodology in their study of developmental problems. In the first study, Eron selected a widely available stimulus in our society, television, and recorded the frequency with which third grade children attended to it. In this assessment he noted the length of viewing time, which programs the subject watched, and the extent to which violence was characteristic of the child's favorite programs. Confirming the fears of many observers of the television scene, Eron found that there was a positive correlation between the violence ratings of favorite programs and aggression as rated by peers in the classroom situation. It is important, however, to qualify this relationship: It held for boys but not for girls. Thus, as Sarason and Harmatz (Part II) showed in studying a quite different problem, the variable of sex can be an extremely important one. It probably merits explicit analysis in any study involving both male and female subjects.

Eron's research provides a stimulus for further study. How might one proceed in an effort to elucidate the relationship between television viewing and aggressive behavior? One way would be to examine those individual difference variables which might bear on this relationship, e.g., social class, age, and the level of aggression. Television viewing conceivably might show quite different relationships to aggressive behavior depending upon the socio-economic background of groups of individuals. It could have different impacts on preschool and elementary school children. It is also conceivable that highly aggressive children respond to televised aggression but that less aggressive children do not. Finally, one must confront the chicken-and-the-egg question. Does television viewing bring about aggressive behavior or do aggressive people seek out for viewing programs rich in aggressive themes? Eron's approach was correlational in nature and, therefore, could not be expected to answer this question of causality. Future research of experimental nature will be needed to reveal cause and effect relationships.

Mussen's study illustrates nicely the nature and value of long-term longitudinal research. He eliminated the variable of sex differences by confining the sample to males. Mussen was interested in the long-term consequences of masculinity of interests and the subjects were a group of men who, during their adolescent years, had been assessed as being either high or low in terms of masculine identification and interests. The technique employed in studying each adult was a lengthy interview carried out by a clinical psychologist. Subsequently, an analysis of the content of the interviews was performed. The results provide a caution to simple ideas about the continuity and meaning of personality characteristics. Other things being equal, all would agree that a strong masculine identification is desirable in boys and men. But what are the limits of and qualifiers to this generalization? It would appear from Mussen's study that interests and characteristics deemed desirable and seemingly effective at one period of life may not necessarily continue to be effective at others. It may be that we delude ourselves when we ask the simple question, what are the characteristics of the effective and well-adjusted individual? This question implies that characteristics desirable at one point in time are also desirable at others. Mussen's continuation of the Adolescent Growth Study suggests the importance of evaluating "delayed effects" of characteristics assessed at a given point in time.

The article by Kolb illustrates how an experimental approach to behavior can complement an assessment approach. This investigator identified a group of boys as being academic under-achievers. He then sought to find if a specially devised experimental procedure could modify the attitudes and behavior of under-achievers. Using both an experimental group which received a special motivational program and a comparable control group which did not, Kolb was able to show that a program directed toward the arousal of achieving motivation can lead to better academic performance among under-achievers. As he points out in his article, the success of the experimental group was not unqualified and a simple and unambiguous explanation for the success which was attained is not immediately obvious. It is clear, though, that Kolb has succeeded in demonstrating that a psychological training program aimed at increasing achievement motivation in under-achievers can bear fruit. While his experiment did not attempt to create a final form of a new education approach to under-achievement, it did represent a first step in that direction. His experiment might be described as a feasibility study to discover the practical value of increasing achievement through broadening the psychological perspectives of under-achievers. It suggests one way in which the personality researcher can contribute to the educational process through the development of learning situations tailor-made to specific needs, problems, and potentialities of students.

Kolb's research is related to a number of articles in this book. Its connection with the work of McClelland (Part I) is obvious since both are interested in developing programs of social and personal change which will influence need for achievement. It also seems related to studies of modeling (Part II) since modeling may be a potent technique in arousing need for achievement. The articles by Rosenthal (Part II) and Betz and Goldstein (Part IV) deal with the experimenter and therapist as variables and it seems likely that these could influence the response of children to motivational procedures such as those used by Kolb. Finally, the need to attend to both assessment and experimental variables, illustrated in many articles in each part of this book, seems especially applicable to Kolb's work. He found that his motivational training program was more effective with high than with low social class boys. This indicates that tailor-made motivational programs may be required for people with particular characteristics or disabilities.

Kolb's inability to obtain as much apparent change with low as with high social class boys reflects a major challenge of our times. Whereas lower social class people are most in need of retraining programs they also may be most refractory to them. The concept of work is a distinctly positive one for middle and upper class parents and their children. Quite the contrary is often the case among lower social class members. The need for intensification of psychological study of what has been called the culture of poverty seems pressing. As this study proceeds, clues as to how retraining programs can be optimally effective may present themselves. The article by Moles in Part IV provides several valuable insights into the psychology of poverty.

The contribution of Harlow is an experimental one and, like the study by Lindzey, Lykken, and Winston in Part II, suggests the relevance of animal studies to a psychology of personality. Harlow and his colleagues creatively devised a series of experiments and demonstrations dealing with aspects of child rearing and development which could not be approached in any sort of a controlled way at the human level. Using monkeys as subjects, they isolated some of the variables which contribute to the complex usually referred to as the mother-child relationship. Paraphrasing what was said above about personality characteristics, development cannot be adequately dealt with by the vague statement that the mother-child relationship is of crucial importance. It is necessary to go beyond this statement of a macro-relationship to the delineation, in as specific a manner as possible, of the many factors involved in that relationship. For example, Harlow's delineation of the mother as a source of food represents one step in unraveling the dimensions of the mother-child relationship. Existing evidence suggests that the need by the infant for food and for cuddling should be regarded, tentatively at least, as separate in order that their independent effects can be empirically assessed. In a similar fashion in Harlow's paper here, we see an attempt to delineate relationships between the nature of early affectional experiences in monkeys and later heterosexual adjustment.

The Kelly article and the Riegel, Riegel, and Meyer article, like the Mussen article, suggest some of the practical problems which beset the researcher interested in going beyond the more usual longitudinal study. These two articles are not representative in that most longitudinal research involves the study of children. For example, it will be remembered that the Mussen study, while using adults as subjects, really had its beginnings in the assessment of subjects when they were adolescents. Both Kelly and Riegel, Riegel, and Meyer followed up subjects who were initially assessed as adults. Their papers are included here because they reflect a growing interest in studying development, not just during childhood, but during the years of maturity as well.

Kelly's research presents data on the degree of consistency in the personality characteristics of the adult and on the degree of consistency in the characteristics of marital mates. His findings, together with those of Mussen, present a strong argument for the belief that despite many noteworthy consistencies in adult characteristics over the years, there are important changes in the adult personality. Kelly's and Mussen's evidence remind us that each person, at any given point in his life, is in a formative state of development. Does this evidence cast doubt on the widely-held belief in the importance of the early years of life in shaping basic and enduring patterns of personality? Unfortunately, the word "basic" may reflect value judgments rather than empirically-derived information. But the question does remain: What are the meanings and implications of observed changes in adults' behavior, attitudes, and values?

Because of the lengthening life span within the population, increased attention is being given to the process of aging. One result of this attention is a growing awareness of the significance of late-maturing behavior. Riegel, Riegel, and Meyer, in planning their work, considered the possibility that there might be discriminable psychological correlates of longevity. They were also interested in obtaining data relevant to the oft-assumed decline in the older adult's intellect. Their work shows the utility of psychological factors in predicting the occurrence of death and also in analyzing some of the methodological problems confronting the student of development interested in following up groups of old persons.

The concluding paper in Part III reminds us of a fact which is often ignored or forgotten. It is that most research on development tends to be individual-oriented, be the research cross-sectional or longitudinal in character. The subjects in developmental studies have typically been individuals rather than social groups. Handel's paper, while in no way denying the importance of studying the individual, strongly emphasizes the points that the individual cannot be meaningfully regarded as an isolated entity and that he must be regarded as a component of several interacting systems, of which the family is probably the most important.

Handel makes a strong case for increased emphasis on the family as an object of investigation. As many crucial processes occur primarily within the structure of the family, there is much support for his position. For example, the process of modeling, which was described in Part II within the context of the psychological laboratory, is probably most potent within the family. The child's observations of parental behavior, together with reinforcement contingencies within the family, help shape his personal identification and the roles which he takes on in social relationships. Perhaps the most dramatic support comes from the field of family psychotherapy. Clinical workers seem to be increasingly convinced that to understand and change deviant behavior, the concept of the patient must be expanded from the individual to significant social groups which influence him and the family is often the group which exerts the most pervasive influence.

Study of the family, as Handel suggests, can occur on a number of levels. One to which developmentally-oriented personality researchers can contribute involves concepts and methods of assessment. Assessment methods can be of considerable value in describing patterns of personality within families and longitudinal application of these methods can shed light on the nature of family change over the years.

The developmental process is a highly complex one. Its components include intellectual, emotional, biological, and social variables. The study of personality development requires inquiry into these components. As these components are identified, it will be possible to investigate the bearing they may have on behavioral differences both among individuals at any given point in time and over time for a given individual.

RELATIONSHIP OF
TV VIEWING HABITS
AND AGGRESSIVE BEHAVIOR
IN CHILDREN *

LEONARD D. ERON [1]

Since the advent of television, popular writers and journalists have linked increased rates of crime and delinquency to the increased production of TV sets, much as, in the past, the same effects have been ascribed to radio, movies, dime novels, and comic books. Television executives have stoutly maintained at the same time that, "there is no direct relationship between action or the physical contact that occurs in television and activity of children who are viewing—except in deviant cases, of course" (Aubrey, 1962). However, little convincing research evidence has been amassed either to substantiate or refute the assertion that TV is the cause of an increase in delinquency or is in any way related to overt behavior in real life. An extensive, well designed survey study carried out in England (Himmelweit, Oppenheim, and Vance, 1958) provided no conclusive answer. This study found no more aggressive or delinquent behaviors among children who viewed TV than among their control group who did not watch TV at all. However, these authors, on the basis of their study of the television habits of over 5,000 youngsters in England, did state that they felt the important question was not how long a child watches television but rather what he sees. Schramm, Lyle, and Parker (1961) in a study of American children came to a like conclusion and Newton

Minow, Chairman of the Federal Communications Commission, has made similar statements about the quality of TV programing, especially for children.[2] Although in the laboratory it has been possible to demonstrate that exposure of children to aggressive behavior portrayed in a film increases the probability of aggressive responses to an immediately subsequent frustration (Bandura, Ross, and Ross, 1963); evidence as to the long-term effect of TV programing on real-life behavior has not been forthcoming.

It has been possible, in a larger investigation of the psychosocial antecedents of aggressive behavior in children (Eron, Laulicht, Walder, Farber, and Spiegel, 1961), to accumulate data which indicate that there is a relationship between such TV habits and aggressive behavior in real life.

METHOD

Subjects and Procedure

Two groups of subjects were included. The first consisted of 367 boys and 322 girls who were in the third grade in a semirural county of New York's Hudson Valley in the spring of 1960. They comprised all children whose mothers had been interviewed in a study of aggressive behavior of all third graders in the county (875). Also included were 277 boys and 245 girls whose fathers had been interviewed in this same study. There is a large degree of overlap between the two samples and thus separate analyses were done for mother and father.

The measures of aggressive behavior and TV viewing were obtained independently of each other. The former was a peer rating measure. (Guess Who?) in which each child rated every other child in his classroom on 10 items having to do with specific aggressive behaviors. A description of the scale and a detailed account of its derivation, scoring, reliability, and validity are contained in a monograph by Walder, Abelson, Eron, Banta, and Laulicht (1961) and in an article by Banta and Walder (1961). Information about TV habits was taken from three questions in a 286-item interview administered individually in the respondent's home. This interview is an extension and refinement of the one described in an

* Reprinted with permission from the American Psychological Association. In *Journal of Abnormal and Social Psychology*, 1963, Vol. 67, pp. 193–196.

[1] The data on which this article is based derive from a larger study, "The Psychosocial Development of Aggressive Behavior," which has been generously supported by Grant M1726 from the National Institute of Mental Health, United States Public Health Service, and the Columbia County Tuberculosis and Health Association, Incorporated, New York. Thanks are due also to the IBM Watson Scientific Computing Laboratory at Columbia University for making computer time available without charge and to the elementary schools in Columbia County for their continued cooperation in this study.

[2] Address to the Radio and Television Executives Society, New York, September 22, 1961.

article by Eron, Banta, Walder, and Laulicht (1961). The specific questions were:

> How often does [Name] watch TV during the week?
> How often does [Name] watch TV during the weekend?
> What are [Name's] three favorite TV programs?

Two scores were obtained: total number of hours spent in viewing TV; and amount of violence in programs watched. Independent estimates by fathers and mothers of hours watched correlated .54 with each other. While information from father thus cannot be substituted for information from mother and vice versa, this is a sufficiently high relationship to indicate that there is some degree of validity in the reports of viewing hours noted by these independent observers and they were not answering randomly. To obtain the violence score, all TV programs mentioned by the respondents were categorized as to whether or not they emphasized antisocial aggression. No classification was permitted on the basis of the title alone. The raters had to be familiar with the content of the programs mentioned before assigning a rating. This was not difficult since the majority of inhabitants of this area can receive only one channel, and at most three, and the raters were familiar with the programs mentioned. Indication that the raters were not influenced by the program titles, but responded only to the content, is seen in the classification of some westerns as violent and some as nonviolent, of some mysteries as violent and some as nonviolent. For example, the *Lone Ranger* and *Perry Mason* were classified as nonviolent

while *Have Gun-Will Travel* and *77 Sunset Strip* were classified as violent.

As one check on the validity of the information itself, i.e., whether the parents were actually giving us the children's three favorite programs or just making it up, we compared the programs mentioned independently by the fathers and mothers for those 509 children both of whose parents were interviewed. Average percentage agreement in naming the child's three favorite programs was 63 which, although again not permitting substitution of father information for mother information, is surprisingly high, considering the number of choices possible. Further evidence of the validity of the violence rating (as well as of the number of hours watched) is seen in the similarity of results whether the mother or father is the informant, which is discussed in the Results section below. Agreement between two independent raters in the categorization of all programs mentioned was 94%.[3] With the remaining 6%, discussion between the raters resolved the differences. On the basis of these ratings each subject was then assigned a score indicating extent of violence observed in TV viewing: 1, no violent programs mentioned; 2, one violent program mentioned; 3, two violent programs mentioned; 4, three violent programs mentioned. For the first measure a threefold classification of hours watched —0–4, 5–9, 10 and over— was used. Since these two variables, hours watched and extent of violence, are not completely independent, two simple randomized analyses of variance (Lindquist, 1953)

[3] Thanks are due Irene Quinn and Anne Yaeger for their aid in making these ratings.

TABLE 1

ANALYSIS OF VARIANCE RELATING TV HABITS OF BOYS AS REPORTED BY PARENTS TO AGGRESSION
AS RATED BY PEERS

Informant	TV variable	Source	df	MS	F
Mothers	Violence rating	Treatments	3	980.07	
		Within groups	363	233.54	4.196**
Fathers	Violence rating	Treatments	3	550.59	
		Within groups	273	198.22	2.925*
Mothers	Hours watched	Treatments	2	731.57	
		Within groups	364	236.96	3.087*
Fathers	Hours watched	Treatments	2	19.95	
		Within groups	274	203.38	<1.00

$*p < .05.$
$**p < .01.$

were then done with aggression score as the dependent variable and, in one case, hours watched and, in the other case, violence ratings of programs as the independent variables. These analyses were done separately for boys and girls, mothers and fathers.

RESULTS AND DISCUSSION

The results of the analyses of variance are summarized in Table 1. There is a strong positive relationship between the violence rating of favorite programs, whether reported by mothers or fathers, and aggression of boys as rated by their peers in the classroom. There is also a significant negative relationship between amount of time spent in viewing TV as reported by mothers and aggression of boys. Although the results for fathers of boys are in the same direction for number of hours watched, they are not significant. There were no significant relationships when TV habits of girls were reported either by mothers or fathers. The magnitude and direction of the differences for boys can be seen in Tables 2 and 3. As the amount of violence increases, the aggression rate of the boys also increases; however, as total amount of time watched increases, aggression scores decrease.

Aside from the fact that definite relationships are thus established between TV viewing habits and aggressive behavior in real life, these findings are interesting for a number of other reasons important in child rearing research.

1. They substantiate the assertions of Himmelweit et al. (1958), Schramm et al. (1961), and Minow (see Footnote 2) that the relationship of behavior to the quality of programing is of a different order than is relationship of behavior to the sheer amount of time spent in watching TV. In general, boys who watch TV more are not as aggressive as boys who watch it less. Is this because they are by temperament less active; is it because they discharge their aggressive impulses in this fantasylike way and thus do not have to act them out in real life; or is it because their time is taken up in watching TV

TABLE 2
MEAN AGGRESSION SCORES ACCORDING TO VIOLENCE RATING OF TV PROGRAMS WATCHED

Informant	1	2	3	4
Mother	14.44	14.97	18.32	28.54
Father	12.44	14.23	18.92	20.67

TABLE 3
MEAN AGGRESSION SCORES ACCORDING TO NUMBER OF HOURS WATCHED

Informant	Hours		
	0–4	5–9	10+
Mother	24.26	16.48	15.25
Father	16.00	14.17	14.75

and they have less opportunity to act out aggression? On the other hand, boys who watch more violence on TV are more likely to be aggressive than boys who watch less violence. Is this because aggressive boys prefer violent programs; or is aggressive drive increased by such viewing; or are the subjects modeling their behavior after that of the characters on the TV programs? This survey study of real-life behavior cannot furnish definitive answers as to cause and effect relationships by itself. It can only demonstrate that a relationship exists. However, buttressed by manipulative laboratory studies, such as that of Bandura et al. (1963), we can speculate with some confidence that TV viewing does affect real-life behavior, and that the modeling variable is a crucial one. The drainage hypothesis, as an explanation for the lowered aggression of children who watch TV for longer hours, is unlikely in light of the results of other manipulative studies which show a direct relationship between aggression expressed in fantasy and overt behavior (Buss, 1961).

2. This study contributes further evidence that mothers and fathers are not equally good observers in all areas of child behavior. A previous article demonstrated areas in which fathers gave us better information than mothers (Eron, Banta, Walder, and Laulicht, 1961). However, for the present purposes, it seems, fathers do not have as good information as mothers. They very likely do not know about the child's daytime TV behavior and thus cannot give accurate details of total time watched. However, they are usually home in the evening hours and perhaps watch TV along with their children and thus are familiar at least with programs viewed then. Also their children are likely to talk to them about what they see on TV but not give them accurate reports of just how much time is spent in front of the TV. Mother, however, is on hand and can observe for herself; thus her estimates are more relevant. At any rate,

when mother and father agree as to what they tell us about their children, we can be more certain we are approximating the truth, especially when the observations of each relate in the same way to an independent criterion.

3. A final observation is the difference in results obtained with boys and girls. This is another indication that it is impossible to generalize from boys to girls in research on socialization, especially as far as the variable of aggression is concerned. This was pointed out by Sears, Whiting, Nowlis, and Sears (1953) a decade ago and is not due merely to the fact that boys score higher on all kinds of measures of aggression than do girls which has been a monotonous finding for even more years (Levin and Wardwell, 1962).

SUMMARY

Information about TV habits, (a) length of time watched and (b) extent of violence in favorite programs, was obtained from 689 mothers and 522 fathers in individual interviews having to do with the psychosocial antecedents of aggressive behavior in their children. This information was related to ratings of aggressive behavior of 3rd-grade children made by their peers. It was found that there was a significant positive relationship between the violence ratings of favorite programs as reported by both mothers and fathers and aggressive behavior of boys as rated in school. Also there was a significant negative relation between total time watched by boys as reported by mothers and aggressive behavior. The results for fathers' reports in this latter case were in the same direction, although not significant. No consistent relationships were noted between girls' TV habits as reported by either mother or father and aggression as rated in school by the peers.

REFERENCES

Aubrey, J. T. Testimony before Federal Communications Commission. N. Y. Times, January 26, 1962.

Bandura, A., Ross, Dorothea, and Ross, Shelia A. Imitation of film-mediated aggressive models. J. abnorm. soc. Psychol., 1963, 66: 3–11.

Banta, T. J., and Walder, L. O. Discriminant validity of a peer-rating measure. Psychol. Rep., 1961, 9: 573–582.

Buss, A. H. The psychology of aggression. New York: Wiley, 1961.

Eron, L. D., Banta, T. J., Walder, L. O., and Laulicht, J. H. Comparison of data obtained from mothers and fathers on childbearing practices and their relation to child aggression. Child Develpm., 1961, 32: 457–472.

Eron, L. D., Laulicht, J. H., Walder, L. O., Farber, I. E., and Spiegel, J. P. Application of role and learning theories to the study of the development of aggression in children. Psychol. Rep., 1961, 9: 291–334. (Monogr. Suppl. No. 2–V9)

Himmelweit, Hilde T., Oppenheim, A. N., and Vance, Pamela. Television and the child: An empirical study of the effect of television on the young. New York: Oxford Univer. Press, 1958.

Levin, H., and Wardwell, Elinor. The research uses of doll play. Psychol. Bull., 1962, 59: 27–56.

Lindquist, E. F. Design and analysis of experiments in psychology and education. Boston: Houghton Mifflin, 1953.

Schramm, W. A., Lyle, J., and Parker, E. B. Television in the lives of our children. Stanford: Stanford Univer. Press, 1961.

Sears, R. R., Whiting, J. W. M., Nowlis, V., and Sears, Pauline S. Some child rearing antecedents of aggression and dependency in young children. Genet. Psychol. Monogr., 1953, 47: 135–234.

Walder, L. O., Abelson, R. P., Eron, L. D., Banta, T. J., and Laulicht, J. H. Development of a peer-rating measure of aggression. Psychol. Rep., 1961, 9: 497–556. (Monogr. Suppl. No. 4–V9)

LONG-TERM CONSEQUENTS OF MASCULINITY OF INTERESTS IN ADOLESCENCE *

PAUL H. MUSSEN [1]

Among the presumed consequents—and specific manifestations—of substantial parental identification, adequate sex typing of behavior, and strong

* Reprinted with permission from the American Psychological Association. In Journal of Consulting Psychology, 1962, Vol. 26, pp. 435–440.

[1] This study was supported in part by the National Institute of Mental Health, United States Public Health Service, under Research Grant M-3217. The author gratefully acknowledges the cooperation of the late Harold E. Jones, Director of the Institute of Human Development, University of California, Berkeley, in making these data available for this research.

conscience development in children have been the most frequent foci of research (e.g., Levin and Sears, 1956; Mussen, 1961; Mussen and Distler, 1959; Sears, Maccoby, and Levin, 1957). Yet, according to both clinicians and theoreticians, such identifications also have a broader and long-lasting result, namely, the development of basic and durable characteristics of personal adequacy and emotional stability.

The relationship between strength of parental identification and personal adjustment has been examined in a few systematic studies in which indices of identification have been correlated with measures of *contemporaneous* (usually childhood or adolescent) adjustment (Cava and Rausch, 1952; Gray, 1959; Mussen, 1961; Payne and Mussen, 1956; Sopchak, 1952). These studies generally show that, as hypothesized, strong parental identification is accompanied by high levels of personal and social adjustment, but they provide no evidence on the possible long-term or enduring consequents. The latter can be adequately investigated only by means of longitudinal studies.

The late Harold E. Jones' longitudinal Adolescent Growth Study (Jones, 1938, 1939a, 1939b, 1940) supplied data that were used in an earlier study comparing the adolescent and adult personality structures of two groups of males, who, during late adolescence, manifested different degrees of masculinity of interests (as evaluated by the Strong Vocational Interest Blank) (Mussen, 1961). During their senior year of high school, the subjects filled out an "adjustment inventory" and were rated by a staff of professional observers and by peers on a large number of personality characteristics. Fourteen years later, when they were in their early thirties, many of the subjects completed the California Psychological Inventory and the Edwards Personal Preference Schedule.

The results indicated that, as had been predicted, a high degree of masculine identification during adolescence is generally associated with concurrent emotional security. Thus, compared with boys with relatively feminine interests, the highly masculine subjects gave more evidence of positive self-conceptions and self-confidence in their TAT stories and scored higher in overall adjustment on the adjustment inventory. Moreover, they were rated by staff observers as more carefree, more contented, more relaxed, more exuberant, happier, calmer, and smoother in social functioning than those with less masculine interests.

Peers considered the highly masculine boys to be less restless than the other group, i.e., they appeared to manifest fewer overt signs of conflict and tension.

Analysis of the data from adult personality tests administered to the subjects yielded equivocal results and failed to confirm any hypothesized relationship between masculinity of interests during adolescence and good adult adjustment. Thus, while there was evidence that highly masculine boys became adults with greater than average ego control and with typically masculine attitudes and beliefs, they appeared to be relatively lacking in dominance, capacity for status, and self-acceptance (as measured by the CPI) and were relatively high in needs for abasement (EPPS). "On the basis of these . . . findings, these men might be described as poorly adjusted and inadequate individuals, strikingly changed from what they had been during adolescence" (Mussen, 1961, p. 20).

It should be noted, however, that several of the differentiating scales of the adult tests are highly correlated with "emotional-expressive" characteristics, such as sociability and gregariousness, in which highly masculine subjects had been rated low during adolescence. Hence, it is possible to interpret some of the relatively low scores of the highly masculine subjects on the CPI scales of dominance and capacity for status as evidence of the continuity of adolescent personality traits and social orientations rather than of poor personal adjustment.

On the other hand, it is at least equally tenable to assume that the adult test scores are, in fact, valid measures of the personal characteristics they purport to measure. In this case, the test results may be interpreted to mean that many subjects experienced radical shifts in personality structure after adolescence. It is quite possible, for example, that some of the social and personal characteristics of the adolescents low in masculinity—especially their sociability, friendliness, and outgoingness—fostered more satisfactory interpersonal relationships and greater social success in adulthood than they did during adolescence. As a result, boys having relatively feminine adolescent interests may have increased in self-confidence, self-acceptance, and social poise and ascendance as they became adults. In contrast, the apparently highly adequate adjustment of the more masculine boys may have actually deteriorated after adolescence, presumably because they may have failed to develop certain social skills and orientations that are pre-requisite to good adult social and personal adjust-ment.

The present investigation was designed to ex-plore further the long-range consequents of high and low masculine identification during adoles-cence, and if possible, to clarify the equivocal findings of the earlier study. The evaluations of adult personality were based on intensive inter-views with some of the subjects about 20 years after masculinity of interests had been assessed, i.e., when they were in their late thirties.

METHOD

Between 1958 and 1960, over 100 subjects of the Adolescent Growth Study were intensively in-terviewed. Among these were 26 of the 39 male subjects of the original study of the correlates of masculinity of adolescent interests (Mussen, 1961). These 26—14 of them with highly masculine inter-ests during adolescence and 12 of them with relatively feminine interests—were the subjects of the present study. The two groups did not differ significantly from each other in either intelligence or social class status.

The interviews, which lasted from 2 to 6 hours, covered a broad range of topics, including adoles-cent memories, vocational and marital adjustment, and child rearing practices. After completion of each interview, the interviewer, a highly trained clinical psychologist, wrote a detailed report on the session(s). In addition, he made a total of 86 impressionistic ratings of the subject's status in the following major categories: self-expressiveness, so-ciability and social prestige, poise, emotional ten-sions, drives, cognitive attributes, and a series of "manifest traits" (e.g., sexual and work adjust-ment, introspection, self-sufficiency). A seven-point scale was used for each characteristic, a rating of 7 indicating a very high degree of the characteristic, a rating of 1, its opposite extreme. Since the ratings were impressionistic—based on the subject's general reactions to the interview and his manner of discussing topics, as well as on the content of his responses—it was impossible to ob-tain interrater reliability coefficients. It should be noted, however, that there could be no systematic biases in the ratings for, prior to the interviews, the interviewers had no knowledge of the inter-viewees' developmental histories, scores on the various psychological tests, or ratings made during the subjects' adolescence.

Thirty-one of the rated variables, listed in Table 1, were considered to be directly relevant to the assessment of adult general adjustment and mas-culinity of personality and interests. The ratings assigned to the two groups of subjects on these variables constituted the basic data of this study.

RESULTS AND DISCUSSION

Each of the 31 distributions of the ratings, based on all 26 subjects, was dichotomized at the median or as close to this point as possible and ratings above the dichotomization point were considered high. Table 1 gives the number of subjects high and low in masculinity of adolescent interests, who, as adults, were rated high in the 31 variables. Fisher's (1938) test of exact probability was ap-plied to each distribution of high and low ratings in order to determine whether or not high ratings occurred significantly more frequently in one group than in the other. The probability values obtained are listed in the final column of the table.

The two groups were significantly, or nearly significantly, differentiated in 8 of the 31 vari-ables. Compared with the number of differentiat-ing adolescent personality characteristics (Mussen, 1961), the number of significant differences be-tween the adult groups was relatively small. Clearly, then, degree of masculinity of adolescent interests is more highly correlated with (i.e., has more pervasive effects on) adolescent personality structure than it is with adult adjustment status. Nevertheless, closer examination of the *kinds* of differences between the two adult groups may help to delineate the enduring consequents of ap-propriate and inappropriate sex typing of interests during adolescence.

Several aspects of the personalities of the sub-jects of the two groups appeared to be constant over the 20-year period. For example, during adolescence, boys with relatively feminine interest patterns were considered, by trained observers and by peers, to be more dependent, but more sociable and socially active—i.e., they manifested more characteristics of the "emotional-expressive" or feminine role (Parsons, 1955)—than their peers with more masculine interests (Mussen, 1961). In adulthood, as Table 1 indicates, the former seemed to show similar characteristics. Thus, the inter-viewers felt that these subjects were less self-

TABLE 1

NUMBER OF SUBJECTS IN TWO GROUPS RATED HIGH IN PERSONALITY CHARACTERISTICS

Rating dimension	Highs with high scores ($N = 14$)	Lows with high scores ($N = 12$)	p
Spontaneity	6	7	ns
Extroversion	6	5	ns
Masculinity of behavior	8	5	ns
Sociability (versus detachment)	5	9	.05
Pleasantness	11	7	ns
Enjoyment of social activities	10	7	ns
Submissiveness (versus self-assertiveness)	6	3	ns
Social initiative	4	5	ns
Social leadership	5	10	<.01
Unihibitedness (versus timidity)	6	5	ns
Social assuredness	6	8	.13
Matter-of-factness	7	6	ns
Unaffectedness	8	6	ns
Lack of concern about making a good impression	9	6	ns
Relaxedness	8	5	ns
Cheerfulness	8	7	ns
Carefreedom	3	4	ns
Constancy of mood	7	5	ns
Objectivity, logicality	4	6	ns
Work adjustment	5	6	ns
Sexual adjustment	10	3	.03
Satisfaction from relation to wife	6	5	ns
Security feelings	7	7	ns
Introspectiveness	5	10	.02
Self-sufficiency	8	4	.10
Maturity of ego identity	7	6	ns
Insightfulness (into own motives)	6	6	ns
Openness of handling anxiety and conflicts	7	7	ns
Overcontrol of needs and impulses	6	6	ns
Adaptability to stress or trauma	10	6	.15
Self-acceptance (versus distortion of personal qualities)	4	7	.11

sufficient (more dependent) but more sociable (more interested in others) and more self-assured socially (less self-conscious), and more likely to be social leaders.

In contrast, during adolescence, boys with more masculine interests were seen as less socially oriented but more independent, i.e., having more so-called instrumental characteristics (Mussen, 1961; Parsons, 1955). The present data show that, as adults, they continued to be relatively more self-sufficient (independent) and less socially oriented (more detached). In addition, they appeared to be relatively nonintrospective, another characteristic consistent with the "instrumental," active functions related to the external world. From these data, it may be concluded that the "instrumental"

and "emotional-expressive" characteristics associated, respectively, with masculine and feminine sex typing of interests during adolescence tend to be relatively stable over the period of two decades.

One other relevant finding, not summarized in the table, indicates that the two groups differed markedly in masculinity of their actual adult occupations. Two psychologists [2] rated all the occupations represented in the group on a three-point scale: 1. Primarily masculine, 2. Appropriate for either sex, or 3. Primarily feminine. Fifteen of the originally highly masculine subjects, but only six of the low masculinity group, were in occupations

[2] I am indebted to Joseph Heller and the late Judy Chang for their participation in this aspect of the study.

assigned average ratings of 1 or 1.5. The exact probability of obtaining this set of cell frequencies (or all other possible, more extreme sets), calculated by Fisher's (1938) method, was $p = < .01$. Clearly, masculinity of adult occupation is strongly related to masculinity of vocational interests during adolescence. In view of the general validity of the Strong Vocational Interest Blank as a predictor of future occupation (Strong, 1943), this is hardly a surprising finding. Nevertheless, if it is assumed that working at a traditionally masculine occupation is a reflection of masculinity of interests (and perhaps of instrumental characteristics), the finding may be interpreted as additional evidence that certain aspects of interest patterns (and of personality structure correlated with such interests) are consistent over a period of two decades.

There was much less congruence between the adolescent and adult statuses of the two groups in certain other characteristics, however. Thus, it will be recalled that during adolescence, the highly masculine boys, compared to the more feminine ones, gave more evidence of positive self-concepts and high levels of self-confidence and they were regarded by others as more carefree, happier, and smoother in social functioning. On the basis of the present data it may be inferred that these subjects no longer manifested such characteristics when they became adults. Their characteristic detachment and self-consciousness in social situations during adulthood, mentioned above, may be indicative of basic feelings of inadequacy, which hardly seems consistent with being self-confident, carefree, and contented.

The interviewers' ratings showed that they were also lacking in leadership qualities, a finding that supports the CPI data indicating that this group was less dominant and had relatively little "capacity for status" (Mussen, 1961). Moreover, according to the CPI, the originally highly masculine subjects became less self-accepting adults and, on the EPPS, they showed greater needs for abasement than the others. These findings are further substantiated by the interviewers' ratings of this group as less "self-accepting of both positive and negative qualities" than the other group and more likely to "distort [their] personal qualities" (see Table 1). In addition, in distorting, they tended more often to emphasize negative, self-derogatory characteristics. Thus, of the 10 highly masculine subjects who were judged likely to "distort personal characteristics," 8 were described as "giving negative qualities," while, among subjects in the other group, only 3 emphasized negative characteristics. The probability of obtaining this distribution of positive and negative distortions, calculated directly, is $p = .05$. The feelings of self-depreciation and inadequacy among the originally highly masculine subjects indicate that the self-evaluations of this group have changed markedly by adulthood. During adolescence, these subjects gave more evidence of positive self-concepts and self-confidence than their peers with relatively feminine interests (Mussen, 1961).

The self-perceptions of the latter group, in contrast, improved markedly as they grew older. As adolescents, the subjects of the relatively feminine interest group manifested relatively strong feelings of insecurity and inadequacy, but as adults, they were, according to test and interview data, relatively more self-accepting, and more self-confident, and, in addition, they had more leadership characteristics and greater "capacity for status" (Mussen, 1961).

In spite of the general evidence that the subjects of the originally highly masculine group felt inadequate and insecure during adulthood, they possessed a few attributes that might be interpreted as manifestations of emotional stability. There were some tendencies for interviewers to rate more of these subjects as well adjusted sexually and high in self-sufficiency and adaptability in stress situations. The ratings in sexual adjustment are difficult to interpret because they were, of necessity, made entirely on the basis of the subjects' self-reports. Since these men tended to be nonintrospective, they probably did not analyze or examine the subtler aspects of their sexual relationships but simply accepted—and reported—the more superficial satisfactions and tension reduction of sexual activity. In addition, since they regarded themselves as highly masculine, they may have found it extremely threatening to admit or discuss any sexual problems or dissatisfactions. For these reasons, their sexual adjustments may appear to be highly adequate, although more intensive investigation may reveal underlying difficulties in this area.

In brief, certain adolescent instrumental characteristics of the highly masculine subjects—and, similarly, certain emotional-expressive characteristics of those with more feminine interests—seem to be maintained in adulthood, but the statuses of the two groups in self-confidence shifted considerably in the 20-year period. The data from adult personality tests and impressionistic ratings, based on interview data, seem to be consistent and lend support to the hypothesis that the self-assurance and positive self-conceptions of the highly masculine subjects decreased after adolescence, while correlatively, the less masculine group changed in a favorable direction.

The antecedents of these changes cannot be determined from the present data, but it seems reasonable to postulate that they are at least partially due to differences between the groups in social interests and skills that foster adjustment in adulthood. More specifically, it may be that, because of the strong peer and adult emphasis on sex typing and traditional stereotyped masculine behavior during adolescence, boys with highly masculine interests are accorded considerable prestige and acquire self-confidence and general emotional stability. While they are relatively lacking in social initiative and orientation, these adolescents seem to be well adjusted and well liked and hence may have little motivation to develop attributes such as gregariousness and sociability. However, these attributes may be essential for the achievement of satisfactory interpersonal relationships and vocational success in adulthood, especially in the middle-class group to which most of the subjects belonged. Failure to develop these characteristics may therefore have adverse long-term consequences, perhaps resulting in important personal, social, and vocational frustrations which weaken self-confidence, self-acceptance, and underlying emotional security and increase feelings of inadequacy and negative self-evaluations.

Subjects with relatively feminine adolescent interest patterns may experience the opposite sequence of events. That is, their characteristic sociability and friendliness may not be enough to assure personal security and self-confidence during adolescence, but may provide substantial bases for social and vocational success—and consequently for increased self-confidence, self-acceptance, and more adequate adjustment—during adulthood.

It may be concluded that high masculine identification during adolescence, as measured in this study, is conducive to the development of feelings of adequacy and contentment at that time but is insufficient per se to ensure enduring favorable consequents. In fact, it appears that the development of strongly masculine interests, if unaccompanied by the certain social characteristics, may have some deleterious long-range results. The extent to which this conclusion may be generalized is, of course, limited by the nature of the sample (only high and low extremes of the distribution of masculinity of interests) and by the criterion of identification employed.

SUMMARY

This investigation was designed to explore the long range consequents of high and low masculinity of adolescent interests. There were two groups of adult subjects drawn from the University of California's longitudinal Adolescent Growth Study. One included 14 subjects who had had highly masculine interests during late adolescence; the other group, 12 subjects, revealed relatively feminine interests at that time. A series of impressionistic ratings of personality and social characteristics, based on intensive interviews with the subjects when they were in their late thirties, constituted the basic data of this study.

Comparison of the ratings assigned to the two groups showed that in adulthood, as during adolescence, those who had had relatively feminine interest patterns manifested more of the "emotional-expressive" role characteristics—e.g., they were rated as more dependent but more social in orientation. In contrast, those with highly masculine adolescent interest patterns possessed, in their late teens and in their late thirties, more active, "instrumental" characteristics: greater self-sufficiency, less social orientation and, in adulthood, less introspectiveness.

There was little congruence between the adolescent and adult statuses of the two groups with respect to several other characteristics, however. During adolescence, highly masculine subjects possessed more self-confidence and greater feelings of adequacy than the other group, but as adults, they were relatively lacking in qualities of leadership, dominance, self-confidence, and self-acceptance. In general there seems to have been a shift in the self-concepts of the two groups in adulthood, the originally highly masculine boys apparently feeling less positive about themselves after adolescence, and, correlatively, the less masculine group changing in a favorable direction. It is suggested that these marked changes may be due to the differences in the extent to which social characteristics such as gregariousness and friendliness were developed by the subjects in the two groups. As adolescents, the highly masculine interest subjects were socially successful and apparently emotionally well adjusted, but failed to develop attributes of sociability and out-goingness which may be essential for the achievement of satisfactory interpersonal relationships and vocational success in adulthood. As a result, they may encounter important social, vocational, and personal frustrations which weaken their previously established self-confidence and underlying emotional security. In contrast, subjects with relatively feminine adolescent interest patterns tend to develop characteristics of social orientation during adolescence and, while these characteristics do not seem to be related to emotional stability at that time, they may provide the bases for future social and vocational success and, consequently, for greater feelings of adequacy and positive self-concepts.

REFERENCES

Brim, O. G., Jr. Family structure and sex role learning by children: A further analysis of Helen Koch's data. *Sociometry,* 1958, 21: 1–16.

Cava, E. L., and Rausch, H. L. Identification and the adolescent boy's perception of his father. *J. abnorm. soc. Psychol.,* 1952, 47: 855–856.

Fisher, R. A. *Statistical methods for research workers.* (7th ed.) Edinburgh: Oliver and Boyd, 1938.

Gray, Susan W. Perceived similarity to parents and adjustment. *Child Develpm.,* 1959, 30: 91–107.

Jones, H. E. The California adolescent growth study. *J. educ. Res.,* 1938, 31: 561–567.

Jones, H. E. Principles and methods of the adolescent growth study. *J. consult. Psychol.,* 1939, 3: 157–159. (a)

Jones, H. E. Procedures of the adolescent growth study. *J. consult. Psychol.,* 1939, 3: 177–180. (b)

Jones, H. E. Observational methods in the study of individual development. *J. consult. Psychol.,* 1940, 4: 234–238.

Levin, H., and Sears, R. R. Identification with parents as a determinant of doll play aggression. *Child Develpm.,* 1956, 27: 135–153.

Mussen, P. Some antecedents and consequents of masculine sex-typing in adolescent boys.

Psychol. Monogr., 1961, 75: (2, Whole No. 506).

Mussen, P., and Distler, L. Masculinity, identification, and father-son relationships. *J. abnorm. soc. Psychol.,* 1959, 59: 350–356.

Parsons, T. Family structure and the socialization of the child. In T. Parsons and R. F. Bales (Eds.), *Family, socialization, and interaction process.* Glencoe, Ill.: Free Press, 1955. Pp. 35–131.

Payne, D. E., and Mussen, P. H. Parent-child relations and father identification among adolescent boys. *J. abnorm. soc. Psychol.,* 1956, 52: 358–362.

Sears, R. R., Maccoby, Eleanor E., and Levin, H. *Patterns of child rearing.* Evanston, Ill.: Row, Peterson, 1957.

Sopchak, A. Parental "identification" and "tendency toward disorders" as measured by the MMPI. *J. abnorm. soc. Psychol.,* 1952, 47: 159–165.

Strong, E. K., Jr. *Vocational interests of men and women.* Stanford: Stanford Univer. Press, 1943.

ACHIEVEMENT MOTIVATION TRAINING FOR UNDERACHIEVING HIGH-SCHOOL BOYS *

DAVID A. KOLB [1]

A substantial body of research using widely differing measurement techniques has indicated that underachieving students are low in their motivation and/or concern for achievement (Bur-

* Reprinted with permission from the American Psychological Association. In *Journal of Personality and Social Psychology,* 1965, Vol. 2, pp. 783–792.

[1] This research was carried out with funds granted by the Carnegie Foundation of New York to David C. McClelland of Harvard University, under whose auspices this study was conducted. Thanks are also due to the Department of Education and officials of Brown University whose cooperation and support made this study possible. George Litwin, Stephen Seigel, and Anthony Davids all made significant contributions in the development, execution, and analysis of this program. The statements made and views expressed are solely the responsibility of the author.

gess, 1956; Garrett, 1949; Gebhart and Hoyt, 1958). In addition, a number of studies have demonstrated a small but positive significant relationship between achievement motivation and academic performance in high school (Atkinson, 1958; McClelland, Atkinson, Clark, and Lowell, 1953; Uhlinger and Stephens, 1960). The present study tests the effect of a training program designed to increase concern for academic achievement in a group of underachieving high-school boys. The content of the training program derives from the research on achievement motivation carried on by McClelland and his associates (Atkinson, 1958; McClelland, 1961; McClelland et al., 1953). A study by Burris (1958) suggests that counseling centered around a student's n Achievement score can produce significant changes in his academic performance. Burris found that the grades of college underachievers who received n Achievement counseling improved significantly more than those of similar students who received nondirective counseling.

The training techniques used in this program stem from four different experimental backgrounds.

1. Identification: The identification models of Kagan (1958) and Hill (1960) maintain that learning takes place through emulation of effective role models, this learning being reinforced through vicarious affective experience. Goldberg (1959) has found that identification with a positive role model seems to be associated with academic improvement in underachieving boys.

2. Expectation: There is a growing body of research which indicates that the expectations held by the experimenter and subject (Orne, 1962; Rosenthal, 1963) or the therapist and patient (Goldstein, 1962) can measurably affect the outcome of the experiment or therapy. In this study the research team model developed by Schwitzgebel and Slack (1960) was adapted. Schwitzgebel (1962) has found the research team model useful in reducing juvenile delinquency.

3. Ideomotor response: The hypothesis that thought determines action has a long history in psychology. Braid maintained that an idea firmly implanted in the mind during hypnosis later issues into behavior. Through the influence of Herbart, nineteenth century educational psychology promoted the copybook to implant in children's minds the "right ideas" which would lead to "right ac-

tions" (Allport, 1954). William James formulated a think-talk-act model recently elaborated by Leary (1961b). Perhaps the most sophisticated modern statement of this theory is George Kelly's (1955) role construct theory. He maintains that behavior is determined in large measure by the way a person construes the world. The Burris (1958) study suggests that teaching underachievers achievement constructs and encouraging them to think in achievement terms can lead to better performance in school. In the current study the technique is to implant the idea of achievement by teaching the students the n Achievement scoring system and to observe the results in action, that is, academic performance.

4. Games: The use of games to simulate life situations is becoming more and more prevalent in the training of managers and administrators, military leaders, diplomats, and others requiring complex skills (Bensen, 1962; Kibbe, Croft, and Nanus, 1961; Sprowls, 1962). These games provide a well-defined psychologically safe situation where men can try out new ways of thinking and behaving. In this study the game concept was used in two ways: in actual games designed to teach achievement skills (e.g., Litwin and Ciarlo, 1961) and as an analytic device in counseling to aid in understanding real-life problems (Leary, 1961a).

METHOD

Setting

The Achievement Motivation Training Program (AMTP) was carried out as part of a summer school for underachieving high-school boys held at Brown University. The summer school was designed to give stimulating instruction using outstanding teachers and exciting subject matter. In addition, the planners of the program hoped that exposure to college living and positive college role models (counselors were chosen to be outstanding in both scholarship and athletics) would increase the underachievers' desire to go to college.

The project was 6 weeks long, beginning in late June and ending in the first week of August. The schedule was a 5-day week of classes in history, English, and mathematics, with weekend recreation at various parks and beaches in the area. The boys lived together on three floors of a college dormitory on the campus and ate in the college dining hall.

Subjects

Fifty-seven boys drawn mainly from public and private schools in New Enlgand were enrolled in the project. These were selected from 95 applicants on the basis of IQ (120 or higher) and school grade average (C or lower). Boys with serious reading defects were generally not admitted. Attempts were made to screen out applicants with serious psychiatric problems. Two general classes of students were recruited: boys from homes where sufficient interest, parental background, and finances favored college entrance and boys from homes where these were lacking. Parents of the first type were requested to pay tuition, room, and board. Lower-class boys were granted scholarships to cover their expenses. About half of the participants received scholarships.

A breakdown by social class based on occupation (Warner, Meeker, and Eells, 1949) shows 14 boys in Class 1, 11 in Class 2, 11 in Class 3, 5 in Class 4, 6 in Class 5, 2 in Class 6, and 1 in Class 7. The mean IQ score (WISC) of the boys was 126 (range: 109–149) and their mean school grade average was D to D+ (range: F–C+). The average year in school was 9.0 (range: 7–11) and their average age was 14 years (range: 12–16). Stanford Achievement Test scores showed them to be at an average grade level of 10.9 (range: 8.8–12.7).

Experimental Design

Twenty of the 57 students were randomly assigned to the fourth floor of the dormitory. This group received the AMTP in addition to their regular summer school schedule. The remaining 37 students received only the regular summer school program.

Subjects were tested in the following manner.

Pretesting. On the second day of the summer school, 57 subjects were given the following tests: the Test of Insight, Form A (this test was an adaptation of the form used by French, 1958, and was scored for n Achievement according to the published scoring manuals—Atkinson, 1958); the Stanford Achievement Test; the Taylor Manifest Anxiety (*MA*) scale; and the Mandler-Sarason Test Anxiety Scale (TAS). In addition the following data were collected for each subject: age, year in school, IQ (WISC), 1961 school grade average, and parents' socioeconomic status based on father's occupation (Warner et al., 1949).

August 1961 posttest. On the next-to-last day of the project, subjects were given the following tests: the Test of Insight, Form B, a parallel form; the Stanford Achievement Test; the *MA* scale; and the TAS. In addition all subjects received grades in each of the three subjects taught in the summer school. AMTP members were ranked on their participation in the AMTP and assessed in moderate risk-taking ability using the Litwin-Ciarlo (1961) Business Game.

January 1962 follow-up. The midyear school grades were collected for all boys who completed the project.

April 1962 follow-up. At this time 33 of the summer-school participants were selected on the basis of proximity to Brown University to return for a testing session. Twenty-seven boys returned (experimentals = 10, controls = 17) and were given the Test of Insight, Form A.

January 1963 follow-up. School grades were collected for the Spring 1962 semester. Unfortunately these were available for only 37 boys (experimentals = 12, controls = 25).

The initial, posttest, and follow-up Insight tests scored for n Achievement were included to determine whether experimental subjects would learn and retain the achievement scoring categories better than controls. School grades and Stanford Achievement Test scores were chosen as indicators of achievement-oriented performance. WISC scores, social class, *MA* scale, and TAS scores were included as potential predictors of change, for example, high *MA* scale subjects might change more than low *MA* scale subjects, though no specific hypotheses were made.

To check for n Achievement scoring reliability, a sample of 30 Tests of Insight (10 from each testing period) was scored by a trained scorer not connected with the training program. Scores thusly obtained correlated (rho) .85 with the experimenter's scores.

School grades were all converted to a numerical scale: A = 95, B = 85, C = 75, D = 65, E or F = 55.

Experimental Condition: The Achievement Motivation Training Program

The experimenter lived in the dormitory with the AMTP boys and served as their counselor. The experimenter behaved in a manner consistent with the behavior of a person with high n Achievement, so that the subjects would have a visible high n Achievement role model to imitate.

The procedure changed from the use of external rules and discipline to internal control and personal responsibility: Structured classes and required meetings gradually gave way to individual appointments made at a subject's request and optional group meetings. Responsibility for running the fourth floor and the AMTP was gradually given to the boys themselves. After a few initial required meetings the boys were free to choose how much they wanted to participate in the program. This policy reflected the research team contract (see below) and was further encouraged by the time limitations of the experimenter. It was felt that time would be more profitably spent working with interested students than trying to involve those who were not interested.

Initially the boys met with the experimenter in a classroom twice a week for 1 hour. As the weeks progressed this meeting time was changed to better fit the summer-school schedule and meet the needs of the boys. The program is described below in detail.

First session. The first session was concerned with negotiating a contract. The role relationship emulated was that of a team doing collaborative research on the problem of underachieving. The aim was to involve the students in the hypothesis that the course would improve academic performance and achievement motivation thereby creating in them the expectation that the course would work. The essence of the contract was this:

> We at Harvard have some ideas about how to help the underachiever play the school game better. Our goal is to try out these ideas to see if they work, and to discover new ways to prevent the problems associated with underachievement. If you will work with us we think that we can, in return, introduce you to some strategies which will help you in school and, more generally, in life. Whether you want to do this or not is entirely your decision. Your involvement with this program is not required; you can participate to the extent to which you feel it is useful to you.

After negotiating the contract, the characteristics of a person with high achievement motivation were described. Subjects were told that the person with high n Achievement has three major characteristics: he likes and chooses to take personal responsibility for his actions, he takes moderate risks, and he likes and attempts to obtain knowledge of the results of his actions (Atkinson, 1958; McClelland, 1961; McClelland et al., 1953). The remainder of the session was spent describing the racing car game the subjects would play in the next session and suggesting how the characteristics of the person with high achievement motivation would be valuable to a racing driver.

Second session. The entire second session was spent playing the race game. The game consisted of a miniature race track around which small electric cars could be driven. The "racers" each had a transformer which controlled the speed of his car. The boys raced against the clock two at a time. The boy in each pair with the fastest time was declared the winner. If by going too fast the boy left the track three times he was disqualified. As they raced the boys were asked to keep in mind the characteristics of the achieving personality in relation to the race, for example, (a) personal responsibility—How involved am I in the race? Do I care if I win or not? (b) moderate risk taking—How much of the time did I take too much of a risk? How often was I too cautious? (c) using knowledge—of results—How well did I use my practice trials to judge my ability?

Third session. This session began with an introduction to the process of assessing motivation by analysis of thought (Atkinson, 1958). The boys were then shown how their n Achievement scores related to their performance in the racing game (boys with low n Achievement tended to be disqualified).

The discussion then turned to time orientation. During the previous evening the boys had estimated a 30-second interval on a stopwatch. Subjects with high n Achievement tended to see time as passing more quickly than subjects with low n Achievement. Further discussion centered around future orientation, delay of gratification, and ability to control impulses.

Fourth session. This session marked the beginning of the shift from structured lecture meetings to a program oriented more toward the individual. In essence the session was a renegotiation of the contract. The group's commitment to the "research team" model was reaffirmed, emphasizing the boy's role in determining the nature of the course. The follow-up and the experimenter's interest in knowing the boys' future grades were discussed.

The last half of the session was spent discussing

how thought influences action. The think-talk-act model was explained: If you think and talk in a certain way you will act that way. In particular the direct relationship of achievement thinking to achievement behaviors was discussed. At the end of this session the boys were given n Achievement scoring manuals.

Fifth session. This session was devoted to a group discussion on the analysis of Test of Insight stories. Example stories from the protocols of control students were read to the class and discussed. Following this discussion the students were given their own Insight test protocols. They were offered help in scoring their protocols for n Achievement. The expert scoring was given to them upon request. The remainder of the hour was spent in teaching the n Achievement scoring system.

Sixth session. A major theme that occurs over and over in the Insight Tests is a conflict between achievement and affiliation goals (see Parsons, 1959). One of these stories is quoted below. (Written to Test of Insight, Form A, Story 4, "Bill may not be the best student in his class, but he is the friendliest and the best-liked.")

> He fools around a lot to make friends and doesn't do his school work the best he can. He didn't take school seriously and just had a lot of fun. He thinks more about making friends than about getting his homework done. He probably wants to be a mechanic. His marks will keep slipping down and he won't get a good job when he gets out of school.

The session was focused on this conflict and on learning to take realistic risks. An article on how to assess risks was given to the class members. The group discussed risk taking in terms of planning goals and strategies in life situations, making conscious decisions, taking action to attain desired goals, and knowing one's own ability. The Litwin-Ciarlo Business Game (discussed below) which they would all play later that week was described.

Informal sessions. Beginning on Thursday of the fifth week, the group began meeting every evening on the lawn on an informal basis. Attendance at these sessions was not required and subjects could come and go as they pleased. The boys wanted this arrangement so they could discuss how the techniques they had learned could be applied to specific problems in their lives. These discussions were intense and seemed to be of considerable benefit to those who attended. Approximately 12 out of the 20 boys attended regularly. The remainder had more or less dropped by the wayside.

Individual counseling sessions. Counseling on an individual basis was done informally. The problems discussed in individual sessions were usually concerned with the application of principles talked about in class to the life of the boy. These ranged from using the principles of moderate risk taking to play a better tennis game, to setting realistic goals in study tasks, to staying out of arguments at home.

Litwin-Ciarlo Business Game. This training device was perhaps the most popular aspect of the whole project. It is designed to train a person to take moderate risks and use knowledge of results, and to assess his capacity to do so. The subject in this game plays the role of a manufacturer and actually builds the products he contracts for with tinkertoys. He is told that he is the head of a company just starting to manufacture three new products—a missile, an atomic cannon, and an airplane. He must order sufficient parts to build each of these products and actually try to assemble them in three separate 5-minute production periods. Only completed units are purchased, so if he orders too many he loses what is invested in the leftover parts, and if he orders too few his profit is lower than it should have been. The subject makes his decisions and assesses risks using two types of information: printed statistics giving prices, profits, and average construction times for each product and his own timed practice construction trials for each product. The game takes an hour to play and gives scores on risk taking and use of past performance as an indicator of future performance. A couple of boys learned to run the game and did a large part of the administration for the other boys.

RESULTS

Eight of the original 57 boys were not included in the final data analysis. Five of these boys (4 controls and 1 experimental) were dropped from the summer school for either disciplinary or emotional problems. The other 3 boys (2 experimentals and 1 control) completed the school but were so withdrawn or rebellious that they were rated unsatisfactory in all three of their courses.

Initial Comparison of Experimental and Control Groups

To determine the success of random assignments, the experimental and control groups were compared on all variables in the study. Using the Mann-Whitney U test, p values were greater than .20 (two-tailed) on the following variables: year in school, age, IQ (WISC), n Achievement, 1961 school grade average, average Stanford Achievement Test score, MA scale, and TAS. A chi-square comparison of the two groups by social class (Classes 1 and 2 versus Classes 3–7) yielded a p value of .50.

Comparison of Experimental and Control Group Changes

In Table 1 the n Achievement change scores are reported for experimental and control subjects, pretest to August posttest and pretest to April posttest for the 27 subjects who attended that follow-up. It is assumed that this latter group represents an unbiased sampling of the total summer-school population since they were selected on nonacademic criteria—proximity of their home to the testing site. Note that the experimental group shows significantly greater increases in n Achievement score in both periods, indicating that experimentals both learned and retained the n Achievement scoring system better than the untrained controls.

Comparison of experimental and control changes on the Stanford Achievement Test from the pretest to August posttest indicated no significant differences either for total score or any subtest score although in most cases experimentals tended to improve more than controls. The two anxiety scales (TAS and MA) also showed no significant differential changes. An analysis of the final grades that the boys received in the summer school showed no significant differences.

In comparing changes in school grades, each boy received, whenever possible, a change score for five subject areas: English, science, foreign language, mathematics, and history/civics, plus a change score for his total semester grade average. Change scores for the subject areas were the average grade that the boy received in the courses he took in that area. Many times these subject change scores were not available because the boy would not have taken a given course in both the

pretest and the follow-up periods. In Table 2, change scores for experimental and control groups are compared for the January 1962 follow-up and the January 1963 follow-up. Note that while in the January 1962 follow-up experimental boys had not improved significantly more in grade average than the control boys, by the January 1963

TABLE 1

CHANGE IN n ACHIEVEMENT

Testing intervals	M change		p[a]
	Experimental group	Control group	
Pretest to August 1961 posttest	6.72 ($n=18$)	−.34 ($n=32$)	<.005
Pretest to April 1962 follow-up	4.4 ($n=10$)	−3.8 ($n=17$)	<.025

[a] Mann-Whitney U test, one-tailed probability.

TABLE 2

CHANGE IN SCHOOL GRADES: ALL BOYS

School subjects	M change		p[a]
	Experimental group	Control group	
Pretest to January 1962 follow-up			
Total grade average	6.3 ($n=18$)	4.1 ($n=31$)	
English	8.3 ($n=18$)	3.1 ($n=30$)	<.03
Science	−4.0 ($n=10$)	7.0 ($n=21$)	<.02[b]
Foreign language	8.1 ($n=12$)	5.1 ($n=14$)	
Mathematics	6.1 ($n=17$)	4.8 ($n=28$)	
History/civics	6.3 ($n=7$)	2.9 ($n=20$)	
Pretest to January 1963 follow-up			
Total grade average	7.1 ($n=12$)	2.6 ($n=24$)	<.05
English	8.7 ($n=12$)	4.7 ($n=23$)	
Science	3.5 ($n=6$)	9.2 ($n=15$)	
Foreign language	7.8 ($n=7$)	−0.9 ($n=10$)	
Mathematics	1.7 ($n=12$)	3.8 ($n=20$)	
History/civics	9 ($n=8$)	4.9 ($n=15$)	

[a] Mann-Whitney U test, one-tailed probability.
[b] Contrary to prediction; two-tailed probability.

follow-up the experimental group's improvements in grade average were significantly greater than the control group's improvements. In addition, the mean experimental improvement increased from 1962 to 1963 while the mean control group improvement decreased in this period. In the subject areas, experimentals improved significantly more than controls in English while controls improved significantly more than experimentals in science in the January 1962 follow-up (contrary to prediction). None of these differences held in the January 1963 follow-up.

In the 1963 follow-up, grades were available for only 73% of the subjects in the 1962 follow-up. One might question the validity of the 1963 change score since ordinarily one would expect students who improved least to drop out in later follow-ups. An analysis of the 13 dropouts' change scores in the 1962 follow-up showed a nonsignificant trend in this direction—8 were below the 1962 total mean change and 5 were above. These boys, however, were evenly divided between the experimental and control groups (experimental = 2/4, control = 3/4). Thus we would suspect that any artificial increase in average change scores would not affect the experimental and control groups differentially.

Effect of Social Class

As described in the section on method, the boys in the project were of two types—boys from homes where interest, parental background, and finances favored college entrance (i.e., high SES boys) and boys from homes where these were

TABLE 3

CHANGE IN n ACHIEVEMENT BY SOCIAL CLASS

Testing interval	M change		p^a
	Experimental group	Control group	
High social class (1 and 2)			
Pretest to August posttest	8.4 (n = 9)	−0.3 (n = 9)	<.05
Pretest to April follow-up	5.7 (n = 7)	−5.8 (n = 5)	<.025
Low social class (3 through 7)			
Pretest to August posttest	5.0 (n = 9)	−.6 (n = 20)	<.01
Pretest to April follow-up	0.3 (n = 3)	−3.2 (n = 12)	<.10

a Mann-Whitney U test, one-tailed probability.

lacking (low SES boys). Because of these differences, all of the change comparisons were made by social class (high SES = Classes 1 and 2, low SES = classes 3–7). In Table 3 are reported the changes in n Achievement score divided by social

TABLE 4

CHANGE IN SCHOOL GRADES: HIGH SOCIAL CLASS BOYS

School subjects	M change		p^a
	Experimental group	Control group	
Pretest to January 1962 follow-up			
Total grade average	9.5 (n = 10)	1.8 (n = 13)	<.005
English	9.4 (n = 10)	0.7 (n = 13)	<.01
Science	0.5 (n = 3)	4.4 (n = 8)	
Foreign language	10.5 (n = 8)	10.0 (n = 3)	
Mathematics	13.0 (n = 10)	−12.0 (n = 11)	<.01
History/civics	7.2 (n = 4)	4.6 (n = 7)	
Pretest to January 1963 follow-up			
Total grade average	11.9 (n = 6)	1.9 (n = 11)	<.05
English	9.5 (n = 6)	3.7 (n = 11)	
Science	8.8 (n = 5)	7.1 (n = 8)	
Foreign language	9.8 (n = 5)	−2.0 (n = 8)	
Mathematics	11.2 (n = 6)	3.0 (n = 10)	
History/civics	6.0 (n = 4)	5.2 (n = 6)	

a Mann-Whitney U test, one-tailed probability.

class. In both lower- and upper-class groups, experimental subjects increase significantly more than control subjects.

While Mann-Whitney U tests indicated no significant differential changes in Stanford Achievement Test scores, MA scale, TAS, or summer-school grades, there were differential changes in school grades in both the January 1962 and January 1963 follow-up periods. These effects are reported in Tables 4 and 5 for the high SES and low SES groups, respectively.

The total grade average of high SES experimentals improved significantly more than controls in the January 1962 follow-up and in the January 1963 follow-up. In addition, high SES experimentals improved significantly more than controls in English and mathematics in 1962. No subject areas were significant in the 1963 follow-up.

The trend reported for high SES experimentals was reversed for low SES experimentals. In most cases they improved less than control subjects although these improvements only approached significance in science and mathematics in the 1963 follow-up. Low SES subjects showed no significant differential changes in total grade average in either follow-up period.

In Figure 1 the total grade averages are plotted for high SES and low SES experimentals and controls for the initial pretest and the two follow-up periods. The data reported in Figure 1 do not correspond exactly with that presented in Tables 4 and 5 since the tables use only subjects

TABLE 5

CHANGE IN SCHOOL GRADES: LOW SOCIAL CLASS BOYS

| School subjects | M change | | p^a |
	Experimental group	Control group	
Pretest to January 1962 follow-up			
Total grade average	2.4 ($n = 8$)	5.7 ($n = 18$)	
English	7.0 ($n = 8$)	4.8 ($n = 17$)	
Science	−10.7 ($n = 4$)	15.8 ($n = 14$)	<.10
Foreign language	−3.2 ($n = 4$)	3.7 ($n = 11$)	
Mathematics	−3.7 ($n = 7$)	8.6 ($n = 17$)	<.10
History/civics	5.0 ($n = 3$)	3.4 ($n = 11$)	
Pretest to January 1963 follow-up			
Total grade average	2.3 ($n = 6$)	3.2 ($n = 13$)	
English	7.8 ($n = 6$)	6.5 ($n = 13$)	
Science[b]			
Foreign language[b]			
Mathematics	−7.6 ($n = 6$)	4.4 ($n = 10$)	<.05
History/civics	12.0 ($n = 4$)	4.7 ($n = 9$)	

[a] Mann-Whitney U test, two-tailed probability (contrary to prediction).
[b] Not enough cases for comparison.

for whom change scores were available whereas the figure uses all subjects in each testing period to obtain the mean score. The high SES experimental group is the only group to show an improvement in grade average in the 1963 follow-up.

This group shows a 12-point increase in grade average in the 1963 follow-up, moving from a D— to a C average.

Similar change comparisons were made with the data divided into high MA and low MA, high TAS and low TAS, high IQ and low IQ, but no significant differences were found.

Analysis of Change within the Experimental Group

To analyze patterns of change within the experimental group, seven variables were intercorrelated: three predictor variables—social class, initial n Achievement score, and WISC IQ score; three participation variables—ranking on course participation by the counselor, a moderate risk-taking score from the Business Game, and the change in n Achievement score from the pretest to the August posttest; and the criterion variable —change in school grades. Changes in grades in the January 1962 follow-up were used since using 1963 changes would too much reduce the already small sample. These correlations are reported in Table 6.

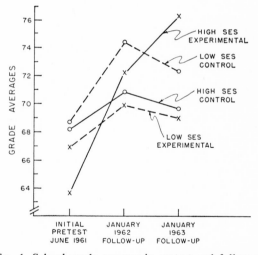

FIG. 1. School grade average in pretest and follow-up periods.

None of the three predictor variables showed significant correlations with change in school grades although when SES was divided into high and low groups as was done for control group comparisons, a median test showed that high SES boys tended to improve more than low SES boys

TABLE 6

EXPERIMENTAL GROUP INTERCORRELATIONS $(n = 18)$

	Social class	Initial n Achievement	IQ	Participation	Business Game	n Achievement change	Change in grades
Predictor variables							
Social class[a]	—						
Initial n Achievement	22	—					
WISC IQ	−32	−31	—				
Participation variables							
Course participation[b]	−03	−02	−01	—			
Business Game score	−15	06	34	15	—		
Change in n Achievement[c]	11	02	35	58**	25	—	
Criterion variable							
Change in grades[d]	32	−30	20	27	63***	42*	—

[a] Scores inverted for ease of interpretation: 7 = high SES, 1 = low SES.
[b] All rank-order correlations.
[c] Change to August posttest.
[d] Change to January 1962 follow-up.
  * $p < .10$, one-tailed.
  ** $p < .02$, one-tailed.
  *** $p < .01$, one-tailed.

$(\chi^2 = 7.29, p < .01)$. None of the predictor variables were significantly related to participation variables, although there was a weak relationship between IQ and Business Game and IQ and n Achievement change.

Two of the participation variables can be seen as measures of how well the boys learned major themes of the course. The Business Game score gives an indication of the boy's ability to take moderate risks and use the results of his previous experience (i.e., feedback) at the end of the course. This score correlated .63 with change in school grades. The change in n Achievement score gives an indication of how well the boy learned to think like a person with high need for achievement. This score correlated .42 with change in grades. The multiple correlation coefficient of Business Game score and change in n Achievement with change in school grades was .68 ($p < .025$, one-tailed). The third participation variable, the participation ranking by the counselor, did not correlate significantly with the criterion, although it did with change in n Achievement.

DISCUSSION

The fact that improvement in experimental group grades differs significantly from control group improvement in the 1963 but not the 1962 follow-up seems to be based mainly on a decrease in the control group improvement score in 1963. This would suggest that while the summer school alone gave some boost to the grades, there is a tendency for this effect to decay over time, while the addition of the AMTP to the summer program seems to promote a more permanent and perhaps increasing improvement in school grade average. This effect is seen most strikingly when the data are analyzed by social class (see Figure 1).

The significant differences in subject areas, especially when controls improve more than experimentals, are difficult to explain with the data available.

The strong differential effect that social class had on change in grades requires some examination. The fact that only high social class experimental boys seemed to benefit significantly from the AMTP might be explained in two ways.

One might reason that the course was designed to appeal more to boys from the upper classes where education is valued more than to lower-class boys (Kahl, 1952). The course was, in fact, pitched at a rather intellectual level and expounded high educational values—Harvard, research, and good grades. But if this argument were so, one would expect social class to be positively correlated with the participation variables—course participation ranking, Business Game score, and change in n Achievement. As is indicated in Table 6, this is not the case. In addition, *both* high and low SES experimentals increased significantly more than controls in n Achievement score.

The alternative explanation is not based on the differential reaction of high and low SES boys to the AMTP but on the different environments to which they returned. An underachieving upper-class boy finds himself in sharp dissonance with his subculture. There is constant pressure for him to achieve and do well in school. The under-achiever from the lower classes is not pushed by such strong values on achievement and hence he is more likely to be in harmony with his subcul-ture. Hence when the boys returned home after learning new techniques for achieving, the high SES boys used these techniques to alleviate the tensions their failure to achieve had created. Al-though we would have to assume that the low SES boy also felt some of these tensions (his par-ents did care enough to send him to the summer school), the aspirations that the subculture holds for the boy are not so high (Kahl, 1952) and thus he need not improve his performance as much to bring himself in harmony with his subculture.

The experimental group's improvement over controls in school grades lends encouraging sup-port to the hypothesis that teaching underachiev-ing boys the characteristics of the person with high achievement motivation can lead to better academic performance. The hypothesis is further supported by the high correlation of change in n Achievement and Business Game score with improvement in school grades in the experimental group.

This experiment, however, does not allow any conclusions about what techniques produced the experimental group's improved academic perfor-mance. The improvements could theoretically be a result of any or all of the following: the experi-menter's particular personality (identification theory), learning n Achievement thought categor-ies (ideomotor response theory and n Achievement theory), learning to take moderate risks and use feedback (n Achievement theory), learning to take personal responsibility for actions (n Achieve-ment theory), and expectations of improvement created by participation in a research project and by the research team contract (expectation the-ory). Further research should attempt to measure and/or isolate the differential effects of these factors.

SUMMARY

An experiment testing the effect of a training program in achievement motivation on the aca-demic performance of underachieving high-school boys. 20 boys with IQs above 120 and school grades below C received the training program de-signed to teach characteristics of the person with high n Achievement in addition to an academic summer-school program. They were compared to a control group of 37 similar boys who received only the academic program. A 6-mo. follow-up revealed no significant differences between the groups in improvement in school grade average. In a 1.5 year follow-up, however, the total grade average of experimental Ss improved significantly more than the grades of controls ($p < .05$). Large social class differences were found. The grades of high social class (SES) experimentals improved significantly more than those of high SES controls ($p < .005$) while low SES experi-mentals did not increase more than low SES controls. In the experimental group, improvement in school grades was significantly correlated with participation variables—change in n Achievement and a Business Game performance score.

REFERENCES

Allport, G. W. The historical background of modern social psychology. In G. Murphy (Ed.), *The handbook of social psychology*. Vol. 1 Reading, Mass.: Addison-Wesley, 1954. Pp. 3–56.

Atkinson, J. W. (Ed.) *Motives in fantasy, action, and society*. Princeton, N. J.: Van Nostrand, 1958.

Bensen, O. Stimulation of international relations and diplomacy. In H. Borko (Ed.), *Computer applications in the behavioral sciences*. New York: Prentice-Hall, 1962. Pp. 574–595.

Burgess, Elva. Personality factors of over- and under-achievers in engineering. *Journal of Educational Psychology*, 1956, 47: 89–99.

Burris, R. The effect of counseling on achieve-ment motivation. Unpublished doctoral disserta-tion, Indiana University, 1958.

French, Elizabeth G. Development of a measure of complex motivation. In J. W. Atkinson (Ed.), *Motives in fantasy, action, and society*. Prince-ton, N. J.: Van Nostrand, 1958. Pp. 242–248.

Garrett, H. F. A review and interpretation of in-vestigations of factors related to scholastic suc-cess in colleges of arts and sciences and teachers colleges. *Journal of Experimental Education*, 1949, 18: 91–158.

Gebhart, G. G., and Hoyt, D. P. Personality needs

of under- and overachieving freshmen. *Journal of Applied Psychology*, 1958, 42: 125–128.

Goldberg, Miriam. A three year experimental program at Dewitt Clinton High School to help bright underachievers. *High Points*, Jan. 1959, 5–35.

Goldstein, A. *Therapist-patient expectancies in psychotherapy*. New York: Pergamon Press, 1962.

Hill, W. F. Learning theory and the acquisition of values. *Psychological Review*, 1960, 67: 317–331.

Kagan, J. The concept of identification. *Psychological Review*, 1958, 65: 296–305.

Kahl, J. A. Adolescent ambition. Unpublished doctoral dissertation, Harvard University, 1952.

Kelly, G. *The psychology of personal constructs*. Vol. 1. New York: Norton, 1955.

Kibbe, M., Croft, C., and Nanus, B. *Management games: A new technique for executive development*. New York: Rinehold, 1961.

Leary, T. How to change behavior. Paper read at the XIVth International Congress of Applied Psychology, Copenhagen, 1961. (a)

Leary, T. Thinking, talking, and doing. Unpublished manuscript, Harvard University, 1961. (b)

Litwin, G. H., and Ciarlo, J. A. *Achievement motivation and risk-taking in a business setting, technical report*. Ossining, N. Y.: General Electric Company, Behavioral Research Service, 1961.

McClelland, D. C. *The achieving society*. Princeton, N. J.: Van Nostrand, 1961.

McClelland, D. C., Atkinson, J. W., Clark, R. A., and Lowell, E. L. *The achievement motive*. New York: Appleton-Century-Crofts, 1953.

Orne, M. T. On the social psychology of the psychological experiment: With particular reference to demand characteristics and their implications. *American Psychologist*, 1962, 17: 776–783.

Parsons, T. The school class as a social system— Some of its functions in American society. *Harvard Educational Review*, 1959, 29: 297–316.

Rosenthal, R. On the social psychology of the psychological experiment: The experimenter's hypothesis as the unintended determinant of experimental results. *American Scientist*, 1963, 51: 268–283.

Schwitzgebel, R. Analysis and evaluation of the experimenter-subject role relationship in the reduction of known male adolescent crime. Unpublished doctoral dissertation, Harvard University, 1962.

Schwitzgebel, R., and Slack, C. *A handbook: Reducing adolescent crime in your community*. Cambridge, Mass.: Authors, 1960.

Sprowls, R. C. Business simulation. In H. Borko (Ed.), *Computer applications in the behavioral sciences*. New York: Prentice-Hall, 1962. Pp. 556–573.

Uhlinger, Carolyn A., and Stephens, M. W. Relation of achievement motivation to academic achievement in students of superior ability. *Journal of Educational Psychology*, 1960, 51: 259–266.

Warner, W. L., Meeker, M., and Eells, K. *Social class in America*. Chicago: Science Research Associates, 1949.

THE HETEROSEXUAL AFFECTIONAL SYSTEM IN MONKEYS [*]

Harry F. Harlow [1]

The inspiration for this address came from observational data obtained from seven guinea pigs—two males and three females in a colony and two females brought in temporarily. Observations were provided by my ten-year-old daughter Pamela. These observations were made with love and endearment, and the behavior observed was endearment and love. Furthermore, these observations were made at a level of objectivity difficult for an adult to attain in this field.

Male and female guinea pigs are very fond of each other. They stare blissfully into the limpid pink or ruby or midnight-blue pools of each other's eyes. They nuzzle and they cuddle and the end production is not characterized by rush or rape. After all, one does not have to hurry if there is no hurry to be had. This, Pamela has witnessed several times. A caged, virgin adult female was brought by a friend for mating. Twirp, Pamela's large, black, gentle male, was put into the cage

[*] Reprinted with permission from the American Psychological Association. In *American Psychologist*, 1962, Vol. 17, pp. 1–9.

[1] This research was supported by funds received from the Graduate School of the University of Wisconsin, from the Ford Foundation, and from Grant M-4528, National Institutes of Health.

with the new female. He purred, nuzzled her, brushed up against her, smelled and licked her, and gradually conquered the frightened animal. A half-hour later they were snuggled up next to each other, peaceful and content, and they lived in bliss for several weeks until another friend brought in her female and Twirp repeated his patient, gentle approach. Twirp has convinced me that some male guinea pigs, at least, are endowed with an innate sense of decency, and I am happy to say that this is the way most male monkeys behave. I presume that there are some men who have as deep a depth of dignity as guinea pigs.

The guest stands, unfortunately, ended peaceful coexistence in the colony. For many months the five adult guinea pigs had lived amiably in one large cage, with Twirp in command and the second male playing second fiddle. While Twirp was host to the visiting females, White Patch commanded the permanent harem. When Twirp was reintroduced to the colony cage, it took but ten seconds to discover that he would not be tolerated. White Patch bared his teeth and lunged at Twirp, and to save the males, a new cage was acquired.

This led to various divisions of the females and led Pamela to discover particular male guinea pigs like particular female guinea pigs, and they squeal piteously when separated, even when the female is so bulging with babies that she can offer the male nothing in terms of drive reduction. Particular female guinea pigs like particular male guinea pigs. Tastes seem fairly stable, for even after weeks of peaceful residence with the unfavored male, the female will still attempt to get to her favorite male, and after weeks of quiet residence with unfavored females, the male will still try to get to his favorite female.

The females, like the males, defend their rights. In the happy one-cage days two females were separated from the group to care for their litters. White Thrush, in an advanced stage of pregnancy, lived alone with the males. When Chirp was returned to the colony cage after three weeks of maternal chores, both males approached enthusiastically, making friendly gestures. But Hell hath no fury like a female guinea pig spurned, and White Thrush would not tolerate infidelity. She hissed at Chirp, and lunged, and as Chirp fled from the cage, White Thrush pursued, teeth bared. The males also pursued, clucking and purring in anticipation. The males won, and White Thrush

sulked the rest of the day. Guinea pigs apparently have a well-developed heterosexual affectional system.

Sex behavior in the guinea pig has been intensively investigated, and there are exhaustive studies on what has been called the sex drive, but I know of no previous mention of or allusion to the guinea pig's heterosexual affectional system. No doubt this stems from the paradigm which has been established for research in this area.

In a typical experiment a male guinea pig and a female guinea pig in estrus are taken from their individual cages, dropped into a barren chamber, and observed for 15 minutes. In such a situation there is a high probability that something is going

Fig. 1. Initial response to female sexual-present posture. The male subsequently accepted the invitation.

to happen and that it will happen rapidly and repeatedly. The thing that happens will be reliable and valid, and all that one needs to do to score it is to count. It is my suggestion that from this time onward it be known as the "flesh count." Sometimes I wonder how men and women would behave if they were dropped naked into a barren chamber with full realization that they had only fifteen minutes to take advantage of the opportunities offered them. No doubt there would be individual differences, but we would obtain little information on the human heterosexual affectional system from such an experiment.

Sex is not an adventitious act. It is not here today and gone tomorrow. It starts with the cradle, and as a part of the human tragedy it wanes before the grave. We have traced and are tracing the development of the heterosexual affectional system in monkeys.

Fig 2. Initial response to male sexual-present posture. The female (No. 48) subsequently approached and groomed the male.

We believe that the heterosexual affectional system in the rhesus monkey, like all the other affectional systems, goes through a series of developmental stages—an infantile heterosexual stage, a preadolescent stage, and an adolescent and mature heterosexual stage. Although these stages are in considerable part overlapping and cannot be sharply differentiated in time, we would think of the infantile stage as lasting throughout the first year and being characterized by inadequate and often inappropriate sexual play and posturing. The preadolescent stage, beginning in the second year and ending in the third year in the female and the fourth year in the male, is characterized by adequate and appropriate sexual play and posturing,

Fig. 3. Normal male and female sexual positioning.

but incompleteness. The adolescent and adult stage is characterized by behaviors which are similar in form but give rise to productive outcomes which are also reproductive.

Since in this paper sex is an unavoidable issue, we present illustrations of normal adult macaque monkey sex behavior. Sexual invitation may be initiated by the female, as in Figure 1, by a present pattern with buttocks oriented toward the male, tail elevated, and the female looking backward with a fear-grimace (not threat) pattern involving flattened ears and lip smacking. As you can see, this pattern need not involve rape nor even rush on the part of the male. The male may also solicit, as in the case of the animal in the foreground of Figure 2; this animal has assumed a posture soliciting either grooming or more intimate favors. These patterns seldom elicit violent, uncontrolled, reflex behaviors. Normal male and female overt sex behavior is shown in Figure 3, the male having assumed the complex sex posture involving ankle clasp, dorsoventral mounting, and clasp of the female's buttocks. The partner demonstrates the complete female sexual pattern of elevating the buttocks, lowering the head, and looking backward. There have been millions of rhesus monkeys for millions of years, and there will be more in the future.

We have traced the development of the infantile heterosexual stage during the first year of life in two test situations using observational techniques. One is our playroom, illustrated in Figure 4, which consists of a room 8 ft. high with 36 feet of floor space. In this room are a platform, ladder, revolving wheel, and flying rings to encourage the infants' adaptation to a three-dimensional world, and there is an assortment of puzzles and toys for quieter activities. Two groups of four infants each, half of each group male and half female, have been observed in the playroom daily over many months. The second apparatus is shown in Figure 5. This is the playpen situation, and it consists of four large living cages and adjoining pens. Each living cage houses a mother and infant, and a three-inch by five-inch opening in the wall between cage and playpen units enables the infants to leave the home cage at any time but restrains the mothers. The playpen units are separated by wire-mesh panels which are removed one or two hours a day to allow the infants to interact in pairs during the first 180 days and both in pairs and in groups of four during the next half-year of life. Again, we are referring to data gathered from two playpen setups, each housing four infants and their real or surrogate mothers. Insofar as the infantile heterosexual stage is concerned, it makes little or no difference from which situation we take our data.

The outstanding finding in both the playroom and playpen is that male and female infants show differences in sex behavior from the second month of life onward. The males show earlier and more frequent sex behavior than do females, and there are differences in the patterns displayed by the sexes. The males almost never assume the female sex-posture patterns, even in the earliest months.

thrust at the companion's head in a completely disoriented manner or laterally across the midline of the body, as in Figure 6. However, it is our opinion that these behaviors are more polymorphous than perverse.

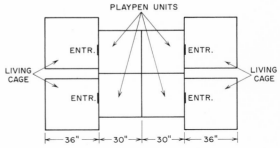

Fig. 5. Playpen test situation.

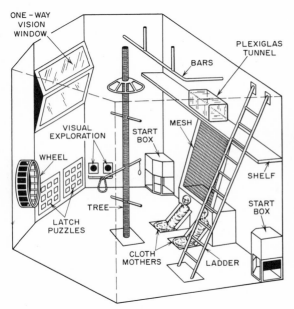

Fig. 4. Playroom test situation.

Fig. 6. Immature male and female sexual posturing, playroom observation.

The females, on the other hand, sometimes display the male pattern of sex posturing, but this is infrequent after ten months of age. Predominantly, females show the female pattern and exceptional instances are to other females, not males. Frequency of sex behavior for both males and females increases progressively with age. There is no latency period—except when the monkeys are very tired.

The early infantile sexual behaviors are fragmentary, transient, and involve little more than passivity by the female and disoriented grasping and thrusting by the male. Thus, the male may

Thus, as soon as the sexual responses can be observed and measured, male and female sexual behaviors differ in form. Furthermore, there are many other behaviors which differ between males and females as soon as they can be observed and measured. Figure 7 shows the development of threat responses by males and females in the playroom, and these differences are not only statistically significant, but they also have face validity. Analysis of this behavior shows that males threaten other males and females but that females are innately blessed with better manners; in particular, little girl monkeys do not threaten little boy monkeys.

The withdrawal pattern—retreat when confronted by another monkey—is graphed for the playroom in Figure 8, and the significance is obvious. Females evince a much higher incidence

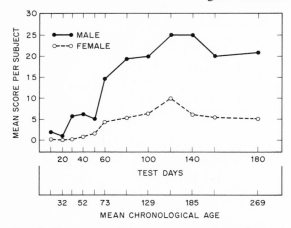

FIG. 7. Frequency of threat responses by males and females in the playroom.

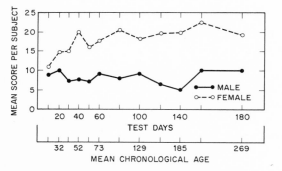

FIG. 8. Frequency of withdrawal responses by males and females in the playroom.

of passive responses, which are characterized by immobility with buttocks oriented toward the male and head averted, and a similar pattern, rigidity, in which the body is stiffened and fixed.

In all probability the withdrawal and passivity behavior of the female and the forceful behavior of the male gradually lead to the development of normal sex behaviors. The tendency for the female to orient away from the male and for the male to clasp and tussle at the female's buttocks predisposes the consorts to assume the proper positions. The development of the dorsally oriented male sex-behavior pattern as observed in the playroom situation is shown in Figure 9 and may be described as a composite yearning and learning curve.

Infant male and female monkeys show clear-cut differences in behavior of far greater social significance than neonatal and infantile sex responses.

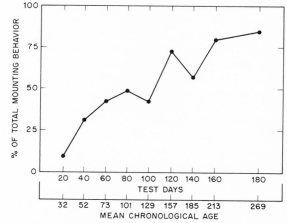

FIG. 9. Percentage of all male mounts (immature and mature) in the playroom that shows dorsal orientation (mature pattern).

Grooming patterns, which are basic to macaque socialization, show late maturation, but as is seen in Figure 10, when they appear, they sharply differentiate the two sexes. Caressing is both a property and prerogative of the females. Basic to normal

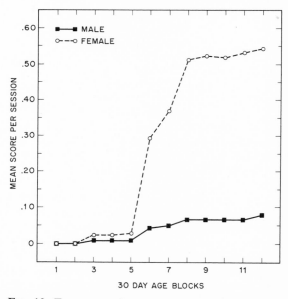

FIG. 10. Frequency of grooming responses made by males and females in the playroom.

macaque socialization is the infant-infant or peer-peer affectional system, and this arises out of and is dependent upon the play patterns which we have described elsewhere and only mention here. As is shown in the solid lines of Figure 11, play behavior in the playroom is typically initiated by males, seldom by females. However, let us not belittle the female, for they also serve who only stand and wait. Contact play is far more frequent among the males than the females and is almost invariably initiated by the males. Playpen data graphed in Figure 12 shows that real rough-and-tumble play is strictly for the boys.

I am convinced that these data have almost total generality to man. Several months ago I was present at a school picnic attended by 25 second-graders and their parents. While the parents sat and the girls stood around or skipped about hand in hand, 13 boys tackled and wrestled, chased and retreated. No little girl chased any little boy, but some little boys chased some little girls. Human beings have been here for two million years, and they'll probably be here two million more.

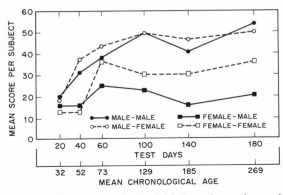

FIG. 11. Frequency of play-initiations by males and females to monkeys of the same (male-male, female-female) and other sex (male-female, female-male). Observations are from the playroom.

These secondary sex-behavior differences probably exist throughout the primate order, and, moreover, they are innately determined biological differences regardless of any cultural overlap. Because of their nature they tend automatically to produce sexual segregation during middle and later childhood, but fortunately this separation is neither complete nor permanent. Behavioral differences may very well make it easy through

cultural means to impose a sexual latency period in the human being from childhood to puberty. We emphasize the fact that the latency period is not a biological stage in which primary sex behavior is suppressed, but a cultural stage built upon secondary behavioral differences.

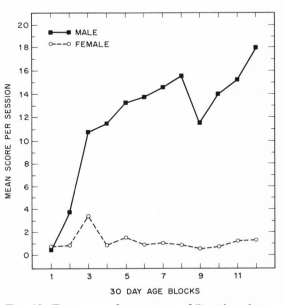

FIG. 12. Frequency of occurrence of "rough-and-tumble" play for two males and two females in the playroom through the first year of life.

We believe that our data offer convincing evidence that sex behaviors differ in large part because of genetic factors. However, we claim no originality for the discovery of intersex behavioral differences. In 1759 Laurence Sterne in his book *Tristram Shandy* described male and female differences at the most critical period in Tristram Shandy's development; indeed, it would not be possible to conceive of a more critical period.

"Pray, my dear, quoth my mother, *have you not forgot to wind up the clock?——— Good G———!* cried my father, making an exclamation, but taking care to moderate his voice at the same time ———*Did ever woman, since the creation of the world, interrupt a man with such a silly question?"* [2]

[2] Sterne, Laurence. *The life and opinions of Tristram Shandy, Gentleman.* J. A. Work (Ed.), New York: The Odyssey Press, 1940, p. 5.

Men and women have differed in the past and they will differ in the future.

It is possible that the listener has been dismayed by the frequent reference to sex and the relatively infrequent reference to affection. Out of these infantile behavior patterns, both sexual and non-sexual, develop the affectional bonds and the social ordering that appear to be important or even essential to the full development of the heterosexual affectional system of macaques. Traumatic affectional errors, both transient and prolonged, may have devastating effects upon subsequent social and sexual behaviors.

For some years we have been attempting to establish experimental neuroses in infant monkeys by having them live on unfriendly and inconsistent mother surrogates. One preparation was a rejecting mother that on schedule or demand separated her baby when a wire frame embedded in her spun-nylon covering was displaced violently upward and backward. The baby was disturbed, but as soon as the frame was returned to its resting position, the baby returned to cling to its surrogate mother as tightly as ever. Next we developed an air-blast mother with a series of nozzles down the entire center of her body which released compressed air under high pressure—an extremely noxious stimulus to monkeys. The blasted baby never even left the mother, but in its moments of agony and duress, clung more and more tightly to the unworthy mother. Where else can a baby get protection? Apparently our infant had never read Neal Miller's theory that avoidance gradients are precipitous and approach gradients gradual and tenuous, for love conquered all.

We next devised a shaking mother, which on schedule or demand shook her infant with unconscionable violence until its teeth chattered. The infant endured its tribulations by clinging more and more tightly. At the present time we believe we may be on the threshold of success through Jay Mowbray's creation of the porcupine mother, which extrudes brass spikes all over its ventral surface. Preliminary studies on two infants suggest that they are emotionally disturbed. Whether or not we eventually succeed, the fact remains that babies are reluctant to develop experimental neuroses, and at one time we even wondered if this were possible.

During the time that we were producing these evil mothers, we observed the monkeys which we had separated from their mothers at birth and raised under various mothered and nonmothered conditions. The first 47 baby monkeys were raised during the first year of life in wire cages so arranged that the infants could see and hear and call to other infants but not contact them. Now they are five to seven years old and sexually mature. As month after month and year after year have passed, these monkeys have appeared to be less and less normal. We have seen them sitting in their cages strangely mute, staring fixedly into space, relatively indifferent to people and other monkeys. Some clutch their heads in both hands and rock back and forth—the autistic behavior pattern that we have seen in babies raised on wire surrogates. Others, when approached or even left alone, go into violent frenzies of rage, grasping and tearing at their legs with such fury that they sometimes require medical care.

Eventually we realized that we had a laboratory full of neurotic monkeys. We had failed to produce neurotic monkeys by thoughtful planning and creative research, but we had succeeded in producing neurotic monkeys through misadventure. To err is human.

Because of housing pressures some of these monkeys and many of our surrogate-raised monkeys lived in pairs for several years while growing to sexual maturity, but we have seldom seen normal sex behavior, and we certainly have not had the validating criterion of newborn baby monkeys. Instead, these monkeys treat each other like brother and sister, proving that two can live in complete propinquity with perfect propriety as long as no one cares.

Their reason for being, as we saw it, was to produce babies for our researches, and so at this point we deliberately initiated a breeding program which was frighteningly unsuccessful. When the older, wire-cage-raised males were paired with the females at the peak of estrus, the introduction only to fighting, so violent and vicious that separation was essential to survival. In no case was there any indication of normal sex behavior. Frequently the females were the aggressors; even the normal praying mantis waits until the sex act is completed.

Pairing such cloth-surrogate-raised monkeys as were sexually mature gave little better end results. Violent aggression was not the rule, and there was attempted sex behavior, but it was unreproductive since both the male and female behaviors were of the infantile type we have already described.

At this point we took the 17 oldest of our cage-raised animals, females showing consistent estrous cycles and males obviously mature, and engaged in an intensive re-education program, pairing the females with our most experienced, patient, and gentle males, and the males with our most eager, amiable, and successful breeding females. When the laboratory-bred females were smaller than the sophisticated males, the girls would back away and sit down facing the males, looking appealingly at these would-be consorts. Their hearts were in the right place, but nothing else was. When the females were larger than the males, we can only hope that they misunderstood the males' intentions, for after a brief period of courtship, they would attack and maul the ill-fated male. Females show no respect for a male they can dominate.

The training program for the males was equally unsatisfactory. They approached the females with a blind enthusiasm, but it was a misdirected enthusiasm. Frequently the males would grasp the females by the side of the body and thrust laterally, leaving them working at cross purposes with reality. Even the most persistent attempts by these females to set the boys straight came to naught. Finally, these females either stared at the males with complete contempt or attacked them in utter frustration. It became obvious that they, like their human counterpart, prefer maturer men. We realized then that we had established, not a program of breeding, but a program of brooding.

We had in fact been warned. Our first seven laboratory-born babies were raised in individual cages while being trained on a learning test battery. William Mason planned to test their social behaviors subsequently, and great care had been taken to keep the babies socially isolated and to prevent any physical contacts. Neonatal baby monkeys require 24-hour-a-day care, and infant monkeys need ministrations beyond a 40-hour week. We had assigned the evening care to Kathy, a maternal bit of fluff who had worked for several years as a monkey tester while studying to become an elementary school teacher.

Checking on his wards one night near 10 P.M., Mason found Kathy sitting on the floor surrounded by seven baby monkeys, all eight of the primates playing happily together. Before the horrified scientist could express his outrage, Kathy had risen to her full height of five feet two. Already anticipating the carping criticisms which he was formulating, she shook her finger in his face and spoke with conviction: "Dr. Mason, I'm an education student and I know that it is improper and immoral to blight the social development of little children. I am right and you are wrong!"

Although we were angry with Kathy, we did think there was a certain humor in the situation and we did not worry about our monkeys. We simply transferred Kathy to an office job. Alas, she could not have been more right and we could not have been more wrong! We have already described the social-sexual life of these 7 monkeys and the next 40 to come.

Two years later we had more than theoretical reasons to be disturbed because Mason tested a group of these isolation-raised monkeys, then between 2.5 and 3.5 years of age, and found evidence of severe social abnormalities, which might be described as a sociopathic syndrome. He matched the laboratory-raised monkeys on the basis of weight and dentition patterns with monkeys that had been born and raised in the wild for the first 12 to 18 months, then captured and subjected to various kinds of housing and caging treatments for the next year or two. In the test situations the laboratory-raised monkeys, as compared with feral monkeys, showed infantile sexual behavior, absence of grooming, exaggerated aggression, and

FIG. 13. Group of cloth-surrogate-raised monkeys on the monkey island in the Madison Zoo.

absence of affectional interaction as measured by cooperation.

We are now quite certain that this sociopathic syndrome does not stem from the fact that the baby monkeys were raised in the laboratory but from *how* they were raised in the laboratory. Our infants raised in the laboratory by real monkey mothers and permitted opportunity for the development of normal infant-infant affection demonstrate normal male and female sexual behavior when they enter the second year of life. Furthermore, our playroom and playpen studies show that infant monkeys raised on cloth mothers but given the opportunity to form normal infant-infant affectional patterns, also develop normal sexual responses.

In a desperate attempt to assist a group of 18 three- to four-year-old cloth-surrogate-raised monkeys, half of them males and half females, we engaged in a group-psychotherapy program, placing these animals for two months on the monkey island in the Madison Zoo, as shown in Figure 13. Their summer vacation on the enchanted island was not without avail, and social grooming responses rapidly developed and were frequent in occurrence. After a few days of misunderstanding, patterns of social ordering developed, and a number of males and females developed friendship patterns. Unfortunately, sexual behavior was infrequent, and the behavior that was observed was completely inadequate—at least from our point of view. In desperation we finally introduced our most experienced, most patient, and most kindly breeding male, Smiley (the male in Figures 1 and 2), and he rapidly established himself as king of the island and prepared to take full advantage of the wealth of opportunity which surrounded him. Fortunately, the traumatic experiences he encountered with unreceptive females have left no apparent permanent emotional scars, and now that he has been returned to our laboratory breeding colony, he is again making an important contribution to our research program. If normal sexual behavior occurred, no member of our observational team ever saw it, and had a female become pregnant, we would have believed in parthenogenesis.

But let us return to the monkeys that we left on the island and the older ones that we left in their cages. A year has passed, and the frustrations that both we and our monkeys experienced

are in some small part nothing but a memory. We constructed larger and more comfortable breeding cages, and we designed a very large experimental breeding room 8 feet by 8 feet by 8 feet in size with appropriate platforms and a six-foot tree. Apparently we designed successful seraglios for I

FIG. 14. Typical behavior of unmothered mother toward her infant. Mother is looking upward while crushing her baby against the cage floor.

can report that not all love's labors have been lost. It does appear that the males are completely expendable unless they can be used in a program of artificial insemination. Certainly we can find no evidence that there is a destiny that shapes their ends unless some Skinnerite can help us with the shaping process. We have, however, had better success with some of the females, particularly the females raised on cloth surrogates.

Even so, one of the wire-cage-raised females is a mother and another is pregnant. Three cloth-surrogate females are mothers and four or five are expectant. We give all the credit to three breeding males. One, Smiley, does not take "no" for an answer. Smiley has a way with females. Patient, gentle, and persuasive, he has overcome more than one planned program of passive resistance. One female did not become pregnant until the fifth successive month of training. Month after month she has changed, and now she is mad about the boy. Male No. 342 behaves very much like Smiley. Even when females threaten him, he does not harm them. Given time, he has been able to overcome more than one reluctant dragon, and he is a master of the power of positive suggestion.

Breeding male No. 496 has helped us greatly, particularly with the younger, cloth-surrogate-raised females. His approach differs from that of Smiley and No. 342. His technique transcends seduction, and in contract bridge terms it may be described as an approach-forcing system.

Combining our human and male-monkey talents, we are winning the good fight and imparting to naive and even resistant female monkeys the priceless gift of motherhood. Possibly it is a Pyrrhic victory. As every scientist knows, the solution of one scientific problem inevitably leads to another, and this is our fate (Figure 14). Month after month female monkeys that never knew a real mother, themselves become mothers—helpless, hopeless, heartless mothers devoid, or almost devoid, of any maternal feeling.

CONSISTENCY OF THE ADULT PERSONALITY *

E. LOWELL KELLY [1]

One of the attractive features of a convention such as this is the opportunity it offers to meet and visit with colleagues whom one has not seen for many years. I don't know how others react to such encounters; my own reaction is typically one of surprise on discovering how much my long unseen friends have aged in the interim! Those of us who

* Reprinted with permission from the American Psychological Association. In *American Psychologist*, 1955, Vol. 10, pp. 659–681.

[1] Address of the President at the Sixty-Third Annual Convention of the American Psychological Association, San Francisco, California, September 4, 1955.

have lived long enough to attend a score or more annual conventions have for the most part accepted the inevitability of aging, and implicitly assume that the passing years will be accompanied by wrinkles, spectacles, additional weight, and grey hair—providing any remains to change its color. These and other changes in the soma are so highly predictable that we take them pretty much for granted. In the realm of behavior we are also accustomed to anticipate certain more general changes: a slowing of pace, less participation in active sports, and fewer late parties.

On the basis of available evidence, psychologists are not likely to anticipate marked changes in the intelligence of their friends—at least, not until relatively late in life. Even though a colleague's intellectual productivity may decline in the middle and later years, we are inclined to give him credit for being about as bright as he ever was.

What about our expectations and anticipations regarding changes in those other aspects of the individual which, for want of a better name, we call personality? Do we expect to find our former colleague pretty much the same sort of person that he was 15 or 20 years before, or are we prepared to find that he has changed markedly with the passing years? William James would have expected little or no change. You will recall the passage from his famous lecture on "Habit" which reads:

> Habit is thus the enormous fly-wheel of society, its most precious conservative agent. . . . Already at the age of twenty-five you see the professional mannerism settling down on the young commercial traveller, on the young doctor, on the young minister, on the young counselor-at-law. You see the little lines of cleavage running through the character, the tricks of thought, the prejudices, the ways of the 'shop,' in a word, from which the man can by-and-by no more escape than his coat-sleeve can suddenly fall into a new set of folds. On the whole, it is best he should not escape. It is well for the world that in most of us, by the age of thirty, the character has set like plaster, and will never soften again (James, 1950, p. 7).

Whether one's thinking about these matters stems from the writings of William James or that of other psychological theorists, the answer is likely to be the same; on perhaps no other major issue do widely variant psychological theories lead to such congruent predictions. Whether one is an extreme hereditarian, an environmentalist, a constitutionalist, or an orthodox psychoanalyst, he is not likely to anticipate major changes in personality after the first few years of life. Not only do psychologists of different theoretical persuasions tend to agree on this issue; it happens to be one on which the layman and the scientist share a common opinion. Perhaps because of the need to believe in consistency of one's self from moment to moment and from year to year, we tend to infer an unwarranted degree of consistency in others. Some consistency is indeed necessary for social intercourse, and it is likely that, as a matter of convenience in remembering and dealing with our associates, we utilize stereotypy to a considerable degree and thus tend to infer greater consistency in others than may be the case.

Although diverse theories and lay opinion lead to the assumption that there will be but little change in personality in adulthood, belief in the possibility of inducing change is implicit in the professional activities of all persons engaged in advertising, public relations, and psychotherapy. While theory underlying these activities is often not explicitly expressed, anyone who attempts to change the attitudes, values, habits, and defense mechanisms of adults may be assumed to hold a position somewhat as follows: "Yes, it is true that the human personality is formed early in life and by late adolescence is quite resistant to change. However, by the skillful application of special techniques, it is possible, though admittedly difficult, to effect significant changes in behavior." Some practitioners go as far as to suggest that it is possible to produce changes in the basic personality structure.

We must pause to note one further exception to the otherwise generally accepted assumption regarding consistency of the adult personality. While assuming that other adults are not likely to change, each of us, I suspect, wants to keep his theory sufficiently flexible to permit the possibility of changes in himself—especially changes in the direction of his ego ideal! Even though in retrospect few of these desired changes may have occurred, it's comforting to think that one *can* change if one tries hard enough.

A more than casual interest on my part in the problem of personality consistency in adulthood began to develop about eight years ago in connection with the VA assessment project, in which Fiske and I were concerned with the prediction of performance of young clinical psychologists after four years of graduate training (Kelly and Fiske, 1951). Since the potential accuracy of our predictions of future performance was limited by the stability of ability and personality variables over the time period involved, we became concerned with the question of consistency of personality over relatively long intervals. A review of the literature revealed but few relevant studies. By all odds, the most extensive evidence available dealt with scores derived from the Strong Vocational Interest Blank. Already in 1943, Strong was able to report relatively stable correlations of vocational interest scores over intervening periods of one, two, three, five, six, nine and ten years. And in 1951, he reported a median correlation of .75 for profiles of vocational interests for college seniors retested after 22 years. A few additional studies, reporting the results of repeated administrations of other psychological tests to college students in one or more successive years of their college careers, have appeared; for example, Whitely (1938) reported correlations for the six scores derived from the Allport-Vernon Scale of Values, based on tests administered to students as freshmen and seniors.

Because of the paucity of studies bearing on the problem of consistency of personality, Fiske and I attempted an evaluation of the consistency of personality variables over four years for the subjects originally assessed by us in the summer of 1947. Since our basic experimental design was not oriented to this particular problem, our results were in no sense definitive. For example, we did not readminister any of the same personality measures four years apart. We did, however, have two sets of comparable data which promised to throw some light on the question. More specifically, all subjects assessed during the summer of 1947 were rated by three peers with whom they were in the closest association during the week-long assessment period. Four years later, the same subjects were rated on the same scales, this time also by peers but not the same judges who rated them in 1947. The interjudge reliability of the first set of ratings ranged from .64 to .92 for 22 variables, with median value of .75. Although not computed, there is every reason to believe that similar reliabilities characterized the second set of ratings four years later. However, somewhat to our surprise, we found that the median correlation between these sets of ratings four years apart was only .21, the range being .00 to .43. In brief, we were confronted with the situation that several judges looking at samples of behavior of a person at the same time agreed reasonably well, but that different judges looking at samples of behavior of the same individual four years apart showed but little agreement in their ratings.

That our subjects *were* somewhat more consistent over this period of time than indicated by these correlations between the two sets of ratings is indicated by the fact that, for each of several criterion variables, one or more objective test scores predicted performance over the four-year time period with validities considerably greater than the above median correlations between these two sets of personality ratings. We were forced to conclude that the relatively low intercorrelation between the ratings by the two sets of judges over this period of time was a function not only of changes in the subjects, but of changes in the frames of reference in the judges themselves, changes associated with the training program that they had undergone during the intervening period.

Since the completion of the assessment project, both Fiske and I have continued to pursue the general problem of intra-individual variability, he concerning himself with relatively short time intervals (Fiske and Rice, 1955) while I have become more interested in time intervals even longer than four years.

In his presidential address to this Association in 1932, Walter Miles lamented the absence of evidence regarding human development during the period of maturity, later maturity, and senescence. He said,

> Psychologists have exhibited great interest in the first two and a half decades of life. Insofar as human behavior has been carefully measured and check-measured, attention has usually been directed to this segment of positive development. . . . Important as this work has been and now is, still it leaves five or six decades of human adult life relatively untouched. Maturity, later maturity, and senescence are still a realm for folklore, anecdote, and personal impression (Miles, 1933, p. 101).

During the nearly quarter of a century following Miles' statement, many psychologists have turned their attention to the field of gerontology, with the result that Shock in his recent bibliography (Shock, 1951) was able to list over 1,000 psychological references. For the most part, attention has been directed to the period of adult life which Miles termed "later maturity." Evidence regarding the course of human maturation during the adult years is still rather limited. In the relatively brief history of psychology, early attention was focused first on children of school age and next on the earlier years of childhood. Still later, a few investigators began to work with infants, while the ready availability of college subjects led to greatly increased knowledge about the period of late adolescence—at least for the selected sample of persons who go to college.

The work of psychologists in the military services during the two World Wars added considerable new knowledge of early adulthood and many current investigations are being conducted in industry and hence on adult subjects. However, for the most part, investigators utilizing adult subjects have been primarily concerned with specific problems which lead to the employment of research designs which, while adequate for the problem at hand, rarely yield definitive data bearing either on the course of development or on intra-individual consistency. Many such studies, however, especially those involving cross-sectional comparisons of different age groups, have provided data which suggest the potential importance of maturational trends in adulthood.

While the data provided by cross-sectional comparisons of different age groups are often highly provocative, they unfortunately are not adequate to permit firm conclusions regarding either developmental trends or intra-individual variability. In a recent monograph reporting one of the few long-term longitudinal studies of mental ability, Owens observes:

> . . . cross-sectional studies demand an excessive number of somewhat unlikely assumptions and are therefore open to varying and ambiguous interpretations. Prominent among the problems involved is that it is extremely difficult to secure comparable samples of the population at successive ages, and to be assured that they are in fact *so* comparable that it is something more than gratuitous to attribute all differences between them to a single variable such as chronological age (Owens, 1953, pp. 7–8).

In the same vein, Kuhlen (1940) notes that unless sampling is so precise that the younger subjects may be truly assumed to *be* what the older subjects once *were,* cultural changes and age changes are almost indistinguishable.

The paucity of longitudinal studies covering any major span of adult years is in no small part due to the fact that appropriate techniques of psychological measurement are themselves just coming of age. A few courageous pioneers such as L. M. Terman, J. W. Anderson, Walter Dearborn, and Jean Macfarlane had enough faith in early intelligence tests to undertake long-term follow-ups of subjects first studied as children. In addition, we have previously mentioned the work of Strong on the stability of vocational interests.

In 1952, Madorah Smith published "A Comparison of Certain Personality Traits as Rated in the Same Individuals in Childhood and Fifty Years Later." While admittedly limited by an *N* of six children of the same family and the absence of any objective measures of personality, this interesting paper pointed to the probability of considerable consistency of several personality variables over a period of nearly half a century.

In 1953, Owens published the results of a study involving the administration of the Army Alpha to 127 freshman males at Iowa State College in 1919, and its readministration 30 years later. In this as yet little known monograph, Owens reports a significant increase in scores for five of the eight subtests of the Alpha as well as for the total Alpha score, of one half sigma of the original distribution. There were no significant decreases in the mean scores on any subtests. More relevant to our present interest is the fact that the test-retest correlation for the total Alpha score over this period of 30 years was .77. Considering the fact that the sample of subjects studied by Owens represented a restricted range of talent, this is indeed convincing evidence of the general stability of adult intelligence over a 30-year time span. Further evidence pointing to the possibility of continuing intellectual maturation during adult years appears in a recently published study by Bayley and Oden (1955). These investigators administered the Concept Mastery test to Terman's gifted subjects and their spouses in 1939–40, and an equivalent form again in 1950–52. Highly significant increases in scores were found for both men and women, for the gifted subjects and their spouses, for all occupational and educational levels and for all age groups. Again, however, the consistency of intellectual level was high, with test-retest correlations of about .90.

THE PRESENT INVESTIGATION [2]

Within the past year I have been fortunate in obtaining a considerable amount of data concerning consistency of selected personality variables in the adult personality. This is because 21 years ago, at the youthful age of 28, I had the temerity to plan a longitudinal study. Lest I seem to take credit for a degree of foresight which I did not have at that time, let me hasten to add that the initially projected duration of this study was only seven years. For a variety of reasons, especially the disturbing effects of World War II, the definitive follow-up stage of this study had to be postponed so that it is only now being completed.

Let me be a little more explicit. In 1943, I began a program of research designed to answer five questions:

1. How do young men and women pair off in marriage?

2. What characteristics of individuals are associated with sexual and marital compatibility?

3. What combinations of characteristics in husbands and wives are associated with sexual and marital compatibility?

[2] In presenting this first major report growing out of this long-term project, I wish to express my appreciation to the many institutions and individuals contributing to it. Only one who has carried out an extended longitudinal study can fully appreciate the many and varied obligations incurred. To the Committee for Research in Problems of Sex of the National Research Council I am indebted for grants which made possible the initiation of the project and collection of the original data between 1934 and 1939. A grant from the Faculty Research Fund of the University of Michigan in 1952 permitted planning the follow-up which was transformed into a reality by grants during the last two years from the Foundations' Fund for Research in Psychiatry. The three universities with which I have been associated have each contributed research facilities and an atmosphere conducive to research. During the last few months the International Business Machines Corporation greatly facilitated the analysis of the data by making available one of its newer electronic computers. A score of research assistants have contributed ideas as well as helping to carry out the actual work of the investigation. Finally, I want to thank the several hundred men and women subjects whose intelligent cooperation over 20 years made this study possible.

4. How do individuals change during the course of marriage?

5. How are these changes related to the nature of the marriage relationship established?

During the years 1935–1938, I enlisted the co-operation of 300 engaged couples. Each of these 600 individuals was assessed with an elaborate battery of techniques including anthropometric measures, blood groupings, a battery of psychological tests, and a 36-variable personality rating scale. In addition, a personally administered questionnaire was used to obtain essential biographical data.

Each of the participating subjects agreed to advise me of the date of his marriage if the engagement eventuated in a marriage, or of the broken engagement if it did not. The original research design called for an annual follow-up questionnaire from each husband and wife for seven years, and retesting at the end of the seven-year period.

The follow-up program was initiated on the anniversary of the first marriage and followed until 1941, at which time it was interrupted by the general dislocation of all civilian activities. The subjects were advised of the writer's intention to return to these studies after the war. In spite of these good intentions I was not able to give serious attention to the project again until 1952–53. That year was spent in re-ordering all previously collected data and planning a full-scale follow-up study to be carried out in 1953–54.

Plans for this follow-up study called for recontacting as many as possible of the original 600 subjects, securing as a minimum a report on the present outcome of the marriage or of the engagement, and inviting all subjects to participate in the final follow-up phase of the study which included (a) retesting on five of the seven psychological tests used in the original battery, and (b) reporting in detail on the marriage between research partners and other intervening life experiences.

In spite of the fact that 16 to 18 years had elapsed between the time of the original testing and the initiation of this major follow-up program, we were successful in securing definitive information regarding the present outcome of all 300 engagements. Parenthetically, it may be of interest to report these outcomes: 278 of the original 300 engagements resulted in marriage of the research partners. There were 22 broken engagements; all but 5 of the 44 individuals involved later married

someone else. Of the 278 marriages, 12 were terminated by death and 39 by divorce. After nearly 20 years, then, 454 of the original 600 persons are still living as husband and wife in 227 marriages.

As might be expected, the subjects, although originally contacted in the New England area, were when recontacted widely dispersed throughout the United States, and several of them live in foreign countries. It was therefore necessary to plan to collect all data in this follow-up phase of the project by mail. Because we planned to ask for approximately six hours of further participation on the part of each subject, it was decided to mail forms to the subjects in two sets. The first of these, mailed in August, 1954, included six forms: the five tests being readministered, and one new instrument, a specially prepared form of Osgood's Semantic Differential. These materials were sent to 521 subjects. The remainder of 1954 was spent in the preparation of two detailed questionnaires, one designed to permit each subject to report on the details of his own life experience during the intervening years, and the other to report the details of his marriage. The second set of forms was placed in the mail about the first of this year. Completed retest forms were returned by 446 of the 521 subjects, or 86%. While this return is not the 100% which we ideally might have hoped for, it is sufficiently large to encourage us to believe that findings based on an analysis of the data will be reasonably representative of the entire sample.

I wish that sufficient time had elapsed since the collection of these new data for me to summarize even tentatively our findings relevant to the five questions asked at the beginning of the project 20 years ago. Such, however, is not the case. In fact, all the data have not yet been coded. Fortunately, the personality retest data was obtained in time to permit a series of analyses concerning the changes in personality variables over this fairly long span of years. At this time, then, I should like to report to you the findings growing out of these analyses. Even with respect to the problem of personality consistency and change, we have not been able to complete all of the detailed analyses needed for a definitive report and interpretation.

I am sure you will want to know a little about the subjects represented in the sample studied. At the time of original testing, all were members of couples with definite anticipations of marriage. The resulting sample is obviously a select one, in that it is composed of persons who responded positively to an invitation to participate in a long-term scientific study of marriage and were willing to contribute initially six to eight hours of their time as well as enter into an agreement to report annually for seven years on the outcome of their marriage. It is not surprising, therefore, that the resulting sample turned out to be superior to the general population in education and intelligence. Only 1% of the men never went to high school and 75% had at least one year of college; nearly 20% had some sort of graduate or professional training. The females were somewhat less selected on the basis of education; nevertheless, approximately two-thirds of them had attended college for varying lengths of time. The IQ equivalent of the mean score on the Otis Self-Administering Test of Mental Ability was 115 for the males and 112 for the females at the time of the original testing. The mean age of the men at the time of the original testing was 26.7 and that of the women 24.7, with nearly 9 out of 10 of the subjects being between the ages of 21 and 30. With respect to religious affiliation, 82% of the males and 89% of the females indicated membership in some church. Approximately 11% of the sample indicated a preference for the Catholic and 8% for the Jewish faith.

We can never know in what manner and to what degree our sample is selected by virtue of its being composed of persons who volunteered to participate in a study of marriage. Admittedly, it does not include, for example, the sorts of people who marry impulsively or those who still regard marriage as a relationship inappropriate for scientific study. However, in a study such as this, one cannot hope for a sample truly representative of the general population. Our goal was that of securing a sample with sufficient variation on each of the variables studied to permit analyses of covariance. In this respect we succeeded. In spite of the operation of known selective factors, the sample studied was characterized by wide individual differences with respect to each of the roughly 200 variables on which the subjects were assessed. And except for education and intelligence, the resulting distributions on the other variables were very similar to those of normative samples.

Since in any study of change it is necessary to obtain measures at two points in time, the retest data which I shall report are based on subsamples of the original samples: those subjects who accepted the invitation to participate in the retest phase of the project. These subsamples included 215 of the original 300 males and 231 of the original 300 females. Furthermore, in order to facilitate the data analyses, I have excluded all cases for whom there was missing any original or retest score on any one of the 103 scores derived from the five tests. The resulting N's are 176 males and 192 females. As might be expected, a comparison of the retested and nonretested samples revealed differences on many of the original measures. While many of these differences are statistically significant and are of interest in themselves as characterizing groups that did and did not choose to participate in the final phase of the project, they are relatively small in magnitude and do not show a systematic pattern of differences for the two sexes. It appeared defensible, therefore, to carry out our analyses of stability and change on those personality variables using the records of the 176 males and the 192 females for whom complete test-retest data were available. Admittedly, our findings will be generalizable only to a population of adults sufficiently cooperative to provide comparable data.

We should also keep in mind that whereas I shall, in most of the analyses, be treating these two samples simply as samples of men and women in general, they are further selected as being primarily the sorts of people who tend to marry. Of the 176 males, 146 were still married at the time of the retest; of the 192 women, 156 were still married at the time of the retest. And, although we shall in these analyses not be primarily concerned with the marriages of these couples, it should be pointed out that 116 of these men and an equal number of women were still married to each other at the time of the retest. To the degree that congruent assortative mating occurred, that is, to the degree that like tend to marry like, any sex differences in the original test scores will tend to be smaller than might be found for samples of men and women not married to each other. Also, since a man and woman married to each other may be assumed to have shared a large proportion of the life experiences intervening between the two testings, it is possible that sex differences in changes in test scores are smaller than

TEST BATTERY

The original assessment battery selected in 1934 included the following standardized instruments: the Otis Self-Administering Test of Mental Ability, the Allport-Vernon Scale of Values, the Bernreuter Personality Inventory, the Bell Adjustment Inventory, Strong's Vocational Interest Inventory, and two of Remmers' Generalized Attitude Scales (Remmers, 1934), one designed to measure Attitude toward any Institution, the other, Attitude toward any Activity. Because it seemed likely (then as now!) that available techniques did not measure adequately all potentially important aspects of personality, we developed a 36-trait graphic personality rating scale; this was used to obtain three sets of ratings for each subject: by self, by research partner, and by five acquaintances.

While we should have liked to have obtained retest scores on all of these measures, limitations in the total amount of time which could be requested of subjects dictated some reduction in the retest battery. The first test to be eliminated was the Otis Self-Administering Test of Mental Ability. Being a timed instrument, it was doubtful that subjects should be asked to administer it to themselves under strict time limits. Furthermore, the definitive results of the 30-year follow-up study of Army Alpha Scores by Owens in 1953 made less essential the inclusion of an intelligence test in this study. Since the original battery had included two adjustment inventories, it seemed reasonable to eliminate one of them; the Bernreuter was chosen over the Bell primarily because the items in the latter are worded primarily for high school students and approximately a quarter of the items deal with adjustment to the parental home. Finally, although we should have much liked to have obtained personality ratings by five present associates of our subjects, we decided to deny ourselves this luxury, primarily because securing such ratings proved to be one of the more difficult aspects of the original assessment program. We did, however, use the original 36-trait rating scale in the retest battery to obtain two additional sets of ratings by self and by partner.

These five instruments provided us with scores on 103 variables. Lest my audience become worried that I am about to discuss changes in each

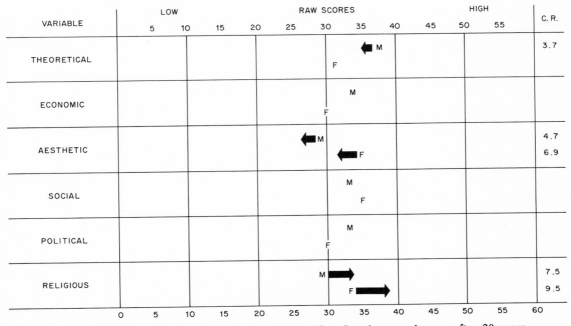

FIG. 1. Allport-Vernon Scale of Values. Means at Time I and mean changes after 20 years.

of these at length, I hasten to assure you that such is not my plan. In fact, because of probable redundancy in these variables, it was not regarded as necessary to analyze all of them in detail. Criteria for selection of variables will be mentioned as we now turn to the results, instrument by instrument. In an effort to enable you to perceive the results more rapidly, I shall present these results in the form of graphs rather than tables, even though some precision is thus lost.

Figure 1 presents the means at Time I and the mean changes after nearly 20 years in scores on the six scales of the Allport-Vernon Scale of Values. Since the Scale of Values is a relatively widely used instrument, I will remind you only that it is designed to measure the relative prominence of six basic interests or motives in personality: theoretical, economic, aesthetic, social, political, and religious. The original form of this instrument published in 1931 was used both for the original and retest.

Inasmuch as the same general format will be used in presenting the data for the other instruments, certain general features of the figure should be noted. The variables are indicated in the left-hand column. The scale over which scores may

range is shown across the top of the figure with the high scores on the right. The letters M and F in each of the rows are placed at points corresponding to the original mean scores of the male and female samples. Mean changes in scores for each variable are indicated by arrows showing the direction and approximate magnitude of the changes. These changes have been indicated in the figure only if the difference was at least 2.5 times its standard error, in which case the critical ratio has been indicated in the column on the right-hand side of the figure.

As will be noted, only 5 of the possible 12 changes on Fig. 1 are significant. By all odds the largest, and in fact the most significant, of all changes to be reported is that for Religious values. Both the men and women score about 5 points higher in their middle years than as young men and women. The change amounts to about one-half sigma of the original score distribution. Since scores derived from the Scale of Values are relative, this shift toward higher Religious values was necessarily accompanied by a downward shift on one or more of the other value scales. For the women, most of this downward shift occurred in Aesthetic values; for the men, it was about equally

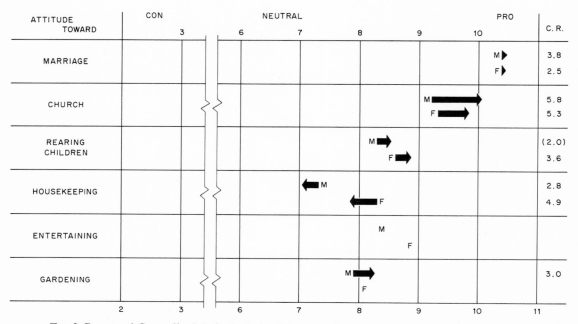

Fig. 2. Remmers' Generalized Attitude Scales. Means at Time I and mean changes after 20 years. (N = 176 males, 192 females.)

divided between Aesthetic and Theoretical values. Quite frankly, I do not know how to interpret this small but significant shift toward higher Religious values. Two alternate interpretations seem equally possible. The shift may merely reflect a cultural change which has taken place in the last 20 years. Perhaps people are generally more religious today than they were during the last part of the great depression. Equally possible and probably a more acceptable interpretation is that in our present-day society people tend to become more religious as they grow older. A recent personal communication from Professor Irving Bender reports a similar enhancement of religious values in a small group of Dartmouth students retested after 15 years.

One additional aspect of this figure deserves your attention, again, because it is also charac-

teristic of those which follow. Note that while small sex differences are reflected in the original means of the men and women on certain of the scales, there is but little evidence of sex differences either in the direction or in the magnitude of the changes in scores. In fact, for the 38 variables to be discussed, the direction of the change was the same for men and women on 32 of the 38.

Figure 2 presents the story for 6 of the 8 attitudes measured. (Two of the attitude scales were omitted from the present analysis because of incomplete data on a number of the subjects.) This figure is to be read in the same way as the previous one. Note that only the upper half of the pro-con continuum is indicated and that the original scores of both the men and women were favorable toward most of these attitude objects and practices. Note,

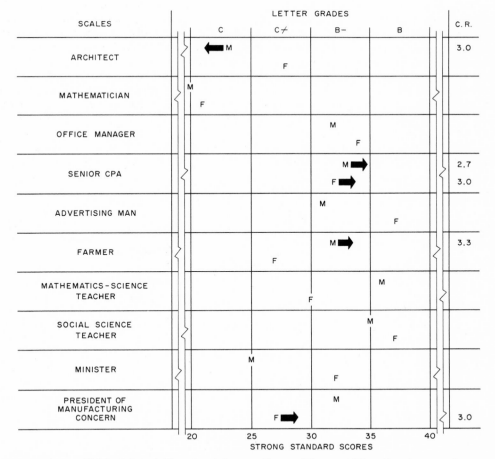

FIG. 3. Strong V.I.B. Selected Vocational Interest Scores. Means at Time I and mean changes after 20 years.

too, that the changes tended to be toward the favorable end after 20 years. The one exception is Housekeeping, shown on the fourth line of the chart. Here we find that men and women, initially mildly favorable in their attitude toward this practice, both shift toward the unfavorable end of the continuum. Whether this reflects a cultural change or the effect of 20 years of married life, we are not able to say with any certainty!

As a measure of interests, the men's form of Strong's Vocational Interest Blank was used for both men and women; this provided comparable measures for each pair of research partners. Both the original and retest responses to Strong's Blank were scored on 47 variables. Figure 3 presents the results for 11 of the vocational interest scores. These particular scales were selected on the basis of two criteria: first, each has a relatively high plus or minus factor loading on one of the five interest factors, and second, the occupation is one which might be followed by either men or women.

While expected sex differences occur in original scores of several of the variables, it is again of interest that there are relatively few sex differences in the changes in scores. Only 5 of the 22 possible changes are statistically significant. In the case of the CPA score, both men and women score significantly higher after 20 years. The men show a small but significant shift toward a lower score on the Architect scale and the women, for reasons

which I shall not attempt to explain, score significantly higher on the scale "President of a Manufacturing Concern." In general, however, note that the picture is again one of few and small score shifts for either sex.

Figure 4 presents the data for five other personality variables. The first two were derived by applying the Flanagan keys to the Bernreuter Personality Inventory, these having been used in preference to the four original keys because the two are relatively uncorrelated and account for practically all of the variance in the other four. Since there are sex differences in the raw score norms for these two scales, the means for the men and women have been located on a percentile scale. While there was no essential sex difference in the original score for either of these scales, the women show a small but statistically significant shift toward greater self-confidence at Time II. I shall not venture an interpretation of this change until we have had an opportunity to determine whether or not it is related to other aspects of married life.

The other three variables shown on this figure are the three nonvocational interest scales derived from Strong's blank. The first is Masculinity-Femininity. As was to be expected, the original means for the men and women are widely separated on this scale, the letters M and F corresponding to the 30th and 3rd percentiles of the male

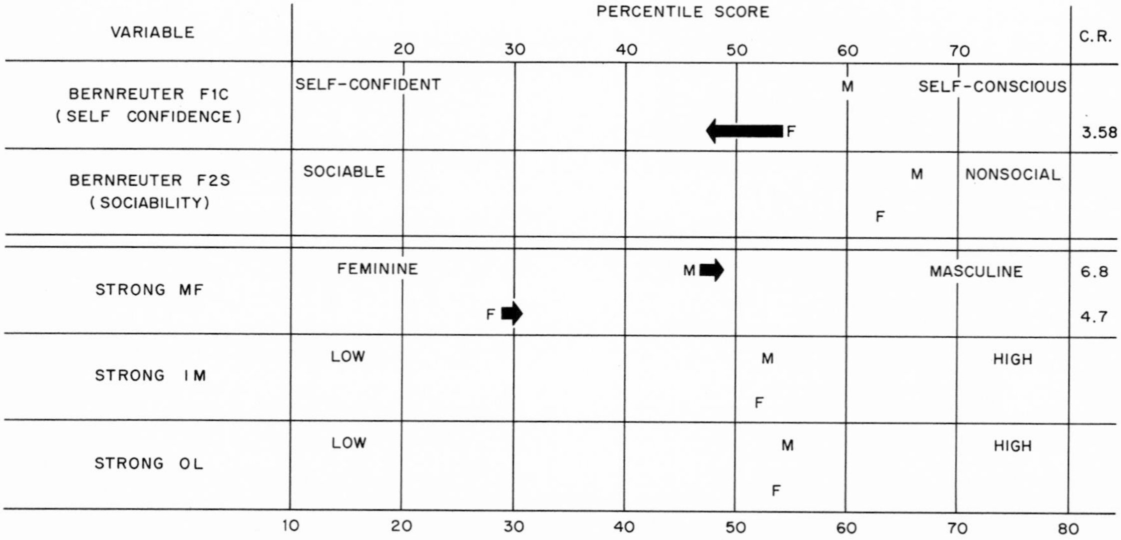

FIG. 4. Other personality variables; means at Time I and mean changes after 20 years.

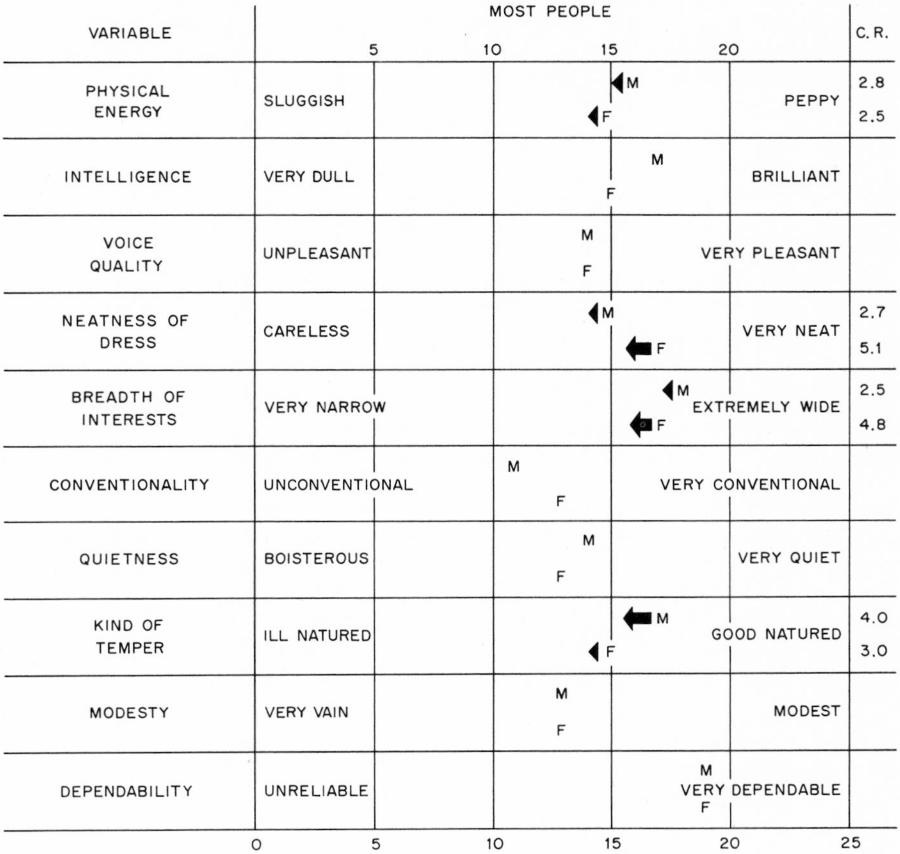

VARIABLE		MOST PEOPLE		C.R.
		5 10 15 20		
PHYSICAL ENERGY	SLUGGISH	◀M ◀F	PEPPY	2.8 / 2.5
INTELLIGENCE	VERY DULL	M / F	BRILLIANT	
VOICE QUALITY	UNPLEASANT	M / F	VERY PLEASANT	
NEATNESS OF DRESS	CARELESS	◀M ◀F	VERY NEAT	2.7 / 5.1
BREADTH OF INTERESTS	VERY NARROW	◀M ◀F	EXTREMELY WIDE	2.5 / 4.8
CONVENTIONALITY	UNCONVENTIONAL	M / F	VERY CONVENTIONAL	
QUIETNESS	BOISTEROUS	M / F	VERY QUIET	
KIND OF TEMPER	ILL NATURED	◀M ◀F	GOOD NATURED	4.0 / 3.0
MODESTY	VERY VAIN	M / F	MODEST	
DEPENDABILITY	UNRELIABLE	M / F	VERY DEPENDABLE	
	0 5 10 15 20 25			

FIG. 5. Self ratings on personality variables; means at Time I and mean changes after 20 years.

adult norms, and to the 1st and 50th percentiles of the female norms. Not expected on the basis of the evidence reported by Strong (1943) was the small but significant shift in the masculine direction for both the men and women, especially not expected by one who had been associated with Lewis M. Terman and Catherine Cox Miles in the research reported in the volume *Sex and Personality* (1936). In fact, all the evidence reported in that volume and by Strong would have led to just the opposite prediction. The data of Terman and Miles, all based on cross-sectional comparisons of groups at different ages and with varying amounts of schooling, show that the peak of masculinity in males is reached in the high school period, and that of the females during the college period, after which time both show a trend toward more feminine scores,

the trend being more pronounced for men than for women.

Again, the interpretation of this finding is hazardous. It may be that our sample studied longitudinally points to meaningful trends which were masked by cultural differences obtaining in the developmental periods of the several age groups sampled by Terman and Miles and by Strong. It may also be true that the last 20 years have been accompanied by cultural changes tending to result in more masculine scores for anyone who has lived his first 20 years of adulthood during this period. To the extent that during this period the home has become more mechanized through modern appliances, and on the assumption that women find that they like the mechanical aspects of home appliances, it is understandable that women should become somewhat more masculine in their likes and dislikes. An equally plausible explanation for the shift in masculinity scores in the men for the same period is not readily available. Perhaps our entire culture is becoming more mechanized all the time, and while both men and women react favorably to these changes, men respond a little more than women. This seemingly simple explanation may well be the correct one. As an hypothesis, it fits both our own findings and those reported by Treman and Miles, providing one is willing to assume that this mechanization of the culture is a process which has been going on gradually for several decades.

The last two scores shown on the figure are two additional personality measures derived from the Strong Blank: Interest Maturity and Occupational Level. It will be recalled that the Interest Maturity score is based on weights corresponding to the differential responses of a representative group of United States males at the ages of 15 and 25 years. At the age of 25 our subjects, both men and women, scored at about the 30th percentile for 25-year-old men and no significant change occurred for either sex over the 20 years.

The Occupational Level scale is based on weights corresponding to the differential responses of representative samples of men between the ages of 18 and 60, representing what might be termed the upper and lower levels of occupations, i.e., professional men vs. unskilled men. Here again, we note practically identical scores for the men and women at the time of the original assessment with no significant shift in these scores at the time of the later test administration. This point on the continuum corresponds to a point about midway between the mean scores of foremen and office workers.

We now turn to a comparison of self ratings made by the subjects at a median age of 25 and again 20 years later. Although the rating scale used for these self ratings included 36 variables, a factor analysis of the ratings of associates showed that not more than 10 relatively independent dimensions were being tapped by the scale. We therefore selected 10 of the 36 variables, each with a relatively high loading on one of these 10 factors and each with relatively low intercorrelations with one another. The findings for these 10 variables are shown in Fig. 5. Since this scale was designed for use by relatively unsophisticated raters, all of the items were originally phrased in terms of sim-

TABLE 1

NUMBER OF PERSONALITY VARIABLES SHOWING
SIGNIFICANT CHANGES IN MEANS

Domain	Total	No Change	For Both Sexes	For One Sex
Allport-Vernon Values	6	3	2	1
Attitudes	6	1	4	1
Vocational interests	11	7	1	3
Other personality variables	5	3	1	1
Self ratings	10	6	4	0
Total	38	20	12	6

ple questions such as: "How peppy is he? How intelligent is he?" etc. The scale was of the graphic type with only three "landmarks": a descriptive phrase at each end of the scale with the phrase "most people" appearing at the center of the line. The high and low ends of the scales were randomly staggered in an effort to reduce halo effect.

We note first the generally comparable means for the men and women in these self ratings. While some of the sex differences in the original mean ratings are statistically significant, none of them are large. Some reason to accept the validity of these self ratings is the slight but significant difference in self ratings of intelligence by the men and women on both occasions, a difference roughly proportional to the measured difference in intelligence of the two groups. Furthermore, self ratings on this simple continuum at Time I correlate about .45 with Otis scores.

Note that significant changes over 20 years occurred for only 8 of the 20 comparisons. Again, too, we find the absence of sex differences with respect to these shifts. For each variable showing a significant shift for the men there is also a significant shift for the women. Certain of these shifts, although small, are in line with general expectations. Thus, both the men and women at the age of 45 rate themselves as somewhat less peppy than 20 years earlier; they also report that they are inclined to be somewhat less neat in their dress and somewhat less broad in their interests. I am not sure what to make of the shift toward an admitted poorer temper. Perhaps by the time one gets to be 45, one is a little more objective in evaluating this aspect of one's personality!

A summary of the findings with respect to ab-

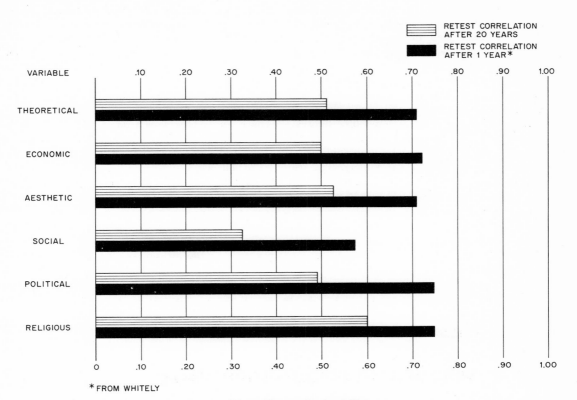

RETEST CORRELATION
AFTER 20 YEARS

RETEST CORRELATION
AFTER 1 YEAR*

* FROM WHITELY

FIG. 6. Allport-Vernon Scale of Values.

solute changes in the mean scores of these 38 personality variables shown in Table 1. We note that:

1. For 20 of the 38 variables, there was no significant change in mean score for either sex.

2. In the case of the 18 variables for which the mean change was statistically significant, the magnitude of the change was still relatively small.

3. These changes, though small, tend to be in the same direction for both sexes.

4. Even though small, each of the significant changes in means is of theoretical interest, but, in the absence of adequate age norms at the two points in time, may be equally well interpreted as due to increasing age or cultural change.

INTRA-INDIVIDUAL CONSISTENCY OF PERSONALITY VARIABLES OVER LONG TIME INTERVALS

We now turn to an analysis of changes in scores on these same 38 personality variables for indi-

viduals. The absence of mean changes could have resulted from either of two states of affairs: for any measure, individuals could have shown little or no change, or alternately, changes in the scores of individuals could have cancelled each other.

In this analysis of change, we shall first compare the retest correlations over the 20-year time span with retest corelations on the same measures for relatively short time intervals. Again, we shall utilize graphical presentation of the results.

Figure 6 presents the findings for the Allport-Vernon variables. For each of the variables shown on the left of the chart, the black bar indicates the retest correlation over a period of 12 months for college students tested by Whitely (1938) as juniors and again as seniors. The striped bar indicates the magnitude of the retest correlation over the approximately 20-year time span for our subjects.

In these charts we have combined the data for

our men and women subjects since the values of these correlations for the men and women were generally within sampling errors of each other. In general, our data lend no confirmation to the popular belief that women are more fickle than men.

Looking again at Fig. 6, it will be seen that for all of the six Allport-Vernon variables, the test-retest correlations over 20 years are considerably smaller than those for the 12-month time interval. Thus, the value for the longer time interval for the Theoretical scale is .51 for our subjects as compared with .71 reported by Whitely. It is also of interest to note that the scores on Social values, which are measured less reliably than the other

over short time periods and, therefore, have plotted the black bar to correspond to the reported Form A–Form B reliability of the scales, i.e., retest correlations over a very brief time interval. It is immediately obvious that the attiude scores of our subjects were much less stable than their value scores on the Allport-Vernon. Thus we note that there is almost no relationship between scores on the attitude toward Marriage at Times I and II. The highest value shown on the figure is .33 for attitudes toward the practice of Housekeeping, as compared with a reported reliability of .79 for this particular scale.

By contrast, over this long time span, vocational interest scores for our subjects were relatively

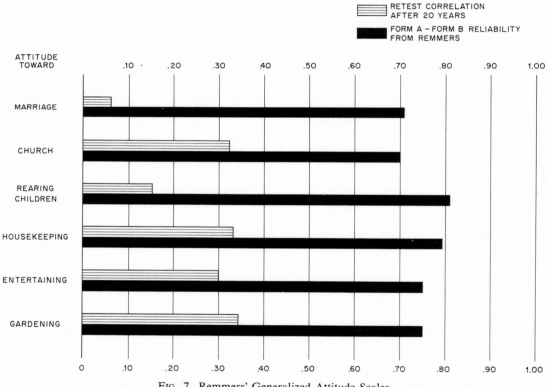

FIG. 7. Remmers' Generalized Attitude Scales.

five values, show the lowest test-retest correlation over the 20-year period.

Figure 7 presents comparable results for the six sets of attitude scores. For these measures, we were unable to obtain any test-retest correlations

stable. Figure 8 presents the essential data for 9 of the 11 vocational interest scores used. Since for several of the scales Strong has provided data showing test-retest correlations for periods of one week and one year (Strong, 1951, p. 78), we have

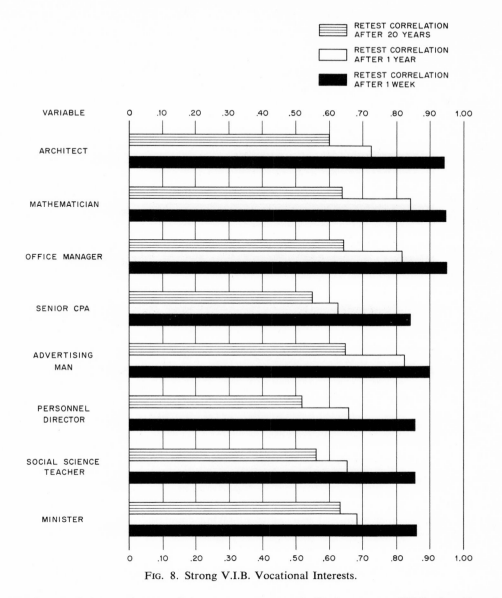

FIG. 8. Strong V.I.B. Vocational Interests.

incorporated both of these estimates of short-term consistency in this chart. The black bars refer to retest correlations over a period of one week and the unshaded bars to correlations for a retest interval of one year.

As was anticipated on the basis of Strong's previously reported findings on the long-term stability of vocational interests, these correlations tend to be relatively high; the median is .62 for men and .57 for women. While for all scales the 20-year retest correlation is somewhat lower than the one-year correlation, the difference in the values for some occupations is rather small.

Turning now to the other personality variables (Fig. 9), we find that the story is much the same. Since no retest correlations over short time intervals were available for the Bernreuter scores, the shaded bars correspond to the reported reliabilities

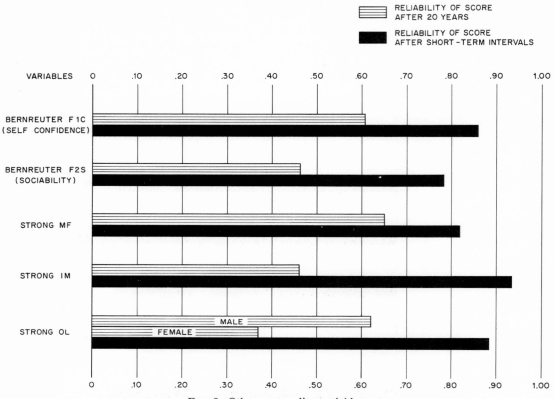

FIG. 9. Other personality variables.

of these scales. It is of interest to note that the retest correlations for the Masculinity-Femininity scores are of about the same magnitude as those for the vocational interest scores on the Strong blank. By contrast, we note a much lower value (.46) for the Interest Maturity scores even though these two Strong scales have about the same reported reliabilities and show the same retest correlations over short time intervals.

The last line of this chart deserves special attention in that it shows the only significant sex difference in consistency of personality measures over this long time span: a value of .62 for our males and .37 for the females. It will be remembered that the Time I scores on this OL variable were approximately equal for the two sex samples and that neither group shifted its mean scores significantly over the 20 years. This little understood scale may measure something less relevant to

women than men, it may measure an aspect of personality which stabilizes later in women than in men, or this may be just a chance difference at the .01 level of significance.

What about the consistency of the self percept as reflected in self ratings on the personality variables at two points widely separated in time? Our findings are shown in Fig. 10. The black bars indicate the retest correlations between self ratings of college sophomores one week apart; the median value is .63. Again, we find our retest correlations after 20 years considerably smaller in magnitude, yet all statistically significant. The median values are .33 for men and .39 for the women.

Just as Strong found the profiles of the Vocational Interest Test scores to show considerably more long-term stability than scores on individual scales, it may be assumed that the stability of the over-all self percept is considerably greater than reflected by the median values of these correlations on single dimensions. As a test of this hypothesis, we computed indices of profile congruency on these 10 self-rated dimensions at two points in time. Using a subsample of 20 cases, and Kendall's tau as an index of congruency, the median profile correlation over 20 years for these 10 traits was found to be .55. By way of comparison, the median value for the Allport-Vernon profile was found to be .65. Strong has reported a median profile cor-

relation of .75 for the Vocational Interest profile over 22 years.

At this point let us summarize the evidence concerning the relative consistency in adulthood of the several domains of personality variables for which data are available. In estimating the relative consistency we first corrected the median retest correlation for attenuation, thus providing an estimate of the most probable correlation between true measures at the two points in time. As an

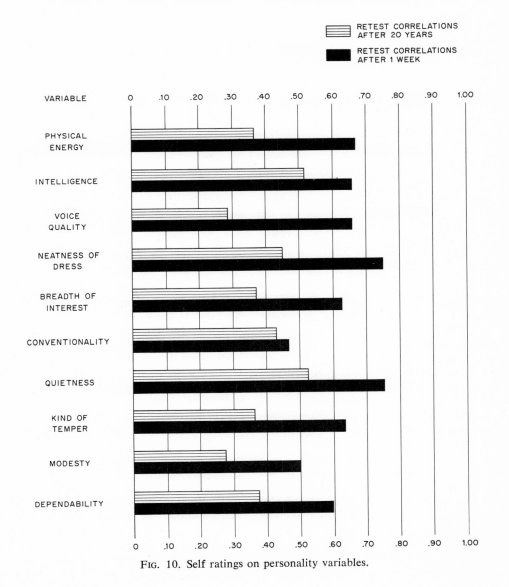

FIG. 10. Self ratings on personality variables.

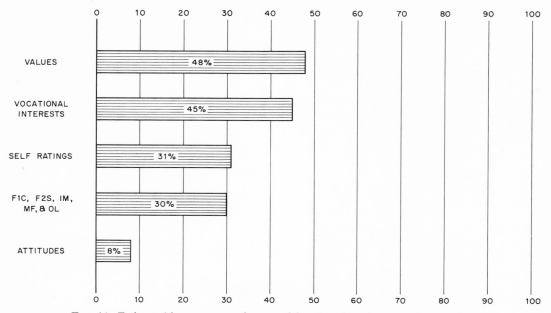

Fig. 11. Estimated long-term consistency of five domains of personality variables.

index of consistency, it seemed most appropriate to utilize the coefficient of determination, i.e., the squared values of those coefficients after correction for attenuation. The resulting values are shown in Fig. 11.

It will be noted at once that the five domains of variables fall into three groups. Values and vocational interests are the most stable, each with an index of approximately .50. Self ratings and the other personality variables are also about equally consistent but with indices about .30. The lowest consistency appears for attitudes, the index being less than .10. While it is essential that any generalizations from these findings be limited to measured variables of the kind here sampled, it is my best guess that this figure fairly accurately summarizes the degree of relative consistency that characterizes the several domains of personality variables.

In view of the considerable evidence for the general constancy of IQ, during the developmental period, and as reported by Owens and by Bayley and Oden for adult groups, it is likely that intelligence would have appeared at the top of this chart, had retest scores been available. Next in order among the personality variables we find values and vocational interests. Apparently these

scores are indicative of relatively deeply ingrained motivational patterns that do not change greatly during the period of middle age. Less stable over this long period of time, but as much so as scores based on many test items, are self ratings on specific personality variables. The relative inconstancy of attitudes during the period of adulthood came as something of a surprise. While it is possible that this relatively low index of constancy is a function of the particular and limited set of attitudes sampled or of the attitude scales utilized, I am inclined to believe that further research will indicate attitudes to be generally less stable than any other group of personality variables. The relative changeability of attitudes is probably a function of their specificity and the fact that alternative attitude objects can easily be substituted one for the other in the service of maintaining an individual's system of values. Thus a person with high social values as measured by the Allport-Vernon scale might shift his attitudes toward and even his allegiance from one to another of several alternative institutions or organizations, each dedicated to the service of humanity.

Although we have thus far been emphasizing the relative consistencies of personality variables, I would call your attention to the fact that Fig. 10

has a "ground" as well as a "figure." Note the relatively wide open spaces to the right of each bar. In effect, these are the relative proportions of variance which may be expected to change during the period of life with which we are here concerned. I venture to say that the potentiality, yes, even the probability of this amount of change during adulthood is considerably greater than would be assumed from any of the current theories of personality. Similarly I suspect that these changes are larger than would be expected by most laymen.

I find it intriguing to speculate as to whether or not these changes in personality variables in adulthood are sufficiently systematic to be predictable for individuals. Conceivably they result from the interaction of so many varied forces in the lives of individuals that prediction of specific changes for individuals may not be possible. To the degree that psychology can develop techniques for predicting the magnitude and direction of change in individual personalities, we should become more effective in the long-term prediction of vocational, marital, and emotional adjustment.

In order to facilitate the analysis of changes in scores, a standard score representing the difference between Time I and Time II scores was computed for each variable, for each of the subjects. In computing these standard scores we utilize the means and standard deviations of the original distribution of scores for each sex. Finally, in order to facilitate computation, these standard scores were transformed into stanine scores. For each individual, then, we had in addition to the original and retest scores, a third set of 38 scores indicative of the direction and magnitude of change over the 20-year period.

Thus far, our studies of change have proceeded along the following lines:

1. an analysis of the relation of change scores to original status scores;
2. an analysis of the degree to which change on specific variables is related to changes on other variables;
3. an analysis of the earlier personality correlates of change scores for a single variable, Interest Maturity as measured by the Strong Blank;
4. an analysis of the relation of changes in paired individuals presumably subject to similar environmental influences.

Time does not permit reporting these studies in

TABLE 2

DISTRIBUTION OF CORRELATIONS BETWEEN ORIGINAL AND CHANGE SCORES FOR 37 VARIABLES
($N = 176$ Males)

r Minus	Obtained Values	Expected on Basis of Statistical Regression Assuming No Change in Variance of Scores
80–89	/	
70–79	//	
60–69	///// //	
50–59	///// ///// //	///
40–49	///// ////	///// ///
30–39	///// /	///// ////
20–29		///// ///// ///// /
10–19		/
Median	−54	−30

detail, but I shall summarize briefly the procedures and findings for each of them.

THE RELATION OF CHANGE TO ORIGINAL STATUS

The first question to which we addressed ourselves was: How are these change scores related to original status scores? For each of the measures, correlations were computed between Time I scores and the corresponding change scores. Since the change scores are indicative of the direction as well as the magnitude of the change, with a mean change score indicative of no change, it was anticipated that statistical regression alone would result in negative values of the status-change correlations. Expressed in less formidable language, subjects who, because of errors of measurement, originally receive scores higher than their true scores tend on a retest to receive lower scores; similarly subjects scoring lower than their true scores are likely to score higher on a retest. For each measure, therefore, it was necessary to estimate, on the basis of the known reliability of the score, the probable value of the status-change correlation that would result from statistical regression alone. Obviously, the lower the reliability of the score, the greater will be the correlation between original and change score; for a test with .00 reliability, the status-change correlation due to statistical regression alone would be .707.

The resulting distributions of obtained and estimated status-change correlations for the male subjects are shown in Table 2. These estimates assume no change in variance from Time I to Time II scores. As will be noted, the obtained values tend to be considerably larger than the expected, the medians being —.54 and —.30. Not shown in the table, but even more pertinent from the standpoint of statistical significance, is the fact that for each of the 37 variables,[3] the obtained value was larger than the expected. It appears, therefore, that we are confronted with a general phenomenon which might be called "maturational regression," a tendency for the retest scores of extreme scoring subjects to regress toward the mean of the group.

This phenomenon of maturational regression appears to account for as much as half the variance of change for some variables and for as little as 5% of the change variance in other variables. It is most dramatically illustrated for the variable "Attitude toward Marriage" which it will be recalled was one of the variables showing a relatively low test-retest correlation over 20 years. Assuming a reliability of .71 for this measure and no reduction in score variance, the status-change correlation that might be expected on the basis of statistical regression alone is —.38; the actual obtained correlation between status and change is —.84 for the men and —.68 for the women. Expressed in nonstatistical terms, our subjects who tended to have extreme attitudes toward marriage at Time I were most likely on the retest to have moved to a much more moderate position on this continuum.

It is my best guess that these regressive changes of extreme scorers are a function of a variety of social forces operative on the individual. If a person finds himself too deviant from his group on a variable subject to change, he apparently finds it easier to shift toward the norm than away from it. Obviously, this statement does not hold for all individuals; strong ego involvement in one's position on the continuum might well lead to "no change" or even to a change in the direction of still greater deviance.

On first thought, it would appear that regression would necessarily result in reducing the variance of retest scores as compared with original scores. This may occur, but not necessarily. Consider the

case of successive administrations of a test of .00 reliability. As noted above, the resulting status-change correlation would be .707, yet the variance of the two distributions of scores would be essentially the same. Consider also the case of filial regression: tall fathers tend as a rule to have sons shorter than themselves, and short fathers sons taller than themselves, yet the means and standard deviation of fathers' heights and sons' heights tend to be quite comparable.

For our data, the fact is that for more than half of the 38 variables studied, the Time II score variances were somewhat smaller than those for Time I. These differences were large enough to achieve statistical significance, however, for less than a fifth of the variables. The most significant reduction in variance occurred in "Attitude toward Marriage," "Attitude toward the Church" and self ratings on "modesty." These were variables for which the status-change correlations were also high—all above .70.

That a highly significant amount of maturational regression may occur without a corresponding decrease in the variance of Time II scores is shown for the variable Interest Maturity. Because of the high reliability of this variable (.93) the status-change correlation expected from statistical regression is only —.19; the actual values are —.49 for the men and —.53 for the women, yet the Time I and Time II variances are almost equal in size. That persons scoring low on Interest Maturity at the age of 25 might be expected to increase their scores 20 years later is hardly surprising. Why persons originally scoring high on this variable should regress and at the age of 45 score more like 15-year-olds than they did at the age of 25 is an intriguing matter to which we will return later.

INTERRELATIONSHIPS OF CHANGE SCORES

Our next attempt to explore the phenomenon of personality change started with the question: if an individual changes on one personality variable, is this change a relatively specific one or is it likely to be accompanied by changes on one or more other variables? For each sex group we computed the 38 × 38 matrix of intercorrelations; note, however, in this case we were dealing not with the usual set of intercorrelations of test scores, but with the intercorrelations of the differences between scores at Time I and Time II.

For obvious reasons, I shall not ask you to look

---

[3] The value of the Time I change correlation for one variable was inadvertently lost in the electronic computer! Because the findings were so consistent, it was not regarded as necessary to compute it separately.

TABLE 3

INTERCORRELATIONS OF CHANGE IN SELF RATINGS
(N = 176 males)

Variables	1	2	3	4	5	6	7	8	9	10
1 Pep	—	09	14	09	18	02	−11	09	00	18
2 Intelligence		—	19	05	11	07	04	02	06	18
3 Voice			—	28	10	−04	−03	19	03	12
4 Dress				—	14	13	−03	17	01	29
5 Interests					—	−04	−06	07	19	18
6 Conventionality						—	13	05	09	20
7 Boisterous-quiet							—	14	21	13
8 Temper								—	11	21
9 Modesty									—	16
10 Dependability										—

TABLE 4

INTERCORRELATIONS OF CHANGE ON
SIX ATTITUDE SCORES

(N = 176 males)

	1	2	3	4	5	6
1 Marriage	—	24	07	01	−06	08
2 Church		—	10	07	10	13
3 Rearing children			—	20	12	11
4 Housekeeping				—	21	05
5 Entertaining					—	−01
6 Gardening						—

at the resulting matrices. I do, however, wish to call your attention to certain of their features. First of all, as has been generally true for the previously reported analyses, the values tended to be very similar for the men and women subjects. Secondly, the values of the intercorrelations tended to be low: of the 703 intercorrelations in each matrix, less than 20% were significant at the 1% level. Thirdly, changes on approximately half of the variables were found to be unrelated to changes on any of the other 37 variables. All of these facts point to the conclusion that personality changes as reflected in these difference scores tend to be relatively specific.

As examples of this specificity, I shall present two small segments of the total correlational matrix for the men. Table 3 presents the intercorrelations of changes in self ratings on the 10 personality variables. Of these 45 correlations only 5 are significant at the 1% level, and these are relatively small in magnitude. Even though these 10 variables were selected from the original 36 as relatively uncorrelated, I had fully expected evidence for one common factor in this little matrix —a factor reflecting a shift over the 20 years in the general level of self esteem. If such a factor is operative its contribution to variance of changes in self ratings is extremely small.

As a second example, we now turn to that section of the matrix showing the intercorrelations of changes in attitude scores. It will be recalled that these scores had a relatively low index of consistency over the 20-year interval, hence the changes on them might well covary. The facts are shown in Table 4. Again the intercorrelations are generally low, only 3 of the 15 reaching a value of .20.

In view of the generally low correlations among the change scores, our original plan of factoring the entire matrix was not carried out. Further inspection showed significant correlations of change scores among the six value scores; these were anticipated because of the manner in which the scores are derived, i.e., one can increase his score on a single scale only by decreasing it on one or more of the other five. Even under these circumstances the highest intercorrelation (for the males) was −.39 indicating a tendency for Economic and Aesthetic value scores to change in opposite directions.

Similarly, in view of the fact that many items on the Strong Blank contribute to several scores derived from it, significant intercorrelations of change scores were expected and found. In general, these were the same sign and magnitude as the correlations reported by Strong among the scales. For example, score changes indicating a subject's interests becoming more like those of Personnel Manager correlated +.73 with changes in the direction of higher Interest Maturity. The correlation reported by Strong between these two scales is +.75.

Inspection of the intercorrelations between changes in Allport-Vernon and Strong scores showed more than a chance number of significant relationships but not as many as might have been expected on the basis of the common factors shown to underlie these two sets of measures in studies by Ferguson, Humphreys, and Strong (1941) and by Duffy and Crissy (1940).

Had relatively high intercorrelations been found among these change scores, we would have attempted to identify the one or few common factors and their early personality correlates. However, the relatively marked specificity of these change scores suggests the fallacy of current attempts to posit and assess a global trait of personality rigidity. Our findings are in line with those of a number of recent studies reporting generally low and insignificant correlations among so-called measures of rigidity (Applezweig, 1954; Cattell and Winder, 1952).

CORRELATES OF CHANGES IN
INTEREST MATURITY

Had the interrelationships among the change scores pointed to the existence of one or more general factors, we had planned to describe the sorts of people who do and do not tend to show marked personality changes in adulthood. In view of the lack of evidence for any general factor of change, we decided to carry out a more limited study of the earlier background correlates of one set of change scores, those for the Strong variable, Interest Maturity. It will be recalled that this variable was one for which there were no sex differences in original scores and no significant change in means or variances over the years for either sex. Furthermore it was a variable for which Time II scores showed considerably more regression toward the mean than was expected from statistical regression alone. These facts posed the interesting question: what kinds of people tend between the ages of 25 and 45 to change their scores on the continuum, reflecting, on the one end, the modal interests of 15-year-old boys, and on the other, the modal interests of 25-year-old men?

In this analysis, carried out for the men only, Interest Maturity change scores were correlated with 66 measures obtained at Time I. Included were Time I scores on the 38 variables treated throughout this report, age, height, Otis IQ, education, church membership, and similar background variables.

Here again the results can be summarized very briefly: only 8 of the 66 correlations were significant at the 1% level. Six of these 8 were negative correlations with Time I Strong scores: Interest Maturity and occupational scores for Personnel Manager, Mathematics-Physical Science Teacher, Social Science Teacher, Minister, and Senior CPA. In general, those men who showed early interests similar to men in the above professions were more likely to score more like 15-year-olds at age 45 than they did at age 25. Conversely, the less our

subjects were like men in these professions at Time I, the more they tended to score higher on the Interest Maturity Scale at Time II.

There were two other significant correlates of Interest Maturity change scores: age at the time of the first test, and attitude toward rearing children. Increase in Interest Maturity scores tended to go with younger age and with more favorable attitudes toward rearing children at time of first testing.

Taken together, these findings suggest the possibility that for some men, there occurs an early (and perhaps premature) development of vocational interests characteristic of professional persons who work with and try to help people; this may lead to later disillusionment and a tendency to develop interest patterns more characteristic of persons who prefer to work with ideas and things rather than directly with other human beings. Changes in the direction of lowered maturity of interests were found to be significantly associated with interest changes toward those of an architect, a mathematician, and a president of a manufacturing concern. Lest it be assumed that I am making a value judgment regarding such changes of interest, let me remind you that members of these three professions may do fully as much for their fellow men as members of professions who prefer to help people through interpersonal relationships. Furthermore, the fact that change scores on Interest Maturity do not correlate significantly with changes in the Allport-Vernon value scores suggests that one may change his vocational interests without necessarily shifting his basic system of values.

RELATIONSHIP OF CHANGES IN PAIRED
INDIVIDUALS PRESUMABLY SUBJECT TO
COMMON SOCIAL FORCES

In our last exploration of changes in the 38 personality variables, we capitalized on the fact that 116 of the male subjects and an equal number of the women had been members of a close diadic group through the time span. As husband and wife, each subject had presumably filled a relatively prominent role in the social environment of another. Was there any systematic relationship between the changes in one and the original scores of the other member of the pair?

To answer this question, correlations were computed between each set of change scores and the original scores of the spouse. The results can be summarized very briefly: for both cross-spouse comparisons, the correlations were all relatively low indicating but little tendency either for the husband to change toward the original score of his wife or the wife to change toward that of her husband. In fact, although the magnitude of most of the correlations was not large enough for them to be individually significant, nearly three out of four were negative, indicating a slight trend for changes for both the husband and wife to be away from the original score of the other. Since the directions of these relationships tended to be similar to those between status and change for men and women separately, it seemed likely that the change scores of husbands and wives, presumably subject to many of the same social forces, would be positively related. While these correlations were found to be generally positive, they were also small, achieving statistical significance for only 4 of the 38 variables: economic, social and religious values, and attitude toward marriage.

It is commonly believed that persons married to each other tend with the passing years to become more and more similar; in fact, I have even heard it said that this principle holds for physical appearance. Obviously, our data provided for a direct test of this hypothesis. For the 116 couples, husband-wife correlations were computed between Time I scores for each of the 38 variables and again at Time II. In line with our preliminary report on assortative mating for the 300 engaged couples (Kelly, 1937) of which these 116 constitute a subsample, the Time I correlations were found to be positive for practically all variables, ranging from −.02 to .58. In other words, we found no evidence [4] to support the opinion that "opposites attract."

What about the Time II correlations? In general, they proved to be no different than those at the time of original testing! Actually they were slightly smaller for 21 of the 38 variables and the few statistically significant shifts were in the direction of the couples becoming less similar with the elapse of 20 years. However, since some of the Time II correlations were attenuated because of slightly reduced variances of measures on the re-

test, the most conservative generalization seems to be that the initial similarity between husbands and wives becomes neither greater nor less with the passing years. Apparently the initial similarity is adequate for most husbands and wives to establish and maintain a cohesive relationship without the need to become more alike. And while we can readily think of many forces tending to promote increasing congruence between mates, we must not overlook the apparently equal impact of centrifugal forces associated with maintaining the many kinds of role differentiation expected of husbands and wives in our culture.

This completes the report of our explorations of personality consistency and change in adulthood. The sample of variables studied was necessarily limited to the techniques available 20 years ago, but the results for the several variables are so consistent that we may accept them as pointing to generalizations that are likely to be confirmed in later research.

With respect to personality consistency, our results can and probably will be used to support very different theoretical positions. Absolute changes in personality scores tended to be small but similar in direction and magnitude for men and women. We found evidence for considerable consistency of several variables, in spite of fallible tools and a time span of nearly 20 years. But we also found evidence for considerable change in all variables measured. These changes were shown to be relatively specific rather than reflecting any over-all tendency to change. While measurable changes occurred on most variables, it appears that correlates of these changes are many and elusive, and hence changes in scores are likely to be difficult to predict for individuals. Finally, we found that the measurable changes showed little or no relation to known forces assumed to be dominant in an individual's immediate social environment; this finding points to the probable difficulty of obtaining firm knowledge concerning the mechanisms of effecting change.

The intensive study of any aspect of growth and development cannot but serve to increase one's respect for the integrative capacities of the human organism. Beginning with the complex structures and functions provided by its unique genetic constitution, each organism, while maintaining its organic integrity and a considerable residue of its original nature, moves through its maturational

[4] Note, however, that our personality variables did not include any measures of "needs" which Winch, Ktsanes, and Ktsanes (1954) believe to be negatively correlated in assortative mating.

cycle adapting to and permitting itself to be modified by selected aspects of its immediate environment. These adaptive changes, occurring most rapidly in the years of infancy and childhood, are so appropriately timed that they do not threaten the organism either physiologically or psychologically. Our findings indicate that significant changes in the human personality may continue to occur during the years of adulthood. Such changes, while neither so large nor sudden as to threaten the continuity of the self percept or impair one's day-to-day interpersonal relations are potentially of sufficient magnitude to offer a basis of fact for those who dare to hope for continued psychological growth during the adult years.

REFERENCES

Applezweig, Dee G. Some determinants of behavioral rigidity. *J. abnorm. soc. Psychol.*, 1954, 49: 224–228.

Bayley, Nancy, and Oden, Melita H. The maintenance of intellectual ability in gifted adults. *J. Geront.*, 1955, 10: 91–107.

Cattell, R. B., and Winder, A. E. Structural rigidity in relation to learning theory and clinical psychology. *Psychol. Rev.*, 1952, 59: 23–39.

Duffy, Elizabeth, and Crissy, W. J. E. Evaluative attitudes as related to vocational interests and academic achievement. *J. abnorm. soc. Psychol.*, 1940, 35: 226–245.

Ferguson, L. W., Humphreys, L. G., and Strong, F. W. A factorial analysis of interests and values. *J. educ. Psychol.*, 1941, 32: 197–204.

Fiske, D. W., and Rice, L. Intra-individual response variability. *Psychol. Bull.*, 1955, 52: 217–250.

James, W. *The principles of psychology.* New York: Dover Press, 1950.

Kelly, E. L. A preliminary report on psychological factors in assortative mating. *Psychol. Bull.*, 1937, 34: 749. (Abstract)

Kelly, E. L., and Fiske, D. W. *The prediction of performance in clinical psychology.* Ann Arbor: Univer. Michigan Press, 1951.

Kuhlen, R. G. Social change; a neglected factor in psychological studies of the life span. *Sch. and Soc.*, 1940, 52: 14–16.

Miles, W. R. Age and human ability. *Psychol. Rev.*, 1933, 40: 99–123.

Owens, W. A., Jr. Age and mental abilities: a longitudinal study. *Genet. Psychol. Monogr.*, 1953, 48: 3–54.

Remmers, H. H., *et al.* Studies in attitudes. In *Studies in higher education, XXVI.* Lafayette, Ind.: Purdue Univer., 1934.

Shock, N. W. *A classified bibliography of gerontology and geriatrics.* Stanford: Stanford Univer. Press, 1951.

Smith, Madorah E. A comparison of certain personality traits as rated in the same individuals in childhood and fifty years later. *Child Develpm.*, 1952, 23: 161–180.

Strong, E. K., Jr. *Vocational interests of men and women.* Stanford: Stanford Univer. Press, 1943.

Strong, E. K., Jr. Permanence of interest scores over 22 years. *J. appl. Psychol.*, 1951, 35: 89–91.

Terman, L. M., and Miles, Catherine C. *Sex and personality.* New York: McGraw-Hill, 1936.

Whitely, P. L. The constancy of personal values. *J. abnorm. soc. Psychol.*, 1938, 33: 405–408.

Winch, R. F., Ktsanes, T., and Ktsanes, Virginia. The theory of complementary needs in mate selection. *Amer. soc. Rev.*, 1954, 19: 241–249.

A STUDY OF THE DROPOUT RATES IN LONGITUDINAL RESEARCH ON AGING AND THE PREDICTION OF DEATH *

KLAUS F. RIEGEL, RUTH M. RIEGEL, AND GUNTHER MEYER [1]

During recent years, an increasing number of longitudinal studies of adult and aged subjects have been reported in the psychological literature. Most of these studies are based on special subsamples of the population and have applied restricted sets of psychological measures only. Owens (1953) retested the intelligence of a group of superior adults, and Bayley and Oden (1955)

* Reprinted with permission from the American Psychological Association. In *Journal of Personality and Social Psychology,* 1967 Vol. 5, pp. 342–348.

[1] This study has been aided by the Foundations' Fund for Research in Psychiatry, New Haven, Connecticut. The analysis has been completed at the Computing Center, the University of Michigan.

reported on the longitudinal analysis of Terman's subjects. At the other end of the continuum, Kaplan (1943, 1956) and Bell and Zubek (1960) retested mentally inferior persons. In both cases it would be inappropriate to generalize the reported findings since there is, most likely, an interaction between the rate of change and the original level of functioning. This has been emphasized by Foster and Taylor (1920), Jones and Conrad (1933), and Miles (1933).

More recently, Jarvik, Kallman, and Falek (1962), Jarvik, Kallman, Falek, and Klaber (1957), Jarvik and Falek (1963), and Falek, Kallman, Lorge, and Jarvik (1960), in a number of joint publications, reported on a longitudinal investigation of intellectual functioning and longevity of senescent twins. Kleemeier (1962) and Kaplan, Rumbaugh, Mitchell, and Thomas (1963) retested the intelligence of residents in a home for the aged after various time intervals, and observed sudden and marked performance decrements preceding the death of the subjects. Among the best-matched samples of the aging population were those by Berkowitz and Green (1963), Eisdorfer (1963), and by Schaie and Strother (1964). The former two studies were restricted to the measurement of intelligence, while the latter also included some attitudinal scales applied to stratified samples ranging from 20 to 70 years of age.

In most of these studies, developmental psychologists have never questioned the superiority of the longitudinal over the cross-sectional design. Only very recently has the complementary nature of both strategies been recognized. In particular, Schaie (1959, 1965) and Schaie and Strother (1964) have provided a thorough discussion of the experimental strategies in gerontological research, in emphasizing more general designs in comparison with which the two traditional approaches are merely specialized and incomplete cases.

In a more concrete sense, the limitations of the traditional research strategies have long been recognized. In their cross-sectional study, Jones, Conrad, and Horn (1928) analyzed the performance of subjects who had originally refused to participate in their study, thus biasing the sample. More recently, Sussman (1964), Damon (1965), and Rose (1965) discussed the representativeness of samples in longitudinal research primarily concerned with the health of the subjects.

Because of systematic factors, of which sickness and death are the most obvious, the problem of sample bias is equally important for longitudinal and cross-sectional studies in psychological gerontology. Indeed, if systematic selection by dropout factors (such as selective death rates) can be detected, the concept of psychological development based on observed trends would itself be seriously challenged, because then cross-sectional or longitudinal research would represent averages for sets of systematically biased age samples only; therefore any inferences about general developmental trends would be questionable.

The present analysis has been undertaken primarily to determine the psychological characteristics of subjects who either did not survive the time period between the two testings, were too ill, or refused to be retested. Since significant differences between the subgroups were detected, attempts have also been made to predict the ensuing death of the subjects on the basis of sociopsychological factors. The present analysis is restricted to major comparisons between the four subgroups mentioned. (In a supplementary technical report—Riegel, Riegel, and Meyer, 1967—statistical details on the 43 variables and five age groups at both testings have been provided, and differences in the distributions of test scores and the effect of multiple testing have been discussed.)

METHOD AND PROCEDURE

Subjects

The present analysis is based on the results of the first testing of a study on sociopsychological factors of aging, conducted in Germany in 1956–57 and a retest study in 1961–62.

The original sample consisted of 190 females and 190 males. These cases were drawn from a group of about 500 subjects, and were subdivided into five age levels of 38 females and 38 males each. The five age levels were 55–59, 60–64, 65–69, 70–74, and over 75 years (average age = 79.0 years). Aside from controlling for age and sex, each age level was matched against census statistics on the following criteria: occupation, source of income, marital status, refugees versus nonrefugees, and religious affiliation. The samples can be regarded as representative for the population of northern Germany. Fuller descriptions of the samples and the procedures are given elsewhere (Riegel and Riegel, 1959; Riegel, Riegel, and Skiba, 1962).

At the time of the second testing all subjects had moved into the next higher age levels. Of the 380 persons originally tested, 202 participated in the second testing, 62 had died during the intervening 5 years, 32 were too ill to be retested (were in hospitals or had to remain in bed during the weeks of the testing), and 84 refused to be retested. A comparison of these four categories of subjects by age levels is given in Table 1 and shows that the number of subjects retested decreased rather regularly with age, whereas the number of deceased subjects increased. The num-

TABLE 1

Fate of Subjects from the Original Samples at the Time of the Second Testing

	55–59	60–64	65–69	70–74	75 +	Sum
Retested	51	48	44	34	25	202
Deceased	2	8	12	17	23	62
Too ill	4	2	6	11	9	32
Refusals	19	18	14	14	19	84

ber of sick subjects increased irregularly. No systematic differences in the number of noncooperative subjects existed between the age levels.

Method

The following measures were used:

1. Short forms of the Hamburg Wechsler Intelligence Test for Adults. These scales were administered to all subjects and the full test to a random subsample of 128 (see K. F. Riegel and R. M. Riegel, 1962; R. M. Riegel, 1960; R. M. Riegel and K. F. Riegel, 1959, 1962).

2. Five multiple-choice verbal tests (synonyms, antonyms, selections, classifications, analogies) as described by Riegel (1959, 1967). Though subjects were under no time stress, the duration of the test performances were recorded. Half of the items of the antonyms, selections, and classifications tests were mixed (m); the others were presented each in separate forms (s).

3. Four attitude and interest scales of the Likert type (rigidity, dogmatism, attitude toward life, interests) as described by Riegel and Riegel (1960).

4. A general questionnaire on the social and living conditions of the subjects, including inquiries on the following topics: education, financial status, health, physical activities, leisure-time activities, social activities, itemized activities, expressions of well-being, comparisons of situations, as well as many single items dealing with the conditions and habits of daily life (see Riegel et al., 1962).

Results and Discussion

Developmental Trends of Subsamples

The main problems to be analyzed can be outlined in reference to Figures 1 and 2, which represent the average scores of the various subgroups on the scale of behavioral rigidity (see Riegel and Riegel, 1960). According to Figure 1, which includes the data from the first testing only, rigidity increased rather steadily with age. Subjects who were later retested were less rigid than the total group, but the rate of increase was about the same for both. Subjects who died during the following 5 years were much more rigid than both the total group and the subjects to be retested. Age differences were small for nonsurvivors. The scores of subjects who were ill at the time of the second testing varied rather markedly between the age levels, but generally were far above those of the other groups. The same held for the subjects who later refused to be retested. However, this group did not deviate as much from the general trend as did the ill subjects.

Figure 2 compares the mean scores obtained at the second testing with total scores of the first test. Again the rigidity of the retested subjects increased with age. The trend of the means was closely parallel to that of the first testing, though the means were significantly higher ($p < .01$). Of greater importance, however, was the fact that the retest means were still below the averages of the total group at the first testing. This may be attributed to the absence of those subjects who died, became ill, or refused to be retested. If one reinstated these subjects by averaging their scores from the first testing with the second scores from the retested group, artificially complete samples would be created on the rather disadvantageous assumption that the scores of the subjects not re-tested would have remained unchanged during the intervening 5 years. The means of these artificial groups were comparable to those of the total group at the time of the first testing. As Figure 2 shows, they were above those of the first testing as well as above all other subgroups; that is, rigidity was higher during the later years than estimated in any of the other analyses. Of major concern in our discussion below will be the question of which of the various curves of Figure 2 would represent most appropriately the developmental trend.

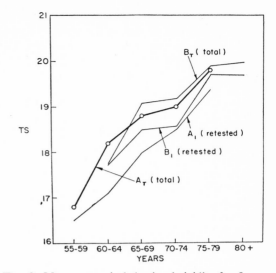

FIG. 2. Mean scores in behavioral rigidity for five age levels of the total group and the group of retested subjects at the first (A) and the second (B) testing.

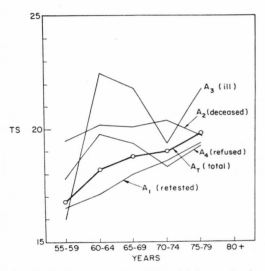

FIG. 1. Mean scores in behavioral rigidity at the first testing for five age levels and four subgroups of subjects.

Dropout Rates

Since at the younger age levels some of the four subgroups did not include enough cases to allow for reliable estimates, the five consecutive age samples were pooled using the retirement age of 65 years as the cutting point. The significance of the retirement age for changes in behavior has been strongly suggested by the authors' as well as by earlier investigations. But aside from any such considerations, the age of 65 years subdivided the group of retested subjects in nearly equal sections of 99 and 103 subjects, respectively, and was selected primarily for this reason.

In the following analysis, the 43 variables tested are being regarded as a sample of measures not

all of which are independent of one another but whose interdependencies—though slightly increasing with age—do not yield different correlation matrices at the two age levels. The variability in scores did not change markedly with age even though the dropout of subjects at the earlier age levels seemed to depend on systematic rather than random factors. These results justify the following comparisons in the numbers of significant differences between the subgroups.

For each variable the differences between the means of the four subgroups at the two remaining age levels have been tested for significance by analyses of variances. Subsequently, the most important *t*-test comparisons between the subgroups have been made and are explained in the footnote to Table 2. Signs are given whenever the differences are significant at or beyond the .05 level. In particular, positive signs indicate that the direction of differences in the first group of comparisons leaned toward greater intelligence, superiority in verbal abilities, more rigidity, more negativism in their attitude toward life, less interested, better education and financial support, poorer health, greater activity, feeling of well-being, and a favorable comparison of their present situation with the past.

By adding all the significant signs for each of

TABLE 2

SIGNIFICANCE OF DIFFERENCE IN MEAN SCORES BETWEEN VARIOUS SUBGROUPS OF THE ORIGINAL SAMPLE[a]

Item	Age group 55–64						Age group over 65					
	1−2	1−3	1−4	2−3	A−2	1−N	1−2	1−3	1−4	2−3	A−2	1−N
Age							−		−			−
Intelligence		+					+	+	+			+
Verbal		+				+	+	+	+	+		+
Performance							+	+	+			
Verbal tests	+	+		+			+	+	+			+
Synonyms							+	+	+	+		+
Antonyms	+	+		+		+		+	+			+
Selections								+	+			+
Classifications												+
Analogies						+		+	+			+
Rigidity		−					−	−				−
General	−						−	−				
Personal		−		−			−	−				
Dogmatism		−										
Anxiety	−	−										
Intolerance	−											
General				+			−		+		−	
Attitude toward life	−											
Proretrospect						−						−
Contemporary	−					−						+
Interests												
Receptive activity												
Productive activity								+	+	+		+
Physical activity												
Education						+		+		+		
Financial status												
Health	−					−						
Physical activity							+					+
Social activity												
Leisure-time activity			−				+		+			+
Itemized activity							+		+			+
Well-Being									+			
Competitive situations							+			−		
Σ signs	7	8	2	1	6	11	12	13	14	5	1	18

[a] The subgroups are denoted by the numbers and letters in the heading of the table in the following way: 1 = retested subjects, 2 = deceased subjects, 3 = subjects too ill, 4 = subjects refusing to be retested, A = alive subjects (retested + ill + refusing subjects), N = not retested subjects (deceased + ill + refusing subjects). Thus, the denotation 1 −2 indicates the differences between subgroup 1 and 2, etc. If any of the differences was significant ($p < .05$) and positive, a positive sign (+) was used; if negative, a negative sign (−) was given.

the two age groups, it is evident that the sub-samples deviated increasingly from one another. Below 65 years there were 35 significant differences, whereas for those over 65 there were 63 significant signs. This difference was particularly marked for the three intelligence measures, where the ratio of the signs for the two age groups was 3:12, as well as for the battery of verbal tests (ratio of 8:19) and the questionnaire scales (ratio of 5:13). An equal number of significant signs occurred for the two age groups on the various attitude scales (ratio of 19:19). Similar results were obtained by comparing the retested and non-retested subjects (1 − N). Eleven of the 32 variables listed in Table 1 were significant for the younger, but 18 for the older age group.

In particular, both the deceased and the sick subjects deviated on a rather large number of variables from the retested subjects. Below 65 years, seven and eight variables, respectively, differed significantly. Above 65 years, the corresponding figures were 12 and 13. For variables discriminating between noncooperative and retested subjects there was also a rather marked age difference. Below 65 years these two groups differed only on two scales (dogmatism and leisure-time activity). Above 65 years, however, 14 variables were significantly different. For both age groups, there were few significant differences between deceased and sick subjects. Only one variable was significant for subjects below 65, and five for subjects above 65 years of age.

Undoubtedly of greatest importance was the finding that in the younger group the deceased subjects differed from all the survivors (including those retested or not retested) on six variables, whereas there was only one significant difference at the higher age level. This finding encouraged a search for systematic differences that might have allowed the prediction of the subjects' death on the basis of their sociopsychological functioning at the time of the first testing.

Prediction of Death

Multiple-regression predictions of death were calculated on an IBM 7090 computer. Age and sex were excluded from the predictions since both of them—being known as good predictors—could have covered up the more interesting psychological variables, even though their elimination would necessarily reduce the overall degree of correlation.

The predictions were made by successively reducing the F level at which variables would enter into the equations. The F levels were set at .05 and .10, but for each variable the F values were also empirically determined. This was necessary because under the more lenient conditions of $p = .10$ the F values for some of the variables already entered could have changed, depending on their correlations with the newly entering measures. Indeed, in some cases, high-ranking predictor variables have been dropped altogether from the equations. Generally, in a new field of investigation it seems reasonable to go somewhat beyond the conventional level of $p = .05$ because additional variables will pick up unaccounted portions of the variance. Even though they will increase the likelihood of Type 2 errors, it seems more appropriate to retain hypotheses-initially, which after

TABLE 3

RANKS AND *F* LEVELS FOR THE PREDICTION OF DEATH AT TWO AGE LEVELS

Variable	55 to 64		Over 65	
	Rank	F	Rank	F
Personal rigidity	11	4.51*		
General rigidity	10	3.10*		
General dogmatism	2	6.91	2	9.48
Productive activities	4	5.48	4	3.13*
Classifications m			5	3.74*
Antonyms T	3	9.37		
Classifications T	5	4.42		
Total testing time m	7	4.48		
Financial status	9	.3.01*		
Health	1	11.94		
Physical activity			1	8.80
Free time	8	3.16*		
Yrs. married			3	4.81
No. acquaintances	12	3.57*		
Itemized activities	6	3.91		
Widow(er) or not	13	2.76*		

* $p = .10$.

sufficient further research turn out to be false, rather than to reject hypotheses too early that may turn out to be true.

As shown in Table 3, 13 variables entered into the equation for the 55- to 64-year-old subjects at an F level of .10, but only five for the subjects above 65 years. Moreover, one of these five variables correlated highly with age, namely, the number of years married, and thus may have been excluded for the same reason for which age has been eliminated. Only two of the five variables were also predictors for the younger age group, namely, general dogmatism and productive activities (interests). The remaining variables were different for both groups. Even though the best single predictors were health for the younger, and the amount of physical activity for the older group, both the attitude and the intellectual measures entered strongly into the regression equations. Because the various inter-correlations were taken into account, the variables selected and shown in Table 3 were not necessarily identical with those significantly different in means between deceased and live subjects (see Table 2).

The point-biserial multiple correlations at the F level of .05 were .47 for the seven variables selected into the equation of the younger, and .31 for the three variables of the older subjects. When the *F* level was lowered to .10, the multiple correlations were raised to .60 and .35, respectively. In further lowering the *F* level to .50, the correlations could have been increased to .68 and .46, respectively, but at the same time the errors of estimate would have grown considerably so that this gain would not have been beneficial.

Conclusions

The present analysis was based on five cross-sectional samples of consecutive age groups above 55 years. Five years after the first testing, attempts were made to retest all subjects. However, success was not possible in these attempts because, in numbers increasing with age, some subjects had died or had become sick. Others refused to be retested, but their numbers seemed to be independent of age. If the biological determinants of death and disease interact with psychological or sociological factors—as has been shown in the present study—a number of far-reaching conclusions can be drawn.

First, a concept of development as represented by curves of growth and decline is questionable, regardless of whether these curves are based on longitudinal or cross-sectional data.

Development as reflected by trends of average test or rating scores would be a meaningful concept only if the dropout of subjects in consecutive age groups is strictly a random process. However, biologically weak subjects will die earlier or will become increasingly unable to participate in the testings. A particular occupational, financial, educational and/or social status may increase the risks and may decrease the chances of survival. According to the present study, groups of dropouts (particularly the younger ones) are also psychologically different in their abilities and attitudes.

Age samples drawn for cross-sectional studies or followed up in longitudinal studies become increasingly biased, the further one moves upward in the age scale, and thus the generalized trend will be confounded by the increasing degree of sample bias.

Second, older reports on the decline of intelligence have been received with shock or suspicion. Relief was felt when some longitudinal studies (Bayley and Oden, 1955; Owens, 1953) reported higher stabilities than originally observed, even though these studies were restricted to subjects with superior capacities. According to the present findings and aside from other psychological factors, less-able persons die earlier or are more likely to become seriously ill. Thus, the samples are increasingly loaded with highly able persons. If it had been possible to retest all of the subjects originally involved in the study, the decline would have been more marked than either cross-sectional or longitudinal studies have revealed.

A third conclusion can be added concerning the determinants of death. Even though the groups of dropouts differed on an increasing number of variables, prediction of death was more successful at the earlier than at the later age levels. This should be attributed to slightly lower intercorrelations between the predictor variables, and to the larger differences in average scores between the groups of subjects who were either sick, refused to be retested, or had died. The differences in accuracy of predictions indicate that at lower age levels nonsurvivors can be described as a subgroup which differs sociopsychologically from the rest in almost the same sense as victims of cancer or heart attacks may differ from healthy persons. At the higher age levels, however, death seems to strike at random, and psychological predictions become less valid. Using again the biological analogy, nonsurvivors resemble persons with general syndromes of aging rather than specific diseases which cause their death.

Summary

Intelligence, verbal abilities, attitudes, interests, and social conditions of 380 Ss above 55 yr. of age were measured. Five yr. later Ss were retested. Some refused to cooperate again, and others had died or become ill. Retested Ss differed significantly from the total group, but in particular from the other subgroups. The prediction of death on the basis of sociopsychological variables was more successful for Ss below than above 65 yr. of age. It was concluded that developmental trends are based on increasingly biased samples, that previous studies have underestimated the amount of attrition, and that nonsurvivors under 65 yr. form a sociopsychological subgroup of different characteristics than survivors.

REFERENCES

Bayley, N., and Oden, M. H. The maintenance of intellectual ability in gifted adults. *Journal of Gerontology,* 1955, 10: 91–107.

Bell, A., and Zubek, J. P. The effect of age on the intellectual performance of mental defectives. *Journal of Gerontology,* 1960, 15: 285–295.

Berkowitz, B., and Green, R. F. Changes in intellect with age: I. Longitudinal study of Wechsler-Bellevue scores. *Journal of Genetic Psychology,* 1963, 103: 3–21.

Damon, A. Discrepancies between findings of longitudinal and cross-sectional studies in adult life: Physique and physiology. *Human Development,* 1965, 8: 16–22.

Eisdorfer, C. The WAIS performance of the aged: A retest evaluation. *Journal of Gerontology,* 1963, 18: 169–172.

Falek, A., Kallman, F. J., Lorge, I., and Jarvik, L. F. Longevity and intellectual variation in a senescent twin population. *Journal of Gerontology,* 1960, 15: 305–309.

Foster, J. C., and Taylor, G. A. The application of mental tests to persons over 50. *Journal of Applied Psychology,* 1920, 4: 39–58.

Jarvik, L. F., and Falek, A. Intellectual stability and survival in the aged. *Journal of Gerontology,* 1963, 18: 173–176.

Jarvik, L. F., Kallman, F. J., and Falek, A. Intellectual changes in aged twins. *Journal of Gerontology,* 1962, 17: 289–294.

Jarvik, L. F., Kallman, F. J., Falek, A., and Klaber, M. M. Changing intellectual functions in senescent twins. *Acta Genetica et Statistica Medica,* 1957, 7: 421–430.

Jones, H. E., and Conrad, H. S. The growth and decline of intelligence: A study of a homogeneous group between the ages ten and sixty. *Genetic Psychology Monographs,* 1933, 13: 223–298.

Jones, H. E., Conrad, H. S., and Horn, A. Psychological studies of motion pictures: II. Observation and recall as a function of age. *University of California Publications in Psychology,* 1928, 3: 225–243.

Kaplan, O. J. Mental decline in older morons. *American Journal of Mental Deficiency,* 1943, 47: 277–285.

Kaplan, O. J. *Mental disorders in later life,* Stanford: Stanford University Press, 1956.

Kaplan, O. J., Rumbaugh, D. M., Mitchell, D. C., and Thomas, E. D. Effects of level of surviving abilities, time of day, and test-retest upon psychological performance in seniles. *Journal of Gerontology,* 1963, 18: 55–59.

Kleemeier, R. W. Intellectual changes in the senium. In, *Proceedings, Social Statistics Section, American Statistical Association.* Washington, D. C.: American Statistical Association, 1962. Pp. 290–295.

Miles, W. R. Age and human ability. *Psychological Review,* 1933, 40: 99–123.

Owens, W. A., Jr. Age and mental abilities: A longitudinal study. *Genetic Psychology Monographs,* 1953, 48: 3–54.

Riegel, K. F. A study on verbal achievements of older persons. *Journal of Gerontology,* 1959, 14: 453–456.

Riegel, K. F. Changes in psycholinguistic performance with age. In G. A. Talland (Ed.), *Human behavior and aging: Recent advances in research and theory.* New York: Academic Press, 1967, in press.

Riegel, K. F., and Riegel, R. M. A study on changes of attitudes and interests during later years of life. *Vita Humana,* 1960, 3: 177–206.

Riegel, K. F., and Riegel, R. M. Analysis of differences in test performance and item difficulty between young and old adults. *Journal of Gerontology,* 1962, 17: 97–105.

Riegel, K. F., Riegel, R. M., and Meyer, G. Sociopsychological factors of aging: A cohort-sequential analysis. *Human Development,* 1967, 10: 27–56.

Riegel, K. F., Riegel, R. M., and Skiba, G. Untersuchung der Lebensbedingungen, Gewohnheiten und Anpassung älterer Menschen in Norddeutschland. *Vita Humana,* 1962, 5: 204–247.

Riegel, R. M. Faktorenanalysen des Hamburg-Wechsler-Intelligenztests für Erwachsen (HAWIE) für die Altersstufen 20–34, 35–49, 50–64 und 65 Jahre und älter. *Diagnostica,* 1960, 6: 41–66.

Riegel, R. M., and Riegel, K. F. Standardisierung des Hamburg-Wechsler-Intelligenztests für Erwachsen (HAWIE) für die Altersstufen über 50 Jahre. *Diagnostica,* 1959, 5: 97–128.

Riegel, R. M., and Riegel, K. F. A comparison and reinterpretation of factorial structures of the W-B, the WAIS, and the HAWIE on aged persons. *Journal of Consulting Psychology,* 1962, 26: 31–37.

Rose, C. H. Representatives of volunteer subjects in a longitudinal aging study. *Human Development,* 1965, 8: 152–156.

Schaie, K. W. Cross-sectional methods in the study of psychological aspects of aging. *Journal of Gerontology,* 1959, 14: 208–215.

Schaie, K. W. A general model for the study of developmental problems. *Psychological Bulletin,* 1965, 64: 92–108.

Schaie, K. W., and Strother, C. R. The effect of time and cohort differences on the interpretation of age changes in cognitive behavior. *American Psychologist,* 1964, 19: 546.

Sussman, M. B. Use of longitudinal designs in studies of long-term illness, some advantages and limitations. *Gerontologist,* 1964, 4: 25–29.

PSYCHOLOGICAL STUDY OF WHOLE FAMILIES *

GERALD HANDEL

In his article, "Abnormalities of Behavior," White (1959) introduces a group of references on schizophrenia with this comment: "It is reassuring to find that several workers are using the concept of interaction patterns in families rather than the questionable cause-effect model of parent influencing child [p. 279]." The implied rarity of this concept in the psychological literature is indicated by the fact that four of the five publications White mentions are of psychiatric origin, while only one is psychological; the rarity is underscored by the fact that Hoffman and Lippitt's (1960) entire presentation of family research methods in child psychology is cast explicitly within the cause-effect framework of parent influencing child.

There is an ambiguity in White's term "interaction patterns in families." On the one hand, it may be taken to mean interaction between some but not all members of a family, such as interaction between husband and wife (Tharp, 1963), mother and child, father and child, or child and child. Hoffman and Lippitt report that studies of parent-child interaction are increasing and they suggest that this is partly because of the failure of the simple parent-child cause-effect model.

White's term may, on the other hand, be taken to refer to interaction of all the family members,

* Reprinted with permission from the American Psychological Association. In *Psychological Bulletin,* 1965, Vol. 63, pp. 19–41.

whether the whole family be defined as the nuclear or conjugal family whose members share a common household or the extended family residing in one or more households. The concept of family interaction in this broader sense has scarcely gained notice in psychology, although psychiatry (Group for the Advancement of Psychiatry, 1954), anthropology (Lewis, 1950, 1959, 1961), sociology (Hill, 1949; Parsons and Bales, 1955), and social work (Voiland, 1962) are giving it increasing attention. Psychology has been concerned with events within the family but has made little effort to conceptualize and study the family as a unit.

This paper reports the progress made thus far in studying whole families. Attention is given to work by investigators and thinkers in psychology and related fields. The paper does not deal with two-person interaction, partly because discussions of work in this area are already available (Eisenstein, 1956; Hoffman and Lippitt, 1960; Tharp, 1963), but mainly because moving beyond the two-person framework has proved to be an especially difficult problem. The discussion is not restricted, however, to interaction in the sense of studies of face-to-face behavior. The problem focus is the psychological study of the family as a whole, and observation of face-to-face interaction is only one of the procedures that have been used. If the parent-child, cause-effect model has been only slightly successful, there are grounds for believing that studies of two-person, parent-child interaction, which omit observation of other family members, will also prove of limited value for understanding child personality. But quite apart from evaluations of the merit of two-person interaction studies in child psychology, the psychological study of whole families is of interest in its own right.

The adequacy, though not the utility, of the interaction concept—regardless of whether the data be obtained by direct observation of face-to-face behavior or by subject reports—is itself problematic, even for the study of whole families. One of the many reasons the burgeoning field of small group study has scarcely concerned itself with the family is perhaps the recognition that the ahistoric framework appropriate for ad hoc laboratory groups is not well suited to the family, which is constituted by enduring interpersonal relationships. Strodtbeck (1954), in one of the few small-group studies using families as subjects, tested propositions derived from ad hoc groups and found important differences which he explained on the basis of these enduring relationships (pp. 28–29). Later work by Strodtbeck (1958) seems clearly to indicate that family interaction can only be understood in conjunction with the family's prevailing interpersonal relationships. The question may be put, then, whether interaction or interpersonal relationship will prove the more fruitful concept in understanding families or, indeed, whether adequate investigation will not require data on both kinds of phenomena as reciprocally determining. (To use both concepts interchangeably as though they were equivalent, as is sometimes done, can only lead to obscuring important problems.)

Thus far, we have been using the term whole family as a means of differentiating a field of study that lies beyond the traditional study of subfamily pairs such as the mother-child pair. For our purposes the term serves adequately, but notice must be taken that its referent is not precise. An issue centers on whether it is fruitful to select the nuclear family as a unit of study or whether adequate understanding requires study of the extended family. Some investigators (Handel and Hess, 1956; Hess and Handel, 1959) have argued that, regardless of the ties that link a nuclear family to kin and wider social groups, there is a sense in which the nuclear family is a bounded universe. The nuclear family is a meaningful unit of study because, typically, its members inhabit a common household which is not shared with relatives; within these boundaries—the home—the family members develop long-sustained, relatively more intense and meaningful relationships among each other than with outsiders, including kin residing in other households. Spiegel and Bell (1959), on philosophical and anthropological grounds, consider this viewpoint too narrow for understanding psychopathology. They consider it essential to view the nuclear family as a component of the extended family and the entire family network as embedded in a larger social and cultural network, if the emotional disturbance of a particular family member is to be adequately understood. The problem of defining the unit of study is discussed briefly by Leichter (1961) who concludes that "the family unit may shift according to the purpose of analysis [p. 143]."

In passing, it may be noted that Spiegel and Bell make common cause with White (1959), Hoffman and Lippitt (1960), Ackerman (1958), and others in questioning the adequacy of the cause-effect model of parent influencing child. Most of the work reviewed in this article has similar import. Some studies focus on the extended family (e.g., Cleveland and Longaker, 1957; Fisher and Mendell, 1956; Mendell and Fisher, 1956) while others focus on the nuclear family (e.g., Ackerman and Sobel, 1950; Frenkel-Brunswik, 1955; Hess and Handel, 1959).

EMERGENCE OF THE PROBLEM

Any discussion of the problem of conceptualizing and investigating whole families must begin with Burgess's (1926) formulation: "The Family as a Unity of Interacting Personalities." [1] From the perspective of contemporary psychology this is a remarkable phrase, as far reaching in its implications as it is compact in expression. It provides a basic orientation that can guide many research programs, regardless of how the unit of study be defined.

First, we may note that the formulation calls attention to the fact that a family is made up of persons, each with an individuality of his own, a personality. By implication, it seems to call in question the cause-effect model which locates independent variables exclusively in the parents and dependent variables exclusively in the children. At the very least, it suggests an alternative perspective in which each family member is regarded as a source of some relatively autonomous action. A child, as well as a parent, is construed as having individuality. Sufficient ground for this assumption is provided by the fact that each child in a family has a unique ordinal position. (The question of whether children in a particular ordinal position differ systematically from children in other ordinal positions is irrelevant here. The point is that within any given family, the first-, second-, and third-born, etc., can be expected to be different from each other in significant ways.) Other grounds for

[1] Most of the studies cited in this paper descend from the seminal thinking of Freud, G. H. Mead, Cooley, and others. Since a full genealogy of ideas is not attempted here, Burgess's formulation is the most appropriate starting point. Further, no effort is made to show the relevance of the work of such significant investigators as Lewin, Sullivan, Erikson, and others; attention is restricted to writers who addressed themselves fairly explicitly to the study of whole families.

the assumption can be adduced, though one would also like to have studies of such dimensions as perceptual sensitivity and activity level of infants (Bergman and Escalona, 1949; Escalona and Heider, 1959; Escalona and Leitch, 1952; Fries and Woolf, 1954) conducted on infants in the same family. However, it is apposite to point out that one of the research problems immediately suggested by the Burgess (1926) formulation is the problem of how different children in the same family develop different identities. The problem is implicit in any effort to understand why one child develops a mental illness while other children in the same family do not. Uniqueness of ordinal position provides a basis for expecting that the personalities of children in the same family will differ from each other in some way, but what those differences will turn out to be and the processes by which they come about require research on whole families. One process is indicated in Harris's (1959) study, where he reports that:

> Both the mothers and the fathers in our study invariably showed evidence of using their parenthood to continue or to resolve, through their children, some aspects of their own growing up, and therefore each of their several children might represent a somewhat different aspect of their past [p. 39].

The same child can, of course, represent different things to the two parents.

By characterizing the family as a unity of interacting personalities, Burgess points to the problem of understanding interaction and interpersonal relationships in terms of the personalities of the participating members. A recent attempt by Miller (1961) to present an organized framework for dealing with the problem is a valuable contribution and perhaps the most explicit statement yet available. It is, however, framed in terms of two-person relationships, and modifications would undoubtedly be required in order for it to be applicable to family groups.

It should be noted that the central research problem raised by Burgess is not that of socialization, child training, or transmission of personality characteristics from parent to child but a problem that is in a sense anterior to these, while also having social psychological interest in its own right. The problem may be phrased: *How do the several personalities in a family cohere in an ongoing structure that is both sustained and altered*

through interaction? Regarded in this way, Burgess's formulation may be seen as, in effect, a charter for the study of whole families. As such, it demands research which (*a*) is directed to conceptualizing the family as a unit; (*b*) studies the personalities of the several members and the interrelationships among them; (*c*) obtains data from each member of the family. The Burgess formulation thus points to a unified psychological approach in which the intrapsychic processes and personality structures of family members are considered in conjunction with the interrelations among the members. This is a tall order, and it cannot be said that the nature of such a psychology is now at all clear. Nonetheless, some definite steps in this direction have been taken, as this article hopes to indicate. The problems are formidable, and the writings of workers in this field often contain confessions of burdensome difficulty. It seems clear that the application of widely accepted concepts of methodological rigor in psychology must, in this field, be adapted and perhaps deferred pending the development of both a minimally adequate conceptual framework and hypotheses that seem fruitful enough to warrant rigorous testing. Due recognition must be made of the recency of effort in this field. It is hoped that the survey presented here contributes a sufficient sharpening of focus to make possible a more concentrated and rigorous research.

Burgess's (1926) concept has received great veneration and reiteration in family sociology, but for about a quarter of a century little effort seems to have been made to pursue its implications. In his study of family adjustment to the stresses of war separation and reunion, Hill (1949) referred to thinking at the family level as third-dimensional in contradistinction to thinking at the level of the individual and the pair—one- and two-dimensional, respectively. He noted that third-dimensional thinking had only recently been attempted.

A beginning of psychoanalytic attention to the whole family is evident in the 1930s. The International Congress of Psychoanalysis in 1936 was devoted to the topic "The Family Neurosis and the Neurotic Family" (Grotjahn, 1959). Ackerman's (1938) first paper on family unity came soon after. Oberndorf (1938) and Mittelman (1944, 1948) broke with the orthodox psychoanalytic rule that the analyst should treat only one person in a family and avoid contact with the relatives; each was analyzing concurrently both partners to a marriage.

Psychiatric attention is now beginning to move from two-person relationships in the family to the whole family. Several considerations prompt this shift. One is that the disordered behavior of the patient is coming to be viewed as involving a certain stabilization of relationships with other family members so that changes in the patient's behavior resulting from therapy disrupt these relationships, often with untoward consequences for other family members. Improvement in the patient is sometimes accompanied by the development of symptoms in other family members; the symptoms are transitive, but the therapeutic effects often are not (Jackson, 1957; Jackson and Weakland, 1959, 1961). However, Fisher and Mendell (1958) report instances of a spread of therapeutic effect from patient to family members not in therapy. One of the tasks of family study is to discover the conditions that favor the spread of symptoms and those that favor the spread of therapeutic effects.

Another consideration is that improved behavior in family relationships is seen as a criterion of therapeutic progress, but such progress cannot always be effected if other parties to the relationship are not engaged in the therapy. Ackerman (1956) states that he finds it increasingly difficult to carry therapy to successful completion without dealing directly with other family members so as to restore healthy family relationships (p. 140).

It is evident that in the thinking of Ackerman (1954) and others the concepts of mental health and illness are changing. These workers view the family, and not the individual, as the primary locus of mental health or illness. Bowen (1960), reporting research on a treatment program in which the families of schizophrenic patients lived with the patients in the hospital, states his view that "The schizophrenic psychosis of the patient is, in my opinion, a symptom manifestation of an active process that involves the entire family [p. 346]." Similar views are found in the work of Jackson and his colleagues and Lidz and his colleagues, which will be discussed below.

These newer psychiatric concepts have led to various innovations in therapy. The newer techniques include: (a) outpatient treatment of the whole family as a group by one therapist, which Jackson (1961) calls conjoint family therapy; (b) diagnostic evaluation of the whole family in order to select one member as the most suitable candidate for therapy in order to induce change in the whole family; (c) residence of the immediate family of the schizophrenic patient in the hospital with him, with individual therapy of the patient and group therapy of the family proceeding concurrently; (d) family group counseling (Freeman, Klein, Riehman, Lukoff, and Heisey, 1963). In addition, concurrent but individual therapy of husband and wife or parent and child by two therapists who compare notes increases in prevalence. Although clinical reports of this work grow in frequency as therapists report their efforts to devise more effective therapies, no systematic evaluations are yet available, so far as this writer is aware. Discussions of the various family therapies and their rationales are presented by Ackerman (1958, 1961) and Grotjahn (1960). Grotjahn's book includes a historical overview of developing psychoanalytic interest in family therapy, while Ackerman's (1958) book contains a discussion of changing concepts of personality which underlie this trend.

CONCEPTUAL VANTAGE POINTS

In recent years, several workers have addressed themselves to the psychological problem raised by the Burgess (1926) formulation, the problem of family unity. They have approached it in several ways; a review of them will form the subject of this section. First, however, a conceptual and terminological clarification is necessary. The term family unity is not in vogue these days, having been replaced by several terms which distribute its meaning: family homeostasis (Jackson, 1957), equilibrium (Parsons and Bales, 1955), integration, and solidarity. All of these terms involve viewing the family as a system, and there is overlap among them, but the first two seem more appropriate for describing interaction and its short-range shifts, while the latter two seem more appropriate for describing interpersonal relations in their more enduring aspect. One further distinction needs to be made. Bossard and Boll (1950) state: "We use the term 'family integration' to mean the welding or unification of its diverse elements into a complex whole or harmonious relationship [p. 199]." It is evident that this definition commingles two elements which are not only analytically distinct but the relationships between which pose empirical problems. Harmonious relationships refer to feelings of well-being or absence of deep conflicts, whereas the welding of diverse elements into a complex whole carries no such connotation. In fact, the work on families of psychiatric patients reveals that such families are often tightly integrated in such a way as to preclude harmony. One of the tasks of psychological research on families can well be to discover which kinds of integration lead to harmony and feelings of well-being among the members and which do not. It is clearly useful to distinguish integration, a construct that can deal with family systems in a non-evaluative way, from harmony, a term that refers to a widely valued family goal. Instead of harmony, however, it seems better to adopt the term solidarity which, as defined by Cousins (1960), can be operational. Integration and solidarity refer to somewhat different aspects of family life; the relationships between them constitute a subject worthy of research. Further, studies can be designed to show how various kinds of interaction (such as, e.g., in conjoint family therapy) affect both integration and solidarity.

We consider now the various conceptual vantage points that have been used in studying whole families.

Family and Culture

Psychologists have become increasingly familiar with the anthropological concept of culture. The importance of the anthropological perspective in understanding personality development was dramatized by Margaret Mead's (1928) pioneering study of adolescence in Samoa and received increased recognition with the publication of Kluckhohn and Murray's (1948) collection of papers in personality and culture. Kaplan's (1961) recent collection indicates that this approach has developed greatly in sophistication.

Until recently, it has been customary to regard the culture or some particular general feature of it—notably the child-rearing practices typical in the culture—as an independent variable and personality as a directly dependent variable. Attention is beginning to shift—very slightly—toward consideration of the individual family as mediating agent of the culture. Cleveland and Longaker (1957) examined the impact of cultural factors on individual mental health by analyzing the transmission and mediation of values in a family setting. In a report deriving from the Stirling County study directed by Alexander Leighton, they studied one kinship group which contributed several patients to the caseload of a small-town clinic in Nova Scotia. On the basis of data derived from psychotherapy, psychological tests, and home visits with relatives, they conclude that the neurotic patterning found in the family is a function of two processes: (a) value conflict within the culture; (b) a culturally recurrent mode of self-disparagement, with roots in the child-rearing methods, linked to the failure of individuals to adjust to incompatible value orientations. The value clash was between a striving orientation, involving personal ambition, acceptance of a rational money economy, and emphasis on personal responsibility for success and failure, and, on the other hand, a traditional being orientation, emphasizing physical labor in an outdoor setting, strong desires for personal independence and integrity, and currently meaningful activities as opposed to longer-range goals. According to the authors' analysis, self-disparagement develops when: (a) the parents, oscillating between the conflicting value orientations, present contradictory models of behavior to their children; (b) the child devalues one of the orientations which he has incorporated in his personality; (c) an obstacle to learning develops in a life area relevant to the already vulnerable and devalued personality segment. In terms of this process, they report a case in which a father, his son, and the father's first cousin developed neurotic behavior disorders.

From the standpoint developed in the present paper, the study just described is incomplete since it does not explore the reasons why other family members did not become neurotic. Presumably some family process is operating selectively. The study is useful, however, because it explicitly interposes the family, as an element of analysis, between the culture and the individual. It suggests the necessity of more microscopic studies of socialization, raising new questions. Instead of the broad question—How are children socialized in this culture?—it suggests that we must ask the more specific question of how a child is socialized into a particular family or—hopefully—type of family. Relevant to this point is a study under way directed by Spiegel and F. Kluckhohn, described by Spiegel and Bell (1959) but not yet reported in detail. Their study closely parallels the Cleveland-Longaker study (1957)—the approach to value analysis used by both pairs of investigators was in fact developed by Kluckhohn (1950) —but Spiegel and Kluckhohn seem to be pushing their clinical analysis further than did Cleveland and Longaker.

Spiegel and Kluckhohn, though moving in a new direction by comparing families with and without an emotionally disturbed child in three subcultural groups, work with the prevailing framework that locates values in the culture (or ethnic and social class subculture). They then analyze family behavior as a response to these external standards. There are, however, signs of a more radical view which is stated by J. Henry (1951), an anthropologist interested in personality development and clinical problems: "every family is almost a different culture [p. 800]." Roberts (1951) studied three neighboring Navaho households and judged that they constituted discrete local cultures, though interlocking. Bott (1957), in her study of family roles and norms in London, states that she started out with the idea of first determining cultural definitions of family roles and then seeing how the members' personalities governed their role performances. But she found so much variation not only in role performance but in role definition, because the environment permits wide latitude of choice, that she was obliged to adopt a more psychological and family-centered view.

These anthropologists thus espouse the view that each family, as a small group, develops its own norms, values, and role definitions. The general case for such a viewpoint has been familiar to psychologists since the early work of Sherif (1936), but its application to families is relatively recent. It is not a widely disseminated view among anthropologists, nor has it received much attention in social psychology as practiced by both psychologists and sociologists, although Frenkel-Brunswik (1955) adopted and exemplified it in her comparison of the social outlooks of an authoritarian and an equalitarian family. Whether it is useful to consider each individual family as having a culture of its own in any strict sense is open to question. But the effort to do so is nonetheless worthwhile in sensitizing us to the fact that analyses of values and norms that are useful at a macrosocial level need refinement when applied at the microsocial level. In the series of midwestern American families reported by Hess and Handel (1959) and

Handel (1962), there are four upper-middle-class families all of whom can be regarded as manifesting the striving orientation defined by Kluckhohn. This orientation takes different forms in the four families: one emphasizes responsibility; one, independence; one, competition; and one reveals marked conflict between independence and responsibility. It is useful to consider them as similar when comparing them with families from a non-striving society, but these four families have different consequences for the personalities of their respective component members.

Family Structure as Personality Component

It is customary to regard identification as a process in which the developing child models his behavior on that of his parents, particularly on that of the same-sex parent. This view implicitly assumes either that the child has no cognizance of the interpersonal relationships prevailing between the parents and between them and their other children, or that such cognizance constitutes no more than a condition which affects the identification of the child with the parent who serves as model.

Exemplifying some of the newer thinking in psychoanalysis is the view of Josselyn (1953) who states that:

> an analysis of the interpersonal relationships between child and mother, child and father, and child and siblings only partially reveals the significance of the family. The intermeshing of these multiple relationships creates a structure that has meaning over and above the meaning of its parts [p. 337].

Josselyn stops just short of saying that the structure of interpersonal relationships in the family is internalized by the child to constitute a part of his ego. This next step is taken by Parsons and Bales (1955) who present a theory of socialization in which personality development is construed as a process of inner differentiation brought about by the child's participation in and identification with a system of intrafamilial social relationships that are, from his point of view, also becoming progressively differentiated. Initially, the child does not differentiate himself from his mother; the mother-child identity is the first system the child internalizes. Next, when the child differentiates himself from his mother, a 2-role system has been formed from the previously undifferentiated system. Corresponding to this process in the external, interactive world, the simple object internalized in the child's personality during the primary identification also becomes differentiated into an object whose complexity matches that of the 2-role system. Next, according to the theory, the 2-role system is succeeded by 1 of 4 roles: father, mother, son, and daughter. The authors propose that the 4-role system is succeeded by an 8-role system and then a 16-role system, accomplished by each role being divided into functional role components so that each person performs multiple roles. They term this division process binary fission and aver that the same process occurs concurrently within the child's personality in terms of need-dispositions. The child's first need-disposition is that of dependency. By binary fission, this primary need-disposition becomes differentiated into dependency and autonomy need-dispositions. As the child becomes involved in the 4-role system, dependency divides into a nurturance need and a conformity need, while autonomy divides into a security need and an adequacy need.

The account just given is a great oversimplification of an uncommonly abstruse theory which attempts to account for some familiar phenomena and some never yet observed through a series of deductions that are alternately logical, rigid, and arbitrary. The concept of binary fission strains credulity, though the same can be said for some earlier concepts that later proved influential as well as for some that did not. To the present writer, the theory makes a suggestive contribution in its proposal that personality differentiation is, to an important degree, a function of involvement in a progressively complex series of systems of social interaction and that the child internalizes not only a parental model but also systems of family behavior. Important also is the emphasis on studying the meanings which family members have for one another; studies which pursue this direction can cast light not only on how self-concepts and identities are formed but also on how the personalities in a family form an interlocking structure.

Family Interaction, Interpersonal Relationships, and Personality

Burgess, in the article referred to, says that he was tempted to call the family a superpersonality. Although this term has since been carefully avoided, some of the work devoted to the study of whole families in fact involves an attempt to characterize them in personality terms. These characterizations are arrived at either through an analysis of family interaction or through an analysis of the personalities of the several family members or through a combination of these approaches. The idea that groups, including families, each have a distinctive psychological character is implicit in earlier work. Lewin, Lippitt, and White's (1939) concept of social climate is an important forerunner. Their categorization of groups as authoritarian, democratic, and laissez-faire has found its way into discussions of the effects of the family on children's behavior. In the latter context, however, these categories are categories of parent behavior rather than of families.

Recent work frequently shows several features which differentiate it from previous practice: (a) Instead of using predetermined categories such as authoritarian and democratic, no assumption is made in advance as to which dimensions are likely to prove most significant for a particular family. A meaningful system or set of family categories is seen as lying in the future, present efforts being exploratory steps toward that goal. Although the importance of categories referring to how power is exercised in the family is indisputable, the familiar dimensions such as power and warmth quite obviously do not exhaust the range of significant family phenomena, and to focus on the effects of these dimensions at the expense of searching out and formulating others can only result in premature closure. (b) Instead of using the cause-effect model of parent influencing child, the family is conceptualized as a group. (c) The personalities of the component members and/or the interplay between intrapsychic and group processes constitute the data matrix from which the concepts are built. This conceptual procedure does not usually take the route of analyzing the personality of each family member in detail before proceeding to the group characterization. Rather, personality materials are examined in order to move directly to characterization of group processes. Family interaction is thus conceived as occurring at the personality level.

A pioneering study exemplifying this viewpoint is that of J. Henry (1951) who proposed that a neurosis can be considered a rigid intrafamilial interaction pattern that is pathogenic in quality. The transmission of the neurosis in the family is the transmission of this pathogenic interaction pattern. Henry studied records of a psychiatric social worker's interviews with the mother of a boy referred to a child guidance clinic. He recognized the limitations imposed by using data obtained only from one member of the family, but at the time of his study these were the best data available for the task he set himself. Using ad hoc categories, he coded every intrafamilial interaction reported by the mother in interviews extending over a period of about 2 years, including interactions between the mother and her own mother and brother, as well as within the nuclear family. The coding procedure enabled him to summarize the interaction pattern of each pair and triad of family members. On the basis of this analysis of family interaction episodes reported by the patient's mother, Henry diagnosed the family as one in which tendencies to dominance, provocation, and clinging are worked out. This family is contrasted with one reported earlier the same year by Henry and Warson (1951) and diagnosed as narcissistic. Henry makes an observation that is important in any attempt to conceptualize families in psychological terms. He points out that family traits are scattered unevenly among family members and may not occur at all in some members. Each family member may embody the pathology in a different way, and some may be free from it. This scatter phenomenon is found repeatedly in the studies reported in this paper and it can safely be assumed that all families will manifest psychologically significant intermember diversity. If there is to be any successful psychological classification of families, it cannot rest upon any simple search for personality similarity among members but will have to be founded upon some conception of dynamic interplay among members, a conclusion which is clearly implied also by Hoffman and Lippitt (1960).

Interaction is a diffuse concept, as yet insufficiently analyzed. It is used to refer to a variety of phenomena which may be regarded as not yet codified components or levels of interaction. Among these are: *physical contacts* such as those of mothering; *cognitive interchanges* in which information is exchanged and which proceed toward a definition of reality (as in Sherif's autokinetic experiments) or toward decision making (as in Bales's interaction-process analysis); behavior in which *norms* and *roles* are created and validated,

or in which *selves* are discovered and created (predominantly a sociological usage but also exemplified in such diverse psychological writers as Piaget, Rogers, and Sullivan); *affective behavior,* in which feelings and emotions are transmitted or exchanged (as in much psychiatric writing, perhaps most explicitly in that of Sullivan). There are various concepts of interaction which cross-cut or are at a higher level of abstraction than the categories just named, such as G. H. Mead's theory of symbolic interaction (Rose, 1962) or other theories of communication, of which that advanced by Bateson, Jackson, and their colleagues will be discussed below.

Although in no way attempting to codify interaction phenomena, Hess and Handel (1959) offered some rudiments of a framework for analyzing family interaction and interpersonal relationships, a framework which is psychologically relevant, which seems capable of fruitful development, and which is capable of encompassing a number of other studies already published. On the basis of their study of nonclinical midwestern American families, they advanced a number of concepts which simultaneously refer to the personalities of the individual family members and the character of the family as a group. First, they postulate that *separateness and connectedness are the underlying conditions of a family's life* and that *a basic family process is the effort to achieve a satisfactory pattern of separateness and connectedness.* As each member of a family develops his own personality, adapts to changes through the life cycle, seeks gratification and, generally, creates an individual life space, he also is involved in more or less binding ties with other family members, ties which he endeavors to create and ties which the other members endeavor to create with him. These ties are likewise expressions of the several personalities involved, as well as of many other kinds of factors.

In the course of establishing patterns of separateness and connectedness each member of a family develops an image of each other member. That is, each family member comes to invest each other member with particular cognitive and affective meaning and significance. These images have certain stable aspects but they also change as the family members move through the life cycle. A second process which these authors identify is that *behavior in a family may be viewed as the family's effort to attain a satisfactory congruence of images through the exchange of suitable testimony.* This family interaction comes to be centered around a particular theme in each family. Themes found in the families reported include: flight from insecurity, equanimity and its vicissitudes, dynamics of disconnectedness, demonstration of constructive independence, and comforts and crises of companionship. A family's theme does not, of course, find identical expression in the personalities of each member; this is implied by the two processes previously described. The theme describes the centering of the family's interaction. Although the concept of theme was developed from qualitative data, the concept has a logical foundation analogous to concepts of central tendency used for quantitative data. By implication and further analogy, therefore, a family's interaction may be considered to have a dispersion. Eventually, it may be possible to compare families both qualitatively and quantitatively in terms of dispersion as well as the centering of their interactions.

Hess and Handel (1959) identify another family process which is, in a sense, a qualitative formulation of dispersion: *establishing boundaries of the family's world of experience.* As each family maps its domain of acceptable and desirable experience it raises signposts for goals and signals for danger. But these boundaries, which lie within persons as well as among them, are continually tested as new experiences occur, new feelings arise, and new actions are taken. Limits to experience are established in a variety of ways and along several dimensions. Four particularly important dimensions are: the differentiation of individual personality, the intensity of experience, the extensity of experience, and the tendency to evaluate experience.

The last process which these writers identify is: *dealing with significant given biosocial issues of family life,* particularly sex, generation, and birth order. These issues include not only sexuality and authority but, more broadly, how each generation and each sex is defined in terms of feelings, rewards, and restraints.

Interaction gives rise to interpersonal relationships within the family. These relationships do not merely follow the intrinsic lines of sex and age but derive from the interlocking meanings which the members have for one another. Hess and Handel propose the term pattern of alignment to refer to the distribution of ties among members of a family. This concept is broader than that of coalition as it is used in small-group research. Whereas coalition refers to the phenomenon of teaming up to exercise power, pattern of alignment includes any basis on which family members line up with each other, unconsciously as well as consciously, in fantasy as well as in action, for reasons of comfort or affection as well as those of power, to enhance each other as well as to defeat each other. From a psychological point of view, the intrapsychic bases of affiliation are as important as the fact of it, both for the persons affiliating and for the group as a whole. Redl's (1942) study of group emotion in school classrooms has useful implications for the study of families. Clearly the phenomena included under pattern of alignment require differentiation and codification just as do those subsumed under interaction. Just as clearly, the concept points to needed areas of research. To name but one, we require research on sibling support (including identification of siblings with one another) that will balance our research into sibling rivalry. It is not unreasonable to suppose that the relative primacy of sibling support as against sibling rivalry is a factor affecting mental health, and personality formation generally. But sibling relationships are part of the total pattern of alignment in a family and they will be adequately understood only if studied in that context. It is evident from everything that has been said thus far in this paper that the personalities of the parents and the motives and meanings they bring to bear in their interaction with their children contribute to the kind of sibling relationships their children will develop.

Hess and Handel (1959) developed their concepts in the course of studying nonclinical families. Several reports of clinical research suggest that these concepts are potentially fruitful for understanding behavior disturbances of various kinds. Distortions in the separateness-connectedness pattern are seen as contributing to clinical behavior pathology. Wynne, Ryckoff, Day, and Hirsch (1958) take as their basic assumption that every human being strives both to form relationships with others and to develop a sense of personal identity. They conceive that the effort to solve this dual problem leads to two main kinds of solutions, mutuality and pseudomutuality. (They also recognize a third category, nonmutual complementarity, which is not relevant in the present context.) Mutuality entails recognition and appreciation of divergence of self-interests. Pseudomutuality is characterized by preoccupation with fitting together at the expense of the identities of the people in the relationship. Drawing on their work with families of late adolescents and young adults who have suffered acute schizophrenia, the authors develop the hypothesis that the relationships in these families that are acceptable and may be openly acknowledged are intensely and enduringly pseudomutual. Although they do not claim either that pseudomutuality in itself produces schizophrenia or that it is unique to the relations of schizophrenics, they do find that it is significant feature of the setting in which reactive schizophrenia develops. Pseudomutuality is sustained by various mechanisms all of which make it difficult for the potential schizophrenic to differentiate himself as an individual with his own identity. Following Parsons and Bales, the authors propose that the potential schizophrenic internalizes the system of family relationships that keeps him from differentiating himself and that he thereby collaborates in maintaining the family pattern in which he is caught. Pseudomutuality requires concealment at the expense of openness, so that communication is distorted and perception blurred. A further result is that the roles enacted by the family members vis-à-vis each other are dissociated from subjective experience.

Bowen (1960) and Lidz, Cornelison, Fleck, and Terry (1957) also found that disturbed separateness-connectedness patterns play a part in the genesis of schizophrenia. Bowen found a relationship much like pseudomutuality in some of the schizophrenic families he studied intensively. These families are characterized by conventionalized and controlled relationships without sharing of personal feelings, thoughts, and experiences. This, however, is only one of the two types of emotional divorce that he found. The other type is hostile and argumentative. He also discovered an interesting pattern of alignment. At the outset of his work, he believed that all the family members were involved in the processes which led to schizophrenia in one member. As time went on, however, he concluded that father, mother, and patient constitute an interdependent triad from which normal siblings withdraw. This is a challenging finding which points to the need to under-

stand more fully how alignments are formed and how some members manage to escape from pathological involvements. Clausen and Kohn (1960) pointed out that systematic data on the siblings of schizophrenics had not been presented in any of the intensive family studies reported to date. However, subsequent to their survey of the literature on social relationships in schizophrenia, Lu (1961) reported a study directed to just this problem. On the basis of participant observation and interviews with 50 schizophrenics in a state hospital and with their siblings and parents she found certain differences between the schizophrenics and their siblings: (a) From early childhood the mother-patient relationship was far more intense than the mother-siblings relationship. (b) Although the mother attempted to dominate all the children, the eventual patient was highly submissive and dependent whereas the patient's siblings rebelled at the domination; the patient thus reciprocated the mother's demands while the siblings did not. (c) The greater inner freedom of the siblings allowed them to develop a wider range of social relationships than was true of the eventual schizophrenics; the schizophrenic grows up in a more constricted world than do his siblings. Lu announces her intention of publishing further, more detailed reports from this project and we may anticipate further specification and elucidation.

Somewhat akin to Bowen's concept of emotional divorce is the Lidz group's finding of marital schism and marital skew. In families characterized by marital schism, coercion, threat, provocation, and distrust are pronounced; satisfaction in marriage is lacking; and both parents compete for the children's affection. Marital skew is a situation in which the psychopathology of one parent is the focus around which family relationships are organized.

Pseudomutuality is a pathologically exaggerated form of connectedness which is established at the cost of the schizophrenic's failure to achieve a distinctive identity (Ryckoff, Day, and Wynne, 1959). Vogel and Bell (1960) described a pathological form of separateness in which a child is pushed into the role of family scapegoat and becomes emotionally disturbed (diagnosis unspecified). Their paper is an interim report from the Spiegel-Kluckhohn study described earlier. On the basis of intensive data from nine families—three

Irish-American, three Italian-American, and three old American, all working class—they concluded that a characteristic pattern of events leads to emotional disturbance in a child. The elements of the pattern are as follows: (a) Between the parents major unresolved tensions exist, based on deep fears about their marital relationship. (b) The tensions are so severe that some discharge is necessary, but for various reasons the parents dare not seek a scapegoat outside the family. The powerlessness of the children invites selection of one of them as a scapegoat. (c) One particular child in the sibship most readily symbolizes the variety of social and psychological problems impinging on the family. He is "selected" as the scapegoat, and his subsequent behavior provides suitable testimony to the appropriateness of the initial selection. Selection of the particular child is governed by such factors as his sex, position in the birth order, intelligence, physical characteristics, and other factors which have a particular emotional meaning to the parents. The other children remain free of emotional disturbance. (d) The child is inducted into and sustained in the scapegoat role by the application of inconsistent parental expectations. Behavior which is explicitly criticized is implicitly encouraged. Or behavior discouraged by one parent is encouraged by the other. Or the parental expectations are inconsistent in their severity. (e) The scapegoat role is further sustained by several mechanisms. These include parental denial that the child is emotionally disturbed and parental definition of themselves as victims rather than the child. Further, preoccupation with the child serves the function of enabling the parents to avoid directly confronting their own problems.

Vogel and Bell's (1960) paper is an important one. If their analysis of the scapegoat process be regarded as a particular instance of a general process, we are provided with a new avenue to understanding personality formation. Their model invites us to look at the ways in which the child's own characteristics and behavior are processed in the family by having meanings attached to them by others, meanings which the child variously resists, modifies, or cooperates in sustaining. In the process of growing up, the child endeavors to create new meanings for himself which the other family members are more or less willing to share

with him. His perceptual, cognitive, affective, and motivational capacities and propensities mesh with or collide with the corresponding capacities and propensities of the other members in such a way that the child is encouraged or induced to grow into the particular kind of person he is to become. Murphy's (1962) concept of coping is relevant in this context because from birth the child is faced with the task of coping with the meanings which his parents and sibs impute to him and his behavior, while he works at imputing meanings to them and their behavior. Vogel and Bell do not present as full a description as we would like of how the scapegoat copes with the meanings his parents assign to him, but Wynne and his collaborators present some vivid examples of how the young schizophrenic resists the meanings assigned by the members of his family. Lidz, Fleck, Cornelison, and Terry (1958) illustrate how the parental personalities influence the meanings they assign to the behavior of children who become schizophrenic.

Wynne (1961), following Hess and Handel (1959), adopted the concept of alignment pattern in his study of schizophrenics. One of his main findings is that, in the families of schizophrenics, alignments are highly unstable; this finding is at variance with that reported by Bowen (1960). Neither writer reports sufficient data to enable the reader to discern what might account for the difference. Another finding by Wynne indicates a situation in families of schizophrenics which seems to be rather different from that in the families studied by Vogel and Bell. He found it a great oversimplification to consider the schizophrenic child a victim of schizophrenogenic parents. Rather, all family members are engaged in reciprocally victimizing—and rescuing—processes. The difference between this conclusion and that of Vogel and Bell may be more apparent than real, for the tension between the parents that they discuss suggests that the scapegoat child is not the only victim in the families they studied. Further, Vogel and Bell's analysis reveals the reciprocating effects which the scapegoat child has upon his parents, effects which sustain their own personality and marital difficulties.

Cumulatively, the foregoing discussion strongly suggests that the processes of personality formation and the processes of family integration are, to an important extent, the same phenomena. While Parsons has made the point that personality, culture, and social system are three different conceptualizations of the same basic data, the point being made here is that when the family is the focus of study it is necessary and possible for some purposes to have a unified conceptualization which encompasses both the individual and the group. As the child copes with the meanings attributed to his behavior by the other family members, he both shapes his own personality and contributes to defining the pattern of separateness and connectedness in the family. The meanings assigned set limits, perhaps, to the coping behavior he will be able to attempt, and in the course of accepting, modifying, or resisting these limits the child both works toward his own identity and builds particular kinds of ties to other members. His ways of coping are at the same time an important part of his contribution to his ties to other members. The child's perceptual and cognitive adjustments, his cathexes, identifications, fantasies, acting out, and all other emotional and behavioral manifestations are at one and the same time constitutive of his own personality, constitutive of his ties to other members in a proactive sense (to use Murray's term), and constitutive of the meaning he has as an object for the other members.

Analysis of interpersonal relationships in the family is bound to raise questions about the usefulness of the concept of role. This is a vast topic in itself, and space limitations preclude an adequate discussion. Suffice it to say in the present context that, if the concept is to prove useful for psychological study of families, we require more highly refined analyses than are yet available. Categories such as male and female roles or parent and child roles are, though necessary as a starting point, simply too gross for adequate understanding. One dimension of the problem is suggested by the Vogel and Bell study. The emotionally disturbed child may be said to occupy a scapegoat role. But do all emotionally disturbed children have comparable roles in their families? If so, how are we to distinguish in role terms between different kinds of emotionally disturbed children, or do these differences have nothing to do with role? An answer to this question does not seem to be available at the present time. Also, since a role is fully understandable only as part of a role system,

we need to know what parental and sibling roles complete the system of which the scapegoat (or other roles of emotionally disturbed children) is a part. Further, we have yet to develop an adequate analysis of the various kinds of family roles of normal children—and, for that matter, of mother-wives and husband-fathers. Much greater effort has been made to codify the phenomena of role (see, e.g., Goffman, 1961; Neiman and Hughes, 1951; Sarbin, 1954; Sargent, 1951) than the phenomena of interaction, but much remains to be done. Ackerman (1951, 1958) presents some ideas about role that are particularly useful for psychology, but neither he nor anyone else has yet given us systematic studies of whole families, making use of these ideas.

The detailed study of personalities of the several members of a family and the interrelationships built up among them is important for a great many purposes. In addition, however, we would also like to have ways of classifying, on a psychological basis, families as groups. A useful classification should eventually enable us to understand the psychological properties of various kinds of families. This task is not altogether distinct from those discussed so far, but it does involve a somewhat different level of analysis. As noted earlier, Hess and Handel (1959) have proposed that the identification of family themes may be a useful procedure for understanding some of the binding forces in families. Search for themes may also serve the purpose of directing attention to relationships in many different behavioral modalities (e.g., thinking, perception, motivation, etc.) among the family members.

Paralleling Hess and Handel's finding of themes in nonclinical families, Fisher and Mendell (1956) and Mendell and Fisher (1956, 1958) have detected themes in neurotic families, 6 of them consisting of 3 generations and 14 of 2 generations. On the basis of Rorschach and TAT data they found in 1 family, for example, that all 7 members, spanning 3 generations, were preoccupied with exhibitionism and self-display. Another family was concerned with death or destructive loss of self-control. The projective responses are often strikingly similar. The Rorschach protocols from the members of the self-display family, for example, included the following responses: a boy referred for treatment for exposing himself to young girls saw a "peacock" and a "medallion" in the cards; his mother's most clear-cut human response was that of a "dandy"; his father perceived exposed genitals of women; his maternal grandmother perceived a "man coming out from between clouds or curtains, stepping out nicely on a stage [Fisher and Mendell, 1956, p. 43]." These investigators also report thematic congruence between projective and interview data. Their work leads them to a conclusion completely in keeping with that reached by Ackerman, Bowen, Vogel and Bell, and others, namely, that the central problems of the patient must be understood in terms of how they are embedded in the total family process. The projective data cited by these investigators are intriguing and point to the need to understand how such striking thematic similarity of response comes about.

Elles (1961) presented a case study of a delinquent family, utilizing psychiatric, medical, and extensive field data. She found a central theme which she characterized as the family's feeling of being futureless. The family's overt behavior and fantasy revealed three subthemes which exemplified the larger one: an oral theme involving difficulties of eating, starving, addiction, and drunkenness; a violence theme focused on fighting and sexual attack; and a theme of death involving both killing and a fear of not being able to stay alive. Her study also provides a particularly good illustration of how a family contracts the boundaries of its experience as a defensive maneuver. In contrast, Bell (1962) finds that disturbed families (by which he means families with an emotionally disturbed child) are distinguished from well families by the fact that the former have a deficiency of family boundaries that leads them to become highly embroiled with extended kin.

In a detailed case analysis of a family in which one son developed ulcerative colitis, Tichener, Riskin, and Emerson (1960) present a new approach to psychosomatic research. As their starting point, they accept a view proposed by some leading investigators in this field that the main psychological factor in the etiology of ulcerative colitis is helplessness and despair arising from actual, threatened, or imagined loss of a key object relationship. This view further holds that this affective state is the result of the patient's fruitless efforts to reinstate the kind of intensely symbiotic

relationship he had in early childhood with a controlling mother who gave love conditionally. This research team's innovation consists in showing that the patient's emotional state derives not merely from his relationship with his mother but is a product of the whole family's effort to deal with a conflict between frustrated dependency needs and the family ideal of independence, respectability, and avoidance of selfishness. They conclude that the family was integrated in a fashion they term anxious cohesion which required each member to give suitable testimony of his adherence to the ideal while vigorously suppressing his needs for emotional contact.

Fleck, Lidz, Cornelison, Schafer, and Terry (1959) and Fleck (1960) report that incestuous and homosexual themes are quite pronounced in the families of schizophrenic patients that they studied. The patient's intrapsychic conflicts over these kinds of sexual impulses reflect flagrantly seductive behavior by the parents.

The concept of family theme seems a useful one for a number of reasons. It provides a way of briefly summarizing the central psychological processes in a family group. Perhaps even more important, it is a stimulus to, and an avenue for, breaking out of the constraint of seeing families only in terms of power (authoritarian-democratic; dominant-submissive) and affection (strict-permissive; warm-cold). Power and affection as concepts constitute entirely too narrow a base for comprehending the rich psychological diversity of family life. Searching for themes prompts the investigator to gather a richer variety of data and to be more open to what the data reveal. At the same time, it must be recognized that the search for themes entails the potential (but as yet undemonstrated) disadvantage of endlessly idiosyncratic findings. Consequently, while some such summarizing concept seems useful for many purposes, it also appears necessary to develop some basis on which families may be systematically compared. A solution to this problem proposed by Handel (1962) and influenced by Kluckhohn's mode-of-value analysis involves moving down one level of abstraction to focus on certain core dimensions which may be regarded as constituent elements of themes. Analyzing individually obtained TATs from each member of five four-person families, Handel found that the family themes obtained could be dissected to yield five orientation categories, so-called because they refer to the family's orientation or stance to the world. These were: nature of the external world, nature of the self, the source of goals, nature of action, and nature of heterosexuality. This list is not considered exhaustive.

Another important attempt to characterize whole families grows out of a social work context and is reported by Voiland (1962); the project began in St. Paul and was later extended to six other cities. A survey of social agency services in St. Paul showed that there was a small group of multiproblem families that made unusually heavy demands on the resources of many agencies. Initially, these disturbed families were classified in terms of marital axes—interaction patterns of the marital partners. Efforts to correlate other family problems with these axes were not successful.

The study then moved to a broader framework utilizing four main dimensions: (a) types of disorder in the family, including personality disorders of any member, financial disorders such as irregular income production, and family dissolution disorders due to desertion, divorce, separation, placement of children; (b) family social functioning, including marital, child rearing, child development, and financial; (c) individual characteristics of each member—personality, intellectual, and physical; (d) development of each parent in his family of origin.

On the basis of this framework, four types of disordered family were identified: perfectionistic, inadequate, egocentric, and unsocial. The types are presented as being supported by statistical analysis of systematically coded, case data. These data are not presented in the book but are said to be available from the organization which sponsored the research.

Each family type is characterized by its own syndrome of disorders. For example, the perfectionistic family tends to involve parental concern about habit-training practices and concern about guiding self-reliance in the child; anxiety and guilt-ridden behavior in the child; problems of emotional give and take between the spouses and problems of maintaining mutual self-esteem; anxiety-dominated behavior patterns in one or both parents. These disorders are described as distorting realistic handling of problems without interfering

with good social conduct. In contrast, the unsocial family's disorders tend to be child neglect and fostering of disrespect for social authority; delinquency, truancy, psychosis, or other serious personality disturbances of the child; multiple symptoms and rapidly changing attitudes in the marital relationship which often bring the parents into court or evoke complaints to police; divorce often followed by remarriage of the partners to each other; hospitalization for mental illness; crime; addictions; sexual deviations common in adult members.

Although the framework for analysis is heterogeneous, this study is notable in two respects. First, it is the only study known to the writer which attempts a psychosocial typology of whole families oriented to total family functioning rather than to some specific life area. Secondly, the study explicitly rejects interaction as a basis for family classification in favor of interpersonal relationships as the basis.

Family Communication and Schizophrenia

Interaction and communication are sometimes loosely used as equivalent concepts. Although, as noted earlier, it does not seem possible at the present time to formulate a definition of interaction that is at once both rigorous and comprehensive, it seems clear that interaction is a term of broader scope than communication. The referents of the latter term are not easily delimited, but generally communication may be said to refer to the process of organizing and transmitting messages. Bateson, Jackson, and their associates consider this process to play a significant part in the development of schizophrenia.

The central concept of their approach is that all communication takes place on at least two levels, and often on more than two. One level is that of the content itself—what is said. The second level in some way qualifies what is said: affirms it, denies it, indicates that what is said is serious or a joke, is a suggestion or a command, etc. The first level of communication is ordinarily the level of words; the second is ordinarily the level of vocal intonation and bodily gesture. The schizophrenic is a person who grows up in a family in which what is said is typically qualified in such a way as to be utterly incongruent. To take a simple example, the mother may characteristically address her child as "Dear" but in a tone of voice which conveys hostility. If the child attempts to note and comment upon the incongruence between these two levels, the mother may resort to a third level of communication, namely, deny that there was any incongruence in her mode of address (Weakland, 1960). The child, because of his dependency and need for love, cannot leave the field and escape from the extreme pain of having to cope continually with these incongruent messages, but neither do his parents allow him to comment on their communication behavior in a way that would induce them toward greater level-congruence. The child is caught in a double bind (Bateson, Jackson, Haley, and Weakland, 1956). As a result of growing up in this prevailing double-bind situation, the child who later becomes schizophrenic suffers an impaired capacity to discriminate correctly communication modes within himself and between self and others.

The concept of multiple levels of communication has been pushed several steps further. The concept that every message necessarily involves some form of qualification is expanded to encompass the idea that families develop implicit rules for qualifying messages (Haley, 1959b). Such rules arise from the fact that all communications are necessarily efforts to define a relationship.

Haley proposes that families govern their behavior by establishing rules for communication and that it would be fruitful to develop a typology of families based on the nature of these rules. On the basis of his research group's extensive study of families of schizophrenics and preliminary observations of families containing children without symptoms, children with asthma and children who are delinquent, he concludes that the family with a schizophrenic is a unique type of family. Briefly, he finds that: The members in a family with a schizophrenic consistently manifest an incongruence between what they say and how they qualify what they say, the members consistently disqualify what each other says, and the consistent disqualification prevents the development both of clear leadership in the family and of stable alliances either between family members or between any family member and someone outside the family. The inability of the schizophrenic to relate to other people, as well as his general withdrawal, is understandable in terms of his being raised in a learning situation where his actions were always disqualified and where he was not permitted to relate to other people so that he could learn to behave differently (Haley, 1959a).

Finally, we should note that this theory proposes an explanation of the schizophrenic break with reality in terms of family communication rules.

This approach to analysis of communication within the family is intriguing. It focuses attention on observable behavior, and the analysis of this behavior reveals something of the complexity of family interaction. Among other merits of this approach is the demonstration of the way in which absence of family arguments can be a pathologic sign (Jackson, 1959), and this is surely a needed corrective to oversimplified notions regarding the nature of family integration. Jackson also, however, states that one of the merits of communication theory as an approach to family interaction is that it avoids the necessity of attributing affects to the subjects. In fact, it does no such thing. In a later report which demonstrates how to analyze a taped family interview, not only is attention paid to the communication pattern but inferences about affect and motivation are also made; the two modes of analysis are said to be complementary (Jackson, Riskin, and Satir, 1961). And, in fact, the ways in which communications of hostility and affection are qualified are staple illustrations in many of the writings of this research group.

Cognitive Processes

A comprehensive view of how a family functions would seem to require that we direct attention not only to the structure of communication but as well to the cognitive structures of the senders and receivers. If, for example, one parent is highly given to thinking in generalities (overproduction of Ws, in Rorschach terminology) and the other is very practical (perceiving the world in terms of D and with a high $F\%$ and $F+\%$), what problems does this pose for their children and how do the children solve them? What style of thinking do they develop? Do different children in the same family develop different styles of thinking? If so, why? Do factual fathers have problems with imaginative daughters, or is the contrast in styles of thought mutually gratifying and growth promoting—or does it depend upon the presence of suitably factual sons or the nature of the mother's input? In short, how are families integrated at a cognitive level? What part do cognitive processes play in family integration? The range of meaningful questions that can be asked is enormous, but the writer is not aware of any systematic effort to develop a social-personological psychology of cognitive processes in the family. Here and there one finds occasional papers that touch upon this problem area. Flavell (1957), for example, in a speculative paper suggests that an adequate explanation of the etiology of schizophrenic thinking must show specifically how cognitive development becomes affected by pathogenic early interpersonal relations. He refers to a suggestion by Powdermaker (1952) to the effect that one factor may be the parents' intolerance for the child's presocialized autistic ideas so that the child is forced to think realistically rather than being allowed to grow more slowly into socialized thinking. The child's loss of self-esteem thereby incurred is suggested as a predisposing factor for a later abandonement of reality in a psychotic episode. A very similar point of view is taken by Lidz, Cornelison, Terry, and Fleck (1958) who argue that a theory of schizophrenia must explain the patient's ability to abandon reality testing as well as his need to do so. The basic point that emerges from their study of the families of 15 upper-middle and upper-class schizophrenics is that these patients had been in various ways trained in irrationality in their families. Working on quite a different problem, Frenkel-Brunswik (1955) found various kinds of systematic constriction of thought processes in all members of the family of an extremely ethnocentric boy.

Getzels and Jackson (1962) suggest that creative children come from families that differ in important ways from the families of high IQ, noncreative children. Whatever be the limitations of their study, they have surely raised a significant question which merits social psychological attention. How do family processes affect cognitive structure and cognitive freedom? In one aspect, the problem is similar to that tackled by Vogel and Bell: Do families select one child as creative innovator much as they might select one to be an emotionally disturbed scapegoat?

RESEARCH METHODS

There are as yet no established methods for studying whole families. Nonetheless it is worthwhile calling attention, however briefly, to some of the most common procedures and some issues

that are raised. The discussion can be no more than suggestive.

Therapy

Psychiatrists have increasingly been using family therapy as a research method. Various clinical research teams are filming and tape recording family therapy sessions and analyzing these in a search for significant relationships. As noted earlier, there are also attempts to study whole families on an in-patient basis (Bowen, 1960). In terms of volume, family therapy is probably the largest single source of data for whole family study at the present time. Should this situation continue, the psychological study of whole families may well repeat the history of personality study; conceptions of abnormal functioning will be dominant for a long time until, belatedly, studies of nonclinical families will be undertaken in an effort to achieve a more rounded view of how families function. The value of obtaining data from family therapy not only to develop more effective therapies but also to increase general understanding of the psychosocial dynamics of family life is not in dispute. The issue is whether studies of families in therapy should be the major source of knowledge in this field, to the relative neglect of other kinds of research. There can be little doubt that psychiatry now leads the way (although admittedly sometimes in collaboration with psychologists and other social scientists) in attempting to understand the family from a psychosocial point of view. If psychology as a discipline does not soon address itself more vigorously to this problem, the result may be that a generation hence psychologists will be devoting their time to trying to verify propositions originating in family psychiatry, just as in the field of personality study they have been significantly preoccupied with the merits of propositions originating in psychoanalysis.

Field Methods

As here used, this is an omnibus term which includes any procedure for obtaining data in the home of the subjects. Thus, interviewing, psychological testing, and observation of family interaction are field methods which have been used. These are, to be sure, diverse procedures, but the point of grouping them under this rubric is to call attention to the fact that the task of studying whole families that are normal or nonclinical poses a challenge for psychology, accustomed to dealing with easily accessible subjects in laboratories, clinics, nursery schools, and other captive or controlled environments. Useful discussions of some fieldwork problems and procedures in studies of whole nonclinical families will be found in Robb (1953), Bott (1957), and Hess and Handel (1959).

Projective Methods

Rosenzweig appears to have been the first psychologist to propose that close relatives of psychiatric patients, as well as the patients themselves, be given projective tests so that the diagnostician can understand the full psychodynamic setting of the patient's life (see Rosenzweig and Cass, 1954; Rosenzweig and Isham, 1947). Although projective techniques have been used before and since for the purpose of studying personality similarities, Rosenzweig and Isham's proposal is the first recognition that these techniques, particularly the TAT, can provide an avenue to understanding the psychic life of the family as a functioning unit. As noted earlier, Fisher and Mendell also used projective techniques in studying whole families, as did Hess and Handel.

Sohler, Holzberg, Fleck, Cornelison, Kay, and Lidz (1957) attempted to predict family interaction from analysis of a battery of projective tests, which included the TAT, Rorschach, Draw-A-Person, and Rotter Sentence Completion, individually administered to each member of a four-person family in which the son was hospitalized for schizophrenia. Over a 2-year period, the patient had been seen for 3 or 4 therapeutic hours per week; both his parents had been seen once a week; and his sister had been interviewed 29 times. All of this psychiatric-interview material constituted the criterion against which the psychological test interpretations were judged. The psychological report was dissected into 333 discrete interpretive statements about each family member and about family interaction. Although, overall, two thirds of these statements were found to agree with the psychiatric material, the individual personality descriptions contained the highest proportion of agreements, while predictions of attitude of one family member toward another and statements about family interaction were the most likely source of disagreements. Even so, some measure of success in this area is reported. Considering the novelty of the attempt, the results seem encouraging.

The interpretive approaches used by Rosenzweig and his associates, Fisher and Mendell, and Sohler et al. entail certain limitations which seem neither necessary nor desirable. First, all of these workers conceive of the family as a group of interrelated individuals but they do not also conceive of the family as having psychological properties of its own that are not explicitly attached to a specific member or pair of members. This restriction means that interpretations about family behavior are always from one person to another (e.g., how patient and mother relate to each other) and never from person to group or group to person. This latter type of conceptualization would seem to be necessary if, for example, one hoped to be able to use TAT data to make a diagnosis such as family scapegoat. Assessments of this order require thinking in group dynamic terms and not simply from person to person in point-to-point fashion, however necessary this way of thinking also is. In addition, of course, conceptualizing at the group level is also necessary if one wishes to use projective data to diagnose families in such terms as Voiland uses or Handel's orientation categories. Conceivably, although this remains to be determined, one might discover from the protocols obtained individually from each family member the family's communication rules as delineated by Haley—or other kinds of rules that might be thought of such as affective rules, defensive rules, rules for dealing with esteem-lowering events, etc.

A second limitation, found in the work of Fisher and Mendell, is the emphasis on responses which are unusual and yet are also similar among members, as in the example cited earlier. Focusing only on highly similar responses among family members leads one to ignore useful, perhaps necessary, data. Further, striking similarities of response among members are not always to be found; neither are highly unusual responses. It is necessary to have a procedure that is free of such limitations.

Handel (1962) proposed a method of TAT analysis for family study, called analysis of correlative meaning, which is not dependent upon the occurrence either of unusual responses or of similarity of members' responses, and which also makes possible analysis of psychological characteristics of a family as a group. The method, which makes use of W. E. Henry's (1951) horizontal-thematic analysis, rests upon three interlocking assumptions: (a) Each card of the TAT has a latent stimulus demand which is "the emotional problem or focus most generally raised by the picture. . . . It will vary from group to group somewhat [W. E. Henry, 1956, p. 100]." (b) The meaning of any individual's stories is not exhausted by reference to his own personality; on the contrary, a part of the meaning of any individual's stories is discovered by reference to the stories of the other family members. (c) Family interaction gives rise to certain general problems and outlooks which involve each family member, each individual's response to a TAT picture in part derives from his interaction with the other family members around the issues tapped by the picture, and the correlativity of meanings of the members' individually-told stories derives from the prolonged interrelations of their experiences.[2] The orientation categories mentioned earlier were obtained by use of this method of interpretation. Its validity remains to be established, but the assumptions underlying it seem reasonable working assumptions.

Hess and Handel attempted a procedure in which a family as a group told stories to a set of specially designed, TAT-type pictures, an idea borrowed from W. E. Henry and Guetzkow (1951) who had successfully used this technique with nonfamily groups. In addition, the interaction of the families as they made up the joint stories was recorded with the aim of relating the overt interaction to the story material. Although some of this material is cited illustratively in Hess and Handel (1959), the technical and interpretive problems of relating the two kinds of data were not solved by the time their project was concluded. The potentiality of this method remains undetermined.

Controlled Experiment

Few controlled experiments using family groups are known to the writer. Certainly one of the few

[2] I thank William E. Henry for suggestions which improved upon my initial concatenation of these assumptions. If the linkage remains unclear, or is proved untenable, the responsibility is mine alone. I express also my appreciation to Sidney J. Levy and Lee Rainwater for their lively and helpful interest in my efforts to use these assumptions in the interpretation of data.

adequately reported ones, and perhaps the first, is that of Strodtbeck (1954). A unique aspect of this experiment is that it was carried out in the homes of the families rather than in a laboratory. Employing as subjects family groups consisting of father, mother, and adolescent son, Strodtbeck devised a procedure termed the revealed difference technique. Each family member was individually presented a list of 47 described situations and for each situation was asked to pick one of two alternatives. One such situation, for example, described two fathers discussing their sons: one a brilliant student and the other an outstanding athlete. The respondent was asked to decide which father was the more fortunate. After each family member had made his 47 choices, the investigator selected three items on which mother and father took one alternative and the son the other; three items on which mother and son had agreed but not the father; and three items on which father and son had agreed but not the mother. The family was then set to discussing these nine issues and urged to reach an agreement on each one. Their discussion was recorded and subsequently scored using the categories of Bales' interaction-process analysis. The interaction data were then analyzed in terms of the relationship between amount of activity in the discussion and number of decisions won. The experiment provides material for another form of analysis not pursued, namely, the symbolic meanings of agreement between each pair of members on different types of item. What, for example, is the difference between a family in which the mother and father but not the son agree that the father with the athletic son is the more fortunate and a family in which one parent and the son but not the other parent agree on this? Do we have any sound reason for believing that this type of analysis would be less illuminating than the interaction-process analysis? What is revealed by revealed differences? Would not the two types of analysis together be more informative than either alone?

Haley (1962) makes a strong plea for experiments with families and discusses some of the special problems involved in experimenting upon groups whose members have a long history of relationship. He argues that the goal of family experiments must be different from the goal of experimenting with ad hoc groups. Whereas the aim of experiments in social psychology is usually to demonstrate the effect of a particular set of conditions upon group performance, the goal of family experiments, as he sees it, is to describe and measure the way family members typically respond to each other, that is, outside the experimental situation. Although experiments with families do present certain difficulties, many discussed by Haley, it is questionable whether the logic underlying such experiments differs from the logic underlying other types of group experiment as radically as Haley believes it does. In this same paper he reports two experiments in which, all told, 30 families with a schizophrenic member were compared with 30 normal families. The experiments showed that families with a schizophrenic member had a harder time forming coalitions within the family than did normal families. However, he himself questions whether the results can be taken as demonstrating the typical behavior of these families outside the experimental situation. He suggests, however, that this latter problem can be solved by running the same families several times in the same experiment and by running them through different types of experiments designed to test the same basic processes. More generally, Haley sees experimentation as the procedure that will yield a suitable classification of families, and he suggests that whereas the first half of this century has been largely devoted to classifying and describing individuals, the second half of the century will likely be devoted to classifying families and other ongoing organizations. Needless to say, he, like every worker studying whole families, does not underestimate the magnitude of the task, but neither does he overestimate its importance.

SUMMARY

Analysis of whole families is delineated as a field of psychological study. Importance of this field is indicated by growing sentiment that a simple parent-child cause-effect model is proving inadequate to the tasks of both child psychology and abnormal psychology. Relevance to psychology of personality and social psychology is also shown. Emergence of the field is traced, and major current approaches are examined. A general conceptual framework, growing out of and integrating data from psychology and other behavioral sciences, is shown to be developing. Evidence suggests that a great range of psychological phenomena, including, illustratively, social attitudes, psychosomatic symptoms, cognitive functioning, identity formation, affiliative behavior, can be illuminated by psychological study of whole families. Principal current research methods are briefly discussed.

REFERENCES

Ackerman, N. W. The unity of the family. *Archives of Pediatrics,* 1938, 55: 51–62.

Ackerman, N. W. Social role and total personality. *American Journal of Orthopsychiatry,* 1951, 21: 1–17.

Ackerman, N. W. Interpersonal disturbances in the family: Some unsolved problems in psychotherapy. *Psychiatry,* 1954, 17: 359–368.

Ackerman, N. W. Interlocking pathology in family relationships. In S. Rado and G. E. Daniels (Eds.), *Changing conceptions of psychoanalytic medicine.* New York: Grune and Stratton, 1956. Pp. 135–150.

Ackerman, N. W. *The psychodynamics of family life.* New York: Basic Books, 1958.

Ackerman, N. W. Emergence of family psychotherapy on the present scene. In M. I. Stein (Ed.), *Contemporary psychotherapies.* New York: Free Press of Glencoe, 1961. Pp. 228–244.

Ackerman, N. W., and Sobel, R. Family diagnosis: An approach to the pre-school child. *American Journal of Orthopsychiatry,* 1950, 20: 744–753.

Bateson, G., Jackson, D. D., Haley, J., and Weakland, J. Toward a theory of schizophrenia. *Behavioral Science,* 1956, 1: 251–264.

Bell, N. W. Extended family relations of disturbed and well families. *Family Process,* 1962, 1: 175–193.

Bergman, P., and Escalona, Sibylle. Unusual sensitivities in very young children. *Psychoanalytic Study of the Child,* 1949, 4: 333–352.

Bossard, J. H. S., and Boll, Eleanor. *Ritual in family living.* Philadelphia: Univer. of Pennsylvania Press, 1950.

Bott, Elizabeth. *Family and social network: Roles, norms and external relationships in ordinary urban families.* London: Tavistock, 1957.

Bowen, M. A family concept of schizophrenia. In D. D. Jackson (Ed.), *The etiology of schizophrenia.* New York: Basic Books, 1960. Pp. 346–372.

Burgess, E. W. The family as a unity of interacting personalities. *Family,* 1926, 7: 3–9.

Clausen, J. A., and Kohn, M. L. Social relations

and schizophrenia: A research report and a perspective. In D. D. Jackson (Ed.), *The etiology of schizophrenia.* New York: Basic Books, 1960. Pp. 295–320.

Cleveland, E. J., and Longaker, W. D. Neurotic patterns in the family. In A. Leighton, J. A. Clausen, and R. N. Wilson (Eds.), *Explorations in social psychiatry.* New York: Basic Books, 1957. Pp. 167–200.

Cousins, A. N. The failure of solidarity. In N. W. Bell and E. F. Vogel (Eds.), *A modern introduction to the family.* Glencoe, Ill.: Free Press, 1960. Pp. 403–416.

Eisenstein, V. W. (Ed.) *Neurotic interaction in marriage.* New York: Basic Books, 1956.

Elles, G. W. The closed circuit: The study of a delinquent family. *British Journal of Criminology,* 1961, 2: 23–39.

Escalona, Sibylle, and Heider, Grace. *Prediction and outcome: A study in child development.* New York: Basic Books, 1959.

Escalona, Sibylle, and Leitch, Mary. Early phases of personality development. *Monographs of the Society for Research in Child Development,* 1952, 17: (1, Whole No. 54).

Fisher, S., and Mendell, D. The communication of neurotic patterns over two and three generations. *Psychiatry,* 1956, 10: 41–46.

Fisher, S., and Mendell, D. The spread of psychotherapeutic effects from the patient to his family group. *Psychiatry,* 1958, 21: 133–140.

Flavell, J. H. Some observations on schizophrenic thinking: Observation and onset. *Canadian Journal of Psychology,* 1957, 11: 128–132.

Fleck, S. Family dynamics and origin of schizophrenia. *Psychosomatic Medicine,* 1960, 22: 333–344.

Fleck, S., Lidz, T., Cornelison, Alice, Schafer, Sarah, and Terry, Dorothy. The intrafamilial environment of the schizophrenic patient: Incestuous and homosexual dynamics. In J. H. Masserman (Ed.), *Individual and familial dynamics.* New York: Grune and Stratton, 1959. Pp. 142–159.

Freeman, V. J., Klein, A. F., Riehman, Lynne, Lukoff, I. F., and Heisey, Virginia. "Family group counseling" as differentiated from other family therapies. *International Journal of Group Psychotherapy,* 1963, 13: 167–175.

Frenkel-Brunswik, Else. Differential patterns of social outlook and personality in family and children. In Margaret Mead and Martha Wolfenstein (Eds.), *Childhood in contemporary cultures.* Chicago: Univer. Chicago Press, 1955. Pp. 369–402.

Fries, Margaret, and Woolf, P. J. Some hypotheses on the role of the congenital activity type in personality development. *Psychoanalytic Study of the Child,* 1954, 8: 48–62.

Getzels, J. W., and Jackson, P. *Creativity and intelligence.* New York: Wiley, 1962.

Goffman, E. *Encounters: Two studies in the sociology of interaction.* Indianapolis, Ind.: Bobbs-Merrill, 1961.

Grotjahn, M. Analytic family therapy: A survey of trends in research and practice. In J. Masserman (Ed.), *Individual and familial dynamics.* New York: Grune and Stratton, 1959. Pp. 90–104.

Grotjahn, M. *Psychoanalysis and the family neurosis.* New York: Norton, 1960.

Group for the Advancement of Psychiatry. *Integration and conflict in family relations.* (Report No. 27) Topeka, Kans.: GAP, 1954.

Haley, J. The family of the schizophrenic: A model system. *Journal of Nervous and Mental Disease,* 1959, 129: 357–374. (a)

Haley, J. An interactional description of schizophrenia. *Psychiatry,* 1959, 22: 321–332. (b)

Haley, J. Family experiments: A new type of experimentation. *Family Process,* 1962, 1: 265–293.

Handel, G. A study of family and personality. Unpublished doctoral dissertation, University of Chicago, 1962.

Handel, G., and Hess, R. D. The family as an emotional organization. *Marriage and Family Living,* 1956, 18: 99–101.

Harris, I. *Normal children and mothers.* Glencoe, Ill.: Free Press, 1959.

Henry, J. Family structure and the transmission of neurotic behavior. *American Journal of Orthopsychiatry,* 1951, 21: 800–818.

Henry, J., and Warson, S. Family structure and psychic development. *American Journal of Orthopsychiatry,* 1951, 21: 59–73.

Henry, W. E. The thematic apperception technique in the study of group and cultural problems. In H. H. Anderson and Gladys L. Anderson (Eds.), *An introduction to projective techniques.* New York: Prentice-Hall, 1951. Pp. 230–278.

Henry, W. E. *The analysis of fantasy.* New York: Wiley, 1956.

Henry, W. E., and Guetzkow, H. Group projection sketches for the study of small groups. *Journal of Social Psychology,* 1951, 33: 77–102.

Hess, R. D., and Handel, G. *Family worlds: A psychosocial approach to family life.* Chicago: Univer. Chicago Press, 1959.

Hill, R. *Families under stress: Adjustments to the crises of war separation and reunion.* New York: Harper, 1949.

Hoffman, Lois, and Lippitt, R. The measurement of family life variables. In P. H. Mussen (Ed.), *Handbook of research methods in child development.* New York: Wiley, 1960. Pp. 945–1013.

Jackson, D. D. The question of family homeostasis. Part 1. *Psychiatric Quarterly Supplement,* 1957, 31: 79–90.

Jackson, D. D. Family interaction, family homeostasis and some implications for conjoint family therapy. In J. H. Masserman (Ed.), *Individual and familial dynamics.* New York: Grune and Stratton, 1959. Pp. 122–141.

Jackson, D. D. Family therapy in the family of the schizophrenic. In M. I. Stein (Ed.), *Contemporary psychotherapies.* New York: Free Press of Glencoe, 1961. Pp. 272–287.

Jackson, D. D., Riskin, J., and Satir, Virginia. A method of analysis of a family interview. *Archives of General Psychiatry,* 1961, 5: 321–339.

Jackson, D. D., and Weakland, J. Schizophrenic symptoms and family interaction. *Archives of General Psychiatry,* 1959, 1: 618–621.

Jackson, D. D., and Weakland, J. Conjoint family therapy: Some considerations on theory, technique and results. *Psychiatry,* 1961, 24: (2, Suppl.), 30–45.

Josslyn, Irene. The family as a psychological unit. *Social Casework,* 1953, 34: 336–343.

Kaplan, B. *Studying personality cross-culturally.* Evanston, Ill.: Row, Peterson, 1961.

Kluckhohn, C., and Murray, H. A. *Personality in nature, society and culture.* New York: Knopf, 1948.

Kluckhohn, Florence. Dominant and substitute profiles of cultural orientations: Their significance for the analysis of social stratification. *Social Forces,* 1950, 28: 276–293.

Leichter, Hope J. Boundaries of the family as an empirical and theoretical unit. In N. W. Ackerman, Frances L. Beatman, and S. N. Sherman (Eds.), *Exploring the base for family therapy.* New York: Family Service Association, 1961. Pp. 140–144.

Lewin, K., Lippitt, R., and White, R. K. Patterns of aggressive behavior in experimentally created "social climates." *Journal of Social Psychology,* 1939, 10: 271–299.

Lewis, O. An anthropological approach to family studies. *American Journal of Sociology,* 1950, 55: 468–475.

Lewis, O. *Five families: Mexican case studies in the culture of poverty.* New York: Basic Books, 1959.

Lewis, O. *The children of Sanchez.* New York: Random House, 1961.

Lidz, T., Cornelison, Alice, Fleck, S., and Terry, Dorothy. The intrafamilial environment of the schizophrenic patient: II. Marital schism and marital skew. *American Journal of Psychiatry,* 1957, 114: 241–248.

Lidz, T., Cornelison, Alice, Terry, Dorothy, and Fleck, S. Intrafamilial environment of the schizophrenic patient: VI. The transmission of irrationality. *Archives of Neurology and Psychiatry,* 1958, 79: 305–316.

Lidz, T., Fleck, S., Cornelison, Alice, and Terry, Dorothy. Intrafamilial environment of the schizophrenic patient: IV. Parental personalities and family interaction. *American Journal of Orthopsychiatry,* 1958, 28: 764–776.

Lu, Yi-chuang. Mother-child role relationships in schizophrenia: A comparison of schizophrenic patients with non-schizophrenic siblings. *Psychiatry,* 1961, 24: 133–142.

Mead, Margaret. *Coming of age in Samoa.* New York: Morrow, 1928.

Mendell, D., and Fisher, S. An approach to neurotic behavior in terms of a three-generation family model. *Journal of Nervous and Mental Disease,* 1956, 123: 171–180.

Mendell, D., and Fisher, S. A multi-generation approach to treatment of psychopathology. *Journal of Nervous and Mental Disease,* 1958, 126: 523–529.

Miller, D. Personality and social interaction. In B. Kaplan (Ed.), *Studying personality cross-culturally.* Evanston, Ill.: Row, Peterson, 1961. Pp. 271–298.

Mittelman, B. Complementary neurotic reactions in intimate relationships. *Psychoanalytic Quarterly,* 1944, 13: 479–491.

Mittelman, B. The concurrent analysis of married couples. *Psychoanalytic Quarterly,* 1948, 17: 182–197.

Murphy, Lois. *The widening world of childhood.* New York: Basic Books, 1962.

Neiman, L. J., and Hughes, J. W. The problem of the concept of role: A re-survey of the literature. *Social Forces,* 1951, 30: 141–149.

Oberndorf, C. P. Psychoanalysis of married couples. *Psychoanalytic Review,* 1938, 25: 453–465.

Parsons, T., and Bales, R. F. *Family, socialization and interaction process.* Glencoe, Ill.: Free Press, 1955.

Powdermaker, Florence. Concepts found useful in

the treatment of schizoid and ambulatory schizophrenic patients. *Psychiatry,* 1952, 15: 61–71.

Redl, F. Group emotion and leadership. *Psychiatry,* 1942, 5: 573–596.

Robb, J. H. Experiences with ordinary families. *British Journal of Medical Psychology,* 1953, 26: 215–221.

Roberts, J. M. Three Navaho households: A comparative study in small group culture. *Papers of the Peabody Museum of American Archaeology and Ethnology,* Harvard University, 1951, 40: (3).

Rose, A. A systematic summary of symbolic interaction theory. In A. Rose (Ed.), *Human behavior and social processes.* Boston: Mass.: Houghton Mifflin, 1962. Pp. 3–19.

Rosenzweig, S., and Cass, Loretta K. The extension of psychodiagnosis to parents in the child guidance setting. *American Journal of Orthopsychiatry,* 1954, 24: 715–722.

Rosenzweig, S., and Isham, A. C. Complementary Thematic Apperception Test patterns in close kin. *American Journal of Orthopsychiatry,* 1947, 17: 129–142.

Ryckoff, I., Day, Juliana, and Wynne, L. C. Maintenance of stereotyped roles in the families of schizophrenics. *Archives of General Psychiatry,* 1959, 1: 109–114.

Sarbin, T. R. Role theory. In G. Lindzey (Ed.), *Handbook of social psychology,* Vol. 1. Cambridge, Mass.: Addison-Wesley, 1954, Pp. 223–258.

Sargent, S. S. Conceptions of role and ego in contemporary psychology. In J. H. Rohrer and M. Sherif (Eds.), *Social psychology at the crossroads.* New York: Harper, 1951.

Sherif, M. *The psychology of social norms.* New York: Harper, 1936.

Sohler, Dorothy Terry, Holzberg, J. D., Fleck, S., Cornelison, Alice, Kay, Eleanor, and Lidz, T. The prediction of family interaction from a battery of projective tests. *Journal of Projective Techniques,* 1957, 21: 199–208.

Spiegel, J., and Bell, N. W. The family of the psychiatric patient. In S. Arieti (Ed.), *American handbook of psychiatry.* New York: Basic Books, 1959. Pp. 114–149.

Strodtbeck, F. L. The family as a three-person group. *American Sociological Review,* 1954, 19: 23–29.

Strodtbeck, F. L. Family interaction, values and achievement. In D. McClelland, A. Baldwin, U. Bronfenbrenner, and F. L. Strodtbeck, *Talent and society.* Princeton, N. J.: Van Nostrand, 1958. Pp. 135–194.

Tharp, R. Psychological patterning in marriage. *Psychological Bulletin,* 1963, 60: 97–117.

Titchener, J., Riskin, J., and Emerson, R. The family in psychosomatic process: A case report illustrating a method of psychosomatic research. *Psychosomatic Medicine,* 1960, 22: 127–142.

Vogel, E. F., and Bell, N. W. The emotionally disturbed child as the family scapegoat. In N. W. Bell and E. F. Vogel (Eds.), *A modern introduction to the family.* Glencoe, Ill.: Free Press, 1960.

Voiland, Alice L. *Family casework diagnosis.* New York: Columbia Univer. Press, 1962.

Weakland, J. H. The "double-bind" hypothesis of schizophrenia and three-party interaction. In D. D. Jackson (Ed.), *The etiology of schizophrenia.* New York: Basic Books, 1960. Pp. 373–388.

White, R. Abnormalities of behavior. *Annual Review of Psychology,* 1959, 10: 265–286.

Wynne, L. C. The study of intrafamilial alignments and splits in exploratory family therapy. In N. W. Ackerman, Frances L. Beatman, and S. N. Sherman (Eds.), *Exploring the base for family therapy.* New York: Family Service Association, 1961. Pp. 95–115.

Wynne, L. C., Ryckoff, I. M., Day, Juliana, and Hirsch, S. I. Pseudo-mutuality in the family relations of schizophrenics. *Psychiatry,* 1958, 21: 205–220.

PART IV

Personality, Deviant Behavior, and Social Problems

PERSONALITY RESEARCHERS working on the problem of deviant or abnormal behavior are basically motivated by two factors. The first is that as abnormality is part of the continuum of behavior, it is necessary to understand it in order to achieve a comprehensive analysis of human behavior and its determinants. The second is the desire to contribute to knowledge which may result in the successful rehabilitation of persons who display behavior which is undesirable or unacceptable either to themselves or to society.

Defining deviant behavior, and especially deviant behavior which poses personal or social problems, is a far from simple task. One man might be deviant in the clothes he wears; another in the occupation he chooses. One of the primary professional foci of the personality researcher is to uncover correlates and determinants of behavior that both individuals and society define as deviant, maladaptive, undesirable, or a source of concern.

The study of abnormal behavior requires the use of every research method described in previous parts of this book. For example, assessment and experimental methods contribute to the psychological study of deviancy and developmental approaches explore the genesis of the abnormal personality. The task before the student of deviancy is to apply existing methodology in a creative manner in order that the breadth of human experience can be better understood. This task is particularly challenging in the case of psychological approaches to behavioral abnormality and social problems since so many levels of analysis are required to fill out a comprehensive picture of these phenomena. The problems of the individual and his society can be studied at the level of the person, but they also can be viewed in terms of the functioning of a variety of social groups and agencies which impinge upon the person. These include the family, schools, hospitals, prisons, and neighborhoods.

Examples of behavioral deviations abound in places such as mental hospitals, mental hygiene clinics, and offices of private practitioners, but they can also be found throughout the everyday world. An example of this is found in Seiden's article which deals with the tragic problem of suicide among college students. Seiden asks: Given a group of suiciding and nonsuiciding students, can psychological inquiry shed light on differences between them and thus identify harbingers of suicide?

In his research, Seiden used diverse sources of information to compare suiciding and nonsuiciding subjects. He identified characteristics that suiciding students share as a group and also showed that these students were significantly different from their fellow students in a number of other characteristics. Thus, applying an assessment paradigm to the study of an important epidemiological problem, Seiden was able to obtain indications of the psychological and environmental determinants of suicide. Considering these Seiden unhappily concludes that increasing competition for admission to college and then for high academic ranking within college will lead to an increase in the college suicide rate.

It is important to bear in mind that suicide studies such as Seiden's are post-hoc in nature, i.e., the subjects of investigation are not identified until after they have killed themselves. This makes it impossible to separate neatly cause-effect relationships in suicide. These relationships need to be studied. Might leads such as those provided by Seiden's research be used to develop a set of characteristics of potential suiciders? And then might it be possible to study longitudinally and predictively people with these characteristics? If a predictive study were successful, the next and crucial step would be to develop interventive techniques directed at preventing the occurrence of suicides.

Assessment research may be viewed as an analytical process leading to the classification of persons. It begins with the assessment of behavior, i.e., the isolation of persons' response tendencies. As these are isolated it becomes possible to classify persons with respect to the degree to which they possess these tendencies. On this basis, therapeutic interventions and predictions of future behavior may be attempted. This process, moving from assessment and classification to intervention and prediction, is not as simple as it might seem to be. This is especially true in assessing behavior deviation, with all its many dimensions. When one considers the problems encountered by the botanist in classifying plant life, it does not seem surprising that psychiatrists and psychologists have experienced some setbacks in their efforts to classify persons and to predict their behavior. These setbacks are attributable to imperfections in the techniques of assessment and to the complexity of behavior determination. Nevertheless, the need to pursue the goal of reliable classification of behavior deviations persists. Shakow has stated this need well:

> I do not understand how a psychologist can adopt a professional orientation which does not acknowledge classification as fundamental in dealing with the multiplicity of phenomena involved in the diagnosis of mental disorder. Classification is essential whether it is being made for therapeutic or for research purposes, but it is especially important for the latter. The objections that are directed against a particular classification system usually arise because the criticized form of classification differs from the one used by the critic himself.

No matter how vehemently a psychiatrist or psychologist may oppose an existing system of classification, he almost always has a personal method of categorizing patients.

Science is not possible without classification. It is essential to the objective investigation which is the core of the scientific method. The major objections to the classification of mental disorders that have been raised are the problems that almost inevitably result from any attempt at categorization. Such problems are reification—dealing with the abstract conception of the disorder rather than the actual behavior or symptoms presented by the individual patient; partialization—taking only a part for the total picture; privacy—the use of personal rather than public categories; and simplification—the substitution of a simple, easily comprehensible explanation for the complex of phenomena which are difficult to grasp in their intricacy. With the growing sophistication and critical self-evaluation of workers in the field, however, such obstacles are gradually being overcome. (Shakow, D. The role of classification in the development of the science of psychopathology with particular reference to research, *Bulletin of the Menninger Clinic,* 1966, Vol. 30, pp. 150–151.)

Advances in knowledge often have their beginning in careful and innovative studies of individual cases. Seiden's work was based on a relatively small number of college students who had committed suicide. Isaacs, Thomas, and Goldiamond, in their article, report an in-depth analysis of two chronically psychotic persons. Their approach was essentially experimental as they sought to apply principles of learning in manipulating the verbal behavior of two patients. Specifically, their aim was to reinstate verbal behavior where, for many, many years, it had been absent. Seiden's study of a number of individual cases of suiciding college students illustrates the application of an assessment method to the understanding of deviant behavior. The Isaacs, Thomas, and Goldiamond case studies, while not part of a formal experiment, do represent the application of experimental methodology to individual clinical cases.

While many experimental methodologies contribute to the psychological study of behavioral deviations, those related to the learning process seem especially prominent. The fact that behavior changes as a function of the conditions of life has been well established. Does this fact apply to the phenomenon of deviancy? The evidence provided by Isaacs, Thomas, and Goldiamond illustrates that environmental events which follow responding do influence subsequent behavior. The behavioral analysis of these events represents one of the most flourishing avenues of psychological inquiry concerning deviant behavior.

Deviant behavior may also be perceived as a product of internal disorganization or disturbed thinking. For many years, dating back to Freud's first reference to "talking therapy" and even before that, clinical workers have sought, through verbal means, to understand mental disorganization and to bring about changes in the behavior of maladjusted individuals. Psychotherapy, as traditionally defined, involves an interpersonal relationship between a patient and therapist. The focus of attention in this relationship is the patient's behavior and his problems. Over the years, and especially in recent years, efforts have been made to describe objectively the anatomy of psychotherapy. This research has been directed at uncovering characteristics of patients, therapists, and situations which might contribute to relieving symptoms and achieving behavior change. There are, of course, many imposing questions to be confronted in such investigations: By what criteria does one assess improvement? How much change in behavior should be regarded as significant? If a patient says he feels better, but his overt behavior is unchanged, should he be regarded as changed in any important way?

The articles by Rogers and Betz deal with the nature of the relationship between a patient and his therapist. Rogers' article discusses the qualifications of a psychotherapist: Should they be defined in terms of his education, training, and experience, or in terms of his personal characteristics? Rogers' theoretical position and the research which he reports strongly suggest that the latter, rather than the former, are especially important in defining the effective psychotherapist.

If it is correct to conclude that personal, human qualities, rather than technical knowledge, are among the essentials of the effective psychotherapist, what then are the implications for the training of psychotherapists? For example, would relatively unsophisticated housewives with the requisite personal qualities be as effective as therapists as highly trained professionals? This question follows from the discussion presented by Rogers. It is also relevant to an increasingly pressing social problem, i.e., the great shortage of professional therapists in our society. Can relatively untrained persons with the necessary personal qualities help meet this manpower gap? Fortunately, recent evidence suggests a positive answer to this question.

Betz is also concerned with the characteristics of the therapist. Using assessment techniques, she was able to identify therapists' characteristics which were significantly correlated with their success or lack of success in treating groups of patients by means of psychotherapy. Her findings seem completely consistent with Rosenthal's discussion (Part II) of the experimenter's role as an influencing factor in the experimental situation. A therapist's characteristics as a person, his procedures, attitudes, and goals, can have a measurable impact on a patient's behavior.

Goldstein's article clearly demonstrates the interlocking of seemingly different areas of psychology: social psychology and psychotherapy. The one is interested in the dynamics of social situations and the other in the dynamics of individual lives. In his study dealing with the concept of level of aspiration, Goldstein shows that these interests are to some extent similar. He demonstrated that the personal aspirations and expectancies studied by social psychologists in many laboratory experiments are also operative in the clinical situation of the psychotherapist and his patient. In his article, he analyzes the dependent variable of patient improvement as a function of the goals and expectancies set by both patient and therapist. Thus, the degree of change that a therapist judges a patient to be capable of influences importantly the degree of change which actually takes place. The expectancies of the patient, of course, make their contributions as well.

The value of Goldstein's article is that it demonstrates that the variables at work in the laboratory and in the clinic are not basically different. One major challenge confronting the personality researcher is the need to uncover significant consistencies *across* situations. The writings of Rogers, Betz, and Goldstein also suggest the necessity of thinking of the interaction between patient and therapist as a fluid system, rather than viewing the therapist simply as a dispenser of expertise and emotional support.

While much research concerned with the modification of maladaptive behavior has been carried out in terms of the interpersonal system of psychotherapy, in recent years there has been a strong move toward the development of other forms of therapeutic intervention. The research reported by Bandura, Grusec, and Menlove in Part II showed that maladaptive behavior can be modified through observation of adaptive behavior. While the maladaptive behavior was not extreme—merely a fear of dogs in preschool children—it seems possible that observational and modeling opportunities might be effective behavior change agents in the case of more clinically significant behavior problems. We have seen how Isaacs, Thomas, and Goldiamond, taking a different tack, have shown that manipulation of environmental contingencies can help modify socially maladaptive behavior. These sorts of innovations seem especially desirable, since it well may be that one type of therapeutic intervention, such as insight-oriented psychotherapy, may be of great value only for certain kinds of patients. Reinforcement and observational learning therapies which are not oriented toward providing patients with insight might be best for other kinds of patients. Various special forms of therapy may be appropriate only for patients with particular characteristics.

The articles by Lang and Lazovik, and by Schwitzgebel further illustrate experimental efforts to develop new therapeutic techniques. Lang and Lazovik sought to determine the efficacy of desensitization training as a means of reducing phobic tendencies. Desensitization training involves the gradual introduction to an individual of stimuli which for him are fear-arousing. This introduction occurs at the same time that he is taught how to experience muscular relaxation. It is hoped that the phobic stimuli will become less fear-arousing when the individual receives them in a state of relaxation.

The results reported by Lang and Lazovik suggest that they were successful in eliminating snake phobias among their subjects. These writers interpreted the elimination of this type of phobic behavior as the unlearning of maladaptive responses. Therapists with different orientations have raised questions about the generality of this learning or unlearning approach to behavior change. Are Lang and Lazovik correct in assuming that it is not necessary to delve into the internal workings of the individual in order to achieve behavior change? Is behavior change in the form of elimination of rather discrete maladaptive responses, like snake phobias, the sole concern of the therapist? How does phobic behavior fit into the "psychic economy" of the individual? If a patient "surrenders" phobic behavior will he, then, acquire a new symptom? Lang and Lazovik have contributed valuable empirical evidence towards a new form of therapy. They have also succeeded in raising searching questions about the assumptions underlying insight-oriented psychotherapy. It is now required that these questions be answered.

Schwitzgebel's experiment bears important similarities to the case studies presented by Isaacs, Thomas, and Goldiamond. Both investigations stemmed from the assumption that manipulation of reinforcers in the environment can lead to changes in overt behavior. Whereas Isaacs, Thomas, and Goldiamond studied chronic psychotics, Schwitzgebel focused his attention on youthful offenders and studied the effect of their being reinforced for emitting particular classes of socially appropriate verbal behavior. He found that adolescent offenders reinforced for emitting pro-social responses increased their frequency of emission of the desired verbal responses. In addition, they showed tendencies in the direction of increases in a variety of other forms of pro-social behavior.

Although the population studied by Schwitzgebel was different from previous ones represented in this book, questions which we have already considered are nevertheless applicable. What role did the therapist-experimenter variable play? The therapist-experimenter variables were not specifically varied by Schwitzgebel and there is reason to believe that there are important individual differences among these people in their effectiveness as reinforcers of persons' behavior. What are the personality characteristics of successful reinforcing agents with juvenile delinquents? And what is the correlation between change in verbal behavior and change in other classes of behavior?

The need to understand the determinants of delinquent behavior among juveniles and adults becomes ever more pressing as the number of unlawful acts committed in our society increase. The term delinquency is basically a legal one. It seems clear that behavioral scientists have much to contribute by way of interpreting and modifying the attitudes and behavior of persons who commit unlawful acts. Hopefully, this contribution will have implications for society's response to criminal behavior.

The experimental efforts of Lang and Lazovik and Schwitzgebel were quite specifically directed towards replacing maladaptive with adaptive behavior. In this sense they have direct, practical, as well as theoretical, implications. The article by Hess, Seltzer, and Shlien is a potentially practical experimental contribution, although its aim was not to modify deviant behavior but to increase understanding of a form of behavior commonly judged to be socially objectionable. Their subjects were homosexuals. They employed a perceptual approach to this form of sexual deviation and used an involuntary response as a classification device. It is obvious from the results of their experiment that the heterosexual and homosexual subjects who were compared were markedly different in terms of their pupillary responses to sexually-related stimuli. Although this one experiment involved a relatively small number of subjects, and much more information is needed about the pupillary responses of homosexuals and others, one cannot help wondering whether or not Hess, Seltzer, and Shlien may have hit upon a useful diagnostic technique for discriminating homosexuals. Might a similar procedure be employed for other forms of behavior deviation?

The three articles with which Part IV concludes represent extensions of a psychological approach to deviancy. Students of personality drawn to the study of deviancy have, until recent years, been largely concerned with varying degrees of bizarre behavior in people. They have sought to understand and to treat symptoms and underlying problems of mentally disturbed individuals. We have already seen how efforts are being made to better understand the patient-therapist relationship in psychotherapy and other therapeutic techniques such as those involving desensitization, modeling, and reinforcement. The mental health field is now considering an exciting, broader possibility: the development of modification procedures of relevance to social groups. This social psychological approach to deviancy parallels in many ways the social (family) approach to development described by Handel (Part III).

The paper by Seymour Sarason comes directly to grips with the need for a more comprehensive conception of maladaptation. In it he calls for the development of methods with which social problems can be handled in a direct fashion. Specifically, if social forces either directly or indirectly are determinants of many forms of deviant behavior, then efforts should be directed towards changing these forces.

Sarason's paper also reflects the increased need to extend psychological principles beyond the consulting office and beyond groups usually defined as disturbed, neurotic, or psychotic. It demonstrates the challenges and problems inherent in developing a psychology of change and innovation within existing social frameworks. Beyond this, it also suggests clues that may be valuable in working within social frameworks. For example, Sarason has found that a psychologist wishing to contribute to the program of a social institution such as a school must, at the same time, (1) be deeply involved in the institution in which he is working, and (2) retain objectivity and a measure of detachment.

One well-known social ill and frequent precursor of deviant behavior is an economically and culturally deprived environment. What does such an environment do to a child as he grows up? What is the psychology of poverty? One solution to the problem is simply more money for the poor. Moles' analysis of the problems and attitudes of low income families leads one to conclude that this is an oversimplified solution to a complex problem. Research findings relating personality, socio-cultural status, and the incidence of mental illness also support this conclusion. The articles by McClelland (Part I) and Kolb (Part III) were specifically directed to the concept of achievement motivation within a social context; Moles' paper demonstrates that the lack of a need for achievement is a psychological correlate and consequence of economic and social deprivation. An integrated effort to attack the problem of poverty as a social ill will require insights of the type presented by Moles relating to apathy, low self-esteem, and low achievement motivation among poor people.

Project Re-ED, as described by Hobbs in his article, provides another perspective to a comprehensive analysis of social problems. The subjects studied by this project's personnel were emotionally disturbed children. As Hobbs points out, there are about one and one-half million emotionally disturbed children in the United States. What should be done with these children? How might they be helped? Even if the supply of professional one-to-one therapists were large enough to treat them on an individual basis, many question if this is the soundest approach to the problem.

Many emotionally disturbed children are removed from their usual day-to-day childhood activities and placed in restricted hospital settings. Project Re-ED took a different approach. It was designed to develop a residential school for disturbed children in which educational efforts would continue to be a major ingredient and in which the gaps created by either short or long periods of hospitalization would be greatly reduced.

One of the key persons in the Re-ED Program represents a new breed of individual—the teacher-counselor. The teacher-counselor and a large group of consultants from a variety of disciplines sought to re-educate children, both emotionally and academically. They did this by attending to the complex of factors which influence individual children. Among these factors are the family, the school, the community, the neighborhood in which he lives, and individual figures such as the family physician and clergyman. In a sense, as described by Hobbs, Re-ED is not just concerned with "curing" emotionally disturbed children; it is also concerned with increasing the effectiveness of the social system of which the child is an active participant.

Many of the articles of Part IV reflect a growing impatience with social ills and the problems of deviant behavior. Research on traditional psychotherapy continues, but there is now a strong effort to pin down variables (such as therapist characteristics) which influence behavior change. Other therapeutic approaches, stemming from varying theoretical orientations, are under development. Finally, the focus of attention is enlarging from the individual by himself to social systems ranging from the family to the neighborhood to society in general. Along with this shift there is a clearly detectable intention to attack directly and comprehensively personal and social aberrations at whatever level they may occur. This intention has been described succinctly by Ford and Urban:

> People seem to be less satisfied with traditional goals, even if they are possible to achieve. Simple understanding is not considered enough. The primary emphasis now seems to be on behavior as it is presently occurring, behavior defined to include feelings, thoughts, and images; physiological responses; interpersonal relationships; and motor behavior. That is, to include all facets of human behavior. Presumably the American emphasis on the values of efficiency, productivity, and accomplishment are feeding this. There continue to be voices proclaiming the legitimacy and the desirability of self-improvement, inner contentment, and acceptance of self, but they seem outnumbered by others who argue for rendering persons effective in their daily lives. (Ford, D. H. and Urban, H. B. Psychotherapy. In P. R. Farnsworth

[Ed.] *Annual Review of Psychology,* Vol. 18, Palo Alto, California: Annual Reviews, Inc., 1967, p. 367.)

The maturity of the psychological study of personal and social ills is rapidly increasing. The need to relate problems of personality to problems of society is now evident. The need to question common notions about mental illness, its determinants, and its eradication is recognized on all sides. Finally, the need for multi-faceted approaches to personal and social problems is becoming increasingly clear. The laboratory, the consulting office, and various societal units each have an important role to play in developing an objective psychology of deviancy.

CAMPUS TRAGEDY: A STUDY OF STUDENT SUICIDE *

RICHARD H. SEIDEN [1]

The act of self-destruction rudely challenges our supposed love for life and fear of death. It is always a puzzlement, but in no case is suicide more shocking or bewildering than it is in the college student. For here are a relatively privileged group of persons enjoying valued advantages of youth, intelligence, and educational opportunity. Why should persons, seemingly so rewarded, seek to kill themselves, and, indeed, to commit suicide at a rate significantly in excess of their noncollege peers (Bruyn and Seiden, 1965, p. 76)?

This perplexing question—"Why do students suicide?"—has motivated a great deal of concern among college health authorities leading to several studies and evaluations of the problem in American universities (Braaten and Darling, 1962; Jensen, 1955; Parrish, 1957; Raphael, Power, and Berridge, 1937; Temby, 1961). Unfortunately, these studies have all had an exclusively descriptive approach. They have drawn conclusions about

* Reprinted with permission from the American Psychological Association. In *Journal of Abnormal Psychology,* 1966, Vol. 71, pp. 389–399.
[1] Revision of a paper presented to Psi Chi colloquium, Western Psychological Association, Honolulu, June 1965. This research was supported by Grant #5 T1 MH-8104 from the National Institute of Mental Health.

certain characteristics of suicidal students but, seemingly, without appreciation for the degree to which these same characteristics are shared by the entire student body population. What has been conspicuously omitted is a baseline—a standard of comparison against which the diagnostic value of their findings might be judged. One is reminded of the gentleman who, when asked, "How is your wife?" astutely responded, "Compared to what?" This very question of relative comparison must also be asked in the study of student suicides.

The present study attempted to remedy this situation by applying a reasonable standard of comparison, namely, the great majority of fellow college students who do not commit suicide. By investigating what characteristics significantly differentiate suicidal students from their classmates plus examining those situational-temporal conditions associated with campus suicides, it was hoped to achieve a clearer diagnostic picture. Once the high-risk, suicide-prone student can be identified, a large and necessary step will have been taken toward the ultimate objective of effective prophylaxis.

METHOD

The approach used in the present study was one of analytic epidemiology, that is, comparing for particular characteristics the subset of student suicides with the total student body population from which they were drawn. This particular procedure meets the methodological criteria for selection of comparison groups, as stated by MacMahon, Pugh, and Ipsen (1960):

A comparison group is a group of unaffected individuals believed to reflect the characteristics of the population from which the affected group was drawn. Ideally the comparison group should not differ from the affected group in any respect (other than not being affected) which might be likely to influence the frequency of the variable or variables suspected of being causally connected. This means either that both the patient and comparison groups must be representative of the same population or that if selective factors enter into the choice of the patterns, the same factors ought to enter into the selection of the comparison group [p. 235].

The method of the present study involved a comparison of the sample of 23 University of California at Berkeley (UCB) students who committed suicide during the 10-year period 1952 through 1961, with the entire UCB student body population during this same decade. The objective of this comparison was to determine what special characteristics differentiated the suicide-prone student from his classmates. Within this framework the following working definitions were employed: (a) *Student*—the definition of a student was established by registration on the Berkeley campus of the University of California, in either graduate or undergraduate status, during the regular college semester periods. Summer sessions were not included because of the unreliability of data for these periods and changes in the usual composition of the student body population during summer sessions. (b) *Suicide*—refers to a completed suicide, established by a death certificate stating suicide as the legal cause of death. In one instance, involving a jump from the Golden Gate bridge, this was not possible. Since the body was never recovered, a certificate was not issued; however, the case was well-documented in police and newspaper files. By keeping to this legalistic definition of suicide, one runs the very likely probability that the true number of suicides will be underenumerated. For example, cases of equivocal student deaths, such as by falls or drowning, were regarded as accidental, in keeping with the coroner's findings, even though these deaths, listed as accidents, could have been suicides which were covered up to avoid the social stigma related to suicide. Indeed, it has been estimated that only about 70% of successful suicides are ever recorded as such (Dublin, 1963, p. 3). The advantage in using this definition is that one can be quite certain that deaths recorded as suicide are bona-fide cases since the error is, almost always, in the direction of underreporting. (c) *Exposure to risk*—the period of exposure to risk comprised the 10-year span 1952–1961 inclusive, a total of 10 academic or 7½ calendar years. This important variable, the length of exposure, was to some degree controlled since both the suicidal and non-suicidal students were exposed to the same period of risk. (d) *Population at risk*—population at risk was the total student body of UCB during the 10-year period cited. Case finding procedures were extremely painstaking, requiring several months of effort to detect and verify 23 bona-fide study cases. Numerous sources of information were used, but for the suicidal students the primary source was the standard death certificate, obtained from the state health department. Secondary sources consisted of newspaper clippings, police files, and University records. The source of materials for the baseline data for the total student body population was the UCB Office of the Registrar. Their publication, *A Ten-Year Survey of Certain Demographic Characteristics of the Student Population* (Suslow, 1963), was indispensable.

In terms of research design, the procedures consisted of collecting and analyzing data regarding selected attributes of the total student population. These data were then used as a baseline to which the sample of suicidal UCB students could be compared. Since suicide may also involve a strong volitional component, further analyses were made with respect to certain situational-temporal features of the academic environment.

RESULTS AND DISCUSSION

Results are presented in tabular and graphic form and discussed in the text by order of their appearance. The various comparisons were statistically analyzed by testing the significance of the difference between two proportions (Hill, 1961, pp. 122–132), specifically, the significance of proportional differences between the suicidal sample and expected population values as based upon knowledge of the student universe. All probability statements are two-tailed probabilities.

Incidence and Prevalence

Previous research on the UCB population (Bruyn and Seiden, 1965) investigated the general question of student suicide risk. By comparing the student suicide experience with the suicide incidence among a comparable group of non-college-age cohorts, it was established that the incidence of suicide among students was significantly greater than for non-student-age peers ($p =$ .004). Conversely, the general mortality experience from all causes was significantly more favorable for students when compared to their non-academic-age peers ($p < .001$). In terms of total mortality, suicides accounted for 23 of the 68 student deaths which occurred during the 10-year study period. Proportionally, it ranked as the second leading cause of death (34%), exceeded only by accidents (37%).

percentage of suicides in the older age group is approximately twice their proportional percentage in the population (see Table 1). This distinction is graphically portrayed in Figure 1 which presents the relative frequency of suicidal and non-suicidal students by 5-year age groups. It is notable that only about 6% of all students fall in the 30 to 34-year age category while more than 26% of the suicidal students are found in this interval. In fact, the median age for the student body popula-

TABLE 1

SELECTED DEMOGRAPHIC CHARACTERISTICS OF SUICIDAL AND NONSUICIDAL STUDENTS, UCB, 1952–61

Demographic characteristics	Suicidal students		Total student body population	p
	Frequency distribution ($n = 23$)	% distribution	% distribution	
Age				
Under 25	9	39	70	.001
25 and above	14	61	30˙	
Class standing				
Undergraduate	12	52	72	.033
Graduate	11	48	28	
Sex				
Male	17	74	67	ns
Female	6	26	33	
Marital status[a]				
Married	3	14	23	ns
Never married	19	86	77	
Race				
White	20	87	89	ns
Nonwhite	3	13	11	
Religion				
Protestant	15	65	60	ns
Jewish	5	22	18	
Catholic	3	13	22	
Nationality				
U.S.A.	19	83	96	.002
Foreign	4	17	04	
Major subject[b]				
Mechanical-mathematic	10	50	64	ns
Aesthetic-social	10	50	36	
Grade-point average[c]				
Above average	14	67	50	ns
Below average	7	33	50	
Mental health service				
Psychiatric patient	8	34	10	<.001
Nonpatient	15	66	90	

[a] Excludes one divorced student.
[b] Excludes three students who had not declared majors.
[c] Excludes two students who did not complete a semester.

Age

For the United States as a whole, there is a well-documented positive correlation between age and suicide (Dublin, 1963, p. 22). This same relationship holds for the student population. If the student body is divided on the basis of those who are above and below age 25, one finds that the

tion is 22 years, 6 months, while the median age for the suicidal students, 26 years, 5 months, is greater by almost 4 years.

Class Standing

Directly correlated with, and, indeed, almost identical to, chronological age, is the class standing of individual students. Median class standing for the entire student population was the junior year, for the suicidal subset it was the senior year. When the groups are divided on the basis of graduate or undergraduate standing, one finds that graduate students committed suicide in numbers significantly greater than could be expected from their proportions in the student body at large (see Table 1).

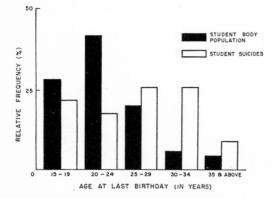

FIG. 1. Age distributions of student suicides and total student body population, UCB, 1952–61.

Sex

Of the 23 student suicides, 17 were male, 6 female, a sex ratio approximating 3:1 (see Table 1). This finding accords with those sex ratios reported in previous studies of completed suicide (Dublin, 1963, p. 23). However, an adjustment is necessary to correctly relate this information to the college population. Whereas the sexes are about equally distributed in the general United States population, they are not equally distributed on campus. For the years under study, males outnumbered females in the student body population by approximately 2:1. Accordingly, the obtained sex ratio of 3:1 must be halved to yield an adjusted student ratio of about 1.5 male suicides for each female suicide. This student sex ratio is considerably narrower than the sex ratio for the country at large. It seems to indicate a heightened risk of suicide among female students as compared to the general female population. However, this indication must remain somewhat speculative since the female suicides were considerably older (median age 30 years, 1 month) than were male suicides (median age 26 years, 1 month). As a consequence one cannot be entirely sure that the constricted ratio is not an effect of confounding

between age and sex. Should further research confirm that there is, in fact, a greater risk of suicide among female students as opposed to female nonstudents, it would follow the predictions of Gibbs and Martin (1964). They proposed a rise in female suicides due to increasing social pressures. According to their status-integration theory, as more women enter the labor force they encounter cross-pressures from conflicting social roles. They postulate that these stresses will lead to increasing numbers of female suicides.

Marital Status

Of the 23 student suicides, it was possible to classify 22 persons into the categories of "married" or "never married," which corresponded to the available student population data. One divorced student was thereby excluded from the analysis. There was no remarkable disparity between the suicidal and nonsuicidal students on the basis of marital status (see Table 1). For the entire United States population, suicide is less common among married persons (Dublin, 1963, p. 26), but this was not the case for campus suicides. Only three of the student suicides were married, and only one of those married had children. The remaining two cases, both females, committed suicide shortly after their marriages.

Race

Of the 23 known suicides, only three were nonwhite and all three of these nonwhite students were Chinese. There were no suicides among Negro, East Indian, or American Indian students who, at any event, comprised only about 3% of the student body population. The distribution of suicides by race corresponded closely to the racial proportions found in the student population (see Table 1). It should be mentioned, however, that there is good reason to question the adequacy of these racial data. Since University records do not ask for nor indicate students' race, these breakdowns, furnished by the University Dean of Students Office, were presumably obtained from simple headcounts with all the imprecision that this method implies.

Religion

Religion was not a significant factor in differentiating suicidal students from the general campus population (see Table 1). As was the case with racial statistics, the religious data, likewise, must be regarded with great skepticism. The University does not conduct a religious census of its students. Consequently, the religious population figures were estimated from student residence information cards on which "religious affiliation" is an optional item. Very frequently it is left unanswered.

Nationality

Only 4 of the 23 student suicides were foreign students. Nonetheless, their representation in the student body was so negligible (only 4%) that they appear among the suicides in approximately four times the magnitude one would expect from their proportions in the student population (see Table 1). As a group, these four "international student" suicides were characterized by some striking similarities. As youngsters, all of the four had known and suffered from the ravages of war, and three of them were forced to flee from their childhood homes. Two of the students, natives of mainland China, had been dispossessed by the Communist revolution; another student, born in Austria, lost his family in the horrors of the Nazi concentration camps and subsequently migrated to Israel. The fourth student, a native Israeli, had grown up amidst the Arab-Jewish war over the Palestine partition.

Moreover, they shared a similar pattern of conflicts, centering to a large degree around strong feelings of shame. These feelings were reflected in a deep dread that they would not meet expectations that others had set for them. There was some reality to these fears, in that other persons had sent them abroad, were paying their expenses, and probably did expect from them some measure of academic achievement. Still, their excessive concern about "what others would think" was unduly frenetic. All four of them were known to the Student Mental Health Service where they had been seen for psychiatric treatment. These find-

TABLE 3
GRADE-POINT AVERAGES FOR GRADUATE AND
UNDERGRADUATE STUDENT SUICIDES

GPA	Suicidal students		Student population %	p
	n	%		
Class standing				
Undergraduate				
Above mean	10	91	50	
Below mean	1	09	50	.006
Graduate				
Above mean	4	40	50	
Below mean	6	60	50	ns

Note.—Excludes two students; one graduate, one undergraduate, who suicided during their first semester.

ings, however, must be interpreted with some caution since the median age of foreign students (26 years, 1 month), exceeded the median age of American students (24 years), raising the possibility that the differences were due in some degree to age rather than nationality.

Major Subject

For this comparison, the suicidal subjects were divided into two categories, corresponding somewhat to William James' distinction between the "tough" and "tender minded." Of the 20 suicidal students who had declared majors, the breakdown was 10 students in the "tough-minded" or mechanical-mathematics group (Engineering, Professional, Physical Sciences, Biological Sciences, Agricultural majors) and 10 students in the "tender-minded" or esthetic-social group (Arts, Social Sciences, Language and Literature majors). Relative to their population proportions, there was a greater incidence of suicides in the tender-minded group, but not a large enough imbalance to achieve statistical significance. Further analysis, by individual subject groups, revealed that suicides were significantly more frequent among students majoring in languages and literature (five cases), espe-

TABLE 2
SUICIDES AMONG LANGUAGE AND LITERATURE
MAJORS VS. ALL OTHER SUBJECT MAJORS

Major subject group	Suicidal students		Total student body population %	p
	n	%		
Language and literature	5	25	9	
All other majors	15	75	91	.012

Note.—Excludes three students who had not declared major subjects.

TABLE 4
OBSERVED AND EXPECTED GPA OF STUDENT
SUICIDES BY CLASS STANDING

Class standing	GPA	
	Observed	Expected
Undergraduate	3.18	2.50
Graduate	2.90	3.35

cially English majors, who comprised three of the five cases (see Table 2).

Grade-Point Average

Grade-point analysis required some basic adjustments since graduate and undergraduate grading systems are not directly comparable. In practice, an undergraduate "C" is approximately equivalent to a graduate "B." For the student population, the grade-point average (GPA) for undergraduates was 2.50, while for graduates it was 3.35 (calculated to the scale: A $= 4$, B $= 3$, C $= 2$, D $= 1$, F $= 0$). Given this discrepancy, it is obviously necessary to separately compare undergraduate and graduate students with reference to their respective grade-point distributions. When the suicidal students (excluding two who did not complete a full semester at UCB) are ranked by means of achievement above or below their population GPA, we find that two-thirds of them were above average while, by definition, only half of the general student body achieved this mark. Although suggestive of a tendency toward higher grades among suicidal students, the difference, in fact, did not achieve statistical significance. However, further analysis, distributing GPA by class standing, revealed a marked discrepancy between graduate and undergraduate students. This breakdown is detailed in Table 3 and reveals that of the 11 undergraduate students who committed suicide (after one complete semester at the University), 10 of them had surpassed the undergraduate GPA. For graduate student suicides, only 4 of the 10 who had completed a semester exceeded the graduate GPA. Despite the differential grading system that rewards the graduate student with more grade points for a similar level of work, the suicidal undergraduate students received a higher overall GPA than the graduate student suicides (see Table 4).

This finding seems to indicate that undergraduate and graduate suicides differ markedly from one another in terms of academic achievement. The undergraduate suicides performed on a level well above their fellow classmates and performed considerably better than did graduate suicides. Looking at the personal histories of these undergraduate students one discovers an interesting paradox. To an external observer, say someone viewing their transcripts, these students achieved splendidly in their academic pursuits. They had all been A or B students in high school since a B or better average is required for undergraduate admission, a policy which is estimated to limit entrance to the top 10–12% of graduating high school seniors. Reports from family and friends, however, reveal that self-satisfaction was not the case with these students. Rather, they seemed filled with doubts of their adequacy, dissatisfied with their grades, and despondent over their general academic aptitude. This exacerbated fear of failure was tempered somewhat by the fact that in every case of undergraduate suicide the final semester's GPA was lower ($\bar{x} = 2.53$) than the previous cumulative GPA ($\bar{x} = 3.34$). Another consideration is whether these students aspired to graduate school which requires a higher than average GPA (2.50–3.0 at UCB). Unfortunately, these exact data are not available; however, a check of those students in major subjects which definitely indicated future graduate work, for example, premedicine, revealed academic achievement in excess of grade requirements. Nevertheless, on balance, they were still achieving loftily above the average of their classmates. How can one explain their deep self-dissatisfaction despite contrary and objective indications of their competence? Two possible explanations suggest themselves: (a) The internal standards these students applied to themselves were so Olympian, the demands they imposed upon themselves so exacting, that they were destined to suffer frustration and disappointment no matter how well they fared; and/or (b) Whereas they had previously been crackerjack students in high school or junior college, excelling without much difficulty, the precipitous drop in grade points over the final semester threatened their feelings of self-esteem. Thus, faced by a sudden loss of status, they may have suicided as a response to this egoistic conflict. In any case, the discrepancy between perceived self-concept and objective reality indicates that a purely objective approach often obscures more than it reveals. What one needs to try and understand is the phenomenological response of the individual student. What is necessary to know is what inner standards, what idealized fantasy he uses to judge himself and his own personal worth. For the graduate student suicides as a group, there was no discrepancy between their academic achievements and what might be expected on the basis of the general population of graduate students. While they produced slightly below their population mean, the variation in this instance was primarily due to two students who were in considerable scholastic straits. Contrary to the undergraduates, graduate suicides showed no pattern of decline in their terminal semester GPA. Confirmation of the scholastic disparity between graduate and undergraduate suicides is further revealed by the irregular distribution of academic awards. Inspection of Table 5 indicates that undergraduate students garnered scholarship honors at a rate well beyond the general undergraduate population, while the graduate student suicides did not differ significantly from their classmates in earning academic awards. Even though graduate student awards were far more plentiful, the great majority of awards (10 of 11) were held by undergraduate student suicides.

Mental Health

Of the 23 student suicides, 8 had been referred to the student mental health service for psychiatric treatment (of the 8 students, apparently only 2 were diagnosed as psychotic reactions). These

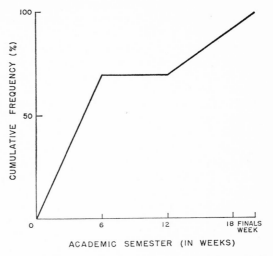

Fig. 2. Time distribution of student suicides, UCB, 1952–61.

TABLE 5

SCHOLASTIC AWARDS BY CLASS STANDING

Class standing	Suicidal students		Student population	
	n	%	%	*p*
Undergraduate				
Scholarship	7	58	05	<.001
Nonscholarship	5	42	95	
Graduate				
Scholarship	1	10	23	
Nonscholarship	10	90	77	*ns*

8 cases comprised better than one-third of the student suicides, significantly exceeding the approximately 10% of the total student body population seen at the mental health facilities (see Table 1). Besides the 8 students known to the student psychiatric service, an additional 3 students were in private psychiatric treatment, making a total of almost 50% of the suicidal group who gave this particular indication of prior mental disturbance.

Temporal-Situational Relationships

Among all causes of death, suicide allows for the greatest degree of volition. The suicidal person

is in a position to choose the date, place, and method of his death, and it has long been speculated that there may be a special psychological significance to these choices. Through tracing the time, place, and method of student suicides, the following particular patterns were observed:

Time. When student suicides were charted by calendar months they formed a bimodal curve with peaks occurring during February and October. A more meaningful comparison obtained when the academic semester was used as the time interval. This distribution, as illustrated in Figure 2, challenges a frequently held belief about campus suicides. Academic folklore often explains student suicides as a response to the anxieties and stresses

TABLE 6

METHODS OF SUICIDE USED BY UCB AND YALE STUDENTS

Method	UCB (1952–1961)		Yale (1920–1955)[a]	
	n	%	*n*	%
Firearms	8	35	10	40
Poisonings	6	26	3	12
Asphyxiation	4	17	5	20
Hanging	2	09	6	24
Jumping from high place	2	09	1	04
Cutting instruments	1	04	—	—
Total	23	100	25	100

[a] Source: Parrish, 1957, p. 589.

of final examinations. Yet, surprisingly, the data showed that almost the reverse relationship held. Only 1 of the 23 student suicides was committed during finals. (Even that single instance may be dubiously related to final exams since this student was doing well in school and had expressed satisfaction with his "finals" performance.) Most of the suicides occurred at the beginning of the semester. When the semester is divided into three equivalent parts, the vast majority of cases, 16 out of 23, are found to occur during the first 6-week segment. (Actually, the period is only 5 weeks from when instruction begins; the first week is confined to registration procedures.) No cases were found during the second 6-week period which includes the mid-term examinations. Over the remaining third of the semester there were seven cases, just one of which occurred during finals week itself (always the last week of the semester). This irregular time distribution of student suicides departed significantly from uniform expectations ($x^2_2 = 16.8$, $p < .001$). Clearly, the old saw about suicides and finals was not supported. Instead, the danger period for student suicide was found to be the start, not the finish, of the school semester. Incidentally, the day of the week departed significantly from the null hypothesis of uniformity ($x^2_1 = 4.18$, $p < .05$) with almost one-half the cases occurring on Monday or Friday, terminals of the school week. Unfortunately, the data were none too precise since some cases were based on coroner's estimates as to the date of death.

The unexpectedly low correspondence between final examinations and the commission of student suicide bears some resemblance to a parallel phenomenon involving student mental health during the recent free speech activities on the UCB campus. In the course of these supposedly stressful times, there was a striking drop in admissions to the student mental health service (20% below average) and no recorded student suicides during the 1965 academic year. (Such behavior corresponds to the drop in suicides, psychosomatic illness, and neurotic conditions observed during both World Wars.) Why, in the midst of all the controversy, turmoil, and tempest was student mental health apparently enhanced? One possibility is that some students who had previously been grappling with internal problems now had the opportunity to act out, to ventilate their inner conflicts, and to displace their intrapunitive anger and hostility

by redirecting it toward an external symbol, namely, the University. Perhaps it was the galvanized and heightened sense of community that facilitated mental well-being. Certainly many students felt involved in a common cause; probably, for some it imparted meaning to their lives where previously they had felt alienated and purposeless. If so, it was also a perfect antidote to the kinds of feelings that often drive people to self-destruction.

Place. Most of the students, 12 of 23, committed suicide at their residences. The next most frequent location was the University itself, upon whose grounds 4 students ended their lives. Three students were found dead in parked autos on isolated suburban roads. Another 3 suicided in out-of-town hotel rooms, and 1 student leaped from the San Francisco Golden Gate bridge. It is difficult to determine any significance to the site of these suicides, except for the 4 cases who killed themselves on the university grounds. Of these, the most symbolic suicide was the 1 student who jumped from the Campanile, an architectural landmark of the Berkeley campus.

Method. The most frequent agent of choice was firearms, followed by ingestions and asphyxiations. A comparison with the methods used by Yale student suicides (see Table 6) revealed considerable similarity in the methods employed by the two groups of students. The relatively larger number of poisonings among UCB students is most likely due to the more recent availability of tranquilizers and barbiturates.

For only two of the Berkeley cases was there the least equivocation about assigning suicide as the cause of death. These two cases, both involving ingestions of poisonous substances, were qualified as "probably suicide" but routinely coded as "deaths due to suicide." In at least 10 instances, suicide notes were left by the decedents. These notes ranged from simple instructions concerning the disposal of personal belongings to lengthy, literary dissertations, one of which finished by tersely quoting Camus: "Life as a human being is absurd."

Psychological Factors

A statistical approach, per se, can go just so far in describing the suicide-prone student. The additional use of case history materials provides a fuller, more clinically oriented dimension to the portrayal. As such, the following inferences were derived from anecdotal reports of friends and acquaintances of the students, along with those members of the University community whose lives they touched. From a preventive standpoint, the most pertinent questions which might be asked are, "What prodromal signs, what clues to suicide could be discerned from the personal lives of these students? Specifically, were there any indications or harbingers of their ultimate destinies?" Lastly, "Was there a characteristic conflict which precipitated their self-destructive actions?" The question of prodromal indications can be flatly answered "yes." There were numerous warnings in almost every case. At least five of the students had made past suicide attempts. Warnings of a more subtle nature could be discovered in the histories of the remaining students. For example, the pupil who went out of his way to modify an item on the medical history form. Where it had requested, "Whom shall we notify in case of emergency?" he crossed out the word "emergency" and substituted "death." Or the student who confided that he sometimes takes 10 or so nembutals because "I am an adventurer." Other students evidenced a longstanding infatuation with death, often initiating "bull sessions" about the futility of life, or making wry jokes about killing themselves. Prior to their suicides a disproportionately large number of these students were involved in psychiatric treatment. As a group, they presented similar symptomatic patterns featuring symptoms of insomnia, anorexia, and extreme moodiness, especially moods of despondency; in all, it was a psychological picture compatible with the general diagnosis of agitated depression.

Although their prodromal response to stress was very similar, the particular crises that precipitated their suicides were not. Bearing in mind that each individual case was unique, for purposes of description, the main prodromal conflicts could be classified into the following three categories:

1. *Concern over studies*—In many cases acquaintances of the students made such judgments as "he pushed himself too hard," "worried over grades," "felt his grades were not as good as he thought they should be," or similar scholastic anxieties which, they felt, triggered the suicidal crisis. It is difficult to evaluate these inferences since "worry over grades" is often seen by informants as a most likely explanation. At any event, if true, their exaggerated concern over studies contrasted vividly with generally excellent academic grades.

2. *Unusual physical complaints*—A number of the students complained of inability to eat or sleep, one student warranting a diagnosis of "avitaminosis." Others worried about possible deterioration such as the student who feared that his "failing sight" might ruin a prospective medical career. A few pupils, however, presented physical complaints of a bizarre semidelusional quality, for instance, the young man whose stomach literally persecuted him. From childhood on he had suffered from anorexia and "stomach ache." Although an exploratory laparotomy did not disclose anything, by the time he entered the University he was at least 50 pounds underweight, still wracked by chronic stomach pains. He then moved from his fraternity house, in the hope of gaining weight by selecting his own food. This plan proved to no avail, nor did extensive medical testing at the student health service, all of which proved negative. He finally ended his torment, perhaps symbolically, by ingesting cyanide.

3. *Difficulties with interpersonal relationships*—Combined under this heading were two different types of conflicts, both reflecting problems in personal relationships. First were the students involved in stormy love affairs. Here the critical stresses were feelings of rejection which had been engendered by broken romances. In the one recorded instance of double suicide, the precipitating event was parental opposition to the youngsters' marriage. Much more typical, however, was the essentially asocial, withdrawn student. These particular students were uniformly described as terribly shy, virtually friendless individuals, alienated from all but the most minimal social interactions. Frequently they had compensated for their personal solitude by increased study and almost total absorption in schoolwork. The most calamitous example of such human isolation was the student, dead for 18 days before he was found in his lonely room. It is a tragic commentary to his existence, and perhaps a cause for his suicide, that there were no friends, no people involved enough in his life to know, or to care, that he had been missing for well over 2 weeks.

Interpretation

Reviewing the results of the present study, one can reasonably conclude that significant associations between student suicide and numerous variables, both personal and environmental, have been demonstrated. Nonetheless, one cannot, with certitude, infer that these relationships are causal ones. This type of inference would require procedures more exacting than the limited epidemiological methods herein employed. For instance, the total student body population, used as a matched control or comparison group, included a number of students who had unsuccessfully attempted suicide. Quite possibly their inclusion diluted the significance of the obtained differences between suicidal and presumably nonsuicidal students. This is a relatively minor concern, compared to other more cautionary limitations. A primary concern is to what degree the observed relationships were spuriously increased by a common variable. For example, the correlation between student suicide and declining terminal GPA may very well be due to a third factor—emotional disturbance—which both depressed scholastic grades and led to self-destruction. As a corollary, it should be recognized that not all of the selected variables were independent of one another. It is known for one that age and class standing are highly dependent, and it was observed, also, that the variable of age probably confounded to some degree the comparisons by sex and by nationality. Another area of uncertainty concerns the time-order sequence of student suicide. One is unable to state, with certainty, which comes first, the disturbed student or the stresses of student life. Are the suicides due to selection into colleges of mentally unstable individuals or are they due to competitive pressures of the academic environment? The fullest answer to these questions will only come from further research. Toward this goal some salient lines of inquiry could include: the investigation of student suicide attempters and student accident cases, postcollegiate follow-up studies, and the use of "psychological autopsy" procedures, as described by Shneidman and Farberow (1961).

Within the expressed limits of the study design, what predictions about the future suicide problem are warranted? Extrapolating from results of the present study, it appears that a future increase of student suicides may be expected. This increase should occur as a function of two variables, that is, age and academic competition, both of which are directly correlated to student suicides, and both of which are slated to increase in future student body populations. Average student age is already rising as a result of ever increasing proportions of graduate students in the American university system.

For example, architects of the UCB educational master plan are considering an ultimate 50:50 graduate-undergraduate ratio. The second variable, academic competition, will likely increase as a result of mounting public demands for quasi-universal college education. As a case in point, the enrollment demands at UCB have already exceeded the available academic supply. Consequently, it has been necessary to restrict enrollment to the upper-most fraction of high school graduating classes. If accepted, the pressure on the student to achieve and maintain very high GPAs gives no indication of abatement. In fact, the situation ominously resembles a suicidal problem which prevails among the youth of Japan. In the Japanese case there are tremendous pressures to attend college, and those students who fail to gain entrance frequently turn to suicide as a solution to their dilemmas. Such conflicts, in addition to a more accepting cultural attitude, have probably helped to make Japan "a country of youthful suicides where suicide has become the number one cause of death in individuals under 30 [DeVos, 1964, p. 6]."

SUMMARY

The purpose of this study was to identify distinctive attributes of the suicidal student, and to determine those environmental conditions which heighten his susceptibility to suicide.

Using an epidemiological approach, demographic comparisons were made between the sample of 23 UCB students who committed suicide during the years 1952–1961 inclusive, and the total student body population for those years. As an additional procedure, the temporal-situational characteristics of student suicides were described and analyzed.

The main findings of the research were:

1. Suicidal students could be significantly differential from their classmates on the variables of age, class standing, major subject, nationality, emotional condition, and academic achievement. Compared to the student population at large, the suicidal group was older, contained greater proportions of graduates, language majors, and foreign students, and gave more indications of emotional disturbance. In addition, the undergraduate suicides fared much better than their fellow students in matters of academic achievement.

2. Contrary to the popular belief that suicides

frequently occur during final examinations week, time relationships indicated that the peak danger period for student suicides was the beginning (first 6 weeks), not the midterm, nor end of the semester.

3. Most of the students gave recurrent warnings of their suicidal intent. Many of them presented a similar prodromal pattern marked by anorexia, insomnia, and periods of despondency.

4. Major precipitating factors were: Worry over schoolwork, chronic concerns about physical health (sometimes of a decidedly bizarre nature), and difficulties with interpersonal relationships. This last category contained some students who had reacted to romantic rejections but, for the most part, comprised the emotionally withdrawn and socially isolated student.

5. A future increase of student suicides was predicted on the basis of changes taking place in the age structure of college populations and in the competitive pressures of student life.

REFERENCES

Braaten, J., and Darling, C. Suicidal tendencies among college students. *Psychiatric Quarterly,* 1962, 36: 665–692.

Bruyn, H. B., and Seiden, R. H. Student suicide: Fact or fancy? *Journal of the American College Health Association,* 1965, 14: 69–77.

DeVos, G. Role narcissism and the etiology of Japanese suicide. Berkeley, Calif.: Institute of International Studies, University of California, 1964. (Mimeo)

Dublin, L. I. *Suicide: A sociological and statistical study.* New York: Ronald, 1963.

Gibbs, J. P., and Martin, W. T. *Status integration and suicide.* Eugene: Oregon University Press, 1964.

Hill, A. B. *Principles of medical statistics.* New York: Oxford University Press, 1961.

Jensen, V. W. Evaluating the suicidal impulse in the university setting. *Journal Lancet,* 1955, 75: 441–444.

MacMahon, B., Pugh, T. F., and Ipsen, J. *Epidemiological methods.* Boston: Little, Brown, 1960.

Parrish, H. M. Epidemiology of suicide among college students. *Yale Journal of Biology and Medicine,* 1957, 29: 585–595.

Raphael, T., Power, S. H., and Berridge, W. L. The question of suicide as a problem in college

mental hygiene. *American Journal of Orthopyschiatry,* 1937, 7: 1–14.

Shneidman, E. S., and Farberow, N. L. Sample investigations of equivocal deaths. In N. L. Farberow and E. S. Shneidman (Eds.), *The cry for help.* New York: McGraw-Hill, 1961. Pp. 118–128.

Suslow, S. *A ten-year survey of certain demographic characteristics of the student population.* Berkeley: Office of the Registrar, University of California, 1963. (Mimeo)

Temby, W. D. Suicide. In G. B. Blaine and C. G. McArthur (Eds.), *Emotional problems of the student.* New York: Appleton-Century-Crofts, 1961. Pp. 133–152.

APPLICATION OF OPERANT CONDITIONING TO REINSTATE VERBAL BEHAVIOR IN PSYCHOTICS *

WAYNE ISAACS, JAMES THOMAS, AND ISRAEL GOLDIAMOND [1]

In operant conditioning, behavior is controlled by explicitly arranging the consequences of the response, the explicit consequence being termed reinforcement. For example, a lever-press by a rat activates a mechanism which releases food. If the rat has been deprived of food, lever-pressing responses will increase in frequency. If this relation-

* Reprinted with permission from the American Speech and Hearing Association. In *Journal of Speech and Hearing Disorders,* 1960, Vol. 25, pp. 8–12.

[1] This report stems from projects connected with a weekly seminar on operant conditioning conducted at the hospital by the third author. Responsibility for the authorship and the *post hoc* analysis is the third author's; the first two authors are responsible for application of experimentally based procedures to shape the verbal behaviors of the patients.

The authors wish to express their appreciation to Dr. Leonard Horecker, Clinical Director of Anna State Hospital, and to Dr. Robert C. Steck, Hospital Superintendent, for their encouragement and facilitation of the project. This investigation was supported in part by a grant from the Psychiatric Training and Research Fund of the Illinois Department of Public Welfare.

ship between food and response holds only when a light is on, the organism may discriminate between light on and light off, that is, there will be no lever-pressing responses when the light is turned off, but turning it on will occasion such responses. From this simple case, extensions can be made to more complicated cases which may involve control of schedules of reinforcement. These procedures have recently been extended to the study of psychopharmacology (5), controlled production of stomach ulcers (4), obtaining psychophysical curves from pigeons (3), conditioning cooperative behavior in children (2), programming machines which teach academic subjects (11), analyzing the effects of noise on human behavior (1), and decreasing stuttering (7), to mention a few examples.

The following account is a preliminary report of the use of operant conditioning to reinstate verbal behavior in two hospitalized mute psychotics. Patient A, classified as a catatonic schizophrenic, 40, became completely mute almost immediately upon commitment 19 years ago. He was recorded as withdrawn and exhibiting little psychomotor activity. Patient B, classified as schizophrenic, mixed type, with catatonic features predominating, was 43, and was committed after a psychotic break in 1942, when he was combative. He completely stopped verbalizing 14 years ago. Each S was handled by a different E (experimenter). The E's were ignorant of each other's activities until pressed to report their cases. This study covers the period prior to such report.

CASE HISTORIES

Patient A

The S was brought to a group therapy session with other chronic schizophrenics (who were verbal), but he sat in the position in which he was placed and continued the withdrawal behaviors which characterized him. He remained impassive and stared ahead even when cigarettes, which other members accepted, were offered to him and were waved before his face. At one session, when E removed cigarettes from his pocket, a package of chewing gum accidentally fell out. The S's eyes moved toward the gum and then returned to their usual position. This response was chosen by E as one with which he would start to work, using the method of successive approximation (9). (This

method finds use where E desires to produce responses which are not present in the current repertoire of the organism and which are considerably removed from those which are available. The E then attempts to 'shape' the available behaviors into the desired form, capitalizing upon both the variability and regularity of successive behaviors. The shaping process involves the reinforcement of those parts of a selected response which are successively in the desired direction and the nonreinforcement of those which are not. For example, a pigeon may be initially reinforced when it moves its head. When this movement occurs regularly, only an upward movement may be reinforced, with downward movement not reinforced. The pigeon may now stretch its neck, with this movement reinforced. Eventually the pigeon may be trained to peck at a disc which was initially high above its head and at which it would normally never peck. In the case of the psychotic under discussion, the succession was eye movement, which brought into play occasional facial movements, including those of the mouth, lip movements, vocalizations, word utterance, and finally, verbal behavior.)

The S met individually with E three times a week. Group sessions also continued. The following sequence of procedures was introduced in the private sessions. Although the weeks are numbered consecutively, they did not follow at regular intervals since other duties kept E from seeing S every week.

Weeks 1, 2. A stick of gum was held before S's face, and E waited until S's eyes moved toward it. When this response occurred, E as a consequence gave him the gum. By the end of the second week, response probability in the presence of the gum was increased to such an extent that S's eyes moved toward the gum as soon as it was held up.

Weeks 3, 4. The E now held the gum before S, waiting until he noticed movement in S's lips before giving it to him. Toward the end of the first session of the third week, a lip movement spontaneously occurred, which E promptly reinforced. By the end of this week, both lip movement and eye movement occurred when the gum was held up. The E then withheld giving S the gum until S spontaneously made a vocalization, at which time E gave S the gum. By the end of this week, holding up the gum readily occasioned eye movement toward it, lip movement, and a vocalization resembling a croak.

Weeks 5, 6. The *E* held up the gum, and said, 'Say *gum, gum,*' repeating these words each time *S* vocalized. Giving *S* the gum was made contingent upon vocalizations increasingly approximating *gum*. At the sixth session (at the end of Week 6), when *E* said, 'Say *gum, gum,*' *S* suddenly said, 'Gum, please.' This response was accompanied by reinstatement of other responses of this class, that is, *S* answered questions regarding his name and age.

Thereafter, he responded to questions by *E* both in individual sessions and in group sessions, but answered no one else. Responses to the discriminative stimuli of the room generalized to *E* on the ward; he greeted *E* on two occasions in the group room. He read from signs in *E*'s office upon request by *E*.

Since the response now seemed to be under the strong stimulus control of *E, the person,* attempt was made to generalize the stimulus to other people. Accordingly, a nurse was brought into the private room; *S* smiled at her. After a month, he began answering her questions. Later, when he brought his coat to a volunteer worker on the ward, she interpreted the gesture as a desire to go outdoors and conducted him there. Upon informing *E* of the incident, she was instructed to obey *S* only as a consequence of explicit verbal requests by him. The *S* thereafter vocalized requests. These instructions have now been given to other hospital personnel, and *S* regularly initiates verbal requests when nonverbal requests have no reinforcing consequences. Upon being taken to the commissary, he said, 'Ping pong,' to the volunteer worker and played a game with her. Other patients, visitors, and members of hospital-society-at-large continue, however, to interpret nonverbal requests and to reinforce them by obeying *S*.

Patient B

This patient, with a combative history prior to mutism, habitually lay on a bench in the day room in the same position, rising only for meals and for bed. Weekly visits were begun by *E* and an attendant. During these visits, *E* urged *S* to attend group therapy sessions which were being held elsewhere in the hospital. The *E* offered *S* chewing gum. This was not accepted during the first two visits, but was accepted on the third visit and thereafter. On the sixth visit, *E* made receipt of the gum contingent upon *S*'s going to the group room and so informed *S*. The *S* then altered his posture to look at *E* and accompanied him to the group room, where he seated himself in a chair and was given the gum. Thereafter, he came to this room when the attendants called for him.

Group Sessions 1–4. Gum reinforcement was provided for coming to the first two weekly sessions, but starting with the third, it was made contingent upon *S*'s participation in the announced group activity. The group (whose other members were verbal) was arranged in a semicircle. Then *E* announced that each *S* would, when his turn came, give the name of an animal. The *E* immediately provided gum to each *S* who did so. The *S* did not respond and skipped his turn three times around. The same response occurred during the fourth session.

Group Session 5. The activity announced was drawing a person; *E* provided paper and colored chalk and visited each *S* in turn to examine the paper. The *S* had drawn a stick figure and was reinforced with gum. Two of the other patients, spontaneously and without prior prompting by *E,* asked to see the drawing and complimented *S*. Attendants reported that on the following day, *S,* when introduced to two ward visitors, smiled and said, 'I'm glad to see you.' The incident was followed by no particular explicit consequences.

Group Session 6. The announced activity was to give the name of a city or town in Illinois. The *S,* in his turn, said, 'Chicago.' He was reinforced by *E,* who gave him chewing gum, and again two members of the group congratulated him for responding. Thereafter, he responded whenever his turn came.

After the tenth session in the group, gum reinforcement was discontinued. The *S* has continued to respond vocally in the situations in which he was reinforced by *E* but not in others. He never initiates conversations, but he will answer various direct questions in the *group sessions*. He will not, however, respond vocally to questions asked *on the ward,* even when put by *E*.

DISCUSSION

Both *S*'s came from special therapy wards of patients selected because of depressed verbal behavior and long stay in the hospital; tranquilizing drugs were not used. The extent to which reinstatement of verbal behavior was related to the special treatment offered the patients in the special wards set up for them cannot readily be assayed. Among the special treatments accorded them were group therapy sessions. Nevertheless, the similarities between the pattern of reacquisition of verbal behavior by the patients and the patterns of learning encountered in laboratory studies suggest that the conditioning procedures themselves were involved in the reinstatement of verbal behavior.

In the case of Patient A, the speaking response itself was gradually shaped. The anatomical relation between the muscles of chewing and speaking probably had some part in E's effectiveness. When a word was finally produced, the response was reinstated along with other response members of its class, which had not been reinforced. The economy of this process is apparent, since it eliminates the necessity of getting S to produce *every* desired response in order to increase his repertoire. In this case, E concentrated on one verbal response, and in reinstating it, reinstated verbal responses in general. On the stimulus side, when the response came under the stimulus control of E, the stimulus could be generalized to other members of E's class of discriminative *stimuli*, namely, people. This may have relevance for the clinical inference of the importance for future interpersonal relations of prior identification with some person. In the case of Patient B, the stimulus control involved a *given setting*, the rooms where he had been reinforced. The discrimination of E in one case, and not in the other, may be explained in terms of the establishment of operant discrimination, which also involves extinction (9). Operant discrimination is established when a response in the presence of S^D, a discriminative stimulus, is reinforced, and a response in the presence of S^Δ, a stimulus other than S^D, is not. After some time, the response will occur when S^D is presented, but not when S^Δ is presented; the response discriminates S^D from S^Δ, it having been extinguished when S^Δ was presented. In the case of Patient A, E was with S on the ward, in the group room, and privately. Reinforcement occurred in all occasions. But S was on the ward (and other rooms) without E, and therefore without reinforcement for those responses which were occasioned by the ward and which only E reinforced. Hence, these responses would extinguish in the ward alone, but would continue in the presence of E, defining discrimination of E

from other stimuli. In the case of Patient B, this process may have been delayed by the fact that E and the other patients reinforced only in a specific room. It will be recalled that attendants rather than E brought S to the group room.

Interestingly, in the group sessions, when Patient B emitted the responses which E reinforced, other psychotic patients also reinforced Patient B. They were thereby responding, on the occasion of S's responses (discriminative stimuli for them), in the same way that E did. The term *identification*, used as a label here, shares some behavioral referents with the term as used in the preceding paragraph and might be explained behaviorally in terms of the *generalized reinforcer* (10). These behaviors by the patients are similar to behaviors reported in client-centered group sessions, where clients increase in reflective behaviors as counseling progresses, and in psychoanalytic group sessions, where patients increasingly make analytic interpretations of each other. Here, the patients are also behaving like the therapist. While this parallel lends itself to the facetious thought that operant group sessions may produce operant conditioners, it does suggest that psychotics are behaving, with regard to responses by the major source of reinforcement in the group, according to the same laws which govern such group behaviors of nonhospitalized S's.

The various diagnostic labels applied to psychotics are based to a considerable extent upon differences between responses considered abnormal, for example, hallucinations, delusions of persecution, and the like. The therapeutic process is accordingly at times seen in terms of eliminating the abnormal behaviors or states. Experimental laboratory work indicates that it is often extremely difficult to *eliminate* behavior; extinction is extremely difficult where the schedule of reinforcement has been a variable interval schedule (6), that is, reinforcement has been irregular, as it is in most of our behaviors. Such behaviors persist for considerable periods without reinforcement. Experimental laboratory work has provided us quite readily with procedures to *increase* responses. In the case of psychotics, this would suggest focusing attention on whatever *normal* behaviors S has; an appropriate operant, no matter how small or insignificant, even if it is confined to an eye movement, may possibly be raised to greater probability, and shaped to normal behavior (8).

Stated otherwise, abnormal behaviors and normal behaviors can be viewed as reciprocally related, and psychotics as exhibiting considerable abnormal behavior, or little normal behavior. Normal behavior probability can be increased by decreasing probability of abnormal behaviors, or abnormal behaviors can be decreased by the controlled increase of normal behaviors. This preliminary report suggests that a plan of attack based upon the latter approach may be worth further investigation.

SUMMARY

Verbal behavior was reinstated in two psychotics, classified as schizophrenics, who had been mute for 19 and 14 years. The procedures utilized involved application of operant conditioning. The relationship of such procedures, based on controlled laboratory investigations with men and animals, to procedures based on clinical practice with human patients was discussed and was considered as directing our attention to shaping and increasing the probability of what normal behaviors the psychotic possesses.

REFERENCES

1. Azrin, N. H. Some effects of noise on human behavior. *J. exp. Anal. Behavior,* 1958, 1: 183–200.
2. Azrin, N. H., and Lindsley, O. R. The reinforcement of cooperation between children. *J. abnorm. (soc.) Psychol.,* 1956, 52: 100–102.
3. Blough, D. S. A method for obtaining psychophysical thresholds from the pigeon. *J. exp. Anal. Behavior,* 1958, 1: 31–44.
4. Brady, J. V. Ulcers in 'executive' monkeys. *Sci. Amer.,* 1958, 199 (4): 95–100.
5. Dews, P. B. The effects of chlorpromazine and promazine on performance on a mixed schedule of reinforcement. *J. exp. Anal. Behavior,* 1958, 1: 73–82.
6. Ferster, C. B., and Skinner, B. F. *Schedules of Reinforcement.* New York: Appleton-Century-Crofts, 1957.
7. Flanagan, B., Goldiamond, I., and Azrin, N. H. Operant stuttering: the control of stuttering behavior through response-contingent consequences. *J. exp. Anal. Behavior,* 1958, 1: 173–178.
8. Goldiamond, I. Research which can be done in a mental hospital. Address delivered to Illinois State Mental Hospitals Conference, Giant City State Park, Illinois, 1958.
9. Keller, F., and Schoenfeld, W. *Principles of Psychology.* New York: Appleton-Century-Crofts, 1950.
10. Skinner, B. F. *Science and Human Behavior.* New York: Macmillan, 1953.
11. Skinner, B. F. Teaching machines. *Science,* 1958, 128, 969–977.

THE THERAPEUTIC RELATIONSHIP: RECENT THEORY AND RESEARCH *

CARL R. ROGERS [1]

I have long been interested in the elements which account for change in personality and behaviour. I have tried to seek out and discover some of the lawful order which exists in this complex and subtle realm. A number of years ago I became interested in the conditions which fostered constructive psychological change, or psychological development or growth toward maturity. I wanted to find the commonalities—if any existed—between different ways of helping people, different orientations to psychotherapy. I tried to abstract from my experience in therapy, and from my observations of others who were carrying on therapy, and from recordings of therapists with quite divergent views, and from the meagre research available, the conditions which facilitate psychological growth.

As I worked on and pondered over this problem, I gradually developed a decidedly unorthodox cluster of hypotheses. It seemed to me that the only way of explaining the divergent modes of being of help to individuals, was that the helpers or therapists had certain basic attitudes in common. I will try to describe in a few moments the

* Reprinted with permission from Melbourne University Press. In *Australian Journal of Psychology,* 1965, Vol. 17, pp. 95–108.
[1] Based on a lecture given to a joint meeting of the British Psychological Society (Victorian Group) and the Australian and New Zealand College of Psychiatrists (Victorian Branch), at the University of Melbourne, on 6 February 1965.

way these attitudes seem to me. After I had formulated these ideas for myself, I decided to put them out to obtain the reactions of others, and also with the hopeful thought that some research on this issue might be stimulated. So I published an article on the necessary and sufficient conditions of therapeutic personality change (1957). The response convinced me that many people were eagerly looking for some answer to the perplexing question as to what it is that facilitates psychological change. The formulation aroused considerable interest and, even more importantly, it has stimulated a number of research investigations.

I think I would like to say at the outset that the radical nature of the formulation I proposed was primarily in what it omitted. I hypothesized that personality change in the client or patient in psychotherapy came about not because of the professional qualifications and training of the therapist, not because of his special medical or psychological knowledge, not because of his ideological orientation to psychotherapy—psychoanalytic, Jungian, client-centred, Adlerian, Gestalt, etc., not because of his techniques in the interview, not because of his skill in making interpretations, but primarily or solely because of certain attitudinal characteristics in the relationship. It is these characteristics that I would like to describe.

Individuals come to psychotherapy with a bewildering diversity of problems and an enormous range of personal characteristics. They are met by therapists who show an almost equally wide range of diversity of views as to what will be helpful in therapy, and these therapists exhibit also very diverse personality characteristics in meeting their clients. Yet underneath all of this diversity, it seemed to me that I could discern an underlying process which might even be cast in terms of some sort of psychological equation. It could be phrased in this fashion, that if certain definable conditions exist in the psychological relationship between client and therapist, then constructive or therapeutic personality change will occur in the client.

Perhaps first I should indicate very briefly what I mean by constructive or therapeutic personality change. I am using here a very simple and common-sense definition. I mean any change in the personality structure, and in the behaviour of the individual, which clinicians would agree implies greater integration, less internal conflict, more

energy utilizable for effective living. I mean a change in behaviours away from those generally regarded as immature and toward those regarded as mature, responsible and socialized.

A HYPOTHESIS

It is my hypothesis that such changes will come about if there exist in the therapist three attitudinal patterns. In addition to this there is one condition which must exist in the client if change is to come about.

The Three Essential Conditions in the Therapist

In the first place, it is hypothesized that personal growth is facilitated when the psychotherapist is what he *is,* when in the relationship with his client he is genuine and "without front" or facade, openly being the feelings and attitudes which at that moment are flowing in him. We have coined the term "congruence" to try to describe this condition. By this we mean that the feelings the therapist is experiencing are available to him, available to his awareness, that he is able to live these feelings, be them, and able to communicate them if appropriate. It means that he comes into a direct personal encounter with his client, meeting him on a person-to-person basis. It means that he is *being* himself, not denying himself. No one fully achieves this condition, yet the more the therapist is able to listen acceptantly to what is going on within himself, and the more he is able to *be* the complexity of his feelings without fear, the higher the degree of his congruence.

I think that we readily sense this quality in our everyday life. We could each of us name persons whom we know who always seem to be operating from behind a front, who are playing a role, who tend to say things they do not feel. They are exhibiting incongruence. We do not reveal ourselves too deeply to such people. On the other hand each of us knows individuals whom we somehow trust, because we sense that they are being what they *are,* that we are dealing with the person himself, and not with a polite or professional facade. This is the quality of which we are speaking, and it is hypothesized that the more genuine and congruent the therapist in the relationship, the more probability there is that change in personality in the client will occur.

I have received much clinical and research confirmation for this hypothesis in our work in recent years with randomly selected hospitalized schizophrenic patients. The individual therapists in our research programme who seemed to be most successful in dealing with these unmotivated, poorly educated, resistant, chronically hospitalized individuals, are those who are first of all *real,* who react in a genuine, human way as persons, who exhibit their genuineness in the relationship, and who are perceived as real by the patients. Being congruent may mean at times expressing a real annoyance, or concern or frustration in the relationship. It always means expressing these feelings as something existing in the therapist, not as an accusation about the client.

It is this aspect of my hypothesis which seems to explain why people as divergent as Dr. John Rosen, Dr. Carl Whitaker, Dr. Albert Ellis and myself, can each in our own way be effective with clients. Rosen (1953) challenges, Whitaker indulges in mutual fantasy [see Whitaker and Malone (1953)], Ellis (1962) shakes a didactic finger, I (1951) try to understand. To the extent that each of us is a real person, and able to let the realness show through, we tend I believe to reach our clients, even though in very different ways.

Now the second condition, I hypothesize that when the therapist is experiencing a warm, positive and acceptant attitude toward what is in the client, this facilitates change. It involves the therapist's genuine willingness for the client to be whatever feeling is going on in him at that moment—fear, confusion, pain, pride, anger, hatred, love or courage. It means that the therapist cares for the client in a nonpossessive way, as a person with human potentialities. It means that he prizes the client in a total, rather than a conditional way. By this I mean that he does not simply accept the client when he is behaving in certain ways and disapprove of him when he behaves in other ways. It means an outgoing, positive feeling, without reservations, without *evaluations.* The term we have come to use for this is "unconditional positive regard," and we believe that the more this attitude is experienced by the therapist, and perceived by his client, the more likelihood there is that therapy will be successful and that change and development will take place.

It is clear that one does not have to be a professional to experience this attitude. In a therapy group I held at a hospital, a woman who had been hospitalized for many years, but who had shown much improvement during the preceding two years, and who has now left the hospital, gave a moving account of what had helped her. I had been much impressed by her improvement, which clearly began before she entered group therapy, and one day when she said, "This is the first year I have *felt* like leaving the hospital," I said, "Gladys, why is this? What has made the difference?" She said, "Well, what changed it was when the Morses began taking me home—the ones I call Mom and Dad, although they are not. I want to get out mostly to show my appreciation to them for what they have done."

And then she told how, by chance, through their daughter, a nurse at the hospital, this middle-aged couple had become interested in her. They brought a picnic lunch for their daughter and included Gladys. They took her home. "I just sat. Wouldn't move. I was real scared." But they continued to take her to their home. Gladys says, "They've stood an awful lot. Even when I was unruly and snotty to them, they stood by me, they didn't let me down." Little by little this educationally retarded girl who could not even read, who had always been unstable, who had been psychotic, hallucinated, and for years a difficult patient, began to respond. She says, "They helped me more than any doctor," and then adds, " 'Course, doctors help too. But they stood by me even when I was disgusting an' that, and saying things I shouldn't."

In one sense this is not an unusual story. Probably each of us could report some similar incident. But I want to point out its significance. Little by little their nonpossessive love for this young woman, their caring, got through to her and transformed her from a hallucinated psychotic to a positive and realistic person who now has a good chance of success outside the hospital walls. This older couple made it clear to the patient that they cared for her no matter how bizarre her behaviour, no matter how much she rejected them. It was an unconditional positive regard, and it gradually changed her life and her personality. It is this kind of attitude, I believe, which also exists in the therapist when he is effective. It produces results. Gladys says, "Now when I go home they can't tell me from their other children. If Mom has a washing to do, I don't ask her. I just go ahead and do it." [2]

The third essential condition of change is that the therapist is experiencing an accurate empathic understanding of the client's private world. To sense the client's inner world of private personal meanings as if it were your own, but without ever losing the "as if" quality, this is empathy, and this seems essential to therapeutic change. To sense his anger or his fear or his feeling of being persecuted as if it were your own, and yet without your own anger, fear or suspicion getting bound up in it, this is the condition we are endeavouring to describe. When the client's world is clear to the therapist and he can move about in it freely, then he can both communicate his understanding of what is already known to the client, and he can also voice meanings in the client's experience of which the client is scarcely aware. It is this kind of highly sensitive empathy which seems essential to therapeutic change.

I suspect that each of us has discovered that this kind of understanding is extremely rare. We neither receive it nor offer it with any great frequency. Instead we offer another type of understanding which is very different, such as "I understand what is wrong with you," or "I understand what makes you act that way." These are the types of understanding which we usually offer and receive—an evaluative understanding from the outside. But when someone understands how it feels and seems to be me, without wanting to analyze me or judge me, then I can blossom and grow in that climate. I am sure I am not alone in that feeling. I believe that when the therapist can grasp the moment-to-moment experiencing occurring in the inner world of the client, as the client sees it and feels it, without losing the separateness of his own identity in this empathic process, then change is likely to occur.

A Fourth Condition in the Client

Unless some communication of the sort of attitudes I have been describing has been achieved,

[2] A very clear example of the way in which a non-possessive caring can get through to a hospitalized schizophrenic patient is provided in the tape recording of two interviews with Mr. Vac. This tape is available (with transcript) from the Tape Library of the American Academy of Psychotherapists, 6420 City Line Avenue, Philadelphia 51, Pennsylvania.

they do not exist in the world of the client and thus cannot be effective. Consequently, it is necessary to add one more condition to our equation. When the client perceives to a minimal degree the genuineness of the therapist and the acceptance and empathy which the therapist experiences for him, then change in personality and behaviour is predicted. It is necessary that the therapist's behaviours and words are perceived by the client as meaning that to some degree the therapist is real; that the therapist does care, that the therapist does seem to understand something of his inner feelings and personal world.

The Essential Hypothesis

Let me restate very briefly the essentially simple but somewhat radical hypothesis I have set forth. I have said that constructive personality change comes about only when the client perceives and experiences a certain psychological climate in the relationship. The elements of this climate do not consist of knowledge, intellectual training, intellectual orientation in psychotherapy, or techniques. They are feelings or attitudes which must be experienced by the therapist and perceived by the client if they are to be effective. The three I have singled out as being essential are: the realness, genuineness, or congruence of the therapist; a warm, acceptant prizing of the client, an unconditional positive regard; and a sensitive, empathic understanding of the client's feelings which is communicated to the client.

Another aspect of the hypothesis is that it has been stated in such a way that it is testable. Operational definitions of these qualities can be formulated, and indeed have been formulated, and thus we can begin to discover empirically whether qualities such as this in the relationship are indeed causal factors in bringing about change in psychotherapy.

EMPIRICAL STUDIES OF THE HYPOTHESIS

I would like to digress for just a moment, to say how personally rewarding the consequences have been when I have been able and willing to set forth a testable hypothesis. In regard to the conditions I have been describing, for example, I can well remember how uneasy and insecure I felt in making the first presentation of the unorthodox hypothesis I have formulated, to a group at the University of Michigan. I not only felt that I was sticking my neck out; I felt that I was sticking it out a long way. The discussion which followed made it very clear that other people felt the same way. But when a hypothesis is set forth in terms which can be made operational, then the situation does not need to end in argument or difference of opinion. It can be settled by a recourse to the facts. And the most exciting thing about the hypothesis about the therapeutic relationship which I have briefly sketched, is not its newness—for in many ways it is not entirely new—but the fact that it has led to a very considerable amount of empirical investigation to test whether it is true, partly true, or false. I would like to try to tell you in summary form of some of these researches and what they seem to mean.

The Hypothesis as Tested by Observer Judgments

The first study I wish to report is one completed by Halkides (1958). Her study was based on 20 recorded cases, 10 of which could be classed by several objective criteria as more successful, and 10 of them categorized as less successful. She took an earlier and a later recorded interview from each of these cases. On a random basis she picked nine client-counsellor interaction units (that is, a client statement and a counsellor response) from each of these interviews. She thus had nine early interaction and nine later interaction units from each case. These interview samples were then placed in a random order for judging. Three judges worked together during a training period in which they tried to become sensitive to the attitudinal qualities of the therapist by listening to interview recordings and making ratings of them. They then were ready to turn to the interview samples for this study. Working independently and with no knowledge of the case or the degree of success or the source of any given unit, the judges listened to these counsellor-client interactions and rated each unit on a seven-point scale as to the counsellor's empathy. When they had completed this work they went through the samples again, rating the degree of the counsellor's unconditional positive regard for the client, and again for the counsellor's genuineness. Finally they went through the samples once more to rate the degree to which the counsellor's response matched the emotional intensity of the client's expression. This was a condition which Halkides hypothesized to be as important as the three conditions I had formulated.

There seemed a very remote possibility of any positive findings, considering all the sources of unreliability in the study and the smallness of the interview samples. Yet the reliability of the judges' ratings was high, in the neighbourhood of .90. It was also found that a high degree of each of these attitudinal conditions—empathy, unconditional positive regard, and congruence—was associated with the more successful cases, and this association was highly significant at the .001 level. Thus the data tended strongly to confirm the hypothesis. The matching of the client's affective intensity by the therapist did not correlate significantly with the other conditions or with the degree of success.

The Hypothesis as Tested by Client Perceptions and Therapist Perceptions

A series of investigations of the hypothesis regarding the therapeutic relationship have been completed by Barrett-Lennard (1962).[3] Rather than using objective observers and rather than using the interview material, he proposed to study the essential qualities in the relationship by measuring the manner in which it was perceived by the client and the therapist. He developed a Relationship Inventory which has different forms for client and therapist, and which was designed to study five dimensions of the relationship. To give you the flavour of the instrument he developed, I will give a few items from his inventory.

For example, in trying to measure the extent to which the client was empathically understood, he included items such as the following to be evaluated by the client on a six-point scale from "strongly true" to "definitely untrue."

He generally senses or realizes how I am feeling.
When I do not say what I mean at all clearly he still understands me.
He understands my words, but does not realize how I feel.

For the items in the therapist form, these were changed to:

I generally sense or realize how he is feeling.
When he does not say what he means at all clearly, I still understand him.
I understand his words, but not how he feels.

Barrett-Lennard divided the dimension of unconditional positive regard into two aspects. First

[3] This section also discusses Barrett-Lennard's further analysis of his data (details from a personal communication).

he wished to measure the level of regard, the degree of liking of the client by the therapist. For this purpose there were items such as these, each one again to be rated by the client from "strongly true" to "definitely untrue."

He likes seeing me.

He cares about me.

He is indifferent to me.

To measure the unconditionality of the regard, the extent to which there were "no strings attached" to the counsellor's liking, items of this sort were included:

Sometimes he responds to me in a more positive or friendly way than he does at other times.

He likes me better when I behave in some ways than he does when I behave in other ways.

In order to measure the genuineness, or congruence, of the therapist in the relationship, there were items of this sort:

He does not try to mislead me about his own thoughts or feelings.

He behaves just the way that he is in our relationship.

He pretends that he likes me or understands me more than he really does.

Barrett-Lennard also wished to measure a fifth variable which he regarded as important, the therapist's psychological availability or willingness to be known. For this purpose he included items of this kind:

He will freely tell me his own thoughts and feelings when I want to know them.

He is unwilling to tell me how he feels about me.

He is uncomfortable when I ask him something about himself.

Using this Relationship Inventory, Barrett-Lennard studied first a series of 42 clients dealt with by 21 therapists, in which he had several objective measures of the degree of change in the client. He administered the Relationship Inventory to each client and therapist after the fifth interview and again at the termination of therapy. I find the results of his study to be of real interest. Let me try to summarize them.

1. Those clients who eventually showed more therapeutic change, perceived more of the four hypothesized attitudinal conditions in their relationship with their therapist at the time of the early interview than did those who eventually showed less change. The fifth condition, the willingness of the therapist to be known, was not significantly associated with later success. The meaning of this finding is that where the client perceived these qualities in the relationship early in therapy the prognosis was good. It was a clear confirmation of the hypothesis that if the client perceives the therapist as experiencing liking and understanding of him, and if he perceives the therapist as being a real and genuine person, then change is facilitated.

2. The correlation between the *client* perception of these attitudinal conditions and the degree of change is higher than the correlation between therapist perception and degree of change. This finding too is in accord with the theory. If the therapist is experiencing these attitudes in himself toward the client early in therapy, this is a reasonably good prediction that constructive change will occur. But if the client *perceives* the therapist as holding these attitudes, this is an even better predictor of constructive change. It is not enough that the therapist hold these attitudes. They must also be perceived by the client.

3. There are two additional findings in his study which deserve consideration, though they are a little more complicated. Those clients who at the time of beginning therapy are better adjusted, as measured by different psychological tests, tend to perceive more of these therapeutic conditions in the relationship than do those clients who are less well adjusted. This was an unexpected finding. On first thought it might seem to indicate that these perceived conditions are not a *cause* of movement toward better adjustment, but an *effect* of better adjustment. Perhaps only those individuals who are already well adjusted can be nondefensive enough to perceive such attitudes on the part of the therapist.

To pursue this issue further, Barrett-Lennard divided the 21 therapists into a more-experienced and less-experienced group. That this was a meaningful division seems indicated by the fact that the clients of the more experienced therapists showed more personality change. Now when he compared the clients in these groups he found that the clients of the more experienced therapists perceived more of the therapeutic conditions than did the clients of the less experienced therapists. Hence it seems reasonable to conclude that the behaviours of the more experienced therapists communicated more of these attitudinal qualities than the behaviours of less experienced therapists. But it is also true that the ability to perceive these qualities is in part a function of the client's openness or adjustment. Thus these findings seem to point up to the fact that this is an interactional situation in which, as therapists grow more skilful, they are more able to experience and provide the conditions which make for therapy. On the other hand, these conditions can only be effective in the relationship to the extent that the client perceives them, and to some degree his ability to perceive them depends on his own adjustment.

Testing the Hypothesis in Psychotherapy with Schizophrenics

I would like to bring you one other line of evidence from our current and just completed investigation of the therapeutic relationship with schizophrenics (Rogers, Gendlin, Kiesler, and Truax, 1967). Here we have been dealing largely with unmotivated schizophrenics, mostly of lower socio-educational status and more or less chronic in their condition. Though this investigation is not yet published we already have findings which bear on the hypothesis I have advanced. Drawing on the work of Gendlin, Kiesler, van der Veen and others, I will mention a few of our findings very briefly.

First of all, schizophrenic patients perceive a much lower level of these attitudes in their therapists than do neurotic clients, though there is good reason to believe that the therapists are experiencing much the same attitudes with each group. This confirms Barrett-Lennard's finding that the more disturbed person can less easily perceive and trust the positive attitudes of the therapist.

In the second place, the more the schizophrenic patient perceived of these attitudes in the relationship, and especially if he saw his therapist as real, the more evidence he gave of therapeutic movement as measured by our process scales. Briefly this means that he showed a greater degree of self-experiencing and self-exploration, a greater openness to what was going on within himself, greater evidence of being involved in a process of changing.

A third finding is that the greater the degree of the therapist's empathy and congruence, the higher the level of process indices in the patient's

interaction with a *third* person, the sampling interviewer, who saw him every three months. In other words, the more satisfactory the relationship in therapy, the more likely it is that the client will show an openness to his own experience, less rigidity, more spontaneity, more capacity for communicating himself, in a relationship with another person.

Finally there are a number of findings which indicate that patients involved in a relationship high in these growth-promoting qualities show the greatest degree of constructive personality change. For example, the most striking of these findings is that those patients who received the highest degree of sensitively empathic understanding in their therapeutic relationship, as judged by unbiased raters, showed the greatest decrease in schizophrenic pathology as measured by the MMPI. Conversely (and this is a disturbing finding), those patients in relationships low in empathic understanding showed an actual worsening in their schizophrenic pathology. At the conclusion they were worse off than the matched control individuals who had no individual therapy.

Without trying to go further into this very complex research, I will simply say that it indicates that the attitudinal qualities I have described are provided largely by the therapist, but elicited partly by certain characteristics in the patient. Thus therapy is an interactional event. When, however, the relationship exhibits these qualities to a high degree, indices of movement or changingness are evident in the patient, and an improved inner integration, a reduction in pathological behaviour, and an improvement in social adjustment follow.

SIGNIFICANCE OF THESE STUDIES

As I mull over the various studies which I have briefly summarized, they seem to me to have a number of rather deeply significant meanings. In the first place they indicate that it is possible to study cause and effect in psychotherapy. These are actually, so far as I know, the first studies to endeavour to isolate and measure the primary change-producing influences in psychotherapy. Whether they are still further confirmed by later research, or whether they are contradicted or modified by future studies, they represent pioneering investigations of the question, "What really makes the difference in psychotherapy?" And the answer they give is that it is the attitudes provided by the therapist, the psychological climate which he is largely responsible for creating, which *really* makes the difference, which really induces change. In the second place, the findings do tend to support in general the theory advanced as to the equation of psychotherapy. Thus we can now say with some assurance and factual backing that a relationship perceived by the client as characterized by a high degree of congruence or genuineness in the therapist, by sensitive and accurate empathy on the part of the therapist, by a high degree of regard, respect and liking for the client by the therapist, and by an absence of conditionality in this regard, will have a high probability of being an effective therapeutic relationship. This statement holds, whether we are speaking of neurotic individuals who come of their own initiative seeking help, or whether we are speaking of chronically schizophrenic persons, with no conscious desire for help. This statement also holds whether these attitudinal elements are rated by impartial observers who listen to samples of the recorded interviews, or whether they are measured in terms of the client's perception of the relationship. To me it seems to be quite a forward stride to be able to make statements such as these in an area as complex and subtle as the field of psychotherapy.

Another significant element of these studies is that they have shown that the individual's perception of a relationship, the relationship as it exists phenomenologically, has a meaningful association with objective measures of change. In view of some of the trends taking place in psychological thought and research today, this is an important instance of movement toward "a science of inner experience," as Bergin (1961) has called it. Research in psychotherapy is bringing back into the world of psychology the subjective experiences of the individual by its approaches to the objective measurement of the cues which point toward such subjective experience. Thus, to measure reliably such an inner, subjective experience as the degree of positive liking the therapist feels toward his client, or the degree to which he is genuine in his feelings, may in the long run be very important for psychology in general.

There is another highly practical significance to these studies. They each indicate quite clearly that, by assessing a relationship early in its existence, we can to some degree predict the probability of its being a relationship which makes for growth.

There is another and broader significance which these studies carry. They would, if further confirmed, seem to have profound implications for the training of therapists and counsellors. It means that if we wish workers to be effective in their helping relationships, we would focus less on courses in abnormal psychology and psychopathology, theories of different therapeutic orientations, theories of personality, training in psychiatric and psychological diagnosis, and would concentrate more on two elements. We would endeavour to select individuals for such training who already possess a high degree of the qualities I have described, in their ordinary relationships with other people. We would want people who were warm, spontaneous, real, and understanding. We would also endeavour so to plan the educational programme for these individuals that they would, in their training courses, come increasingly to experience empathy and liking from others and for others, and that they would find it increasingly easier to be themselves, to be real, to be spontaneous and expressive. When I ask myself whether the training programmes I know, either in psychology or psychiatry, approach this goal, I come up with a strong negative. It seems to me that most of our professional training programmes make it *more* difficult for the individual to be himself, and more likely that he will play a professional role. Often he becomes so burdened with theoretical and diagnostic baggage that he becomes *less* able to understand the inner world of another person as it seems to that person. Also, as his professional training continues, it all too often occurs that his initial warm liking for other persons is submerged in a sea of psychiatric and psychological evaluation, and hidden under an all-enveloping professional role.

SPECULATION

I would like to grow speculative for a moment, going well beyond the specific findings of these studies. I am sure that the hypothesis proposed as to the attitudes which facilitate psychological growth and development will, in the course of time, be modified. I am sure that the studies thus far completed will be qualified by the findings of further studies. Yet it does seem to be quite within the range of possibility that in the not too distant future we will acquire an increasingly accurate knowledge of the elements which make for constructive psychological development, just as we have in the realm of nutrition acquired an increasingly accurate knowledge of the elements which promote physical growth. As this knowledge accumulates, and as our instruments grow sharper, then there is the exciting possibility that we may be able, relatively early in the game, to predict whether a given relationship will actually promote individual psychological growth and development, just as we can assess the diet of a child in India or the Congo, and predict the extent to which it will promote or inhibit physical growth. This opens some astonishing vistas. Suppose we could measure a given parent-child relationship and not only predict whether it is likely to be growth promoting, but could also assess the deficiencies which keep it from being as helpful as it might be. Suppose that in like manner we could assess a given teacher-pupil relationship in the classroom, or the relationship between an executive and the men who report to him, or the relationship between a doctor and his patients. In short, what I am suggesting is that we may have the beginning here of a significant flowering of psychological knowledge to a point where we can encourage those relationships in which individual development toward psychological maturity is most probable, and where we can help to remedy those relationships in which at the moment psychological growth seems less likely. Enough pilot work has been done with the Relationship Inventory in teacher-pupil situations and in some parent-child relationships to make this seem not a far-off dream but a real possibility.

In concluding I cannot resist reading a paragraph from a letter from a psychotherapist friend in which he states very well a viewpoint which I deeply share. He says:

> I do not believe that even therapists are fully aware of how novel and unique is the relationship in which they are engaged. In all the long history of man, in the centuries and centuries that he has existed, for the first time in this long stretch of time, there are human beings who have made a profession and calling of listening to other human beings with sympathy, with understanding, with acceptance; and in many instances making no effort to alter these other human beings, to change them, push them around, persuade them. There has never been a relationship even remotely resembling this, a relationship in which a person makes no demands for himself. For hostile, judgmental, egotistical, self-loving and self-seeking man, this is indeed a radical and revolutionary relationship. And it represents, also, probably the hardest and strangest role for man to provide.

What I have been saying in this paper is that we are making progress in understanding the nature of this unique therapeutic relationship. I have been saying that the essential elements appear to be not technical knowledge nor ideological sophistication, but personal human qualities— something the therapist *experiences,* not something he *knows.* And I have said that the empirical knowledge we have gained thus far confirms this view. In a variety of clients, normal, neurotic and psychotic, with many different therapists, and studying the relationship from the vantage point of the client, the therapist, or the uninvolved observer, the answer tends to come out the same: attitudes of realness, genuine liking, of sensitive empathy, help to create a climate which produces constructive personal growth and change. And the ramifying implications of these findings are great indeed.

SUMMARY

Constructive personality change in the client during psychotherapy is hypothesized as being dependent upon three essential attitudes in the therapist. These are held to be more important than the therapist's professional qualifications, his therapeutic orientation, or his interview techniques. These attitudes are: congruence or genuineness in the relationship; acceptance or prizing of the client; an accurate emphatic understanding of the client's phenomenal world. A number of research investigations bearing on this hypothesis are briefly reported. The evidence is to a considerable extent confirmatory. Some implications for psychology, for psychotherapy, and for the training of therapists, are pointed out.

REFERENCES

Barrett-Lennard, G. T. Dimensions of therapist response as causal factors in therapeutic change. *Psychol. Monogr.,* 1962, 76: No. 43 (Whole No. 562).

Bergin, A. Worknotes toward a science of inner

experience. Paper read at New Jersey Psychol. Assn., December, 1961.

Ellis, A. *Reason and emotion in psychotherapy.* New York: Lyle Stuart, 1962.

Halkides, G. An experimental study of four conditions necessary for therapeutic change. Unpublished doctoral dissertation, Univer. of Chicago, 1958.

Rogers, C. R. *Client-centred therapy.* Boston: Houghton Mifflin, 1951.

Rogers, C. R. The necessary and sufficient conditions of therapeutic personality change. *J. consult. Psychol.,* 1957, 21: 95–103.

Rogers, C. R., Gendlin, E. T., Kiesler, D. J., and Truax, C. B. *The therapeutic relationship and its impact: a study of psychotherapy with schizophrenics.* Madison: Univer. of Wisconsin Press, 1967.

Rosen, J. M. *Direct analysis.* New York: Grune and Stratton, 1953.

Whitaker, C. A., and Malone, T. P. *The roots of psychotherapy.* New York: Blakiston, 1953.

STUDIES OF THE THERAPIST'S ROLE IN THE TREATMENT OF THE SCHIZOPHRENIC PATIENT *

Barbara J. Betz [1]

The complex nature of events between people is a source of fascination for all students of human behavior. The psychiatrist in this century, in his role as clinician and investigator, has become a major contributor to new viewpoints regarding these complexities and to new methods of exploring them. The psychotherapeutic relationship, in particular, has provided a potent means for influencing clinical progress and outcome, and as a consequence has itself become an important focus for study. Although the psychotherapist's task is complex, his aim is simply stated: to assist a patient with a psychiatric disability to a state of improved personality functioning.

The task of the investigator of psychotherapeutic events is to seek to identify the variables which facilitate or hinder good patient outcome. Levinson (11), at Harvard, has provided a framework for the investigator in the field of individual psychotherapy by summarizing seven major domains contributing relevant variables to the patient's treatment "career."

Three of these domains which have occupied my attention for a number of years are: 1) the characteristics of the therapist, 2) the characteristics of the patients (the two independent variables in the research design), and 3) the outcome of treatment (the dependent variable). A closely related fourth domain is the "match" between the patient's and the therapist's characteristics. Variables from this domain are currently under study by a number of investigators with interesting preliminary findings.

My studies have not been concerned with psychotherapy in an abstract sense. Since I began them, about 1942, the *aim has been to attempt to establish with reliability what makes a difference in the treatment of schizophrenic patients.* The research focus is on the schizophrenic patient in actual therapeutic contact with his doctor. Some progress was made in carrying out this aim in a series of studies with Dr. John Whitehorn at the Henry Phipps Clinic of the John Hopkins Hospital, Baltimore, Md., over a period of several years. I shall give a brief account of some of these studies and their substantive results.

Early Studies

During the first several years, the research approach was that of participant-observation, with the investigator working as psychotherapist with a series of schizophrenic patients. Twenty-five years ago the underlying personal problems of which the clinical phenomena were indicators were still little understood. Early studies of schizophrenia, as is well known, had led primarily to descriptive statements focused on morbid phenomena. Dynamically oriented clinicians (Kempf, Sullivan, Federn, Fromm-Reichmann, and others) had begun to report success in establishing relationships with schizophrenic patients, with concomitant clinical improvement, but the body of knowledge was still slight.

* Reprinted with permission from the American Psychiatric Association. In *American Journal of Psychiatry,* 1967, Vol. 123, pp. 963–971.

[1] Read at a meeting of the New York Society for Clinical Psychiatry—New York County District Branch, American Psychiatric Association, New York, N. Y., February 10, 1966.

My early interest was to learn more about the underlying conditions in the patient which give rise to and sustain the schizophrenic reaction, and to identify what conditions in the treatment situation facilitate the reduction of the schizophrenic mode of reaction and its replacement by more satisfactory personal and social capacities. In the course of these studies (1, 2, 3) the characteristic aloofness of the schizophrenic patient became increasingly intelligible as a sensitive pattern for the maintenance of psychological distance, motivated by fearful and hateful distrust of self and of others.

A common theme, centered about the issue of "authority," was noted to underlie the clinical phenomena. Much of the symptomatology and behavior became meaningful as an expression of a special orientation toward "authority" as external and imposed—its source in others, not in the self. The classical inward experience of feeling "controlled" or "influenced" by outside forces is an indicator of a dominant concern with imposed authority.

The issue of "influence" would not arise, of course, without a sense of ego weakness in relation to the ego strength of others. Since the patient feels vulnerable and helpless, safety rather than communication becomes his primary goal, although attained at a high price of frustration, loneliness, and the negation of further ego growth through emotional experiences with others. The patient does not act from "leads" arising within himself, and he is wary of any leadership initiated by others. This barrier confronts all persons who come in contact with him and presents itself as a formidable obstacle to the therapist.

It was possible, in these early studies, to see this autistic barrier resolve: 1) as the patient developed a trusting relationship with the therapist, and 2) as he began to locate and rely on his own inner resources as guides for personal and social behavior. These developments were associated with the disappearance of clinical "schizophrenia." The actual experience of the relationship with the therapist, rather than psychological insights about the morbid pathology, seemed itself to be the crucial factor in effecting the favorable change.

The establishment of such a trusting relationship is not readily accomplished. Why is it so difficult to achieve? Do some physicians achieve it more readily and frequently than others? If so, why

and how? Questions such as these sharpened interest in focusing more intensively on the person of the therapist as an important source of influence in the treatment of these patients.

This idea was explored between 1950 and 1963 in a series of studies (4, 5, 6, 7, 8, 16, 17, 18) focused on resident psychiatrists and their schizophrenic patients. In this new approach the investigator is not a therapist of the patient but studies the events which take place between other doctors and their patients. This method brings a much larger sample of doctors and patients under study. Similarities and contrasts—in styles of clinical transactions and in personal characteristics—can be looked for and systematic comparisons made designed to reveal any differential effects on the patient's progress and outcome.

Two methods of study were successfully utilized. The first was a study of data recorded in the individual case records by physicians and by nurses during the time when treatment was in progress. This method yielded characterizations of physicians in terms of differences in their clinical "styles" in therapeutic transactions with their schizophrenic patients.

The second method was to study the personal interest patterns of the physician by the use of an independent instrument, the Strong Vocational Interest Inventory. By the use of this second method, as will be described, it was possible to predict successfully, in advance of therapeutic performance, that physicians with one kind of personal interest patterns would have a high proportion of their schizophrenic patients improve, and that physicians with an opposite kind of interest pattern would have a lower proportion improve.

DIFFERENCES IN CLINICAL STYLE

The first step, however, was to see *whether* physicians differ in the improvement rates achieved with schizophrenic patients. That they do differ, only some consistently obtaining high improvement rates, was demonstrated in the following way. A list of 35 resident physicians was assembled, selected to be comparable in range of clinical experience with schizophrenic, depressed, and neurotic patients. The success rate of each with his patients was then calculated by dividing the number of patients "improved" at discharge by the number treated. (The validity of the designation "improved" or "unimproved"—the important dependent variable—has been tested in detail in studies which will not be reported here.) Only patients treated by psychotherapy without insulin or electric shock were included.

The physicians were then listed in order of descending rank. In an initial study, the top seven physicians—for convenience designated A doctors —were selected as a sample for comparison and contrast with the seven low-ranking physicians who were designated B doctors. The A doctors had an average improvement rate of 75 percent with their 48 schizophrenic patients, while the B doctors had an average improvement rate of only 27 percent with their 52 schizophrenic patients.

Why did the patients of the A doctors improve almost three times as frequently as those of the B doctors? The possibility that the A doctors' patients were clinically "easier" cases than those of the B doctors was ruled out by a detailed comparison of the two patient groups, which established that the groups were, initially, clinically comparable. The possibility that the A doctors were "better therapists," with greater general therapeutic aptitude, was ruled out by demonstrating that both physician groups did equally well with other types of patients than schizophrenics.

The possibility that the A doctors carried out their therapeutic transactions in a different style than did the B doctors, and that these differences were related to differences in therapeutic outcome, remained to be explored. When this was done by a detailed analysis of the individual case records, differences in clinical "style" between A and B doctors were demonstrated by the chi square test at high levels of statistical significance (.001). Methodological details will be omitted; the empirical findings will be summarized briefly for the present purpose.

It was found that the A doctors, more frequently than the B doctors, grasped the personal meaning and motivation of the patient's behavior, going beyond mere clinical description and narrative biography. Likewise, they more frequently selected personality-oriented rather than psychopathology-oriented goals in the treatment of a particular patient, i.e., goals aimed at assisting the patient in definitely modifying his adjustment patterns and more constructively using his assets, rather than merely decreasing symptoms or correcting faulty "mechanisms."

Finally, while the B doctors tended to be passively permissive, or to point out to a patient his mistakes and misunderstandings and to interpret his behavior in an instructional style, the A doctors did little of this. Rather, they more freely expressed attitudes toward problems being talked about, manifested initiative in sympathetic inquiry, expressed honest disagreement at times, sometimes challenged the patient's self-deprecatory attitudes, set realistic limits, and avoided getting caught permissively in the patient's patterns of control.

These characteristics are recognizable as manifestations of an attitude of respectful and sympathetic independence on the part of the doctor toward the patient combined with the expectation that the patient also has a potential for respectful independent action. The patients of the A doctors were those with whom trustful communication was most frequently established. They were also the patients whose improvement reached the highest levels of excellence.

The above study, in its entirety, was cross-validated on an independent sample of 18 resident physicians and 109 schizophrenic patients.

In summary, these studies provided data to support the conclusion that differences exist among doctors, manifest in differences in their clinical "styles" with schizophrenic patients and highly associated with differences in patient outcome.

PHYSICIAN CHARACTERISTICS

This correlation was next explored with a view to discovering more about how psychiatrists might differ as persons as well as in their clinical style. Much of the preliminary work consisted of trying out various means of characterizing physicians, testing how reliably such characterizations could be determined, and then testing whether the reliably determinable characterizations were, in fact, correlated with patient improvement rates.

From preliminary work of this type, an "objective" psychological test procedure—the use of the Vocational Interest Inventory devised by Strong—proved definitely superior to any other tried in that it did show a correlation of physician characteristics with patient improvement rates and was quite free of any observer bias regarding the physicians. The Strong test is self-administered and mechanically scored. (For those not familiar with this test, it is a well standardized research tool, not psychopathologically oriented but focused on human interests. It selects out from a fairly wide range interests highly shared by an individual with some groups of his fellow beings, and interests only slightly shared with other groups of persons. The inventory matches the interest patterns of any given individual with known interest patterns of individuals in 45 vocations, by a scoring scale ranging from high to low matching.)

Strong Interest Test scores were available on 26 residents whose success rates with their schizophrenic patients were known. Fifteen residents whose individual success rates were 68 percent or higher were designated A doctors, and the remaining 11 residents whose success rates fell below this criterion comprised the B group.

Some interesting findings emerged from a comparison of the Strong test scores of these two groups. Both groups scored high in three vocations: physician, psychologist, and public administrator. In 38 other vocations, score differences discriminating between the two groups were not found. By the scores on four vocations, however, it was possible to detect differences in the interest patterns of the A and B physicians, at levels of statistical significance between .10 and .02. These four vocations are: lawyer, Certified Public Accountant (As high; Bs low); printer, and mathematics and physical science teacher (As low; Bs high). These empirical findings are independent data constituting a source of possible clues to some distinguishing personal characteristics of each physician group.

The next consideration was how these data might be utilized as a predictive device to indicate which physicians, whose therapeutic success with schizophrenic patients was not yet known, would have high improvement rates with their patients and which would not. Such a predictive study, if successful, would serve as a rigorous check on the validity of the differences observed in the initial sample.

Furthermore, the level of predictive accuracy might serve as an indicator as to whether the crucial determinants of successful interaction lay in the doctor or in the patient. The possibility had been kept in mind that the A doctors might have owed their success to the good luck of getting patients who, for some reason not detected in the studies, had the knack of establishing confidential relationships, etc. Such an hypothesis had not seemed probable, but it did seem possible. If,

however, success in therapy with schizophrenic patients could be predicted in advance, with reasonably high reliability, from indicators of the doctor's characteristics, such a result would support the idea that the crucial determinants of success lay in the doctors.

A five-point screening device was developed from the four vocational scores discussed above. The highest point, 4, on this screen indicates a full four-point matching of an individual's interest patterns with the constellation of vocations characteristic of the A doctor (high for lawyer and C.P.A., low for printer and mathematics and physical science teacher); the intermediate points (3, 2, and 1) indicate matching this constellation in 3, 2, or 1 of these vocational categories. The lowest point (0) indicates matching in none of these categories.

Points 4 and 3 on the screen would be expected to predict A doctors. Points 1 and 0 on the screen would be expected to predict B doctors. Point 2 (weighted equally between characteristic A and B patterns) would not be predictive.

To check the predictive accuracy of this screen, an independent sample of resident physicians, 46 in number, was used. Strong test scores were available on each of these physicians. Using the screening device, predictions were made for each of them as to whether or not they would achieve improvement rates of 68 percent or more with their schizophrenic patients.

ACCURACY OF PREDICTIONS

These predictions were then compared with the actual improvement rates achieved with schizophrenic patients. The A predictions turned out to be 80 percent correct and the B predictions 67 percent correct. More specifically, out of 25 physicians predicted to meet the A criterion, only five failed to do so; out of 12 physicians predicted to fall below this criterion, eight did so.

These results thus support the idea that determinants of success in the treatment of schizophrenic patients lie in the physicians. The cluster of interest patterns represented by high scores for lawyer and C.P.A., and low scores for printer and mathematics and physical science teacher, presumably point to special qualities in the physician's personality more likely to evoke favorable clinical response from schizophrenic patients. And the inverse constellation of interest patterns (high for printer and mathematics and physical science teacher; low for lawyer and C.P.A.) presumably point to special personal qualities less likely to evoke acceptance as an effective working partner.

Next, a more detailed characterization of the personal qualities of A and B doctors was attempted. This was done by examining their responses to each of the 400 items composing the Strong Vocational Interest Inventory. The initial examination was made on the 15 A and 11 B doctors comprising Sample 1 in the preceding study. The second, independent sample of 46 residents was again used for purposes of cross-validation.

This examination led to the identification of 23 test items which differentiated the two doctor groups at levels of statistical significance. The 23 items are listed in Table 1.

A second predictive screen was devised from the data in Table 1. This screen was tested on the independent sample of 46 doctors mentioned above. It performed with 77 percent accuracy in predicting A doctors and 83 percent accuracy in predicting B doctors. Specifically, out of 26 doctors predicted to meet the A criterion in treating their schizophrenic patients, only six failed to do so; out of 12 doctors predicted to fall below this criterion, ten did so.

It is thus apparent that this second screen, based on the individual items from the Strong inventory, performed with even greater accuracy than the first screen, based on the final scores in the four vocational categories. The 23 items in Table 1 are currently proving to be the findings from these studies most actively utilized by other investigators in studies of the therapist variable.

I should also like to refer briefly to one other validation study. The following question had presented itself: Were the results obtained particular in some way to the psychiatric milieu and working points of view prevalent in the Phipps Clinic? Or did they have a more general validity? That is, would A and B doctors (by the Strong inventory criteria) working in *any* clinical setting with schizophrenic patients have the same kind and degree of differential therapeutic results?

An opportunity for examining this matter was provided by a neighboring psychiatric hospital, the Sheppard and Enoch Pratt Hospital. This hospital has its own residency training program, which is psychoanalytically oriented, and has had a traditional interest in the treatment of the schizo-

TABLE 1

Strong Vocational Interest Test Items Which Differentiate A and B Physicians

Item No.				
17	Building contractor	L	*I	*D
19	Carpenter	L	*I	*D
59	Marine engineer	L	I	*D
60	Mechanical engineer	L	I	*D
68	Photoengraver	L	I	*D
87	Ship officer	L	*I	*D
90	Specialty salesman	L	I	*D
94	Toolmaker	L	I	*D
121	Manual training	L	*I	*D
122	Mechanical drawing	L	*I	*D
151	Drilling in a company	*L	*I	D
185	Making a radio set	L	I	*D
187	Adjusting a carburetor	L	*I	*D
189	Cabinet making	L	*I	*D
216	Entertaining others	L	*I	*D
218	Looking at shop windows	L	*I	*D
290	Interest public in a new machine through public addresses	*L	*I	D
311	President of a society or club	*L	I	D
356a	Many women friends	*L	I	D
367	Accept just criticism without getting sore	*Yes	?	No
368	Have mechanical ingenuity	Yes	?	*No
375	Can correct others without giving offense	*Yes	?	No
381	Follow up subordinates effectively	*Yes	*?	No

L—Like, I—Indifferent, D—Dislike.
* Signifies characteristic A physician response.

phrenic patient. Information on the improvement rates achieved by the individual doctors treating patients in this hospital was available. Eleven doctors were selected for study, five who met the A criterion of improvement rate (68 percent or better) and six who had not met this criterion. Strong Vocational Interest Inventory scores were obtained on each of these 11 doctors and the position of each on the two predictive screens was ascertained. Both screens performed in the expected direction. The second screen, based on the individual test items, again performed outstandingly—with 80 percent accuracy in regard to the A doctors and with 100 percent accuracy in regard to the B doctors.

The results of these studies [2] support the thesis that crucial determinants of therapeutic outcome of schizophrenic patients lie in certain personal qualities in the physician. It would be useful to seek further corroboration of the general validity of these findings by studies using other samples of doctors working in several other hospitals.

DISCUSSION

What inferences can be drawn concerning the meanings of these findings? One line of thought is that the As, with interests resembling lawyers and C.P.A.s, have more of a problem-solving and less of a mechanical approach than the B doctors, with attitudes resembling printers and mathematics and physical science teachers.

In the A doctor the patient would find the values of responsible self-determination more honored and exemplified than those of deference and conformity—an emphasis providing an avenue of progress out of his own entanglements in mutinous

[2] These studies utilized schizophrenic patients and resident physicians at the Phipps Clinic between 1944 and 1955. The possibility of drawing on the patient-resident sample in the next five years (1955–1960) for further studies was surveyed, but this material was found not suitable. Between 1955 and 1960 the number of patients in the "unimproved" outcome group had become too low to make comparisons between the "improved" and "unimproved" outcome groups possible. (The average annual improvement rate after 1954 remained above 70 percent; prior to that date it had not exceeded 62 percent and prior to 1952 it had not exceeded 57 percent.) There were correspondingly too few physicians whose success rates met the B criteria for a comparative study of the personality variable with the sample in the A group. Also, for reasons not readily explained, between 1955 and 1960 only a few of the new residents entering training scored, by the Strong test criteria, as predictive Bs. There was therefore in this period an unusually homogeneous group of "A" residents, so far as personal interest patterns and success rates with schizophrenic patients were concerned. This is also the period when the ataractic drugs were introduced. The task of selecting a "psychotherapy only" patient sample, corrected for this variable, did not seem practicable, and a sample without this correction would not correspond with the earlier studies. A recent study by Stephens(14) utilizes patient-resident material in the 1950–1960 decade, without critical attention to these considerations which indicate the unsuitability of the 1955–1960 segment of the material for a study of the doctor variable. The negative findings in his study with reference to the doctor variable must, accordingly, be weighed with this fact in mind which, indeed, they appear to reflect.

commitments toward authoritative influences, seen as imposed from external sources. The A doctors, in their clinical styles, reveal a capacity to be perceptive of the individualistic inner experiences of the patient while functioning themselves in responsibly individualistic roles.

This is acceptable to the distrustful patient, who is likely to respond to restrictive pressures by more withdrawal, and to mere permissiveness by inertia. With the A doctors, solutions to the patient's problems are worked out through collaborative exploration of possibilities rather than through authoritative instruction.

In the B doctors, on the other hand, the patient would find an emphasis on value systems weighted more heavily toward exactness and critique. A particular set of attitudes implied by the mechanically inclined interests may constitute an actual hindrance to the development of self-trust and social spontaneity in the schizophrenic patient.

The larger significance of the findings in these studies is in their challenge to the customary view that a physician's effectiveness rests exclusively in his technical skills—the pills, shocks, manipulations, and other therapeutic technics which he utilizes.

The personality of the physician has long been recognized in a general way as a factor in medical treatment. That it may be a prime source of influences on therapeutic response, and therefore an area of potential scientific importance, is of recent and growing interest to colleagues from as disparate disciplines as psychopharmacology and psychoanalysis. The era of systematic study of the phenomena of interpersonal relationships, and of the factors governing events among individual persons and among groups of persons, is still in its infancy. Indications are that the lawful factors governing events among individual persons and among groups of persons will be identified and their modes of operation clarified. Studies of imprinting; of operant conditioning; of transference, countertransference and corrective emotional experience (in education, as well as in the clinic); of communication (with attention to both the manifest and the covert message); of perceptual variations, challenging static definitions of what is "so" and "not so"; and of adaptive capacities and potentialities for constancy and for flexibility—these are a few of the current areas under intensive investigation. Studies of psychotherapy are a part of a broader trend, and only a few have yet been made.

It may be of interest to report that in the past three years the 23-item A-B scale has been in active use in a number of investigations. McNair, Callahan, and Lorr (12), in a well-designed study at the Veterans Administration, divided 55 therapists into A and B groups, treating neurotic outpatients for a four-month period. In this study the patients of B therapists improved significantly more than did those of A therapists. This diametrically opposite finding from the Phipps studies with schizophrenic inpatients suggested to Carson and others (9, 10) at Duke University the operation of a patient type X therapist-type interaction in determining outcome. This suggestion received strong support in a number of therapy analogue studies.

Results in the Duke studies point to specific patient attributes which are relevant to differences between experimentally demonstrated behavior of persons with A-type and B-type interest patterns. They support the assumption that A- and B-type persons are differentially sensitive to "avoidance behavior" (schizoid) and to "turning against the self" (neurotic) behavior in other persons.

The hypothesis which emerges is that it may be the "fit" between therapist characteristics and patient characteristics, and not the therapist's personality alone, which determines the therapist's mode of therapeutic behavior. This hypothesis is receiving confirmatory support from studies in process by Uhlenhuth(15) at Johns Hopkins.

I shall mention one other study, an experimental study of perception done by Pollack and Kiev (13) at Johns Hopkins. Their postulate was that A-type therapists could be differentiated from B-type therapists by their mode of spatial orientation in a perceptual task designed to measure the relative reliance on body or field cues. Forty male psychiatrists with known A-B ratings on the Strong test items were studied, using Witkin's Rod and Frame apparatus. The results found the B group extremely field-independent compared to the A group (.025 level of significance).

This study confirms, by an independent method, that there are significant differences between the A- and B-type therapists, and it suggests that the style of perceptual process of the therapist may be significantly related to the therapeutic interactions, although the exact association remains to be studied. They state:

It is of interest that spatial orientation and other perceptual processes are a focal point in the training of psychotherapists who must learn to utilize information, *viz.*, transference and countertransference cues, which are not ordinarily recognized outside the psychotherapeutic situation. Such training thus effectively involves increasing awareness of spatial (situations) as well as internal proprioceptive (therapist) information for purposes of therapy. This study suggests that there may perhaps be certain constitutional or psychological limits beyond which such training may not be effective and points to the need for further investigations of the perceptual processes of individual therapists before, during, and after training in therapy, as a fruitful avenue of approach to the physician variable in the psychotherapeutic relationship.

Although the emphasis in this presentation has been on *contrasts* between therapists with known high and low success rates with schizophrenic patients, the data point to a continuum of therapist characteristics between the A-B polarities. Therefore it may be expected that some physicians in the borderline group may move from a B position to an A position in their therapeutic performance if appropriately motivated and guided along the lines of understanding and technic which have been presented.

Physicians whose attitudes expect and respect spontaneity tend to evoke self-respectful social participation more effectively than those whose attitudes tend to restrict spontaneity by preference for conventional expectations. This appears to be the basic difference in attitude between the A and B physicians.

SUMMARY

The relationship between the personality of the physician and that of the patient in determining the outcome of psychotherapy has been of interest to many investigators. Primary attention in this paper is paid to studies designed to identify qualities in the physician's personality that seem most likely to evoke favorable clinical response from schizophrenic patients. In one study, utilizing the Strong Vocational Interest Inventory, it was found that physicians scoring high in interest patterns for lawyer and Certified Public Accountant and low for printer and mathematics and physical science teacher were more successful in treating schizophrenic patients than physicians with inverse scores. A rationale for such findings is considered.

REFERENCES

1. Betz, B. J. Experiences in the psychotherapy of the obsessive-schizophrenic personality, *Southern Med. J.,* 1946, 39: 249–257.

2. Betz, B. J. A study of tactics for resolving the autistic barrier in the psychotherapy of the schizophrenic personality, *Amer. J. Psychiat.,* 1947, 104: 267–273.

3. Betz, B. J. Strategic conditions in the psychotherapy of persons with schizophrenia, *Amer. J. Psychiat.,* 1950, 107: 203–215.

4. Betz, B. J. Experiences in research in psychotherapy with schizophrenic patients, in H. H. Strupp and L. Luborsky (Eds.), *Research in Psychotherapy,* Vol. 2, Washington, D. C.: American Psychological Association, 1962, pp. 41–60.

5. Betz, B. J. Bases of therapeutic leadership in psychotherapy with the schizophrenic patient, *Amer. J. Psychother.,* 1963, 27: 196–212.

6. Betz, B. J. Differential success rates of psychotherapists with "process" and "non-process" schizophrenic patients, *Amer. J. Psychiat.,* 1963, 119: 1090–1091.

7. Betz, B. J. Validation of the differential treatment success of "A" and "B" therapists with schizophrenic patients, *Amer. J. Psychiat.,* 1963, 119: 883–884.

8. Betz, B. J. and Whitehorn, J. C. The relationship of the therapist to the outcome of therapy in schizophrenia, in American Psychiatric Association, *Research Techniques in Schizophrenia.* Washington, D. C.: American Psychiatric Association Psychiatric Research Report No. 5, 1956.

9. Carson, R. C., Harden, J., and Shows, W. D. A-B distinction and behavior in quasi-therapeutic situations, *J. Consult. Psychol.,* 1962, 28: 426–433.

10. Carson, R. C., and Klein, S. J. The A-B distinction and perception of patient characteristics. Paper read at the Southeastern Psychological Association, April, 1965.

11. Levinson, D. J. The psychotherapist's contribution to the patient's treatment career, in H. H. Strupp and L. Luborsky (Eds.), *Research in Psychotherapy,* Vol. 2. Washington, D. C.: American Psychological Association, 1962, pp. 13–24.

12. McNair, D. M., Callahan, D. M., and Lorr, M. Therapist "type" and patient response to psychotherapy. *J. consult. Psychol.,* 1962, 26: 425–429.

13. Pollack, I. W., and Kiev, A. Spatial orientation and psychotherapy: An experimental study of perception. *J. Nerv. Ment. Dis.,* 1963, 137: 93–96.

14. Stephens, J., and Astrup, C. Treatment outcome in "process" and "non-process" schizophrenics treated by "A" and "B" types of therapists. *J. Nerv. Ment. Dis.,* 1965, 140: 449–456.

15. Uhlenhuth, E. H. States of subjective distress and their modification, Personal communication on studies in process, 1965.

16. Whitehorn, J. C., and Betz, B. J. A study of psychotherapeutic relationships between physicians and schizophrenic patients, *Amer. J. Psychiat.,* 1954, 111: 321–331.

17. Whitehorn, J. C., and Betz, B. J. A comparison of psychotherapeutic relationships between physicians and schizophrenic patients when insulin is combined with psychotherapy and when psychotherapy is used alone, *Amer. J. Psychiat.,* 1957, 113: 901–910.

18. Whitehorn, J. C., and Betz, B. J. Further studies of the doctor as a crucial variable in the outcome of treatment with schizophrenic patients, *Amer. J. Psychiat.,* 1960, 117: 215–223.

PSYCHOTHERAPY RESEARCH BY EXTRAPOLATION FROM SOCIAL PSYCHOLOGY *

Arnold P. Goldstein [1]

The psychotherapy researcher engaged in the development of psychologically meaningful and experimentally testable research hypotheses has several broad classes of hypothesis-generating material available to him. Broadly speaking, the source materials most frequently utilized include, singly or in combination, (1) the researcher's own clinical experience or that reported by others, (2) theories of psychotherapy, (3) personality theories and (4) findings from other investigations of psychotherapy. This partial listing, it appears, ac-

* Reprinted with permission from the American Psychological Association. In *Journal of Counseling Psychology,* 1966, Vol. 13, pp. 38–45.

[1] Presented at the American Psychological Association convention, Los Angeles, August, 1964. This paper has been prepared in conjunction with research supported in part by MH-107201, from the National Institute of Mental Health, U. S. Public Health Service.

counts for a very large proportion of the hypothesis development sources used by contemporary investigators of the psychotherapeutic process. Much less frequent recourse is made to yet another broad class of psychological literature, material which the present paper will attempt to suggest represents a potentially fruitful source of hypotheses relevant to psychotherapy. We refer here to social-psychological research focusing upon several diverse types of two-person interactions. More concretely, we will examine what appear to be important ways of advancing our understanding of individual psychotherapy by having recourse in hypothesis building to research findings in such areas as level of aspiration, role expectations, interpersonal attraction, authoritarianism and cognitive dissonance. In a directly parallel manner, we have given expression to this research philosophy elsewhere, as it applies to group psychotherapy (Goldstein, Heller, and Sechrest, 1966). In that instance, we sought to illustrate several ways in which the focus of social psychology upon member and leader behavior and interaction in problem-solving groups appears to have much to offer the researcher interested in group psychotherapy. With reference to individual psychotherapy, however, a very small number of other non-clinical research domains have not been ignored in this extrapolatory sense, the prime example being studies of verbal operant conditioning. Krasner (1962) has provided an excellent overview of this important, if segmented development in therapy research of recent vintage, and we need not explore it further here. It may be observed, however, that while such verbal conditioning and social reinforcement findings have begun to gain the stature of an important force in some circles of contemporary therapy research, the absolute number of such studies is small, their acceptance by both practitioners and "naturalistic" therapy researchers is, unfortunately, even smaller and, more to the point of the present paper, there still remains a host of other nonclinical research areas basically untouched by the hypothesis—seeking forays of present day therapy researchers.

Thus, for the most part, researchers interested in psychotherapy and their colleagues studying social psychological phenomena have gone their separate ways, making scant reference to one another's work and, in general, ignoring what

appear to be very real opportunities for mutual feedback and stimulation. While the present paper will speak primarily to the issue of therapy researchers drawing upon findings uncovered by their social-psychologist research counterparts, we would hold that a more active two-way exchange would serve to sharpen *both* classes of research hypotheses. A few voices have been raised by others interested in improving the effectiveness of psychotherapy via recourse to extrapolation from social psychological research findings. Frank (1961), for example, comments:

> all research that deals with the dynamics of any one-to-one interpersonal relationship, such as with hypnosis, non-clinical studies of attitude change, etc., are relevant for an understanding of psychotherapy. One can reason that all these are but special instances of the dyadic relationship, therefore, the phenomena pertinent to one should be pertinent to the other. (Frank, 1961, pp. 89–90.)

Heller (1963), Krasner (1962) and Rotter (1954) have espoused a similar viewpoint, as has Shoben (1953) who raises the issue in more general terms:

> for all their important contributions, the various types of psychoanalysts and the client-centered group have, in the main, worked apart from their experimental confreres. What this means is that the "applied" science of psychotherapy has been essentially divorced from the "pure" science that presumably should most nourishingly feed it, general psychology. . . . This seems most unfortunate. Certainly medicine would not have made the striking advances it has were it not for underlying developments in physiology and biochemistry, nor would engineering be capable of its dramatic accomplishments were it not for the growth of physics. (Shoben, 1953, p. 121.)

While a limited number of therapy investigations have been responsive to the research philosophy championed by these writers, such studies have been inordinately rare—particularly in light of both the dire need for more effective means of changing patient behavior and the very slight impact to date of psychotherapy research upon clinical practice. Let us now turn, therefore, to an examination of these relevant individual therapy investigations as a first approximation toward delimiting investigative areas appropriate for such extrapolation.

EXTRAPOLATION FROM EXPECTANCY RESEARCH

Therapist and patient expectancies about the eventual therapeutic outcome (prognostic expectancies) and about the nature of their therapeutic interaction (role expectancies) form the class of process variables we wish to consider first. It is instructive to note in passing that the very choice of expectancies as a variable of interest for psychotherapy research was, for this writer, largely a function of demonstrations of its powerful influence in social-psychological and other non-clinical areas of interest. We refer here to studies of perceptual hypothesis theory (Bruner, 1941; Postman, 1951); the personality theories propounded by Kelly (1955) and Rotter (1954); level of aspiration research (Irwin, 1944; Lewin et al., 1944); Biddle's (1957) and Stogdill's (1959) expectational approach to group organization; the work of Johnson (1937), Wischner (1952) and others on stuttering; Rosenthal's (1963) experimenter bias research; Orne's (1959) studies of hypnosis; and Masling's (1960) research on situational and interpersonal aspects of psychological testing. At the most general level of abstraction, these several and diverse studies combine to clearly indicate that expectations are a powerful and far reaching determinant of human behavior.

A few early and inconclusive studies (Brady et al., 1960; Goldstein, 1962) of expectations in psychotherapy attempted to ascertain the degree of association between the amount of change which a patient anticipates will follow from his therapeutic participation, and the amount of change in himself which he or some independent source later reports as having taken place, i.e., between patient expected and perceived improvement. Level of aspiration research also seeks to describe relationships between expected and achieved performance on a task. Several LOA studies (e.g., Frank, 1941; Irwin, 1944; Kausler, 1959; Lewin et al., 1944) combine to implicitly suggest a curvilinear relationship between these two classes of variables, one in which *moderate* goal settings are associated with higher task performance than either low or high aspiration levels. Extrapolating to the therapeutic context, Goldstein and Shipman (1961) predicted and found a significant curvilinear relationship between expected and perceived patient change. Moderate prognostic expectors reported the greatest change; patients anticipating little or great change, changed least.

Our studies of the degree of patient improvement expected by the therapist, or therapist prognostic expectancies, illustrate the predictive usefulness of other social-psychological and related non-clinical research domains. Our chief interest in therapist prognostic expectancies has been in the degree to which they influence patient progress. We speak here not of "accuracy" of prognosis, but, instead, of the manner in which the therapist's anticipations regarding patient movement are communicated to the patient, influence his within therapy behavior, and in turn, the therapeutic outcome. Studies in a number of areas have rather conclusively demonstrated the degree to which persons are responsive to what is overtly or covertly expected of them. Rosenthal (1963), in his extended study of experimenter bias and, in his terms, the "social psychology of the psychological experiment" has examined the unplanned influence an experimenter's expectancies may have upon his subjects in an experimental setting. His general design involves two groups of experimenters. One group is told to expect high (or good, rapid, etc.) performance from their experimental subjects; the second set of experimenters are told to anticipate low (poor, slow, etc.) task performance from their subjects. Several of his studies indicate that subjects achieve on the experimental task at a level clearly consistent with their experimenter's expectations for their achievement—in spite of the fact that all experimenters read identical instructions to their subjects. Rosenthal's repeated demonstration of this finding across numerous types of subjects and experimental tasks makes the experimenter bias phenomenon a secure finding indeed.

Masling has demonstrated much the same phenomenon in the psychodiagnostic context. In one recent study (Masling, 1965), for example, all testers administered the Rorschach to subjects in a standardized manner. One group of experimenters had been led to believe that A (animal) responses are "good"; the other experimenters were biased in favor of H (human) responses. In spite of standardized test administration, the two groups of S's differed significantly in the number of their A and H responses, such responses being more or less frequent in a manner related to their tester's bias.

An investigation by Uhlenhuth et al. (1959) yielded essentially comparable results in the area of drug therapy. This study examined the effect of two "active" medications and placebo on anxiety reduction. Those differences in effectiveness of the three agents which did emerge were closely related to corresponding differences in expectation regarding such effectiveness which were held by the psychiatrists who administered the agents.

This same type of treatment-receiver (subject, patient, etc.) responsiveness to treatment-giver (experimenter, physician, etc.) expectancies has been demonstrated by Orne (1959) in his studies of demand characteristics associated with hypnosis induction, by Hyman et al. (1954) in their studies of interview bias effects in survey research, and by Drayer's (1956) study of reactions to the impact stage of disaster.

The generality of this expectancy-pull effect across a spectrum of research areas seems established. The question then becomes obvious, does it extend to psychotherapy? Our single attempt to date to answer this question experimentally (Goldstein, 1962) has provided confirmation of the predicted influence. We divided our experimental group patients (those receiving individual therapy) into those who perceived their problems as improving over the course of therapy and those who felt their problems had intensified. The therapists for these two patient groups were then compared in terms of their initial prognostic expectations for their patients. This comparison yielded a significant difference in favor of the therapists of the improved patients. That is, the therapists for those patients who perceived positive change in themselves over therapy, had expected significantly more patient improvement than had the therapists for those patients who perceived negative change in themselves. Thus, we find a series of research findings derived in non-therapeutic contexts converging on a prediction about the same variable as it operates in therapy, and subsequent confirmation of the prediction.

Role expectations, long a major area of research interest to the social psychologist, form the second broad class of variables focused upon by our research. Role expectation compatability or congruence between two participants in various types of interactions has been demonstrated by Cottrell (1933), Goffman (1959), Linton (1945) and others to exert a major influence on the interper-

sonal quality and outcome of the interaction. In the psychotherapy context, investigations by Appel (1960), Chance (1959) and Lennard and Bernstein (1959) all provide evidence that the therapist-patient relationship, and continuance in therapy itself, is directly influenced by the degree of role expectation compatability between therapist and patient.

Our focus thus far on investigations of expectancies in psychotherapy has attempted to illustrate two broad advantages of a research philosophy which relies for hypothesis development largely upon extrapolation from social-psychological research findings. First, there is the matter of *selection* of therapy variables for investigation. It was noted earlier that our choice of expectancies as a research variable was in large part a function of its prominence in several non-clinical research domains. Second, and at the heart of hypothesis development, is the process of *prediction*. The present paper to this point has, we feel, satisfactorily begun to demonstrate the predictive value of social-psychological and other non-clinical expectancy studies for expectancy research in psychotherapy. A third manner in which non-clinical research findings may prove useful to the therapy researcher concerns *explanation* of research findings. That is, regardless of the source of a researcher's hypotheses, his subsequent findings may best be interpretable by recourse to results derived from non-therapy studies. The finding noted earlier of an influence of therapist prognostic expectancies upon patient improvement meant, if the finding was something other than simple accuracy of prognosis on the therapist's part, that his expectancies had to be communicated to the patient. Operant conditioning research, combined with studies indicating that interpersonal attraction facilitates interpersonal communication and influence provided us with a reasonable initial explanation of the manner in which such expectational communication from therapist to patient was taking place (verbal operant conditioning) and why the patient was receptive to the therapist's expectational messages (interpersonal attraction). Naturally, matters should not be left at this point, as has often been done by learning theory explanations of psychotherapy. The non-clinical explanation must then be supported or refuted by direct research examination. In the case of the communication of expectancies explanation outlined above, a subsequent investigation (Heller and Goldstein, 1961) did, in fact, supply partially confirming evidence.

It is clear, however, that of the three related uses which the therapy researcher can make of social-psychological research findings—selection, prediction and explanation—the predictive function is the most consequential. Let us then leave the expectancy area and turn to a brief consideration of other investigations of individual therapy, all of whose hypotheses grew from social psychological research.

EXTRAPOLATION FROM OTHER INVESTIGATIVE AREAS

Several sub-areas of research interest to the social psychologist have focused attention upon the variable of interpersonal attraction. Among other uses, the small group researcher has more and more come to rely upon measures of interpersonal attraction among group members as the means of operationally defining group cohesiveness. Libo's (1953) Group Picture Impressions Test is but one of the several concrete forms this operationalization has taken. Reasoning that the therapist-patient relationship in individual psychotherapy could be conceptualized in interpersonal attraction terms, Libo (1957) modified the Picture Impressions Test and attempted to demonstrate its predictive usefulness with regard to a behavioral consequent of therapy relationships varying in quality. The Picture Impressions is a projective test consisting of four cards depicting therapy-like situations to which the client is requested to respond in a manner analogous to TAT administration. The test was administered to a series of patients immediately following their initial psychotherapeutic interview. Each story was reliably rated in terms of degree of patient attraction toward the therapist and a total attraction score derived. As Libo hypothesized, the attraction score predicted with a statistically significant degree of accuracy whether or not a patient would return for his second interview. The more attracted a patient was, in Picture Impressions terms, the more likely he was to return. Thus, not only does Libo's finding provide a degree of predictive validity for his Picture Impressions Test but, more important for our purposes, it demonstrates the fruitfulness of predicting to a therapy criterion which is a behavioral consequent of the therapy

relationship from what has been an essentially social psychological construct, i.e., interpersonal attraction.

Heller and Goldstein (1961) provided a second such demonstration with the interpersonal attraction variable. In this study support was obtained for the prediction of a significant positive relationship between patient attraction toward the therapist, defined in Picture Impressions terms, and (a) patient pre-therapy dependency and (b) patient over-therapy movement toward independence. With the therapist-patient relationship occupying such a central role at the heart of almost all psychotherapeutic approaches, these two studies are perhaps a beginning at indicating that defining relationship partly in terms of interpersonal attraction brings to bear upon the psychotherapy relationship a wide range of potentially useful and clarifying social-psychological research.

An investigation reported by Vogel (1961) examined the influence of therapist and patient authoritarianism upon their interpersonal relationship. This extrapolatory effort, derived from the work of Adorno et al., failed to find support for the hypothesis that therapist-patient similarity along an authoritarianism-equalitarianism dimension would enhance their therapeutic relationship. It is to be noted that although this is the only negative result we will have to report, we are not at all necessarily proposing that such failure of prediction is an infrequent event. As with any other class of research, negative results are very infrequently reported, thus the proportion of unsuccessful to successful attempts at extrapolation is unknown. Our reason for its inclusion here is to emphasize the need for extrapolation to be a selective process, and the need, when one has successfully predicted to psychotherapy from social-psychological research, to exercise caution in generalizing to other implications derived from the social-psychological area in question.

There is a second, and at least equally important, implication to be derived from Vogel's study. We noted earlier that under ideal circumstances, attempts at predicting to psychotherapeutic effects from social-psychological research would yield information which, in turn, would feed back to and aid in the clarification of the original non-therapy predictive source. Vogel's second hypothesis illustrates this feedback effect. A major, and as yet unresolved, issue in authoritarianism research concerns the behavioral consequents of authoritarian attitudes. Does a high F scale score, for example, have direct predictive significance for overt authoritarian behavior? Titus and Hollander (1957) are among the investigators of authoritarianism who raise serious doubts over the relatedness of these two classes of authoritarian expression. Christie (1954), in contrast, presents evidence indicating a marked degree of congruence in certain situations between F scale scores and overt authoritarian behavior. In a direct attempt at clarification, Vogel hypothesized that F scale scores obtained from therapists and patients would predict the extent of their within-therapy authoritarian behavior. The hypothesis was clearly supported in the case of the therapists, with results being somewhat equivocal as far as patient authoritarian attitudes and behavior were concerned. Thus, while less revealing than would have been true for more consistent results, Vogel has delimited for the social psychologist certain circumstances under which the predicted attitudinal-behavioral relationship holds.

In an analogous extrapolatory manner, Bergin (1962) has examined certain important aspects of psychotherapeutic interpretation from the perspective of cognitive dissonance research, Cutler (1958) has confirmed his predictions about counter-transference effects, using perceptual hypothesis theory as his predictive base, and Lennard and Bernstein (1960) have fruitfully brought a host of social-psychological findings and concepts to bear in their extensive investigation of psychoanalytic psychotherapy.

While there are relatively few additional therapy studies which have made predictive use of social-psychological research findings, it is of interest to note that several therapy researchers have recently begun to formulate and outline research programs of this extrapolatory type. For example, Pepinsky and Karst (1964) have underway a series of studies which center upon the variable of convergence, i.e., the gradual lessening of attitudinal and related discrepancies between patient and therapist. As the investigators note, their hypotheses derive directly from the early research on convergence and group norm setting conducted by Sherif and Asch. In analogous ways, and also oriented toward relationship aspects of the therapeutic process, Pilisuk (1963) writes of research

plans based upon cognitive balance and primary group research, Heller (1963) is utilizing research broadly describable as studies of social influence, Krasner (1959) is having recourse to investigations of role taking and related role constructs, and the present writer has underway investigations in which patient attraction to the therapist is manipulated, and later examined as it affects patient receptivity to therapist influence attempts.

In all, therefore, one can note a new brand or class of individual therapy research taking shape, research whose predictions grow in full or in part from social psychological findings. Throughout this presentation, it has been made abundantly clear that our personal conviction holds that such an extrapolatory approach offers a particularly promising path for the advance of psychotherapy. It will be further empirical findings responsive to this research approach, however, which will determine whether this substantial promise leads to an equally substantial payoff for researcher and practitioner alike.

SUMMARY

This article seeks to examine the potential usefulness of social-psychological research findings for purposes of developing research hypotheses of relevance to psychotherapy. A number of studies of individual psychotherapy are considered, particularly with regard to the manner in which they illustrate the possible rewards and hazards of such an "extrapolatory" research orientation.

REFERENCES

Appel, V. H. Client expectancies about counseling in a university counseling center. Paper presented at Western Psychol. Assoc., San Jose, Calif., April, 1960.

Asch, S. E. *Social psychology.* New York: Prentice-Hall, 1952.

Bergin, A. E. The effect of dissonant persuasive communications upon changes in a self-referring attitude. *J. Pers.,* 1962, 30: 423–438.

Biddle, B. Social expectation theory. Unpublished manuscript. November, 1957.

Brady, J. P., Reznikoff, M., and Zeller, W. W. The relationship of expectation of improvement to actual improvement of hospitalized psychiatric patients. *J. nerv. ment. Dis.,* 1960, 130: 41–44.

Bruner, J. S. Personality dynamics and the process of perceiving. In R. R. Blake and G. V. Ramsey

(Eds.) *Perception: an approach to personality.* New York: Ronald Press, 1941. Pp. 123–142.

Chance, E. *Families in treatment.* New York: Basic Books, 1959.

Christie, R., and Jahoda, M. (Eds.) *Studies in the scope and method of the authoritarian personality.* Glencoe, Ill.: Free Press, 1954.

Cottrell, L. S. Role and marital adjustment. *Publ. Amer, sociol. Soc.,* 1933, 27: 107–112.

Cutler, R. L. Countertransference effects in psychotherapy. *J. consult. Psychol.,* 1958, 22: 349–356.

Drayer, C. S. *Disaster fatigue.* Committee on Civil Defense, Amer. Psychiat. Assoc., 1956.

Frank, G. H. On the history of the objective investigation of the process of psychotherapy. *J. Psychol.,* 1961, 51: 89–95.

Frank, D. J. Recent studies of the level of aspiration. *Psychol. Bull.,* 1941, 38: 218–226.

Goffman, E. *The presentation of self in everyday life.* New York: Doubleday, 1959.

Goldstein, A. P. *Therapist-patient expectancies in psychotherapy.* New York: Pergamon Press, 1962.

Goldstein, A. P., Heller, K., and Sechrest, L. B. *Psychotherapy and the psychology of behavior change.* New York: John Wiley, 1966.

Goldstein, A. P., and Shipman, W. G. Patient's expectancies, symptom reduction, and aspects of the initial psychotherapeutic interview. *J. clin. Psychol.,* 1961, 17: 129–133.

Heller, K. Experimental analogues of psychotherapy: the clinical relevance of laboratory findings of social influence. *J. nerv. ment. Dis.,* 1963, 137: 420–426.

Heller, K., and Goldstein, A. P. Client dependency and therapist expectancy as relationship maintaining variables in psychotherapy. *J. consult. Psychol.,* 1961, 25: 371–375.

Hyman, H. H., Cobb, W. J., Feldman, J. J., Hart, C. H., and Stember, C. H. *Interviewing in social research.* Chicago: Univer. Chicago Press, 1954.

Irwin, F. W. The realism of expectations. *Psychol. Rev.,* 1944, 51: 120–126.

Johnson, W., and Sinn, A. Studies in the psychology of stuttering: 5. Frequency of stuttering with expectation of stuttering controlled. *J. sp. hear. Dis.,* 1937, 2: 98–100.

Kausler, D. H. Aspiration level as a determinant of performance. *J. Pers.,* 1959, 27: 346–351.

Kelly, G. A. *The psychology of personal constructs.* New York: W. W. Norton, 1955.

Krasner, L. Role taking research and psychotherapy. *VA res. rept.,* Palo Alto, November, 1959, No. 5.

Krasner, L. The therapist as a social reinforcement machine. In H. H. Strupp and L. Luborsky (Eds.) *Research in psychotherapy.* Washington, D. C.: American Psychological Association, 1962. Pp. 61–94.

Lennard, H. L., and Bernstein, A. *The anatomy of psychotherapy.* New York: Columbia University Press, 1960.

Lewin, K., Dembo, T., Festinger, L., and Sears, P. Level of aspiration. In J. McV. Hunt (Ed.) *Personality and the behavior disorders.* New York: Ronald Press, 1944. Pp. 333–366.

Libo, L. M. *Group-Picture-Impressions.* Ann Arbor: Univer. of Mich. Press, 1953.

Libo, L. M. The projective expression of patient-therapist attraction. *J. clin. Psychol.,* 1957, 13: 33–36.

Linton, R. *The cultural background of personality.* New York: Appleton-Century, 1945.

Masling, J. The influence of situational and interpersonal variables in projective testing. *Psychol. Bull.,* 1960, 57: 65–68.

Masling, J. Differential indoctrination of examiners and Rorschach responses. *J. consult. Psychol.,* 1965, 29: 198–201.

Orne, M. T. The nature of hypnosis: artifact and essence. *J. abnorm. soc. Psychol.,* 1959, 58: 277–299.

Pepinsky, H. B., and Karst, T. O. Convergence, a phenomenon in counseling and in psychotherapy. *Amer. Psychol.,* 1964, 19: 333–338.

Pilisuk, M. Cognitive balance, primary groups, and the patient-therapist relationship. *Behav. Sci.,* 1963, 8: 137–145.

Postman, L. Toward a general theory of cognition. In J. H. Rohrer and M. Sherif (Eds.) *Social psychology at the cross roads.* New York: Harper, 1951. Pp. 242–272.

Rosenthal, R. On the social psychology of the psychological experiment. *Amer. Scientist,* 1963, 51: 268–283.

Rotter, J. B. *Social learning and clinical psychology.* New York: Prentice-Hall, 1954.

Shoben, E. J. Some observations on psychotherapy and the learning process. In O. H. Mowrer (Ed.) *Psychotherapy, theory and research.* New York: Ronald Press, 1953. Pp. 120–139.

Stogdill, R. M. *Individual behavior and group achievement.* New York: Oxford Univer. Press, 1959.

Titus, H. E., and Hollander, E. P. The California F Scale in psychological research: 1950–1955. *Psychol. Bull.,* 1957, 54: 47–64.

Uhlenhuth, E. H., Canter, A., Neustadt, J. O., and Payson, H. E. The symptomatic relief of anxiety with meprobamate, phenobarbital and placebo. *Amer. J. Psychiat.*, 1959, 115: 905–910.

Vogel, J. L. Authoritarianism in the therapeutic relationship. *J. consult. Psychol.*, 1961, 25: 102–108.

Wischner, G. J. An experimental approach to expectancy and anxiety in stuttering behavior. *J. sp. hear. Dis.*, 1952, 17: 139–154.

EXPERIMENTAL DESENSITIZATION
OF A PHOBIA *

PETER J. LANG AND
A. DAVID LAZOVIK [1]

In recent years there has been increasing interest in the development of psychotherapeutic techniques based on learning theory models. These efforts are not limited to the translation of accepted psychotherapeutic practice into a laboratory language, in the manner of Shoben (1949) and Dollard and Miller (1950), but are attempts to extrapolate from laboratory findings to new methods of treatment. The most promising of these techniques with respect to clinical findings, is Wolpe's (1958) systematic desensitization therapy of phobic reactions. In a recent article Wolpe (1961) reported that desensitization was effective in the treatment of 35 of 39 phobic patients. Similar results have been reported by Lazarus (1961) utilizing group desensitization.

In a pilot project Lazovik and Lang (1960) demonstrated that desensitization could be successfully carried out under controlled laboratory conditions. This result opens the way not only to a more precise evaluation of treatment outcomes, but also makes it possible to test conflicting theories of the treatment process.

* Reprinted with permission from the American Psychological Association. In *Journal of Abnormal and Social Psychology*, 1963, Vol. 66, pp. 519–525.

[1] This research is supported by Grant M-3880 from the National Institute of Mental Health, United States Public Health Service. The main content of this paper was presented by A. David Lazovik at the meeting of the American Psychological Association in New York, September 1961.

According to Wolpe (1958), desensitization is effective to the extent that subjects learn to make responses to phobic objects which reciprocally inhibit (are incompatible with) fear. Specifically, the treatment is designed to substitute muscular relaxation for anxiety. It is assumed that this process—not suggestion, "hello-goodbye" effects, or transference—is the agent of behavior change. It is further assumed that explorations with the patient of the genesis of the fear are not necessary to the elimination of a phobia. Wolpe proposes that the unlearning of a phobia follows the rules of what is generally called association learning theory. He therefore expects that therapy will be more difficult, the more generalized the anxiety response, but that "symptom substitution" is not a consequence of successful behavior therapy.

A very different set of predictions would be made by psychoanalytic therapists. This frame of reference expects little positive result unless the background of the phobia and its symbolic meaning, is elucidated and worked through with the subject. If this approach is not employed, only a temporary, "transference cure" may be anticipated. It is further assumed that the difficulty of the case is related to the importance of the symptom in the individual's "psychic economy," and that its temporary removal can only lead to the substitution of some new symptom.

The current experiment is designed to evaluate these two interpretations of desensitization therapy. The procedure developed previously (Lazovik and Lang, 1960), while it submits to the rigid control of the laboratory, is nevertheless sufficiently flexible that it can be employed in the treatment of actual phobic behavior. In this experiment snake phobic individuals served as subjects. This fear was chosen because it is frequent in a college population, approximately 3 in 100 students are to some degree snake phobic, and also because of the symbolic, sexual significance attributed to this fear by psychoanalytic theory (Fenichel, 1949, p. 49). The fact that snake phobias are held to reflect conflict in more fundamental systems of the personality, suggests that this is good ground for a stringent test of behavior therapy.

Specifically, the study is designed to: evaluate the changes in snake phobic behavior that occur over time, particularly the effects of repeated exposure to the phobic object; compare these changes with those that follow systematic desensitization therapy; determine the changes in behavior that are a direct function of the desensitization process, as opposed to the independent effects (when not part of desensitization) of hypnosis, training in deep muscle relaxation, and the establishment of a good patient-therapist relationship. In addition, an attempt is made to isolate factors which determine the success or failure of this method with individual subjects.

METHOD

Systematic Desensitization

The experimental treatment consists of two sequential parts, training and desensitization proper (Lazovik and Lang, 1960). The former procedure requires five sessions of about 45 minutes each. At this time an *anxiety hierarchy* is constructed. This is a series of 20 situations involving the phobic object, which each subject grades from most to least frightening. The actual items vary from subject to subject. However, the following scenes are typical: "writing the word snake," "snakes on display at the zoo (moving within a glass case)," "stepping on a dead snake accidentally."

The subject is then trained in deep muscle relaxation, following the method presented by Jacobson (1938). He is further instructed to practice relaxation 10–15 minutes per day at home. In the final phase of the training period the subject is introduced to hypnosis, and an effort is made to teach him to visualize vividly hypnotic scenes.

Following training, there are 11 45-minute sessions of systematic desensitization. In this, the subject learns to respond with relaxation to stimuli that originally evoked anxiety. At the beginning of the first session the subject is hypnotized and instructed to relax deeply. He is then told to imagine the hierarchy item which he previously rated as least distressing—the smallest "dose" of anxiety. If relaxation is undisturbed by this experience, the subsequent item is presented. Items which induce small amounts of anxiety are repeated, followed by deep relaxation, until the subject reports he is undisturbed by the scene. In this way successive items are presented from session to session. The goal of treatment is the presentation of the item originally ranked as most frightening without impairing the individual's

calm state. At this point a new response (relaxation) has been attached to the imagined representative of the fear inducing stimulus, and clinicians working with the method assume that it will readily transfer to actual life situations.

In the experimental treatment described here, just these operations were carried out. No attempt was made to induce change through direct hypnotic suggestion, nor was an effort made to alter motivation. Subjects were informed that the experimenter was trying to evaluate a new method of treatment, and that he was much more interested in accurate findings than therapeutic successes. A majority of the therapist's actual verbalizations, as well as the step by step description of the training and desensitization procedures, was contained in a mimeographed program which guided the treatment of all subjects.

Subjects

A total of 24 subjects participated in this research. They were all college student volunteers, attending undergraduate psychology courses. The experimental groups included a total of four males and nine females. The control groups consisted of three males and eight females. None of these subjects presented evidence of a severe emotional disturbance on the basis of MMPI and interview data.

Subjects were selected on the basis of a classroom questionnaire which asked students to list their fears and rate them as mild, moderate, or intense. All subjects who participated in this experiment were afraid of nonpoisonous snakes, and rated this fear as "intense." Furthermore, the two authors interviewed all subjects who met this criterion. If despite the high self-rating on the screening questionnaire the subject's fear was judged to be weak, he was not asked to participate in the project. Subjects who formed the final experimental sample were characterized by most of the following behaviors: They reported somatic disturbance associated with the fear—"I feel sick to my stomach when I see one." "My palms get sweaty. I'm tense." They habitually avoided going anywhere near a live snake. They would not enter the reptile section of the zoo or walk through an open field. They became upset at seeing snakes at the motion pictures or on the television screen, and would leave, close their eyes, or turn off the set. Even pictures in magazines or artifacts such as a snake skin belt were capable of evoking discomfort in many of these subjects.

Measures of Phobic Behavior

All subjects filled out a Fear Survey Schedule (FSS) at the beginning and end of the experiment, and again at a 6-month follow-up evaluation. The FSS is a list of 50 phobias each of which is rated by the subjects on a 7-point scale. An estimate was thus obtained not only of the subject's snake phobia, but of other related and unrelated fears.

A direct estimate of the subject's avoidance behavior was obtained by confronting him with the phobic object. The subject was informed that a nonpoisonous snake was confined in a glass case in a nearby laboratory. He was persuaded to enter the room and describe his reactions. The snake was confined at a point 15 feet from the entrance to the room. On entering the room with the subject, the experimenter walked to the case and removed a wire grill that covered the top. The subject was assured that the snake was harmless. The experimenter then requested that the subject come over and look down at the snake as he was doing. If the subject refused, he was asked to come as close as he felt he could and the distance was recorded. If the subject was able to come all the way to the case, he was asked to touch the animal (a 5-foot black snake) after he had seen the experimenter do this. If the subject succeeded in this, the experimenter picked up the snake and invited the subject to hold it. After the avoidance test, the subject was asked to rate his anxiety on a 10-point "fear thermometer" (Walk, 1956). The subject's degree of anxiety was also rated on a 3-point scale by the experimenter.

In addition to the subjective scales and the avoidance test, all subjects were extensively interviewed concerning their fear. These interviews were tape recorded. The experimenter who conducted the interview and administered the avoidance test participated in no other phase of the project.[2]

Procedure

Following an initial interview and the administration of Form A of the Stanford Hypnotic Susceptibility Scale (SHSS; Weitzenhoffer and

[2] The authors would like to thank David Reynolds, who acted as interviewer and conducted the snake avoidance test.

Hilgard, 1959), subjects were placed in the experimental or control groups. Assignment was essentially random, although an effort was made to balance roughly these groups in terms of intensity of fear and motivation to participate in the experiment. All subjects were administered Form B of the SHSS when the experimental subjects completed the training period, and before desensitization began.

The basic plan of the study is described in Table 1. It consisted of two experimental and two control groups. The subgroups were created so that the effects of repeating the avoidance test, pretherapy training, and desensitization itself could be separately evaluated. Thus, the experimental groups E_1 and E_2 both experienced the laboratory analogue of desensitization therapy already described. However, subjects assigned to E_1 were administered the avoidance test before the training period, prior to desensitization, and again at the end of the experiment. E_2 subjects, on the other hand, were tested before desensitization and after, but did not participate in the initial evaluation. The control subjects did not participate in desensitization, but the C_1 and C_2 groups were evaluated at the same time as their opposite numbers in the

TABLE 1

DESIGN OF THE EXPERIMENT, SHOWING THE TIMES AT WHICH SUBJECTS WERE EVALUATED (the Snake Avoidance Test, Experimenter's Rating, Fear Thermometer, and Taped Interview)

Group	Experimental procedures				
E_1	Test 1	Training	Test 2	Desensitization	Test 3
E_2		Training	Test 2	Desensitization	Test 3
C_1	Test 1	—	Test 2	—	Test 3
C_2		—	Test 2	—	Test 3

experimental series. All available subjects were seen and evaluated 6 months after the termination of therapy.

Four replications of this experiment are reported here. They varied only in the therapists who were assigned to the experimental groups. Four experimental subjects and five controls participated in the first replication. The authors each saw two of the experimental subjects. In the second, third, and fourth replications (which included three, four, and two experimental subjects and two, three, and one control subjects, respectively) three other therapists participated.[3] While two of these individuals are engaged in full-time private practice, they had never before attempted desensitization therapy. The third therapist was an advanced clinical graduate student, who also had his initial experience with the desensitization method in this project.

RESULTS

Avoidance Test

The results of this test were evaluated in two ways: an absolute criterion in which touching or holding the snake constituted a test pass, and scale scores based on the subject's distance in feet from the snake. Table 2 presents the number of subjects from the separate experimental and control groups who met the former criterion.

Note that the reliability of this test is high. The control subjects show no appreciable change, even with three exposures to the snake. Furthermore, the pretherapy training period does not affect the performance of the experimental subjects: no more E_1 subjects pass at Test 2 than at Test 1. However, following therapy, the incidence of test passes goes up significantly in the experimental

TABLE 2

NUMBER OF SUBJECTS WHO HELD OR TOUCHED THE SNAKE DURING THE AVOIDANCE TEST

Group	N	Test 1	Test 2	Test 3
E_1	8	1	1	5
E_2	5	—	1	2
C_1	5	0	0	0
C_2	6	—	1	2
E_1 and E_2	13		2	7
C_1 and C_2	11		1	2

group. The percentage of increase from Test 2 to Test 3 yielded a t of 2.30, $p < .05$. A similar test of the control subjects was not significant.[4]

The above analysis does not, of course, measure subtle changes in behavior. In an attempt to increase the sensitivity of the avoidance test, subjects were assigned scores on a 19-point scale which roughly corresponded to their closest approach in feet to the phobic object. Holding the animal was equal to a scale score of 1; touching, 2; the 1-foot mark, 3; 2 feet, 4; and so on up to a score of 19 for subjects who refused to go to the testing room. The correlation between the first two presentations of the avoidance test ($N = 19$) yielded an r of $+.63$.[5] Although this statistic suggests some degree of reliability, nothing is known about the relative distance between values at different places on the scale. The control sample employed in the experiment is too small to make an adequate analysis. Nevertheless, it is logical that the probability of a positive increase in approach lessens the closer the subject is to the phobic object, i.e., movement from a score of 15 to 12 is more likely or easier than movement from a scale score of 4 (2 feet away) to a score of 1 (holding a live snake). Thus, a simple difference score does not appear to be the best estimate of change.

The change score used in the following analysis was the difference between pre- and post-therapy scale scores divided by the pre-therapy score. For example, a subject who achieved a scale score of 12 on Test 2 and a score of 5 on Test 3 was assigned a change score of .58—the solution to the equation:

$$\text{change score} = \frac{12 - 5}{12}.$$

The mean change score for the first two avoidance tests ($N = 19$) was only $+.03$. This suggests that the score has considerable stability, and tends to minimize chance fluctuations. The mean change scores for the experimental and control subjects from Test 2 to Test 3 may be found in Table 3. Note that the Mann-Whitney U test of the difference between groups is significant.

[3] The authors would like to thank Robert Romano, Richard Miller, and James Geer, who participated as therapists in this project.

[4] A live snake varies to some extent in activity, and this appears to be related to its effectiveness as a stimulus. In order to determine whether this factor influenced our results, the experimental assistant's ratings of the snake's activity during tests of the control and experimental subjects were subjected to a t test. No significant difference in snake activity for the two groups was found.

[5] The sample ($N = 19$) used in estimating the reliability of the avoidance scale and the other fear measures includes the members of the control sample plus the eight subjects of the E_1 group. Although the training period does intervene between the first and second presentations of the fear measures for the E_1 group, it appears to have no appreciable effect on the phobia. The E_2 subjects could not, of course, be included in a reliability estimate, as actual therapy intervenes between their first and second fear evaluation.

Fear Thermometer and the FSS Snake Item

The correlation between the first two tests for the reliability sample ($N = 19$) was $r = + .75$. The average difference score (obtained by subtracting the second fear thermometer score from the first) was only $+ .63$. As in the case of the avoidance test, no significant change was associated with the pre-therapy training period. The mean difference score for the E_1 group from Test 1 to Test 2 was $+.38$, less than the group mean cited above.

The difference between Test 2 and Test 3 scores for the experimental and control groups are presented at the top of Table 4. While the therapy

TABLE 3

Mean Snake Avoidance Scale Scores at Test 2 and 3, Mean Change Scores, and the Mann-Whitney U Test

Group	Test 2	Test 3	Change score	U
Experimental	5.35	4.42	.34	34.5*
Control	6.51	7.73	−.19	

*$p < .05$.

TABLE 4

Mean Rating Scale Measures of Phobic Behavior Before (Test 2) and After (Test 3) Desensitization Therapy

Group	Test 2	Test 3	Difference
	Fear thermometer		
Experimental	7.62	5.15	2.47
Control	6.45	5.45	1.00
	FSS-subject's rating of snake fear		
	Test 1[a]	Test 3	Difference
Experimental	6.69	5.31	1.38
Control	6.27	5.73	.54

[a] The FSS was not administered at Test 2. The difference score is between a pretherapy interview and Test 3.

groups show a greater mean change than the control subjects, this difference did not attain statistical significance on the Mann-Whitney U test. The same trend and statistical findings were obtained for the snake item on the FSS. The experimenter's rating of the subject's level of anxiety during the avoidance test did not differentiate between ex-

perimental and control groups. In this case, the failure to discriminate may be attributed to the selection, prior to the experiment, of a 3-point rating scale. The experimenter reported that this measure was too gross for the behavior under observation.

Follow-Up Study

All subjects who were still available ($N = 20$) were re-evaluated approximately 6 months after the experiment was completed. This included 11 members of the original experimental group, 6 of whom touched or held the snake at the final avoidance test. Two of these subjects no longer met this criterion 6 months later. However, neither subject indicated an increase in self-rated fear and one actually showed improvement on this dimension. Furthermore, because of gains by others, the mean avoidance test change score for the entire experimental group indicates a slight reduction in phobic behavior from Test 3 to the 6-month follow up.

The therapy group showed even greater gains on the fear thermometer. The increase was sufficient that the difference between experimental and control subjects from Test 2 to the follow up was statistically significant ($U = 16.5$, $p < .05$). Subjects who had experienced therapy also showed a significant reduction in their overall estimate of the intensity of their phobia as measured by the snake item of the FSS. The change in this score from pre-therapy to the 6-month follow up was significantly greater for experimental than control subjects ($U = 8.5$, $p < .02$).

Therapy Terminated and Unterminated

The design of the current experiment arbitrarily limited therapy to 11 sessions. This resulted in subjects being tested for change at varying points in the therapeutic process. Fortunately, in desensitization therapy it is possible to define a subject's degree of progress by referring to the number of hierarchy items successfully completed. It will be recalled that all subjects started with a 20-item hierarchy. This represented the combined efforts of the therapist and the subject to build an equal-interval scale, extending from a remote point where the subject felt little or no fear to a maximum fear involving close contact with the offending object. Normally, therapy would be terminated when the twentieth item had been passed. In the present experiment four subjects achieved this goal. Seven subjects completed 16 or more items and six subjects completed 14 or less items.

All subjects who completed their hierarchies touched or held the snake at the final avoidance test. Furthermore, subjects who completed over 15 items ($N = 7$) showed significant improvement on nearly all measures employed in this experiment: subjects who completed under 15 items differed little from controls. Table 5 presents the difference between the two therapy groups on the snake avoidance scale and the fear thermometer. Note that the improvement of the over 15 items group is significantly greater than that of subjects completing less than 15 items. Similar results were obtained for the FSS snake item and they are presented in Table 6. Note in this same table that the

TABLE 5

Avoidance Test Behavior Change from Test 2 to Test 3 for Therapy Subjects Who Completed More than 15 Hierarchy Items, for Those Who Completed Less than 15, and for the Mann-Whitney U Test

Number of hierarchy items successfully completed	Test 2	Test 3	Change score	U
	Snake avoidance scale			
More than 15[a]	6.71	3.93	.49	5.0**
Less than 15[b]	4.17	5.00	−.07	
	Fear thermometer			
More than 15[a]	7.57	4.00	3.57	8.0*
Less than 15[b]	7.67	6.50	1.17	

Note.—All scores are mean values.
[a] $N = 7$.
[b] $N = 6$.
* $p < .08$.
** $p < .03$.

mean rank of the FSS also shows a significantly greater reduction in the over 15 items group, than in the group completing fewer items. This finding suggests that the elimination of snake phobic behavior does not initiate an increase in other fears, but in fact leads to a significant reduction in overall anxiety.

Discussion

The results of the present experiment demonstrate that the experimental analogue of desensitization therapy effectively reduces phobic be-

TABLE 6

Changes in the Fear Survey Schedule (FSS) Following Desensitization Therapy for Subjects Who Completed More than 15 Hierarchy Items, for Those Who Completed Less than 15, and for the Mann-Whitney U Test

Number of hierarchy items successfully completed	Pre-therapy	Post-therapy	Difference	U
	Fear survey schedule			
More than 15[a]	2.34	1.85	.49	4.5*
Less than 15[b]	3.21	3.20	.01	
	FSS-subject's rating of snake fear			
More than 15[a]	6.71	4.14	2.57	3.0**
Less than 15[b]	6.67	6.67	0.00	

Note.—All scores are mean ranks or mean rank differences.
[a] $N = 7$.
[b] $N = 6$.
* $p < .02$.
** $p < .01$.

havior. Both subjective rating of fear and overt avoidance behavior were modified, and gains were maintained or increased at the 6-month follow up. The results of objective measures were in turn supported by extensive interview material. Close questioning could not persuade any of the experimental subjects that a desire to please the experimenter had been a significant factor in their change. Furthermore, in none of these interviews was there any evidence that other symptoms appeared to replace the phobic behavior.

The fact that no significant change was associated with the pre-therapy training argues that hypnosis and general muscle relaxation were not in themselves vehicles of change.[6] Similarly, the basic suggestibility of the subjects must be excluded. The difference between the SHSS Form A scores of the experimental and control groups did not approach statistical significance ($U = 58$). Clearly, the responsibility for the reduction in phobic behavior must be assigned to the desensi-

[6] While these findings indicate that hypnotizing subjects or training them in muscle relaxation are not effective independent of desensitization, we do not yet know if they are a necessary part of the desensitization process, itself. Research currently underway, in which these procedures are included or omitted in different therapy groups, is designed to answer this important question.

tization process itself. This is evidenced not only by the differences between experimental and control subjects but also by the relationship within the experimental groups between degree of change and the number of hierarchy items successfully completed.

One must still raise the question, however, why desensitization therapy could be accomplished in 11 sessions with some subjects and barely gotten underway with others. The intensity of the phobia is obviously not a relevant factor. The mean avoidance Test 2 score is actually higher for the experimental subjects who completed more than 15 items than for those who completed less (see Table 5). The base FSS snake item rank and the fear thermometer scores are almost exactly the same in both groups. On the other hand, a negative relationship ($r = -.58$) exists between the total FSS score at the first testing and the number of hierarchy items completed by individual members of the experimental group. The FSS is in turn positively related to the Taylor (1953) Manifest Anxiety (MA) scale ($r = +.80$ for the experimental group). Thus, the degree of progress attained in therapy in a constant period of time (11 sessions) appears to be a function of generalized anxiety, as measured by both the MA scale and FSS. These data suggest that desensitization therapy is more difficult, or at least slower, when many stimuli in the subject's environment are capable of eliciting anxiety responses. This is of course consistent with the clinical findings of Wolpe (1958) and the prediction of a learning theory model.

The present experiment also reveals an interesting connection between changes in overt avoidance behavior and the subject's verbal report. The relationship between these two dimensions is generally positive. However, even when precisely the same event is being evaluated, it is sometimes surprisingly low (Test 3 avoidance scale and fear thermometer $r = +.40$). Furthermore, initial changes in phobic behavior seem to occur in either one dimension or the other, rather than in both simultaneously. Most frequently subjective report lags behind overt behavior. Thus, avoidance test scores differentiated between experimental and control subjects immediately following the experiment, but it was not until the follow-up interview that the subjective scales yielded the same finding. It will be interesting to observe in future studies if this pattern continues, and to what extent it is

characteristic of any reduction in phobic behavior, or simply a function of the desensitization technique.

The question of whether learning theory, specifically counterconditioning, best explains the desensitization process is not completely answerable by the present investigation. Certainly the theory is consistent with the results, and some of the other possible explanations have been eliminated. However, further research, particularly the direct measurement of changes in muscular tension during the presentation of hierarchy items, is necessary to an evaluation of theory.

But of the greatest immediate interest are the implications of the present research for traditional theories of clinical practice. The findings suggest the following important conclusions:

1. It is not necessary to explore with a subject the factors contributing to the learning of a phobia or its "unconscious meaning" in order to eliminate the fear behavior.

2. The form of treatment employed here does not lead to symptom substitution or create new disturbances of behavior.

3. In reducing phobic behavior it is not necessary to change basic attitudes, values, or attempt to modify the "personality as a whole." The unlearning of phobic behavior appears to be analogous to the elimination of other responses from a subject's behavior repertoire.

SUMMARY

Twenty-four snake phobic Ss participated in an experimental investigation of systematic desensitization therapy. Ss who experienced desensitization showed a greater reduction in phobic behavior (as measured by avoidance behavior in the presence of the phobic object and self-ratings) than did nonparticipating controls. Ss tended to hold or increase therapy gains at a 6-month follow-up evaluation, and gave no evidence of symptom substitution.

REFERENCES

Dollard, J., and Miller, N. E. *Personality and psychotherapy: An analysis in terms of learning, thinking and culture.* New York: McGraw-Hill, 1950.

Fenichel, O. *The psychoanalytic theory of neurosis.* New York: Norton, 1945.

Jacobson, E. *Progressive relaxation.* Chicago: Univer. of Chicago Press, 1938.

Lazarus, A. A. Group therapy of phobic disorders by systematic desensitization. *J. abnorm. soc. Psychol.,* 1961, 63: 504–510.

Lazovik, A. D., and Lang, P. J. A laboratory demonstration of systematic desensitization psychotherapy. *J. psychol. Stud.,* 1960, 11: 238–247.

Shoben, E. J. Psychotherapy as a problem in learning theory. *Psychol. Bull.,* 1949, 46: 366–392.

Taylor, Janet A. A personality scale of manifest anxiety. *J. abnorm. soc. Psychol.,* 1953, 48: 285–290.

Walk, R. D. Self ratings of fear in a fear-invoking situation. *J. abnorm. soc. Psychol.,* 1956, 52: 171–178.

Weitzenhoffer, A. M., and Hilgard, E. R. *Stanford Hypnotic Susceptibility Scale.* Palo Alto, Calif.: Consulting Psychologists Press, 1959.

Wolpe, J. *Psychotherapy by reciprocal inhibition.* Stanford: Stanford Univer. Press, 1958.

Wolpe, J. The systematic desensitization treatment of neuroses. *J. nerv. ment. Dis.,* 1961, 132: 189–203.

SHORT-TERM OPERANT CONDITIONING OF ADOLESCENT OFFENDERS ON SOCIALLY RELEVANT VARIABLES *

ROBERT L. SCHWITZGEBEL [1]

The elimination or modification of unwanted behavior is a frequent goal of psychotherapy. Although assessment of psychotherapeutic effectiveness is an extremely complex matter, there seems to be rather general agreement that orthodox clinical procedures have not proven very effective in dealing with adolescent behavior disorders. One

* Reprinted with permission from the American Psychological Association. In *Journal of Abnormal Psychology,* 1967, Vol. 72, pp. 134–142.

[1] The author is indebted to the Society for the Psychological Study of Social Issues for financial assistance and to numerous graduate students at Brandeis and Harvard Universities, where this study was conducted, for volunteering their time as experimenters or judges.

of the most well-known, extensive, therapeutic and research efforts, the Cambridge-Somerville project (McCord, McCord, and Zola, 1959; Powers and Witmer, 1951), had but marginal success. An evaluation of results based on psychological tests, school adjustment reports, and court records 3 years after termination showed no significant difference between treatment and control groups.

The recidivism rate for juvenile parolees in the United States ranges from 43% to 73% of the original reformatory commitments (Arbuckle and Litwack, 1960, p. 45). Southerland and Cressey (1960, p. 43), for example, noted that about 72% of the offenders admitted to reformatory in Massachusetts in 1957 had been in correctional institutions previously. Teuber and Powers (1951) found that psychiatric treatment of delinquents resulted in no significant difference in the number of court appearances. Meese (1961) conducted a study involving younger adolescent offenders in weekly conferences with a counseling and guidance orientation. After treatment, the experimental group did significantly poorer than the control group in terms of measurable anxiety, academic achievement, and reading skill. Apparently the treatment procedures were not only unhelpful but to some extent iatrogenic. A review by Shannon (1961) concludes that

> research indicates that no group or profession has demonstrated the ability to effectively deal with deviant behavior; research shows that treatment results in no greater improvement than that which accrues by simply leaving persons with a behavioral problem alone [p. 35].

There are now over 100 published studies which have used the free operant method with humans. Several comprehensive reviews are readily available (e.g., Bandura, 1961; Bandura and Walters, 1963; Krasner, 1958). The most common S populations have been college students and psychiatric patients. The outstanding exceptions, from the point of view of the present research, have been the rare reports of studies involving criminal offenders as Ss (e.g., Cairns, 1960; Johns and Quay, 1962; Kadlub, 1956; Lykken, 1957). All of the experimental Ss in these studies were incarcerated at the time of the research, and none of the procedures had a therapeutic orientation. The large majority of human operant studies to date have been conducted in "artificial" settings (e.g., laboratory cubicles, hospital wards). This, of course, raises the question as to what extent the results and principles can be generalized to common social interactions; although Azrin, Holz, Ulrich, and Goldiamond (1961) have dramatically demonstrated that "the importance of extending the procedures of operant conditioning to 'real life' situations should not be allowed to override the elementary considerations of experimental control [pp. 29–30]." With but few exceptions, the behaviors which have been most frequently studied (e.g., plural nouns, lever pulling) may also be considered rather "nonsocial."

In 1958 a small clinical research project studying the dynamics of hostility hired seven adolescent male delinquents to participate in interviews and to take a series of psychological tests (Slack, 1960). A mutual acquaintance of the E and the delinquent, in most cases a social worker, served as a referral contact. Once the delinquent could be persuaded to come to the office a few times the probability of establishing a treatment relationship was fairly high. How to initiate cooperative attendance without the use of referrals, however, remained a problem. For this reason, the original procedure was altered by going directly into areas of high crime rate and hiring Ss from amusement centers, pool halls, and street corners (Schwitzgebel and Kolb, 1964). A storefront was established as a meeting place.

The responses of Ss were tape-recorded during each interview session, and Ss were paid the customary wage of $1.00 an hour. After six or seven interviews, it was noticed that most Ss seemed to enjoy the interviewing and testing, and thus the procedure was gradually modified toward therapeutic ends. Each S participated in an interview procedure involving psychoanalytic, client-centered, or a directive counseling orientation. The Ss were seen an average of three times a week for a period of approximately 9 months. A follow-up study of the first 20 Ss (Schwitzgebel, 1964), 3 years after termination of employment, showed that the number of arrests and months of incarceration of the employees was about one-half that of a matched control group. Casual inspection of the data suggested that the degree of "unorthodoxy," directness, and concrete expression of feelings on the part of the E—regardless of professed theoretical bias—seemed to bring about the most substantial change in S behavior. The present study was designed as a partial test of

this observation. It was hypothesized that therapeutic intervention which provided planned differential consequences for typical interview behaviors would result in different "treatment" outcomes.

METHOD

Subjects

The initial contact to recruit Ss was made by two Es who met prospective Ss, without prior knowledge or arrangement, on a street corner. The nature of the contact was informal but direct. prospective S was told that Es were from a university, that they were doing research, and that they needed people to help them with their work. It was explained that the purpose of the research was to find out what teenagers think and feel about things, how they come to have certain opinions, and how they change.

In the course of this explanation, Es would offer to take the prospective S and several of his friends to a nearby restaurant of their choice and buy them refreshments. It was made explicit, however, that one of the "qualifications" for the job and for going to the restaurant was that the person had a court or police record and, preferably, had spent some time in prison. (At this point, some Ss voluntarily produced probation cards, tattoos, knives, bicycle chains, and an accurate knowledge of the state penal system as evidence of their qualifications to serve as research Ss). Although Ss were often suspicious that Es were policemen, detectives, homosexuals, gangsters, or even escaped mental patients, they would usually go to the restaurant. Informal conversation in the restaurant about topics of the boys' interest would be followed by an invitation to visit the office.

Forty-eight Ss were employed and assigned to one of three matched groups: two experimental groups and a control group. The Ss in the experimental groups participated in 20 interviews over a period of 2–3 months. Control Ss ($N = 14$) participated in only two interviews spaced over the same amount of time. Due primarily to the inability to locate control Ss for the final interviews, the final effective N was 35. The mean age for these 35 Ss was 16.2 years with 9.1 years of completed schooling and an average of 1.4 years probation. Seven Ss had been incarcerated an average of 1.6 years.

Definition of Response Categories

To determine what specific effects social reinforcers might have, Experimental Group I ($N = 9$) received positive consequences for statements of concern (positive statements) about other people and for dependable and prompt arrival at work. Experimental Group II ($N = 12$) received negative consequences for hostile (negative) statements about people and positive consequences for socially desirable nonverbal behavior giving evidence of tact or employability.

1. Positive statements. "Positive statements" or "statements of concern" were interpreted as any verbalization of sympathy for another person or any comment raising another person's status (cf. Bales, 1950) directed toward a specific individual or individuals. For example, a general statement, such as "Us crooks are good people" (which was, in fact, made), was not scored as a positive statement. However, "Joe is a good guy," did satisfy the criterion. The scoring was done in terms of "units" rather than separate sentences or general topics. Sentences were assumed to be too difficult for a judge to count accurately, and general topics occured so infrequently that they could not provide a discriminative measurement. A "unit" was defined as any continuous series of statements (disregarding the usual conversational interruptions). If, for example, an S talked about Joe's being a "good guy" for 5 minutes, it was scored only as one unit. If, on the other hand, the S talked about Joe for several minutes, changed the topic, and then later reverted to talking about Joe, he would receive a score of two units.

2. Negative statements. Negative or hostile statements were defined as expressions showing antagonism, or which decreased another person's status. Again the verbalizations were required to refer to a particular person or persons, and were scored in units. The intention and meaning of a statement was taken into account in scoring, and not merely its structure. A statement negative in structure might be made, for example, toward a friend, but the intention and tone of it might clearly imply playfulness or even admiration. Such statements were not scored as hostile units.

3. Arrival at work. "Arrival at work" was measured by the regularity and promptness with which an S arrived at the laboratory for his interview. The Ss who arrived within 5 minutes of the appointed time were considered as having arrived on time. For Ss who arrived later, a record was made of the difference between the appointed time and the arrival time. Failure to arrive at all was assigned a value of 60 minutes, since Es were not required to wait longer than 1 hour. On this basis, an average time discrepancy was computed for each S.

4. Socially desirable behavior. "Socially desirable behavior" was measured by a standardized series of test situations presented to each S while having refreshments at a restaurant. The purpose was to measure S's social behavior in terms of general employability. The test situations included the following:

(a) Each S was told that he could order a maximum of $1.00's worth of food. The amount of food ordered and the attitude of S was observed.

(b) The E would begin playing with a small Chinese puzzle. At S's request, the puzzle would be given to S, and the total amount of time spent working on the puzzle was recorded.

(c) A small sum of money (between 25 and 40 cents) was secretly placed on the floor by E. The Ss were ranked on the basis of the amount of money retained.

(d) The S was offered the last stick of gum or the last cigarette of a pack. The Ss were grouped as to whether or not they accepted the offer.

(e) The E purchased, in addition to individual requests, food which could be shared by the group (e.g., French fried potatoes, a large pizza, potato chips). The proportion which S ate of the total amount was noted.

(f) During the initial and final interviews, Ss were invited to play what was called "the poker chip game." This game required that within a 5-minute period an S thinks of all the "bad" things he could do. For each item he named he was given a poker chip, which could be cashed in at the end of the game for 3–5 cents each. After 5 minutes had passed, the chips were counted and the earnings tallied. The S was then required to think of all the "good" things he could do. (The tasks were assigned in this order since the latter was more difficult.) One rule of the game was that negative suggestions (e.g., *don't* let the air out of tires) did not cout as a "good" behavior. It was necessary for S to think of something positive or constructive, not simply prohibitive. Again, a 5-minute limit was set, and the chips counted.

This provided, for experimental purposes, a

measurable index of *S*'s ability to "free associate" and to verbalize possible actions related to the concepts of "good" and "bad" behavior. The *S*s appeared to enjoy the game and often asked to play it again during work sessions. This was not permitted since practice effects had not been determined. A comparison of the number of chips received for each of the two tasks gave what was referred to as a "thought-count ratio." Variations in this ratio were observed before and after the employment period.

During the actual treatment or employment period, desirable social behaviors were not sharply defined in advance. The *E*s observed individual *S*s and attempted to reinforce those operants which indicated cooperativeness, tact, or sustained effort at a task. Behaviors specifically rewarded by *E*s included, for example, voluntarily picked up Coke bottles around the laboratory, leaving a note in advance when unable to come to work, returning change when accidentally overpaid, unexpectedly bringing food to share with *E,* and helping to repair a tape recorder.

Schedule and Types of Consequences

The main task assigned to each experimental *S* consisted of his talking into a tape recorder about anything he wished. The tone of the work sessions was informal and friendly, but *E*s tried to avoid giving direction to the content of the conversation. Ideally, *S* and *E* interacted in a manner best described as "client-centered counseling." The single purposeful exception to this procedure was the differential consequences following the specific behaviors previously indicated. Control *S*s received no special, planned consequences except a cash bonus following the initial interview. All experimental *S*s came to the laboratory two or three times a week for 1 hour for the required total of 20 hours.

When an *E* consciously attempted to alter the frequency of a specific behavior of an *S* by the delivery of a prescribed consequence, this constituted for this experiment a legitimate reinforcement attempt. Positive consequences consisted of verbal praise, small gifts (e.g., cigarettes, candy bars, and cash bonuses in amounts varying from 25 cents to $1.00); negative consequences were inattention and mild verbal disagreement. All reinforcement attempts were delivered on a variable interval—variable ratio schedule. It was assumed that this would be the most convenient and natural

schedule to administer, and possibly the only feasible schedule to use where *E* was also required to maintain an active interest in the content and feelings expressed by the *S* (cf. Azrin et al., 1961).

The attempt to shape dependable and prompt attendance at work among Experimental Group I *S*s may serve to illustrate the reinforcement procedure. An *S* might arrive, for example, 30 minutes late for the third meeting. The *E* would welcome him and mention that this was much better than 2 days before when he was an hour late. For the "good effort" the *S* was given a 50-cent bonus. The next appointment might find *S* arriving within 15 minutes of the scheduled time—hoping perhaps for a 75-cent bonus. The *E* would be likely to say nothing about his arrival, but the *S* might call attention to the fact and ask about his bonus. It would then be explained that an employee could always expect to receive the basic wage, but that bonuses depended entirely on the amount of money the *E* happened to have and on his feelings at the time. The *S* might be disappointed until, later that hour, he received a 50-cent bonus for, say, mentioning that he was worried about his aunt in the hospital. He might then realize that he could never be sure what he might receive a bonus for, or what the bonus would be, but the whole thing seemed to be an interesting game.

Each *S* received an average of six explicit reinforcement attempts on each of two variables. This average was depressed by the fact that many fewer negative consequences were given than positive (cf. Figures 1 and 2). At least two factors combined to account for this unintentional discrepancy. First, since the participation of the *S*s depended on their willingness to return for additional interview

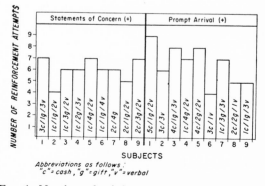

FIG. 1. Number of reinforcement attempts, Group I.

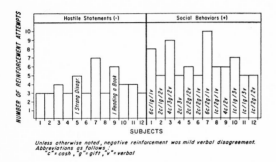

FIG. 2. Number of reinforcement attempts, Group II.

sessions, interviewers were hesitant to risk antagonizing Ss. Second, Es usually became favorably disposed toward Ss and were not inclined to intentionally apply aversive sanctions. The following excerpt, taken from an interview with a 15-year-old Negro S (Experimental Group II) several days after President Kennedy's assassination, may serve to illustrate an E's rather weak attempt to suppress an S's hostile statements.

S: I had a book report in school. We had to write about him [President Kennedy]. Now I wrote—let me see if I can remember what I said—Oh, there should have been no reason in the world why the President should have been assassinated.
E: Yes.
S: Then I said, Lee Oswald must have been crazy, you know.
E: Yes.
S: Then I put it this way. On the morning when Kennedy went to make his speech at Dallas, Texas, I myself had no idea that later on in the day he would be . . . be, you know, dead.
E: That's right, nobody did.
S: Then I said to myself, it was a blow to everybody; it was a big blow, you know what I mean?
E: Yes.
S: It hurt everybody. I wrote, Lee Oswald is dead now, right? . . . O.K., he's dead. He paid for his punishment, right?
E: No.
S: O.K., wait. Let me finish. I said to myself, he paid for his punishment. . . .
E: Yes.
S: . . . but he paid for it too easy. (S then describes various tortures he would like to have inflicted on Oswald.)
E: Yes, the other night I was thinking about that. That's the way you feel even though you know better; you still feel like this.

S: Yes. I know how his brothers feel and his wife especially. (This leads to a discussion about the Kennedy family and the funeral.)

Transfer

In order to test the effects of the attempted conditioning procedure outside the laboratory situation, various behaviors of the Ss were recorded while in a restaurant of their choosing. One of the two Es who made initial contact with a prospective S served as a "judge." The judge was primarily responsible for noting the frequency of positive and negative verbal statements of the S. The judge was expected to participate in the group, but to remain distant enough to obtain the necessary count. The other E had the major responsibility for group interaction and for noting the responses of the S to the nonverbal test situations. Postemployment testing was again done in a restaurant, the S's particular E (who served as a judge on the initial contact) was replaced by another judge. It was assumed that the presence of the S's E would be less duplicative of natural situations than the presence of a stranger. Judges were randomly assigned to Ss for postemployment testing. Theoretically, no judge was to know S's group assignment. This was practicable with experimental Ss, but since meeting control Ss was often a matter of searching, their group assignment was more obvious.

In order to test interjudge scoring reliability, eight persons who served as judges or Es were instructed in advance as to the scoring procedure. A composite tape recording was made from excerpts from the work sessions of five different pilot Ss. The length of the excerpts varied from 5 to 7 minutes and they were selected to yield different frequency counts (between 0 and 9) of positive or hostile verbal units for each S. Judges listened to the tape and independently noted the occurrences and the topics of hostile and positive statements. On the basis of the frequency of these verbal units, each judge then ranked the five Ss on the amount of expressed hostility or expressed concern. The ranking procedure aided in proving some internal check on the validity of scoring, since judges could recognize any discrepancy between the total of scored units and their general impression of a given S. On two occasions such discrepancies arose, but, for purposes of ranking, the original or uncorrected scores were utilized.

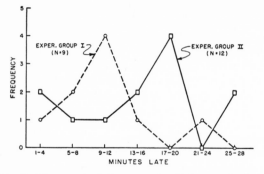

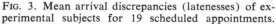

FIG. 3. Mean arrival discrepancies (latenesses) of experimental subjects for 19 scheduled appointments.

The rankings of the five Ss by the eight judges permitted an estimate of interjudge reliability as expressed by the Kendall (1948) coefficient of concordance. The Kendall W coefficient was .84 ($s = 542$) for positive units and .69 ($s = 440$) for negative units, both significant below .01 (Siegel, 1956). Informal periodic spot checks requiring two interviewers to count the number of hostile and positive units from a randomly selected 15-minute interview segment of a single S showed no significant change in reliability. In general, it was not difficult for judges to agree on what constituted a positive or a hostile statement. This particular S population is not usually given to subtlety of expression. The most difficult decisions (accounting perhaps for the somewhat lower W coefficient for hostile units) involved statements which were hostile in content but not in tone or affect. Consider, for example, the following exchange:

S_1: (Describing his being stopped by a policeman for a stolen motor scotter) . . . I told him we didn't need no permit to drive in Alabama, but he didn't believe me.

S_2: (Slowly, each word emphasized) You dumb ——! (Both laugh)

This type of expression would not formally qualify as a hostile statement although some interviewers would initially tend to score it so. This source of variance was never completely eliminated.

RESULTS

The results of the present investigation will be described by noting the effect of the conditioning procedure on (a) arrival time, (b) verbal behavior, and (c) "nonverbal" social behavior.

(a) Arrival Time. The early sessions with almost all Ss brought wide fluctuation in attendance behavior. By the sixth or eighth session differences became more apparent. On the basis of the average time discrepancy computed for each S, Experimental Group I Ss showed an average time discrepancy of 11.2 minutes. Experimental Group II Ss, not conditioned on this variable, showed a 15.6-minute discrepancy. The difference in promptness arrival between the two groups was significant in the predicted direction (Fisher test, $\alpha < .025$). Figure 3 shows the distribution of the Ss based on their mean arrival time for 19 scheduled appointments (the first hour, the initial contact, was unscheduled.) The majority of Ss from Experimental Group I lie within the first three ranges; in contrast, the majority of Experimental Group II Ss lie within the last three ranges.

(b) Verbal Behavior. The mean number of verbal units for each group of both positive and negative statements is presented in Table 1. The most clear change occurred in Experimental Group I where an average of 1.9 positive statements was made during the test period prior to employment, and an average of 4.0 statements was made after employment. A comparison of changes

TABLE 1

AVERAGE FREQUENCY OF POSITIVE AND NEGATIVE VERBAL UNITS FOR A
2–HOUR TEST PERIOD BEFORE AND AFTER EMPLOYMENT

Group	Positive				Negative			
	Before		After		Before		After	
	M	SE	M	SE	M	SE	M	SE
Experimental I	1.9	±0.6	4.0	±0.9	5.1	±0.8	3.6	±0.7
Experimental II	2.5	±0.6	2.9	±0.5	5.8	±0.7	3.8	±0.6
Control	1.8	±0.4	2.1	±0.4	5.4	±0.6	4.8	±0.5

within each group, using the Mann-Whitney test (Siegel, 1956), showed that Experimental Group I Ss had a significantly ($U = 22$, $\alpha = .047$) larger increase in positive statements after employment than did Experimental Group II Ss. A similar comparison of Experimental Group I Ss with Control Ss showed an even more significant ($U = 94.5$, $\alpha = .017$) gain for the Experimental Ss conditioned on this variable.

Experimental Group II Ss, who received negative consequences for hostile statements, showed some decrease in the average frequency of such statements. Although this decrease (from a mean of 5.8 to 3.8) was somewhat larger than in the other two groups, a comparison of the changes within the groups (Mann-Whitney test) did not permit rejection of the Null hypothesis at a significance level equal to or less than .05.

(c) Social Behaviors. Only two tests yielded significant results: the amount of food ordered and the "thought-count ratio." No other measured variable was found to distinguish the groups. The amount of time Ss spent working on a puzzle showed a wide variance (from 10 seconds to 6 minutes and 20 seconds) and no clear trend. The majority of Ss in all groups prior to employment did not accept the last cigarette or last stick of gum; this was reversed to about the same extent in all groups on the second testing. Similarly, it could not be predicted on the basis of group assignment what percentage of the money found on the floor would be appropriated by S. And the estimate of the proportion of shared food taken by S proved to be too unreliable to serve as a measure.

The average amount of food ordered by Ss before and after employment is shown in Table 2. All groups showed some increase in the amount of food ordered on the second testing; however, Experimental Group II Ss who were conditioned on social behaviors showed the least amount of increase. A comparison of changes within the groups revealed that the increase among Group II Ss was significantly less (Fisher test, $\alpha < .05$) than the increase among Control Ss.

The other measure which was apparently influenced by the treatment procedure was the "thought-count ratio." The mean scores for each group on this test are presented in Table 3. Experimental Group II Ss conditioned on socially desirable behaviors increased from 10.2 thoughts about "good" things they might do to an average of 15.6 such thoughts during the 5-minute game-like situation. This gain was significantly greater than that in the Control group ($U = 36$, $\alpha < .05$), and it also differed significantly from the slight loss which occurred in Experimental Group I ($U = 25$, $\alpha < .05$). Seemingly, the treatment procedure which rewarded positive social behaviors was capable of influencing the ability of Ss to think of ways in which they might act to another person's benefit. The treatment procedures used in the present study had no apparent effect on the frequency of thoughts about "bad" behaviors.

In summary, the treatment procedure as applied

TABLE 2
Average Amount of Food Ordered before and after Employment

Group	Before		After	
	M	SE	M	SE
Experimental I	$.65	±.05	$.77	±.07
Experimental II	.61	±.06	.64	±.06
Control	.55	±.08	.74	±.07

TABLE 3
Mean Frequencies of Thoughts about "Good" and "Bad" Behaviors as Tested in a Game Situation

Group	"Good" behaviors				"Bad" behaviors			
	Before		After		Before		After	
	M	SE	M	SE	M	SE	M	SE
Experimental I	8.8	±1.6	8.5	±1.8	18.0	±2.1	17.3	±1.8
Experimental II	10.2	±1.0	15.6	±1.6	18.3	±1.6	18.5	±1.1
Control	10.1	±0.9	11.1	±1.0	16.7	±1.3	16.9	±1.1

in this investigation resulted in significant modifications in two of the four major reinforcement categories; namely, positive statements and arrival time. The frequency of positive statements was significantly increased, and arrival at work sessions became significantly more prompt among Ss specifically conditioned on these variables. The categories of social behaviors related to employability and of hostile statements gave some indication of conditioning effects; however, they were not judged to be significant. Measurement and other procedural difficulties unfortunately complicate the interpretation of these results.

DISCUSSION

Since the frequency of positive statements and of attendance behavior was altered with an average of only six reinforcement attempts, one of the issues raised by the present study would seem to be the adequacy of a "reinforcement" interpretation of the results. It is possible that control over these two operants could have been accomplished by the informative or instructional properties rather than the rewarding or incentive properties of the prearranged consequences. Unfortunately, these alternative hypotheses were not explicitly investigated. It seems somewhat unlikely however that the instructional aspects alone account for the observed changes. The very nature of the S population suggests that these are individuals who do not respond readily to adults' instruction to be prompt for appointments or to talk kindly about other people. Both experimental groups were informed as to the next scheduled appointment and were generally aware of the desire on E's part for promptness, yet performance was significantly improved only in the group receiving consequences. Furthermore, the "burst" of appropriate behavior which often occurs when meaningful instruction or information is initially given to well-motivated Ss, did not occur in this study at the onset of the treatment phase.

The procedures of the present experiment did not permit us to specify with any certainty or preciseness what the effective variables of change were, although several other studies seem to indicate the kind of functional relationships which might be profitably investigated in the future. Ayllon and Azrin (1964), for example, investigating the differential effects of instruction and reinforcement, found that adult psychotic patients would show a sharp rise in appropriate social behavior (i.e., use of silverware at meals) when first instructed. Performance would then gradually deteriorate. Consequences without any instruction yielded steady but marginal improvement. Instruction plus contingent consequences produced a high, steady rate. Other work (e.g., Goldiamond, 1962) has demonstrated the importance of contingency relationships between operant and consequence. Speilberger, Bernstein, and Ratliff (1966) have claimed that some awareness of the correct response is necessary for verbal conditioning in adults, but that once this awareness occurs, most change is attributable to motivational factors.

The failure to obtain a more profound reduction in hostile statements or clearer transfer effects is believed to be largely a result of procedural inadequacies. Many of the tests or observations in the restaurant proved to be unreliable, and Es were somewhat hesitant to apply aversive sanctions to hostile verbal behavior during the interviews for fear that S might become angry or not return (cf. excerpt previously cited).

The results of the present study would seem to indicate the therapeutic feasibility of an environmentalistic interpretation of behavior disorders. Anna Freud (1958) has written that, among other things, adolescents are very difficult to get into treatment because they do not cooperate, they miss appointments, they are unpunctual, they cannot or will not introspect, and their rapidly changing emotional patterns leave little energy available to invest in the analyst. These behaviors may be typical, but, in this writer's opinion, can be modified without extreme difficulty. Informal observation after the present study indicated that in a few cases "trying to attend work" had not been completely extinguished even 2 months after termination of employment. One Experimental Group I S, for example, a month and a half after termination, left the following note at the laboratory.[2]

Don
    I would like you to call me Phone [deleted]. Because I would like to know if I could Get back into the Business if its okay with you
                                            Dingo

It should be noted that by the twentieth interview the attention of the E and participation in the

---

[2] Punctuation and capitalization as in original.

project seemed to become very important reinforcers for most *S*s. Arrival became more prompt in both groups, and this tended to wash out earlier group differences presumably caused by differential treatment. On the other hand, aversive sanctions (when *E*s dared to give them) seemed to become more effective, although significant group differences were never achieved.

The characteristic impulsivity ascribed to juvenile delinquents is likely influenced or determined by the particular type and schedule of reinforcements in the individual's history. To some extent, these may be explicitly programmed. Pigeons, rats, dogs, and other organisms which might normally be considered impulsive "by nature" have been successfully trained on slow-down schedules to inhibit gratification for relatively sustained periods of time. And this has been done, of course, without the advantage of any symbolic verbal control.

The fact that a series of interviews with an operant-conditioning orientation could develop dependable and prompt attendance and certain other social behaviors in juvenile delinquents may not surprise therapists familiar with experimental analysis of human learning. What is more difficult to explain, however, is why this knowledge has not been put to systematic use in the large majority of treatment programs. This may be related to a still broader problem; namely, the extent to which usual clinical assumptions about the "character structure" of delinquency is an artifact of the traditional clinical procedure itself. This should be a problem of continued and judicious investigation.

SUMMARY

Two matched groups of adolescent male delinquents, informally recruited from street corners, were differentially treated during the course of 20 tape-recorded interviews on 4 classes of operants: hostile statements, positive statements, prompt arrival at work, and general employability. Hostile statements were followed by a mild aversive consequence (i.e., disagreement or inattention) while the other selected operants were followed by a positive consequence (i.e., verbal praise or a small gift). Results in both a laboratory and a natural setting showed a significant increase in the frequency of behaviors followed by positive consequences. Attempted punishment of hostile statements, however, resulted in no significant decrease. Some clinical implications of the operant procedure are discussed.

REFERENCES

Arbuckle, D. S., and Litwack, L. A. A study of recidivism among juvenile delinquents. *Federal Probation,* 1960, 24: 44–46.

Ayllon, T., and Azrin, N. H. Reinforcement and instructions with mental patients. *Journal of Experimental Analysis of Behavior,* 1964, 7: 327–331.

Azrin, N. H., Holz, W., Ulrich, R., and Goldiamond, L. The control of the content of conversation through reinforcement. *Journal of the Experimental Analysis of Behavior,* 1961, 4: 25–30.

Bales, R. F. *Interaction process analysis.* Cambridge, Mass.: Addison-Wesley, 1950.

Bandura, A. Psychotherapy as a learning process. *Psychological Bulletin,* 1961, 58: 143–159.

Bandura, A., and Walters, R. H. *Social learning and personality development.* New York: Holt, Rinehart and Winston, 1963.

Cairns, R. The influence of dependency-anxiety on the effectiveness of social reinforcers. Unpublished doctoral dissertation, Stanford University, 1960.

Freud, A. Adolescence. In, *The psychoanalytic study of the child.* (Vol. 13) New York: International Universities Press, 1958. Pp. 255–277.

Goldiamond, I. The maintenance of ongoing fluent verbal behavior and stuttering. *Journal of Mathematics,* 1962, 1: 57–95.

Johns, J. H., and Quay, H. C. The effect of social regard on verbal conditioning in psychopathic and neurotic military offenders. *Journal of Consulting Psychology,* 1962, 26: 213–220.

Kadlub, K. The effects of two types of reinforcement on the performance of psychopathic and normal criminals. Unpublished doctoral dissertation, University of Illinois, 1956.

Kendall, M. G. *Rank correlation methods.* London: Griffin, 1948.

Krasner, L. Studies of the conditioning of verbal behavior. *Psychological Bulletin,* 1958, 55: 148–170.

Lykken, D. T. A study of anxiety in the sociopathic personality. *Journal of Abnormal and Social Psychology,* 1957, 55: 6–10.

McCord, W., McCord, J., and Zola, I. K. *Origins of crime.* New York: Columbia University Press, 1959.

Meese, B. G. An experimental program for juvenile delinquent boys. Unpublished doctoral dissertation, University of Maryland, 1961.

Powers, E., and Witmer, H. *An experiment in the prevention of delinquency.* New York: Columbia University Press, 1951.

Schwitzgebel, R. *Streetcorner research: An experimental approach to the juvenile delinquent.* Cambridge, Mass.: Harvard University Press, 1964.

Schwitzgebel, R., and Kolb, D. A. Inducing behavior change in adolescent delinquents. *Behavior Research & Therapy,* 1964, 1: 297–304.

Shannon, L. W. The problem of competence to help. *Federal Probation,* 1961, 25: 32–39.

Siegel, S. *Nonparametric statistics for the behavioral sciences.* New York: McGraw-Hill, 1956.

Slack, C. Experimenter-subject psychotherapy. *Mental Hygiene,* 1960, 44: 238–256.

Southerland, E., and Cressey, D. *Principles of criminology.* New York: Lippincott, 1960.

Spielberger, D. C., Bernstein, I. H., and Ratliff, R. G. Information and incentive value of the reinforcing stimulus in verbal conditioning. *Journal of Experimental Psychology,* 1966, 71: 26–31.

Teuber, H., and Powers, D. The effects of treatment of delinquents. *Research Publication of the Association of Nervous Mental Disorders,* 1951, 31: 139–147.

PUPIL RESPONSE OF HETERO- AND HOMOSEXUAL MALES TO PICTURES OF MEN AND WOMEN: A PILOT STUDY [*]

Eckhard H. Hess, Allan L. Seltzer, and John M. Shlien [1]

Change in the size of the pupil of the human eye has been reported to vary with a subject's interest in various pictorial stimuli (Hess and Polt,

[*] Reprinted with permission from the American Psychological Association. In *Journal of Abnormal Psychology,* 1965, Vol. 70, pp. 165–168.

[1] This research was supported in part by a grant from Social Sciences Research Committee of the University of Chicago and in part by Interpublic, New York, New York.

1960). Male subjects had a larger pupil while looking at pictures of women than when looking at pictures of men. The reverse was true for female subjects: they had larger pupils looking at men. Unpublished work with a large number of subjects has continued to substantiate the finding of this difference between the sexes.

If this difference in pupil response is truly a reflection of interest in the male or female figure as a sexual object then homosexuals would be expected to show a larger pupil response to pictures of their own sex. In the course of our work a few subjects have given a larger response to pictures of their own sex; as measured by pupil size, same-sex pictures seemed more interesting to them. Review of these anomalous cases increased the plausibility of the idea that this same-sex response might be typical of homosexuals. The present report, a pilot study of a small group of overt male homosexuals, strongly supports that hypothesis.

METHOD

Subjects

Ten young adult male subjects were tested. Five of these, students or workers in our laboratory—the heterosexual group—were well known to us over a period of several years. Their sexual outlet was judged to be exclusively heterosexual. The other five were known, through observation, interview, and in every case by their own voluntary admission to one of the authors who had gained their trust, to have overt homosexuality as their sole or primary sexual outlet. All 10 were of roughly the same age (between 24 and 34 years), same education (all but one were graduate students), and same social level. None was hospitalized or in therapy.

Procedure and Apparatus

In a dimly-lit room, a subject was seated before a viewing aperture, fitted with a headrest, which was inserted in a large plywood panel. The panel concealed the working of the apparatus from the subject. Resting his head against the aperture, the subject faced a rear-projection screen, set in an otherwise black box, at a distance of 2½ feet from his eyes. A 35-millimeter slide projector behind this screen projected a 9 × 12-inch picture onto it. Changing of slides was controlled by the experimenter from his position behind the panel where he also operated a concealed 16-millimeter camera fitted with a frame counter. As the slides were being viewed a half-silvered mirror placed at a 45-degree angle across the subject's line of vision permitted unobtrusive filming of the eye, at the rate of two frames per second. Illumination for this photography was furnished by a 100-watt bulb on rheostat control.

Stimuli

Fifteen picture slides, representations of the human figure, were shown in the following order:

Slide Content	Scoring Category
A. Painting, cubist, five figures	Art
B. Painting, realistic, crucifixion	Art
C. Painting, two nude males	Male
D. Painting, reclining female nude	Female
E. Photograph, nude man, head and upper torso	Male
F. Painting, seated nude female, rear view	Female
G. Painting, sailor, nude upper torso	Male
H. Painting, nude male and nude female	Art
I. Photograph, nude female torso	Female
J. Photograph, nude man, rear view	Male
K. Painting, nude female, head and upper torso	Female
L. Painting, two partly clothed males	Male
M. Painting, nude female, head and torso	Female
N. Painting, abstract, three figures	Art
O. Painting, cubist, three figures	Art

The presentation of each of these stimulus pictures was preceded by the presentation of a medium gray "control" slide. The total sequence was 30 slides in this order: Control A, Stimulus A, Control B, Stimulus B, etc., each shown for 10 seconds, with a total viewing time of 5 minutes for the entire sequence.

From the list of slides it can be seen that five were scored as being pictures of females and five were scored as pictures of males. The "male" pictures (C, E, G, J, and L), considered to be the homosexual equivalent of pinups, were culled from physique magazines and were generally more crude artistically than the pictures of females. These latter (D, F, I, K, and M) represented a rather lush concept of the female figure: for example, "D" was a Titian "Venus," "K" an Ingres "Odalisque."

The five "art" slides (A, B, H, N, and O) ranged in style and period from a Michelangelo to a Picasso. None of these was a clearly male or clearly "female" picture; the abstracts (A, N, and O) were ambiguous sexually, "H" showed both sexes, "B" had a strong religious connotation. This group of slides was included in the series for several reasons. Firstly, it was deemed desirable to place the sexual pictures in an artistic setting to reduce the threat to some subjects that might inhere in the obviously sexual material. Secondly, an abnormally high response is frequently given to the first stimulus shown to a subject. By placing art slides "A" and "B" first in the sequence, the male and the female slides, which were of major interest, were protected from this artifact. Thirdly, homosexuals are often thought to have artistic interests and, indeed, most of the homosexuals in this study did verbally indicate such interests. It was useful, therefore, to include a group of slides which would permit appraisal of response to the artistic quality of pictures separate from their representation of sexual objects. Such a separation of pictorial content from its artistic mode of expression appears feasible since (*a*) the homosexuals, as a group, showed a high response to the artistically good but sexually ambiguous art slides but (*b*) they also showed a high response to the artistically crude male pictures yet (*c*) they showed a low response to the artistically good female pictures. Thus, in addition to the use made of it in this report, the data point also to the potential value of the pupil technique in esthetics research.

Measurement and Scoring

The processed 16-millimeter film was projected, frame by frame, onto the underside of an opal-glass insert in a table, to a magnification of approximately 20 times. The diameter of the pupil in each frame was measured with a millimeter rule and recorded, giving a set of 20 measurements for each control presentation and a set of 20 for each stimulus. Averages were then computed for each stimulus set and for each preceding control set. In order to compare average pupil size during viewing of a picture to the pupil size during the preceding control this method was used: for each control-stimulus pair the percentage of increase or decrease in average pupil size was computed by dividing the difference between stimulus average and control average by the control average. A positive percentage indicated a larger pupil size when the subject was viewing the stimulus than when he viewed the preceding control. A negative percentage meant a smaller average pupil size during stimulus viewing. For each subject, the five percentages of his response to each of the male pictures (C, E, G, J, and L) were added together to give his "response to 'male' picture" score (Table 1, first column). The total of percentages of his response to the female pictures (D, F, I, K, and M) gave his "response to 'female' picture" score (Table 1, second column). The algebraic subtraction of each subject's male picture total from his female picture total (column two minus column one) gave each subject's relative male-female response measure (Table 1, third column). Using this order of procedure for the table, a positive figure in the third column indicates that the subject had a greater total response to pictures of females than to pictures of males; a negative figure indicates lesser response to pictures of females but greater response to pictures of males.

RESULTS

These male-female response measures clearly discriminate between the subject groups, as is shown in the last column of Table 1. Figure 1 shows this last column graphically. There is no overlap between the groups in that the lowest heterosexual response is $+06.3$ while the highest homosexual response is no higher than $+05.7$. All heterosexual males show a larger response to pictures of women than to pictures of men (positive scores). Four of the homosexuals show a larger response to pictures of men (negative scores).

DISCUSSION

Some of the female pictures drew a high-positive response from some of the homosexuals and some of the male pictures drew a high-positive response from some of the heterosexuals. Therefore, response to any single stimulus did not serve to categorize individuals. The total response of a

TABLE 1

PUPIL SIZE INCREASE OR DECREASE WHEN COMPARING STIMULI TO CONTROLS EXPRESSED IN PERCENTAGE TOTALS

Subject	Total response to 'male' pictures	Total response to 'female' pictures	Relative 'male-female' response score
Heterosexuals			
1	−00.4	+05.9	+06.3
2	−54.5	−22.4	+32.1
3	+12.5	+19.2	+06.7
4	+06.3	+39.0	+32.7
5	−01.5	+23.1	+24.6
Homosexuals			
6	+18.8	+11.2	−07.6
7	−04.6	−38.0	−33.4
8	+18.9	+18.1	−00.8
9	+18.2	−05.6	−23.8
10	+15.8	+21.5	+05.7

group of subjects to any single stimulus, however, usually served to categorize that stimulus. Total heterosexual response to three of the five female pictures was positive. Total homosexual response to each of the five male pictures was positive. The pictures used in this pilot study were chosen on an a priori basis. The information they have given us and more recent advances in our technique—especially in the matter of brightness matching of pictures—may now permit the formulation of a test battery of pictorial stimuli designed to give a more absolute reflection of a single subject's sex-object interest. It should be emphasized, however, that since *all* subjects in this study saw identical stimuli, the brightness factor could not in any way account for the reported difference between individuals and the resultant groups.

The cooperation of the homosexual subjects, it should be noted, was an unusual relaxation of their customary defense against identification as homosexuals. They were all effectively operating in a normal living environment, in school, at work, with friends. Their sexual preferences were not obvious, and they were ordinarily most reluctant to talk about or reveal them, yet the pupil technique, using a response that is nonverbal and beyond voluntary control, was able to differentiate them from the heterosexual subjects. This is not to say that the pupil response as an index of preference is a predictive substitute for the ultimate criterion of the behavior itself. It does mean that where both preference and behavior are

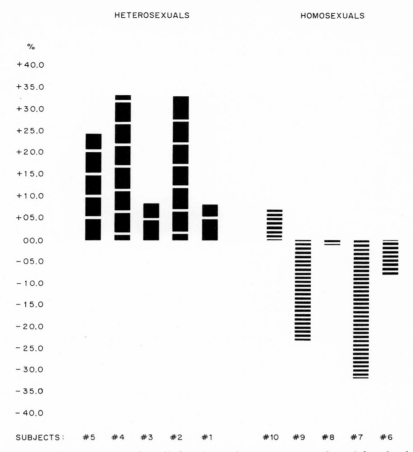

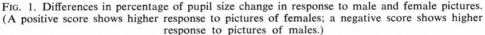

Fig. 1. Differences in percentage of pupil size change in response to male and female pictures. (A positive score shows higher response to pictures of females; a negative score shows higher response to pictures of males.)

homosexual, even though socially concealed, the pupil response has been shown in this sample to have discriminating power.

Pupil response has already seen application in the area of studies of cognition (Hess and Polt, 1964). In the study of some aspects of personality, compared with projective tests and other instruments and techniques that have been used, this technique appears to us to open up entirely new dimensions.

SUMMARY

The pupil response of each individual in a group of heterosexual males was greater when looking at pictures of women than when looking at pictures of men. Homosexual male Ss responded in the opposite direction. Measurement of changes in pupil size permitted clear-cut discrimination between the 2 groups.

REFERENCES

Hess, E. H., and Polt, J. M. Pupil size as related to interest value of visual stimuli. *Science,* 1960, 132: 349–350.

Hess, E. H., and Polt, J. M. Pupil size in relation to mental activity during simple problem-solving. *Science,* 1964, 143: 1190–1192.

TOWARD A PSYCHOLOGY OF CHANGE AND INNOVATION *

SEYMOUR B. SARASON [1]

There is an increasing number of psychologists who are interested in how organizations or social systems work and change. One of the factors in this development is the realization that all psychologists, like the rest of humanity, are affected by the different social systems of which they may be a part. This realization is frequently not due to considerations of theory or training but an awareness forced on one by virtue of day-to-day living. I suppose it is possible for a psychologist to live his days unaware that his thinking, teaching, practices, and relationships (personal or professional) bear in some way the stamp of his past and present immersion in what may be termed organizations or social systems. It is possible, and it may even be that such a person is involved as a psychologist with problems upon which this unawareness has no particular effect. Such a psychologist would likely be a researcher who at the same time that he views his research as unaffected by the workings of social systems—such as the particular department or university of which he is a member—can usually talk loud and long about how the conduct of his research has in some measure been affected by grant-giving agencies which are, after all, organizations or social systems. There are probably no important facets of a psychologist's existence which do not reflect the influence of his relationship to one or another type of organization.

I have not made the above comments because I happen to think that psychologists should have a keen sensitivity to the world in which they live. That would be as presumptuous as it would be ineffective. My comments were by saying that as psychological theorists move in the direction of stating comprehensive formulations about the determinants of human behavior they will become increasingly concerned with the nature of social

organizations, the ways in which they change, and the consequences of these changes. This development will not be a matter of choice but rather of necessity in that in reality the relationship between the individual and "organized settings" is not a matter of choice. The problem for theory is how to go beyond token gestures to these relationships, how to study and understand the extent of variations in these relationships, and how to begin to formulate generalizations which do justice to the complexities involved.[2]

Several years ago a number of colleagues and myself became interested in the processes of change in a certain social system. In the course of studying this system we became aware, as might have been predicted, how complex the processes of change were to understand and how little there was in psychological theory and practice to guide

* Reprinted with permission from the American Psychological Association. In *American Psychologist*, 1967, Vol. 22, pp. 227–233.
[1] Psi Chi (National Honor Society in Psychology) invited address at American Psychological Association, New York, September 1966.

[2] It is important to note that the problem which I am stating generally is one quite familiar to the industrial psychologist, as Stagner (1966) has made clear. "Industrial psychology has since its inception dealt with problems of man in an organization, but in its early stages gave consideration only to part of the man, and took the organization for granted. . . . Decided changes began to appear after 1950. . . . Only within the past ten years, however, has this transformation of industrial psychology been completed. People like Haire and Simon began to write about the total organization as a network of human interactions; Likert and McGregor applied new ideas of psychodynamics to the managerial role. The Survey Research Center and other research institutes began to pile up empirical evidence for the reciprocal effects of organizations and individuals.

"A look at a clutch of recent books dealing with the behavior of human beings in industrial organizations confirms my feeling that industrial psychology is no longer the step-child of theoretical and research efforts. Instead there is a good deal of sophisticated work in both theory and data-gathering. Undoubtedly some industrial psychologists of what we may call 'the old school' will protest that this new baby is no legitimate offspring of their specialty. Certainly its parentage is in doubt. Social psychology, sociology, and anthropology have made important genetic contributions; even a few psychoanalytic genes seem to have been incorporated. I would hold, nevertheless, that this new growth is truly industrial psychology, in the sense that it represents the best application of theoretical and empirical psychology to the understanding of human behavior in industrial settings." It is my point that the need for, and the problems involved in, conceptualizing comprehensively man-system relationships is not a necessity for one kind of psychologist (e.g,. school, industrial, etc.) but for any psychologist concerned with human behavior.

us. The complexity of the problem would have been more tolerable were it not for the fact that we had no conceptual framework which could serve, however tentatively, as a basis for thinking, planning, and action. It has been said that there is nothing more practical than a good theory. There are times when we would have settled for the illusory comfort of a bad theory. In any event, what follows in this paper is no more than a variety of thoughts which may serve only to convince others that the problem is important and requires thoughts better than our own.

THE PSYCHO-EDUCATIONAL CLINIC

Several years ago a Psycho-Educational Clinic was started at Yale as an integral part of our clinical training program. The origins, purposes and activities of the Clinic have been described in detail elsewhere (Sarason, Levine, Goldenberg, Cherlin, and Bennett, 1966). For the present paper it is necessary to state very briefly two of the purposes which have increasingly become the focus of our interest and concern. The first of these purposes is to describe and understand the educational setting as a social system, i.e., to view and study this setting as a subculture possessing a distinctive pattern of traditions, dynamics, and goals (Sarason, 1966). We are quite aware that this is a task far beyond the capacities of any single group of investigators. We are acutely aware that it is a task which involves almost every important problem and field in psychology. The complexity of the task in part reflects the fact that in the educational setting these problems have to be conceptualized in a way which erases artificial or arbitrary distinctions (e.g., learning, social psychology, clinical psychology, child development, etc.) and which truly reflects actual relationships. For example, it apparently (but inexplicably) makes sense to some people to talk of "curriculum" independent of who teaches it, why he teaches it, to whom he teaches it, his conceptions of children and the nature of learning, and whether or not he has had any voice in its selection or is given the freedom to depart from it. Elsewhere (Sarason, 1966) I have illustrated and discussed this problem in relation to the "new math," emphasizing the point that how a curriculum is introduced to (and even foisted upon) teachers affects children, teachers, supervisors, and the "curriculum." What I am saying is obvious to any thinking graduate student, i.e., any graduate course is a function not only of the formal curriculum for that course and the particular instructor but also of the particular department, relationships within it, and characteristics of the particular university.

The second purpose which I must briefly discuss is that we are interested in two kinds of change: that which is introduced and executed by those indigenous to the school, and that which represents primarily forces outside the social system we call a school. We know far more about the latter than the former kind of change and this is symptomatic not only of our lack of knowledge about what goes on in a school but also of the implicit assumption that it is a static and not particularly complicated kind of setting. There are many people, including most psychologists who should know better, who view the school as they do (or would) a so-called primitive society, i.e., life in it is simple, the people in it relatively uncomplicated and easy to understand, and the surface appearance of order and purpose can be taken pretty much at face value. There are times when those of us at the Psycho-Educational Clinic wish that such a view of the school setting could indeed be justified because the more we have gotten into the problem the more impressed we have become with its complexity. We sometimes look back nostalgically at the days when we could think of studying the school in terms of what seemed to be discrete problems such as learning, socialization, intellectual development, the process of teaching, the formal curriculum, and the like. This is not to say that one cannot study these discrete problems in a profitable way, but one runs the risk of becoming a prisoner of one's limited theories and methodologies. It is not always made clear that theories—containing as they do a defined but limited set of variables and their presumed relationships—constrict one's scope at the same time that they expand it. Nowhere is this more true than in the literature on the school setting.

But the school is only one of several settings in which we have been able to observe processes of change. In relation to all these settings we have also been in the role of "advice givers," a role which illuminates not only the processes of change as they are reflected in the "advice seeker" but in the advice giver as well. The remainder of this paper contains observations and thoughts about processes of change as we have seen them in the role of observer and advice giver.

Change and Implementation

Some of the most interesting and important aspects of the processes of change are revealed before the point of implementation of proposals for change. The importance of these aspects resides not only in how they affect implementation *but in the degree to which they result in no implementation at all.* It is not enough for the person interested in processes of change in various types of organizations or social systems to focus on ongoing or planned changes, although there is no question that such a focus can be a productive one. It is my contention, however, that an equally important part of the problem is the frequency of, and the contexts which surround, proposals for change which either do not get a hearing or never reach the stage of implementation. I have no doubt that these instances are far more frequent than those which reach the stage of implementation. Organization—such as a university department, a professional school, a social agency—vary tremendously among and between themselves in the degree to which proposals and ideas for change never reach the stage of discussion or implementation.

In recent months I have taken to asking members of various types of organizations what their estimate was of the relationship between proposals made and proposals implemented. The most frequent response was embarrassed silence. In some instances the embarrassment stemmed from the feeling that the question touched on something which, if pursued, would be quite revealing of that organization, and the revelation would not be very pleasant. In other instances the embarrassment was a consequence of the realization that the individual had never been aware of what was implied in the question, although I tried to ask the question without stating what I thought its implications were.

The significance of the question I have been putting to individuals may be gleaned in the following opinion: the greater the discrepancy between the frequency of proposals for change which are never implemented, and the number of proposals which are implemented, the more likely that the implemented changes over time will increasingly lose whatever innovative characteristics they may have had or were intended. In other words, the more things change on the surface the more conditions remain basically the same.

The basis for this opinion brings us back to one of the major interests of the Psycho-Educational Clinic, i.e., the culture of the school and the processes of change. It has been in relation to our work in various school systems that we have become acutely aware of how implemented changes quickly lose their innovative intent.[3] Elsewhere (Sarason, 1966) I have indicated that one of the major reasons for this self-defeating process is the tendency for change proposals to emanate from on high without taking into account the feelings and opinions of those who must implement the changes, i.e., the teachers. What I emphasized was the interpersonal turmoil which such tendencies engender and its effect on the content and goals of change. My comments, however, were in relation to the history and consequences of a single proposal for change (e.g., new math, bussing, etc.) and neglected what I now think is the more general characteristic of the system: the marked discrepancy between the number of proposals to change the system and the number of proposals actually implemented. Put in another way: The fate of any single proposal for change will be determined in part by the number of changes which have been proposed but never implemented. If this is true, my observations suggest that it is because those who have to implement any single proposal for change react to it in terms of their knowledge of and experiences with other proposals (implemented or not) for change in the system. If they are aware, rightly or wrongly, that there is a discrepancy between proposals made and implemented, and particularly if this awareness is associated with feelings of dissatisfaction, it often affects the implementation of the single proposal for change in a way so as to fulfill the prophecy that the more things change the more they remain the same. The fate of a single proposal for change cannot be understood apart from all other proposals for change if only because those who do the implementing do not understand or react to it in that way—and any theory of change and innovation must face this inescapable fact.

The above observations and formulations stemmed in part from repeated experiences in the role of advice giver in relation to personnel in the

[3] A colleague, Albert Myers, has well characterized urban school systems as the "fastest changing status quos."

school system. More candidly, they stemmed from a variety of frustrating and failure experiences in which, as I look back over them, I underestimated how much of an advice seeker's behavior reflected the system of which he was a part. I could, of course, be criticized as naïve. The point is that my naïveté reflects well the naïveté of psychological theories (e.g., learning, psychoanalytic) which do not face the fact that individual behavior always takes place in the contexts of organizations or social systems. I am not maintaining that social systems "cause" behavior. I am only maintaining that any theory which purports to explain behavior and which does not come to grips with man-system relationships is a naïve, incomplete, and mischief-producing theory.

The Advice Seeker and Advice Giver

The behavior of advice givers, like that of advice seekers, reflect man-system relationships. With increasing frequency, in ours as well as other societies, the advice giver is outside the system of the advice seeker, a fact which can markedly influence change and innovation. Put in its most concrete form the question which I would like to raise is: If somebody is interested in studying a social system (e.g., a school, a company, police department, etc.) with the intent of devising ways of changing it in some ways, and that somebody comes to you for advice and guidance, how would you go about deciding how to respond? Let us assume that you are relatively unfamiliar with the particular setting the individual wishes to study and ultimately change in some large or small way. This assumption provides an easy out for many people who feel uncomfortable thinking about problems with which they are not familiar. It may well be that these are the kinds of people who discourage students and others from getting into unfamiliar territory. I do not intend this as an *argumentum ad hominem* but as a way of stating that an unfamiliar problem—be it unfamiliar to a single advice giver or to the field at large—tends to engender reactions which serve to change the problem or to discourage the advice seeker. It is not all necessary for the unfamiliar to be threatening in some personal way to the establishment. It is often sufficient that the proposal be unfamiliar, i.e., not capable of being assimilated by prevailing attitudes toward "important" problems.

Am I straying from the question by focusing initially on the response of an individual advice giver or field to an unfamiliar problem? There are at least two reasons why I do not think I have strayed. The first reason is that the fate of any proposal for change is not unrelated to the prevailing attitudes of the field to which the advice giver belongs. Although these attitudes may not always be decisive—the situation is much too complicated to permit one to focus exclusively on a single source or variable—they can or do play a role well before the time when the proposal for change reaches the point of implementation. It needs hardly to be pointed out that these prevailing attitudes can abort the proposed change even though the change involves a setting different from that in which the prevailing attitudes are found. The second reason I do not think I have strayed from the original question is, I think, less of a glimpse of the obvious than is the first reason. The relationship between the advice seeker, on the one hand, and the advice giver or field, on the other hand, is frequently identical to the relationship between the advice seeker and the setting which is the object of change. The point here is that a proposal for change far more often than not encounters an obstacle course and its ultimate fate, by whatever criteria this may be judged, must be viewed in terms of how the proposal changed as a function of each hurdle. We are far more aware of what happens once a proposal reaches the stage of implementation than we are of what happens to the proposed change (and changer) before that stage. A psychology of change and innovation cannot neglect these preimplementation events which, in my experience, frequently have the effect of insuring that changes will take place in a way so as to preclude innovation.

An Illustrative Case

A number of years ago in New Haven an organization was started the major aim of which was to develop programs and services for the inner city or poverty population. The name of this organization is Community Progress Inc. (CPI). Anyone familiar with community action programs is well aware that CPI was one of the first of such programs and is regarded as one of the, if not *the,* most successful and comprehensive of these ventures. CPI antedates many of the Federal programs and, in fact, a number of Federal programs are modeled on what CPI has done. In our recent book (Sarason et al., 1966) we described two of CPI's most pioneering and intriguing programs and the relationship of our clinic to these programs. One of these programs is the Neighborhood Employment Center and the other is the Work Crew Program for school dropouts. Most of the employees in these programs are nonprofessional personnel who are indigenous to the area and the population served. With very few exceptions no employee had previous experience in or training for the job he was doing. It is obviously impossible for me here to describe in any detail the nature of and rationale for these programs. Suffice it to say that the titles "Neighborhood Employment Center" and "Work Crew Programs" are distressingly ineffective in communicating the seriousness, variety, and complexity of the human problems which these programs encounter, cope with, and effectively handle. By "effectively handle" we mean that there is no reason to believe that the rate of success is any less than that in more traditional helping agencies. Our opinion is that when one takes into account the nature of the population served, the rate of success is somewhat short of amazing. It sometimes has offended some of our colleagues in the mental health professions when we have said that these two programs are truly mental health programs. But how can you call them mental health programs if they do not employ psychiatrists, clinical psychologists, and social workers? The obstacles to change or innovation—both in thinking and action—are many, and words and categorical thinking will be found high on the list.

How did these programs, reflecting as they do change and innovation, come about? Before answering this question I must tell you two things about CPI. First, the mental health professions had nothing to do with the beginnings of CPI. It would be near correct to say that CPI was begun and developed by a small group of individuals who had no previous formal training to do what they subsequently did. The second fact I must tell you is that today, a few years after CPI's existence, there is not a single mental health agency in New Haven whose thinking and practices have not been changed by what CPI has developed. This is not to say that these agencies have changed in a fundamental way but rather that to a limited extent they have adapted their way of thinking to new problems and new settings. This is not true for the Psycho-Educational Clinic and I hope it will not be taken as an expression of arrogance or

presumption when I say that as in the case of those at CPI we at the Clinic are involved in problems and settings in ways which represent a deliberate break with our own pasts and professional training—as a result of which we have become quite knowledgeable about the interactions among the unfamiliar, anxiety, and resistances to change in self and others. I must add that the consequences of resistance are much less lethal to change, by which I mean here engaging in an activity one has not done before, than they are to innovation by which I mean sustaining the spirit or intent of change so that one recognizes that one has unlearned part of one's past and that the direction of one's future has thereby been influenced.

Now let us return to the original question via a fantasy I have sometimes had. Reformulated, the question is: what if CPI, as an advice seeker, came to me as an advice giver to respond to their initial plans to develop programs and services for the school dropouts and poverty population? In point of fact CPI did circulate a document containing a general statement of its aims in relation to its view of the problems with which it was to deal. This document was sent to me and I confess that I saw a lot in there that I considered presumptuous, if not grandiose, particularly in light of the fact that a program in "human renewal" was going to be attempted by people possessing no particular expertise in the dynamics of human behavior and the ways in which one goes about helping problem people. The fantasy I have had centers around the situation in which CPI learns that I think what they are planning to do is probably for the birds and that I was not prepared to give them my blessings. (In reality, of course, nobody was asking for my blessings or anything else I had to give them.) CPI comes running to my door and says, "O.K., you don't like what we want to do. You don't like the way we are thinking about the problems. What would *you* do?" That would have been the polite way they would phrase the question. The more legitimate way of phrasing the question—and fantasy is not noted for its close relation to reality—would have been: "What do you or your mental health colleagues who have not been involved with the poverty population have to suggest to us?" It is not important to relate in detail what I would have told them. Suffice it to say that what I would have recommended would have been an instance of translating an unfamiliar problem into familiar terms. I would have told them about clinics, diagnostic and treatment services, mental health professionals, and research and evaluation. The result, of course, would have been quite different from what they intended and subsequently implemented. Had they taken my advice some innovative programs which have had a pervasive and sustained effect around the country would have been scuttled, to the detriment of the populations served *and* the mental health fields.

SOME CONCLUDING COMMENTS

Social systems, large or small, are fantastically complicated. To describe and understand a single school, let alone a school system, presents staggering problems for methodology and theory. What I have attempted to do in this paper is to suggest that the complexity of these systems as well as some of their distinctive characteristics become quite clear as one focuses on how these systems change over time, particularly in relation to innovations which are sustained, or aborted, or in one or another way defeating of the aims of change. Perhaps the major import of this view is that at the same time that it illuminates features of the system it also makes clear how understanding of the behavior of the individual requires, in fact demands, conceptualization of man-system relationships. This is as true for the individual we call a psychologist as it is for anyone else. I tried to illustrate the point by focusing on the psychologist in the role of advice giver not only because the psychologist is so frequently related to processes of change in individuals or groups but because he so often is the contact point between different social systems or organizations, i.e., he illustrates the fact that processes of change frequently (if not always) involve interacting systems. An additional factor in focusing on the psychologist is that it is too easy to overlook that whatever conceptualizations we develop will have to be as relevant for psychology and psychologists as for any individual in any other social system.

At the beginning of this paper I ventured the opinion that there are probably no important facets of a psychologist's existence which do not reflect the influence of his relationship to one or another type of organization. I would at this point venture the additional hypothesis that there is not a single psychologist who has not at some time or another been involved in initiating or administering proposals for change in some organization. Whatever his role, I would predict that if we ever studied the psychologist in relation to processes of change in various types of organizations we would be impressed by two findings. First, psychologists are as good as anybody else in initiating change and as bad as everybody else in sustaining it in a way such that "the more things change the more they remain the same." Second, in relation to these changes the behavior of most psychologists will be found to be remarkably uninfluenced by knowledge of or concern for relationships between change and innovation, on the one hand, and complexity of social systems, on the other.

The distinction between processes of change and innovation as they occur in organized settings is fundamental to understanding how these settings work. It is a distinction which has profitably occupied the thinking of those interested in child development, e.g., the concept of stages implies a distinction between change and innovation. As this distinction is applied to the most important social systems with which we are or have been related, our understanding of these systems *and* the individuals in it will take on an innovative characteristic. I have no doubt that this will be particularly true in the case of the social system we call a school.

The last point brings me, finally, to a consideration to which I have only alluded earlier in this paper. One can characterize our society as one in which massive and deliberate attempts are being made to change aspects of the nature of groups, settings, and regions within as well as beyond our society. The schools, the Negro, the poverty population, Appalachia, the public mental hospital—these are only some of the more important objects of change. Being, as most of us are, for virtue and against sin we applaud and support these programs for change. We know something is being done because billions are being spent. For what it is worth, it is my opinion, based on some extensive observations, that much is being done but little of it in a way calculated to bring about changes which sustain the intent to innovate. I do not say this in the spirit of criticism, but rather as a way of suggesting that, among many reasons, two of them are: the absence of a psychology of change and innovation, and the tendency within psychology to develop molecular theories about molecular-sized problems. In relation to the latter reason it is necessary to state that however necessary it may be at times to restrict the scope of theorizing by grasping a part of the problem and sticking with it, there is the distinct danger that over time the part unwittingly becomes the whole of the problem.

REFERENCES

Sarason, S. B. The culture of the school and processes of change. Brechbill Lecture, University of Maryland School of Education, January, 1966.

Sarason, S. B., Levine, M., Goldenberg, I. I., Cherlin, D., and Bennett, E. *Psychology in community settings: Clinical, educational, vocational, social aspects.* New York: Wiley, 1966.

Stagner, R. Book review. *Contemporary Psychology,* 1966, 11: 145–150.

EDUCATIONAL TRAINING IN LOW-INCOME FAMILIES *

Oliver C. Moles, Jr.

The poor educational performance of children from low-income families has recently received much attention. They are more often retarded in subject matter comprehension and in grade level than their better-off counterparts. More of them eventually drop out of school (Lee, 1963). The possible lifetime consequences of such poor educational performance are clear in light of the increasing demand for workers with a high level of education and declining opportunities for the less educated.

Workers in various helping professions draw on a common body of knowledge about children in low-income families,[1] but tend to put different emphases on selection and interpretation. For example, educators tend to view the child's background as it affects his ability to learn, and social workers tend to view it in terms of social disabilities and social adjustment.

Since variations do exist within the low-income stratum, the findings to be reported represent general tendencies. While they do not reflect the position of all low-income families, still they point to general differences from more favored groups. This discussion will cover some of the family background factors and the child's personal characteristics which affect his educational performance. It will be organized around the impact of various lower-class child training practices on the child's intellectual skills and achievement motivation which he brings to school, and his opportunities to learn at home. Several important family educational problems are identified and intervention strategies for them are suggested. But first, it will be helpful to survey briefly the performance of children from the low-income stratum as they proceed through the educational system and out into the world of work.

The Scope of the Problem

A number of studies have shown that children from low-income families make lower scores on standardized achievement tests and are retarded in grade placement more often than their better-off counterparts.[2] As poor children grow older, their performance levels frequently decrease. They drop out of school in larger numbers than higher status children even when allowance is made for differences associated with sex, race, parents' education, and rural-urban residence. Amid this distressing picture apparently the preschool and early school years offer the greatest possibilities for intervention.

Dropouts face increased difficulties finding employment and moving to better jobs. Poor children who remain in school and want to attend college still may lack the needed financial resources and academic achievement levels. Clearly, many of the poor never reach their full potential because of educational retardation. Our society also is the loser for lack of their full productive contribution.

---

* Reprinted with permission from the author. In Irelan, Lola M. (Ed.) *Educational Training and Low Income Life Styles.* Washington, D.C.: U. S. Dept. of Health, Education, and Welfare, Welfare Administration, Division of Research, 1966.

[1] For a recent review of the child training practices of low-income families affecting child behavior in several areas including educational achievement, see Chilman, C. S., 1965. For a discussion of childhood deprivation, see Coll, B. D., 1965.

[2] The points covered in this section are discussed at greater length in Moles, O. C., Jr., 1965.

Some Dimensions of the Child's World

While it is true that many conditions contribute to the educational plight of poor children—ill health, cultural deprivation, inadequate home preparation for school, inadequate school facilities, less talented teachers, racial discrimination, diversion from school achievement by peer pressures, to mention just a few—the following discussion focuses primarily on the role of parents in molding selected characteristics of poor children which affect their educational achievement. The dimensions of the child's world which are of concern here are certain intellectual skills, motivation to succeed, and opportunities for educational training afforded by the parents. These appear to constitute an essential and interlocking set of dimensions: motivation provides the drive, and intellectual skills the technique for mastering school work, but without opportunities for practice and additional stimulation at home the best intentions and abilities cannot be completely fulfilled.

Intellectual Skills

Intellectual skills pertain to the capacity for acquiring, retaining and restructuring knowledge. This capacity may be expressed in such forms as general level of intelligence, problem-solving ability, creativity, verbal ability, and cognitive style. Among the variety of intellectual skills, none has received more attention than general intelligence. The effect of intelligence on achievement in school subjects is generally recognized, although much debate continues over the dimensions of intelligence,[3] the relative contributions of heredity and environment (Hunt, 1961) and how sound an estimate of one's intellectual ability can be obtained from intelligence tests (Davis, 1961; Sexton, 1961). Several dimensions of intelligence and kinds of intelligence tests will be discussed, but the influence of heredity and maturation are beyond the scope of this paper.[4]

Although the evidence is not all in agreement, most studies find that children who score low on intelligence tests are more likely to drop out of school than brighter students (Lee, 1963; Bowman and Matthews, 1959). Over the long term, low intelligence undoubtedly contributes to academic failure at all grade levels and to a reduced attraction to school after such failure. But what does low intelligence have to do with the low-income family?

A number of studies have shown repeatedly that after the first year or two of life children from families of lower socioeconomic status score lower on a variety of intelligence tests (Eells, Davis, Havighurst, Herrick, and Tyler, 1951; Harlem Youth Opportunities Unlimited, Inc., 1964; Sexton, 1961; Tyler, 1965). What is not so apparent is the process at work in these families which leads to differences in intelligence level. A recent study (Wolf, 1964) throws some new light on this question. Parents of fifth graders from different social classes were rated on a number of kinds of implicit and explicit educational training given to children. These included emphasis on achievement motivation, emphasis on language development, and provisions for general learning. Important variables in each area, respectively were the nature of intellectual expectations for the child, opportunities provided for enlarging his vocabulary, and other opportunities provided for learning in the home. Each cluster of variables was more highly related to I.Q. than were the social class variables—not surprisingly, since child-training practices should have more effect on children than the more remote measures of social class itself.

Deficiencies in each of these child-training areas can be found among low-income families. Low levels of education discourage parents from reading to their children. Provisions for general learning in the form of good books, travel, or even the usual household articles which impart aspects of the general American culture are restricted by inadequate income. In poverty-ridden households family conversations tend to focus on the tangible and immediate. Goals to be achieved are necessarily scaled down, and with this narrowing of outlook come reduced expectations for children's achievement.

The net effect of lower-class home environments has been described as a kind of "stimulus deprivation" in the sense of a less systematically organized and more restricted variety of stimulation. For example, adults are less likely to be competent sources of information and less inclined to encourage questions. And while there may be much noise nearby as in the urban slum, a great deal of it is not meaningful to the child and may actually promote inattention on his part. Circumstances

[3] For two views on the dimensions of intelligence see Guilford, J. P., 1956.

[4] For a discussion of the relationship of heredity to intelligence, see Hunt, J. McV., 1961.

such as these serve to inhibit intellectual growth.

Even the style of language more common to the lower working class tends to be different. In contrast to the elaborate language structure of the middle class, theirs more frequently consists primarily of short, simple, often unfinished sentences. Because it does not convey nuances of meaning, it has been termed a "public" language (Bernstein, 1961). Interaction between the lower-class child and his typically middle-class teacher is apt to be greatly hampered by the child's inability to structure ideas as precisely as is expected of him. His training simply leaves him unable to comprehend the full meaning of what the teacher says.

The restricted nature of much lower-class language may originate in the disadvantaged position of the class itself. For those who must work with their hands and usually take orders from others, there is not much inducement for abstract thinking or nuances of speech. But their children frequently pay the heavy price of isolation from the mainstream of American society. One result is a more limited ability to comprehend many intelligence tests.

Since verbal comprehension differs so much between the middle class and the lower working class, it has been suggested as a "middle-class bias" and a key to success on intelligence tests (Eells, Davis, Havighurst, Herrick, and Tyler, 1951). One experiment to test this notion demonstrated that when verbal tests were used the difference in scores between middle-class and lower-class sixth graders was greater than when non-verbal tests were used (Siller, 1957).

Besides the element of verbal comprehension, another dimension of intelligence is the ability to form concepts which refer to a number of objects in the same category. In the study just mentioned the tests concerned ability to conceptualize and to form analogies. The middle-class students performed better on both verbal and non-verbal forms of the concept formation test and used more abstractions in a vocabulary test (Siller, 1951). Other research also testifies to the greater ability of middle-class students to think abstractly.[5] This deficit of lower-class students appears to be directly associated with the concrete verbal style more generally used by their elders.

[5] Reviewed by Tyler, 1965.

The intelligence test scores of low-status children seem to decline somewhat as they grow older. Comparing third and sixth graders in Harlem, the median measured I.Q. was four points lower for the older group (Harlem Youth Opportunities Unlimited, Inc., 1964). A decrease in I.Q. was also noted between first and fifth grade samples in another study of lower-class Negro boys in New York City, although for white boys there was a slight increase (Deutsch and Brown, 1964). Other work with a great variety of intelligence test questions has demonstrated that, for white children aged 9–10, half the questions favored middle-class children, and for slightly older children (ages 13–14) this tendency was found for about 85 percent of the questions (Eells et al., 1951). Since there are more verbal items in tests for older children, the deficits in verbal comprehension and ability to form abstractions of many poor children may especially inhibit their later test performance. This may also help to explain why more poor children are retarded in the upper grades, where such abilities are more important. It should be noted, however, that the quality of teaching and school facilities has also been attacked as a source of poorer performance by older school children (Sexton, 1961; Harlem Youth Opportunities Unlimited, Inc., 1964).

Several kinds of efforts have been made to raise the I.Q. scores of poor children. In one series of experiments, test questions were rewritten so that the subject matter was more familiar to all children with the result that low-status children performed better. The tests were also read aloud to minimize reading problems, again with some effect. Short-term practice sessions likewise influenced later performance, but the reward of a theater ticket for a good score produced the most marked improvement in I.Q. scores (Haggard, 1954). Thus it appears that simply revising test questions will not produce dramatic effects, whereas tangible incentives may have more power.

In general, sustained programs with young children appear to be needed in order to capitalize on these findings and promote continued growth in intelligence. One type of program is the nursery school. In a recent study, even mentally retarded children benefited from nursery school experience tailored to their individual needs, regardless of whether the children were living in an institution or in the community (Kirk, 1958). More important, their greater acceleration in intelligence test scores continued over a period of 3–5 years after the nursery school experience, suggesting that preschool programs can have lasting effects even for children with subnormal mentality perhaps especially when educational efforts are maintained over a period of time. Since there are some indications that enrichment programs produce marked changes only among children who are disadvantaged (Tyler, 1965), more research along these lines is indicated before general conclusions can be drawn.

Still in its first year, Project Headstart has provided preschool training to many thousands of poor children across the country. While this is a much shorter and less intensive kind of training than the retarded children experienced and a systematic evaluation of the program is not yet available, early reports suggest improvement in social skills and readiness for school tasks occurring for at least some of the children.

At the school-age level, results are not so clear-cut, although many innovative programs have been started. Some are directed toward making the teacher more effective with her class through various kinds of inservice training. Other programs provide special school services to the most educationally disadvantaged, and still others operate outside of the regular school through summer classes and contacts with families at home (Research Council of the Great Cities Program for School Improvement, 1964; Passow, 1963). Most of the evaluations of these programs are still in progress. Evaluation is complicated by the variety of activities, often going on at once, which makes it difficult to isolate specific activities or practices associated with increases in measured intelligence. While these new activities are encouraging, much remains to be studied before optimal school learning environments can be designed to counteract the inadequacies of family and school, and hence lift the intellectual level of culturally disadvantaged children.

ACHIEVEMENT MOTIVATION

Children who do not perform up to the level of their intellectual capacities, the underachievers, call attention to the need to study the motivation of poor children—their motives for action, their values, goals, and the means they use to attain educational goals. While many motives may influence academic performance, one of the most relevant and best understood is the need for achievement. It has been defined by McClelland, the psychologist who has studied it most, as "competition with a standard of excellence" or behavior guided by past and prospective satisfactions or dissatisfactions over achievement (McClelland, 1953). Need for achievement is usually measured by scoring the achievement content of stories written in response to a series of ambiguous pictures. Because most of the work on the achievement motive has been done with boys we know much less about the need for achievement in girls. A few of the studies to be discussed included girls, but otherwise, the circumstances surrounding their need for achievement remained relatively unexplored.

Competition with a standard of excellence suggests competition for good grades in school. The relationship between need for achievement and school grades has been demonstrated at different ages with both sexes (Rosen, 1956; Arnold, 1962). Given this relationship, the question arises whether need for achievement is more or less prevalent among the poor. The answer is clear. Need for achievement has been found to vary by social class for adults, adolescents, and younger children (Veroff, Atkinson, Feld and Gurin, 1960; Rosen, 1956; Rosen, 1959); the poor are less motivated by need for achievement than are the middle classes. But in order to understand how being poor affects the need for achievement it is necessary first to see how need for achievement is learned and then to see how these learning situations compare to the situations common to poor families.

McClelland has summarized and interpreted a series of studies concerning the sources of need for achievement (McClelland, 1961). One study of middle-class families showed that mothers of sons with high need for achievement expected them to display independence and mastery at an earlier age than did mothers of sons with low need for achievement. Mastery was measured by asking them questions like when they expected a son to have learned "to be active and energetic in climbing, jumping and sports." The mothers of sons with high need for achievement placed fewer demands on them, but what few they did place they expected the boys to meet at an earlier age. On the other hand, the mothers of boys with low need for achievement imposed more restrictions and did not expect their sons to show independence and mastery as early.

Later work has underscored the relatively greater importance of achievement or mastery training in comparison with independence training in promoting need for achievement. In addition, mothers and fathers of boys with high need for achievement have been actually observed to set higher standards for them and to reward good performance with more supporting comments than did parents of low achieving boys (Rosen and D'Andrade, 1959).

Going one step further, there seems to be a direct relationship between the achievement values held by mothers and their own social class position: Mothers at the lowest level in each of six different ethnic groups had lower measured achievement orientations than did their higher level counterparts (Rosen, 1959). The same relationship has been observed for fathers in two different ethnic groups (Strodtbeck, 1958). But within the lower class, McClelland found no relationship between achievement training and need for achievement. Apparently when mothers stress the son's looking after himself before they stress the mastering of tasks, the boy's need for achievement is lower than when achievement is stressed first.

McClelland concluded that early mastery training promotes high need for achievement only when it does not signify generalized restrictiveness, authoritarianism, or "rejection" by parents. Thus if a boy is expected to "make decisions for himself" at an early age, this may mean either that the parents help him to become self-reliant and masterful or that they push him to take care of himself and not be a burden to the family. When it is the latter he is not apt to develop a high need for achievement because the parents are not primarily interested in his mastering tasks, only in his being out of the way.

Likewise, excessive demands and domination inhibit the development of need for achievement, probably because they frustrate the boy's own efforts toward independence achievement. This seems to be especially true for fathers although not so much the case for demanding mothers (Berkowitz, 1964). Apparently the boy feels more power-

less in dealing with a demanding father, whereas the demanding mother does not make him feel so incompetent and hence her demands promote need for achievement.

The optimum time for stressing achievement standards seems to lie between 6 and 8 years of age—not too early for the boy's ability and not too late for him to internalize the standards as his own. Meaningful differences in level of need for achievement have, however, been observed as early as five years of age.

Both domination and a push for children to take care of themselves are more common among lower status families. Over at least a twenty year period it has been observed that middle-class parents tend to be more accepting and equalitarian, and working-class parents more concerned with neatness and obedience in the children (Bronfenbrenner, 1959). Fathers who are themselves less well educated or engaged in lower status occupations are frequently more autocratic than their better-off counterparts (Elder, 1962), so the lower-class boy is more likely to have the kind of demanding father who inhibits the development of his need for achievement—although many others also report more equalitarian relations with fathers.

An earlier emphasis on having children take care of themselves also seems likely among lower-class families, especially those living in cities, for a number of reasons. Broken homes are more common, and in such homes, other things being equal, the mother must assume extra responsibilities and the children must do more for themselves. In the larger lower-class family the parents also have less time to help each child as an individual. Irregular employment and unusual working hours make it difficult for parents to develop a routine in the home and to help children at important times such as when they are getting ready for school. Finally, overcrowding forces children onto the streets to play without supervision at an early age. These kinds of conditions do not promote supervised training, let alone achievement. Instead they force children to fend for themselves—exactly the kind of situation which McClelland found produced low need for achievement.

Negroes are especially subject to these conditions, particularly the poor jobs available to them, broken homes, and overcrowded housing. These factors may in turn help to account for the fact the Negro lower-class children have scored the lowest of six different racial and ethnic groups tested on need for achievement (Rosen, 1959). But the limited opportunities for advancement probably affect all low-income families to some extent, creating an atmosphere of defeat and alienation. In a study of Italian and Jewish families, the lower the socioeconomic status of the family, the lower were the fathers' achievement values. Their values were in turn directly related to the sons' need for achievement (Strodtbeck, 1958).

The process of motivating the pupil to perform school work is sufficiently complex to necessitate some discussion of how need for achievement fits into the larger picture of overall achievement motivation. On games of skill it has been repeatedly observed that children with high need for achievement try more often to accomplish the moderately difficult task (McClelland, 1961). The children classified as low on need for achievement more often try the very easy or very hard tasks. Their successes come either with little satisfaction because the task is very easy or infrequently because the task is very difficult. Apparently a higher level of need for achievement accentuates the choice of moderately difficult tasks which provides a reasonable combination of success and satisfaction (Atkinson, 1957). On the basis of their lower need for achievement, lower-class children are likely to set less satisfying standards for themselves, aiming either too low or too high for their potential.

Another source of differences in achievement-oriented behavior is the extent to which test situations arouse need for achievement. In a comparison of working-class and middle-class seniors of both sexes in a midwestern city high school, tests of ability were administered to some who were offered money for doing well and to others who were not. For the middle-class students there was no difference in need for achievement whether the reward was present or absent, but for the working-class students the presence of the reward was associated with higher need for achievement scores. Working-class students who thought of themselves as being middle-class were not affected by the reward and behaved as the middle-class students did (Douvan, 1956). It seems that working-class students who do not identify with the middle class are likely to need additional incentives in the form of more tangible rewards before their need for achievement is fully aroused. But once it is aroused the working-class students have almost as high need for achievement scores as middle-class students.

How lasting the effects of later training might be is debatable. The general assumption with need for achievement and other motives is that they are learned early in life and thereafter remain at a relatively constant level for most people. Recent findings suggest, however, that situations can be created which will raise, perhaps for a sustained period of time, the motivation level for educationally disadvantaged children. The technique involves teaching individuals to use the same cognitive patterns as are used by others with high need for achievement. Self-confidence is reinforced while achievement motivation-related thinking is encouraged and then applied to life problems in a supportive atmosphere. The results, although not fully evaluated, point to increased striving for achievement (McClelland, 1965), and the technique is currently being applied with some culturally disadvantaged youth.[6]

Speaking abstractly, the conditions thought to produce need for achievement include an attractive goal, a moderate risk concerning the possibility of attaining it, a sense of being responsible for success or failure, and knowledge of the results of one's efforts (Atkinson, 1964). Two of these conditions, the attractiveness of different goals and a sense of personal responsibility for the outcome of one's actions, pose special problems for many lower-class youth, and sometimes for others as well.

The desirability of high academic marks is a good example. From a study of students in ten high schools in widely varying communities, being remembered as a very good student was less often seen as important than being remembered as a star athlete for boys or a popular leader for girls. Having good grades was felt less essential to getting into leading crowds than such things as being friendly, good looking and having a good reputation. When good grades were seen as important for access into the leading crowds, it ap-

[6] Personal communication from Mr. George R. Fritzinger, Human Resources Development Corporation, 56 Boylston St., Cambridge, Mass., which is promoting the Achievement Motivation Development Programs.

pears that students with ability (higher I.Q.) were more likely to achieve well in school because this behavior was rewarded by their peers (Coleman, 1961). While these findings apply to adolescents across a range of social class levels, lower status youths have additional pressures against good school performance. Their parents tend to exert less control and supervision over their activities in later childhood than do middle-class parents (Campbell, 1964). The youths themselves frequently find school work less interesting, parents less interested in their performance, and school social life less satisfying (Coster, 1958). Instead, their activities with peers seem to emphasize boy-girl relations and independence from the home (Phelps and Horrocks, 1958).

The second important obstacle to achievement motivation is a sense of personal responsibility for success or failure. A strong argument can be built to show that lower-class people feel relatively powerless to control the direction of their lives, and that this sense of powerlessness arises from the objective conditions of deprivation under which they live. The result is often a weakened sense of personal efficacy and an increased resignation and trust to chance or good luck for getting ahead (Irelan and Besner, 1966).

This is not to deny that many parents and children from lower-class families see higher education and better jobs than parents have as desirable (Chinoy, 1952; Empey, 1956; Phelps and Horrocks, 1958). They frequently do even though their middle-class counterparts more often have high aspirations (Sewell and Straus, 1957; Hyman, 1953). The aspirations of lower status parents for upward mobility for their children may serve as a substitute for parents whose own careers have fallen short of the American Dream (Chinoy, 1952). These parents are often keenly interested and sometimes more concerned than are middle-class parents about their children's achievement in early years of school (Sears, Maccoby and Levin, 1957; Greenleigh, 1965).

But the means of attaining the goal of educational achievement are likely to become eroded through the years by a number of factors including the scant opportunities for home study to be discussed in the next section. Other factors include the inability of many poor parents to supervise children, their greater distrust of intellectual pursuits (Miller and Riessman, 1961), their tendency

to emphasize job security rather than advancement (Hyman, 1953) and their children's more frequent alienation from the school and the value of good grades. As children mature but do not attain the education they need, another tragic aspect of powerlessness unfolds.

OPPORTUNITIES TO STUDY

The child's behavior is also shaped by the situation in which he finds himself. This situational dimension pertains to his opportunities for study and learning in the home. Parents have no direct influence over the child when he is at school and must depend on whatever skills and motivation he has acquired, plus the school situation, to sustain his educational performance. But in the home parents can exert much influence on the situation. Even for a child with high ability and motivation, disruptive family conditions may make study and learning difficult.

Some of the handicaps more characteristic of poor parents, such as their tendency to lack verbal ability, and the inadequate provisions for teaching children at home continue to exist long after they have made their greatest impact on the child's motivation and abilities. These and other characteristics more frequently found in low-income families are likely to act as continuing restraints against the child's use of his talents to best advantage. Even the well-motivated and skillful child from a low-income family still must contend with more limited home opportunities to practice what he is learning.

In many localities parents must buy school books and supplies for their children. On a low income this is not easy, and important supplies for studying, such as sufficient paper and pencils in the home for school work, may not be purchased. Moreover, various supplementary home learning tools such as dictionaries, educational games, and story books are beyond the reach of parents who must be concerned first with subsistence (Deutsch, 1963). At a later stage the problem looms larger when the cost of college is considered.

The size of the home is likely to impose further restraints on the opportunities to study afforded poor children. In urban slums the problem of overcrowded living space is complicated by the tendency of families to share their homes with others when finances become tight (Schorr, 1963).

Space in which children can study is scarce, and space in general is so crowded that children are apt to spend much of their time outside of the home; all this detracts from their studying.

Poor children are further handicapped in doing homework by their parents' lack of education. It is clear that poorly educated parents will have more difficulty helping their children with school work and guiding them in the use of educational resources in the community, especially in the high school years. As part of their general isolation from the rest of society, they join parent organizations less often (Sexton, 1961). With fewer voluntary school contacts by means of parent organizations and teacher conferences, low-income parents are generally less informed about both school resources and home techniques to help their children.

SUMMARY AND IMPLICATIONS

Children from low-income families are more likely to display a number of interrelated educational problems: more pupils retarded in achievement and grade placement, more school drop-outs, and fewer college students than among their better-off counterparts. Among the contributing factors, these aspects of the child's world affect educational performance: his intellectual skills, his achievement motivation, and home opportunities for study. Each tends to be underdeveloped among the lower classes.

A higher level of measured intelligence is linked to parental emphasis on the child's achievement, language development, and general learning. The limited nature of much lower class language often restricts the range of verbal comprehension, but incomplete comprehension does not fully explain the social class differences observed in intelligence test scores. Sustained programs with young children may well offer the most promising avenue toward growth in intelligence for the culturally disadvantaged.

Achievement motivation is closely tied to the need for achievement which prompts people to work for realistically difficult tasks. This need appears to be fostered by early yet supportive parental expectations for the child to master aspects of his environment. The press of other responsibilities may force lower status parents to demand self care of children in a way which does not promote need for achievement. Competing goals and a

sense of powerlessness also work to limit the educational performance of lower-class youth. New training programs offer the possibility of increasing the need for achievement even among older children and adults.

Finally, opportunities to study at home also are more likely to be limited among the lower classes by the lack of money for home educational tools, crowded living quarters, and the parents' own foreshortened education. Intellectual skills, motivation and home study opportunities are all essential to a full utilization of the instruction provided by the schools.

This is a period of experimentation with new programs designed to extricate people from the web of poverty. Fortunately, government and citizens groups have already joined hands in a number of these programs to help the poor. This is greatly needed. In a very real sense only a broad attack which helps parents to obtain dignified work, social skills, and a sense of power over their own individual and collective lives is likely to give them the money, the goals and values, the skills, and control needed to prepare their children for school more adequately.

But in a more limited sense this review also points to certain problem areas and suggests some strategies which might be employed to help low-income parents and children in the immediate area of education.[7]

1. Poor parents often lack an adequate education. Literacy programs and classes in basic communications skills can do much more than simply making people more productive and economically independent. Recent national figures suggest that the breadwinner's education is an even stronger factor than family income in predicting which children will drop out of school (Cowhig, 1960). Better educated and more self-confident parents can do a much better job of stimulating the intellectual development of their children.

2. The pre-school years can be a period of rapid intellectual growth. In order to assist parents, the provision of kindergartens, Operation Headstart,

---

[7] Some of the programs cited have already been instituted in large or small measure. For a brief summary of the Federal government's recent support of public welfare services furthering education, see: Moles, 1965. This source also describes current research on the education of lower-class children being supported by the Welfare Administration.

and at younger ages nurseries and day care centers for children of working mothers can be very useful. Here verbal comprehension can be expanded and middle-class language introduced. Even if there is no formal educational program, a variety of new learning experiences can be provided to compensate for some of the deficit of early training. As children demonstrate their competence and learn new skills from supportive teachers, their need for achievement may be strengthened. Those who have been pushed by parents to excel or who suffer from physiological defects of course cannot be helped much by this approach. Where mothers can serve as aides the transfer of learning to home situations should be increased.

3. Children from the lower classes are more apt to need additional incentives to maintain interest in school and school work. The use of tangible short-term rewards has been shown to increase both intelligence and need for achievement scores. If rewards are valued by the student's peer group they stand an even better chance of improving his educational performance. The lack of adequate school clothes and money for ordinary school activities experienced by many children from low-income families strongly detracts from willingness to continue schooling (Moles, 1966). Drop-out campaigns have been mounted, even on a national scale, with counseling to provide special services to motivate returning students. To hold culturally disadvantaged youth in school will require a new look at the opportunities which affect the different facets of achievement motivation.

4. The use of group work techniques as a means of maximizing peer support has proved helpful as part of remedial programs for older low-income children. Neighborhood action programs where mothers organize and work as leaders of other groups of mothers have shown results in bringing about reentry of school dropouts, in home-school communication, and in stimulating the educational interest of mothers.

5. Continuing interest of the caseworker in the educational achievement of the children in the family offers support and direction to the mother. Casework references to community resources are essential, as well as social work efforts in mobilizing new and needed resources for enriched social-educational experiences.

6. Innovative approaches to reach fathers in intact families are needed. Low-income family patterns make this difficult and will require new and different modes of programming.

REFERENCES

Arnold, M. B. *Story sequence analysis*. New York: Columbia University Press, 1962.

Atkinson, J. W. Motivational determinants of risk-taking behavior. *Psychological Bulletin*, 1957, 64: 359–372.

Atkinson, J. W. *An introduction to motivation*. Princeton, New Jersey: Van Nostrand, 1964.

Berkowitz, L. *The development of motives and values in the child*. New York: Basic Books, 1964.

Bernstein, B. Social class and linquistic development: A theory of social learning, in A. H. Halsey, J. Floud and C. A. Anderson (Eds.) *Education, economy and society*. New York: Free Press, 1961, pp. 288–314.

Bowman, P. H., and Matthews, C. V. *Motivations of youth for leaving school*. Chicago: University of Chicago, 1959. Mimeographed report to U. S. Office of Education on Cooperative Research Project #200.

Bronfenbrenner, U. Socialization and social class through time and space. In E. E. Maccoby, T. M. Newcomb and E. L. Hartley (Eds.) *Readings in social psychology*. New York: Holt, 1959, pp. 400–424.

Campbell, J. D. Peer relations in childhood, in M. L. Hoffman and L. W. Hoffman (Eds.) *Review of child development research*. New York: Russell Sage Foundation, 1964.

Chilman, C. S. Child-rearing and family relationship patterns of the very poor, *Welfare in Review*, 1965, 3: 9–19.

Chinoy, E. The tradition of opportunity and the aspirations of automobile workers, *American Journal of Sociology*, 1952, 62: 453–459.

Coleman, J. S. *Social climates in high schools*. Cooperative Research Monograph No. 4, Office of Education, U. S. Department of Health, Education, and Welfare, 1961.

Coll, B. D. Deprivation in childhood: Its relation to the cycle of poverty, *Welfare in Review*, 1965, 3: 1–10.

Coster, J. A. Attitudes toward school of high school pupils from three income levels, *Journal of Educational Psychology*, 1958, 49: 61–66.

Cowhig, J. D. *Characteristics of school dropouts and high school graduates, farm and non-farm,*

1960. Agricultural Economic Report No. 65. Economic Research Service, Economic and Statistical Analysis Division, U. S. Department of Agriculture, 1964.

Davis, A. Socio-economic influences upon children's learning. Speech delivered at Midcentury White House Conference on Children and Youth, Washington, D. C., December 5, 1950.

Deutsch, M. The disadvantaged child and the learning process, in A. H. Passow (Ed.) *Education in depressed areas*. New York: Columbia University, Teachers College, 1963, pp. 163–179.

Deutsch, M. and Brown, B. Social influences in negro-white intelligence differences, *Journal of Social Issues*, 1964, 20: 24–35.

Douvan, E. Social status and success strivings, *Journal of Abnormal and Social Psychology*, 1956, 52: 219–223.

Eells, K., Davis, A., Havinghurst, R. J., Herrick, V. E. and Tyler, R. *Intelligence and cultural differences*. Chicago: University of Chicago Press, 1951.

Elder, G. H. Structural variations in the child rearing relationship, *Sociometry*, 1962, 25: 241–262.

Empey, L. T. Social class and occupational aspirations: A comparison of absolute and relative measurement, *American Sociological Review*, 1956, 21: 703–709.

Greenleigh, A. *Home interview study of low-income households in Detroit, Michigan*. New York: Greenleigh Associates, Inc., 1965. Mimeographed.

Guilford, J. P. The structure of intellect, *Psychological Bulletin*, 1956, 267–293.

Haggard, E. A. Social status and intelligence: An experimental study of certain cultural determinants of measured intelligence, *Genetic Psychology Monographs*, 1954, 49: 141–186.

Harlem Youth Opportunities Unlimited, Inc. *Youth in the ghetto*. New York: Orans Press, 1964.

Hunt, J. McV. *Intelligence and experience*. New York: Ronald Press, 1961.

Hyman, H. H. The value systems of different classes, in R. Bendix and S. M. Lipset (Eds.) *Class, status and power*. Glencoe, Illinois: Free Press, 1953.

Irelan, L. and Besner, A. Low-income outlook on life in L. M. Irelan (Ed.) *Low-income life styles*, Washington, D.C.: Superintendent of Documents, U. S. Government Printing Office, 1966.

Kirk, S. A. *Early education of the mentally re-*

tarded. Urbana, Illinois: University of Illinois Press, 1958.

Lee, B. C. *Project: school dropouts*. Washington, D. C.: National Education Association, 1963. Mimeographed.

McClelland, D. C. *The achieving society*. Princeton, N. J.: Van Nostrand, 1961.

McClelland, D. C. Toward a theory of motive acquisition, *American Psychologist*, 1965, 20: 321–333.

McClelland, D. C. and others. *The achievement motive*. New York: Appleton-Century-Crofts, 1953.

Miller, S. M. and Riessman, F. The working-class subculture: A new view, *Social Problems*, 1961, 9: 86–97.

Moles, O. C., Jr. Training children in low-income families for school, *Welfare in Review*, 1965, 3: 1–11.

Passow, A. H. (Ed.) *Education in depressed areas*. New York: Columbia University, Teachers College, 1963.

Phelps, H. R. and Horrocks, J. E. Factors influencing informal groups of adolescents, *Child Development*, 1958, 29: 69–86.

Research Council of the Great Cities Program for School Improvement. *Promising practices from the projects for the culturally deprived*. Chicago: 1964.

Rosen, B. C. The achievement syndrome: A psychocultural dimension of social stratification, *American Sociological Review*, 1956, 21: 203–211.

Rosen, B. C. Race, ethnicity, and the achievement syndrome, *American Sociological Review*, 1959, 24: 47–60.

Rosen, B. C. and D'Andrade, R. G. Psychosocial origins of achievement motivations, *Sociometry*, 1959, 22: 185–218.

Schorr, A. L. *Slums and social insecurity*. Research Report No. 1. Division of Research and Statistics, Social Security Administration, 1963.

Sears, R. R., Maccoby, E. E. and Levin, H. *Patterns of child rearing*. New York: Row, Peterson, 1957.

Sewell, W. H., Haller, A. O. and Straus, M. A. Social status and educational and occupational aspirations, *American Sociological Review*, 1957, 22: 67–73.

Sexton, P. C. *Education and income*. New York: Viking Press, 1961.

Siller, J. Socioeconomic status and conceptual thinking, *Journal of Abnormal and Social Psychology*, 1957, 55: 365–371.

Strodtbeck, F. L. Family interaction, values and achievement, in D. C. McClelland, A. L. Baldwin, U. Bronfenbrenner and F. L. Strodtbeck, *Talent and society*. Princeton, N. J.: Van Nostrand, 1958.

Tyler, L. E. *The psychology of human differences*. New York: Appleton-Century-Crofts, 1965.

Veroff, J., Atkinson, J. W., Feld, S. C. and Gurin, G. *The use of thematic apperception to assess motivation in a nationwide interview study*. Psychological Monographs, Vol. 74, No. 12, No. 499, 1960.

Wolf, R. M. *The identification and measurement of environmental process variables related to intelligence*. Chicago: University of Chicago, unpublished doctoral dissertation, 1964.

HELPING DISTURBED CHILDREN: PSYCHOLOGICAL AND ECOLOGICAL STRATEGIES *

Nicholas Hobbs [1]

Honoring a long tradition, I have the privilege tonight to present to you, my colleagues in psychology, an account of my own work in recent years.[2]

I wish to present a case study in institution building, an account of a planful effort at social invention to meet an acute national problem, the problem of emotional disturbance in children.

I should like to cast this account in large con-

* Reprinted with permission from the American Psychological Association. In *American Psychologist*, 1966, Vol. 21, pp. 1105–1115.

[1] Address of the President to the Seventy-Fourth Annual Convention of the American Psychological Association, New York, September 3, 1966.

[2] The work here reported was made possible by Grant No. MH 929 of the United States Public Health Service, and by funds provided by Peabody College, the State of Tennessee, and the State of North Carolina. We are grateful for the support and wise counsel of Commissioner Joseph J. Baker and Commissioner Nat T. Winston, Jr., of Tennessee, Commissioner Eugene A. Hargrove and Sam O. Cornwell of North Carolina, Leonard J. Duhl and Raymond J. Balester of NIMH, and Paul W. Penningroth and Harold L. McPheeters of the Southern Regional Education Board.

text as an example of the kind of responsibility psychologists must assume in order to respond to a major challenge of our time: to help increase the goodness of fit between social institutions and the people they serve. This commitment demands that we invent new social arrangements designed to improve the quality of human life, and, in doing so, to adhere to the exacting traditions of psychological science: that is, to be explicit about what we are doing, to assess outcomes as meticulously as possible, to relate practice and theory to the benefit of both, and to lay our work open to public and professional scrutiny.

Let me acknowledge here that the work I report is the product of a cooperative effort to which a number of psychologists have contributed, notably Lloyd M. Dunn, Wilbert W. Lewis, William C. Rhodes, Matthew J. Trippe, and Laura Weinstein. National Institute of Mental Health officials, mental health commissioners, consultants, and especially the teacher-counselors, have invented the social institution I shall describe. If on occasion I seem unduly enthusiastic, it springs from an admiration of the work of others.

The Problem

"Project Re-ED" stands for "a project for the reeducation of emotionally disturbed children." Re-ED was developed explicitly as a new way to meet a social need for which current institutional arrangements are conspicuously inadequate. It is estimated that there are some 1½ million emotionally disturbed children in the United States today, children of average or superior intelligence whose behavior is such that they cannot be sustained with normal family, school, and community arrangements. There is one generally endorsed institutional plan for the care of such children: the psychiatric treatment unit of a hospital. But this is not a feasible solution to the problem; the costs are too great, averaging $60 a day, and there are not enough psychiatrists, psychologists, social workers, and psychiatric nurses to staff needed facilities, even if the solution were a good one, an assumption open to question. There is a real possibility that hospitals make children sick. The antiseptic atmosphere, the crepe sole and white coat, the tension, the expectancy of illness may confirm a child's worst fears about himself, firmly setting his aberrant behavior.

But worse things can happen to children, and

do. They may be sent to a state hospital to be confined on wards with psychotic adults. They may be put in a jail, euphemistically called a detention home, or committed to an institution for delinquents or for the mentally retarded; or they may be kept at home, hidden away, receiving no help at all, aggravating and being aggravated by what can become an impossible situation.

The problem is further complicated by the professional advocacy of psychotherapy as the only means of effecting changes in behavior and by the pervasive and seldom questioned assumption that it takes at least 2 years to give any substantial help to a disturbed child. Finally, the availability of locks and drugs makes children containable, and the lack of evaluative research effectively denies feedback on the adequacy of approved methods. We became convinced 8 years ago that the problem of the emotionally disturbed child cannot be solved by existing institutional arrangements. The Re-ED program was developed as one alternative, surely not the only one or even the most satisfactory one, but as a feasible alternative that deserved a test.

THE RE-ED SCHOOLS

The National Institute of Mental Health made a test possible by a demonstration grant in 1961 to Peabody College to develop residential schools for disturbed children in which concepts of reeducation could be formulated and tried out. The States of Tennessee and North Carolina, represented by their departments of mental health, joined with Peabody College to translate a general idea into an operational reality. The grant further provided for a training program to prepare a new kind of mental health worker, called a teacher-counselor, and for a research program to evaluate the effectiveness of the schools to be established.

Cumberland House Elementary School in Nashville received its first students in November of 1962, and Wright School of Durham in January of 1963. The schools are located in residential areas not far from the universities (Vanderbilt and Peabody, Duke and North Carolina) that provide personnel and consultation. They are pleasant places, open, friendly, homelike, where children can climb trees and play dodge ball, go to school, and, at night, have a good meal, and a relaxed, amiable evening.

Both schools have nearby camps that are used in the summer and on occasion throughout the year. The camps are simple, even primitive, with children erecting their own shelters, preparing their own meals, making their own schedules. For staff and children alike there is a contagious serenity about the experience. Cooking is a marvelously instructive enterprise; motivation is high, cooperation is necessary, and rewards are immediate. Children for whom failure has become an established expectation, at school and at home, can learn to do things successfully. Nature study is a source of unthreatening instruction. And there is nothing quite like a campfire, or a dark trail and a single flashlight, to promote a sense of community. In this simpler setting, where avoidant responses are few or weakly established, the child can take the first risky steps toward being a more adequate person.

At capacity each school will have 40 children, ages 6 to 12, grouped in five groups of 8 children each. Each group is the responsibility of a team of two teacher-counselors, carefully selected young people, most of whom are graduates of a 9-month training program at Peabody. The two teacher-counselors, assisted by college students and by instructors in arts and crafts and physical education, are responsible for the children around the clock. Each school has a principal and an assistant principal, both educators, a liaison department staffed by social workers and liaison teachers, and a secretarial and house-keeping staff, who are full partners in the reeducation effort. The principal of a Re-ED school has an exacting job of management, training, interpretation, and public relations. The two schools have developed under the leaderships of four able men: John R. Ball and Neal C. Buchanan at Wright School and James W. Cleary and Charles W. McDonald at Cumberland House.[3]

Of course, the teacher-counselors are the heart of Re-ED. They are young people, representing a large manpower pool, who have had experience in elementary school teaching, camping, or other work that demonstrates a long-standing commitment to children. After careful screening, in which

---

[3] So many people have worked to make Re-ED a reality it is impossible even to record their names. They will have received recompense from seeing children flourish in their care. Yet Alma B. McLain and Letha B. Rowley deserve special recognition for long service and uncommon skill and grace in managing many problems.

self-selection plays an important part, they are given 9 months of training in a graduate program leading to the Master of Arts degree. The program includes instruction in the characteristics of disturbed children, in specialized methods of teaching, including evaluation and remediation of deficits in reading, arithmetic, and other school subjects, in the use of consultants from mental health and educational fields, and in arts and crafts and games and other skills useful on the playing field, on a canoe trip, in the living units after dinner at night. They get a thorough introduction to child-serving agencies in the community and to the operation of a Re-ED school through an extensive practicum. Finally they are challenged with the task of helping invent what Re-ED will become.

But most of all a teacher-counselor is a decent adult; educated, well trained; able to give and receive affection, to live relaxed, and to be firm; a person with private resources for the nourishment and refreshment of his own life; not an itinerant worker but a professional through and through; a person with a sense of the significance of time, of the usefulness of today and the promise of tomorrow; a person of hope, quiet confidence, and joy; one who has committed himself to children and to the proposition that children who are emotionally disturbed can be helped by the process of re-education.

The total school staff, and especially the teacher-counselors who work directly with the children, are backed by a group of consultants from psychiatry, pediatrics, social work, psychology, and education, an arrangement that makes available to the schools the best professional talent in the community and that has the further attractive feature of multiplying the effectivenes of scarce and expensive mental health and educational personnel.[4]

THE CHILDREN

What kind of children do the teacher-counselors work with? It can be said, in general, that diagnostic classification has not been differentially re-

lated to a successful outcome; that the children are normal or superior in intelligence but are in serious trouble in school, often retarded 2 or 3 years in academic development; that they do not need continuing medical or nursing care, and that they can be managed in small groups in an open setting. Re-ED is not a substitute for a hospital. There are children too disturbed, too out of touch, too aggressive, too self-destructive to be worked with successfully in small groups in an open setting. However, Re-ED schools do take many children who would otherwise have to be hospitalized.

Susan was 11, with a diagnosis of childhood schizophrenia. She had attended school 1 day, the first day of the first grade, and had been in play therapy for 4 years. She was a pupil at Cumberland House for a year, staying longer than most children. She has been in a regular classroom for 3 years now, an odd child still but no longer a prospect for life-long institutionalization. Ron was a cruelly aggressive child, partly an expression of inner turmoil and partly an expression of class values and habits; he is much less destructive now, and is back in school. Danny was simply very immature, so that school was too much for him; his problem could be called school phobia if that would help. Dick was extremely effeminate, wearing mascara and painting his nails. Both boys responded to masculine activities guided by a trusted male counselor. Billy was a gasoline sniffer and an ingenious hypochondriac; he returned to a reunion recently much more mature though still having trouble with school work. Larry, age 12, was quite bright yet unable to read; nor were we able to teach him to read. So we failed with him. It is such children as these that we aspire to help. To call them all "emotionally disturbed" is clearly to use language to obscure rather than to clarify. Nonetheless, they are all children who are in serious trouble, for whom the Re-ED idea was developed.

During the past summer, under the direction of William and Dianne Bricker and Charles McDonald, we have been working at Cumberland House with six of the most severely disturbed children we could find, mostly custodial cases from state institutions. Regular Re-ED activities are supplemented by a 24-hour schedule of planned behaviors and contingent rewards, the staff being augmented to make such individualized programming possible, but still using inexpensive and available personnel, such as college students. While it

4 The consultants have meant much more to Project Re-ED than can be recorded in this brief account. We here inadequately recognize the invaluable contribution of our colleagues: Jenny L. Adams, MSW, Gus K. Bell, PhD, Lloyd J. Borstelmann, PhD, Eric M. Chazen, MD, Julius H. Corpening, BD, Jane Ann Eppinger, MSW, John A. Fowler, MD, Ihla H. Gehman, EdD, W. Scott Gehman, PhD, Maurice Hyman, MD, J. David Jones, MD, and Bailey Webb, MD.

is too early to assess the effectiveness of this effort, we are pleased with the progress that most of the children are making, and we are certain we are giving them more of a chance than they had when their principal challenge was to learn how to live in an institution.

ECOLOGICAL CONCEPTS

Let us turn now to an examination of the theoretical assumptions and operational procedures involved in the process of reeducation. We do not, of course, make use of the principles involved in traditional psychotherapy; transference, regression, the promotion of insight through an exploration of inner dynamics and their origins are not a part of the picture. The teacher-counselor is not a psychotherapist, nor does he aspire to be one.

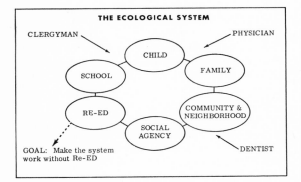

FIG. 1. Chart of ecological system, the smallest unit in a systems approach to working with a disturbed child.

We have become increasingly convinced that a major barrier to effective national planning for emotionally disturbed children is the professional's enchantment with psychotherapy. Everything in most model institutions revolves around getting the child to his therapist 1, 2, or maybe 3 hours a week. A few superb treatment centers combine psychotherapy with a program of daily activities conducive to personal growth and integration. But these are rare indeed. It is not uncommon to find children locked 15 stories high in steel and glass, with a caged roof to play on, drugged to keep them from doing too much damage to the light fixtures and air conditioning, while they await their precious hour, guarded by attendants who think disturbed children must scream, fight, climb walls, cower in a corner. Most frequently, of course,

therapy is not available; most hospitals hold children hoping somehow they will get better.

An overcommitment to individual psychotherapy seems to us to stem from an uncritical acceptance of "cure" as the goal in working with a child, a consequence of defining the problem initially as one of "illness." That some disturbed children are "ill" in the usual sense may be accepted, but to define them all as such leads, we think, to a host of unvalidated and unquestioned assumptions; to a preoccupation with the intrapsychic life of the child, with what goes on inside his skull; to an easy use of drugs without knowledge of their long-term effects on character development; to the extended isolation of children from their families, the presumed source of contagion; to a limitation of professional roles; to the neglect of schools and of schooling; and so on. The preemptive character of a definition and the semantic sets that ensue are major barriers to innovation in working with disturbed children.

Of course we have our own ways of talking about the problem, and our metaphors are no less preemptive, making it all the more important for us to be explicit about definitions. We prefer to say that the children we work with have learned bad habits. They have acquired nonadaptive ways of relating to adults and to other children. They have learned to perceive themselves in limiting or destructive terms and to construe the world as an uncertain, rejecting, and hurtful place. We also recognize that the child lives in a real world that often falls short in giving him the affection, support, and guidance he needs. So we deal directly with social realities as well as with private perceptions.

This kind of thinking has led us gradually to a different way of defining our task, a definition of considerable heuristic merit (see Figure 1). For want of a more felicitous phrase, we have been calling it a systems approach to the problem of working with a disturbed child. We assume that the child is an inseparable part of a small social system, of an ecological unit made up of the child, his family, his school, his neighborhood and community. A social agency is often a part of the picture when a child has been designated emotionally disturbed, and other people—a physician, a clergyman—may be brought in as needed. The system may become "go" as a result of marked improvement in any component (the father stops drinking and goes back to work, a superb teacher becomes available, the child improves dramatically), or it may work as a result of modest improvement in all components. The effort is to get each component of the system above threshold with respect to the requirements of the other components. The Re-ED school becomes a part of the ecological unit for as brief a period of time as possible, withdrawing when the probability that the system will function appears to exceed the probability that it will not. We used to speak of putting the child back into the system but we have come to recognize the erroneous assumptions involved; the child defines the system and all we can do is withdraw from it at a propitious moment.

Once we abandoned cure as a goal and defined our problem as doing what we can to make a small social system work in a reasonably satisfactory manner, there ensued a number of operational patterns that contrast sharply with the practices of existing residential treatment centers for children.

For one thing, parents are no longer viewed as sources to contagion but as responsible collaborators in making the system work. Parents are involved in discussion groups and are helped to get assistance from mental health centers. They actively participate in the ongoing program of the school. They organize an annual reunion, publish a parent's manual, sew for the children, and in many ways assume responsibility for reestablishing the child as quickly as possible in his own home, school, and community.

The children go home on weekends to keep families and children belonging to each other, to avoid the estrangement that can come from prolonged separation, and to give the child and his parents and brothers and sisters an opportunity to learn new and more effective ways of living together. Visitors ask "Aren't your Mondays awful?" They are, indeed, but we cherish their chaos as a source of new instruction; we try to keep in mind that our goal is not to run a tranquil school but to return the child as quickly as possible to his own home and regular school.

The ecological model requires new strategies to involve home, neighborhood, school, agency, and community in a contract with us to help a child. It requires new patterns for the deployment of personnel, and it has led to the development of a new kind of mental health worker: the liaison teacher. The liaison teacher is responsible for maintaining communication with the child's regular school, again to prevent alienation and to arrange optimum conditions for the child's early return to a regular classroom. For example a liaison teacher may personally accompany a child to a new school to which he has been transferred in order to increase the probability that that component of the ecological system will function effectively.

The social worker in Re-ED honors an early heritage of his profession, before the lamentable sit-behind-the-desk-and-do-psychotherapy era got established. He reaches out to the family, to community agencies, and to individuals—to any reasonable source of help for a child in trouble. Again, the goal is to make the system work, not simply to adjust something inside the head of the child.

THE PROCESS OF REEDUCATION

Now, let us turn to the child himself, to our relationships with him, and to what is meant operationally by the process of reeducation. Here are an even dozen underlying concepts that have come to seem important to us as we try to talk about what goes on in a Re-ED school.

Item 1: Life is to be lived, now. We start with the assumption that each day, that every hour in every day, is of great importance to a child, and that when an hour is neglected, allowed to pass without reason and intent, teaching and learning go on nonetheless and the child may be the loser. In Re-ED, no one waits for a special hour. We try, as best we can, to make all hours special. We strive for immediate and sustained involvement in purposive and consequential living. We constantly test the optimistic hypothesis that if children are challenged to live constructively, that if they are given an opportunity for a constructive encounter with other children and with decent adults, they will come off well—and they do, most of the time. They learn, here and now, that life can be lived on terms satisfactory to society and satisfying to themselves. Our task is to contrive each day so that the probability of success in this encounter clearly outweighs the probability of failure. I paraphrase Jessie Taft when I say, in the mastery of this day the child learns, in principle, the mastery of all days.

Item 2: Time is an ally. We became convinced, in the early stages of planning the project, that children are kept too long in most traditional treatment programs. The reasons for this are many. The abstract goal of cure through psychotherapy leads to expectations of extensive personality reorganization, of the achievement of adequacy in a wide array of possible life roles. It thus takes a long time either to succeed in this ambitious endeavor or to become aware that one has failed. Staff and children become fond of each other, making separation difficult. The widespread practice of removing the child from his home for extended periods of time causes a sometimes irreparable estrangement; the family closes ranks against the absent member. While everyone recognizes the importance of school in the life of the child, mental health programs have neither operational concepts nor specialized personnel necessary to effect an easy transition for the child from the institution back to his own school. Furthermore, the expectation of a prolonged stay in a treatment center becomes a self-validating hypothesis. A newly admitted child asks "How long do kids stay here?" He is told "about 2 years," and he settles down to do what is expected of him, with full support of staff and parents who also "know" that it takes 2 years to help a disturbed child. Myriad other constraints get established; for example, the treatment center hires just enough secretaries to move children in and out of a 2-year cycle, and it is not possible to speed the process without hiring more secretaries, a restraint on therapeutic progress that is seldom identified. So before we admitted the first child, we set 6 months as the expected, average period of stay, a goal we have now achieved.

Time is an issue of importance in the process of reeducation in yet another way. We work with children during years when life has a tremendous forward thrust. Several studies suggest that therapeutic intervention is not demonstrably superior to the passage of time without treatment in the subsequent adjustment of children diagnosed as emotionally disturbed (Lewis, 1965). Treatment may simply speed up a process that would occur in an unknown percentage of children anyway. There is a real possibility that a long stay in a treatment center may actually slow down this process. Furthermore, in ecological perspective, it is clear that children tend to get ejected from families at low points in family organization and integrity. Most families get better after such periods; there is only one direction for them to go

and that is up. The systems concept may entail simply observing when the family has regained sufficient stability to sustain a previously ejected child. The great tragedy is that children can get caught up in institutional arrangements that must inexorably run their course. In Re-ED we claim time is an ally and try to avoid getting in the way of the normal restorative processes of life.

Item 3: Trust is essential. The development of trust is the first step in reeducation of the emotionally disturbed child. The disturbed child is conspicuously impaired in his ability to learn from adults. The mediation process is blocked or distorted by the child's experience-based hypothesis that adults are deceptive, that they are an unpredictable source of hurt and help. He faces each adult with a predominant anticipation of punishment, rejection, derision, or withdrawal of love. He is acutely impaired in the very process by which more mature ways of living may be acquired. A first step, then, in the reeducation process, is the development of trust. Trust, coupled with understanding, is the beginning point of a new learning experience, an experience that helps a child know that he can use an adult to learn many things: how to read, how to be affectionate, how to be oneself without fear or guilt.

We are intrigued by the possibility, indeed are almost sure the thesis is true, that no amount of professional training can make an adult worthy of the trust of a child or capable of generating it. This ability is prior to technique, to theory, to technical knowledge. After seeing the difference that teacher-counselors in our two schools have made in the lives of children I am confident of the soundness of the idea that some adults know, without knowing how they know, the way to inspire trust in children and to teach them to begin to use adults as mediators of new learning.

Item 4: Competence makes a difference. The ability to do something well gives a child confidence and self-respect and gains for him acceptance by other children, by teachers, and, unnecessary as it might seem, even by his parents. In a society as achievement oriented as ours, a person's worth is established in substantial measure by his ability to produce or perform. Acceptance without productivity is a beginning point in the process of reeducation, but an early goal and a continuing challenge is to help the child get good at something.

What, then, in the process of reeducation, does the acquisition of competence mean? It means first and foremost the gaining of competence in school skills, in reading and arithmetic most frequently, and occasionally in other subjects as well. If a child feels that he is inadequate in school, inadequacy can become a pervasive theme in his life, leading to a consistent pattern of failure to work up to his level of ability. Underachievement in school is the single most common characteristic of emotionally disturbed children. We regard it as sound strategy to attack directly the problem of adequacy in school, for its intrinsic value as well as for its indirect effect on the child's perception of his worth and his acceptance by people who are important in his world. A direct attack on the problem of school skills does not mean a gross assault in some area of deficiency. On the contrary, it requires utmost skill and finesse on the part of the teacher-counselor to help a disturbed child move into an area where he has so often known defeat, where failure is a well-rooted expectancy, where a printed page can evoke flight or protest or crippling anxiety. The teacher-counselor need make no apologies to the psychotherapist with reference to the level of skill required to help a disturbed child learn.

So, in Re-ED, school keeps. It is not regarded, as it is in many mental health programs, as something that can wait until the child gets better, as though he were recovering from measles or a broken leg. School is the very stuff of a child's problems, and consequently, a primary source of instruction in living. Special therapy rooms are not needed; the classroom is a natural setting for a constructive relationship between a disturbed child and a competent, concerned adult.

Much of the teaching, incidentally, is through the unit or enterprise method. For example, a group of boys at Cumberland House was invited to go camping with some Cherokee Indian children on their reservation. The trip provided a unifying theme for 3 month's instruction in American History, geography, arithmetic, writing, and arts and crafts. At Wright School, rocketry has provided high motivation and an entrée to mathematics, aerodynamics, and politics. The groups are small enough to make individualized instruction possible, even to the point of preparing special programmed materials for an individual child, a method that has been remarkably effective with children with seemingly intractable learning disorders. The residential character of the Re-ED school means that the acquisition of competence does not have to be limited to increased skill in school subjects. It may mean learning to swim, to draw, to sing; it may mean learning to cook on a Dakota Hole, to lash together a table, to handle a canoe, to build a shelter in the woods; it may mean learning to talk at a council ring, to assert one's rights, to give of one's possessions, to risk friendship, to see parents as people and teachers as friends.

Item 5: Symptoms can and should be controlled. It is standard doctrine in psychotherapeutic practice that symptoms should not be treated, that the one symptom removed will simply be replaced by another, and that the task of the therapist is to uncover underlying conflicts against which the symptom is a defense, thus eliminating the need for any symptom at all. In Re-ED we contend, on the other hand, that symptoms are important in their own right and deserve direct attention. We are impressed that some symptoms are better to have than other symptoms. The bad symptoms are those that alienate the child from other children or from the adults he needs as a source of security or a source of learning. There is much to be gained then from identifying symptoms that are standing in the way of normal development and working out specific plans for removing or altering the symptoms if possible. The problem is to help the child make effective contact with normal sources of affection, support, instruction, and discipline. We also work on a principle of parsimony that instructs us to give first preference to explanations involving the assumption of minimum pathology, as contrasted to professional preference for deep explanations and the derogation of all else as superficial.

Item 6: Cognitive control can be taught. Though little emphasis is placed on the acquisition of insight as a source of therapeutic gain, there is a lot of talking in Re-ED about personal problems and how they can be managed better. The teacher-counselor relies primarily on immediate experience, on the day-by-day, hour-by-hour, moment-by-moment relationship between himself and the child; he relies on specific events that can be discussed to increase the child's ability to manage his own life. The emotionally disturbed child has fewer degrees of freedom in behavior than the normal child, yet he is not without the ability to shape his own behavior by self-administered verbal instruction. He can signal to himself if he can learn what the useful signals are. The teacher-counselor works constantly to help a child learn the right signals. The focus of this effort is on today and tomorrow, not on the past or the future, and on ways for the child to signal to himself to make each day a source of instruction for the living of the next. At the council ring at night, at a place set apart from the business of living, children in a group are helped to consider what was good about the day just past, what went wrong that might be handled better tomorrow, and what was learned, especially in successes and failures in relationships among themselves. Possibly more important than the solving of particular problems is the acquisition of the habit of talking things over for the purpose of getting better control over events, a habit that can frequently be carried over into the child's home and become a new source of strength for his family.

Item 7: Feelings should be nurtured. We are very interested in the nurturance and expression of feeling, to help a child own all of himself without guilt. Children have a way of showing up with animals and we are glad for this. A child who has known the rejection of adults may find it safest, at first, to express affection to a dog. And a pet can be a source of pride and of sense of responsibility. Anger, resentment, hostility are commonplace, of course, and their expression is used in various ways: to help some children learn to control their violent impulses and to help others give vent to feelings too long repressed. In Re-ED Schools one finds the familiar ratio of four or five boys to one girl, a consequence in part, we believe, of a lack of masculine challenge in school and community today. Thus we contrive situations of controlled danger in which children can test themselves, can know fear and become the master of it. The simple joy of companionship is encouraged. We are impressed by the meaningfulness of friendships and how long they endure. The annual homecoming is anticipated by many youngsters as an opportunity to walk arm-in-arm with an old friend associated with a period of special significance in their lives. And we respect the need to be alone, to work things through without intrusion, and to have a private purpose. Feelings also get expressed through many kinds of creative activities that are woven into the fabric of life in a Re-ED school.

Throwing clay on a potter's wheel gives a child a first sense of his potential for shaping his world. A puppet show written by the children may permit freer expression than is ordinarily tolerable. Drawing and painting can be fun for a whole group. And an object to mold gives something to do to make it safe for an adult and child to be close together.

Item 8: The group is important to children. Children are organized in groups of eight, with two teacher-counselors in charge. The group is kept intact for nearly all activities and becomes an important source of motivation, instruction, and control. When a group is functioning well, it is extremely difficult for an individual child to behave in a disturbed way. Even when the group is functioning poorly, the frictions and the failures can be used constructively. The council ring, or powwow, involving discussion of difficulties or planning of activities can be a most maturing experience. And the sharing of adventure, of vicissitudes, and of victories, provides an experience in human relatedness to which most of our children have been alien.

Item 9: Ceremony and ritual give order, stability, and confidence. Many Re-ED children have lived chaotic lives, even in their brief compass. They may come from homes where interpersonal disarray is endemic. We have stumbled upon and been impressed by the beneficence of ceremony, ritual, and metaphor for children and have come to plan for their inclusion in the program. The nightly backrub is an established institution with the Whippoorwills, a time of important confidences. Being a Bobcat brings a special sense of camaraderie and has its own metaphorical obligations. And a Christmas pageant can effect angelic transformation of boys whose ordinary conduct is far from seraphic.

Item 10: The body is the armature of the self. We are intrigued by the idea that the physical self is the armature around which the psychological self is constructed and that a clearer experiencing of the potential and the boundaries of the body should lead to a clearer definition of the self, and thus to greater psychological fitness and more effective functioning. The Outward Bound schools in England, developed as an experience for young men to overcome the anomie that is the product of an industrial civilization, are built around the concept. Austin Des Lauriers' ideas about treatment of schizophrenia in children emphasize differentiating the body from the rest of the world. Programmatically, in Re-ED, the idea has been realized in such activities as swimming, climbing, dancing, tumbling, clay modelling, canoeing, building a tree house, and walking a monkey bridge.

Item 11: Communities are important. The systems concept in Re-ED leads to an examination of the relationship of the child to his home community. Many children who are referred to our schools come from families that are alienated or detached from community life or that are not sufficiently well organized or purposeful to help the child develop a sense of identity with his neighborhood, his town or city. He has little opportunity to discover that communities exist for people and, while the goodness of fit between the two may often leave much to be desired, an important part of a child's education is to learn that community agencies and institutions exist for his welfare and that he has an obligation as a citizen to contribute to their effective functioning. This is especially true for many of the boys referred to Re-ED, whose energy, aggressiveness, lack of control, and resentment of authority will predispose them to delinquent behavior when they are a few years older and gain in independence and mobility. This idea has a number of implications for program planning. Field trips to the fire, police, and health departments are useful. Memberships in the YMCA, a children's museum, a playground group, or a community center may be worked out for a child. Church attendance may be encouraged and a clergyman persuaded to take special interest in a family, and a library card can be a proud possession and a tangible community tie.

Item 12: Finally, a child should know joy. We have often speculated about our lack of a psychology of well-being. There is an extensive literature on anxiety, guilt, and dread, but little that is well developed on joy. Most psychological experiments rely for motivation on avoidance of pain or hunger or some other aversive stimuli; positive motivations are limited to the pleasure that comes from minute, discrete rewards. This poverty with respect to the most richly human of motivations leads to anaemic programming for children. We thus go beyond contemporary psychology to touch one of the most vital areas of human experiencing.

We try to develop skill in developing joy in children. We believe that it is immensely important, that it is immediately therapeutic if further justification is required, for a child to know some joy in each day and to look forward with eagerness to at least some joy-giving event that is planned for tomorrow.

COSTS AND EFFECTIVENESS

Now, let us turn to the practical questions of cost and of effectiveness.

FIG. 2. Geometric felt figures used in replacement technique (after Weinstein, 1965).

FIG. 3. Human felt figures used in replacement technique (after Weinstein, 1965).

A Re-ED school costs about $20 to $25 per child per day to operate. Thus the per-day cost is about one-third the cost of the most widely accepted model and perhaps four times the cost of custodial care. Cost per day, however, is not the best index to use, for the purpose of a mental health program is not to keep children cheaply but to restore them to home, school, and community as economically as possible. In terms of cost per child served, the cost of a Re-ED program is equivalent to or less than the cost of custodial care. The cost per child served is approximately $4,000. If Re-ED can prevent longer period of institutionalization, this is a modest investment indeed.

Appropriate to the systems analysis of the problem, most of our studies of effectiveness of Re-ED schools have employed ratings by concerned observers: mother, father, teacher, our own staff, and agency staffs, all important persons in the ecological space of the child. However, Laura Weinstein (1965) has been interested in the way normal and disturbed children construct interpersonal space, as illustrated by the accompanying representations of felt board figures. She used two techniques. In the first (the replacement technique), each of two figure pairs—a pair of human figures and a pair of rectangles—is present on a different board and equally far apart (Figures 2 and 3). The child is asked to replace the felt figures "exactly as far apart as they are now." Normal and disturbed children make systematic errors, but in opposite directions: normal children replace human figures closer together while Re-ED children replace human figures farther apart (Figure 4). In the second technique (the free placement technique), human figures are used,

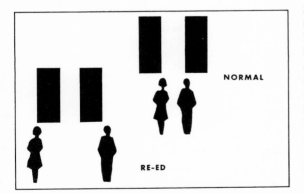

FIG. 4. Placement of geometric and human felt figures by normal and disturbed children (after Weinstein, 1965).

representing mothers, fathers, and children. The children are asked to place the figures on the board "any way you like." Again systematic differences occur. Normal children place the child very close to the mother. Re-ED children place greater distance between the mother and the child than between any other human pair (Figure 5). The mother-child relationship is clearly crucial in the life space of the 6- to 12-year-old children with whom we work. It is gratifying to report that children after the Re-ED experience put the child figure closer to the mother than they did before; that is, they structure interpersonal space as normal children do.

The basic design for evaluating the effectiveness of the Re-ED schools involves observations taken at time of enrollment and repeated 6 months after discharge. Preliminary results present an encouraging picture. A composite rating of improvement, based on follow-up information on 93 graduates provided by all evaluators, gives a success rate of approximately 80%. We are in process of obtaining comparison data from control groups to determine the extent to which the reeducation effort is superior to changes that occur with the passage of time.

Detailed analyses show that mothers and fathers independently report a decrease in symptoms such as bedwetting, tantrums, nightmares, and school fears, and an increase in social maturity on a Vineland type check list. School adjustment as rated by teachers shows the same favorable trends. On a semantic differential measure of discrepancy between how the child is seen and parental standards for him, there is an interesting and dynamically significant difference between fathers and mothers. Both see the child as having improved. For fathers the perceived improvement results in lower discrepancy scores between the child as seen and a standard held for him. For some mothers, however, improvement results in a raising of standards so that discrepancy scores frequently remain high. This is not true of all mothers but it is more frequently true of mothers than of fathers.

But T tests seldom determine the fate of institutions; public and professional acceptance is crucial.

To obtain an informed and mature professional appraisal of Re-ED, we have established a panel of visitors composed of men whose judgment is held in high esteem: Eli M. Bower, psychologist; Reginald S. Lourie, psychiatrist; Charles R. Strother, psychologist; and Robert L. Sutherland, sociologist. Members of the panel have been visiting the schools regularly since their inception and will make public their final appraisal at the end of the project period. It is enough to say now that they are all strong supporters of the Re-ED idea.

A test of public support of the Re-ED idea was adventitiously obtained when the Legislature of the State of North Carolina last June terminated state funds for the support of Wright School after July 1, 1966. Protest from all over the state was immediate and strong; in less than 3 years of operation the school had won impressive public support. Funds have been raised to continue Wright School in operation until the Legislature convenes again.[5] The Governor has assured the mental health officials of North Carolina that he will support legislative measures to restore state funds for the operation of Wright School. Fortunately the Tennessee school has not been put to such public test but professional and political endorsement is evident in the decision to build two new schools, one in Memphis and one in Chattanooga, that will be operated as reeducation centers. Finally, it is encouraging that several other states have committees working to establish Re-ED schools.

Our aspiration and our growing confidence are that the Re-ED model will be replicated in many states, that it will have its influence on the character of more traditional treatment programs, and

---

[5] Among the major contributors are the Wright Refuge Board, the Sarah Graham Kenan Fund, the Mary Duke Biddle Foundation, the Hillsdale Fund, and the Stanley County Mental Health Association. Many gifts have come from churches, mental health associations, civic organizations, and individuals. We gratefully acknowledge their help in keeping Wright School in operation.

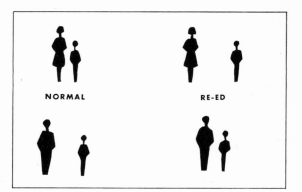

FIG. 5. Mother, father, and child felt figures as placed by normal and disturbed children (after Weinstein, 1965).

that the beneficiaries will be the disturbed children of America.

We further think of Re-ED as an institution that exemplifies, in its development, the contemporary challenge to psychologists to concern themselves with the invention of social arrangements that put psychological knowledge to use to improve the quality of human life.

REFERENCES

Hobbs, N. Mental health's third revolution. *American Journal of Orthopsychiatry*, 1964, 34: 822–833.

Lewis, W. W. Continuity and intervention in emotional disturbance: A review. *Exceptional Children*, 1965, 31:(9), 465–475.

Weinstein, L. Social schemata of emotionally disturbed boys. *Journal of Abnormal Psychology*, 1965, 70: 457–461.

Subject Index

Author Index